Client/Server LAN Programming

Barry Nance

QUE

Client/Server LAN Programming

Library of Congress Catalog Number: 94-67363

ISBN: 1-56529-924-8

97 96 95 94   5 4 3 2 1

Interpretation of the printing code: the rightmost double-digit number is the year of the book's printing; the rightmost single-digit number, the number of the book's printing. For example, a printing code of 94-1 shows that the first printing of the book occurred in 1994.

Publisher: David P. Ewing

Associate Publisher: Joseph B. Wikert

Managing Editor: Michael Cunningham

Marketing Manager: Greg Wiegand

Dedication

To Susan, Scott, Chris, and Joel. In many ways, this book was a family effort!

Bill Sudlow

Credits

Publishing Manager
Joseph B. Wikert

Acquisitions Editor
Angela J. Lee

Acquisitions Coordinator
Patricia J. Brooks

Product Development Specialist
Bryan Gambrel

Production Editor
Thomas Hayes

Copy Editor
Andy Saff

Technical Editor
Bruce Wynn

Cover Designer
Dan Armstrong

Book Designer
Amy Peppler-Adams

Production Team
Steve Adams
Karen Dodson
Joelynn Gifford
Dennis Clay Hager
Bob LaRoche
Elizabeth Lewis
Tim Montgomery
Wendy Ott
Kaylene Riemen
Clair Schweinler
Dennis Sheehan
Michael Thomas
Suzanne Tully
Susan VandeWalle
Mary Beth Wakefield
Angie Ward
Donna Winter

Editorial Assistant
Michelle Williams

Indexer
Michael Hughes

Composed in *StoneSerif* and *MCPdigital* by Macmillan Computer Publishing

About the Author

Barry Nance, a programmer for the past 20 years, is the author of *Using OS/2 2.1* (Que, 1992–1994), *Network Programming in C* (Que, 1990), and *Introduction to Networking* (Que, 1994). Barry is the Exchange Editor for the IBM Exchange on BIX. Barry's Internet e-mail address is barryn@bix.com.

Acknowledgments

All terms mentioned in this book that are known to be trademarks or service marks have been appropriately capitalized. Que cannot attest to the accuracy of this information. Use of a term in this book should not be regarded as affecting the validity of any trademark or service mark.

Screen Reproductions in this book were created using Collage Plus from Inner Media, Inc., Hollis, New Hampshire.

Contents at a Glance

Contents

II Network Programming Techniques 109

4 Shared File Programming 111

7 Testing and Debugging Your Program   215

8 Network Applications   227

III Reference   277

DOS Services for Network Programming   279

DLR and PCLP Programming Services   **299**

Novell's Extended DOS Services   **307**

OS/2 Services 375

NetBIOS Functions (DOS)　　　　　389

IPX and SPX Functions　　　　　427

The LANtastic Programming Interface   453

IV Appendixes   483

Introduction

Client/server computing is perhaps the most important software technology of this decade. Businesses of all sizes are *downsizing* (sometimes called *rightsizing*) their operations, using PCs on local area networks (LANs) to automate and streamline their daily activities. This book explains the programming techniques and strategies that you can use to implement client/server computing in your business.

A network operating system enables workstations to access files on a file server just as if the files existed on the workstation's local hard disk. In a file server environment, however, you need to design the workstation software to share those files cooperatively. In a multiuser environment, many workstations may concurrently attempt to access a file. This book describes exactly how you can manage concurrent access from within the software that you write.

Perhaps you want to use a database manager product on your LAN. If you put the database on a file server and use the network operating system's file redirection feature to access the database from each workstation, your database search operations can take a long time to execute and can cause substantial LAN traffic. Each workstation must read the entire database from the file server to perform a search. For example, if you have a database with a table of 50,000 entries, and you run a query that displays five rows of the table, your workstation must read all 50,000 rows to find the five desired entries. Each of the 50,000 rows becomes a series of LAN messages that flow from the file server to each workstation. You can avoid the extra LAN traffic by using the techniques provided by this book.

Database client/server technology involves sending SQL statements to a database server and receiving acknowledgments and possibly selected table rows from the database. Compared to a file server environment, a client/server environment reduces LAN traffic and manages the server computer more intelligently, thus providing a higher-capacity information processing system. This book identifies and explains the programming statements that you can use to send and receive LAN messages containing SQL entries or other information.

Forward-thinking data-processing departments are currently developing significant, mission-critical systems for LANs. Other systems, in other companies, will soon follow. These systems are cost-effective, put the application closer to the user, take advantage of the PC's excellent capability to interact with users, and distribute the workload across several computers. This book gives you the system design, coding, and debugging skills that you need to take advantage of the information-sharing features of a LAN.

LANs—a New Frontier

Local area networks are a new frontier in software technology. If you are accustomed to working with mainframe computers, you will be pleased with the way that a LAN gets you closer to your users through the screen and keyboard control provided by personal computers. The file- and record-locking tools will seem rudimentary, but you will grow used to them. Also, after having dealt with tools like CICS, you will find that the facilities for communicating information among users are a breath of fresh air. On the other hand, if you have developed PC applications before, you have been in a single-user environment. You must adjust your thinking to account for the extra dimension of having multiple concurrent users of your software. Finally, you will also like the new facilities for user-to-user communications.

A medium-sized LAN represents, collectively, much more raw computing horsepower than a mainframe. Your immediate response is probably, "PCs can't be as powerful as a mainframe!" If this is your reaction, you are thinking of desktop computing in terms of individual people using individual PCs, running off-the-shelf software applications (word processors or spreadsheets, for instance). Until now, this sort of individual usage has been a classic way to look at PCs. But think of 50 personal computers on a LAN, being used by 40 people. Forty workstations are used as data-collection and inquiry vehicles, and the other 10 computers, unattended, run programs that perform calculations, update a database, and work in close harmony with the software on the interactive workstations. These 10 "engines" are fast 80486 or Pentium computers with a total rating of about 200 MIPS. Each has a gigabyte hard disk (or perhaps I should refer to it as *DASD* in this context) with a 10-millisecond or faster average access time. Each engine communicates with the other computers on the LAN at 16 megabits per second.

This picture of a LAN defines an environment *much* more powerful than a mainframe. You can incrementally add even more horsepower by purchasing more personal computers; you don't have to write a check for four million dollars every time that you run out of computing power. This book explains how you can take full advantage of this powerful environment.

The Purpose of This Book

Using networked PCs for more than sharing printers and spreadsheet files requires new systems design techniques and new programming skills. These techniques and skills have been in short supply. Until recently, LANs have been used mostly to keep from wearing out the carpet ("sneakernet"—walking floppy disks around the office). This book gives you the techniques and skills that you need to write LAN-aware applications.

After you read this book, you will be able to design and develop LAN-based systems that share files, communicate directly from workstation to workstation, and perform distributed processing. You will easily be able to program client/server applications.

Who Should Read This Book

This book is for you if you are interested in LANs and are any of the following:

- A systems analyst

- A software designer or software engineer

- A programmer

- A LAN administrator who occasionally writes programs

This book gives you the information that you need to fully understand, design, program, and debug LAN-aware applications.

What Is in This Book

Part I of this book, "Local Area Networks," lays the groundwork for the later discussions on design and programming. Chapter 1, "The Basics of Networking," explores the characteristics and components of a LAN and the differences among various vendors' network products. Chapter 2, "Multiuser Concepts," covers file-sharing and concurrency concepts, emphasizing the features and facilities that the network adds to a single-user operating system such as DOS, Windows, or OS/2 to enable multiple users to coordinate with each other. Finally, Chapter 3, "PC-to-PC Communications Concepts," explains the protocols that the network uses to send and receive LAN messages.

Part II, "Network Programming Techniques," delves deeply into the systems design and programming issues that you face when developing a LAN-aware application, and fully explores the programming techniques that you use to address these issues. Chapter 4, "Shared File Programming," covers file-level topics such as sharing files, record locking, access rights, and network printing. Chapter 5, "PC-to-PC NetBIOS Programming," explains how to send and receive NetBIOS messages from within your DOS, Windows, or OS/2 software. Chapter 6, "IPX and SPX Programming," describes how to use the IPX and SPX protocols popular on NetWare LANs. Chapter 7, "Testing and Debugging Your Program," provides techniques and tools that you can use to make your program work correctly in a LAN environment. Chapter 8, "Network Applications," discusses the six LAN-oriented computer programs supplied on the floppy disk that accompanies this book. You can use the programs as-is, or you can use parts of the programs in your own software. The applications that you get are the following:

- *File and Record Collision Tester*—If you don't have two users who can press the Enter key at *exactly* the same time, this tool is for you. Use it to cause deliberate collisions between files and records to see how your application handles them.

- *NetBIOS Microscope*—This application enables you to choose the NetBIOS functions that you want to learn about and watch them execute, step by step.

- *Remote Program Execution*—This application runs programs and DOS commands on a remote workstation. You queue up the programs and commands, cancel items that are in the queue, and see what is in the queue. The application works similar to the way that jobs are submitted on a mainframe—you even refer to the queued programs and commands by job number.

- *Electronic Mail*—This application sends and receives electronic mail messages from workstation to workstation, without storing the messages on a file server.

- *Token Ring Monitor*—With this application, you can diagnose your Token Ring LAN by watching error events and statistics, provided automatically by the Token Ring adapters and decoded by this computer program.

- *Post Office NLM*—Explore this program to see how to write a NetWare loadable module (NLM). The software implements an electronic mail post office inside a NetWare server.

The source code for these programs appears on the companion disk and in this book's appendixes.

Part III is a technical reference for network programming. Detailed explanations are provided for the following:

- Network-related DOS function calls

- DOS LAN Requester and PC LAN Program function calls

- Novell NetWare function calls

- OS/2 Kernel API calls that are network-related

- NetBIOS function calls

- Novell NetWare IPX and SPX function calls

- LANtastic function calls

What You Need, and What You Need to Know

To use this book effectively, you need access to a LAN (although you can run the File and Record Collision Tester application on a stand-alone computer). You need an IBM personal computer (such as a PC, XT, AT, or PS/2) or close compatible. You should also be aware that I used the Borland C compiler, version 3.1, to produce the workstation applications discussed in Chapter 8. I used the Watcom 32-bit compiler, version 9.5, to compile the Post Office NLM program. Also, because I used the inline assembler facility of Borland C, you need an assembler (such as Microsoft's MASM or Borland's TASM) if you want to compile and link the programs yourself.

Many of the code examples and fragments in Part II, however, consist of fairly standard C code. Where differences exist among the Microsoft, IBM, and Borland C compilers' code, I show specific examples of each.

You should already be somewhat familiar with the C language, although you don't have to be an expert to understand the examples in the book. I keep things simple and avoid language-related issues as much as possible. One of the goals of this book is to make it easy for you to explore network programming.

> **Note**
>
> Code lines that are too long to fit within the margins of this book are joined by the following special line-wrap icon:
>
> ➡
>
> In your programs, you should type the two lines as one.

You will find network programming a fun challenge, and an impressive addition to your resume. Turn the page and get started!

Part I

Local Area Networks

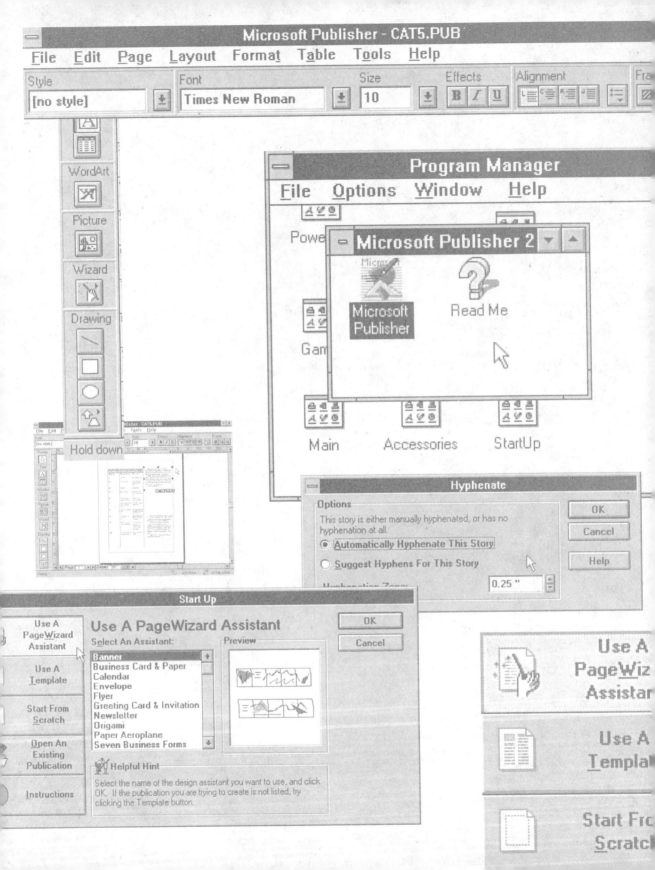

Microsoft Publisher - CAT5.PUB

File Edit Page Layout Format Table Tools Help

Style [no style] Font Times New Roman Size 10 Effects **B** *I* <u>U</u> Alignment

WordArt
Picture
Wizard
Drawing

Hold down

Program Manager

File Options Window Help

Powe

Microsoft Publisher 2

Microsoft Publisher   Read Me

Gam

Main   Accessories   StartUp

Hyphenate

Options
This story is either manually hyphenated, or has no
hyphenation at all.

○ Automatically Hyphenate This Story

○ Suggest Hyphens For This Story

0.25 "

OK
Cancel
Help

Start Up

Use A
PageWizard
Assistant

Use A
Template

Start From
Scratch

Open An
Existing
Publication

Instructions

Use A PageWizard Assistant

Select An Assistant:

Banner
Business Card & Paper
Calendar
Envelope
Flyer
Greeting Card & Invitation
Newsletter
Origami
Paper Aeroplane
Seven Business Forms

Preview

OK
Cancel

Helpful Hint
Select the name of the design assistant you want to use, and click
OK. If the publication you are trying to create is not listed, try
clicking the Template button.

Use A
PageWiz
Assistar

Use A
Templa

Start Fro
Scratcl

Chapter 1

The Basics of Networking

There are different kinds of networks and different ways of programming them. In this chapter, you learn the distinguishing characteristics and the hardware and software components of local area networks (LANs), and the principles on which a LAN operates. You explore different LAN platforms (DOS, Windows, and OS/2) and you look at using different computer languages (C, C++, Pascal, assembler, and BASIC) to develop LAN-aware computer software. Finally, you learn about different LAN hardware and software products.

The chapter begins by looking at a local area network from the inside out, to give you a feeling for what makes a LAN a LAN.

Characteristics

Local area networks vary considerably in size and appearance. Some low-end networks, called *RS-232 LANs* or sometimes *zero-slot LANs*, consist merely of PCs connected by serial (modem) cables between their serial ports. At the other end of the spectrum are computers (not necessarily microcomputers) that contain specialized interface boards connected by thick cables that disappear under a raised floor and that use a mainframe as a file server. Such networks connect mainframes, supercomputers, minicomputers, and fast peripherals. Externally, then, it can be difficult to tell whether a group of computers is part of a LAN and which LAN products might be in use.

Most local area networks, however, consist of a combination of computers, LAN cables, network adapter cards, network operating system software, and LAN application software. You sometimes see the term *network operating system* abbreviated as *NOS*. On a LAN, each personal computer is called a *workstation*, except for one or more computers designated as *file servers*. Each workstation and file server contains a network adapter card. LAN cables connect all the workstations and file servers. In addition to running DOS or other base operating systems, each workstation runs network software that enables it to communicate with the file servers. In turn, the file servers run network software that communicates with the workstations and serves files to those workstations. LAN-aware application software runs at each workstation, communicating with the file server when it needs to read and write files.

Fortunately, from an internal (software) point of view, you can easily distinguish a LAN from the many other mechanisms used to tie computers together. To make categorizing these mechanisms even easier, this book assumes that each workstation on the LAN is an IBM microcomputer—either a PC, XT, AT, PS/2, or close compatible. This book refers to these machines simply as PCs.

Less formally, a LAN is a group of PCs connected to one another by cables. Each PC contains a network adapter card and network support software. Each PC has a unique address on the network and is known as a *node* or *workstation*. The network support software in each workstation typically occurs in layers. The layer at the lowest level talks directly to the network adapter card; the layer at the highest level talks to your application program and provides a programmatic interface that your application can use to access the network. Each layer implements a well-defined method of communicating across the network (a *protocol*).

Now that you know what a LAN is, let's see how a LAN provides PC-to-PC communications and how it lets you access a file server's hard drive.

Message Packets (Frames)

At the lowest level, networked PCs communicate with one another and with the file server using message packets, often called *frames*. The foundation on which all LAN activity is based, these frames are sent and received by the network adapter and its support software. Chapter 3, "PC-to-PC Communications Concepts," discusses frames in detail. This section provides an overview of what frames are and how they work.

The network support software sends frames for many purposes, including the following:

- Opening a communications session with another adapter

- Sending data (perhaps a record from a file) to a PC

- Acknowledging the receipt of a data frame

- Broadcasting a message to all other adapters

- Closing a communications session

PC-to-PC communications are easy to visualize in this way: you programmatically ask a protocol such as NetBIOS or IPX (both of which are described fully in Chapter 3, "PC-to-PC Communications Concepts") to send or receive a message, and the higher-level protocol works with the adapter support software to send or receive the appropriate data frames and acknowledgment frames. Different types of frames serve different purposes. For example, some of the frames used in implementations of NetBIOS are Name Query frames, Session Request frames, frames containing application data, and Close frames.

Figure 1.1 shows the layout of a typical frame. Different network implementations define frames in different ways, but the following data items are common to all implementations:

- The sender's network address

- The destination's network address

- An identification of the frame's contents

- A data record or message

- A checksum or CRC for error-detection purposes

Sender ID	Dest ID	Frame type	Data/message	CRC

Fig. 1.1
The basic layout of a frame.

How are frames used in the context of sharing files on a file server? What happens when an application running on a workstation wants to open a file that resides on the file server? The answer lies in the *redirection of DOS function calls*.

Here is an ordinary program statement that opens a file; I'm sure you have coded something similar many times:

```
char filename[] = "DATABASE.FIL";
int file_handle;

file_handle = open(filename, O_RDWR | O_DENYNONE);
```

The following statements are *exactly equivalent* to the preceding statements, but use the int86x() library function to invoke the DOS Open File service explicitly:

```
union REGS regs;
struct SREGS sregs;
char filename[] = "DATABASE.FIL";
int file_handle;

regs.h.ah = 0x3D;
regs.h.al = 0x42;
regs.x.dx = FP_OFF( (void far *) filename);
sregs.ds  = FP_SEG( (void far *) filename);
int86x(0x21, &regs, &regs, &sregs);
if (regs.x.cflag == 1)
    file_handle = -1;
else
    file_handle = regs.x.ax;
```

I show the longer, more complicated version to introduce the concept of DOS function calls. A DOS function call works as follows: the application loads certain CPU registers with certain values and executes an Interrupt 21 (hexadecimal). For example, to invoke Open File, the hex value 3D is placed in the AH CPU register, the DS:DX register pair is made to point to the name of the file to be opened, and the AL register is set to a value that represents a combination of things—whether or not the file will be written to, and how the file should be shared.

On a stand-alone (non-LAN-attached) computer, Interrupt 21 is a primary entry point into DOS. On a LAN, however, one of the higher levels of the LAN support software intercepts (filters) Interrupt 21. This filtering enables the LAN software to shunt some of the function calls across the LAN to the file server, instead of letting DOS see them. The layer of the LAN support software that intercepts Interrupt 21 is called the *shell* or sometimes the *redirector*.

The shell/redirector software, which "sees" the Interrupt 21 requests first, detects that the file being opened is located on the file server. Thus the software knows to put the contents of the CPU registers into a message packet and send the packet to the file server. The local copy of DOS running on the workstation does not process network requests. Instead, the file server gets the message, opens the file for the workstation, and sends back a response to the workstation saying, in essence, "Okay, the file was opened successfully." The shell/redirector software layer then passes this information back to the application in the appropriate CPU registers, just as though DOS had opened the file on the workstation's local hard disk. The net effect is that the shell/redirector software extends DOS functions (Open, Read, Write, Close, and other functions) across the network in a way that is transparent to an application. Figure 1.2 shows this redirection process.

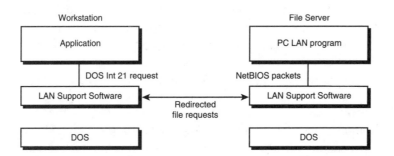

Fig. 1.2
Redirection of DOS functions.

Note that the actual sending and receiving of frames are performed by the network support software and not by you. Your application causes network activity by doing I/O on files that are located on the file server, or by instructing a protocol such as NetBIOS or IPX to give a message record to another PC.

Extending Windows Functions to the Network

Because Windows runs on top of DOS, you usually can use DOS, IPX, or NetBIOS calls to access the network in the Windows environment, just as though Windows were not present. The two exceptions to this general rule involve the use of memory that you allocated and the period of time that can elapse before a network function returns control to your program.

Windows can move and swap to disk memory that your software is using. Programmers who have used the Windows memory management functions are familiar with the moving and swapping of memory, and know that they should manage their use of Windows memory carefully. However, network function APIs (especially those for IPX and NetBIOS) often use memory a few moments after you invoke a network function, not immediately. Therefore, you must take extra precautions. Make sure memory areas for IPX or NetBIOS network functions are in fixed, page-locked Windows memory. For example, when you call the `GlobalAlloc()` (Windows' memory allocation function), you should use the GMEM_FIXED manifest constant. In 386 Enhanced mode, you should then call `GlobalPageLock()` to make sure that you can safely use the memory you have allocated. Additionally, if your program includes call-back functions that you have indicated the network software can call, you should make sure that those functions reside in fixed code segments. Within a DLL's DEF file, for instance, you should declare your code segments FIXED. You should also page-lock your callback functions, to prevent Windows from swapping those functions to disk while they are executing. References to callback functions should also be procedure-instance addresses acquired from a call to `MakeProcInstance()`.

Network function calls that query other workstations or that might take several moments to process are another consideration in the Windows environment. Windows multitasks in a cooperative manner, which means that you must be aware of the CPU time that your Windows program consumes and occasionally surrender use of the CPU to give other software running in the Windows environment a chance to process. In particular, many of the NetBIOS functions that you learn about in Chapter 5, "PC-to-PC NetBIOS Programming," have both wait and no-wait options. In a Windows environment, you should use the no-wait version of a NetBIOS command. After calling NetBIOS with a no-wait command, you will probably program a wait loop that watches for the command to finish executing. You should call `PeekMessage()` in your program's wait loop to let Windows dispatch message queue events while you wait.

When writing LAN-aware Windows programs, you can use the information in this book to invoke the network services that you want to use. The services are part of the network software you already have loaded at your workstation; you simply need to know the calling conventions of those services. Optionally, you can purchase a product such as Novell's NetWare Client SDK (Software Developer's Kit). You can then call the functions in the libraries that Novell supplies and avoid using the lower-level interface that the network software provides. You learn more about such SDKs later in this chapter.

Extending OS/2 Functions to the Network

OS/2 2.x offers the Interrupt 21h interface only to programs running in virtual DOS sessions or programs running in the Win-OS/2 environment. An OS/2 program, running natively in OS/2's 32-bit mode, uses a call interface to invoke network functions. The network operating system software provides these functions in DLLs. When creating your executable file, the linker inserts in the DLLs references to these functions. To insert these references, the linker uses information in your DEF file and import libraries.

Although a DOS or Windows program uses callback functions to let IPX or NetBIOS notify the program that a network event has completed, an OS/2 program uses semaphores. The OS/2 program creates the semaphore, uses it in the call to the network service, and waits on the semaphore. When the network event completes, the network software clears the semaphore and the OS/2 program resumes execution. In other respects, using IPX or NetBIOS from within an OS/2 program is much like using these network services from within a DOS program.

To write an OS/2 program that uses network functions (beyond simple file sharing), you definitely need an SDK. The functions that you invoke are available from the DLL files included in your OS/2-based workstation's network software. The SDK, however, provides the import libraries and header files that you need when you compile and link your program.

Writing LAN Software in Different Computer Languages

If you're accustomed to writing assembler software, you'll be right at home with the services that the network provides. The fundamental interface to the network in both the DOS and Windows environments consists of putting certain values in the CPU registers and performing a software interrupt. Within the OS/2 environment, you perform a far call to a function in a DLL. Assembler programmers can easily construct code that invokes these network services.

For any other language besides assembler, you must discover the extent to which your language enables you to either set up CPU registers and perform software interrupts or, for OS/2, call system functions from within your program.

C and C++ programmers who want to develop DOS or Windows software can take advantage of the int86x() function mentioned earlier in this chapter. This function enables C and C++ programmers to set registers and invoke a software interrupt. In addition to offering the int86x() function, the Borland C/C++ compiler for DOS and Windows also offers direct access to CPU registers and a geninterrupt() function that enables you to invoke a software interrupt without making a library call.

Furthermore, for OS/2 in general and for the SDKs offered by Novell in particular, the calling interface to the network services is one natural to the C language. Novell and IBM can supply you with C header files and import libraries that fit right into a C language development environment.

If you work in C++, you can even create your own objects for the network services that you invoke. As you code the methods within your objects, you must be careful to adhere to the memory and CPU allocation guidelines mentioned earlier. For example, to ensure that your program operates correctly, you may have to page-lock some of your private data in Windows fixed memory.

Pascal programmers can also set CPU registers and invoke software interrupts. For instance, Turbo Pascal offers the MsDos() procedure, which issues Interrupt 21h, and the Intr() procedure, which you can use to issue other interrupts. Turbo Pascal programmers can also write inline assembler statements that invoke network services. If you're a Pascal programmer, however, you need to understand enough assembler or C to translate the calling conventions for a particular network service into a form that you can easily code in your program.

Similarly, most BASIC compilers and BASIC development environments supply programmers with intermediate subprograms (in library or DLL form) that you can use to set CPU registers and invoke network services. BASIC programmers can adopt the same approach as Pascal programmers to translate the calling conventions into a form that they can use in their programs. Unfortunately, BASIC compilers don't offer an easy way to code a callback function that network software can invoke when a particular event occurs. In fact, many BASIC or similar-to-BASIC development environments (such as Visual Basic for Windows, PowerBuilder, and ObjectView) do not compile BASIC statements into executable machine code; instead, they provide an interpreter program that uses a tokenized version of the BASIC program to know what processing to perform at run-time. To produce IPX-aware or NetBIOS-aware computer programs, BASIC programmers usually must use C or assembler to develop static library or DLL functions that their BASIC programs can use.

Types of Networks

Local area networks come in two basic flavors: collision-sensing and token-passing. Ethernet is an example of a collision-sensing network, and Token Ring is an example of a token-passing network.

In the collision-sensing environment, often abbreviated as CSMA/CD (carrier sense, multiple access, with collision detection), the network adapter card listens to the network when it has a frame to send. If the adapter card hears that another card is sending a frame at that moment, it waits for a little while and tries again. Even with this approach, collisions (two workstations attempting to transmit at exactly the same moment) can and do happen. CSMA/CD networks expect collisions and handle them by retransmitting frames as necessary. The adapter card automatically handles these retransmissions, which are transparent to the user and usually occur in less than a microsecond. Although many people blame poor CSMA/CD network performance on the number of network users who are currently sending and receiving messages, over 90 percent of transmission problems on an Ethernet network are caused by faulty cables or malfunctioning adapter cards.

Data is broadcast throughout an Ethernet network in all directions, at the rate of 10 megabits per second. All machines receive every frame, but only those intended to receive a frame (by virtue of the frame's destination network address) respond with an acknowledgment. Figure 1.3 is a diagram of an Ethernet network.

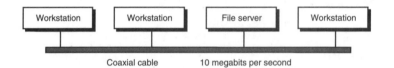

Fig. 1.3
An Ethernet network.

A token-passing network, on the other hand, can logically be viewed as a ring. This is true even though the network may be wired electrically as a star, because data (frames) move around the network from workstation to workstation (see fig. 1.4). Each network adapter card regenerates the signal from its "upstream neighbor" and passes the result along to the next workstation.

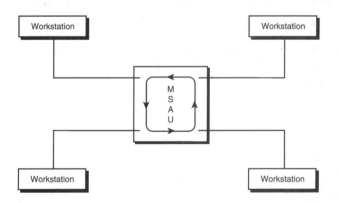

Fig. 1.4
A Token Ring network.

A token is a special type of frame. It contains no message data, but is circulated continuously around the ring during idle periods. When it wants to send a frame, a workstation waits for the token and, if the token is currently free (no one else is transmitting at this moment), the adapter card marks the token "in use" and transmits the frame to the next downstream workstation. The frame passes from adapter to adapter until it eventually reaches its destination, which acknowledges the frame's reception. On receiving an acknowledgment frame that contains its own network address, the sending station relinquishes the token by recirculating a free token. A token-passing network is designed so that collisions never occur on it.

IBM offers Token Ring running at either 4 or 16 megabits per second. Several third-party companies make equipment compatible with IBM Token Ring, including the following:

Gateway Communications
3Com Corporation
General Instrument
Harris Data Communications
Madge Networks
NCR
Proteon
Pure Data
Racore
RAD Data Communications
Siecor
Standard Microsystems
Thomas Conrad
Ungermann-Bass

Some of these companies (such as Proteon and Siecor) make Token Ring hardware that operates at different rates or that uses fiber optics.

Digital Equipment Corporation and 3Com Corporation are major suppliers of Ethernet hardware. Other companies that offer Ethernet equipment include the following:

AST Research, Inc.
Data General
Excelan
Gateway Communications
Intel
Micom-Interlan
Proteon
RAD Data Communications

Ungermann-Bass
Western Digital
Zenith Electronics Corporation

These lists are neither exhaustive nor endorsements. However, they should help you start your research into LAN hardware if you're planning to put together your own LAN.

The Institute of Electrical and Electronic Engineers (IEEE) has defined and documented a set of standards for the physical characteristics of both collision-sensing networks and token-passing networks. These standards are IEEE 802.3 (Ethernet) and 802.5 (Token Ring). Be aware, though, that the frame definitions for "true Ethernet" and "true IEEE 802.3" differ slightly, and that IBM's 16-megabit-per-second Token Ring adapter card is an "802.5 Token Ring Extension." Chapter 3, "PC-to-PC Communication Concepts," defines and describes the layout for these low-level frames.

Of course, some LANs do not conform to either IEEE 802.3 or IEEE 802.5. The most popular of these is Arcnet (which is available from Datapoint Corporation, Standard Microsystems, and Thomas-Conrad); others include the following:

StarLan (AT&T)
VistaLan (Allen-Bradley)
LanTastic (Artisoft)
Omninet (Corvus)
PC Net (IBM)
ProNet (Proteon)

In addition, there is an emerging physical standard called Fiber Distributed Data Interface (FDDI), which uses fiber-optic cable and a token-passing scheme that differs subtly from IEEE 802.5 to transmit data at 100 megabits per second.

The Components of a LAN

Basic LAN hardware components consist of network adapter cards, cables, and access units/repeaters. Depending on the complexity and nature of the network, you may also encounter such components as bridges, routers, concentrators, baluns, hubs, and transceivers. You don't need to understand these items to conceptualize a LAN for programming. One other component—the file server—is discussed later in this chapter.

Diskless Workstations

Imagine a PC that consists of just a keyboard, network adapter, and a monitor—but no floppy drive or hard disk. You turn this PC on and it attaches itself immediately to the network. Also, this PC is fairly inexpensive. Sounds like a great way to save money on LAN workstations, doesn't it?

Don't be fooled; it isn't. A diskless workstation must rely completely on the file server's hard disk, and it therefore increases network message traffic. Furthermore, such a workstation is a single-purpose computer that you cannot upgrade later. You will not be able to run OS/2 on it, or use it as a stand-alone computer.

Although diskless workstations don't save money in the long run, there is a reason for using them: security. If you have a LAN environment in which you need to prevent users from copying files to disk and transporting them, diskless workstations can give you just the security you need.

Network Adapter Cards

As mentioned before, network adapter cards can be either collision-sensing or token-passing. Both kinds of adapters contain enough onboard logic to know when it is okay to send a frame and to recognize frames that are intended for them. With the adapter support software, both types of cards perform seven major steps during the process of sending or receiving a frame. When data is being sent, the steps are performed in the following order; when data is being received, however, the steps are reversed:

1. *Data transfer.* Data is transferred from PC memory to the adapter card or from the adapter card to PC memory by DMA (direct memory access), shared memory, or programmed I/O.

2. *Buffering.* While the network adapter card is processing it, data is held in a buffer. The buffer gives the card access to an entire frame at once, and lets the card manage the difference between the data rate of the network and the rate at which the PC can process data.

3. *Frame formation.* The network adapter must break up the data (or, on reception, reassemble it) into manageable chunks. On an Ethernet network, these chunks are up to 1.5K; Token Ring networks can transmit frames up to about 4K (for 4 mbps rings) or 17K (for 16 mbps rings). Most networks use a size between 1K and 4K. A frame header is prefixed to the data packet; a frame trailer is suffixed to it. At this point, a complete, ready-for-transmission frame has been created. (On reception, the header and trailer are removed at this stage.)

4. *Cable access.* In a CSMA/CD network such as Ethernet, the network adapter ensures that the line is quiet before sending its data. In a token-passing network, the adapter waits until it gets a free token that it can grab and claim. (Cable access is irrelevant to message reception.)

5. *Parallel and serial conversion.* The bytes of data in the buffer are sent or received through the cables in serial fashion, with one bit following the next. The adapter card does this conversion in the split second before transmission (or after reception).

6. *Encoding and decoding.* The electrical signals that represent the data being sent or received are formed. Most network adapters use Manchester encoding, a technique that has the advantage of incorporating timing information into the data by using *bit periods.* Instead of representing a 0 as the absence of electricity and a 1 as its presence, the 0s and 1s are represented by changes in polarity as they occur in relation to very small time periods.

7. *Sending and receiving impulses.* The electrically encoded impulses making up the data (frame) are amplified and sent through the wire. (On reception, the impulses are sent to the decoding step.)

Of course, the execution of all these steps takes only a fraction of a second; as you read about these steps, thousands of frames could have been sent across a LAN.

Network adapter cards and the support software recognize and handle errors, which occur when electrical interference, a collision (in CSMA/CD networks), or malfunctioning equipment corrupts some portion of a frame. Errors are usually detected by a Cyclic Redundancy Checksum (CRC) data item in the frame. The receiver checks the CRC; if the receiver's own calculated CRC doesn't match the value of the one in the frame, the receiver "NAKs the frame," which means that it requests retransmission of the frame in error. If you suspect a malfunctioning adapter card or cable on your LAN, several vendors offer products that perform diagnostic and analytic functions on the different types of LANs.

The different types of network adapters vary not only in access method and protocol but also in the following:

- Transmission speed

- Amount of onboard memory for buffering frames and data

- Bus design (8-bit, 16-bit, or MicroChannel)

- Bus speed (some adapters fail when run at high speed)

- Compatibility with various CPU chipsets

- DMA usage

- IRQ and I/O port addressing

- Intelligence (some adapters use an onboard CPU such as the 80186)

- Connector design

Cabling Systems

At this point, you might imagine that cabling systems for LANs vary widely in their appearance, characteristics, intended purpose, and cost. You're right, as the following discussion explains. The three most popular ways to tie computers together on a LAN are the following:

- The IBM Cabling System

- The AT&T Premises Distribution System

- The DEC cabling concept called DECconnect

The cable systems discussed in this section can be categorized into three distinct cable types:

- Twisted pair (shielded and unshielded)

- Coaxial cable (thin and thick)

- Fiber-optic cable

Twisted pair is just what its name implies: insulated wires with a minimum number of twists per foot. Twisting the wires reduces electrical interference (attenuation). "Shielded" refers to the amount of insulation around the wire and therefore its noise immunity. You're probably already familiar with unshielded twisted pair, because it is often used by the phone company. *Shielded* twisted pair, however, looks entirely different, somewhat resembling the wire used to carry "house current" (110 volts) throughout your home or apartment. But appearances are deceiving, because shielded twisted pair actually carries a relatively low voltage signal; the heavy insulation is for noise reduction, not safety.

Coaxial cable is fairly prevalent in our everyday lives; you often find it connected to the backs of television sets and audio equipment. "Thin" and "thick," of course, refer to the diameter of the coaxial cable. Standard

Ethernet cable (thick Ethernet) is as thick as your thumb. The newer Thinnet cable is about the size of your little finger. The thick cable offers greater noise immunity and is more difficult to damage. To connect thick cable to a LAN, you need a vampire tap (a piercing connector) and a drop cable. Although it carries the signal over shorter distances than the thick cable, Thinnet uses a simple BNC connector, is less expensive, and has become a standard in office coaxial cable.

Finally, fiber-optic cable, as its name suggests, uses light rather than electricity to carry information. Although it can send data farther and faster, fiber-optic cable is expensive and is difficult to install and maintain. Splicing the cable, installing connectors, and using the few available diagnostic tools for finding cable faults are skills that few people have. Fiber-optic cable is simply designed, but unforgiving of bad connections. It consists of a hollow core fiber whose diameter is measured in microns, surrounded by a solid cladding, which in turn is covered by a protective sheath. The first fiber-optic cables were made of glass, but plastic fibers have also been developed. The light source for fiber-optic cable is a *light-emitting diode* (LED); information usually is encoded by varying the intensity of the light. A detector at the other end of the cable converts the received signal back into electrical im-pulses. There are two types of fiber: single mode and multimode. Single mode has a smaller diameter, is more expensive, and can carry signals farther.

IBM Cabling System. The IBM Cabling System, oddly enough, is not manufactured or sold by IBM. Rather, the system consists of a published standard for building wiring systems that defines cabling system components and different cable types. When introducing the IBM Cabling System in 1984, IBM described the system as the intended backbone for its Token Ring Network. The first such cables to be manufactured by third-party companies were tested by IBM itself, verified to IBM specifications, and actually given IBM part numbers. Now, however, cable manufacturers must rely on the independent testing laboratories ETL or UL, or industry-standard manufactur-ers like AMP, to verify compliance with the specifications published by IBM.

The IBM specification defines workstation faceplates, adapters and connec-tors, access units, wiring closet termination methods, and the following cable types:

- Type 1—*data cable.* Used for data connections only, this copper cable is available in nonplenum, plenum, and outdoor varieties. The cable consists of two twisted pairs of 22-gauge solid conductors, shielded with both foil and braid, and covered with a polyvinyl-chloride (PVC) sheath. This cable type is used for connecting terminal devices located in work areas to distribution panels located in wiring closets, and for connecting between wiring closets. The plenum cable is installed in air ducts and other spaces used for environmental air; in case of fire, this cable type emits less-toxic fumes than the nonplenum cable. The outdoor cable is protected in a corrugated metallic shield with a polyethylene sheath, and the core is filled with a jellylike compound to keep out moisture.

- Type 2—*data and telephone cable.* Used for both data and voice (telephone) applications, Type 2 is similar to Type 1, but has four additional twisted pairs (22-gauge). Type 2 cable comes in plenum and nonplenum varieties.

- Type 3—*telephone twisted pair cable.* Consisting of four-pair 24-gauge wire in polyvinyl-chloride plastic, Type 3 wire is equivalent to the IBM Rolm specification and available in plenum. The cable is unshielded and not as immune to noise (when used for data) as Type 1 cable.

- Type 5—*fiber-optic cable.* This cable contains two 100/140-micron (100-micron core surrounded by 140-micron cladding layer) multimode optical fibers.

- Type 6—*patch panel cable.* This cable is used for connecting a workstation to a wall faceplate or making connections within a wiring closet. Type 6 is more flexible than Type 1 cable (hence its use as patch cable). It consists of two twisted pairs of 26-gauge stranded conductors.

- Type 8—*undercarpet cable.* An undercarpet cable useful for open office or workstation areas where there are no permanent walls, Type 8 consists of two pairs of 26-gauge solid conductors in a flat sheath.

- Type 9—*low-cost plenum cable.* An economy version of Type 1 plenum cable, Type 9 can transmit only about two-thirds the distance that Type 1 can. This cable consists of two twisted pairs of 26-gauge stranded conductors.

(Types 4 and 7 are not defined by IBM.)

AT&T Premises Distribution System. The AT&T Premises Distribution System is similar in many ways to the IBM Cabling System, but relies much more heavily on unshielded telephone twisted pair. It also integrates voice and data wiring. Connections are based on modular jacks and plugs and the cross-connect techniques originally designed for voice PBX to telephone-set wiring, which use multipair cable. PDS expands on the extensive base of this type of cable, which is already installed in many office buildings. The AT&T

PDS parts usually cost less than those of the IBM system, but installation is more labor intensive.

DECconnect. The DECconnect cabling concept is based on the use of 50-ohm thin coaxial cable (Thinnet), which is commonly used in Ethernet networks. The DECconnect system has standardized much of the connecting hardware used in major DEC installations of VAX systems. DECconnect also defines a line of protocol converters, line drivers, and "satellite closet" rack and termination hardware. A DECconnect system consists of an Ethernet backbone (a central cable to which all other cables connect) wired through-out a building, with taps (connection points) provided at VAX computer sites and the satellite closets. The system provides for the connection of Thinnet cables and other data lines to the Ethernet backbone at the closet.

Access Units and Repeaters

In a token-passing network, the cables from the workstations (or from the wall faceplates) are centrally connected to a Multi-Station Access Unit (MSAU, or MAU). The MSAU keeps track of which workstations on the LAN are neigh-bors and which neighbor is upstream or downstream. This is an easy job; you usually don't even have to plug the MSAU into an electrical power outlet. The exception to this is an MSAU that provides for longer cable distances or the use of unshielded twisted pair (Type 3) cable in high-speed LANs. In ei-ther case, the externally powered MSAU helps the signal along by regenerat-ing it.

An MSAU has eight ports for connecting one to eight Token Ring devices. Each connection is made with a "genderless" Data Connector (as specified in the IBM Cabling System). The MSAU has two additional ports labeled RI (Ring-In) and RO (Ring-Out) that are used to link several MSAUs together (in a daisy-chain) when you have more than eight workstations on the LAN.

It takes several seconds to open the adapter connection on a Token Ring LAN (something that you may have noticed). During this time, the MSAU and your Token Ring adapter card perform a small diagnostic check, after which the MSAU establishes you as a new neighbor on the ring. After being estab-lished as an active workstation, your computer is linked on both sides to your neighbors (as defined by your position on the MSAU). In its turn, your Token Ring adapter card accepts the token, regenerates it, and gives it a swift kick to send it through the MSAU in the direction of your downstream neighbor.

In an Ethernet network, the number of connections (taps) and their interven-ing distances are limiting factors. Repeaters are used to regenerate the signal every 500 meters or so. If these repeaters were not used, "standing waves" (additive reflections) would distort the signal and cause errors. Because collision detection depends partly on timing, only five 500-meter segments and four repeaters can be placed in series before the propagation delay becomes longer than the maximum allowed time period for detecting a collision— otherwise, the workstations farthest from the sender could not detect any collisions. Computer systems designers, who usually hate limitations, made it possible to create Ethernet networks in star, branch, and tree designs that overcome these basic limitations. Thousands of workstations are possible on a complex Ethernet network.

In general, the limits on distances and numbers of workstations specified in both IEEE 802.3 Ethernet and IEEE 802.5 Token Ring are being overcome through the technologies of optical fiber, intelligent fast-acting repeaters, active bridges, routers, hubs, and gateways.

File Servers

You need a place to store the files that you want to share among the PCs. You can turn one of the PCs into a file server, or use a different kind of computer as the server. Either way, your server must provide the following:

■ Fast access to the files

■ Capacity to hold files and records for many users

■ Security for the files

■ Reliability

If you choose a computer other than a PC for your file server, you also must verify that the machine can be connected to the LAN and function as a file server.

On the other hand, if you use a PC as a file server, you should choose a PC that is faster and has larger, faster disks than its brothers and sisters. Why do you need the file server to be a faster computer if the software applications run on each of the individual PCs on the LAN and not some central machine? During busy periods, the server receives many requests for disk files and records; it takes a certain amount CPU effort as well as disk rotation and access time to respond to each request. You want the requests to be serviced quickly so that each user has the impression that he or she is the only one using the file server at that moment.

File Server Hard Disks. The access speed and capacity of a server's hard disk are the most important criteria for a file server. The most common bottleneck in the average LAN is disk I/O time at the file server. And the most common complaint of LAN users is that the file server has run out of free disk space.

Several factors determine the disk access speed, including the following:

- The recording method (MFM, RLL, ESDI, IDE, or SCSI)

- The type and onboard intelligence of the controller

- The type of hard disk (stepper band or voice coil)

- The interleave factor

- The location of the files on the disk (location affects how far the Read-Write head must move to get to the file)

Disk access speed is measured by two variables: data transfer rate and average seek time. The *data transfer rate* is the number of bytes of data that the hard disk or controller can deliver to the computer in one second. The *average seek time* is the time that it takes the disk to move the Read-Write head a small distance and then wait about a half-revolution of the disk platter for a given sector to appear under the head. The type of disk that IBM installed as standard equipment in the IBM PC/AT computer gives a data transfer rate of about 180K per second and an average seek time of 40 milliseconds. Third-party disks from companies like Core, Maxtor (Storage Dimensions), Connor, Seagate, Fujitsu, and Western Digital are faster, with average seek times in the 5- to 20-millisecond range. IBM offers speedy drives in the current crop of high-end PS/2 machines.

Disk capacity tends to go hand in hand with speed; the larger drives are also the faster drives. The designers of 600 to 2,200M (2.2 gigabyte) drives are obviously thinking "file server!" as they engineer their latest, technologically advanced products. However, some of these huge beasts cost as much as the computer in which you install them. So how much space do you need on *your* file server? How many drives should you buy, and how many file servers will you need? A significant factor is that you are limited in the number of drives that can be installed in a given file server machine. (SCSI drives are less limited in this respect; they can accommodate as many as seven devices on a disk controller.) A related consideration: it's usually better to have several medium-sized disks in multiple servers than one huge disk in one server, because you then have more Read-Write heads, more controllers, and more CPUs responding to user requests for files. This is only a general observation, of course; your situation may differ.

Optical disks are another alternative for file servers. They use light to store data, or sometimes a combination of light and magnetism. With the proper software drivers, optical disks can be made to behave just like any other file server drive. These disks are extremely durable and reliable. Until recently, optical disks had two major drawbacks that kept them from being more popular: they tended to have slower access times than magnetic disks and could not erase files. (These are "Write Once, Read Many" WORM drives.) However, companies such as IBM and Storage Dimensions have overcome these shortcomings and now offer rewritable optical disks that are network-compatible.

File Server CPU, Memory, and Network Adapters. After capacity and access speed, the other considerations for the file server are CPU speed, amount of memory, network adapter speed, and dedicated versus nondedicated use.

Unless a LAN will have very few users and will never grow (that's hard to imagine!), a file server with an 80486 or Pentium CPU and with plenty of memory is a wise investment. You can realize significant performance gains with a faster CPU and ample RAM, which make possible something called *caching*. With sufficient memory installed, the file server can "remember" those portions of the hard disk that it previously accessed and send these to the next user without actually having to access the hard disk for that subsequent user. Because it can avoid going to the hard disk, the file server can do its job quicker.

One of the characteristics of network adapter cards mentioned earlier in this chapter is buffer size. Some adapter cards have bigger buffers than others, and thus can hold more frames at one time. Such cards are ideal candidates for installation in a file server, which can be thought of as the Grand Central Station for message frames.

You can often set up a file server so that it can be used as a workstation while acting as a file server. You should avoid using such *nondedicated* file servers, however, because if a user is running an application at the server and the software crashes, the entire network will crash with it. Also, although not a common practice (especially in larger LANs), some networks are designed so that *every* workstation's hard drive can be accessed by the other workstations on the network. Conceptually, though, every workstation is a file server, and vice versa.

Network Support Software

You have covered a lot of ground so far. Take a moment to review what you would have if you had been building a LAN as you read. You chose an access method—collision-sensing or token-passing—and installed the proper network adapter cards in several PCs. You also connected the PCs together with the appropriate cabling. If you needed additional support hardware, you obtained and installed it. You designated one or more of the PCs as a file server and ensured that it is sufficient for your needs.

What can you do with the LAN you have assembled so far? Absolutely nothing.

To enable the computers to talk to one another, you must add network software. Of course, the software that you use must be compatible with the hardware that you have acquired. (You can imagine the talk you would have with your boss if you bought Ethernet hardware and Token Ring LAN Support software—not to mention the troubleshooting you would have to do to make it work!)

The network support software must

- Provide access to the network adapter card

- Enable PC-to-PC communications

- Emulate DOS (or OS/2) so that the file server's disks are available to the applications running on the workstations

PC-to-PC Communications

Many vendors have created their own proprietary protocols for peer-level communications on LANs. Although most vendors have endorsed the standard created by the International Standards Organization (ISO), called the *Open System Interconnection (OSI) Model*, this standard hasn't yet been fully implemented. The seven layers of the OSI Model are explained in Chapter 3, "PC-to-PC Communication Concepts," as are the internal formats and conventions used in some of the more popular vendor-created protocols.

Regardless of how each particular vendor's protocol is designed, certain basic functions and features are common:

- *Initiating communications.* Each protocol provides the means to identify a workstation by name, by number, or both. This identification scheme is made available to both the shell/redirector layer and to an application. Point-to-point communications are activated by one workstation identifying a destination workstation (often a file server) with which it wants to carry on a dialog. The originating workstation also designates the type of dialog: a *datagram*, in which frames are addressed and sent to the destination without guarantee or verification of reception, or *session*, in which a connection (or "pipe") is established with the delivery of message data guaranteed.

■ *Sending and receiving data.* Each protocol provides the means for originating and destination workstations to send and receive message data. A protocol-specific limit on the length of a given message is imposed, and each participant in a session-type dialog is given the means to determine the status of the dialog. For example, a workstation may inadvertently power down in the midst of a dialog—perhaps someone kicked the power cord—and the other participants are notified that an error has occurred.

■ *Terminating communications.* The protocol provides the means for the participants to end a dialog gracefully.

DOS Redirection and Emulation

As stated earlier, redirection of DOS function calls makes file sharing possible. An application running on a workstation goes through the motions of asking DOS for some part of a disk file, but the network software intercepts the request and sends it to the file server. The file server does the actual disk I/O to obtain that part of the disk file and returns the result to the workstation. The network software on the workstation hands the disk file contents to the application, and in doing so makes it look as though the local copy of DOS had been the one to obtain the file contents.

To send the request to the server and get back the response, the network software performs several steps.

The first thing the network software does is determine whether it should handle a DOS File Read request or pass the request to DOS. The software does this by noting at File Open or File Creation time whether a network drive letter is in effect for the Open or Create call. The network software maintains an internal table of which drives are network devices, so it is fairly easy for it to determine whether an Open or a Create applies to a network drive. As the file is opened or created, the network software assigns a file handle (just as DOS would have done) or, if the old-style File Control Blocks (FCBs) are being used, it remembers the address of the FCB. When a File Read call occurs, the network software examines the file handle or FCB address to determine whether the request should be shunted across the network to the file server or passed along for DOS to handle.

Suppose that the network software detects that the File Read request is for a file on the file server. The software puts the contents of the appropriate CPU registers into a control block. The format and size of this control block varies among the different vendors' protocols, but its basic purpose, to request some file material from the file server, is the same for all protocols. The shell/redirector then passes this control block to a PC-to-PC communications program or module running on the workstation so that the network adapter card can turn the block into one or more frames, which in turn are transmitted to the server.

At the server, the network adapter card and its supporting software process the frames back into a File Read request. If the server is currently processing another user's request (a common occurrence on a busy LAN), the File Read request is queued for scant-moments-later handling. In its turn, the request is processed by the File Service portion of the network software running on the server; the desired sectors of the file are found in the server's cache memory or, if not in memory, accessed directly from the server's hard disk.

During the I/O operation, the file server encounters one of three typical situations for a disk-read: the requested bytes are read, the end-of-file is detected, or only some of the requested bytes are read (this happens if more bytes are requested than actually exist). The file server creates a control block that contains an indication of which of these three situations was encountered, appends the file data (if any) to the control block, and then hands the result to the network support software to be transmitted back to the appropriate workstation.

After receiving the response from the file server, the workstation reverses the steps that it took to send the File Read request. The network adapter processes the frames that contain the response, the frame headers and frame trailers are removed, and the shell/redirector emulates DOS by putting the file data into the application's buffer, setting the CPU registers to indicate the number of bytes actually read, and returning to the application at the next instruction after the DOS function call.

Vendor-Specific Protocols

Someday, perhaps, the OSI Model will be the only protocol that the different LAN manufacturers use. Until that day, you face a kaleidoscope of proprietary protocols from IBM (NetBIOS and APPC), Novell (IPX/SPX), DEC, AT&T, Sun (NFS), Apple (Appletalk/AFP), and other companies. The Department of

Defense developed another protocol, TCP/IP, for use over large networks. This protocol is popular for tying together networks from diverse vendors.

IBM sells several software products that implement IBM's LAN protocols. DOS-based products include the LAN Support Program, PC LAN Program, DOS LAN Requester, and Advanced Program-to-Program Communications (APPC). OS/2 LAN Server, a complete network operating system environment, turns an OS/2-based PC into a file server. Novell currently offers NetWare 2.2, NetWare 3.12, NetWare 4.0, and Novell's own APPC product, NetWare for SAA.

Not only are the protocols from IBM and Novell the most popular, they also represent fundamentally different approaches to managing communications on a LAN. In general, IBM's network products use the NetBIOS programming interface, which sends and receives frames using either the NetBEUI (NetBIOS Extended User Interface) protocol or the TCP/IP protocol, while Novell's network products use the IPX protocol. IBM's LU 6.2 APPC protocol is an easy-to-program message-passing protocol that you might select for a client/server application. Remote Procedure Calls (RPC) provide a high-level approach to client/server computing. Finally, some network products from various companies use the public domain TCP/IP protocol. The next few sections of this chapter look at these protocols and architectures.

IPX and SPX

Novell NetWare workstations and file servers use the Internetwork Packet Exchange (IPX) protocol to send and receive LAN messages. IPX, the underlying protocol used by Novell NetWare's file redirection modules, is an adaptation of a protocol developed by Xerox Corporation called XNS (Xerox Network Standard). The protocol supports only datagram messages (it is said to be connectionless). IPX corresponds to the network layer of the OSI Model, performing addressing, routing, and switching to deliver a message (packet) to its destination. IPX is speedier than the session-oriented SPX protocol. Although delivery is not guaranteed, IPX packets are correctly received about 95 percent of the time.

The Sequenced Packet Exchange (SPX) is a session-level, connection-oriented protocol. Before SPX packets are sent or received, a connection must be established between the two sides that want to exchange information. After this connection is established, messages within a session can be sent in either direction, and delivery is guaranteed. SPX also guarantees that packets arrive in the correct order (if multiple packets are sent at once). Novell NetWare uses IPX to send and receive file service packets, but NetWare uses SPX to allow access to its internal diagnostic and network management functions. You learn more about IPX and SPX in Chapter 3, "PC-to-PC Communications Concepts."

APPC—Advanced Program-to-Program Communications (LU 6.2)

APPC is an IBM-designed programmatic interface that fundamentally changes the way that PCs communicate with larger computers. This interface replaces the technique of talking to a host computer through a terminal emulator with a technique that is conversation (peer-to-peer) based. IBM designed APPC to be a programmer's view of the Systems Network Architecture (SNA) standard LU 6.2. Before LU 6.2, PC and mainframe communications were accomplished by loading a terminal emulator program on the PC and forcing the emulator to pretend that each byte of data being sent was a keypress from the keyboard. Similarly, receiving data from the mainframe involved intercepting 3270 screen data before it reached the terminal emulator screen. The technique was workable, but primitive.

APPC, on the other hand, assumes that two *computers* are talking to each other; both sides of the conversation can be "smart." APPC dispenses with 3270 keypress and screen-at-a-time transmissions, and instead provides that only the LU 6.2 verbs and raw data move through the communications link.

Because of the peer-to-peer nature of LU 6.2 (accessed through APPC), it can be used as the basis for communications between workstations on a LAN as well as between a workstation and a mainframe (in fact, it can be used between any two computers on an SNA network). Application programs are unaware that the communications medium is Token Ring, an SDLC mainframe link, or even a direct computer-to-computer link.

Under LU 6.2, two types of conversations are possible: basic conversations and mapped conversations. With *mapped* conversations, the protocol converts the data into a standard *generalized data stream* for sending and converting the data back into its original form on reception. With *basic* conversations, the application must handle any necessary conversions. Programs that use basic conversations also have some responsibility for recovering errors.

LU 6.2 implements a set of verbs. Think of these as a programming language for developing the communications capabilities of an application. Each verb is a specifically formatted record with a particular purpose. The major verbs are the following:

- ALLOCATE initiates a conversation with a remote application. Parameters include the following:

  > LU_NAME, which gives the name of the logical unit that represents the remote program

  > TPN, which gives the name of the remote program

  > MODE_NAME, which specifies session properties for the conversation

  > SYNC_LEVEL, which specifies a synchronization level between the two conversants

- GET_ATTRIBUTES returns information about the conversation, such as the mode name, partner LU name, and synchronization level.

- DEALLOCATE terminates a conversation.

- CONFIRM asks the remote computer to confirm that the data was successfully received.

- CONFIRMED is the reply sent in response to a CONFIRM verb.

- SEND_DATA causes data to be sent.

- RECEIVE_AND_WAIT notifies a remote application that it is okay to send data. The issuer of RECEIVE_AND_WAIT then waits for a response.

You can see from this description of APPC and LU 6.2 that these tools are powerful. They also have some disadvantages, however. The PC implementation of APPC occupies a sizable chunk of memory (a resident program that offers a subset of APPC can be as small as 70K to 80K; full APPC takes a little less than 200K of resident code) and, under DOS, this is a big concern. Under OS/2, however, such memory constraints are not a consideration. IBM's Communications Manager/2 (CM/2) product includes an APPC implementation that makes it easy for OS/2-based PCs to send and receive information in the form of message records that flow through LAN cables or other physical media.

TCP/IP—Transmission Control Protocol/Internet Protocol

The Department of Defense designed TCP/IP for ARPANET, a geographically large network (not a LAN) that connects the various sites of the DoD Advanced Research Projects Agency. TCP/IP is a layer of protocols, not a LAN operating system. The Internet Protocol (IP) provides datagram communications between nodes on a network (like Novell's IPX does); the Transmission Control Protocol (TCP) is like NetBIOS in that it provides point-to-point, guaranteed-delivery communications between nodes. TCP/IP usually comes with a set of fairly standard utilities designed to work with TCP/IP. These utilities transfer files (FTP), do simple remote program execution (TELNET), and send electronic mail (SMTP). The set of utilities is not a DOS shell/ redirector, and the remote computer is not a file server. To create a file- and printer-sharing environment on top of TCP/IP, you need a product such as Sun Microsystems' NFS (Network File System).

Because TCP/IP is a public, not proprietary, protocol, it has become extremely popular as the basis for interconnecting LANs from different vendors. However, the popularity is bound to wane, because the federal government decreed that after August 1990 all major computer and network acquisitions must comply with the Government OSI Profile (GOSIP), and proposed that OSI protocols replace TCP/IP products by the late 1990s. Yet several years after the government ban, government agencies continue to purchase TCP/IP-based products.

RPC—Remote Procedure Calls

RPC enables programmers to treat a heterogeneous network of computers as though it were one big computer. With RPC, each part of an application can be targeted for the kind of computer that best suits that part. RPC is sometimes the tool of choice for building client/server systems.

What does a programmer have to do to use RPC? He or she codes each module in C, as usual, and designates each program module as either a server or a client. Server modules typically are the back-end of the application (calculations, report generation, and storage of permanent database records), and client modules manage the front-end user interface. The programmer creates an RPC compiler script that identifies the server and client modules. He or she then runs the RPC compiler to generate the C source code that ties the modules together as if they were one executable program. The generated code creates a communication session between the client and server modules on the different computers. To the programmer, though, the server modules are called in the same way as any other subroutines that the client code calls. The fact that the client and server modules execute on different computers becomes invisible to the application.

When an application makes a subroutine call to a program module on a different computer, the RPC-generated code creates a new communications session between the computers or uses an existing session. The subroutine call becomes a Send operation and, on completion, a Receive operation.

The generated program code for each subroutine call is a stub with the same name as the remote subroutine. The stub manages the communications session with the actual code module on the remote computer. RPC itself consists of a network-specific library of LAN communication services and the RPC compiler for generating the C language communications code.

The following is an example of an RPC in action:

```
/* CLIENT MODULE  */
struct  DATA_REC data_record;
main ()
    {
    gather_input();
    calc_results(&data_record);
    }


/* CLIENT STUB*/
calc_results();


/* SERVER MODULE  (actual subroutine) */
calc_results(struct DATA_REC *data_record)
      {
data_record->result = 5;
      }
```

When calling the `calc_results()` subroutine, the computer program running on the client actually is invoking a local stub routine written by the RPC compiler. This client stub uses the communications session with the server stub to invoke the real `calc_results()` routine on the remote server computer. Data, in the form of passed parameters or global data items residing in the client, are sent to the server computer to be processed by the real (server) `calc_results()` module. After the remote routine finishes, results are sent back to the originating computer. The data is made to look as if the local machine had executed the module.

Distributed client/server processing is not a new software technology. Code-named Courier, it was developed by Xerox at the Palo Alto Research Center (PARC) about the same time that Xerox invented windows and mice. Sun Microsystems later created the first commercial instance of RPC on top of its Network File System (NFS). RPC tools are now available from such companies as H/P-Apollo, Sun, Novell, and Netwise. (Novell's RPC is a repackaged version of the Netwise RPC Tool for SPX.)

Different computers represent data differently. RPC handles these internal representations by packing and unpacking the data into *protocol data units*, or PDUs. Once packed, the contents conform to an ISO standard, the Specification of Basic Encoding Rules for Abstract Syntax Notation (ASN.1, ISO 8825).

Byte-flipped machines like the Intel-equipped IBM PC can thus communicate with Apple, DEC, and Sun computers.

Each time that a client stub is called, the stub performs the following tasks:

1. Places the parameters and appropriate external variables into a request PDU

2. Sends the request PDU to the server

3. Waits for the server's response PDU

4. Updates the parameters and external variables with the received values

5. Returns program control to the calling client code

The code running on the server behaves as you would expect: the server receives the request PDU, unpacks the data, calls the appropriate (actual) subroutine, packs the results into the response PDU, and sends the response to the client. The data encapsulated in a PDU can be of any type. Even an item referenced through a pointer is sent or received as an entity, and the pointer relationship is reestablished on the server. Pointers themselves, however, cannot usefully be transferred.

Floating-point numbers are another potential problem. RPC converts floating-point numbers as best it can between different computers, but a less precise server CPU cannot always preserve the exact numeric value of floating-point data across the call.

As you design client/server systems, be careful when passing large data structures or many external variables. Remember that the data must be sent and received between the different computers, and it takes time to transfer the data from one computer's memory space to another's.

Depending on the complexity of your application, you can choose one of three basic server control procedure bindings. *Single-binding* supports one client at a time, and denies other clients access to the server. *Multiple-client binding* also processes only one client request at a time but puts subsequent requests in a queue. *Multitasking* can handle multiple requests from many clients by establishing a separate thread for each.

Why would you ever choose single-binding? You might have multiple server machines and design the client to do a "round-robin" search of available servers to handle a request. Be aware that not all RPC implementations support multitasking; you must use a server computer with an operating system that understands multiple process threads.

It's technically possible to use RPC to transform any application into a client/server system. You don't want to put small, fast-executing routines in a server, though; the time spent in communicating the data back and forth would overwhelm the application and cause it to degrade severely. Calculation-intensive or I/O-intensive routines are good candidates for server modules, if you have computers on your network that are better at handling such tasks.

The next sections of this chapter look at several network products from IBM and Novell.

IBM PC LAN Support Program

A prerequisite for DOS-based Token Ring LANs, the IBM PC LAN Support Program implements the network adapter support software, as well as NetBIOS, in a set of device drivers (.SYS files) that are loaded when the system boots. Typically, three driver files are used. Although memory usage depends on how the drivers are configured, typical memory usage is from 40K to 50K. The file DXMC0MOD.SYS is the layer of adapter support software that talks directly to the IEEE 802.5 chipset on the Token Ring card—and the file DXMT0MOD.SYS is NetBIOS.

NetBIOS accepts communications requests from an application program or from the PC LAN Program (described in the next section). These requests fall into four categories:

- *Name support.* Each workstation on the network is identified by one or more names. NetBIOS maintains these names in a table; the first item in the table is automatically the unique, permanently assigned name of the network adapter. The user can assign to the table optional user names (such as "BARRY") to make it easier to identify each user. These names can be unique, or, in a special case, can refer to a group of workstations.

- *Session support.* A point-to-point connection between two names (work-stations) on the network can be opened, managed, and closed under NetBIOS control. One workstation begins by listening for a call, and the other workstation calls the first. The workstations are peers; both can send and receive message data concurrently during the session. At the end, both workstations hang up on each other.

- *Datagram support.* Message data can be sent to a name, a group of names, or to all names on the network. A point-to-point connection is not established and there is no guarantee that the message data will be received.

■ *Adapter or session status.* Information about the local network adapter card, about other network adapter cards, and about any currently active sessions is available from NetBIOS.

IBM used to offer NetBIOS as a separate program product that was implemented as a terminate-and-stay-resident (TSR) file named NETBEUI.COM. This TSR is now obsolete. If you have an older Token Ring network that uses NETBEUI.COM, you should strongly consider replacing the low-level network support software on each workstation, including NETBEUI.COM, with the later IBM PC LAN Support Program's device drivers.

IBM PC LAN Program

The PC LAN Program is a DOS-shell/redirector that can be configured as a file server, a simple workstation redirector, a receiver, or a messenger. Before you can use this program, NetBIOS must already be running on the workstation. The PC LAN Program creates and uses NetBIOS sessions to transfer file data and messages from workstation to workstation.

When configured as a file server, the PC LAN Program consumes the most memory; as a simple redirector, it consumes the least (about 46K on a workstation). The other configurations, receiver and messenger, are in the middle, enabling users to send small notes back and forth, almost like an electronic mail system. Frankly, no one ever really sets up a workstation as a messenger or receiver. The note-passing facility is simply not worth the extra memory that these configurations consume. (Because you bought this book, you now have a full-featured electronic mail product, so you can safely forget about receivers and messengers.)

The PC LAN Program is flexible. Not only can you set it up to act as a file server or as a simple workstation redirector, you can install it (network-wide) to provide base services or extended services. *Base services* enable users to share resources in a simple manner, without the need for user IDs and passwords. *Extended services* implement the following concepts:

■ The *system administrator* is a user with special privileges on the network. He or she can set up domains, define servers, define remote-IPL machines, assign user IDs, assign passwords, and assign user access levels.

■ A *domain* is a group of network resources (servers, server directories, or printers) and the mapping of users to these resources.

■ The *user ID and password* mechanisms provide user identification and security.

- A *fileset* is a named, shared disk resource (directory) that is part of a domain. Users are allowed Read-Only or Read-Write access to a fileset. A *home fileset* is unique to a user; when a user logs in, information in a user's home fileset is used to create that user's environment.

- A *remote IPL MACHINE* is a workstation whose network adapter contains special program code. This code loads PC DOS and the network support software directly from a file server (the program server) at boot time.

- The *application selector* is a menu-driven, friendly looking program launcher that presents each user with a unique list of applications that he or she runs. Initially the system administrator sets up this list, but the user can maintain it.

Whether base services or extended services are installed, the PC LAN Program manages the sharing of files between workstation and file server in the same manner. The PC LAN Program uses what IBM calls *server message blocks* (SMBs) as a vehicle for shunting DOS function calls across the network. After a NetBIOS session is established between a workstation and a server, SMBs are sent to the file server to request remote DOS services and to send the response from the file server to the workstation. A field in the SMB, SMB_Function, identifies the network request represented by a particular SMB. Usually, each value of SMB_Function corresponds to a different DOS function call. Chapter 3, "PC-to-PC Communciation Concepts," discusses SMBs, including the format of the SMB itself, in greater detail.

IBM LAN Server

While the PC LAN Program is a relatively old network operating system for DOS-based PCs, IBM's LAN Server product enables DOS, OS/2, and even Macintosh computers to share files and printers on the LAN. When installed on a machine that runs OS/2, the LAN Server product turns that machine into a file server. Like the PC LAN Program, LAN Server uses NetBIOS and SMBs to share files and printers.

LAN Server is an excellent environment for client/server computing. It's relatively easy to program an OS/2 computer, even one that is already running as a file server. If you have a staff of programmers, or if the application software that you buy already supports it, client/server architecture becomes a possibility. SQL Server, ORACLE, and DB2/2 are examples of relational database managers that work well on OS/2-based LANs. LAN Server (and its distant cousins, Microsoft's LAN Manager and Windows NT Advanced Server) offer file sharing and printer sharing in an environment that encourages custom programming and efficient use of network resources.

To explain OS/2 fully is beyond the scope of this chapter. If necessary, though, you should read some background material on IBM's newest PC-based operating system. OS/2 is an excellent base for advanced, high-end PC networking. Its multitasking facilities make it a good candidate for distributed processing, it eliminates the memory-crunch problems that LANs so often face, and it is part of IBM's System Application Architecture (SAA) standard.

From a user's perspective, the LAN Server network environment is much like that provided by the PC LAN Program's extended services. The environment includes the concepts of system administrator, domains, and other aspects of extended services. From a programmer's perspective, however, OS/2 LAN Server is altogether different from PC DOS and the PC LAN Program. Besides the usual facilities for file sharing, printer sharing, and PC-to-PC communications through NetBIOS, OS/2 LAN Server offers built-in support for remote program execution and various kinds and levels of interprocess communications, including APPC (discussed earlier) and named pipes.

Named Pipes on OS/2 LANs

A *pipe* is a stream of data between two programs. One program opens the pipe and writes data into it; the other opens the pipe and reads the data from the first program. Sound easy, and simple to program? It is. A *named pipe* is a file whose name has a particular format:

```
\PIPE\path\name.ext
```

OS/2 provides a set of functions for opening, using, and closing named pipes. The application that wants to create the pipe (called the *server*, but don't confuse it with a file server) does so by calling DosMakeNmPipe. The application can then use DosConnectNmPipe to wait until another application (called the *client*) opens the pipe with DosOpen. Both the server and the client can use a simple DosWrite to put data into the pipe or DosRead to get data from the pipe. DosPeekNmPipe can be used to inspect data in the pipe without removing it. Finally, the server can close the pipe and destroy it with DosDisConnectNmPipe.

The programmer can treat named pipes as simple data streams or as message pipes. In the latter case, each call to DosRead fetches one message at a time from the pipe.

Because they do so much work but require a programmer to code only a few simple program statements, named pipes are extremely popular on OS/2 LANs.

LAN Server Characteristics

In LAN Server parlance, a *requester* is the software that enables a workstation to log on to a domain and use network resources. Users have access to the network through the OS/2 LAN Requester program from OS/2 workstations and through the DOS LAN Requester program from DOS workstations. A server can share its files, printers, and even serial devices (such as modems) across the LAN. DOS requesters cannot access a shared modem, but OS/2 requesters can.

During installation, the network administrator specifies a server to be a domain controller or an additional server. Each domain has only one domain controller. A domain is a group of file servers and workstations with similar security needs. You can set up several domains on a large LAN Server network. On a small LAN, a file server can also act as a domain controller. Domains provide a simple way for you to control user access to the network and its resources. A network user can have accounts in multiple domains, but he or she can log on in only one domain at a time. Additional servers cannot be started, and users cannot log on if the domain controller is not running. A LAN can have several domains, each managed separately, but each file server belongs to only one domain. Domains are managed by network administrators who set up, maintain, and control the network, manage its resources, and support its users.

An *alias* is a nickname for a shared resource. For example, on a server named ACCTING, an administrator might create the alias OCTRCPTS to refer to the server's C:\RECEIPTS\OCTOBER directory. Workstations equate the OCTRCPTS alias to a drive letter, perhaps G:, to gain access to the files in that directory. The alias specifies the server in which the directory is located and the path to the directory, so the users at workstations don't have to remember server names and directory structures. An alias remains defined after the domain controller is stopped and restarted, but a netname does not.

An administrator assigns a *netname* to a resource (a disk directory, printer, or serial device) to define the resource temporarily. Like an alias, a netname identifies a shared resource on a server. However, to use a resource through its netname, you specify the server name in addition to the netname. Unlike an alias, a netname does not remain defined if the domain controller is stopped.

A *UNC* (universal naming convention) name consists of a server name and a netname, which together identify a resource in the domain. A UNC name has the following format:

`\\servername\netname\path`

Note the double backslash characters that precede the server's name.

If you assign LPT1 to a shared LAN Server print queue, you override your local printer port and your print jobs go to the network printer. However, you cannot override local drive letter assignments. If your computer has a C: drive, for example, you must use other drive letters besides C: to refer to LAN Server's file server disk resources.

User-level security on a LAN Server network consists of logon security and permissions. Each user account has a password; the user specifies a user ID and the password to gain access to the network through a domain. A network administrator can limit a particular user's access to certain times of the day or the workstations from which the user can log in. Permissions limit the extent to which a user can use shared resources. The network administrator, for example, can create a COMMON directory that all users can use, and the administrator can create an UPDATE directory with files only certain users can modify but which all users can read.

The network administrator grants, restricts, or denies access to a shared resource by creating an access control profile. Each shared resource can have just one access control profile. An administrator can put individual logon accounts in an access control profile, or the administrator can set up named groups of accounts and insert group names in the access control profile. Group names are more convenient and help keep the profile's size manageable. Each individual or group name has a list of permissions and security restrictions that the administrator can use. The access permissions allow or disallow the following operations:

- Run programs

- Read and write data files

- Create and delete subdirectories and files

- Change file attributes

- Create, change, and delete access control profiles

Novell NetWare

NetWare is the most popular network operating system in use today. More than half of all LAN installations run a version of NetWare. People like it because it performs well, runs on several different kinds of hardware, and offers a useful, comprehensive set of security features. Novell NetWare also supplies a rich set of services and facilities to the programmer who develops a Novell-specific LAN-aware application.

The NetWare File Server and the File System

Although it looks like a regular IBM AT or PS/2 from the outside, a NetWare file server is actually a minicomputer in disguise. The hard disk (or disks) in the file server are formatted with a file system structure completely foreign to DOS; you cannot, for example, boot a NetWare file server with a DOS disk and then access the hard disk with DOS commands, especially a file system oriented command such as CHKDSK. A user at a workstation, however, can nonchalantly view the file server as just another DOS disk drive. The magic that allows this, of course, is the redirection of DOS function calls discussed earlier in this chapter. Novell has simply carried the principle a bit further.

The proprietary format of a Novell file server disk contains more information about files and subdirectories than is possible under DOS. Not only can a file have the DOS attributes READ-ONLY, HIDDEN, and MODIFIED-SINCE-LAST-BACKUP, it can also be marked SHAREABLE or NON-SHAREABLE (a property that allows or disallows simultaneous access by multiple users). Each file is also tagged with its original creation date, the identification of the user who created the file (its owner), the date on which the file was last accessed, the date last modified, and the date and time last archived. Directories also have special properties, which are described in the "NetWare Security" section.

From this description of the file system used on a NetWare file server, you probably have guessed that the operating system software running on the server is not DOS, and you're right. NetWare operates in protected mode (something that OS/2 also does, although NetWare did it first) and literally takes control of the entire computer. Because protected mode enables the 80286 or higher CPU chip to address 16M of memory, NetWare uses what-ever extra memory you install in the file server for caching (see the section "File Servers," earlier in this chapter).

NetWare Security

Novell NetWare implements four types of security to restrict or provide access to a file server, its directories, and its files:

- A user ID and password are required for file server access.

- *Trustee rights*, granted to a user or group of users, can allow or disallow various levels of access to a directory and its subdirectories.

- Each directory has security restrictions that apply to that specific directory.

- A file can be marked Read-Only to prevent inadvertent modification of the file.

Each directory has a *maximum rights mask* that is the highest level of privilege that any of the directory's trustees can be granted. Each directory can have as many as five trustees, and each trustee can have the following eight rights expressed by the rights mask. These rights enable the user to do the following:

- Read from open files

- Write to open files

- Open existing files

- Create new files

- Delete existing files

- Act parentally, by creating, renaming, or erasing subdirectories and setting trustee rights and directory rights in the directory and its subdirectories

- Search for files in the directory

- Modify file attributes

NetWare Fault Tolerance

Realizing that reliability is an important trait of a file server, the designers and programmers at Novell have gone to some lengths to protect the data stored on the server. NetWare can employ strategies and techniques to minimize and handle transparently the failure of the disk surface to record data correctly. SFT (system fault tolerant) NetWare goes a step further and provides *disk mirroring* and *disk duplexing*, software mechanisms for maintaining duplicate copies of disk data.

The NetWare operating system is also programmed to recognize signals from an uninterruptible power supply (UPS), through UPS monitoring. NetWare knows when the UPS is supplying power and notifies users of how much time they have left before the UPS batteries run down. If commercial power is not restored within the time period, NetWare closes any open files and shuts itself down gracefully.

Finally, SFT NetWare offers the NetWare Transaction Tracking System (TTS). An application programmed to use TTS can treat a series of database updates as a single, atomic operation—either all of the updates take place or none of them do. A system failure in the midst of a multiple file update does not cause inconsistencies between the files.

A NetWare Workstation

Both of the software components running on each Novell NetWare workstation are TSR programs. *IPX* manages the PC-to-PC and PC-to-file server communications by implementing Novell's IPX/SPX communications protocol. *NETX* is the shell/redirector that shunts DOS file requests to and from the file server by issuing commands to IPX. Together, IPX and NETX make the file server's disks and printers look like DOS-managed peripherals. IPX usually takes about 20K of memory; NETX takes about 50K.

You don't have to run NetBIOS on a NetWare workstation (unless you have applications that use its protocol), because the NetWare shell software uses IPX to communicate with the file server. If you want both protocols, Novell supplies a NetBIOS emulator that can be loaded on top of IPX and that converts NetBIOS commands into IPX commands for transmission across the network. This emulator adds roughly 20K of memory to the resident portion of NetWare.

NetWare Programming Aids

To help programmers manipulate the NetWare environment more easily, Novell offers software developer's kits (SDKs). These kits consist of programming documentation, C language header files, and libraries of LAN-related functions and subroutines. You can obtain the NetWare Client SDK if you want to do NetWare-specific programming in a DOS, Windows, or OS/2 environment. The NetWare C Interface for Macintosh and MacIPX products provide programming support for Apple Macintosh computers. Novell also offers NetWare RPC. RPC (remote procedure calls) is described earlier in this chapter, in the "Remote Procedure Calls" section.

Novell currently offers NetWare versions 2.2, 3.12, and 4.0.

Novell NetWare 2.2

Novell consolidated all earlier versions of 80286-based NetWare (NetWare 2.0a, 2.15, SFT Advanced NetWare, and Entry Level System [ELS]) into a single product when it released NetWare 2.2. Version 2.2 is quite similar to SFT Advanced NetWare.

NetWare 2.2 supports value-added processes (VAPs), which are separate program modules that link with NetWare and enable the file server to provide extra services. Novell's BTRIEVE file access method is a good example of a VAP. BTRIEVE is a keyed sequential access method. Instead of using DOS redirection to ask the file server for various portions of a file, an application running on a workstation sends the key of the record that it desires directly to BTRIEVE, which looks up the record on the server and returns the appropriate record to the application.

As many as 100 workstations can be concurrently logged into each NetWare 2.2 file server, depending on the license that you buy from Novell.

Novell NetWare 3.12

NetWare 3.12 takes advantage of the 80386 CPU chip to extend the limits of NetWare. It supports up to four gigabytes of memory for caching; as many as 250 users can be logged into a server; as many as 32 terabytes (32 trillion bytes) of disk storage can reside on a single server; each file can be up to 4 gigabytes in size; and a file can span multiple physical drives. As many as 100,000 files can be open concurrently. Up to 250 workstations can access a NetWare 3.12 file server. NetWare 3.12 includes the features of SFT NetWare and adds enhanced security facilities. Also new is the concept of *NetWare loadable modules* (NLMs)—software modules that can be loaded into (or unloaded from) the file server even while the server is still running.

Novell NetWare 4.0

Novell began selling the core NetWare 4.0 product in March 1993, after showing it at the Interop/Spring trade show in Washington, D.C. In 1993, Novell also released NetWare System Fault Tolerance (SFT) III, a version of NetWare 4.0 that incorporates software techniques to ensure fail-safe operation of the LAN. Novell also offers NetWare 4.0 for UNIX and OS/2 2.x. The versions of NetWare 4.0 for UNIX and OS/2 are completely rewritten network operating systems, based more on the core NetWare 4.0 product than on the older Portable NetWare. NetWare for UNIX relies on technology provided by UNIX System Laboratories (USL), which Novell acquired from AT&T late in 1992.

The most significant feature of NetWare 4.0 is Novell's new NetWare Directory Services (NDS), a hierarchically organized database that replaces the bindery that versions 2.2 and 3.12 use. Several network utility software products use the Novell API to access the bindery. By default, NetWare 4.0 turns on bindery emulation, so you don't have to throw away those utilities. Version 4.0 also includes a new named directory service. The new named service is the key that enables users to log on local servers in a single operation. Users also can easily access servers located in geographically dispersed LANs, called wide area networks (WANs).

NetWare 4.0 has the same limits on the number of volumes and total disk space as version 3.12, and version 4.0 also supports NLMs. As many as 1,000 workstations can be concurrently logged into each NetWare 4.0 file server.

Other Environments

Most LANs offered by other vendors look different externally than those of IBM and Novell, but internally they work pretty much the same. Most, like IBM's PC LAN Program, are based on NetBIOS. Of course, these LANs strive to give the user speedy PC-to-PC communications along with transparent PC DOS-like access to a file server. Some, like 3Com Corporation's 3+, offer easy-to-use system administration utilities and an enhanced NetBIOS that can route message packets across bridges (a *bridge* ties together two file servers or two LANs). Artisoft's LANtastic has become a popular peer-to-peer network operating system, and Banyan's StreetTalk is an easy-to-use naming convention for LAN resources.

Summary

This chapter covers the basics of local area networking. LANs are based on the exchange of message packets (frames) by the workstations on the network. You have seen how a file server shares its resources through the redirection of DOS function calls. Also, you are familiar with the different types of networks and their components, and understand the different LAN environments offered by the popular IBM and Novell products.

Chapter 2

Multiuser Concepts

Chapter 1, "The Basics of Networking," discussed the software products that create the LAN environment on a group of interconnected PCs. This chapter explores that environment more closely.

This chapter explains the concepts on which multiuser network programming is based, and describes what the network software does to enable multiple users to coexist peacefully on a LAN, sharing files and printers. Chapter 4, "Shared File Programming," discusses network programming techniques in detail.

This chapter shows how the various versions of DOS provide LAN support, and discusses how DOS, the IBM PC LAN Program, and Novell NetWare transform a group of PCs into a multiuser setting for LAN-aware application programs. The role of the program SHARE.EXE is described, and the concepts of workstation identification, file sharing, and record locking are introduced. Printing to a shared network printer is also discussed. The chapter concludes with a brief look at how network security affects programs running on a LAN.

DOS, DOS-plus-Windows, and OS/2 by themselves are single-user operating systems. On a LAN, however, several users must be able to run the same application on different workstations. The application coordinates the efforts of each user and workstation by understanding and manipulating the environment presented by the LAN. Network software adds an entirely new dimension to programming a PC.

The Multiuser DOS Environment

From a programming perspective, a multiuser operating system must provide three things:

- The system must offer some way to identify which user is which, so that programs can know who they're talking to.

- The system must enable an application to share files and control whether a file can be shared among several users or accessed exclusively by the application.

- For those files that are being shared, the system must let an application *lock records*—to gain exclusive access momentarily to all or a part of a file, update the file without possibly colliding with another application, and then release its temporary ownership.

In addition to these standard multiuser facilities, a LAN needs a fourth mechanism—a way to determine whether the PC is on a LAN.

The functions that Microsoft, IBM, and (in a completely separate way) Novell added to DOS provide these capabilities and a little more. Microsoft and IBM, who obviously control what goes into DOS, placed these new and extended functions directly in DOS itself. Because Novell is not a partner in the maintenance and programming of the DOS operating system, Novell originally supported these capabilities with functions provided by the NetWare *shell* (originally called ANET2, ANET3, NET2, NET3, or NET4, depending on the version of DOS and NetWare, and now simply called NETX). The NetWare shell supports these capabilities by intercepting the primary entry point into DOS (Interrupt 21 hex). Besides offering its own proprietary set of multiuser functions, Novell also recognizes and supports the Microsoft and IBM DOS functions.

NetWare, the IBM PC LAN Program, LAN Server, LANtastic, and other network operating systems can share an entire file server disk drive or certain subdirectories on it. In NetWare, the MAP command sets up drive mappings that specify the relationship between the drive letters and directories that a workstation sees on the network and the actual drive and directory structure on the file server. Similarly, the commands NET SHARE (at the file server) and NET USE (at a workstation) are used with LAN Server and the IBM PC LAN Program to specify the drive and directory relationships. Note that the drive letters and the directory structure that are visible to your application depend on how these commands are used. In the installation section of your user documentation, you might want to mention how you expect the user to set up these drive mappings. In any case, try to make your software as flexible as possible when it comes to drive and directory naming conventions. Note also that you can enable your program to determine which drives are network drives. Chapter 4, "Shared File Programming," provides more detail and some source code examples that demonstrate how to determine local versus network drives.

DOS Versions

Microsoft and IBM added LAN-related function calls to versions of DOS starting with version 3.0. File-access control (exclusive and shared modes) and record locking are available to programs running under DOS 3.0. Version 3.1 added the capability to obtain the identification of individual workstations, to determine which disk drives are remote (that is, redirected or shared) and which are local, and to find out the network name of a remote disk drive. Version 3.2 coincided with the release of IBM's Token Ring network adapter cards. Version 3.3 added a function that enables programs to commit file data to disk (a sort of *temporary close* action). DOS 4.0 made the loading of the SHARE.EXE program mandatory rather than optional (the SHARE program is described momentarily). Finally, DOS versions 5 and 6 made SHARE optional again.

You probably will want to determine the DOS version early in your program. You then can decide whether to continue or to warn the user to upgrade to a later version to run your application. In fact, if you detect a DOS version earlier than 5.0, you should *definitely* tell the user to upgrade.

You can use DOS function call 30 (hex), Get Version, to determine which version of DOS is running on a workstation and therefore which network-related programming services are available. This question is so frequently asked inside application programs that C compilers typically offer major and minor DOS version information as a prefilled data item that application programs can access. Borland C and Microsoft C both place DOS version information in the global variable _osmajor (the minor part of the version information is in _osminor).

If you want to perform DOS function call 30 (hex) yourself, you can do so as follows:

```
regs.h.ah = 0x30;
int86 (0x21, &regs, &regs);
dos_major = regs.h.al;
dos_minor = regs.h.ah;
```

A few years ago, version 2.1 was the most popular version of DOS. The version's popularity lasted far beyond the release of DOS 3.0. Because of the approach that Novell took to create a LAN environment, based on a separate layer of software above DOS, users of DOS 2.1 who had the appropriate NetWare shell software could gain access to a LAN without upgrading to a new operating system. This capability is one of the reasons Novell got an early toehold in the LAN marketplace. Today, of course, the capability is no longer a significant factor; most users have a later (LAN-compatible) version of DOS.

The LAN-related services provided by OS/2 are conceptually similar to those of DOS. Support for file sharing and record locking has been a part of OS/2 from the beginning (version 1.0 of OS/2). Although OS/2 by itself is a single-user environment, it is also a multitasking environment. The same file-sharing and record-locking facilities that you use on a LAN are used to control concurrently running OS/2 tasks that need to access and share the same files. If you have OS/2 and want to see an example of these facilities in action, go to the directory where your SWAPPER.DAT file resides (if you have OS/2 version 1.1, the file is located in the \OS2\SYSTEM directory). Try to copy another file (it doesn't matter which one) over SWAPPER.DAT by using the following syntax:

```
COPY <anyfile> SWAPPER.DAT
```

This command results in a file-sharing error.

The SHARE.EXE Program

SHARE.EXE, which enables file sharing on a LAN, is distributed on the IBM DOS distribution disks and consists of a terminate-but-stay-resident (TSR) program that inserts hooks deep into DOS. These hooks are so deep that you cannot remove SHARE from memory without rebooting the computer.

If SHARE is not loaded, DOS ignores the special file-access modes that you specify when you open a file (to acquire exclusive access to a file, for example). In fact, you can thoroughly correct a network disk if SHARE is not in effect. This is one of the reasons that, beginning with version 4.0, DOS automatically loads SHARE so that users can no longer forget to run the program. (SHARE is also automatically in effect under OS/2.)

In the user documentation for your application (perhaps in the installation section), you should remind the user to make sure that SHARE is run before starting your software. For versions of DOS that don't load SHARE automatically, the best time to invoke the SHARE program is when the user types in the sequence of commands for logging on to the network. This sequence is often a .BAT file (and could likely be the AUTOEXEC.BAT file). If you are a cautious programmer who wants to double-check whether users are following instructions, Chapter 4, "Shared File Programming," presents a technique for detecting the presence of SHARE.

One interesting aspect of SHARE is that it enables file sharing even on a stand-alone, single-user PC. SHARE identifies the current owner of a file by the address at which the program is loaded. This address is the program's *process ID* (PID). The PID consists of the segment address of the program's program segment prefix. This segment address uniquely identifies different processes running on the same computer. Because you can have several TSR-type programs loaded underneath a running application program, DOS must keep separate track of the file I/O performed by each program—background and foreground. DOS does this by using the PID. If SHARE is loaded on a single-user computer, the same file sharing that occurs across the network can occur between two TSRs, or between a TSR and a foreground application. This aspect of SHARE enables the File/Record Collision Test software described in Chapter 8, "Network Applications," to work on a single-user computer.

Is This PC on a LAN?

When your program starts up, one of the first things it should do is determine whether it is running on a LAN. If you design a program to run exclusively in a LAN environment and a user tries to execute the program on a stand-alone computer, you would want to terminate processing and display to the user a message like "Did you know that your computer isn't on the LAN right now?" On the other hand, your program may be sophisticated enough to run in both LAN and stand-alone environments; such a program might do things one way on a LAN and a different way off the LAN.

If you scan the "NetBIOS Extended DOS Services" section of Part IV, "Reference," IBM's *DOS Technical Reference Manual*, or any other DOS reference, you will find functions for opening files in shared mode, locking records, and other network-related operations. One thing that you will *not* find, however, is a unique, standard mechanism for programmers to use to determine whether their programs are running on a LAN or on a stand-alone PC. Different vendors have provided different "Am I installed?" schemes, and the programmer must code a series of tests and infer the presence or absence of the LAN by checking the results. Chapter 4, "Shared File Programming," shows how to make this inference.

Identifying the Workstation

Multiuser programming on a LAN differs from programming under "big computer" operating systems such as UNIX or MVS. On a mainframe or mini-computer, each user runs a copy of the application program on the same computer. On a LAN, each copy of the application runs on a different computer (the workstation). The LAN application may even be designed so that unattended computers acting as slaves (often called *engines*) perform some of the work.

Mainframes and minicomputers identify the user with a login identifier, user ID, or account ID, which is then internally associated with the unique terminal address assigned to the terminal being used. On a LAN, each workstation can be given a *machine name* that identifies the workstation (not necessarily the user). To further complicate matters, on some LANs, it is possible to have the same machine name assigned to more than one workstation, or to have no machine names at all. Chapter 4, "Shared File Programming," describes ways to avoid these situations, because having unique machine names for all workstations can help your application.

Your program must distinguish the machine on which it is running from the other workstations on the network. DOS function call 5E00 (hex), Get Machine Name, is used to determine whether a machine name exists and to obtain the name. Chapter 4, "Shared File Programming," presents techniques for obtaining and using machine names.

IBM PCLP, DLR, and LAN Server Workstation IDs

The IBM PC LAN Program (PCLP), the DOS LAN Requester (DLR), and LAN Server use machine names automatically; the NET START command that loads and runs PCLP requires a machine name as part of the command line. The DOSLAN.INI and IBMLAN.INI configuration files contain machine name entries on machines running DLR and LAN Server. The reason for this requirement is that NetBIOS is a name-oriented PC-to-PC communications service. PCLP, DLR, and OS/2 LAN Requester use NetBIOS to shuttle file data to and from the server. The machine names used by PCLP are always present and unique.

If you use the NetBIOS Microscope program (see Chapter 8, "Network Applications") on a LAN running PCLP or DLR, you can examine (but don't delete) the NetBIOS names that PCLP or DLR establishes on each of the workstations.

Novell NetWare Workstation IDs

Novell NetWare, on the other hand, more closely resembles the minicomputer environment. Each of the users must log in to the network with a user ID, but internally NetWare refers to each user (workstation) with a number that identifies the connection made to the file server. In fact, unless specifically disallowed by the system administrator, the same user ID can be logged in to the network from two or more workstations.

Although you can code your program to use NetWare-specific mechanisms for identifying workstations and users (by using either the connection number or the user ID), NetWare provides a facility for setting up machine names on a NetWare LAN. To establish a machine name under NetWare, you use the SYSCON utility to create for each user a *login script*, as in the following example:

```
machine name = "BARRY"
```

Login scripts are similar to .BAT files. They consist of a series of NetWare commands and, if you want, program invocations for one or more programs that you want to run each time a user logs on to the network. The scripts are interpreted and executed as part of the processing done by the login command.

If you create such NetWare login script entries, both user identifiers (the connection number and the machine name) are available to application programs. If you use connection numbers, however, be aware that your code will run only on NetWare networks. Also note that, under NetWare, the same machine name can be associated with more than one workstation. The best way to avoid nonunique machine names on a NetWare network is to have a system administrator assign them carefully.

File Ownership and Locking

On a file server, every open file is owned by the workstation that opened it. The ownership can be possessive ("No one touches this file but me!") or communal ("If we cooperate, we can all own this file"). There are gradations between these extremes. Applications specify how they want to share a file when it is opened.

What happens if two workstations ignored file-sharing concepts and tried to change the contents of the same file? If two workstations open the same file and attempt to update it at the same time, the results can be messy, to say the least. Here's an example of what can happen:

When a workstation reads a file or a portion of a file, the data is transferred from the file server into workstation memory. Writing the data transfers it back to the file server. Suppose that Workstation A reads the file and displays the data to the user. While User A is looking at the screen and keying in changes, Workstation B also reads the file into its memory and displays the file's data to User B. User B, typing faster than User A, saves Workstation B's changes first. User A, after pondering a few minutes, then saves Workstation A's changes (by writing the data from workstation memory to the file server). The changes that User B made are now lost; they have been overwritten by those of the slower typist, User A.

An even more complicated situation arises when several *interrelated* files must be updated. Because the contents of one file are supposed to have a certain correspondence to the contents of the other files, a helter-skelter series of updates from multiple workstations would be disastrous. Any relationships that existed before the several updates took place would be quickly destroyed.

Deadlocks

Deadlock is a gruesome but well-chosen word for a situation you very much want to avoid. Suppose that Workstation A and Workstation B are both running different programs, but both programs need to update the same two files on the file server. Each program must lock the two files so that it can update the files with consistent data. At about the same moment, both programs reach the point in their execution at which they need to acquire the locks. The sequence of events goes like this:

1. Program A locks file 1.

2. Program A writes data to file 1 that absolutely *must* also be reflected in file 2.

3. Program B locks file 2.

4. Program B writes data to file 2 that absolutely *must* also be reflected in file 1.

5. Program A tries to lock file 2—the request is denied.

6. Program B tries to lock file 1—a Mexican standoff.

Another term for this situation is *deadly embrace*—a term just as gruesome as *deadlock*, and perhaps a bit more descriptive. Untangling the participants in a deadlock usually requires rebooting both workstations, which leaves inconsistent data in the files that were open at the time. Chapter 4, "Shared File Programming," tells how to avoid deadlocks.

File Sharing

Beginning with version 3.0, facilities were built into DOS that enable the programmer to control file sharing. These same facilities, although specified through a calling interface rather than a CPU register value interface, are also available under OS/2. Novell NetWare supports the DOS function calls that involve file sharing and access, and also offers its own set of facilities (unique to NetWare) under the category of *Synchronization Services*.

When an application opens a file, either by calling DOS directly or by performing an open() call, the application specifies three things to DOS: *access mode*, *sharing mode*, and *inheritance*. How DOS handles the file also depends on whether the file has a Read-Only attribute.

Let's first discuss inheritance, and then dismiss it, because it isn't directly related to LAN programming. If you are spawning one or more child processes that need access to a file opened by the main program, you can set the Inheritance flag to File is Inheritable. Setting this flag enables the child process to use the same file handle that the open() call issued to the main program.

Access mode indicates to DOS whether you intend to write to the file. You should use this flag conservatively; if you need only to read from a file, open it with an access mode of Read-Only. This mode gives you a better chance of successfully opening the file, because DOS and the network software allow multiple readers of a file but reject a Read-Write open if others already have the file open in Read-Only mode. Similarly, if a workstation has opened a file for Read-Write access and other workstations subsequently try to open the file for Read-Only access, the subsequent attempts will fail.

The value of sharing mode lets you control how other workstations can open the file after your workstation successfully opens the file. Sharing mode is expressed in terms of denying certain capabilities to the other workstations that attempt to open the file. The restrictions that you can specify are DENY_NONE, DENY_READ, DENY_WRITE, and DENY_READ_WRITE. In addition, there is a special mode called compatibility mode.

DENY_READ_WRITE Mode (Exclusive Access)

When you open a file in DENY_READ_WRITE mode, you gain exclusive access to the file. While you have the file open, no other workstation can read from the file or write to it. The file belongs to you until you close it. However, your attempt to open the file will fail if another workstation already has the file open in any other mode.

DENY_WRITE Mode

Opening a file in DENY_WRITE mode enables other workstations to open and read from the file but not to write to it. The other workstations must open the file for Read-Only access in DENY_NONE mode; otherwise, their attempts to open the file will fail. Likewise, an attempt to open a file in DENY_WRITE mode fails if any other workstation has the file open in a DENY_WRITE or DENY_READ_WRITE (exclusive) mode.

DENY_READ Mode

You can cause other workstations to fail to open a file for reading if you open it first in DENY_READ mode. Oddly enough, this mode lets multiple work-stations write to a file but not read from it. This mode is perhaps less useful than the others, at least in common practice.

DENY_NONE Mode

DENY_NONE is the "communal ownership" mode previously mentioned. It lets multiple workstations open a file for Read-Write access, and defers control of concurrent reads and writes to the record-locking functions described later in this chapter.

Compatibility Mode

Compatibility mode confers exclusive control of a file. This mode is set auto-matically when you create a file (not when you open a file) or when you use file control blocks (FCBs) rather than file handles. When you open a file, you should avoid this mode, and you should also avoid using FCBs in LAN-aware software. FCBs are a holdover from DOS 1.X, and DOS continues to support them only so that users can run older programs (which is how this mode got its name). For most compilers, compatibility mode is also in effect when you open a file with a call to fopen() rather than the more explicit open().

In certain cases, DOS changes compatibility mode to a different file-sharing mode while opening the file. If a file has an attribute of Read-Only (as indicated by its directory entry), DOS replaces compatibility mode with DENY_WRITE. If other workstations try to open the file, access is allowed or denied based on the rules mentioned for DENY_WRITE.

If a newly created file falls into the compatibility mode category, giving the creating workstation exclusive control of the file, how can you change the mode so that other workstations can share the new file? Unfortunately, there is no mechanism for changing sharing mode on the fly; you have to close the file and then open it with a suitable sharing mode.

File-Sharing Situations

Because these file-sharing modes use "negative logic" to control what happens when workstations try to open files, these modes can be pretty confusing. Figure 2.1 summarizes how access mode and sharing mode work together. The following examples should also help explain the interactions.

Workstation A (already open)		Sharing/Access modes Workstation B can use			
Sharing	Access	DENY ALL	DENY WRITE	DENY READ	DENY NONE
DENY ALL	R/W	fail	fail	fail	fail
DENY WRITE	R/W	fail	fail	fail	READ
DENY READ	R/W	fail	fail	fail	WRITE
DENY NONE	R/W	fail	fail	fail	R/W
DENY ALL	READ	fail	fail	fail	fail
DENY WRITE	READ	fail	READ	fail	READ
DENY READ	READ	fail	WRITE	fail	WRITE
DENY NONE	READ	fail	R/W	fail	R/W

Fig. 2.1
Access mode and sharing mode.

Exclusive Access Example

Suppose that your application uses a B-Tree access method. Each file of data records is paired with a file of index entries that point into the various data records in the first file. Occasionally, a user (perhaps the system administrator) must run a utility program that rebuilds (reorganizes) the index file and physically deletes from the data file any records that are marked as logically deleted. In this case, the utility program should open both the data and index files in DENY_READ_WRITE mode. If the open fails, the utility program detects the error and informs the user that another user is currently using the file. If the open succeeds, the utility program can go about its business, secure in the knowledge that no other user can open the file during the rebuilding process.

For another example, suppose that your application has a file that it opens, reads, and displays on the screen for a user to view and update. After the user keys any changes, the application writes the data back to the file and closes it. The application enables other workstations to read and view data even while an update is pending. Should you open the file for exclusive (DENY_READ_WRITE) access, or perhaps DENY_WRITE, and leave the file open for the duration of the update? Probably not. A user can spend several minutes keying the update.

In this situation, the best approach is what I call the *library card* scheme. The application first puts in a separate file a note indicating that the file is "charged out," and then proceeds with the open and read operations. After the update occurs, the application removes the entry from the ChargedOut file. For any user, the application first checks the ChargedOut file against the type of operation that the user has indicated. The application informs the user of what it finds in the ChargedOut file, if that information conflicts with the intended operation. If you record the machine name (discussed earlier in this chapter) in the ChargedOut file, the application not only can inform users of the pending update but also can tell *who* has the file charged out. Chapter 4, "Shared File Programming," presents some pseudocode that shows how to implement this scheme.

A DENY_NONE Example

A multiuser environment commonly has two or three central files that all the workstations need to be able to update concurrently, while the contents of these files must remain consistent. Each time that a user at a workstation starts up a copy of the application software, the common files are opened in DENY_NONE mode (with Read-Write access) so that all workstations can have the files open simultaneously. The control of concurrent access is then designed into the part of the program that performs the record-level updates. The concept of record locking is discussed later in this chapter.

Sharing Retry Count and Delay

DOS and OS/2 are smart enough to realize that many file-sharing conflicts are only momentary. Both environments implement a *retry* mechanism that attempts to resolve sharing errors by delaying a certain length of time before reexecuting the file-open request. If the conflict cannot be resolved after a certain number of retries, DOS or OS/2 gives up and signals to your program that a sharing error has occurred.

Your application can use a function call (IOCTL, hex 44; subfunction Set Sharing Retry Count/Delay, hex 0B) that changes the number of retries and the delay time between them. The delay itself consists of a simple "do nothing" loop. The default values used by DOS are *1 loop = 1 delay period* and *retries = 3*. If you expect your application to cause frequent but brief collisions, you can increase the retry count and the delay period. Note, however, that OS/2 does not let you change its count or delay values. Chapter 4, "Shared File Programming," shows source code techniques for setting these values in the DOS environment.

The DOS "do nothing" loop executes quicker on faster computers. However, DOS does not take into account the difference between a PC/XT and a PS/2 Model 95, for example. As you fine-tune the Sharing Retry Count/Delay parameters, you must take into account the processing speed of the workstation computer as well as the estimated number of collisions and their duration. These parameters affect not only file locking, but also the way that DOS processes record-locking conflicts (discussed later in this chapter).

NetWare Synchronization Services for Files

Besides supporting the access mode and sharing mode concepts just discussed, Novell NetWare offers its own set of services that your program can use to control access to shared files. Novell calls these services *Synchronization Services*. They can be used to lock specific files individually or together, as a set. Chapter 4, "Shared File Programming," describes specific techniques for using these services.

Unlike the built-in DOS functions, the NetWare file-locking services let you treat a group of files as a related set. Novell suggests that you think of these services as four separate tasks that you insert into your code at strategic points:

1. *Logging*—Your program first issues a LogFile request for each file that you are about to lock. This request informs the file server of what's to come.

2. *Locking*—Next, your program uses LockFileSet to lock all the files as a group. If the file server cannot successfully lock the entire set of files within a time period that you specify, your program receives an error.

3. *Releasing*—After part or all of an update is complete, you can call ReleaseFile to release the lock on an individual file, or ReleaseFileSet to release all the locks associated with the group of files.

4. *Clearing*—Finally, you undo the LogFile operation by using either ClearFile (one file at a time) or ClearFileSet (the entire group).

As you can see, Novell designed these services to help programmers avoid deadlocks.

DOS Commands versus File Sharing

DOS is not immune to file-sharing problems—even something as simple as issuing a COPY command to DOS can cause problems on a network. Fortunately, such problems do not occur often. However, COMMAND.COM is not particularly LAN-aware. A file collision occurs if you tell DOS to copy a file that another workstation currently has open. It doesn't matter that the other workstation might only be reading from the file and the COPY command just wants to share the file by also reading from it. To execute the COPY command, COMMAND.COM opens the input (source) file in compatibility mode, which, unless the file's directory entry is marked with the Read-Only attribute, asks for exclusive access to the file. What the COPY command *should* do is open the input file with a mode that denies other workstations the capability to write to the file.

Novell supplies NetWare users with a file-copy utility of its own, called NCOPY. Not only is NCOPY LAN-aware, but it also has a special feature for avoiding unnecessary message traffic across the LAN. If the feature detects that the source and destination files both reside on a file server, NCOPY performs the file copy directly at the file server instead of transmitting the file to a workstation, which in turn would have to transmit the file back to the file server under the destination file name.

Record Locking

Because a file lock affects the entire file and lasts from the time that a file is opened until the time it's closed, file locking can be an awkward inconvenience to the users of your application. You can choose instead to implement locking at the record level; a record lock lasts only long enough to ensure that consistent data was written to the files, and usually affects only a small portion of the file.

A record lock specifies a certain region of a file by giving the region's location in the file (its offset) and its size (length). If the specified region cannot be successfully locked (another workstation opened the file in a mode other than DENY_NONE, or locked the same record), your program receives an error. The locked region can encompass a portion of a data record, one data record, several physically adjacent data records, or the entire file. If each data record in a file is independent of all the others, simply locking the affected data record is appropriate. However, if there are relationships among the records in a file (perhaps one record contains a pointer to another, or the updating of the file implies that several records may have to be physically moved in the file), the correct approach is to lock the entire file as if it were a single large record.

Don't forget to unlock the record when you finish with it.

Deadlocks

The same sort of situation described earlier for file-level deadlocks can happen at the record level.

DOS and OS/2 Record Locks

DOS function call 5C (hex), Lock/Unlock File Region, is used to lock or unlock a range of bytes in a file. All workstations using the file should have opened it in DENY_NONE mode. If DOS cannot acquire the lock, it returns an error to your program. If another workstation tries to read from or write to a locked region, DOS generates a critical error situation by invoking Interrupt 24 (hex), the Critical Error Handler (which produces an `Abort`, `Retry`, `Ignore`, or `Fail?` message at the other workstation). In the OS/2 environment, you call `DosSetFileLocks()` to either lock or unlock a region of a file.

As mentioned in the *DOS Technical Reference* manual, the record lock is expected to last for only a brief duration. If your program must make sure that a portion of the file remains untouched while interacting with the user, you should consider implementing the library-card scheme previously discussed.

A program should not discover that a region of the file is locked by attempting to write a record and then noticing that a critical error has occurred. You must first issue the lock request and then, if the request succeeds, proceed to write the record.

The DOS IOCTL function previously mentioned for setting the duration of the delay loop and the number of retries (Set Sharing Retry/Count) applies also to record locks. DOS uses the same retry mechanism for file locking and record locking.

NetWare Synchronization Services for Records

The record-locking services provided by Novell NetWare are conceptually similar to the NetWare file-locking services previously discussed. The same four tasks of logging, locking, releasing, and clearing apply to record locking. Your application can choose to use either physical record locks or logical record locks.

NetWare's physical record locks work the same as DOS record locks. The protected region of the file is expressed as a given number of bytes, starting at a given position in the file. To use the NetWare method of physical record locking, your program issues one or more calls to `LogPhysicalRecord`, then a call to `LockPhysicalRecordSet`. After the updating is finished, your program issues a `ReleasePhysicalRecordSet` and finally a `ClearPhysicalRecordSet`. If you choose to release or clear records one at a time, you can use `ReleasePhysicalRecord` and `ClearPhysicalRecord`.

NetWare also offers logical record locking—the capability for a program to refer by symbolic name to a record that will be locked. Logical records are logged, locked, released, and cleared just as physical records are, but the lock applies only to the name of the record in a table residing in the file server, not to the actual file region itself. In other words, logical record locks provide a convenient coordination mechanism but no real security for file integrity. When a workstation requests a logical lock, the file server checks only its name table to see whether another workstation previously issued a logical lock against that name. Therefore, if one program uses logical record locks, every program that accesses a file must use them. Both file locks and physical record locks override logical locks.

Building Your Own Server

The preceding sections of this chapter explained how you can take advantage of the network operating system's file redirection to read and write files on the file server. However, working with large files on the server can cause a great deal of LAN traffic. For example, if software at each workstation reads all or most of a large file that resides on a file server, the contents of that file flow through the LAN cable to each workstation. The resulting volume of LAN packets might cause the LAN to slow down. But as you have seen, the work done by the file server merely consists of repeatedly responding to essentially the same pattern of file I/O requests from the workstations. To create a more efficient file I/O environment, you might consider building your own record server.

A *record server* is an unattended computer on the LAN that serves records to the applications running on the other workstations. One of the goals of a record server should be to relieve the file server of some of its workload.

Designing the Record Server

You might put flat files on the file server and keyed (indexed) files on the record server, and then let the workstation concentrate on managing the user interface. Each workstation delegates all its record handling to the record server. The workstation computer need only be powerful enough to handle the user interface. The record server computer handles the record I/O on behalf of the workstations, based on the record requests that it receives from them. To send and receive records to and from the record server computer, you can use a messaging protocol, such as NetBIOS or IPX, with programming techniques demonstrated in this book.

An ordinary application that stores or retrieves records on a file server by using a B-Tree or other record indexing method causes a flurry of LAN traffic during each file access. To retrieve a record, the file I/O portion of the application reads through the tree or index to find the desired key. Each read operation becomes a separate request message to the server and a response message back from the server. The network operating system passes these messages completely independent of your control. Your application is at the mercy of the network operating system and the file server.

The number of requests and responses depends on the depth of the tree associated with the keyed access method. To get an idea of the number of LAN I/O messages required to read and write B-Tree or other keyed index entries, however, you can multiply the typical number of read operations to locate a key by the number of workstations on the LAN. The traffic can accumulate quickly. For instance, 50 workstations sharing a keyed index file containing 1,000 1K records, assuming 10 transactions per minute per workstation, might easily cause 50M worth of LAN traffic each minute. Adding or deleting records causes even more traffic, because the workstation must rebalance or coalesce the tree by manipulating the file indirectly, piece by piece, through the network operating system and through the LAN cable.

In a record server environment, your file access code (not the network operating system) controls the message passing. The application retrieves a record by sending the desired key to the record server as a NetBIOS or IPX message. The record server sends back the desired record (or an indication that the key doesn't exist). Record server technology greatly reduces LAN message traffic. More importantly, a record server places the indexed file I/O burden on a separate machine.

How do you implement your own record server? Basically, you change your application so that the workstation sends all keyed-file activity to the record server. The workstation itself no longer contains any program code to do file accesses. Each `OpenKeyedFile`, `FindKey`, `AddKeyAndRecord`, `DeleteKeyAndRecord`, and `NextRecord` operation becomes a message that you send to the record server. The record server—which might be a fast, OS/2-based, multitasking computer—processes each message by doing the operation locally.

To create the record server component, you link your file-access code to a library of functions that you develop. These functions take the place of the file I/O routines presently in your program. The record server software uses the incoming message requests to drive each operation. When your record server program receives a message request, the program calls the appropriate keyed-file routine and returns the result to the requesting workstation in the form of a return message. The file I/O software module at the workstation is just a message-passing stub. The actual file I/O module resides inside the record server, waiting patiently for request messages from the workstations.

The Advantages of a Record Server

On a busy LAN, a record server helps distribute the processing evenly and fairly. To choose a computer and operating system for the record server, your criteria may differ from that which you used to choose the file server machine. You might even use Macintosh computers for workstations and a high-powered "superserver" as the record server computer. Because the workstation no longer has to contain the actual file I/O logic, you can make your application smaller by saving whatever memory those file I/O routines consume. If your application is DOS-based and must run within the 640K of conventional memory (minus the memory that DOS and the network require), you'll find record server technology tempting for the RAM it saves.

Considerations for the Record Server

Because the message passing adds an extra dimension to your application, you must consider a few new questions in your design. What happens if someone kicks the power cord on the record server just as it gets a message to process? What should the code at the workstation do to handle this situation? Usually, it suffices to have the workstation file I/O stub wait a second or two for a response, retry sending the request a few times, and then signal an I/O error to the application if you hear only silence from the record server. You can design a sequence number into the messages to ensure they are processed in order and that none are lost.

Conversely, what should the record server do if it loses touch with one or more workstations? You want to design carefully around this situation. Generally, if you are not doing related, multiple-record updates, you can assume the last update request from a workstation was a single, atomic transaction. When the workstation reawakens, it can simply carry on with the next transaction. If a set of related record updates is under way, however, you might want to design a "journaling" mechanism into the record server so that you can roll back the files to a previous, known state. Note that you would have to design this sort of file integrity into your application regardless of whether you implement record server technology.

In the record server, do you have to process every Open and Close workstation request by actually opening and closing files as instructed by the workstations? No—you can leave the files open and thus avoid having to reopen the file when the next workstation wants the file. However, you would want to flush the file material out to the disk periodically. The record server can close all its files at the end of the day, when the user chooses a "shut everything down" menu option before going home.

Similarly, at startup time, the record server might anticipate the day's activities by opening certain files and having them ready for processing. You probably know which files to preselect based on your familiarity with the application.

Finally, what happens if several workstations begin clamoring for data at the same time? You can handle such requests by queuing them as they arrive, and you might even design your record server module to be multithreaded. If you choose an OS/2-based computer as the record server, you should have no problem building multithreaded capabilities into your file I/O routines. File sharing and record locking become simple issues in your record server environment. You can build and maintain a table inside the record server that reflects each workstation's ownership of certain files and records. This table can reside in memory; you don't have to write it to disk.

Printing across the LAN

You might think that sending print data to a shared network printer is easy, painless, and not nearly as much trouble as trying to share files and records. Unfortunately, this isn't so.

Suppose that a user on the network runs Lotus 1-2-3 and wants to print a spreadsheet in condensed (small) print because the spreadsheet is several cells wide. The user sends control codes to the printer, prints the spreadsheet, and happily walks away from the network printer with a nicely formatted printout in hand. The next user to print a report (from your application) mutters dark, nasty things about your software when he or she sees that the printout is scrunched on the left side of the page in small characters.

Here's another example. You have a series of programs that each print a section of a lengthy, complex report. You test the programs on a stand-alone, non-networked PC, and everything seems to work perfectly; each report section flows to the next one exactly as it should. Next, you run a test that sends the report to the network printer. To your bewilderment, stray page breaks are inserted throughout the report, destroying the report's appearance. You have to spend an extra day or two to figure out the problem: each of the programs in the series opens and closes the printer to print a given report section, and the network software inserts automatic page breaks each time the printer is closed.

Controlling the Printer

With LAN Server and the IBM PC LAN Program, a special form of the NET USE command is issued at a workstation to indicate that print data should be redirected across the network. For the print redirection to happen, a corresponding NET SHARE command must execute at the file server. With earlier versions of Novell NetWare, the workstation command that turns on print redirection is SPOOL; recent versions use CAPTURE.

The NET SHARE command that you issue to LAN Server or the IBM PC LAN Program at the file server to cause a printer to be shared can have optional arguments that describe how page breaks (form feeds) should occur at the printer. You can specify one of three things:

- A form feed should be automatically issued between printouts.

- The PC LAN Program or DOS LAN Requester should check the end of the print file to see whether it contains a form feed; if no form feed is found, PCLP or DLR sends one automatically.

- The PC LAN Program or DOS LAN Requester should not send any extra form feeds.

Additionally, you can create a file that the PC LAN Program or LAN Server uses to print Job Separator pages between printouts. Both LAN Server and the PC LAN Program support several printer-control options in the Job Separator file, and you can use these options not only to specify what the Separator page should look like but also to reset the printer to a default mode before producing each printout. The default Job Separator file is PQ.SEP. You use the NET SEPARATOR command to specify whether separator pages should be in effect and the name of the Job Separator file.

You can use DOS function call 5E02 (hex), Set Printer Setup String, to designate a string of control characters to be sent to the printer each time that the network printer is opened.

Printer Control under NetWare

With earlier versions of Novell Netware, NetWare offers somewhat more extensive control over the network printer through the use of the CAPTURE command (formerly the SPOOL command). This command enables you to control the following:

- Whether to add automatic form feeds to the end of a file of print data

- Whether to produce a separator page (Novell calls it a banner page)

- Whether to expand tabs into spaces and how many spaces to use

- The number of copies to print

- The type of form that must be mounted in the printer

- The variable text (the user name or job name) that appears on the banner page

- How NetWare is to detect the end of the print job (based on a time-out value or a file-close operation)

- The number of lines per page

- The width of each line

- Other miscellaneous items

Each of these parameters can be programmatically set by calling functions within Novell's Print Services.

Security Issues

As you design a LAN-aware application, you must consider security issues from two different points of view.

First, you want to ensure that your application operates in a secure environment. Your application should instruct users how to make backup copies of the files that your application uses; the application should protect sensitive data in appropriate ways; and, to the extent possible, your application should prevent users from being able to damage each other's work, even inadvertently. Of course, you would have considered each of these issues in your design even if the application were not intended for a LAN environment. But you should revisit each aspect of your design that relates either to security or reliability, anticipating what might happen when multiple users run your software.

Second, the application must conform to the existing environment set up by the system administrator. A shared network drive is not a local hard drive. Especially under Novell NetWare, situations are possible that would never occur on a single-user computer. Chapter 1, "The Basics of Networking," discussed the rights associated with a directory on a NetWare server. A directory can be marked so that a program cannot even search the directory to see what files it contains. The files may actually exist (and be visible to users who

Local Area Networks

have different trustee rights), but other users may be restricted so that certain directories and files are "invisible" to the programs that they run. Because of these rights, your program may function differently when run by different users.

Another example of a situation that is unique to NetWare involves the Shareable/Non-Shareable file attribute that Chapter 1, "The Basics of Networking," also discussed. When created on a NetWare file server, a file is automatically given a default attribute of Readable/Writable/Non-Shareable. Therefore, the files that your application expects to share among multiple users must have their file attributes modified, either with the NetWare FLAG command or by your software. This requirement applies not only to files that your application creates while running, but also to the installation process that copies to the file server your application and the files that it uses.

Checking Return Codes and Handling Errors

Every programmer knows that it is important to check return codes after performing file I/O and to handle error situations correctly, but such error handling is even more important in a LAN environment. For example, programs often display the message File Not Found when the file actually exists but is currently open at a different workstation. The program detected an error at file-open time, but neglected to find out exactly what error occurred. Make sure that your LAN-aware program checks return codes thoroughly, and that it offers users good error-recovery options. You might even want to include retry options in your error-handling code so that users have more control over their access to the LAN. Recognizing that error checking and processing is a concern of many programmers, Microsoft and IBM added function call 59 (hex), Get Extended Error, to versions of DOS beginning with 3.0.

The DOS Critical Error handler, Interrupt 24 (hex), is particularly important to programmers on a LAN. On a single-user PC, the Abort, Retry, Ignore, or Fail? prompt usually pops up only when the printer is out of paper or when true disk drive hardware problems occur, such as Sector Not Found. On a network, however, the DOS Critical Error handler is also invoked for file-access collisions, which occur when a workstation tries to read from or write to a file that another workstation already has either locked or opened for exclusive access.

DOS returns some errors to the program and handles others as critical errors. These critical errors are called *sharing violations*. You should watch out for two situations that cause sharing violations:

- *Files open in compatibility mode*—As mentioned earlier, you should avoid opening a file in compatibility mode. Here's one reason to avoid doing so: If one workstation tries to open a file in compatibility mode and another workstation has already opened the file in one of the other sharing modes, DOS generates an Interrupt 24 (hex) critical error. The error code from Interrupt 24 indicates Drive Not Ready, and a call to the Get Extended Error service (function call 59 hex) returns Sharing Violation.

- *Reading and writing a locked region*—If a properly functioning program opens a file and locks a record in that file, but a rogue program then tries to read from or write into that region of the file (without testing first to see whether the region is locked), DOS generates an Interrupt 24 (hex) with a General Failure error code.

Other actions simply result in your application receiving DOS error code 5, Access Denied. Such actions include attempting to open a file for exclusive access when another workstation already has the file open, or attempting to lock a region of bytes in a file when another user has already locked the region. Some network operating system environments report error code 32 (20h), Sharing Violation, rather than error code 5.

Unless you specially intercept critical network errors, DOS uses the default Abort, Retry, Ignore, or Fail? mechanism to give a user a chance to decide how to handle the situation. Because the message isn't the world's friendliest, you should seriously consider incorporating your own critical error handler in the LAN-aware programs that you develop. Under Novell NetWare, the message's wording differs, but the net effect is the same. Also under NetWare, you can call the function SetNetWareErrorMode(). This function call tells NetWare to let your program handle critical errors instead of having NetWare handle them.

Summary

If you have worked in mainframe- or minicomputer-based multiuser environments, you may already have been familiar with some of the concepts presented in this chapter. But now you understand how the concepts relate to the environment of networked PCs. This chapter discussed how to identify users, share files, lock records, print, and handle the issues associated with security and error checking. The chapter also described the different environments presented by LAN Server, the IBM PC LAN Program, and NetWare. Also, you now know that DOS offers network-related services and functions that are common to almost all network operating system environments.

Chapter 3

PC-to-PC Communications Concepts

Chapter 1, "The Basics of Networking," briefly discussed frames, which form the basis for all activity on the LAN. This chapter describes frames in more detail and shows how they are used for both redirection of file-service functions and PC-to-PC communications. The chapter also explains the basics of the NetBIOS and IPX/SPX protocols.

Frames undergo several stages of processing during their lifetimes. For outbound frames, each processing stage adds information to the frame to help it along; for inbound frames, each stage removes its layer of information and hands the frame to the next stage. The content, length, and usage of frames depend on which protocol the LAN is using. The format of frames differs even between protocols as similar as Ethernet and the IEEE 802.3 protocol. Because vendors have implemented so many different protocols on LANs, you first must understand frames from a general perspective so that you can more easily focus on the individual protocols as you later explore them in depth.

After discussing frames in general, this chapter specifically examines how Ethernet frames, IEEE 802.3 frames, and Token Ring frames are formatted. In addition, the chapter quickly introduces you to using frames on an FDDI fiber-optics network, and to the higher-level protocols IPX, SPX, and NetBIOS.

You may never need this chapter's information on how a low-level protocol's frames are formatted—you shouldn't have to go down to that level for application-level programming—but knowing what they look like and how they are used will help you understand what's happening "underneath" your program so that you can make better use of the LAN's facilities. You may even someday run across an odd-looking piece of data while using a debugger to pore through a memory dump, and you'll be able to say to yourself, "Ah-hah! That's the frame that contains the last message I sent."

General Features

Regardless of the protocol used, frames have certain common characteristics. As defined in Chapter 1, "The Basics of Networking," a frame is a message packet that contains sender and receiver address information that is used to route the message packet. As discussed in that chapter's description of network adapter cards and supporting software, each network adapter knows where to look in the frame for this routing information, so the adapter recognizes message packets intended for the adapter.

Frames are always layered (see fig. 3.1). When you give a message to a protocol such as NetBIOS, for example, and ask that it be sent to another PC on the network, NetBIOS puts an "envelope" around your message packet and hands it to the next lower level, which consists of the network support software and network adapter card. This lower layer in turn wraps the NetBIOS envelope in an envelope of its own and sends it out across the network. After receiving the frame, the network support software on the receiver's computer removes the outer envelope and hands the result upward to the next higher level, NetBIOS. The NetBIOS program running on the receiver's computer removes NetBIOS envelope and gives the message, now an exact copy of the sender's message, to the receiver application.

Fig. 3.1
The layering
of frames.

The OSI Model

How many layers are in a frame? Different vendors split the LAN communications functions in different ways, but all compare themselves to the OSI Model (see fig. 3.2). This "template" standard describes how communications between two computers *should* happen. Perhaps in the future this theoretical standard will become a practical one as more vendors continue to switch to it.

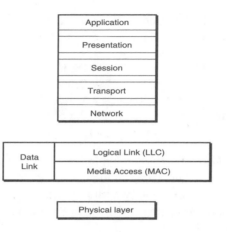

Fig. 3.2
The OSI Model.

The OSI Model declares seven layers and specifies that each layer is insulated from the others by a well-defined interface. The seven layers are the following:

- *Physical (lowest) layer*—This part of the OSI Model specifies the physical and electrical characteristics of the connections that make up the network (twisted pair cables, fiber-optic cables, coaxial cables, connectors, repeaters, and so on). Think of this as the hardware layer.

- *Data Link layer*—At this stage of processing, the electrical impulses enter or leave the network cable. This layer (and only this layer) is aware of bit patterns, encoding methods, tokens, and other such elements. At this stage, errors are detected and corrected (through requests for re-transmission of corrupted packets). Because of its complexity, this layer is often thought of as being subdivided into a Medium Access Control (MAC) layer and a Logical Link Control (LLC) layer. The MAC layer deals with network access (either token-passing or collision-sensing) and network control. The LLC layer, operating at a higher level than the MAC layer, sends and receives the user data messages themselves.

- *Network layer*—This processing step switches and routes the packets as necessary to get them to their destination. This layer is responsible for addressing and delivering message packets.

- *Transport layer*—When more than one packet is in process at any one time, this layer controls the sequencing of the message components and also regulates inbound traffic flow. If a duplicate packet arrives, this layer recognizes it as a duplicate and discards it.

■ *Session layer*—The functions in this layer enable applications running at two workstations to coordinate their communications into a single session (which you can think of as a dialog). This layer supports the creation of the session, the management of the packets sent back and forth during the session, and the termination of the session.

■ *Presentation layer*—When IBM, Apple, DEC, NeXt, and Burroughs computers all want to talk to one another, a certain amount of translation and byte-reordering obviously must be done. This layer converts data to or from a machine's native internal numeric format.

■ *Application (highest) layer*—This is the layer that an application program sees, and therefore is also the interface to the OSI Model that the programmer sees. A message to be sent across the network enters the OSI Model at this layer, travels downward toward Layer 1 (the Physical layer), zips across to the other workstation, and then travels back up the layers until the message reaches the application on the other computer through its Application layer.

Compare the way that these layers function to the U.S. Postal Service:

■ The Application layer is a plain sheet of 8 1/2-inch-by-11-inch paper, folded to fit in an envelope.

■ The Presentation layer is a #10 envelope (9 1/2-inches-by-4-inches) with windows through which the addresses show.

■ The Session layer is the envelope with the names of the sender and recipient showing through the windows.

■ The Transport layer is the post office.

■ The Network layer is the mail carrier.

■ The Data Link layer is your mailbox.

■ The Physical layer is—of course—the mail truck.

Most vendors combine the functions expressed in the seven layers of the OSI Model into two or three layers of proprietary implementation.

Ethernet and IEEE 802.3 Frames

Ethernet is a LAN standard that is based on the Experimental Ethernet network that Xerox designed and built in 1975 (before PCs!). Ethernet operates at 10 megabits per second over 50-ohm coaxial cable. The current Ethernet version is 2.0, established in November 1982. The first edition of a similar LAN standard, IEEE 802.3, was published in 1985. The two standards differ subtly in network architecture and not so subtly in frame formats.

In terms of network architecture, IEEE 802.3 distinguishes between MAC and LLC layers. True Ethernet lumps these layers together into a single Data Link layer. Also, Ethernet defines an Ethernet Configuration Test Protocol (ECTP) that the IEEE 802.3 standard lacks. However, the important differences between the two standards are in the types and lengths of the fields that make up a frame. These differences can cause the two protocols to be incompatible with one another.

Ethernet Frames

Figure 3.3 shows the layout of an Ethernet frame.

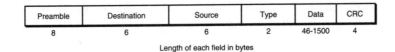

Length of each field in bytes

Fig. 3.3
An Ethernet frame.

The fields of the frame are as follows:

- The eight-byte-long *preamble* field (the standard refers to a byte as an *octet*) is used for synchronization and framing. The preamble always contains the bit pattern 10101010...10101010 in the first seven bytes, with 10101011 in the last (eighth) byte.

- The six-byte *destination* address field contains the address of the workstation that will receive this frame. As a result of a naming scheme administered by the Xerox Corporation, the first three bytes are a group address assigned by Xerox and the last three are assigned locally. If the bit is 0, the destination address is a physical address that is unique throughout the entire Ethernet universe. The first (leftmost) bit of the first byte has a special meaning. If the leftmost bit is a 1, it represents a broadcast frame. In this case, the remainder of the destination address can refer to a group of logically related workstations or to all workstations on the network (all 1s).

- The *source* address field, which is also six bytes long, identifies the workstation sending the frame. The leftmost bit of the first byte is always 0.

- The *type* field contains two bytes of information that identify the type of the higher-level protocol that issued (or wants to receive) this frame. Xerox assigned the type field. Ethernet does not interpret it. This field lets multiple high-level protocols (called *client layers*) share the network without running into each other's messages.

- The *data portion* of the frame, which can be from 46 to 1,500 bytes long, is the data message that the frame is intended to carry to the destination.

- Finally, the frame contains four bytes of cyclic redundancy checksum (*CRC*) remainder, calculated by the CRC-32 polynomial. After receiving this frame, the workstation performs its own CRC-32 calculation on the frame and compares its calculated value to the frame's CRC field. This calculation tells the workstation whether the frame arrived intact or was somehow damaged in transit.

Without a preamble, an entire Ethernet frame is between 64 bytes and 1,518 bytes. The minimum size of a data message is 46 bytes.

IEEE 802.3 Frames

Figure 3.4 shows an IEEE 802.3 frame.

Fig. 3.4
An IEEE 802.3 frame.

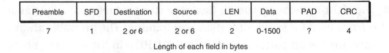

Preamble	SFD	Destination	Source	LEN	Data	PAD	CRC
7	1	2 or 6	2 or 6	2	0-1500	?	4

Length of each field in bytes

The frame consists of the following fields:

- The *preamble* field contains seven bytes of synchronization data. Each byte is the same bit pattern (10101010).

- The *start frame delimiter* (SFD) consists of a single byte that has the bit pattern 10101011. (These two IEEE 802.3 fields, the preamble and SFD, exactly match the single Ethernet preamble field.)

- The *destination address* field, which can be either two or six bytes long, indicates which workstation is to receive the frame. The first bit of the destination address is the Individual/Group (I/G) bit; this bit is 0 if the address refers to a single workstation or 1 if the address represents a group of workstations (a broadcast message). If the destination address is a two-byte field, the remainder of the bits forms a 15-bit workstation address. If the destination address is a six-byte field, however, the bit following the I/G bit is a Universally/Locally (U/L) Administered bit, which is a 0 for universally administered (global) addresses and a 1 for locally administered addresses. The remainder of the six-byte field is a 46-bit workstation address. Note that all addresses on a particular network must be either two-byte or six-byte addresses. The most popular type of IEEE 802.3 frame, 10BASE5, specifies six-byte addresses.

■ In the two- or six-byte *source address* of the sending workstation, the I/G (first) bit is always 0.

■ The two *length* bytes express the length of the frame's data portion.

■ The *data* portion can range from 0 to 1,500 bytes of data. If the length of this field is less than 46 bytes, the next field (PAD) is used to fatten the frame to an acceptable (minimum) size.

■ The *PAD* field consists of enough bytes of filler to ensure that the frame has at least a certain overall size. If the data portion is large enough, the PAD field does not appear in the frame (it becomes a zero-length field).

■ Like that of Ethernet frames, the *CRC* field of an IEEE 802.3 frame contains four bytes of remainder from the CRC-32 algorithm.

Under both Ethernet and IEEE 802.3 (assuming Type 10BASE5), the size of a frame, excluding the preamble and SFD, is the same: between 64 and 1,518 bytes. However, under IEEE 802.3, the application (or an upper-layer protocol) can send a data area that is less than 46 bytes long, because the MAC layer will automatically pad the data area. Under Ethernet, data areas that are too small result in error situations.

Token Ring Frames

Before you learn about actual frame formats, you first need to understand the magic that makes Token Rings work. In 1985, Texas Instruments and IBM jointly developed the TMS380 Chipset (although, ironically, IBM doesn't use the chipset; it builds its own proprietary chipset that is *mostly* compatible with the TI/IBM set). The TMS380 chipset implements the IEEE 802.5 standards for the Physical layer and the Data Link layer of the OSI Model. The chipset supports functions of both the MAC sublayer and the LLC sublayer of the Data Link layer. Originally released as a set of five chips, the TI product can now be produced as a single chip. In relation to the original five chips, the TMS380 functions are the following:

- The *TMS38051 and 38052* chips handle the lowest level, the ring interface itself. The chips perform the actual transmitting and receiving of data (frames), monitor cable integrity, and provide clocking functions.

- The *TMS38020* chip is a protocol handler that controls and manages the 802.5 protocol functions.

- The *ROM* chip has program code burned into it. The permanently stored software performs diagnostic and management functions.

- The *TMS38010* chip is a 16-bit dedicated microprocessor for handling communications. It executes the code in the ROM chip and has a 2.75K RAM buffer for temporary storage of transmitted and received data.

Be prepared for a bit of a letdown at this point, because I now have to tell you that a Token Ring is not a ring at all. Although most people think of a Token Ring as a single piece of cable that all the workstations tap into, a Token Ring actually consists of individual point-to-point linkages. My workstation sends the token (or a frame) to your workstation, your workstation sends the token downstream to the next workstation, and so forth. Only the fact that one of your downstream neighbors happens also to be my *upstream* neighbor makes it a ring. From a communications perspective, the messages go directly from one PC to another.

Not all workstations on the ring are peers, although the differences are invisible to the outside world. One of the workstations is designated the *active monitor*, which means that it assumes additional responsibilities for controlling the ring. The active monitor maintains timing control over the ring, issues new tokens (if necessary) to keep things going, and generates diagnostic frames under certain circumstances. The active monitor, which is chosen when the ring is initialized, can be any one of the workstations on the network. If the active monitor fails for some reason, there is a mechanism by which the other workstations (*standby monitors*) can decide which one becomes the new active monitor.

Tokens, Frames, and Abort Sequences
Three different formats are defined for IEEE 802.5 Token Ring message packets: the token, the data frame, and the abort sequence.

Figure 3.5 shows the format of the *token*. In principle, the token is not a frame but simply a means by which each workstation can recognize when its turn to transmit has arrived.

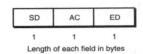

Fig. 3.5
The token format.

The second format, shown in figure 3.6, is a true *data frame*. Data frames can contain messages that applications send to one another on the ring, and they also sometimes contain internal messages used privately among the Token Ring network adapter cards for ring-management purposes.

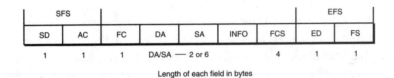

Fig. 3.6
A Token Ring data frame.

Figure 3.7 shows the format of the third type of message that can be transmitted on a Token Ring, the *abort sequence*. This message also is not considered a frame. An abort sequence can occur anywhere in the bit stream and is used to interrupt/terminate the current transmission.

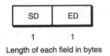

Fig. 3.7
The abort sequence format.

The Token. A token is three bytes long (24 bits) and contains the following three fields:

- Start delimiter

- Access control

- End delimiter

The start delimiter (SD) field appears at the beginning of the token (and also at the beginning of every message or frame that is sent across the network). Because four nondata symbols (each one bit long) and four (normal) 0 bits are in the field, it totals one byte.

Next comes the access control (AC) field, which is divided into four data items:

    P P P   T   M   R R R

in which PPP are the priority bits, T is the token bit, M is the monitor bit, and RRR are the reservation bits.

Every token or frame is prioritized by setting the priority bits to a value from 0 to 7 (7 is the highest priority). A workstation can use the network (that is, change a token into a frame) only if it receives a token with a priority less than or equal to its own priority. The workstation's network adapter sets the priority bits to indicate the priority of the current frame or token. See the descriptions of reservation bits for details on how this works.

The token bit has a value of 0 for a token and 1 for a frame.

The active monitor sets the monitor bit to 1, and any workstation transmitting a token or frame sets the bit to 0. If the active monitor sees a token or frame that contains a monitor bit of 1, it knows that this token or frame has been around the ring once without being processed by a workstation. Because a sending workstation is responsible for removing its own transmitted frames, and because high-priority workstations are responsible for grabbing a token to which they've previously laid claim (see the next paragraph's discussion of reservation bits), the active monitor detects that something is wrong if a frame or a prioritized token circulates without being processed. The active monitor cancels the transmission and circulates a new token.

The reservation bits work hand in hand with the priority bits. A workstation can place its priority in the reservation bits (if its priority is higher than the current value of the reservation bits). That workstation then has dibs on the next use of the network. When transmitting a new token, a workstation sets the priority bits to the value that it found in the reservation field of the frame that it just received. Unless preempted by an even higher-priority workstation, the workstation that originally set the reservation bits will be the next station to turn the token into a frame.

The final field of the token is the end delimiter (ED) field. Like the start delimiter field, this field contains a unique combination of 1s and special nondata symbols that cannot be mistaken for anything else. The end delimiter appears at the end of each token. Besides marking the end of the token, ED also contains two subfields: the intermediate frame bit and the error-detected bit. These subfields are discussed in the following section, because they pertain more to frames than to tokens.

The Data Frame.   A frame consists of several groups of fields—the start frame sequence (SFS), the destination address (DA), the source address (SA), the data itself (INFO), the frame check sequence (FCS), and the end frame sequence (EFS). Together, these fields form a message record (envelope) that is used to carry either ring-management information (MAC data) or user data (LLC data). You already know about user data, which consists of the frames that contain application-oriented data such as PC-to-PC messages or perhaps a portion of a disk file (from a file server) that a workstation is sharing. MAC frames, on the other hand, are used internally by the network software. The IEEE 802.5 standard defines six MAC control frames. The frame control field (defined in the following list) indicates the type of the frame (MAC or LLC) and, if a MAC frame is specified, the field also identifies which one of the six MAC frame types is represented by this particular frame.

Briefly, the six MAC frames are the following:

■ To ensure that its address is unique, a workstation sends a *duplicate address test* frame when it first joins the ring.

■ To let other workstations know that it is still alive, the active monitor circulates the *active monitor present* frame every so often.

■ A *standby monitor present* frame is sent by any workstation other than the active monitor.

■ A standby monitor sends a *claim token* frame when it suspects that the active monitor may have died. The standby monitors then negotiate with one another to determine which one becomes the new active monitor.

■ A workstation sends a *beacon* frame in the event of a major network problem, such as a broken cable or a workstation that is transmitting without waiting for the token. By detecting which station is sending the beacon frame, diagnostic software can localize the problem.

■ A *ring purge* frame is sent after the ring is initialized and a new active monitor establishes itself.

Each frame (MAC or LLC) begins with a *start frame sequence*, which contains the following three fields:

■ The definition of *start delimiter (SD)* is the same for frames as for tokens.

■ The *access control (AC)* is also the same for frames as for tokens.

■ *Frame control (FC)* is a one-byte field that contains two subfields, frame type and MAC control ID:

```
    F F   C C C C C C
```

The two frame type bits (FF) have a value of 00 for MAC frames and 01 for LLC frames. (Bits 11 and 10 are reserved.)

The MAC control ID bits identify the type of ring-management frame (see table 3.1).

Table 3.1   MAC Control ID Bits

Bit Values C C C C C C	Ring-Management Frame Types
0 0 0 0 1 1	Claim Token
0 0 0 0 0 0	Duplicate Address Test
0 0 0 1 0 1	Active Monitor Present
0 0 0 1 1 0	Standby Monitor Present
0 0 0 0 1 0	Beacon
0 0 0 1 0 0	Purge

The *destination address (DA)*, which follows the *start frame sequence* fields, can be either two or six bytes long. With two-byte addresses, the first bit indicates whether the address is a group address or an individual address (just as in the collision-sensing IEEE 802.3 protocol). With six-byte addresses, the first bit is also an individual/group (I/G) bit and the second bit (the U/L bit, which again is the same as in the IEEE 802.3 protocol) expresses whether the address is locally or globally assigned. The remainder of the bits forms the address of the workstation to which the frame is addressed.

The *source address (SA)* is the same size and format as the destination address.

The data portion of the frame (*INFO*) can contain one of the MAC frames just discussed, or a user data message record intended for (or received from) a higher-level protocol such as IPX or NetBIOS. This field has no specified maximum length, although there are practical limits on the size based on the timing requirements of how long a workstation can control the ring.

The *frame check sequence (FCS)* field, which is used for error detection, is four bytes of remainder from the CRC-32 cyclic redundancy checksum algorithm.

The *end frame sequence (EFS)* consists of two fields: the end delimiter and the frame status.

I discussed the *end delimiter (ED)* field briefly in relation to tokens, but in a frame it takes on additional meaning. Besides consisting of a unique pattern of electrical impulses, the field also contains two one-bit subfields. The inter-mediate frame bit is set to 1 if the frame is part of a multiple-frame transmis-sion, and 0 for the last (or only) frame. The error-detected bit starts as a 0 when a frame is originally sent; each workstation that passes the frame checks for errors (verifying that the CRC in the frame check sequence field still corresponds to the contents of the frame, for example) and sets the error-detected bit to 1 if it finds anything wrong. The intervening workstations that see an error-detected bit that is already set simply pass the frame along. The originating workstation notices that a problem occurred and retransmits the frame.

The one-byte *frame status (FS)* field contains four reserved bits (R), and two subfields, the address-recognized bit (A) and the frame-copied bit (C):

```
A   C   R R   A   C   R R
```

Because the calculated CRC does not encompass this field, each of the one-bit subfields is duplicated within the frame status to ensure data integrity. A transmitting workstation sets the address recognized bit to 0 when it origi-nates a frame; the receiving workstation sets the bit to 1 to signal that it rec-ognizes its destination address. The frame-copied bit also starts as 0 but is set to 1 by the receiving (destination) workstation when it copies the frame's contents into its own memory (in other words, when it actually receives the data). The data is copied (and the bit set) only if the frame is received without error. If the originating (source) workstation gets its frame back with both of these bits set, it knows that a successful reception occurred. However, if the address-recognized bit is not set when the frame returns to the originating workstation, the destination workstation is no longer on the network—it must have crashed.

Another situation happens when the destination address is recognized but the frame-copied bit is not set. This tells the originating workstation that the frame was damaged in transit (the error-detected bit in the end delimiter is also set). One other combination of these bits is possible: if the address-recognized bit and the frame-copied bit are both set but the error-detected bit is also set, the originating workstation knows that the error happened *after* the frame was correctly received.

The Abort Sequence. An abort sequence, consisting of a start delimiter followed immediately by an end delimiter, signals that the current transmis-sion of a frame or token is being canceled.

FDDI Frames

The fiber distributed data interface (FDDI) is a much newer protocol than Ethernet or Token Ring. The X3T9.5 Task Group of the American National Standards Institute (ANSI) designed FDDI to pass tokens around a ring of optical fiber at a rate of 100 megabits per second. Purposely designed to be much like IEEE 802.5 Token Ring standard as possible, FDDI differs from Token Ring only where necessary to support faster speed and longer transmission distances.

If FDDI were to use the same bit-encoding scheme employed by Token Ring, every bit would require two optical signals: a pulse of light and then a pause of darkness. Thus FDDI would have to send 200 million signals per second to have a 100-megabit-per-second transmission rate. Instead, FDDI uses a scheme, *4B/5B,* that encodes four bits of data into five bits for transmission so that fewer signals are needed to send a byte of information. The five-bit codes (*symbols*) were chosen carefully to ensure that network timing requirements are met. At a 100-megabit-per-second transmission rate, the 4B/5B scheme actually sends 125 million signals per second (125M baud). Also, because each carefully selected light pattern symbol represents fours (a half-byte, or nibble), FDDI hardware can operate at the nibble and byte level rather than at the bit level, making the high data rate a little easier to achieve.

There are two major differences in the way that FDDI and IEEE 802.5 Token Ring manage the token:

- In Token Ring, a new token is circulated only after a sending workstation gets back the frame that it sent. In FDDI, a new token is circulated immediately by the sending workstation after it finishes transmitting a frame.

- FDDI doesn't use the priority and reservation subfields that Token Ring uses to allocate system resources. Rather, FDDI classifies attached workstations as asynchronous (those that aren't rigid about the time periods that occur between network accesses) and synchronous (those that have stringent requirements regarding the timing between transmissions). FDDI uses a complex algorithm to allocate network access to the two classes of devices.

Figure 3.8 shows an FDDI token. It consists of preamble, start delimiter, frame control, and frame status. These fields have the same definition for FDDI tokens as for FDDI frames.

Fig. 3.8
An FDDI token.

Figure 3.9 shows the layout of an FDDI frame. Notice the similarity to the IEEE 802.5 Token Ring frame just discussed. The FDDI frame, like its slower Token Ring cousin, carries either MAC control data or user data.

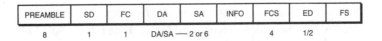

Fig. 3.9
An FDDI frame.

The fields in an FDDI frame are the following:

- The *preamble* field is used for synchronization purposes. Although initially 64 bits (16 symbol-encoded nibbles), the preamble's length can be modified dynamically by subsequent workstations according to their own clocking and synchronization requirements.

- The pattern of the unique two-symbol (one-byte) *start delimiter (SD)* field identifies the start of the frame.

- The two-symbol (one-byte) *frame control (FC)* field consists of the following subfields:

      C   L   F F   T T T T

- The C subfield designates the frame class, which tells whether the frame is being used for synchronous or asynchronous service. The L bit is the frame address length and indicates whether 16-bit or 48-bit addresses are being used (both are possible on the same FDDI network). The FF bits are the frame format subfield, which expresses whether the frame is a MAC frame carrying ring-management information or an LLC frame carrying user data. If this is a MAC frame, the TTTT bits specify the type of the MAC control frame contained in the information field.

- The *destination address (DA)* field, which can be either 16 bits or 48 bits long, identifies the workstation to which this frame is being sent.

- Either 16 or 48 bits long, the *source address (SA)* field identifies the sending workstation.

- The *information (INFO)* data portion of the frame contains either a MAC control record or user data. The length of this field can vary, but cannot cause the frame's overall length to exceed 4,500 bytes.

- The four bytes (eight symbols) of CRC data in the *frame check sequence (FCS)* field are used for error checking.

- In a frame, the *end delimiter (ED)* field is one nibble (one symbol) long. In a token, it is one byte (two symbols) long. It always uniquely identifies the end of the frame or token.

- Of arbitrary length, the *frame status (FS)* field contains the error-detected bit, the address-recognized bit, and the frame-copied bit. These subfields do the same job on an FDDI network as on a Token Ring network.

Higher-Level Protocols

Some of the material just covered on low-level MAC and LLC frames is a bit dry. Fortunately, though, it's time to move on to the higher-level protocols, and learn what goes into the data portion of each of the types of frames described so far. Recall that frames are layered; the data portion of an LLC (user data) frame contains a frame that a higher-level protocol has constructed.

The protocols discussed next are IPX, SPX, and NetBIOS. Each of these protocols is directly programmable by your software. The actual data messages that flow around the network come from either your software (when you do PC-to-PC communications) or from the shell/redirector software that shuttles DOS file-service requests to and from the file server.

Datagrams and Sessions

The two types of PC-to-PC or PC-to-server communications are datagrams and sessions. A *datagram* is a message that the receiver never acknowledges; if message delivery must be verified, the receiver has to supply the verification in a return message. In other words, to use datagrams safely, the sender and receiver must agree on a protocol of their own. Each datagram message stands on its own—if more than one datagram is outstanding, the order in which the datagrams are delivered is not guaranteed. In some cases, the maximum size of a datagram is much smaller than that of a session-related message. However, most networks can send and receive datagrams faster than session-related messages. In contrast to datagrams, a *session* is a logical connection between two workstations in which message reception *is* guaranteed.

Datagrams can be sent at will. For messages to be sent during a session, however, more work must be done: the session must be established, data messages must be sent and received, and at the end of the dialog the session must be closed.

IPX—a Datagram Service

The underlying protocol used by Novell NetWare, Internetwork Packet Exchange (IPX), is a close adaptation of a protocol developed by Xerox Corporation, the Xerox Network Standard (XNS). IPX supports only datagram messages (it is said to be "connectionless"). Corresponding to the network layer of the OSI Model, IPX delivers a message (packet) to its destination by performing addressing, routing, and switching. IPX is speedier than the session-oriented SPX protocol (discussed later in this chapter). While not guaranteeing that IPX always delivers its packets, Novell maintains that IPX packets are correctly received about 95 percent of the time.

Incidentally, NetWare's shell/redirector software uses IPX (not SPX) to send and receive file-service packets to and from the file server. Using IPX is safe and reliable because every such request from a workstation requires a response from the file server. Until the proper response is received, the shell/redirector never assumes that the file server has processed a file-service packet (to write data to a file, for example).

If you use Novell NetWare, you obviously already have IPX. Depending on the version of NetWare that you have, you may also already have SPX. All you need to begin developing DOS or Windows programs that do PC-to-PC communications is a good C compiler and the information in this book.

Recall from Chapter 1, "The Basics of Networking," that if you want to use IPX in your OS/2 programs, you need import libraries from Novell. The import libraries let you reference functions in the DLLs that Novell supplies as part of the NetWare Requester for OS/2.

IPX Destination Address

The destination address in an IPX packet consists of three components: a network number, a node address, and a socket number.

- *Network numbers* identify each segment of a multiserver network. System administrators assign the numbers when the Novell NetWare file servers are initialized.

- *Node addresses* uniquely identify each network adapter card.

- A *socket number* represents the destination application itself, running on the target workstation. Your application opens and closes sockets in much the same way that it opens and closes files.

For IPX packets, the destination address can contain a group (broadcast) address; for SPX packets, the destination address must contain the address of a specific workstation on the network. If your application needs to communicate with a particular workstation, you can use services within IPX to find that workstation's destination address. Chapter 6, "IPX and SPX Programming," includes some examples that show how to obtain a destination address when all you know is the user ID under which the other workstation is logged on. You send IPX packets by specifying a destination address (network, node, and socket), but you receive them by specifying a socket.

IPX Program Services

You can manage PC-to-PC communications by using a set of services that IPX offers to your software. These services rely on three data structures that you construct and pass to IPX:

- The IPX header, which consists of the first 30 bytes of the IPX packet discussed later in this chapter

- The data record or message that you want to send or receive

- An event control block (ECB) that isn't actually transmitted but contains information about a particular IPX operation that you initiate

Chapter 6, "IPX and SPX Programming," covers IPX services in detail; the following sections simply categorize them.

Initialization and Termination Functions. When two PCs on a network want to use IPX to send message records back and forth, the application on each workstation first uses the IPXOpenSocket function to open a socket. The socket number that is open on Workstation A must be known to the application running on Workstation B, and vice versa.

Each workstation needs to know the destination address (the network number, node address, and socket number) of the other workstation. Socket numbers are easy to determine; you simply establish conventions for the sockets that you use. However, your application doesn't automatically know the network number and node address—what you typically know is the other workstation's user ID.

To translate a user ID into a network number and node address, you use the `GetObjectConnectionNumbers` and the `GetInternetworkAddress` functions near the beginning of your program. Be aware, however, that NetWare lets a single user ID log on at several workstations simultaneously. The usual way to handle this situation is by using the first item from the list that is returned to you and ignoring any subsequent items in the list.

After the two workstations finish sending and receiving message records, they each close the open sockets by calling `IPXCloseSocket`.

Functions That Send and Receive Packets. After you open a socket at Workstation A and determine the network number, node address, and socket number at Workstation B (presumably Workstation B has determined the same information regarding Workstation A), you're ready to send and receive message records.

You use `IPXSendPacket` and `IPXListenForPacket` to do the sending and receiving. Each time that you call `IPXSendPacket`, however, you must supply an additional data item called the *immediate address* field. If the message packet must cross a bridge (go through a linkage between two networks) to reach its destination, the immediate address field is the node address of the bridge. To determine the value to be placed in the immediate address field, you call the function `IPXGetLocalTarget`. If the packet doesn't need to cross a bridge, `IPXGetLocalTarget` simply returns the node address of the destination workstation (which still goes into the immediate address field).

IPX does not wait for the packet to be sent or received before returning to your application program; the protocol only initiates the operation. The actual sending and receiving occur in the background. You can handle these operations in either of two ways: the application can go into a loop that repeatedly checks whether the send or receive operation is complete, or it can supply IPX with the address of a routine that IPX executes when the operation completes. Chapter 6, "IPX and SPX Programming," includes examples of these techniques, which are also discussed later in this chapter's description of SPX.

Miscellaneous Functions. Outstanding IPX operations (events) can be canceled with the `IPXCancelEvent` call. Your application can call `IPXScheduleEvent` to ask IPX to schedule a send or receive event to occur later. Especially while polling for the completion of a send or receive operation, you can call `IPXRelinquishControl` to give IPX control of the CPU; this call gives IPX a chance to "breathe" while you wait for the operation to complete.

The IPX Packet Format

Figure 3.10 shows the format of an IPX packet. This packet is the data record that is placed inside an Ethernet frame or Token Ring frame for transmission, or extracted from the frame on reception. An SPX packet (discussed later in this chapter) contains an IPX packet header in its first 30 bytes.

Fig. 3.10
The IPX packet
format.

Length in bytes

Field	Length in bytes
Checksum	2
Length	2
Transport control	1
Packet type	1
Destination network	4
Destination node	6
Destination socket	2
Source network	4
Source node	6
Source socket	2
Data portion	0-546

The fields within an IPX packet are the following:

■ *Checksum*—This two-byte field is a holdover; Xerox defines it in the XNS protocol and so it appears in the IPX packet. Because the lower-level protocol always performs error checking (as mentioned earlier in this chapter), you never need to set this field (IPX always sets it to 0xFFFF).

■ *Length*—This two-byte field expresses the size of the complete packet, including both the IPX packet header and the data portion. The small-est packet length is 30 bytes (just the IPX header itself) and the largest is 576 bytes (30 bytes of IPX header plus 546 bytes of data). IPX calculates the value of this field based on information that you provide when you tell IPX to send a packet; you do not set this field directly.

■ *Transport control*—An IPX packet can cross as many as 16 Novell bridges. IPX sets this one-byte field to 0 when the packet is originally transmit-ted, and increments the field each time a bridge passes along the packet. If the count reaches 16, the packet is discarded, which normally is not a concern. IPX sets and uses this field.

- *Packet type*—Xerox defines various types of packets for various purposes; an application that sends IPX packets should set this one-byte field to a value of 4. This value signifies that the packet is what the Xerox standard calls a packet-exchange packet. Later, when this chapter discusses the SPX session-level protocol, you will see that SPX-oriented applications set this field to a value of 5.

- *Destination network*—This four-byte field, as mentioned previously, identifies the network on which the intended receiver workstation is located. Destination network is the first of three fields that you must specify to tell IPX/SPX where to deliver a packet.

- *Destination node*—The second of the three fields in which you specify where IPX/SPX should deliver a packet, these six bytes identify the target workstation by its unique physical address. Chapter 6, "IPX and SPX Programming," includes examples that show how to obtain both the destination network and destination node.

- *Destination socket*—This field contains a two-byte socket number. Destination socket is the last of the three fields in which you specify where to deliver the packet. The application running on the destination workstation must open the socket. Novell and Xerox have reserved certain socket number values. You can ask Novell to assign a particular socket number to your application, or you can use dynamic socket numbers, which are in the range 0x4000 to 0x8000. In either case, you must establish conventions regarding which socket numbers your IPX/SPX-based software will use.

- *Source network*—The network number of the originating workstation, this four-byte field is set by IPX.

- *Source node*—The physical address of the network adapter card in the originating workstation, this six-byte field is set by IPX.

- *Source socket*—The packet is sent through an open socket, which IPX sets in this field.

- *Data portion*—This field—the data record or message that your application wants to send—can be from 0 to 546 bytes long. A zero-length data area might be appropriate, for example, if the presence of the packet itself is sufficient for a particular purpose, such as acknowledging reception of a previous packet. Also, for SPX packets, using the datastream type field for a single-byte data item may also be sufficient. The datastream type field is discussed in the "SPX Packet Format" section.

All the multiple-byte fields in an IPX packet are ordered so that the high-order byte is first (leftmost) and the low-order byte is last. This differs from the native format for multibyte fields in an IBM-type microcomputer.

SPX—Session-Level Communications

Sequenced Packet Exchange (SPX) is a session-level, connection-oriented protocol. Before SPX packets are sent or received, a connection must be established between the two sides that want to exchange information (SPX assigns a *connection* ID at either end of the connection). After the connection is established, messages can be sent in either direction with the guarantee that they will be delivered. SPX also guarantees that packets will arrive in the correct order (if multiple packets are sent at once). Although IPX operates at the Transport layer of the OSI Model, SPX operates at one layer above that, the Network layer. SPX also has some of the characteristics of the Session layer.

SPX uses IPX to send or receive message packets. If you have Novell NetWare, you know that IPX is available to your software. This is not necessarily true for SPX; early versions of NetWare did not support SPX. If you have version 2.0a of NetWare, you have SPX only if the version of the shell/redirector program (ANET3.COM) is 2.01–4. SPX is present in all later versions of NetWare (2.1 and higher). There is a function call that you can use to determine whether SPX is available.

Chapter 6, "IPX and SPX Programming," covers in detail the functions and services that SPX provides; for now, let's see how they are used.

Establishing and Terminating a Connection

The first thing that both workstations do is initialize SPX with the SPXInitialize call. Each workstation then opens one or more sockets by calling the IPXOpenSocket function. (If the call to SPXInitialize indicates that SPX is not installed, you should terminate your program with a message that tells the user that, to use your software, he or she must upgrade to a later version of NetWare.) To establish a connection, Workstation A issues to SPX an SPXListenForConnection call that specifies an open socket. Workstation B must then issue a subsequent SPXEstablishConnection call that specifies Workstation A's destination address (network, node, and socket).

If it knows the user ID of the listening workstation, the calling workstation (the one that issues the SPXEstablishConnection) can call the NetWare GetObjectConnectionNumbers and GetInternetworkAddress functions to determine the network and node that it needs to use in the SPXEstablishConnec- tion call. As previously mentioned, the socket number portion of the destination address is application-specific.

If the SPXEstablishConnection call is issued first, and if all the retry attempts that SPX performs are exhausted before the other workstation issues an SPXListenForConnection, the connection attempt fails.

To establish a connection, both workstations must issue a set of SPXListenForSequencedPacket calls. There are three reasons for this requirement:

- SPX uses some of the resulting packet buffers internally as it creates the connection.

- A pool of packet buffers must be available to SPX so that the protocol can receive and queue incoming messages.

- SPX sometimes "borrows" some of the packet buffers for its own internal use.

While creating the connection, SPX assigns a connection ID at each workstation. When your application wants to send or receive message packets, it uses the connection ID to refer to this particular connection.

To sever a connection, one of the workstations issues an SPXTerminateConnection call. This call causes SPX to automatically send to the other workstation a packet (which your application must recognize and process) whose datastream type field contains a value of 0xFE. Both workstations should close all open sockets after the dialog finishes.

Does the listening application need to sit idle while waiting for a call? No; if you give IPX or SPX the address of an *event service routine* (ESR) that it can execute when the call occurs, the listening application can continue doing other things. ESRs are most useful when your application is listening and waiting for another workstation to call, but they can also be used in other situations. An ESR can be associated with sending or receiving messages and can be used under both IPX and SPX. If you do not use an ESR, you can simply poll for the completion of the event by going into a loop that waits for IPX or SPX to set a completion code for that event.

Sending and Receiving Packets

Sending a message packet is fairly straightforward: you give SPX the address and length of the message data along with the connection ID that SPX assigns while creating the connection. Receiving a packet, however, is a little more complicated. Because multiple ListenForSequencedPacket calls are outstanding when the message is received (a set of them was issued as part of establishing the connection), you must devise a method for determining which call SPX used. Then you must issue another `ListenForSequencedPacket` call to return the packet buffer to SPX's pool. Otherwise, SPX starves and crashes the machine.

You can attach an ESR to a send or a receive operation. The ESR is awakened and executed when the send or receive finishes. Alternatively, you can simply poll for the event's completion. In a Windows program, remember to use `PeekMessage()` in your polling loop to ensure that Windows can dispatch events in the message event queue. Make sure that your ESR is in a fixed segment, and carefully page-lock any allocated memory that holds ECBs.

Miscellaneous Functions

For a quick, emergency exit, you can call `SPXAbortConnection` to unilaterally end a connection. If you want status information about an existing connection, you can call `SPXGetConnectionStatus`. The `SPXInitialize` function returns information about SPX itself, including an indication of whether the protocol is installed.

The SPX Packet Format

An SPX packet, as shown in figure 3.11, contains 30 bytes of IPX packet header followed by 12 bytes of SPX-specific header fields, for a total length of 42 bytes. The 30 bytes of IPX header have the same meaning for SPX as for IPX, except that the packet type field must be set to 5 to specify what Xerox and Novell call a sequenced packet protocol packet (an SPX packet).

Some of the bits within the one-byte *connection control* field are for your use, and others are for use by SPX. The byte is formatted as follows:

```
S   A   !   E   X X X X
```

where the S bit is the system packet flag, A is the acknowledgment-required bit, ! is the attention bit, E is the end-of-message bit, and the remaining four bits are undefined. SPX uses the system packet flag and the acknowledgment-required flag internally. The attention flag and the end-of-message flag are available for your use. SPX passes them untouched along to the destination workstation.

Length in bytes

Checksum	2
Length	2
Transport control	1
Packet type	1
Destination network	4
Destination node	6
Destination socket	2
Source network	4
Source node	6
Source socket	2
Connection control	1
Datastream type	1
Source connection ID	2
Destination connection ID	2
Sequence number	2
Acknowledge number	2
Allocation number	2
Data portion	0-534

Fig. 3.11
The SPX packet format.

The fields in the SPX portion of the header are the following:

- *Datastream type*—You and SPX share this one-byte field. You can set this field to a value from 0 to 253 (0xFD) in each packet that you send to identify the type of data contained in each packet (SPX does not touch values in this range). SPX uses values of 254 (0xFE) and 255 (0xFF) as follows: when Workstation A tells SPX to terminate a connection, SPX sends to Workstation B a final message packet that contains a datastream type field of 254 (0xFE). On receiving this final packet, the application running on Workstation B knows that Workstation A has ended the dialog. For packets that it uses internally, SPX sets this field to a value of 255 (0xFF); your application never sees these packets.

- *Source connection ID*—SPX sets this two-byte field. It contains the SPX-assigned value of the connection ID that identifies this SPX session at the source workstation.

■ *Destination connection ID*—SPX also sets this two-byte field, which contains the connection ID assigned at the destination. If multiple connections are associated with one socket, SPX uses this field to keep track of which message goes with what connection ID.

■ *Sequence number*—SPX also sets this two-byte field, and uses it to identify and discard duplicate packets. (Such duplications can occur, for example, if SPX resends a packet after failing to receive an acknowledgment from the original transmission, but both packets eventually arrive at their destination.)

■ *Acknowledge number*—This field, also set by SPX, keeps track of the sequence number of the next packet that SPX expects to receive for a particular connection ID.

■ *Allocation number*—This two-byte field is also set internally by SPX, which uses the field to count how many packets that have been sent but have not yet been acknowledged by the other workstation.

The maximum size of the data portion of an SPX packet is 534 bytes (slightly less than that of IPX) to accommodate the SPX-specific fields.

NetBIOS

NetBIOS is IBM's protocol for PC-to-PC transfer of message records. Novell provides a NetBIOS emulator with NetWare (when loaded, it sits on top of IPX/SPX). However, because it uses a different frame format, Novell's NetBIOS software is incompatible with the IBM NetBIOS program layer. Novell's NetBIOS software also is incompatible with the IBM NetBIOS program because both use different formats.

IBM NetBIOS on NetWare LANs

A device driver provides IBM NetBIOS services. Under DOS, the driver file, DXMT0MOD.SYS, is part of the IBM PC LAN Support Program. Under OS/2, IBM's protected mode NetBIOS device driver is NETBIOS.OS2. And (to muddy the waters even more), it is possible to have an IBM Token Ring network on which Novell NetWare is running, and, if DXMT0MOD.SYS is loaded at each workstation, NetBIOS communications can take place just as described in this section. Does this mean that you should forget about IPX and SPX communications and concentrate on using NetBIOS? Not necessarily; NetBIOS (either in the form of the Novell emulator or the IBM device driver) takes up extra memory on a Novell NetWare workstation. A further complication is that a NetWare bridge does not pass IBM NetBIOS messages to a different physical token ring. (Nothing is ever simple, is it?)

NetBIOS (Network Basic Input/Output System) is the protocol that the DOS LAN Requester (DLR) and the IBM PC LAN Program use to send file service requests to and from the file server. The protocol's communications facilities are also available to the programs that you write. NetBIOS corresponds to the Network layer, Transport layer, and Session layer of the OSI Model, operating at a higher level than either IPX or SPX. NetBIOS supports both datagram and session-oriented communications. File service packets sent to and received from a file server are managed under session control instead of being treated as individual datagrams; this is one of many differences between DLR, the IBM PC LAN Program, and NetWare.

Most NetBIOS commands come in both *wait* and *no-wait* flavors. When you use the wait version of a command, NetBIOS completes the operation before returning to your program. If you specify no-wait, you can choose to poll (loop until an operation is complete) or to give NetBIOS the address of one of your routines, which NetBIOS will invoke when it completes the command. This facility is similar to the IPX/SPX event service routine concept discussed earlier. Under NetBIOS, such a routine is called a *POST routine*. When you use the no-wait option, your program must inspect two different return codes to determine whether a command completed successfully. The first is the *immediate return code* (available as soon as NetBIOS returns to your application), and the second is the *final return code* (which holds a value of 0xFF until the operation completes, when NetBIOS sets it to the appropriate value).

For DOS programming purposes, when your application is not running in the Windows environment, you can freely use wait and no-wait versions of the NetBIOS commands. Within Windows, you should use only the no-wait versions and use `PeekMessage()` in the loop that watches for the completion of the NetBIOS event.

NetBIOS Names
NetBIOS is name-oriented. Each workstation (and each file server, if the network is operating under LAN Server or the IBM PC LAN Program) is identified by one or more 16-byte names. A table of these names is kept inside NetBIOS. In addition to this table of names, a *permanent node name* is always present. The permanent node name is formed by taking the six bytes of the network address from the network adapter card and prefixing them with 10 bytes of binary 0s. This name is always unique on the network.

Your program can inspect the names in the name table and, except for the permanent node name, can add or delete names at your application's convenience. A special sort of name, the *group name*, can also be added to the table;

unlike a regular name, a group name does not have to be unique on the network. Several workstations can use the same group name at the same time. The number of names and group names that the table can hold is configurable when the device driver is loaded, and usually defaults to 16 names. When establishing a session, you use names (those that you add or the permanent node name) and group names as the destination address and source address. NetBIOS assigns a *name number* to each name that you add. This name number is used to send datagrams.

Because names are always 16 bytes long, you must pad a short name (such as BARRY) with trailing spaces before adding it to the table. Also, you should not try to add a name that starts with an asterisk (*) or with a binary zero (0x00). One more caution: you should not use names that begin with the three characters "IBM"; such names are reserved.

The NetBIOS commands relating to name management are Add Name, Add Group Name, and Delete Name. The NetBIOS Reset command deletes all names from the name table (the permanent node name remains). You should not use a Reset command when running under DOS LAN Requester or the IBM PC LAN Program; Reset will delete the names being used for DOS file redirection as well as the names that you added.

To ensure that a name being added to the table is unique, NetBIOS searches first its local name table and then the entire network to see whether the name is already being used. To search the network, NetBIOS broadcasts a Name Claim frame. If a Name Claim Response frame is received, NetBIOS knows that another workstation is already using the name. NetBIOS frames are discussed later in this chapter.

NetBIOS Datagrams

As you recall, a datagram is connectionless and not guaranteed to be delivered to the other workstation. NetBIOS support for datagrams enables them to be sent to an individual name, to a group name, or to all workstations on the network. NetBIOS datagrams can carry message records up to 512 bytes long.

The NetBIOS commands used for sending and receiving datagrams are Send Datagram, Send Broadcast Datagram, Receive Datagram, and Receive Broadcast Datagram.

NetBIOS Sessions

You can create a session between any two names on the network. Multiple sessions are possible between the two names, and you can even create a session between two names on the same workstation. While the session is active, you can send and receive message records with the assurance that each will be delivered in the proper destination in the proper sequence.

To create a session, one workstation issues a Listen command (with or without the Wait option). The Listen command specifies whether it is listening for a call from a specific name or from any name. The other workstation then issues a Call command, specifying the name that it is calling. When each command completes on its respective workstation, NetBIOS returns a *local session number* (LSN) to each application. (The LSNs returned to each workstation are not necessarily the same.) Thereafter, each workstation uses the assigned LSN to refer to the open, active session.

Message records sent and received during a session can be up to 65,535 bytes long. The commands that you use are Send, Chain Send (which can be used to send multiple messages back to back), and Receive.

At the end of the dialog, both workstations issue a Hang Up command to close the session.

Miscellaneous NetBIOS Services

You can use the Session Status command to obtain information about all active sessions for a specified name, or for all names in the local name table. Use the Adapter Status command when you want to find out, for example, the permanent node name of a particular workstation.

Network Control Blocks (NCBs)

To invoke a particular NetBIOS command, your application builds a *network control block (NCB)* and then executes an Interrupt 5C (hex). Figure 3.12 shows the format of an NCB.

Fig. 3.12
The network
control block
(NCB) format

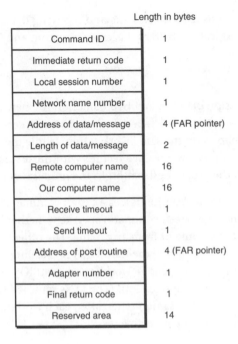

Length in bytes

Field	Length in bytes
Command ID	1
Immediate return code	1
Local session number	1
Network name number	1
Address of data/message	4 (FAR pointer)
Length of data/message	2
Remote computer name	16
Our computer name	16
Receive timeout	1
Send timeout	1
Address of post routine	4 (FAR pointer)
Adapter number	1
Final return code	1
Reserved area	14

Here is a description of each of the fields:

■ You set the one-byte *command* field to tell NetBIOS which command you want it to execute. If the high-order bit is set, the command is executed in no-wait mode.

■ This one-byte *immediate return code* field contains the immediate error code. NetBIOS sets this field when it begins executing the command.

■ After a Listen or Call command is executed, the one-byte *local session number* field contains the LSN assigned to that session. For Send or Receive commands, you put the LSN of the session in this field.

■ NetBIOS returns the one-byte *name number* field after an Add Name or Add Group Name command. You use this number, not the name, when issuing any of the datagram-related commands or the Receive Any command.

■ The four-byte (segment:offset) *data buffer address* field is where you put a pointer to the data buffer associated with a send or receive operation.

■ You set the two-byte *data buffer length* field to indicate the length of the data buffer.

- You set the 16-byte *call name* field to indicate the name of the workstation with which you want to communicate.

- You set the 16-byte *local name* field to indicate which of the names in the local name table (or the permanent node name) you want for your application.

- When you issue a Call or Listen command, you set the one-byte *receive timeout* field to a value that indicates how many half-second intervals NetBIOS should use when waiting for a subsequent Receive command to complete. A value of 0 indicates no time-out.

- When you issue a Call or Listen command, you set this one-byte *send timeout* field to a value that indicates how many half-second intervals NetBIOS should use when waiting for a subsequent Send command to complete. A value of 0 indicates no time-out.

- You put into the four-byte *POST routine address* a far pointer (segment:offset) to a routine that NetBIOS invokes when the command completes. This field is meaningful only when the no-wait option is in effect. If you set this field to 0 (NULL), you should poll the final return code to determine when the command completes and whether it completed successfully. Under OS/2, you put into the POST field the handle of a semaphore that you have created, then wait for the semaphore to clear. NetBIOS clears the semaphore when NetBIOS completes processing the event. The clearing of the semaphore enables the code waiting on the semaphore to resume execution.

- You set the one-byte *adapter number* field to indicate which network adapter you want to use (0 for primary and 1 for alternate). A workstation can contain as many as two Token Ring cards.

- The one-byte *final return* code field contains 0xFF while a command is being processed; when processing finishes, the field's setting shows whether the command was successful.

- Your program does not use the NCB's 14-byte *reserved area*, which is reserved by NetBIOS.

NetBIOS Frames

NetBIOS frames are created and managed exclusively by NetBIOS; you don't have to deal with them directly. To create its frames, NetBIOS uses the contents of the NCB that you build, as well as what it knows about the sessions and names currently in effect. NetBIOS uses several types of frames. The more important ones are the following:

- When you issue a Call command, NetBIOS broadcasts a *name query* frame to find out whether the destination workstation is on the network.

- When you issue an Add Name command, NetBIOS sends an *add name query* frame around the network to ask whether any other workstation is using the name.

- When you issue an Add Group Name command, NetBIOS sends an *add group name query* frame to find out whether another workstation is already using the name as a unique name. Several workstations can use the same group name, but it cannot already have been established as a unique name.

- A listening workstation returns a *name recognized* frame coded to indicate the outstanding listening response to a name query frame. In essence, the frame announces, "I exist, and I am listening."

- If a workstation recognizes that one of its names is the same as the name in an *add name query* frame, that workstation returns an *add name response* frame to tell the workstation executing an Add Name command that the name is already in use.

- A workstation executing a Call command sends a *session initialize* frame to establish the session.

- The calling workstation receives a *session confirm* frame to indicate that the session is established.

- A *data* frame is sent when you give NetBIOS a Send command to process.

- NetBIOS sends the *session end* frame when you issue a Hang Up command.

- A *datagram frame* is similar to a data frame, except that a data frame exists within the context of a session that you have created, and a datagram frame does not require that a session already be established.

- NetBIOS transmits a *status query* frame when you give NetBIOS an Adapter Status command for a remote adapter.

■ Returned by the workstation that received a status query frame, the *status response* frame contains configuration and status information.

Server Message Blocks (SMBs)

As previously mentioned, the DOS LAN Requester and the IBM PC LAN Program intercept network-related DOS function calls and send them across the network to the file server. Both programs use a *server message block (SMB)* protocol to accomplish file redirection. To request that the server perform file operations on behalf of the workstation, DLR and the PC LAN Program open NetBIOS sessions with the file server and then send SMBs to the server. There are four categories of SMBs: session control, file access, print service, and messages.

Session Control

After a NetBIOS session is established between a workstation and the server, the workstation sends a Verify Dialect SMB to the server. This message contains data that indicates the capabilities of the version of DLR or the PC LAN Program running at the workstation. The server examines this message and responds to the workstation with information about itself and the capabilities that the server supports. This exchange is then followed by one or more Start Connection SMBs that are used to create logical connections between the workstation and network resources at the file server. These logical connections are later terminated by the workstation when it sends End Connection SMBs to the server (or when the occurrence of an error aborts the NetBIOS session).

File Access

A workstation uses the SMBs in the file access category to gain remote access to the files on the server's hard disk. The functions included in this category enable the workstation to treat the server disk almost like a local hard drive. The workstation can direct the file server to do the following:

■ Create and remove directories

■ Create, open, and close files

■ Read from and write to files

■ Rename and delete files

- Search for files

- Get or set file attributes

- Lock records

For remote files, these operations are intercepted at the workstation (the local copy of PC DOS never sees them) and turned into SMBs for the file server to execute.

Print Service

The SMBs in the print service category enable a workstation to queue files so that a server can print them, and to obtain print queue status information. The workstation can create a spool file, write data to the spool file, close the spool file, and ask that the server return a Print Queue Status SMB.

Messages

The messages category of SMBs supports simple message-passing through the following functions:

- Send Single Block Message

- Send Broadcast Message

- Send Start of Multiple Block Message

- Send Text of Multiple Block Message

- Send End of Multiple Block Message

- Forward User Name

- Cancel Forward

- Get Machine Name

The messenger and receiver configurations of the IBM PC LAN Program discussed in Chapter 1, "The Basics of Networking," use these functions.

The Format of an SMB

Figure 3.13 shows the layout of a server message block.

Length in bytes

Field	Length
Message type	1
Server type	3
Function ID	1
Return error class	1
Critical error class	1
Return code	2
Direction code	1
Reserved	14
Network path ID	2
Process ID	2
Reserved	4
Parameter count	1
Parameters	?
Buffer length	2
SMB buffer	?

Fig. 3.13

The server message block (SMB) format.

The fields included in the block are the following:

- The *message type* field identifies the type of message that the SMB contains.

- The *server type* field indicates the type of server component that the SMB addresses.

- The *function ID* field indicates the type of the network request that the SMB represents.

- If an error occurs, the *return error class* field indicates where the failure occurred (for example, while executing an Interrupt 21 [hex] function at the server).

- The *critical error class* field provides information about critical errors that occur at the server.

- The *return code* field indicates the command's completion status.

- The *direction code* field indicates whether the SMB is a request to a server or a response to a workstation.

- The 14 bytes of the first *reserved* area are reserved.

- The *network path ID* field contains the computer name, path, and the file name that identify a logical connection between a workstation and a particular file server resource.

- The *process ID* field identifies the program on the workstation that issued the DOS function call which resulted in the SMB.

- The second *reserved* area is another set of reserved bytes.

- The *parameter count* field indicates the number of parameters that the parameters field represents.

- The meaning of the *parameters* field varies with the function of the SMB.

- The *buffer length* field gives the length of the SMB buffer area.

- A variably formatted field containing function-specific data, the *SMB buffer* field can include zero or more variable-length structures. The first byte of each structure identifies the type of the structure, and the next two bytes give the structure's length.

Summary

This chapter explored, literally from bottom to top, how PCs communicate on a LAN. You are now familiar with the different layers of processing that messages and frames undergo as they are prepared for transmission. Also, you now have a good grasp of the underlying differences between Ethernet, Token Ring, and FDDI. IPX, SPX, and NetBIOS are no longer vague, mysterious layers of software on the workstations that you use; you now understand how these protocols operate. And, you have delved into the mechanisms used by NETX, DLR, and the PC LAN Program to enable a file server's resources to be shared across the network.

Part II

Network Programming Techniques

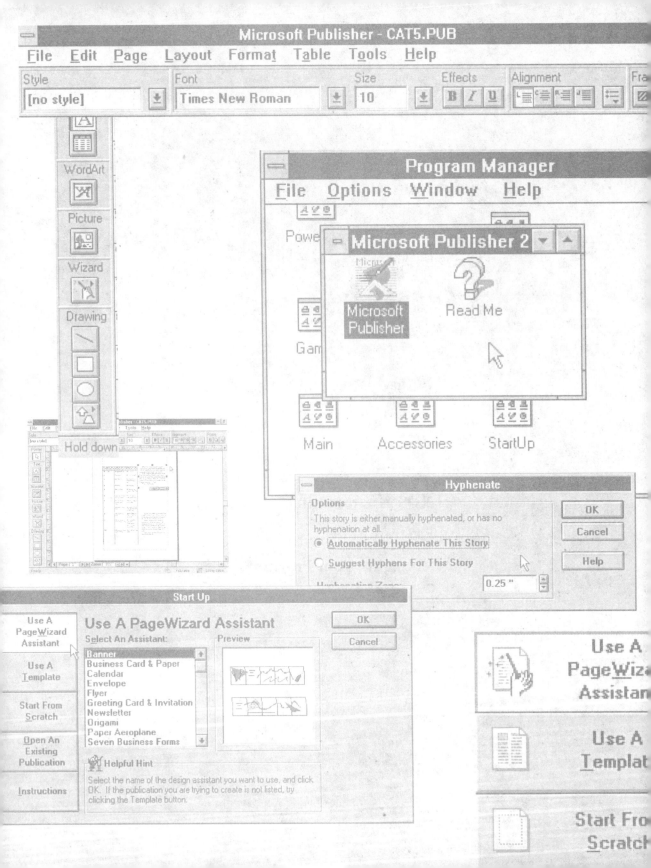

Chapter 4

Shared File Programming

Programming for a multiuser LAN environment is mostly a matter of taking extra care to ensure that users don't bump into each other or destroy each other's files. This is easier said than done; it takes thorough planning and design.

So far, this book has described what the LAN environment looks like. This chapter discusses how to design and program your applications so that they are LAN-aware. The chapter raises several design issues that you need to consider, such as how to choose a file- and record-locking scheme and how to coordinate related file updates. This chapter also includes a series of tests for determining when your application is running on a LAN, and offers coding examples for identifying workstations, sharing files, locking files, printing to a shared printer, and handling file attributes on a network. Finally, this chapter closes with a discussion of the things you *cannot* do on a network, such as sorting directory entries on a file server.

The theme of this chapter is *how to develop programs that run well on many different kinds of networks*. Some of the more specialized features and facilities found on various LANs are touched on, but their full description is deferred to Part IV, "Reference." The aim is to work at the highest possible level that allows the job to get done.

Design Considerations

The extra care that you take in designing your application will really pay off when people begin using it in a LAN environment. Users will not only be glad for the bugs that they don't run into, but they will be impressed by the LAN-aware features that you build into the environment. The following section describes several things to consider.

General Techniques

Whenever possible, avoid writing code that uses facilities specific to a particular LAN vendor. For example, you may find that Novell's Transaction Tracking System (TTS) exactly suits the design of your application. (TTS is a mechanism that Novell provides for grouping sets of database updates into atomic operations.) Be aware that, if you want your application to run on non-Novell LANs, you will have to provide your own substitute for TTS.

When is it impossible to avoid vendor-specific programming? Here are some situations in which vendor-specific coding is required:

- PC DOS does not provide a surefire, standard method of determining the presence of a LAN. Because you almost certainly need to be aware in your application whether it is running on a LAN, you must run several tests (some vendor-specific) and infer from the results whether a LAN is present. Later, this chapter describes some techniques for detecting the LAN.

- When a file is created on a NetWare LAN, the file is automatically given a file attribute of Nonshareable. To modify this NetWare-specific file attribute to make the file shareable, you must call a function within NetWare. The section "Setting File Attributes," toward the end of this chapter, shows the technique for doing this.

- When the NetWare shell detects the termination of a program, the shell releases all locks, closes all files, and performs several general cleanup tasks. Normally, this behavior is exactly what you want. Under NetWare version 2.0a and later, however, the shell sometimes does not distinguish between a program that COMMAND.COM executed and a program that you executed from within your application. If your application expects files to remain open across the spawn() or exec() call, you must use a NetWare function call to disable NetWare's cleanup actions temporarily. You then should reenable them before returning to DOS. This function, SetEndOfJobStatus, which turns the cleanup action off or on, is invoked as follows:

```
regs.h.ah = 0xBB;     /* SetEndOfJobStatus       */
regs.h.al = 0;        /* 0 = disable; 1 = enable */
int86(0x21, &regs, &regs);
```

> **Caution**
>
> In a Windows environment, calling `SetEndOfJobStatus` affects other pro
> grams, including both Windows applications and DOS applications running in
> a DOS session. Be aware that because of Windows' cooperative computing
> environment, your program may sometimes conflict with other software if you
> modify the default behavior of DOS, NETX, or Windows itself.

- Sometimes not enough memory is available to do things at the highest
  possible level. A good example is the choice that you make to support
  NetBIOS or IPX/SPX for PC-to-PC communications (see Chapter 3,
  "PC-to-PC Communication Concepts"); you can run NetBIOS on a
  Novell NetWare network, but the Novell NetBIOS emulator
  consumes extra memory.

- Your application may absolutely *require* that certain things be true. For
  example, you have to be running OS/2 on the file server; in this case,
  you give up compatibility with Novell NetWare. On the other hand,
  you may find that you cannot design or write your application without
  using NetWare's Print Services (see the "NetWare Print Services" section
  later in this chapter); in this case, you give up compatibility with the
  DOS LAN Requester (DLR), the IBM PC LAN Program (PCLP), and LAN
  Server. Of course, you compromise as much as possible in these situations, but (rarely, I hope) the application's requirements may not be at
  all flexible.

One of the most devastating things that you can do on a network is to store
user configuration data inside the executable (.EXE) file itself. This scheme
has two problems: first, you can't store individual user configurations for
everyone on the LAN; second, you can't mark the executable file Shareable,
Read-Only. A better approach is to establish a configuration file for each user,
and this approach is where you can put the machine name (discussed in
Chapter 2, "Multiuser Concepts") to good use. If you tell users that they must
set up a machine name for each workstation (or each user login account), and
also give them guidelines for constructing the name (it must be unique, between one and eight characters long, consist of alphanumeric characters, and
otherwise conform to the requirements for a valid file name under DOS), you
can use the machine name as the basis for the name of each user's configuration file. An example of such a name is BARRY.CFG. Later in this chapter,
you see a method that you can use to ensure that users have set up machine
names.

A common programming technique that makes perfect sense in a single-user environment is for a program to read a control record into memory and hold it there while the program executes. If the control record is one that is modified as the application runs, each workstation will soon have a different copy of the record and lose the capability to coordinate with the other workstations. Make sure that you recognize which files and records in your application the general user population can update, and then maintain these files and records on the file server, not in the workstation's memory.

Chapter 2, "Multiuser Concepts," discusses the importance of checking for I/O errors inside your software. On a LAN, you should offer users more options for handling these errors. For example, you may have to acquire a physical lock on a file and find that DOS returns to your program the error message Access Denied. No matter how you tune Sharing Retry Count/Delay, you must still account for the possibility that a locked region of a file may become inaccessible because of a network operating system bug, file server problem, or other difficulty. To account for this possibility, you should implement your own automatic retry logic in addition to setting Sharing Retry Count/Delay. But what if the lock cannot be acquired, even after a reasonable amount of time? You should abort the current process as gracefully as possible—release any locks in effect, close any open files, and inform the user at the workstation that a significant error has occurred that requires a system administrator's attention. You may even have to broadcast a message telling all the users to log off so that the file server can be restarted.

Deciding on a File- and Record-Locking Scheme

As mentioned at the beginning of this chapter, it takes thorough planning and design to develop programs that work well on a network. The key is knowing how each file is accessed and updated, including database files, help files, user-specific files, and temporary files. For each file or class of file, decide how you want to protect the contents from being damaged by users who are concurrently using the file. The following guidelines should help.

An application usually retrieves records, displays them on the screen, and begins accepting keyboard input from the user. While users are entering input data, physical record locking clearly is an inadequate method of collision protection. Such record locking, during the (relatively) long period of time it takes a user to do keyboard entry, is unfair to the other users. Besides, the method cannot guarantee that the user performing I/O will actually fulfill his or her intention of updating those records.

The best approach is to implement a user-lock facility at the application level. This approach is the essence of the library-card scheme mentioned in Chapter 2, "Multiuser Concepts." Such a facility makes use of a centralized control file on the file server, in which records representing user intentions and fulfillments are placed. This technique makes it possible for an application, running on several workstations simultaneously, to coordinate with all the currently running instances of itself.

The drawback to the library-card scheme is that all programs that access the charged-out files must be designed to look in the control file before opening files. The library-card scheme works well with large, vertical market applications (such as an insurance claims handling system, a stock-market trading system, a shop floor control system, or an airline fleet maintenance system) because the application should be the only one to touch the files. Horizontal market applications, such as word processors and business graphics presentation programs, have a tougher time enforcing this scheme, because users at other workstations can easily use other software—not developed by you—to access files.

Table 4.1 shows some possible fields of a control file.

Table 4.1 An Example of a Control File's Fields	
Field	**Purpose**
User ID	The machine name of the user doing an update
File ID	The file that the user intends to update
Key	Identification of the records affected by the update
Transaction	Code expressing the type of update
Date/Time	Date-and-time stamp
In Progress	Code that gives the status of the update; 1 while in progress, 0 when finished

Of course, you may want to add other fields to this control file so that it supports your application exactly the way you want. And you may want to tie this control file logically to a journal file, discussed later in this chapter.

When a user signals an intention to enter new or changed information, the application performs the following steps (note that the control file is opened in DENY_NONE [shared] mode):

II

Network Programming

1. Physically lock the control file.

2. Check whether it is okay for the user to proceed. (Is there an entry in the control file already that shows that another user has something in progress?)

3. If there is a conflict, unlock the control file and inform the user that the record (or file, or entity) is not now available, perhaps with a message telling the user to try again later. (If the date/time stamp is old, this control file entry may be obsolete. Old entries will need housecleaning, but should not cause conflicts.)

4. If there is no conflict, insert an entry in the control file for the user, unlock the file, and proceed with the update.

5. Read the necessary data files and display the data to the user. Accept the user's input.

6. When the user finishes, acquire a physical lock on the individual data records (or perhaps the entire file) that need to be updated, as prescribed by the following guidelines. After all locks are acquired, do the I/O.

7. After the updates are done and the locks are removed from the affected data records and files, remove the entry from the control file. You can delete the entry simply by marking the entry as unused (finished) or by copying the entry to a separate file for audit trail purposes and then marking the control file entry as unused.

8. If the user cancels the update, simply remove the entry from the control file.

If the data file being updated is a single common database that the application accesses on a record-by-record basis (each record is an independent entity, with no relationships among records), the locking that your application performs when writing a record is rather simple. Because the file is open in DENY_NONE (shared) mode, all users have access to the file and various users may be updating different records within the file at the same time. To write a record, you lock the appropriate region of the file (corresponding to the record about to be written), make sure that the lock is successful, actually write the record, and then unlock that region of the file.

You may have designed your application so that a separate file contains each entity that the application handles. If the file is read into memory, updated, and immediately written back to disk without intervention or input from the

user, it is appropriate for your application to open the file in
DENY_READ_WRITE (exclusive) mode for the duration of the quick update.
On the other hand, if your application accepts input from the user between
reading the entire file and writing it (a good example is the way that a spreadsheet or word-processing program handles files), you can follow these steps to
implement a secure, LAN-aware method of handling concurrent access:

1. Use the previously described library-card scheme to "own the file"
   while the user inputs data. When you put an entry in the control file,
   also record the file's last-modified date, last-modified time, and size.

2. Open the file for DENY_READ_WRITE (exclusive) access, read it into
   memory, and close the file. Present the data to the user and enable the
   user to change it.

3. Before updating the file, first check whether the file's current last-
   modified date, last-modified time, and file size match the values that
   you originally placed in the control file. If you detect a difference, inform the user that the file has changed since he or she first loaded it.
   Then ask whether your software should proceed with the update.

4. If the file was not touched while the user keyed changes, or if the user
   signals that it's okay to overlay the changed file with the more recent
   changes, open the file for DENY_READ_WRITE access, write the
   changes, and close the file. If your application uses the entries in the
   control file for audit purposes, you can mark this entry with a code that
   says "file was overlayed!" if the user authorized it.

Suppose that your application manages an index-type file, in which certain
data records bear a relationship to one another or to the contents of records
in another file. In this case, besides possibly employing the library-card
scheme, you can use the following mechanism:

1. Open the file for DENY_NONE (shared) access from each workstation so
   that everyone can use the file.

2. To do an update, acquire a lock on the entire file (as if it were one big
   record) before writing records.

3. Write the records that contain the related data and release the lock.

Help files and other files that are usually accessed on a Read-Only basis (but
are periodically updated by a special maintenance program or upgrade/instal-
lation process) can benefit from this design approach:

II

Network Programming

1. After initial installation or file creation, use DOS function call 43 (hex), Change File Mode, to mark the file Read-Only.

2. In everyday use, the Read-Only attribute protects the file from being modified (or being inadvertently deleted), and also enables the file to be buffered locally at the workstation rather than remotely at the file server. (Local buffering helps performance.)

3. When the file needs to be updated, the installation or special maintenance program can use that same DOS function call to give the file a Read-Write attribute and then proceed with the update.

4. During the update process, you can protect the file from multiuser access by opening it with a DENY_READ_WRITE (exclusive) mode. After the update or installation finishes, the file should be marked Read-Only again.

Some programming environments provide their own locking schemes, over which you have little or no control. For example, you may find yourself coding *embedded SQL statements* in your C programs (or calling an SQL API directly). In such a situation, the programming manual may discuss *shared locks*, *exclusive locks*, and *isolation levels*. However, the underlying software that performs the actual I/O on the files probably uses one or more of the locking schemes described in this section to protect the data.

Coordinating Related File Updates

A special situation arises when a file contains data fields whose values have certain relationships to data fields in a second file. To handle such a situation, you need to do the following:

- Avoid deadlocks during the process of acquiring locks

- Protect the data in both files while updating takes place

- Prepare for the possibility that the machine may crash (perhaps from a power failure) after one file is updated but before the second update takes place

By using a technique known as *journaling*, you can easily handle this potentially disastrous situation. The following are the steps that you take in your application; note that step 1, which contains the exception-handling logic, is described last:

2. Acquire all locks on the related files before you proceed. This step avoids deadlock.

3. Read the records that will be affected by the update and store their images in a separate file (the journal file). Mark the journal entry "update not yet applied."

4. Write the updated records to the files.

5. Mark the journal entry "update applied."

6. Release the locks.

7. If program execution reaches this point, the updates were fully applied and the journal file was marked accordingly. However, a power failure could have caused processing to halt after any one of the preceding steps, and you need to restore the related files to a consistent condition.

1. This step is described last so that you understand the context in which it executes. When your application starts, it needs to inspect the journal file before letting users make changes to any of the files in the system. If any of the items in the journal file are marked "update not yet applied," you can show these entries to the user, roll back the related files to a consistent state by copying the images from the journal file back to their respective file locations, and mark the journal file entry "rolled back."

Power failures are not the only culprits that can cause inconsistencies. If you are an especially conservative designer or programmer, or you are working on an especially sensitive application, you can take steps in your software, at strategic points, to check for inconsistencies in the data. If your defensive programming turns up an "impossible situation," you can fall back on an enhanced variation of the preceding steps to make the related files consistent again. Naturally, this is a good time to ask the user to notify you that something went wrong.

Incidentally, you may find other uses for the audit trail provided by the journal file.

Far Pointers

Far pointers are commonly used in network programming. IBM microcomputers have a segmented architecture in which the complete address of a structure or function is specified in segment:offset form. Because the network support software exists in a segment different from your application code, you must use far pointers to tell the network support software where your structures and functions are located. The current versions of the Borland and Microsoft compilers support far pointers, but some differences exist in how the compilers' preprocessor macros and library routines handle far pointers. In particular, the process of separating a far pointer into its segment and offset components varies by compiler. The reverse process of creating a far pointer from a segment and an offset is also handled differently.

This book treats far pointers according to the descriptions of the following three macros. Each description is accompanied by a function prototype and a macro definition. If your compiler defines macros or functions that behave differently than the following ones, you can insert the given prototypes and macro definitions into your code.

MK_FP() makes a far pointer. This function (macro) takes two unsigned integer parameters: segment and offset. MK_FP() returns a far pointer that it creates from the segment and offset values. The Borland and Microsoft compilers conform to this definition.

```
Function prototype:
void far *MK_FP(unsigned int segment, unsigned int offset)

Macro definition:
#define MK_FP(seg, ofs)    ((void far *)  \
   (((unsigned long) (seg) << 16) ¦ (unsigned) (ofs)))
```

FP_OFF() obtains the offset portion of a far pointer. This function (macro) takes a far pointer as a parameter and returns the offset portion of the pointer. The Borland compiler conforms to this usage of FP_OFF(), but the Microsoft compiler defines the function differently.

```
Function prototype:
unsigned int FP_OFF(void far *pointer)

Macro definition:
#define FP_OFF(pointer)    ((unsigned) (pointer))
```

FP_SEG() obtains the segment portion of a far pointer. This function (macro) takes a far pointer as a parameter and returns the segment portion of the pointer. The Borland compiler conforms to this usage of FP_OFF(), but the Microsoft compiler defines this function differently.

```
Function prototype:
unsigned int FP_SEG(void far *pointer)

Macro definition:
#define FP_SEG(pointer)    ((unsigned)  \
    (unsigned long) (pointer) >> 16))
```

Detecting the LAN

Because there isn't a standard method for detecting the presence of a LAN, you must conduct a series of tests in your program and infer the LAN environment from the results. The following section describes the tests that you can perform, along with a discussion of what each tells you. After each of the tests is explained, some of them are combined into a custom *LAN-Presence Test* that you can use in your software.

The SHARE Installed Test

One way to detect a LAN is to look for SHARE.EXE. SHARE enables file sharing on a DOS-based workstation. SHARE hooks into DOS Interrupt 2F (hex), the *multiplex interrupt*.

Caution

The multiplex interrupt was added to DOS beginning with version 3.0. If you invoke it under earlier versions of DOS, your program will likely crash.

Also, if you use Windows on a LAN, you should make doubly certain to load SHARE before starting Windows. Windows does not let you run SHARE in one of its enhanced mode DOS sessions. Because SHARE hooks itself into DOS, and because you can use the DOS EXIT command to end a DOS session (which would remove SHARE from memory), Windows prevents SHARE from running by pretending that it is already loaded. When you run SHARE in a Windows DOS session, SHARE reports that it is already running. As an unfortunate side effect, multiuser software running in a DOS session will think that file sharing is enabled, when in fact SHARE is not present. File damage and corruption can result.

Each process that makes use of Interrupt 2F adheres to a general interface for recognizing and accepting function requests. A *multiplex number* identifying the particular interrupt handler is placed in the AH CPU register, and the setting of the AL register indicates the specific function to be performed. For SHARE.EXE, the multiplex number is 10 (hex) and the Get Installed State function code is 0. If installed, SHARE responds to this function code by setting the AL register to FF (hex). Any other value returned in the AL register indicates that SHARE is not installed, as shown in the following example:

```
if (_os_major < 3)
    {
    printf("Can't check for SHARE.\n");
    exit(1);
    }
```

```
    else
        {
        regs.h.ah = 0x10;
        regs.h.al = 0;
        int86(0x2f, &regs, &regs);
        if (regs.h.al != 0xFF)
            {
            printf("SHARE.EXE is not loaded.\n");
            exit(1);
            }
        }
```

To avoid the problem of Windows pretending that SHARE is loaded when in fact it is not, you can use an alternative detection scheme. Open a file with a DENY_NONE sharing mode, use DOS function call 5Ch to lock a region of the file, and note whether the call is successful. If SHARE is in fact not present (Windows, not SHARE, puts 0xFF in the AL register when you invoke interrupt 2Fh), the lock operation returns an error.

The Network Drive Test

Another way to detect a LAN is with a DOS IOCTL call (function 44 hex, subfunction 9). The call tests whether a logical drive is local or remote. To use this function, put the number of the logical drive in the BX register (drive A: is 1, drive C: is 3, and so on) and perform the call. If bit 12 of the DX register is a 1 following the call, the drive is a remote drive. Perform this test for all possible nonremovable drives (C: through Z:) and look for at least one remote drive:

```
    remote_drive_present = 0;

    for (i=3; i<26; i++)
        {
        regs.h.ah = 0x44;
        regs.h.al = 9;
        int86(0x21, &regs, &regs);
        if ( (regs.x.dx & 0x1000) == 0x1000 )
            {
            remote_drive_present = 1;
            break;
            }
        }
```

The IOCTL method has one problem: it doesn't discriminate between a network drive and a CD-ROM drive. The software drivers that Microsoft developed to support CD-ROM machines use the same DOS internals as the network to identify remote drives. However, there are some MSCDEX (Microsoft CD-ROM Extension) function calls that can help. Interrupt 2F (hex) is the entry point for the MSCDEX functions. Function 15 (hex), subfunction 0, returns the number of CD-ROM logical drives in the BX

register. If BX is 0 after this call, you don't have to worry about CD-ROM
drives. If it's nonzero, however, things get complicated. After this call,
the CX register contains the first CD-ROM drive (drive D: is 3, drive E: is 4,
and so on), but multiple CD-ROM drives are possible. Function 15 (hex),
subfunction 0B (hex), checks whether a drive is a CD-ROM drive, and
subfunction 0D (hex) gets a list of all the CD-ROM drive letters. Unfortunately, only the newer MSCDEX versions (2.0 or later) support the additional
query subfunctions 0B and 0D, so they may not be available

If your application detects a CD-ROM drive, you might use an approach that
counts on the almost certain likelihood that any network drives have been
assigned drive letters that come after the CD-ROM drives because of the way
that DOS establishes drive letters. This means you can look for network drives
by starting with a drive letter one position beyond the count (in the BX register) of drives beginning with the first CD-ROM drive (the CX register).

Here's some code that summarizes the situation with CD-ROM drives:

```
start_drive = 3;      /* tentatively start at C: */

regs.h.ah = 0x15;
regs.h.al = 0;
regs.x.bx = 0;
int86(0x2f, &regs, &regs);
if (regs.x.bx != 0)
     start_drive = regs.x.cx + regs.x.bx + 1;
                   /* CD-ROM found.  Start 1 beyond it. */


/*   Now do the 'network drives' test, starting beyond
     any CD-ROM drives that might exist.   */


remote_drive_present = 0;

for (i=start_drive; i<26; i++)
     {
     regs.h.ah = 0x44;
     regs.h.al = 9;
     int86(0x21, &regs, &regs);
     if ( (regs.x.dx & 0x1000) == 0x1000 )
          {
          remote_drive_present = 1;
          break;
          }
     }
```

The NetBIOS Installed Test

Many types of networks are based on NetBIOS. The test for NetBIOS' presence
relies on getting an `Invalid Command` error code back after passing it a deliberately incorrect command. The following code for the Borland C compiler

shows how you conduct such a test. The code uses the network control block
(NCB) data structure, which is explained in Chapter 5, "PC-to-PC NetBIOS
Programming."

```
NCB      test_ncb;
void interrupt  (*int_5C_vector)(void);


int_5C_vector = getvect(0x5C);
if (int_5C_vector == (void far *) NULL)
    {
    printf("ERROR. NetBios not loaded (Int5C not present).\n");
    exit(1);
    }

memset(&test_ncb, 0, sizeof(NCB));
test_ncb.NCB_COMMAND = 0x7F;
NetBios(&test_ncb);
if (test_ncb.NCB_RETCODE != 03)
    {
    printf("ERROR. NetBios not loaded (No response from Int5C).\n");
    exit(1);
    }

/* - - - - - - - - - - - - - - - - - - - - - - - */
/*
 *  Call NetBIOS, via Interrupt 5C.
 */

void    NetBios(NCB far *ncb_ptr)
        {
        ncb_ptr->NCB_CMD_CPLT = 0xFF;
        _ES   = FP_SEG(ncb_ptr); /* Borland C can directly */
        _BX   = FP_OFF(ncb_ptr); /* access CPU registers.*/
        _AX   = 0x0100;
        geninterrupt(0x5c);
        }
```

The NetWare Installed Test

This test asks the NetWare shell for version information. If the shell is not
loaded, your cue is that no information is returned. The function code for this
call is EA (hex) and the subfunction code is 1. These values go into the AH and
AL registers, respectively. BX is set to 0 and the ES:DI register pair is loaded with
a far pointer to a reply buffer (50 bytes of buffer area is enough). After the call, if
the NetWare shell is loaded, the BX register contains major and minor version
information. If the BX register remains 0 after the call, the shell is not loaded.

```
union REGS regs;      /* from <dos.h> with most compilers. */
struct SREGS sregs;
char    reply_buffer[50];
```

```
regs.h.ah = 0xEA;
regs.h.al = 1;
regs.x.bx = 0;
sregs.es  = FP_SEG( (void far *) reply_buffer);
regs.x.di = FP_OFF( (void far *) reply_buffer);
int86x(0x21, &regs, &regs, &sregs);
if (regs.x.bx == 0)
    printf("Not a NetWare LAN.\n");
```

The PCLP and DLR Installed Test

The PC LAN Program and DOS LAN Requester both use the multiplex interrupt. The multiplex number for both products is B8 (hex), and both PCLP and DLR support the same Get Installed State call as SHARE. If the AL register remains 0 after the call to Interrupt 2F (hex), either DLR or PCLP is not loaded.

```
if (_os_major < 3)
    {
    printf("Can't check for PCLP.\n");
    exit(1);
    }
else
    {
    regs.h.ah = 0xB8;
    regs.h.al = 0;
    int86(0x2f, &regs, &regs);
    if (regs.h.al == 0)
        {
        printf("DLR is not loaded.\n");
        exit(1);
        }
    }
```

The Custom LAN-Presence Test

Each of these tests for detecting the presence of a LAN has advantages and disadvantages. The test for SHARE.EXE, for example, is not a good indicator of whether a workstation is on a LAN because DOS 4.0 loads SHARE automatically, even on stand-alone PCs. On the other hand, SHARE *must* be loaded to enable file sharing, so your application should test for its presence before sharing files or locking records.

The test for network drives (with allowances for the possible existence of CD-ROM drives) is an excellent, highly accurate test for the presence of a network. In essence, this test says "yes, there is a file server." The only problem with this test is that some implementors of low-cost networks may overlook this particular IOCTL call in the network support software that they have written. To address this problem, you can formulate a LAN-presence test as follows:

II

Network Programming

- SHARE must be loaded so that the application can share files and lock records.

- The test for network drives must find at least one drive letter to be remote; otherwise, NetBIOS must be operational on the workstation.

Note that this test does not incorporate all the various tests previously mentioned. The other tests, such as the NetWare-present test, are handy for special situations—particularly if you need to perform a vendor-specific function and first want to verify the environment in which your program is running.

Identifying the Workstation

After you are satisfied that your application is running on a workstation and not just a stand-alone PC, you next must identify the workstation in some way. Recall from Chapter 2, "Multiuser Concepts," that the machine name provides a common method of identification that is supported by DOS itself.

However, using the machine name has two drawbacks:

- If the workstation always boots up with a certain machine name, the name actually identifies the workstation, not the user. No matter who sits down at the workstation to use the network, he or she has the same machine name as all the other users who happen to sit down at the same workstation.

- On some LANs, more than one workstation can have the same machine name established, or a workstation may have no machine name at all.

The solution to both these problems is usually administrative. Each user who wants to use your application on the LAN should execute a program that identifies that user with a unique machine name. This program might consist (under DLR or PCLP) of rebooting the workstation and executing a new NET START command, or perhaps (under NetWare) simply telling each user how to use the Login and Logout commands properly so that he or she is correctly identified.

You can also take extra steps to ensure that each machine name is always unique by using the techniques explained in Chapter 5, "PC-to-PC NetBIOS Programming," to route a simple message across the network. Any workstation that recognizes its machine name in the message can respond with a Present! message, thus alerting the new claimant to the presence of the name's current owner. You can use this technique if unique user/workstation identification is critical to your application. You can also set the machine name yourself, from within your program, using an undocumented DOS function call (which is documented later in this section).

The Machine Name

The DOS Get Machine Name function call, hex 5E00, returns a 16-byte machine name. The name is padded on the right with spaces and is null-terminated in the 16th byte (in other words, the name is an ordinary C string). This function also returns the NetBIOS name number, which is meaningful only on NetBIOS-based LANs. NetBIOS assigns the name number when you call either of the NetBIOS functions Add Name or Add Group Name. The NetBIOS name number of the permanent node name (discussed in Chapter 3, "PC-to-PC Communications Concepts") is always 1. Also, this function returns a 0 in the CH register if the machine name is not defined. The following is an example of the function:

```
char            machine_name[16];
unsigned char   netbios_name_number;

regs.x.dx = FP_OFF( (void far *) machine_name);
sregs.ds  = FP_SEG( (void far *) machine_name);
regs.x.ax = 0x5E00;
int86x(0x21, &regs, &regs, &sregs);
if (regs.h.ch == 0)
    {
    printf("ERROR.  Machine name not set.\n");
    exit(1);
    }

netbios_name_number = regs.h.cl;    /* not really useful */
                                    /* in this chapter.  */


/* If you want to use machine name as part of a  */
/* file name, you should remove the spaces.      */

i = strlen(machine_name) - 1;
while (i > 0 && machine_name[i] == ' ')
    {
    machine_name[i] = '\0';
    i--;
    }
```

The following is an undocumented (not mentioned in the *DOS Technical Reference*) variation of the Get Machine Name function call that you can use to set the machine name. You probably wouldn't use this function on a NetBIOS-based LAN, because NetBIOS is already a name-oriented environment. However, you might use this function in lieu of NetWare's login script facility for setting the machine name:

II

Network Programming

```
char      machine_name[16];

/* At this point, set machine_name to a null-terminated,   */
/* 15-byte string that is padded on the right with spaces. */
/* The null terminator should appear in the 16th byte:     */

machine_name[15] = '\0';

regs.x.dx = FP_OFF( (void far *) machine_name);
sregs.ds  = FP_SEG( (void far *) machine_name);
regs.h.ch = 1;
regs.h.cl = netbios_name_number;
regs.x.ax = 0x5E01;
int86x(0x21, &regs, &regs, &sregs);
```

After glancing at this coding example, you probably wonder where you come up with a value for netbios_name_number. Because you should use this function only on a non-NetBIOS-based LAN, you have to fake it; put a value of 1 into the CL register, if you want.

NetWare User IDs

In addition to supporting the machine name (set with a command in the login script), NetWare also has its own mechanism for identifying users. Basically, the process has two steps: you first find out the workstation's *connection number* (assigned by the file server at login time), and then use the result to obtain information about the connection number, including the user ID (which Novell calls the *object name*).

You accomplish the first step with a GetConnectionNumber function call. To perform the call, set the AH register to the function number DC (hex) and do an Interrupt 21 (hex). On return, the AL register contains the connection number (in the range 1–100).

```
regs.h.ah = 0xDC;
int86(0x21, &regs, &regs);
connect_num = regs.h.al;
```

The second step consists of a GetConnectionInformation call. The addresses of two data areas are passed to this function. The first area is a four-byte request buffer:

```
struct
    {
    unsigned int     request_length;
    unsigned char    subfunction;
    unsigned char    buffer_connect_num;
    } request_buffer;
```

The second area is a 63-byte reply buffer:

```
struct
    {
    unsigned int      reply_length;
    unsigned long     object_id;
    unsigned int      object_type;
    char              object_name [48];
    char              login_time [7];
    } reply_buffer;
```

The call sets the AH register to the function code (hex E3), the DS:SI register pair to the address of the request buffer, and the ES:DI register pair to the address of the reply buffer, and does an Interrupt 21 (hex):

```
request_buffer.request_length     = 2;
request_buffer.subfunction        = 0x16;
request_buffer.buffer_connect_num = connect_num;

reply_buffer.reply_length = 61;

regs.h.ah = 0xE3;
sregs.ds  = FP_SEG( (void far *) &request_buffer);
regs.x.si = FP_OFF( (void far *) &request_buffer);
sregs.es  = FP_SEG( (void far *) &reply_buffer);
regs.x.di = FP_OFF( (void far *) &reply_buffer);

int86x(0x21, &regs, &regs, &sregs);
```

Because it is null-terminated, the object name returned in the reply buffer can easily be treated as an ordinary string:

```
printf("The User ID is %s\n",
        reply_buffer.object_name);
```

DLR and PCLP Logon Names

You can ask either DOS LAN Requester or the PC LAN Program for the name of the user logged in at a workstation. The API returns the name or an indication that no one is currently logged in. To use this service, you invoke Interrupt 2Ah after setting the AX CPU register to 0x7802 and setting the ES:DI register pair to point to a nine-byte area of memory. After the call, the AL register is 0 if no one is logged in. If DLR or PCLP set AL to a nonzero value, that program puts the logon name in the area of memory pointed to by the far pointer in ES:DI. The resulting name is blank-padded and the last byte contains a null value.

The following get_logon_id() example is a function that you can call from within your program. The function obtains the logon name and status information from DLR or PCLP and returns the information in the function's parameters.

```
void    get_logon_id(char *logon_name, int *status_ptr)
    {
    union REGS regs;
    struct SREGS sregs;

    regs.x.ax = 0x7802;
    regs.x.di = FP_OFF( (void far *) logon_name);
    sregs.es  = FP_SEG( (void far *) logon_name);
    int86x(0x2A, &regs, &regs, &sregs);
    *status_ptr = (int) regs.h.al;
    }
```

Sharing Files

Earlier this chapter discussed several strategies for sharing files. Chapter 2,
"Multiuser Concepts," explained the concepts behind sharing mode and
access mode, which are specified when a file is opened. This section presents
specific coding techniques that demonstrate how you indicate these modes
from within your application.

First note that the high-level call fopen() is not generally LAN-aware, and
does not provide a means for indicating sharing mode and access mode. For
example, under Borland C and Microsoft C, fopen() results in a *compatibility
mode* open of a file. Avoid using fopen() in your LAN-aware applications; it
simply doesn't give you enough control over the different file-sharing modes.
Use the open(), _open(), or sopen() calls instead, as outlined in the following
sections. Under DOS, these functions ultimately call the same DOS function
call (3D hex, Open File) as fopen(), but enable you to specify the values for
the sharing mode and access mode.

Exclusive Access

The following code shows some examples of calls that open a file named
PRIVATE.FIL for exclusive access. After a particular workstation opens a file in
this mode, no other workstation can open the file. Also, if another workstation already has the file open in any mode, the request for exclusive access
fails. Note that the manifest constants differ among the different compilers,
but these calls all do the same thing.

In Borland C:

```
handle = _open("PRIVATE.FIL", O_RDWR | O_DENYALL);
if (handle == -1)
    {
    if (errno == ENOENT)
        printf("No such file.\n");
    else
```

```
        if (errno == EMFILE)
            printf("Too many open files.\n");
        else
        if (errno == EACCES)
            printf("File is READ-ONLY, or already open.\n");
        else
        if (errno == EINVACC)
            printf("Invalid access mode.\n");
        }

    /* Note that I use UNIX-style error handling */
    /* here, because it's fairly consistent      */
    /* among different compilers.                 */
```

In Microsoft C:

```
    handle = sopen("PRIVATE.FIL", O_RDWR, SH_DENYRW);
    if (handle == -1)
        /* same error handling as for Borland C. */
```

One Writer; Many Readers

Occasionally, you want to update a file so that only one workstation can write to the file but others can concurrently read from it. The following examples show what the open() or sopen() call looks like for the workstation that wants to be the only one to write to the file. These examples omit error handling, but it would be exactly the same as described earlier for establishing exclusive access.

In Borland C:

```
    handle = open("ONEWRITE.FIL", O_RDWR ¦ O_DENYWRITE);
```

In Microsoft C:

```
    handle = sopen("ONEWRITE.FIL", O_RDWR, SH_DENYWR);
```

Of course, the other workstations want to open the file only for reading; their call would look like one of the following:

In Borland C:

```
    handle = open("ONEWRITE.FIL", O_RDONLY ¦ O_DENYNONE);
```

In Microsoft C:

```
    handle = sopen("ONEWRITE.FIL", O_RDONLY, SH_DENYNO);
```

Shared Access

If you want record-level control over concurrent file access, you must open the file in DENY_NONE mode. Here are some examples of how this is coded:

II

Network Programming

In Borland C:

```
handle = open("SHARED.FIL", O_RDWR ¦ O_DENYNONE);
```

In Microsoft C:

```
handle = sopen("SHARED.FIL", O_RDWR, SH_DENYNO);
```

The Sharing Retry Count/Delay

You can fine-tune the way that DOS retries network-related errors before they are returned to your program as failed function calls. The default is that DOS performs three retries, with one delay loop between attempts. You set both the retry count and the number of delay loops with the Set Sharing Retry Count/Delay IOCTL function call. The following example sets the delay period to two loops and tells DOS to retry six times before quitting:

```
regs.h.ah = 0x44;
regs.h.al = 0x0B;
regs.x.cx = 2;          /* number of delay loops into CX */
regs.x.dx = 6;          /* new retry count into DX       */
int86(0x21, &regs, &regs);
```

NetWare File Sharing

NetWare adds several individual function calls to DOS under the general category of *Synchronization Services*. If your software is to be used in a NetWare environment only, these services can give you exactly the control you need.

As mentioned in Chapter 2, "Multiuser Concepts," the basic process of using Novell services consists of *logging* the files that you're about to lock, *locking* that set of files, actually performing the updates, *releasing* the locks, and *clearing* the list of logged files. The following example shows how you do these steps in Borland C for a pair of related files, FILE.ONE and FILE.TWO:

```
void main(int argc, char *argv[])
    {
    char filename1[15] = "FILE.ONE";
    char filename2[15] = "FILE.TWO";
    int  handle1;
    int  handle2;

/* even though NetWare services are being used,      */
/* the file should still be opened in a sharing mode. */

    handle1 = open(filename1, O_RDWR ¦ O_DENYNONE);
    handle2 = open(filename2, O_RDWR ¦ O_DENYNONE);

log_both_files:
    if (nw_log(filename1) != 0)
        abend("Couldn't log file 1.");
    if (nw_log(filename2) != 0)
```

```
            abend("Couldn't log file 2.");

issue_lock:
     if (nw_lock_set() != 0)
          {
          printf("1 or both already locked.  Retry? (Y/N) ");
          gets(string);
          if (string[0] == 'Y' ¦¦ string[0] == 'y')
               goto issue_lock;
          abend("Couldn't lock.  Try later.");
          }

update_the_files:
     perform_update();      /* your routine to write records. */

now_release_files:
     if (nw_release(filename1) != 0)
          abend("Couldn't release file 1.");
     if (nw_release(filename2) != 0)
          abend("Couldn't release file 2.");


clear_log_entries:
     nw_clear_files();

     close(handle1);
     close(handle2);
     printf("Update complete.\n");
     return;
     }


/*   -   -   -   - subroutines  -   -   -   - */

int     nw_log(char *name)
     }
     union REGS regs;
     struct SREGS sregs;

/*
 * Function Call EB, Log File
 * AL = 0 to just log, 1 to log and lock.
 * DS:DX = pointer to drive, path, file name string.
 * BP = number of 1/18ths of a second to keep trying the
 *      lock before timing out.
 * Completion code returned in the AL register.
 */

     regs.h.ah = 0xEB;
     regs.h.al = 0;
     regs.x.dx = FP_OFF( (void far *) name);
     sregs.ds  = FP_SEG( (void far *) name);
     regs.x.bp = 18;
     int86x(0x21, &regs, &regs, &sregs);
     regs.h.ah = 0;
     return regs.x.ax;
```

```
        }


int    nw_lock_set(void)
    {
    union REGS regs;

/*
 * Function Call C2, Lock Physical Record Set
 * AL = 0 to lock with exclusive locks;
 *      1 to lock with shareable, Read-Only locks.
 * BP = time-out limit, in 1/18ths of a second.
 * Completion code returned in AL.
 */

    regs.h.ah = 0xC2;
    regs.h.al = 0;
    regs.x.bp = 18;
    int86(0x21, &regs, &regs);
    regs.h.ah = 0;
    return regs.x.ax;
    }


int    nw_release(char *name)
    {
    union REGS regs;
    struct SREGS sregs;

/*
 * Function Call EC, Release File
 * DS:DX = far pointer to file name.
 * Completion code in AL register.
 */

    regs.h.ah = 0xEC;
    regs.x.dx = FP_OFF( (void far *) name);
    sregs.ds  = FP_SEG( (void far *) name);
    int86x(0x21, &regs, &regs, &sregs);
    regs.h.ah = 0;
    return regs.x.ax;
    }


void nw_clear_files(void)
    {
    union REGS regs;

/*
 * Function Call CF, Clear File Set
 * no parameters.
 * returns nothing.
 */

    regs.ah = 0xCF;
    int86(0x21, &regs, &regs);
```

```
        }

void abend(char *msg)
        {
        printf("%s\n", msg);
        exit(1);
        }
```

OS/2 File Sharing

Borland and IBM offer 32-bit compilers for the OS/2 2.x environment,
and you can use Microsoft C 5.1 or 6.0 to create 16-bit OS/2 software. For
Microsoft C, the code examples for open() and sopen(), given earlier, are also
applicable to the OS/2 environment. If you want even more control over the
way a file is opened, however, you can call the DosOpen() kernel API function
directly, using any one of the three vendors' compilers:

```
char            filename[80];      /* drive, path, name        */
unsigned        handle;            /* returned file handle     */
unsigned        action;            /* action that OS/2 took    */
unsigned long   filesize;          /* file's new size in bytes */
unsigned        file_attribute;    /* used when creating file  */
unsigned        flag;              /* action to take           */
unsigned        open_mode;         /* Sharing Mode; Access Mode */
unsigned long   reserved;
unsigned        return_code;       /* returns 0 if successful  */

strcpy(filename, "SHARED.OS2");
filesize       = 0l;
file_attribute = 0;
flag           = 0x0001;
open_mode      = 0x0042;
reserved       = 0l;

return_code = DosOpen   (filename,
                         &handle,
                         &action,
                         filesize,
                         file_attribute,
                         flag,
                         open_mode,
                         reserved);
```

This example does not create a new file, so the file_attribute and filesize
items are set to 0. The flag value of 0x0001 signifies which action to take.
If the file exists, the call opens the file; the file doesn't exist, the call fails and
returns an error. The open_mode informs OS/2 that the file should be opened
for Read-Write access in DENY_NONE mode. If the file is successfully opened,
OS/2 returns a file handle in the handle field and sets the action field to 1 if
the file exists, 2 if it was created, and 3 if the file was replaced.

II

Network Programming

Setting File Attributes

The function call Change File Mode, hex 43, is used under DOS to set a file's attributes. To mark a file Read-Only, put the new file attribute value in the CX register, make DS:DX a far pointer to the name of the file, and do the call:

```
regs.h.ah = 0x43;
regs.h.al = 1;           /* 1=set mode; 0=return mode     */
regs.x.cx = 0x0001;      /* set bit 1 to indicate Read-Only */
regs.x.dx = FP_OFF( (void far *) filename);
sregs.ds  = FP_SEG( (void far *) filename);
int86x(0x21, &regs, &regs, &sregs);
```

DOS doesn't know about or recognize the Shareable/Non-Shareable attribute, which is specific to NetWare. However, because NetWare intercepts Interrupt 21, Function 43, you can use this function call to control whether more than one workstation can access a file. NetWare turns the request into a Novell-specific function request and sends the result to the file server. Bit 8 of the attribute field, which is marked "reserved" in the *DOS Technical Reference*, is defined as the Shareable/Non-Shareable bit by Novell. In the preceding example, putting 0x8000 into the CX register makes a file Shareable, and 0x8001 makes it Shareable/Read-Only.

Under OS/2, you can set a file to Read-Only with the `DosSetFileMode()` kernel API call:

```
ret_code = DosSetFileMode( (void far *) filename,
                           0x0001,
                           01);
```

Locking Records

Before you look at the techniques that you use for locking individual records, you need to be aware of two important rules:

■ You can have multiple locks in a file, but you should not overlap file regions.

■ Make sure that you unlock all records that you lock.

To lock records, your application must have opened the file for Read-Write access in DENY_NONE mode. You can then freely lock and unlock records within the file. If you want to lock the entire file as one large record, specifying a length for the file region that is larger than the file itself is not an error. You don't have to determine the current length of the file before performing the lock action. Also note that the Sharing Retry Count/Delay parameters discussed earlier in this chapter apply to record locking as well as to file sharing.

The following coding examples show how records are locked for the Borland C and Microsoft compilers. Each of these compilers requires a slightly different syntax for the library calls, but all wind up invoking the DOS function call 5C (hex), Lock/Unlock File Range. In each example, the fifth (counting from 1) record is locked, written, and unlocked. The record is 100 bytes long.

Invoking DOS Function 5C

If you don't mind coding your record-locking routines yourself (instead of using the library routines supplied with the compiler), you can create a fairly generic function that invokes the DOS function 5C and can be used with just about any compiler:

```
int lock_record    (int handle,
                    long file_position,
                    long record_length)
{
union REGS regs;

/* Function 5C */
/* AL = 0 to lock, 1 to unlock */
/* BX = file handle */
/* CX:DX = position in file */
/* SI:DI = byte count to lock/unlock */

regs.h.ah = 0x5C;
regs.h.al = 0;
regs.x.bx = handle;
regs.x.cx = (unsigned) file_position >> 16;
regs.x.dx = (unsigned) file_position & 0x0000ffff;
regs.x.si = (unsigned) record_length >> 16;
regs.x.di = (unsigned) record_length & 0x0000ffff;
int86(0x21, &regs, &regs);
return regs.x.ax;
}
```

The following is an example of file locking that uses Borland C library functions:

```
int   handle;
int   return_code;
int   my_retries;
long  record_length;
long  record_number;
long  file_position;
```

```
handle = _open("SHARED.FIL", O_RDWR | O_DENYNONE);
if (handle == -1)
    /* same error handling as mentioned earlier. */

/* each record is 100 bytes long. */
/* lock the 5th record. */

my_retries    = 0;
record_length = 1001;
record_number = 51;
file_position = record_length * (record_number - 11);

do_the_lock:
return_code = lock(handle, file_position, record_length);
if (return_code != 0)
    {
    if (errno != EACCES)
        {
        close(handle);
        printf("Lock attempt failed; I/O error.\n");
        exit(1);
        }
    /* at this point you know someone else has */
    /* locked the record. */
    my_retries++;
    if (my_retries < 100)       /* app-specific number */
        goto do_the_lock;
    close(handle);
    printf("Lock failed after 100 retries.\n");
    exit(1);
    }

/* lock succeeded; write the record(s) */

/* notice that, if the write() fails, I make sure */
/* to unlock the file region before exiting */

return_code = write(handle, &a_record, (int) record_length);
if (return_code == -1)
    {
    unlock(handle, file_position, record_length);
    close(handle);
    printf("Write attempt failed.\n");
    exit(1);
    }

unlock(handle, file_position, record_length);
close(handle);
printf("All done.  Update successful.\n");
exit(0);
```

The next example is in Microsoft C, which has a library function, locking(), that you use for both locking and unlocking file regions. This function assumes that your application has already positioned the file pointer to the

correct location in the file with an `lseek()` call before issuing either a lock or
unlock operation.

```c
int   handle;
int   return_code;
int   my_retries;
long  record_length;
long  record_number;
long  file_position;

handle = _sopen("SHARED.FIL", O_RDWR, SH_DENYNO);
if (handle == -1)
    /* same error handling as mentioned earlier. */

/* each record is 100 bytes long. */
/* lock the 5th record. */

my_retries    = 0;
record_length = 100l;
record_number = 5l;
file_position = record_length * (record_number - 1l);

do_the_lock:
lseek(handle, file_position, SEEK_SET);
return_code = locking(handle, LK_NBLCK, record_length);
if (return_code != 0)
    {
    if (errno != EACCES)
        {
        close(handle);
        printf("Lock attempt failed; I/O error.\n");
        exit(1);
        }
    /* at this point you know someone else has */
    /* locked the record. */
    my_retries++;
    if (my_retries < 100)     /* app-specific number */
        goto do_the_lock;
    close(handle);
    printf("Lock failed after 100 retries.\n");
    exit(1);
    }

/* lock succeeded; write the record(s) */
/* notice that, if the write() fails, I make sure */
/* to unlock the file region before exiting */

return_code = write(handle, &a_record, (int) record_length);
if (return_code == -1)
    {
    lseek(handle, file_position, SEEK_SET);
    locking(handle, LK_UNLCK, record_length);
    close(handle);
    printf("Write attempt failed.\n");
    exit(1);
    }
```

```
lseek(handle, file_position, SEEK_SET);
locking(handle, LK_UNLCK, record_length);
close(handle);
printf("All done.  Update successful.\n");
exit(0);
```

NetWare Record Locking

In addition to supporting DOS function call 5C, Lock/Unlock File Range (and therefore all the examples you have seen so far), Novell NetWare lets you access its own proprietary functions for locking and unlocking records. Like the NetWare-specific file-sharing functions discussed earlier, the record-level functions also fall under the NetWare category, Synchronization Services.

The approach that you take is exactly the same: log the records that you want to access, lock them as a single entity, perform whatever update is appropriate, release the locks, and clear the list of logged records. You can specify either physical record locks, which are analogous to the record locking discussed so far, or logical record locks, which consist of symbolic references to the actual records. In the latter case, the file server maintains a list of named records and denies or allows access to items in the list according to the logical locks that the application issued against a name.

The use of logical locks requires that all programs accessing the files cooperate by using logical record locks exclusively. An uncooperative program can cause havoc by not adhering to the use of logical locks. For this reason, you should not use logical locks in your software; stick with physical record locking.

Before you see how to code NetWare-specific record locks, be aware that NetWare also provides system calls for manipulating network-wide semaphores. These have many of the same properties as logical record locks; each workstation must cooperate closely in the creation, opening, examination, and closing of semaphores. Each semaphore is a symbolic name for a network resource (a file, record, or set of records). Although logical record locks enable you to control which particular workstation has access to a record, semaphores let you indicate that a certain limited number of workstations can concurrently access a given record or set of records.

The following example is equivalent to the earlier record-locking examples. The code uses NetWare services to lock record number 5 in a file that consists of 100-byte records. Note, however, that you can lock multiple related, interdependent records as a set by using these services. These services thus make it easy to avoid deadlocks.

```
int   handle;
int   return_code;
long record_length;
long record_number;
long file_position;

handle = _sopen("SHARED.FIL", O_RDWR, SH_DENYNO);
if (handle == -1)
    /* same error handling as mentioned earlier. */

/* each record is 100 bytes long. */
/* lock the 5th record. */

record_length = 100l;
record_number = 5l;
file_position = record_length * (record_number - 1l);

log_the_record:
regs.h.ah = 0xBC;
regs.h.al = 0;      /* 0 = log the record */
                /* 1 = log and lock the record exclusively */
                /* 2 = log and lock as shareable, Read-Only */
regs.x.bx = handle;
regs.x.cx = (unsigned) file_position >> 16;
regs.x.dx = (unsigned) file_position & 0x0000ffff;
regs.x.bp = 0;
                /* bp = time-out limit if log-and-lock */
regs.x.si = (unsigned) record_length >> 16;
regs.x.di = (unsigned) record_length & 0x0000ffff;
int86(0x21, &regs, &regs);
if (regs.h.al != 0)
    {
    close(handle);
    printf("Couldn't log the record.\n");
    exit(1);
    }


lock_record_set:
regs.h.ah = 0xC2;
regs.h.al = 0;          /* 0 = lock exclusively */
                /* 1 = shareable, read-only lock */
regs.x.bp = 18;     /* time-out limit, in 1/18ths second */
int86(0x21, &regs, &regs);
if (regs.h.al != 0)
    {
    close(handle);
    printf("Couldn't lock the record.\n");
    exit(1);
    }

/* lock succeeded; write the record(s) */
/* notice that, if the write() fails, I make sure */
/* to unlock the file region before exiting */

return_code = write(handle, &a_record, (int) record_length);
```

```
release_record_set:
regs.h.ah = 0xC3;
int86(0x21, &regs, &regs);

clear_record_set:
regs.h.ah = 0xC4;
int86(0x21, &regs, &regs);

close(handle);

if (return_code == -1)
    {
    printf("Write attempt failed.\n");
    exit(1);
    }

printf("All done.  Update successful.\n");
exit(0);
```

OS/2 Record Locking

The Microsoft 5.1 or 6.0 C compiler emits code for either OS/2 or DOS, so the preceding examples for the Microsoft compiler are equally applicable to OS/2. In a program produced by one of these Microsoft compilers, running under OS/2, the `locking()` and `rlock()` library routines internally call the OS/2 kernel, instead of DOS function call 5CAPI, to lock records.

Within the Microsoft, Borland, or IBM OS/2 compiler environments, you can call the `DosSetFileLocks()` kernel function yourself. The data structures and general calling interface look like this:

```
struct    FILE_REGION
    {
    unsigned long  file_offset;
    unsigned long  region_length;
    };

struct FILE_REGION lock_region;
struct FILE_REGION unlock_region;


return_code = DosSetFileLocks(handle,
                    (void far *) &lock_region,
                    (void far *) &unlock_region);
```

Calling `DosSetFileLocks()` is simple. You should pass a NULL pointer for a parameter if you don't want its corresponding action to be taken.

```
/* to lock a record: */

lock_region.file_offset   = file_position;
lock_region.region_length = record_length;
```

```
return_code = DosFileLocks(handle,
                           (void far *) &lock_region,
                           (void far *) NULL);


/* later, to unlock that record: */

unlock_region.file_offset   = file_position;
unlock_region.region_length = record_length;
return_code = DosFileLocks(handle,
                           (void far *) NULL,
                           (void far *) &unlock_region);
```

Committing Changes to Disk

Under DOS, there are two methods to ensure that records you have written (which are probably sitting in DOS buffers) are actually flushed to the disk. In the first method, you use DOS function call 45 (hex), Duplicate Handle, and then close the resulting duplicate handle. A bit faster than closing the original handle and reopening it, this method also has the advantage that it works with DOS version 2.1 and subsequent versions. In Borland C, you code this method as follows:

```
close ( dup(handle) );
```

The second method—using DOS function call 68 (hex), Commit File—is more explicit. However, this function was not added to DOS until version 3.3. You code this method as follows:

```
regs.h.ah = 0x68;
regs.x.bx = handle;
int86(0x21, &regs, &regs);
```

Under OS/2, the kernel API call `DosBufReset()` performs the same job as the DOS Commit File function. You can call the function with the handle of a single file, or with a handle of –1, which causes the records for all open files to be flushed to disk. The following is an example of its use:

```
DosBufReset(handle);
```

Printing to a Shared Printer

As noted in Chapter 2, "Multiuser Concepts," even something as simple as printing a report takes a little extra care on a network. After you have the print program tested and working on a stand-alone PC, you should run a few tests on the network to make sure that the report looks like you expected. Your two main concerns are the following:

- The mode, font or typeface, pitch, and other printer characteristics used for your report

- The possible insertion of stray page breaks into the report by the network operating system

To address these concerns, DOS, PCLP, DLR, and NetWare all offer services that you can use to control printing (of course, the DLR, PCLP, and NetWare functions are available only if your program is running in that particular environment).

Whether or not you use these operating system services, you must send a setup string of printer commands to the printer at the beginning of each printout that you produce. If you want to be kind to the next printer user, at the end of the printout you can also send a setup string to the printer that resets the printer to a known, default state. Because every printer has a different set of commands, you definitely want to make your setup string file-driven. At some point in your application, ask the user to enter the setup strings and store them in a file; you then do not have to worry as much about supporting the myriad of different printers.

Also, regardless of whether you use the operating system services that this section describes, you should make sure that you open the printer (as a file) only once, at the top of the report. Although usually acceptable on a stand-alone PC, the technique of opening and closing the printer in the middle of a printout is definitely a bad idea on a shared, network printer. The spooler software could insert page breaks into the printout each time that you close the LPT*x* device. If the printer is being used heavily by many users, you could even find another user's printout interleaved with your own.

Setup Strings

DOS function call 5E02 (hex), Set Printer Setup, is used to insert a setup string in front of each printout sent to the printer from a workstation (until a subsequent 5E02 call or the workstation is rebooted). Unfortunately, the function does not send a reset setup string after the printout is produced, so you find using this function less useful than providing your own setup string processing. If you want to use this function, you first must use DOS function call 5F02 (hex), Get Redirection List Entry, to determine the Redirection List Index entry for the printer that you want to use. Perform the function 5F02 call repeatedly until you detect a redirected printer or until the list is exhausted (which returns an error code 18):

```
    int  done, index;
    char local_name[128];
    char network_name[128];
    union REGS regs;
    struct SREGS sregs;

    done  = 0;
    index = 0;

    while (!done)
        {
        regs.x.ax = 0x5F02;
        regs.x.bx = index;
        regs.x.si = FP_OFF( (void far *) local_name);
        sregs.ds  = FP_SEG( (void far *) local_name);
        regs.x.di = FP_OFF( (void far *) network_name);
        sregs.es  = FP_SEG( (void far *) network_name);
        int86x(0x21, &regs, &regs, &sregs);
        if (regs.x.cflag)
            break;
        if (regs.h.bl = 3) /* 3=printer; 4=file device */
            {
            if (strncmp(local_name, "LPT1", 4) == 0)
                done = 1;
            }
        else
            index++;
        }

    /* at this point, if done == 1, the variable "index"     */
    /* corresponds to the Redirection List Entry of the      */
    /* printer whose device name is recorded in "local_name". */
```

Now that you have the Redirection List Entry index value for a redirected
LPT1 printer, you can issue function call 5E02 to tell DOS to begin using a
particular setup string. The string can be up to 64 bytes long.

```
    regs.x.ax = 0x5E02;
    regs.x.bx = index;
    regs.x.cx = strlen(setup_string);
    regs.x.si = FP_OFF( (void far *) setup_string);
    sregs.ds  = FP_SEG( (void far *) setup_string);
    int86x(0x21, &regs, &regs, &sregs);
```

DLR and PCLP Printer Control

DOS LAN Requester (DLR) and the IBM PC LAN Program (PCLP) provide a
service called *Network Print Stream Control* that you can use to specify how you
want to handle page breaks. You invoke this service by doing an Interrupt 2A
(hex) after setting the AH CPU register to 6 and the AL register to a mode
value as follows:

1. *Concatenation mode*—Use this value to tell DLR or PCLP to ignore its normal assumptions about when page breaks should occur. In this mode, DLR and PCLP insert a page break (the formfeed character, hex 0C) into the redirected print stream only when COMMAND.COM regains control after a program ends or after an entire .BAT file of commands is processed.

2. *Truncation mode* (the default mode)—In this mode, DLR and PCLP insert a page break into the print stream in the following instances:

   ■ Whenever a program ends

   ■ When the files LPT1, LPT2, or LPT3 are closed

   ■ When DLR or PCLP sees a transition to or from printing by Interrupt 17 (hex) and printing by DOS files

   ■ When DLR or PCLP detects that a different program or process is using Interrupt 17 to print characters

3. *Truncate print stream*—Use this service to tell DLR or PCLP that a complete print stream has been sent to the printer (when concatenation mode is in effect).

NetWare Print Services

As mentioned in Chapter 2, "Multiuser Concepts," NetWare provides a rich set of programming services for controlling the network printers. To get a sense of how rich this set of services is, examine the following data structure, which is used at each NetWare workstation to manage nonlocal printing:

```
struct     PRINT_CONTROL_DATA
    {
    unsigned char status;
    unsigned char print_flags;
    unsigned char tab_size;
    unsigned char server_printer;
    unsigned char number_copies;
    unsigned char form_type;
    unsigned char reserved1;
    unsigned char banner_text[13];
    unsigned char reserved2;
    unsigned char local_lpt_device;
    unsigned int  flush_timeout_count;
    unsigned char flush_on_close;
    unsigned int  maximum_lines;
    unsigned int  maximum_chars
    unsigned char form_name[13];
    unsigned char lpt_flag;
```

```
        unsigned char file_flag;
        unsigned char timeout_flag;
        char far      *setup_string_ptr;
        char far      *reset_string_ptr;
        unsigned char connect_id_queue_print_job;
        unsigned char in_progress;
        unsigned char print_queue_flag;
        unsigned char print_job_valid;
        unsigned long print_queue_id;
        unsigned int  print_job_number;
        };
```

Note that in this structure, NetWare provides for both a setup string and a reset string. This enables NetWare to "bracket" a stream of print material with printer commands that put the printer into the proper mode for a report and then put the printer back into a default state after printing. The NetWare function call for obtaining the information in this structure, GetSpecificCaptureFlags(), is coded as follows:

```
    struct PRINT_CONTROL_DATA print_data;

    regs.h.ah = 0xB8;
    regs.h.al = 2;
    regs.x.cx = sizeof(struct PRINT_CONTROL_DATA);
    regs.x.bx = FP_OFF( (void far *) &print_data);
    sregs.es  = FP_SEG( (void far *) &print_data);

    regs.h.dh = 0;          /* 0=LPT1, 1=LPT2, 2=LPT3 */

    int86x(0x21, &regs, &regs, &sregs);
    if (regs.h.al != 0)
        printf("Couldn't obtain print data.\n");
```

After performing this call, you can use the far pointers setup_string_ptr and reset_string_ptr, which are returned as part of the data structure, to access the respective control strings. Note that the first two bytes (one word) of each string contain the maximum length to which each string can be set. The actual setup and reset characters follow the length field.

The print_flags field within the structure contains bits that indicate how the end of the print job is detected (see fig. 4.1.)

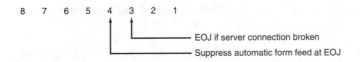

Fig. 4.1.
The bits within the *Print_Flags* field.

You can modify any of the first 42 bytes of the data structure (except for the *status* field) with the `SetSpecificCaptureFlags()` function call:

```
struct PRINT_CONTROL_DATA print_data;

/* any of the fields up through form_name, except */
/* status, may be set here. */

regs.h.ah = 0xB8;
regs.h.al = 3;
regs.x.cx = sizeof(struct PRINT_CONTROL_DATA);
regs.x.bx = FP_OFF( (void far *) &print_data);
sregs.es  = FP_SEG( (void far *) &print_data);

regs.h.dh = 0;              /* 0=LPT1, 1=LPT2, 2=LPT3 */

int86x(0x21, &regs, &regs, &sregs);
if (regs.h.al != 0)
    printf("Couldn't set print data.\n");
```

Things That You *Cannot* Do on a Network

So far, you have seen that redirecting DOS function calls from a workstation to the file server is a powerful concept. However, it just does not make sense to try to do the following things to the file server:

- *Doing sector-level I/O*—You cannot do direct I/O to a shared disk at the sector level with Interrupts 25/26 (hex) or with the Interrupt 13 (hex) ROM BIOS service. There's no way to lock the sectors. Under NetWare, the layout of the server's disk (its *filesystem*) differs completely from the layout of a DOS-formatted disk. (CHKDSK, for example, does sector-level I/O.)

- *Treat directories as files*—Because you cannot lock a directory on the server, you also cannot do such things as reading a directory into workstation memory to sort and then write the directory back to the file server. The other users on the network would find the rug pulled from under their feet by the inconsistencies that would exist in the directory for the duration of the update. (Peter Norton's Utilities Directory Sort utility does not work on a LAN.)

- *Issue illegal FCB operations*—File control blocks (FCBs) are difficult for network software to handle; the usual approach that the shell/redirector takes is to translate each FCB operation into a corresponding file-handle operation and then send the result to the file server. Illegal FCB programming practices—such as constructing an already open FCB, saving an FCB in a disk file for later use, modifying the reserved areas inside an FCB, or closing an FCB and continuing to use it as though it were still open—are strictly forbidden on a network.

- *Turn interrupts off*—Leaving interrupts masked off for any but the briefest moment is always a bad idea on a PC, but in a network environment, this practice is particularly deadly. The network software relies heavily on interrupts.

- *Removing SHARE from memory*—When you run SHARE.EXE, it does much more than just intercept an interrupt vector (as many TSRs do). SHARE actually modifies a set of user-exits inside DOS itself and becomes an integral part of DOS. Removing SHARE then takes an effort analogous to doing brain surgery, which simply is not worthwhile.

Summary

You have covered a lot of ground in this chapter. You now have a good understanding of the design considerations that go into developing a LAN-aware application. You've seen how detecting the presence of a network is a matter of conducting some tests and inferring a LAN environment from the results. You know how to use the machine name to distinguish between workstations. Sharing files and locking records are key operations on a LAN; you now know how to write code that performs these operations properly. You can control file attributes as they relate to the LAN, and you know several techniques for managing a shared network printer. You also know the kinds of programming tactics that you cannot use on a network.

Chapter 5

PC-to-PC NetBIOS Programming

At this point, you might be thinking that the best (and easiest) way to share information among the workstations on the network is to write the data to a file on the file server and make the file available to the other workstations. However, this is not always so. Using the file server has some disadvantages:

- It is relatively slow compared to sending and receiving LAN messages.

- It entails periodic housecleaning and maintenance of the files.

- It takes up disk space.

- It requires that users have the necessary rights and privileges to access the files.

There also are design questions. If you want to pass a message or data record to another workstation and receive a reply, should you append the reply to the original file or should you write the reply to a separate file? How should the other workstation recognize that the message or record is intended for itself and not another workstation? In many applications, direct PC-to-PC message passing is often a better technique than file sharing, and just as easy to design.

I want you to feel perfectly comfortable exploring the techniques outlined in this chapter. You may think that using NetBIOS or IPX/SPX can be dangerous—that it's possible to crash the entire network unless you code things exactly right, according to some magic formula. However, when you finish this chapter, you'll understand that peer-level communications on a LAN are simple and safe, and that it's actually difficult to bring down the entire network from within your program. The techniques and ideas that this chapter presents suggest several useful LAN applications and utilities—try your hand at them!

The most popular protocols for doing PC-to-PC communications on a LAN are NetBIOS, IPX, and SPX. This chapter offers some general design guidelines for developing applications that "talk directly to one another," and you see how to program NetBIOS applications. The chapter first covers the DOS interface to NetBIOS, and then covers the Windows and OS/2 interfaces. Chapter 6, "IPX and SPX Programming," covers the NetWare protocols IPX and SPX.

Designing the Dialog

Peer-level communications on a LAN can be used for simple applications, such as real-time chatting or electronic mail, and as the basis for sophisticated distributed processing systems that allocate a processing workload among several networked PCs. No matter how simple or complex the application, you should consider the communications link as a dialog or conversation between two or more cooperative processes. Think of this dialog as a special kind of file. Receiving a message is equivalent to reading a record; sending a response is akin to writing a record. Your program defines the format and content of the messages just like records in a file.

Simple Dialogs

In a real-time chat facility, the record layout couldn't be simpler—the record needs to hold only a single keypress. When the user presses a key, the chat program echoes it to the screen and sends it to the chat partner. Similarly, when the chat program receives a keypress-record from the chat partner, the chat program displays the incoming data on the screen. The toughest part of designing a chat program is managing two windows on the screen—incoming (remote) keypresses get displayed in the top window; outgoing (local) keypresses get echoed in the bottom window.

Electronic mail programs vary widely in their complexity, but the record layouts that they use have much in common. Each typically contains header ("envelope") data, such as the sender name, subject, and addressee. The remainder of the record is simply the text of the mail message.

Complex Dialogs

At the other end of the spectrum, distributed processing systems send and receive data records that contain highly application-specific information. Each workstation in the system might have a particular task or subtask to do,

in which case a workstation receives (reads) a data record, performs its processing, and sends the result to the next workstation. Or, in a different design, each workstation may run the same software and perform the same task;
the next available (not already busy) workstation receives a set of input data
to be processed. In a *really* complex design, the individual workstations might
share (send and receive) various areas of memory along with the data records.
You could consider this design as a form of parallel processing.

Design Considerations

The following guidelines will help you design a dialog between two or more
workstations.

Each protocol limits the size of the data packet (data record) that you can
send or receive. For NetBIOS datagrams, the maximum length is usually 512
bytes. A NetBIOS session-related Send operation imposes a maximum data
message length of 65,535 bytes, and a Chain Send operation doubles this by
letting you send two data buffers with a single command. The maximum
length of an IPX data packet (excluding the fixed, 30-byte IPX header) is 546
bytes. Because SPX uses a 42-byte packet header, the maximum length of an
SPX data packet is 534 bytes.

There are a couple of ways to handle packet size limitations in your application. One approach is to segment your data—break it into small chunks and
perform a series of Send operations on the segments; on reception, reassemble them. Segmentation is a little harder to design and code, but it has
the advantage of insulating the main part of the program from the packet
size limitation. Another approach is to design the data records deliberately
and explicitly with the packet size limitation in mind. This approach is simpler to program initially, but it implies that, when you want to add new data
fields to existing records, you must create new records to hold the fields.

You usually should not have to worry about the increase in traffic on the
network. You can consider the PC-to-PC communications link to be just
another file that your software manages. The message traffic that occurs on
the LAN is no more than the traffic that would result if the file were located
on a file server (because the shell/redirector layer must send and receive a
flurry of messages to accomplish the file redirection). However, avoid continuously polling another workstation. For example, suppose that you want
to know when a key is pressed at a remote workstation. If you send a constant stream of packets to the remote computer, each one asking whether a
key has been pressed yet, you dramatically and unnecessarily increase message traffic. Design such a dialog so that you ask the remote computer only
once about its keyboard activity (or modem activity, or whatever).

II

Network Programming

When you send a data packet on its outbound journey to a remote work-station, when can you count on it arriving at the destination? The answer can vary somewhat, of course, depending on the type and size of the network, as well as the current message traffic. On an Ethernet or Token Ring network, a 512-byte data packet usually takes only a millisecond or two to reach the application running on the remote workstation. However, even on a heavily loaded network, the sending and receiving of data packets take less time than if the application were designed instead to access files on a file server.

Both NetBIOS and IPX/SPX are very good at supporting point-to-point message delivery. One-to-many and many-to-many communications, however, can be a challenge to design. You can establish multiple NetBIOS sessions (or the equivalent, multiple SPX connections) between workstations, but each protocol limits the number of concurrent sessions (or connections). Even increasing these limits, by setting configuration parameters, may not give you the "elbow room" you want. You usually shouldn't bother reestablishing a session (or connection) each time that you have a data packet to send, because the initial establishment of a session requires significant overhead. If you want to send data packets from one workstation to several other workstations, or have several workstations share the same data packets among themselves, consider using the IPX or NetBIOS facilities for broadcasting the data packets, or devise a table-driven, datagram-based scheme that builds the data packet and then sends it to multiple destinations by repeatedly copying a new destination into the packet and sending each copy.

Session or Datagram?

The preceding discussion brings us to the issue of when sessions are better than datagrams and vice versa. The most important difference between datagrams and the messages that are sent and received in a session is that datagrams sometimes get lost in transit and your program is not notified of the error. Messages sent within the framework of a session are guaranteed to be delivered (the protocol, transparent to your application, automatically detects and retransmits lost messages). If multiple packets are outstanding at one time, session control also guarantees that they are delivered in the same sequence in which they were sent.

Sessions are a good environment for point-to-point dialogs in which several related data packets are passed back and forth between two workstations. Datagrams, however, are a good design choice for applications whose dialogs consist of unrelated messages, only a few messages (brief dialogs), or a series of messages that does not always have to be a complete set. If you don't mind the extra design and coding work that it takes to ensure that lost messages are properly retransmitted, datagrams can be particularly useful. Often all it takes to detect and retransmit lost messages is to add a sequence number field to your data packets, along with some logic to assign and check the sequence number values.

NetBIOS includes functions for doing both datagrams and session-related messages. Because NetBIOS diagrams do not cause return acknowledgments from the copy of NetBIOS running on the dialog partner PC, NetBIOS datagrams are speedier than their session-related counterparts. NetBIOS datagrams are limited in size, as was previously mentioned, but they are very easy to program. The ease of programming is offset somewhat by the need to include some retry logic in your program to detect and handle lost packets. Sessions require that you code a few extra program statements to establish and later dismantle the session itself, but doing so usually requires fewer statements than handling the retransmission of lost packets.

NetWare's IPX protocol supports datagrams only; SPX is required to do connections (sessions). SPX is available in NetWare beginning with version 2.1. IPX is the speediest of the protocols discussed in this book, and, for ease of programming, IPX is comparable to NetBIOS datagrams. SPX, though, is much more difficult to program, as you'll see in Chapter 6, "IPX and SPX Programming."

Polling versus Asynchronous Event Handling

As was mentioned in Chapter 3, "PC-to-PC Communications Concepts," your program can take either of two approaches while you wait for a NetBIOS or IPX/SPX event to complete. Messages are actually sent or received in the background; you can choose to go into a loop that simply waits for an event to finish, or you can specify that NetBIOS or IPX/SPX call one of your program's functions when the event completes. The techniques are a little different for NetBIOS and for IPX/SPX, of course. This chapter and Chapter 6, "IPX and SPX Programming," show you exactly how polling and asynchronous event handling are done. From a design perspective, you should choose your approach based on what best suits your application. The only design constraint to keep in mind is that a program function that NetBIOS or IPX/SPX calls should be coded to execute as quickly as possible and then return. Simply setting a flag that notifies the main program of event completion is often the best design.

Planning for Time-Outs and Errors

With any I/O that your program performs, good error handling is a must. In a NetBIOS or IPX/SPX environment, this means checking return codes to ensure that the PC-to-PC connection is still alive and healthy. If you design and test your application well, some of the possible return codes will never happen (such as "buffer too small," "invalid name," or "socket not open"). However, other return codes can crop up right in the middle of the communications link. Persistent time-out errors usually indicate that the other workstation has crashed or suffered a power failure. If a return code indicates that a network hardware error occurred, your program should handle the situation by telling the user about the error and gracefully terminating itself.

Programming NetBIOS under DOS

A useful way to begin looking at specific NetBIOS programming techniques is to see how similar NetBIOS programming is to disk file programming. In fact, you can treat peer-level communications as a special sort of file. Table 5.1 compares DOS file operations and equivalent NetBIOS functions.

Table 5.1 DOS File I/O Compared to NetBIOS Functions

File Operation	NetBIOS Equivalent
Open	Add Name, then call (or Listen)
Read	Receive
Write	Send
Seek	<none>
Close	Hang Up, then Delete Name

Using NetBIOS datagrams (which lets you dispense with the session-oriented Call, Listen, and Hang Up NetBIOS commands), you send and receive data packets as shown in table 5.2.

Table 5.2 A Data Packet Sequence for NetBIOS Datagrams	
Workstation A	**Workstation B**
1. Add Name A	1. Add Name B
2. Send message to B	2. Receive a message
3. Receive a message	3. Send message to A
4. Delete Name A	4. Delete Name B

The NetBIOS commands Call, Listen, and Hang Up are your tools for managing sessions. Table 5.3 shows the sequence of events that you would use to open a session, exchange messages, and close the session.

Table 5.3 A Data Packet Sequence for NetBIOS Sessions	
Workstation A	**Workstation B**
1. Add Name A	1. Add Name B
2. Listen (wait for call)	2. Call Workstation A
3. Send message to B	3. Receive a message
4. Receive a message	4. Send message to A
5. Hang Up on B	5. Hang Up on A
6. Delete Name A	6. Delete Name B

Invoking NetBIOS

To invoke any particular NetBIOS function, you set up a network control block (NCB), put a far pointer to the NCB in the ES:BX register pair, and execute an Interrupt 5C (hex):

```
void    NetBIOS (NCB far *ncb_ptr)
    {
    struct SREGS sregs;
    union  REGS regs;

    sregs.es  = FP_SEG(ncb_ptr);
    regs.x.bx = FP_OFF(ncb_ptr);
    int86x(0x5C, &regs, &regs, &sregs);
    }
```

The Network Control Block (NCB)

As the preceding description of how to invoke NetBIOS indicates, all that you specify when you call Interrupt 5C is the address of a network control block. The NCB is a self-contained vehicle that tells NetBIOS all it needs to know about each particular operation. The NCB itself is not transmitted across the network; NetBIOS uses the block as a set of directions specifying what you want to do. You should declare a separate NCB for each operation; you'll find this is easier to manage than if you used one or two generic NCBs for multiple purposes. The following typedef'd struct shows the layout of the NCB:

```
typedef unsigned char byte;
typedef unsigned int  word;

/* Network Control Block (NCB)   */
typedef struct
    {
    byte NCB_COMMAND;
    byte NCB_RETCODE;
    byte NCB_LSN;
    byte NCB_NUM;
    void far *NCB_BUFFER_PTR;
    word NCB_LENGTH;
    byte NCB_CALLNAME[16];
    byte NCB_NAME[16];
    byte NCB_RTO;
    byte NCB_STO;
    void interrupt (*POST_FUNC)(void);
    byte NCB_LANA_NUM;
    byte NCB_CMD_CPLT;
    byte NCB_RESERVE[14];
    }
    NCB;
```

Each of these fields is described in Chapter 3, "PC-to-PC Communications Concepts," in the discussion of NetBIOS concepts. As a supplement to that chapter's discussion, table 5.4 briefly describes each field.

Table 5.4 NCB Fields	
NCB_COMMAND	Command ID
NCB_RETCODE	Immediate return code
NCB_LSN	Local session number
NCB_NUM	Network name number
NCB_BUFFER_PTR	Far pointer to a message packet
NCB_LENGTH	Length of the message packet

NCB_CALLNAME	Name of the other computer
NCB_NAME	Your network name
NCB_RTO	Receive a time-out, in 500-millisecond increments
NCB_STO	Send a time-out, in 500-millisecond increments
POST_FUNC	Far (function) pointer to a POST routine
NCB_LANA_NUM	Adapter number (0 or 1)
NCB_CMD_CPLT	Final return code

NetBIOS Commands

NetBIOS commands come in two versions: *wait* and *no-wait*. When you use
the wait option, control does not return to your program until the operation
completes. In contrast, the no-wait option tells NetBIOS to start the operation
in the background and return immediately to your program. You can give
NetBIOS a pointer to a function in your program (a POST routine) that
NetBIOS calls when the event completes, or you can poll for the completion
of the event by looping until the NCB_CMD_CPLT field changes from 0xFF
to an actual return code (NetBIOS return codes are discussed next). You
might want to include the following list of symbolically defined NetBIOS
commands in your program:

```
#define RESET                 0x32
#define CANCEL                0x35
#define STATUS                0xb3
#define STATUS_WAIT           0x33
#define UNLINK                0x70
#define ADD_NAME              0xb0
#define ADD_NAME_WAIT         0x30
#define ADD_GROUP_NAME        0xb6
#define ADD_GROUP_NAME_WAIT   0x36
#define DELETE_NAME           0xb1
#define DELETE_NAME_WAIT      0x31
#define CALL                  0x90
#define CALL_WAIT             0x10
#define LISTEN                0x91
#define LISTEN_WAIT           0x11
#define HANG_UP               0x92
#define HANG_UP_WAIT          0x12
#define SEND                  0x94
#define SEND_WAIT             0x14
#define SEND_NO_ACK           0xf1
#define SEND_NO_ACK_WAIT      0x71
#define CHAIN_SEND            0x97
```

```
#define CHAIN_SEND_WAIT                   0x17
#define CHAIN_SEND_NO_ACK                 0xf2
#define CHAIN_SEND_NO_ACK_WAIT            0x72
#define RECEIVE                           0x95
#define RECEIVE_WAIT                      0x15
#define RECEIVE_ANY                       0x96
#define RECEIVE_ANY_WAIT                  0x16
#define SESSION_STATUS                    0xb4
#define SESSION_STATUS_WAIT               0x34
#define SEND_DATAGRAM                     0xa0
#define SEND_DATAGRAM_WAIT                0x20
#define SEND_BCST_DATAGRAM                0xa2
#define SEND_BCST_DATAGRAM_WAIT           0x22
#define RECEIVE_DATAGRAM                  0xa1
#define RECEIVE_DATAGRAM_WAIT             0x21
#define RECEIVE_BCST_DATAGRAM             0xa3
#define RECEIVE_BCST_DATAGRAM_WAIT        0x23
```

NetBIOS Return Codes

NetBIOS passes back both an immediate return code (NCB_RETCODE) and a final return code (NCB_CMD_CPLT) to your program. If you use the wait option for a command, or if you use a command that does not have a no-wait option, you should check the NCB_RETCODE field to find out whether the command succeeded. If you use the no-wait option, however, NetBIOS sets the NCB_CMD_CPLT field to a value of 0xFF while the operation is under way. NetBIOS puts an actual, final return code in NCB_CMD_CPLT only when the operation completes. Appendix L, "NetBIOS Error Codes," lists the specific error codes.

POST Routines

If you don't want to associate a POST routine with a particular NCB, set the POST_FUNC pointer to NULL. If you are executing a no-wait command, your program should then loop on NCB_CMD_CPLT until it changes from 0xFF to a real return code.

For a no-wait command, you can code a function that NetBIOS will call when the operation completes. Place the address of the routine in POST_FUNC, as a pointer to a function:

```
void interrupt   answer_the_call()
     {
     ...
     }

listen_ncb.POST_FUNC = answer_the_call;
```

As the appearance of the interrupt keyword in the declaration of answer_the_call() indicates, the POST routine must behave as though it were an interrupt service routine. The following conditions are true at the time of the call:

- Interrupts have been masked (turned off).

- The register pair ES:BX contains a far pointer to the NCB associated with the completed event.

- The NCB_CMD_CPLT field contains the final return code.

- The AL CPU register also contains the final return code.

- The other registers, including the data segment (DS), have no particular value.

- Performing DOS function calls (disk file operations, for example) from within the POST routine may not be safe.

You should code the POST routine to execute as quickly as possible. An IRET machine instruction must be used to exit the routine when it completes. The compiler automatically generates the IRET as one of the side effects of using the interrupt keyword. A simple POST routine, coded in Borland C (note the direct reference to CPU registers, as well as the interrupt keyword), looks like this:

```
/*  Borland C POST routine */

unsigned es_reg, bx_reg;
unsigned msg_received_flag;
NCB far *posted_ncb_ptr;

void interrupt post(void)
    {
    es_reg  = _ES;
    bx_reg  = _BX;
    posted_ncb_ptr = MK_FP(es_reg, bx_reg);
    msg_received_flag = TRUE;
    }
```

The following is the same routine coded according to the conventions of the Microsoft C compiler:

```
/*  Microsoft C POST routine */

unsigned msg_received_flag;
NCB far *posted_ncb_ptr;

void interrupt cdecl far post
```

II

Network Programming

```
                              (unsigned es,
                               unsigned ds,
                               unsigned di,
                               unsigned si,
                               unsigned bp,
                               unsigned sp,
                               unsigned bx,
                               unsigned dx,
                               unsigned cx,
                               unsigned ax,
                               unsigned ip,
                               unsigned cs,
                               unsigned flags)
           {
           posted_ncb_ptr = MK_FP(es, bx);
           msg_received_flag = TRUE;
           }
```

If you are using a C compiler that does not offer the interrupt keyword, this
assembler implementation of a POST routine lets you handle the completion
of an NCB event (scavenge the code at will for your own purposes):

```
;  Assembler function whose address (far pointer) you
;   can put in the POST_FUNC field in a NetBIOS NCB.


;  The prototype of the assembler function should appear
;  as follows somewhere near the top of your program.

;      extern void far post_func(void);

;  And you should declare the following two global
;  data items in your C program:

;      NCB far *posted_ncb_ptr;
;      char    msg_received_flag = 0;

;  When this POST routine is invoked, it puts the
;  address of the NCB associated with the POST
;  in the 'posted_ncb_ptr' pointer, and it sets
;  'msg_received_flag' to 1.

;  If you want, you can modify this assembler routine
;  to call one of your C routines, once the registers
;  have been set up correctly.

;  You can change the following line to match the
;  compiler memory model you're using:

     .model small

     public _post_func
        extrn   _posted_ncb_ptr : dword
        extrn   _msg_received_flag : byte
```

```
        .code
_post_func      proc      far
        push    ds
        push    ax

        mov     ax, @DATA
        mov     ds, ax

;  let the C program know which NCB has completed.

        mov     word ptr _posted_ncb_ptr+2, es
        mov     word ptr _posted_ncb_ptr, bx

;  set a flag to indicate the completion of an operation.

        mov     _msg_received_flag, 1


;  if you have a C function declared like this:
;
;       void post_handler(void)
;           {
;           ... do something brief here ...
;           }
;
;  you could call it here:
;
;       extrn   _post_handler : near
;       call    _post_handler

        pop     ax
        pop     ds
    iret
_post_func      endp
        end
```

NetBIOS Names and Workstation IDs

The fields in an NCB that relate to NetBIOS name management are
NCB_NAME, NCB_CALLNAME, NCB_LSN, and NCB_NUM. NCB_NAME represents the name that you are inserting into the local name table (for an Add
Name call) or the name by which you want to be known (for a Listen or Call
command). NCB_CALLNAME, on the other hand, expresses the name of the
other (remote) workstation. Except for when you are performing an Add
Name or Add Group Name command, NCB_NAME should already exist in
the local name table. The name that you add with an Add Name command
must be unique on the network. Group names, on the other hand, do not
have to be unique, but must not already be on the network as a regular name.
For example, you can add the group name TEAM_ONE to the local name
tables of several different workstations as long as TEAM_ONE has not been
added to any local name table with an Add Name command.

Chapter 3, "PC-to-PC Communications Concepts," mentioned that a permanent node name "pre-identified" each workstation. This workstation ID is constructed by obtaining the six-byte identification number that is "burned into" the network adapter, and prefixing the number with 10 bytes of binary 0s. The name thus formed is always unique on the network and always available to you in your software. You cannot add or delete the name, but you can use it to establish sessions with other workstations. The Adapter Status call (described later in this section) returns the six-byte ID number of the network adapter. Be careful how you handle the permanent node name; it is not a normal, null-terminated C string.

The local session number returned from a successful Listen or Call command, NCB_LSN, represents an established session. In subsequent calls to Send, Receive, and Hang Up, you use NCB_LSN to refer to this session.

NCB_NUM is the network name number returned by an Add Name or Add Group Name command. Use the value in NCB_NUM when you send datagrams to other workstations.

One more note about NetBIOS names: for the Adapter Status command, you can specify an asterisk (*) in the first byte of NCB_CALLNAME to indicate that you are interested in the local adapter. For the Session Status command, you can put an asterisk in the first byte of NCB_NAME to tell NetBIOS that you want session status information for all names. Finally, for the Chain Send command, the first two bytes of NCB_CALLNAME specify the length of the second buffer (to be appended or concatenated to the first) and the next four bytes of NCB_CALLNAME specify a far pointer to the second buffer.

The NetBIOS Installed Test

Chapter 4, "Shared File Programming," introduced the NetBIOS Installed test as a useful component of the LAN-Presence test. Here is the same test in Borland C:

```
NCB     test_ncb;
void interrupt  (*int_5C_vector)(void);

int_5C_vector = getvect(0x5C);
if (int_5C_vector == (void far *) NULL)
    {
    printf("ERROR. NetBios not loaded (Int5C not present).\n");
    exit(1);
    }

memset(&test_ncb, 0, sizeof(NCB));
test_ncb.NCB_COMMAND = 0x7F;
NetBios(&test_ncb);
```

```
if (test_ncb.NCB_RETCODE != 03)
    {
    printf("ERROR. NetBios not loaded (No response from Int5C).\n");
    exit(1);
    }

/* - - - - - - - - - - - - - - - - - - - - - - - */
/*
 *  Call NetBIOS, via Interrupt 5C.
*/

void    NetBios(NCB far *ncb_ptr)
        {
        ncb_ptr->NCB_CMD_CPLT = 0xFF;
        _ES     = FP_SEG(ncb_ptr);          /* Borland C can directly */
        _BX     = FP_OFF(ncb_ptr);          /* access CPU registers.*/
        _AX     = 0x0100;
        geninterrupt(0x5c);
        }
```

Adding Names

Each name that you add to the local name table should be "filtered" to ensure that it is both a normal C string that you can easily manipulate in your program and a proper name entry for the table. The name should be 15 bytes long, with a null byte after the last string character, as shown in the following example:

```
char netbios_name[16];

struct SREGS sregs;
union  REGS  regs;

NCB     add_name_ncb;

strcpy(netbios_name, "BARRY");
while (strlen(netbios_name) < 15)
      strcat(netbios_name, " ");
```

To add the preceding name to the local name table as a unique name, follow these steps:

```
memset(&add_name_ncb, 0, sizeof(NCB));
add_name_ncb.NCB_COMMAND = ADD_NAME;
strcpy(add_name_ncb.NCB_NAME, netbios_name);

sregs.es  = FP_SEG( (void far *) &add_name_ncb);
regs.x.bx = FP_OFF( (void far *) &add_name_ncb);
int86x(0x5C, &regs, &regs, &sregs);

while (add_name_ncb.NCB_CMD_CPLT == 0xFF)
      ;

if (add_name_ncb.NCB_CMD_CPLT != 0)
```

```
        {
        printf("Error.  Could not add name %s\n",
                netbios_name);
        exit(1);
        }
```

To add a group name to the local name table, follow the preceding example but use ADD_GROUP_NAME instead of ADD_NAME.

NetBIOS Datagrams

If the preceding Add Name operation completed successfully, NetBIOS assigns a name number and places it in add_name_ncb.NCB_NUM. You use this name number to identify the local workstation when you issue datagram commands. The destination of a datagram is specified simply as a name (or a group name) in the NCB_CALLNAME field.

Datagrams can be sent on a point-to-point basis (Send Datagram, Receive Datagram) or broadcast throughout the network (Send Broadcast Datagram, Receive Broadcast Datagram). The following example sends a point-to-point datagram:

```
    NCB send_ncb;
    char destination[16];
    char sql_message[] =
      "SELECT AIRCRAFT_ID, AGE WHERE AGE GREATER THAN 20";

    strcpy(destination, "DATABASE_ENGINE");
    memset(&send_ncb, 0, sizeof(NCB));
    send_ncb.NCB_COMMAND    = SEND_DATAGRAM;
    send_ncb.NCB_NUM        = add_name_ncb.NCB_NUM;
    send_ncb.NCB_BUFFER_PTR = (void far *) sql_message;
    send_ncb.NCB_LENGTH     = strlen(sql_message);
    strcpy(send_ncb.NCB_CALLNAME, destination);
    sregs.es  = FP_SEG( (void far *) &send_ncb);
    regs.x.bx = FP_OFF( (void far *) &send_ncb);
    int86x(0x5C, &regs, &regs, &sregs);

    while (send_ncb.NCB_CMD_CPLT == 0xFF)
        ;

    if (send_ncb.NCB_CMD_CPLT != 0)
        {
        printf("Error.  Could not send message\n");
        exit(1);
        }
```

Next you want to receive the reply message from DATABASE_ENGINE (which, in this example, retrieved some information from a relational database based on the query that you specified). The Send Datagram command performed by the other workstation is exactly like the preceding example, except that the destination is BARRY and the message itself contains the reply. To do the receive operation, you give NetBIOS an NCB that contains the name number assigned to the name BARRY along with information about where to put the reply:

```
NCB recv_ncb;
struct
    {
    int  aircraft_count; /* number of entries (0-50) */
    int  aircraft_id[50];
    int  age[50];
    } sql_response;

memset(&recv_ncb, 0, sizeof(NCB));
recv_ncb.NCB_COMMAND    = RECEIVE_DATAGRAM;
recv_ncb.NCB_NUM        = add_name_ncb.NCB_NUM;
recv_ncb.NCB_BUFFER_PTR = (void far *) sql_response;
recv_ncb.NCB_LENGTH     = sizeof(sql_response);

sregs.es  = FP_SEG( (void far *) &recv_ncb);
regs.x.bx = FP_OFF( (void far *) &recv_ncb);
int86x(0x5C, &regs, &regs, &sregs);

while (recv_ncb.NCB_CMD_CPLT == 0xFF)
    ;
        /* might want to put a time-out loop here, */
        /* in case there's no response at all.    */

if (recv_ncb.NCB_CMD_CPLT != 0)
    {
    printf("Error.  Could not receive reply.\n");
    exit(1);
    }
```

After you receive the reply that DATABASE_ENGINE sent to BARRY, no further communication is necessary. For example, you don't need to tell NetBIOS that you're finished talking to DATABASE_ENGINE.

NetBIOS Sessions

As mentioned earlier in this chapter, sessions are a good environment for point-to-point dialogs in which several related data packets are passed back and forth between two workstations. This section explains how to establish a session, send and receive session messages, terminate a session, and more.

Establishing a Session

If the dialog that you have designed is going to be longer than the previous datagram example, you may want to consider establishing a session between the two workstations. You create a session by having one workstation issue a Listen command and subsequently causing another workstation to issue a Call command. The Listen NCB that you construct and give to NetBIOS can specify that the workstation listen for a call from anyone or, if your design dictates, listen for a call from a specific name. In the first case, you put an asterisk (*) in the first byte of the NCB_CALLNAME field. When listening for a call from a specific name, that name goes into the NCB_CALLNAME field. Note that all 16 bytes of the names (caller and who-can-call) must match; this is where the previously mentioned convention for padding of the name with spaces comes in handy.

After the Listen command completes on the first workstation, NetBIOS returns a local session number (LSN) that you use in the Send and Receive NCBs to refer to that session. On the other workstation, the same thing happens after the Call command finishes. Additionally, if you are listening for a call from anyone, the caller's name is returned in the NCB_CALLNAME field. At either workstation (Listener or Caller), you can begin sending or receiving messages just as soon as the Listen (or Call) command finishes.

When you fill out the Listen NCB, you specify NCB_CALLNAME as the name for which to listen (* specifies anyone) and NCB_NAME as the name in the local name table by which you want to be known. You also specify the time-out intervals that NetBIOS uses for the Send and Receive commands issued in this session. NCB_RTO is the Receive Time Out and NCB_STO is the Send Time Out. Both are expressed in 500-millisecond (1/2 second) intervals. If you use a value of 0 in either field, NetBIOS does not signal a time-out for that command.

The Listen command itself does not time out (use the wait option carefully!). A Call command times out after a few retries, indicating that the remote workstation has not issued a Listen command. The occurrence of a time-out during a Send operation aborts the session, but the occurrence of a time-out for a Receive operation merely invalidates that particular NCB, so you can reissue the Receive command if that suits your design.

You might code the Listen function like this:

```
/* - - - - - - - - - - - - - - - - - - - - - - - - */
/*
 *    Build the 'listen' NCB and send it out
 *    across the network.  Set the POST address to
 *    point to a 'background' routine to handle a caller.
 */
void    net_listen_post(char *caller, char *us,
                        void interrupt (*post_function)(),
                        unsigned char rto, unsigned char sto)
```

```
        {
        memset(&listen_ncb, 0, sizeof(NCB));
        listen_ncb.NCB_COMMAND = LISTEN;
        strcpy(listen_ncb.NCB_NAME,      us);
        strcpy(listen_ncb.NCB_CALLNAME, caller);
        listen_ncb.POST_FUNC = post_function;
        listen_ncb.NCB_RTO = rto;
        listen_ncb.NCB_STO = sto;
        sregs.es  = FP_SEG( (void far *) &listen_ncb);
        regs.x.bx = FP_OFF( (void far *) &listen_ncb);
        int86x(0x5C, &regs, &regs, &sregs);
        }
```

Then, to invoke this `net_listen_post()` function, you might code the following:

```
    net_listen_post("*", "DATABASE_ENGINE", handle_call, 20, 20);
```

In this function call, `handle_call()` is a POST routine (discussed earlier), DATABASE_ENGINE is the name that was added to the local name table to identify that workstation, * says "listen for a call from anyone," and the `rto` and `sto` values of 20 tell NetBIOS to wait as long as 10 seconds for each Send or Receive operation before timing out.

Similarly, the calling workstation (BARRY) constructs and issues an NCB as follows:

```
    /* - - - - - - - - - - - - - - - - - - - - - - - - */
    /*
     *   "Call" another workstation.
     */
    void    net_call(char *who, char *us,
                    unsigned char rto, unsigned char sto)
            {
            memset(&call_ncb, 0, sizeof(NCB));
            call_ncb.NCB_COMMAND = CALL;
            memcpy(call_ncb.NCB_NAME,      us,  16);
            strcpy(call_ncb.NCB_CALLNAME, who);
            call_ncb.NCB_RTO = rto;
            call_ncb.NCB_STO = sto;
            sregs.es  = FP_SEG( (void far *) &call_ncb);
            regs.x.bx = FP_OFF( (void far *) &call_ncb);
            int86x(0x5C, &regs, &regs, &sregs);
            }
```

The call to this function, elsewhere in the program, is coded as follows:

```
    net_call("DATABASE_ENGINE", "BARRY            ", 20, 20);

    while (call_ncb.NCB_CMD_CPLT == 0xFF)
        ;

    if (call_ncb.NCB_CMD_CPLT == 0)
        local_session_number = call_ncb.NCB_LSN;
    else
        abort("Call was unsuccessful.");
```

Sending and Receiving Session Messages

While a session is under way, you can issue Send and Receive commands (NCBs) to transfer information back and forth. In fact, when sending data, you have a choice of NetBIOS commands: Send, Chain Send, or Send No ACK. The Send command can be used for data packets as long as 65,535 bytes, and the Chain Send command concatenates two send buffers, which you specify, into a message that can be as long as 131,070 bytes. The Send No ACK command is coded just like a Send command, but behaves like a datagram; no (internal) acknowledgment is sent between NetBIOS on the two workstations. This section discusses the plain Send and Receive commands; Part IV of this book, "Reference," describes the Chain Send and Send No ACK commands.

To construct an NCB that causes data to be sent to the other session partner, fill in the NCB_LSN field to identify the session and fill in the NCB_BUFFER_PTR and NCB_LENGTH fields to describe the data message that you want to send. The following is an example of a function that performs a NetBIOS Send:

```
/* - - - - - - - - - - - - - - - - - - - - - - - - - */
/*
 *    Build the 'send' NCB and send it out
 *    across the network.
 *
 */
void    net_send(unsigned char lsn,
                 void far *packet_ptr, int packet_len)
        {
        memset(&send_ncb, 0, sizeof(NCB));
        send_ncb.NCB_COMMAND = SEND;
        send_ncb.NCB_LSN = lsn;
        send_ncb.NCB_LENGTH = packet_len;
        send_ncb.NCB_BUFFER_PTR = packet_ptr;
        sregs.es  = FP_SEG( (void far *) &send_ncb);
        regs.x.bx = FP_OFF( (void far *) &send_ncb);
        int86x(0x5C, &regs, &regs, &sregs);
        }
```

You might call the net_send() function with the following parameter values:

```
net_send(local_session_number,
         &aircraft_age_rcd, sizeof(struct AGE_RECORD));
while (send_ncb.NCB_CMD_CPLT == 0xFF)
    ;
```

The Receive command also uses the local session number to refer to the session. The following example shows how you can specify a POST routine when the Receive is issued:

```
/* - - - - - - - - - - - - - - - - - - - - - - - - */
/*
 *    Build the 'receive' NCB and send it out
 *    across the network.  When the operation completes,
 *    let NetBIOS call the POST routine to handle it.
 */
void    net_receive_post(unsigned char lsn,
                         void interrupt (*post_function)(),
                         void *packet_ptr, int packet_len)

        {
        memset(&receive_ncb, 0, sizeof(NCB));
        receive_ncb.NCB_COMMAND = RECEIVE;
        receive_ncb.NCB_LSN = lsn;
        receive_ncb.NCB_LENGTH = packet_len;
        receive_ncb.NCB_BUFFER_PTR = packet_ptr;
        receive_ncb.POST_FUNC = post_function;
        sregs.es  = FP_SEG( (void far *) &receive_ncb);
        regs.x.bx = FP_OFF( (void far *) &receive_ncb);
        int86x(0x5C, &regs, &regs, &sregs);
        }
```

At the point in your program at which you want to let NetBIOS know you are
ready to receive some data, you invoke `net_receive_post()` as follows:

```
net_receive_post(local_session_number,
    post_handler, &input_buff, sizeof(input_buff));
```

Terminating the Session

When the exchange of data messages is complete, both session partners issue
a Hang Up command to end the session. Before issuing a Hang Up command,
your program should make sure that any pending operations are canceled
with the Cancel command. To cancel an outstanding NCB, you put the address of the NCB into another NCB's NCB_BUFFER_PTR field as a far pointer
and issue the Cancel:

```
/* - - - - - - - - - - - - - - - - - - - - - - - - */
/*
 *    Build the 'cancel' NCB and send it out
 *    across the network.
 *
 */
void    net_cancel(NCB *np)
        {
        memset(&cancel_ncb, 0, sizeof(NCB));
        cancel_ncb.NCB_COMMAND = CANCEL;
        cancel_ncb.NCB_BUFFER_PTR = np;
        sregs.es  = FP_SEG( (void far *) &cancel_ncb);
        regs.x.bx = FP_OFF( (void far *) &cancel_ncb);
        int86x(0x5C, &regs, &regs, &sregs);
        }
```

II

Network Programming

The following is a specific example of how to use net_cancel() to cancel a pending Listen command:

```
net_cancel(&listen_ncb);
while (cancel_ncb.NCB_CMD_CPLT == 0xFF)
    ;
```

To hang up a session, all you need to specify is the local session number. The Hang Up command that both session partners should execute looks like this:

```
/* - - - - - - - - - - - - - - - - - - - - - - - - - */
/*
 *      Build and issue a 'hang up' NCB
 *
 */
void    net_hangup(unsigned char lsn)
        {
        memset(&hangup_ncb, 0, sizeof(NCB));
        hangup_ncb.NCB_COMMAND = HANG_UP;
        hangup_ncb.NCB_LSN = lsn;
        sregs.es  = FP_SEG( (void far *) &hangup_ncb);
        regs.x.bx = FP_OFF( (void far *) &hangup_ncb);
        int86x(0x5C, &regs, &regs, &sregs);
        }
```

Deleting Names

When you finish sending or receiving datagrams, or after you close a session by canceling any outstanding commands and performing a Hang Up, you should delete the names that you added to the local name table. Not only does deleting names keep things neat and tidy, it also prevents users from encountering the error Duplicate Name if they run your software again without rebooting the workstation (because the name is still in the local name table when your software issues its Add Name command). The following is an example of Delete Name:

```
/* - - - - - - - - - - - - - - - - - - - - - - - - - */
/*
 *      Build the 'delete_name' NCB and issue it
 *
 */
void    net_delete_name(char *name)
        {
        memset(&delete_name_ncb, 0, sizeof(NCB));
        delete_name_ncb.NCB_COMMAND = DELETE_NAME;
        strcpy(delete_name_ncb.NCB_NAME, name);
        sregs.es  = FP_SEG((void far *) &delete_name_ncb);
        regs.x.bx = FP_OFF((void far *) &delete_name_ncb);
        int86x(0x5C, &regs, &regs, &sregs);
        }
```

Make sure that the NCB_NAME and NCB_CALLNAME fields are properly set up (using all 16 bytes) so that an exact match for the name you are trying to delete is found in the local name table.

Determining Session Status

The Session Status command returns information about all the sessions for a particular name in the local name table, or for all the names in the local name table. Session Status information is not available for remote sessions. You can use this command to find out the following:

■ The name number assigned to the name

■ The number of sessions associated with the name

■ The number of Receive Datagram and Receive Broadcast Datagram commands that are outstanding

■ The number of Receive Any commands that are outstanding

The remainder of the data is a series of entries, one per session. To determine how many entries are filled in, check the "number of sessions for this name" field to determine how many entries are filled in. The remaining fields are the following:

■ The session's local session number

■ The current state of the session (see table 5.5)

■ The local session partner's name

■ The remote session partner's name

■ The number of Receive commands outstanding

■ The number of Send and Chain Send commands outstanding

Table 5.5 Session Status Codes	
State	Meaning
1	Listen pending
2	Call pending
3	Session established

(continues)

Table 5.5 Continued	
State	**Meaning**
4	Hang Up pending
5	Hang Up complete
6	Session ended abnormally

To issue a Session Status command, set up an NCB so that its
NCB_BUFFER_PTR points to the STATUS_INFO following structure, and put
sizeof(STATUS_INFO) in the NCB_LENGTH field. Specify in the NCB_NAME
field the name in which you're interested, or put an asterisk in the first byte
of NCB_NAME to obtain session status for all local name table items. The
following STATUS_INFO structure allows as many as 40 sessions, but you can
adjust this limit as necessary for your application.

```
typedef struct {
        unsigned char  name_num;
        unsigned char  session_count;
        unsigned char  datagram_count;
        unsigned char  recv_any_count;
        struct {
            unsigned char  lsn;
            unsigned char  state;
            char           local_name[16];
            char           remote_name[16];
            unsigned char  recv_count;
            unsigned char  send_count;
            } session_data[40];
        }
        STATUS_INFO;

STATUS_INFO    session_status_info;
```

Determining Adapter Status

The Adapter Status command, unlike the Session Status command, can
be used to obtain information about a remote copy of NetBIOS and about
the local copy in the requesting workstation. The structure to which
NCB_BUFFER_PTR points returns the following three categories of
information:

■ The six bytes of the network adapter ID, which represent the unique
address of that particular network adapter card

■ A set of statistics that show traffic and error counts

■ A copy of the name table from the remote (or local) workstation,
   including status information about each name

One thing to watch out for is that the implementations of NetBIOS from
different manufacturers may define the information differently, especially in
the traffic-error count category. The following layout shows the information
that the IBM NetBIOS device driver, DXMT0MOD.SYS, returns in the Adapter
Status buffer area:

```
typedef struct {
        unsigned char    card_id[6];
        unsigned char    release_level;
        unsigned char    reserved1;
        unsigned char    type_of_adapter;
        unsigned char    old_or_new_parameters;
        unsigned int     reporting_period_minutes;
        unsigned int     frame_reject_recvd_count;
        unsigned int     frame_reject_sent_count;
        unsigned int     recvd_data_frame_errors;
        unsigned int     unsuccessful_transmissions;
        unsigned long    good_transmissions;
        unsigned long    good_receptions;
        unsigned int     retransmissions;
        unsigned int     exhausted_resource_count;
        unsigned int     t1_timer_expired_count;
        unsigned int     ti_timer_expired_count;
        char             reserved2[4];
        unsigned int     available_ncbs;
        unsigned int     max_ncbs_configured;
        unsigned int     max_ncbs_possible;
        unsigned int     buffer_or_station_busy_count;
        unsigned int     max_datagram_size;
        unsigned int     pending_sessions;
        unsigned int     max_sessions_configured;
        unsigned int     max_sessions_possible;
        unsigned int     max_frame_size;
        int              name_count;
        struct {
            char             tbl_name[16];
            unsigned char    tbl_name_number;
            unsigned char    tbl_name_status;
            } name_table[20];
        }
        ADAPTER_DATA;

ADAPTER_DATA    adapter_data;
```

The layout's fields have suggestive names, but some require further
explanation:

■ The release_level field identifies the major version number of the
   NetBIOS software: 0x00 = version 1.X, 0x02 = version 2.X, and
   0x03 = version 3.X.

- The definition of the `type_of_adapter` field depends on the NetBIOS version. For NetBIOS 1.X, the field always contains 0xFF. For later versions, this field contains 0xFE if the adapter is a PC Network interface card and 0xFF if the adapter is a Token Ring card.

- The `old_or_new_parameters` field contains two subfields, the minor version of NetBIOS (second nibble) and whether NetBIOS was started with old or new parameters (first nibble). For NetBIOS version 1.X, the first nibble is always 0. For later versions, the field contains 0x1 if NetBIOS was started with old parameters and 0x2 if started with new parameters.

- The `exhausted_resource_count` field contains the number of times that data was lost because NetBIOS ran out of buffers. All the count fields roll over from 0xFF..FF to 0 except for `exhausted_resource_count`.

- The last two bytes of each name table entry express the name number assigned to the name (`tbl_name_number`) and the status of the name (`tbl_name_status`). The `tbl_name_status` byte is encoded in the following format:

    G x x x x S S S

    where G, the first bit, is 1 if the name is a group name and 0 if it is a unique name. NetBIOS reserves the xxxx bits for its own use, and they are not necessarily 0. The SSS bits indicate the status of the name. Table 5.6 lists the status values.

Table 5.6 NetBIOS SSS Bits

SSS	Meaning
000	Name registration in progress
100	Registered name
101	Deregistered name (a Delete Name command has been issued, but still has active sessions)
110	Duplicate name detected
111	Duplicate name and deregistration pending

The NCB that you construct for an Adapter Status command must have the NCB_CALLNAME, NCB_BUFFER_PTR, and NCB_LENGTH fields set, as shown in the following example:

```
/* - - - - - - - - - - - - - - - - - - - - - - - */
/* Build and issue an 'adapter status' command
 * for the workstation named "DATABASE_ENGINE"
 */
    memset(&status_ncb, 0, sizeof(NCB));

    status_ncb.NCB_COMMAND = STATUS;
    strcpy(status_ncb.NCB_CALLNAME, "DATABASE_ENGINE");
    status_ncb.NCB_LENGTH = sizeof(ADAPTER_DATA);
    status_ncb.NCB_BUFFER_PTR = (void far *) &adapter_data;

    sregs.es  = FP_SEG((void far *) &status_ncb);
    regs.x.bx = FP_OFF((void far *) &status_ncb);
    int86x(0x5C, &regs, &regs, &sregs);
```

Resetting the Adapter

NetBIOS processes the Reset Adapter command by doing the following:

- Deleting all names from the local name table (the permanent node name is not deleted)

- Aborting all active sessions

- Discarding any outstanding NCBs

If you put a nonzero value in the NCB_LSN field, that value is used as the new maximum number of sessions. A value of 0 tells NetBIOS to use the default (usually 6). If you put a nonzero value in the NCB_NUM field, NetBIOS uses it as the new maximum number of NCBs that can be outstanding at any one time. A value of 0 tells NetBIOS to use the default, which is usually 12.

You should avoid using the Reset Adapter command in such NetBIOS-based environments as DOS LAN Requester or the IBM PC LAN Program. Reset Adapter deletes not only the names and sessions belonging to your application but also the DLR or PCLP names and sessions. Therefore, this command effectively disables DLR or PCLP and kicks you off the network.

The layout for the Reset Adapter command is as follows:

```
/* the Reset Adapter command */

    memset(&reset_ncb, 0, sizeof(NCB));

    reset_ncb.NCB_COMMAND = RESET;
    reset_ncb.NCB_LSN = max_sessions;
    reset_ncb.NCB_NUM = max_ncbs;

    sregs.es  = FP_SEG((void far *) &reset_ncb);
    regs.x.bx = FP_OFF((void far *) &reset_ncb);
    int86x(0x5C, &regs, &regs, &sregs);
```

Programming NetBIOS under Windows

Most of what you just learned about programming NetBIOS in a plain DOS environment also applies to programming NetBIOS in a Windows application. Because Windows manages memory in special ways and occasionally requires your program to relinquish the CPU cooperatively, you must take into account some extra considerations when writing a Windows program that sends and receives NetBIOS messages.

After you load DOS and the network software at your workstation (including NetBIOS), you can program NetBIOS exactly as described earlier in this chapter. However, when you run Windows on top of DOS and the network software, your PC changes from a single-tasking environment to a simple multitasking environment. To the extent that your program processes Windows message queue events efficiently and does not consume the CPU for inordinate amounts of time, your program should behave well in the Windows environment. However, using one of the wait versions of the NetBIOS commands can make your program a CPU bottleneck, as can polling for the completion of a NetBIOS event without giving Windows a chance to use the CPU. Avoid using a wait version of a NetBIOS command in your Windows program. In your polling loops that wait for the completion of a NetBIOS event, you should insert calls to the PeekMessage() Windows function to let Windows handle mouse, keyboard, and other message queue events. Otherwise, your program and the entire Windows environment will occasionally seem unresponsive to the user running your program.

Calling PeekMessage() can enable other Windows applications to process, but PeekMessage() by itself doesn't let programs running in DOS sessions execute. To relinquish the CPU more thoroughly, you must invoke the Interrupt 2Fh function provided by Windows. In your PeekMessage() loop, use inline assembler statements to put 0x1689 into the AX register and 1 into the BL register, and then invoke Interrupt 2Fh. The following code fragment shows this sequence of instructions:

```
if ( !PeekMessage(lpMsg, hWnd, uFirst, uLast, uCommand) )
    {
    _asm mov ax, 0x1689
    _asm mov bl, 1    ; mouse busy flag TRUE
    _asm int 0x2F
    }
```

In a larger, more comprehensive `PeekMessage()` loop, you could invoke `TranslateMessage()` and `DispatchMessage()` to enable Windows to direct message queue events to a particular process. If you provide for the dispatching of messages within your `PeekMessage()` loop, you should make sure your program's event-handling code can be reentered. A user might select one of your program's menu options, for example, while you wait for a NetBIOS NCB to complete.

Windows can move memory areas from location to location in RAM and swap memory areas to disk. From a NetBIOS programming perspective, you must ensure that the memory areas within your program that you give to NetBIOS are in fixed, page-locked memory. When allocating memory for an NCB with `GlobalAlloc()`, for example, use the GMEM_FIXED manifest constant in your call. If you put your NetBIOS code into a Windows DLL, you should call `GlobalPageLock()` and `GlobalPageUnlock()` in your DLL to prevent Windows from moving or swapping the memory area. However, if a call to `GetWinFlags()` indicates that Windows is not running in 386 Enhanced mode, you shouldn't page-lock memory areas.

Programming NetBIOS under OS/2

Programming NetBIOS in the 32-bit OS/2 environment differs only slightly from programming NetBIOS for plain DOS. To invoke NetBIOS, you use a calling interface, `NetBiosSubmit()`, rather than Interrupt 5Ch. You use an OS/2 semaphore to handle POST processing, instead of having NetBIOS call one of your program's functions. Although you can poll for the completion of a NetBIOS event instead of using a POST routine, consider using a separate OS/2 thread for receiving and processing incoming NetBIOS messages. The formats of the NetBIOS data structures, including the NCB, are similar to the data structures that you would use in a DOS program. In all other respects, the principles and concepts that you learned earlier in this chapter apply to both the DOS and OS/2 environments.

> **Note**
>
> If you use the NetBIOS emulator that is part of the NetWare Requester for OS/2, or if you use the OS/2 LAN Server Requester to connect to a LAN Server file server, you can run NetBIOS-aware DOS programs in OS/2's virtual DOS sessions.

From within an OS/2 program, you call NetBIOS functions in a DLL. The DLL comes with the Requester (LAN Server or NetWare) that enables the workstation to access the file server. The NetBIOS function that you will use most often is NetBiosSubmit(). This function lets your program give an NCB to NetBIOS for processing.

Most implementations of NetBIOS for OS/2 are 16-bit device drivers. For this reason, you must pass 16-bit pointers to the functions in the NetBIOS DLL. The following prototype shows one way to tell the IBM C Set/2 or C/C++ Tools compiler to emit the proper 16-bit code for the NetBiosSubmit() function:

```
extern unsigned short _Far16 Pascal
     NetBiosSubmit(short, short, void * _Seg16);
```

The _Far16 keyword informs the compiler to emit a 16-bit call to NetBiosSubmit() in your program, and the _Seg16 keyword instructs the compiler to pass the pointer to the NCB as a 16-bit entity.

To add a name to the NetBIOS name table from within an OS/2 program, you can use the following code fragment:

```
memset(&ncb, 0, sizeof(struct network_control_block));
ncb.ncb_command  = NB_ADD_NAME_WAIT;
ncb.ncb_lana_num = 0;
memcpy(ncb.ncb_name, name, 16);
NetBiosSubmit(0, 0, &ncb);
```

The following code fragment receives a datagram packet; note how the address of the field rcv_buffer is cast into a 16-bit pointer:

```
memset(&recv_ncb, 0, sizeof(struct network_control_block) );
recv_ncb.ncb_command = NB_RECEIVE_DATAGRAM_WAIT;
recv_ncb.ncb_lana_num = 0;
recv_ncb.ncb_num = namenum;
recv_ncb.ncb_length = bufsiz;
recv_ncb.ncb_buffer_address = (char * _Seg16) rcv_buffer;
NetBiosSubmit(0, 0, &recv_ncb);
```

The following code fragment deletes a name from the NetBIOS name table:

```
memset(&ncb, 0, sizeof(struct network_control_block) );
ncb.ncb_command  = NB_DELETE_NAME_WAIT;
ncb.ncb_lana_num = adapter;
memcpy( ncb.ncb_name, name, 16);
NetBiosSubmit(0, 0, &ncb);
```

You can use the following code fragment to send a datagram message packet:

```
memset(&ncb, 0, sizeof(struct network_control_block) );
ncb.ncb_command = NB_SEND_DATAGRAM_WAIT;
memcpy(ncb.ncb_callname, callname, 16);
ncb.ncb_lana_num = adapter;
ncb.ncb_num = namnum;
```

```
      ncb.ncb_buffer_address = (char * _Seg16) buffer;
      ncb.ncb_length = bufsiz;
      NetBiosSubmit(0, 0, &ncb);
```

You should use the following definition of an NCB in your OS/2 programs:

```
struct      network_control_block
{
  byte      ncb_command;                   /* NetBIOS command code       */
  byte      ncb_retcode;                   /* Return code                */
  byte      ncb_lsn;                       /* Local session number       */
  byte      ncb_num;                       /* Number of application name */
  address   ncb_buffer_address;            /* Address of message buffer  */
  word      ncb_length;                    /* Length of message buffer   */
  byte      ncb_callname[16];              /* Destination name           */
  byte      ncb_name[16];                  /* Source name                */
  byte      ncb_rto;                       /* Receive time-out           */
  byte      ncb_sto;                       /* Send time-out              */
  ulong     ncb_post_sem_handle;           /* Semaphore handle           */
  byte      ncb_lana_num;                  /* Adapter number             */
  byte      ncb_cmd_cplt;                  /* Final command status       */
  byte      ncb_reserve[14];               /* Reserved                   */
};
```

The following code defines the structure of data returned by NetBIOS when
you use the adapter status NetBIOS command:

```
struct      ncb_status_information
{
  byte      burned_in_addr[6];             /* Adapter's burned in addr   */
  byte      reserved1[2];                  /* RESERVED always X'0000'    */
  word      software_level_number;         /* X'FFnn' - nn is level num  */
  word      reporting_period;              /* Reporting period (minutes) */
  word      frmr_frames_received;          /* Number of FRMR received    */
  word      frmr_frames_sent;              /* Number of FRMR sent        */
  word      bad_iframes_received;          /* # bad Iframes received     */
  word      aborted_transmissions;         /* # aborted transmits        */
  dword     packets_transmitted;           /* # successfully transmitted */
  dword     packets_received;              /* # successfully received    */
  word      bad_iframes_transmitted;       /* # bad Iframes transmitted  */
  word      lost_data_count;               /* Lost SAP buffer data cnt   */
  word      t1_expiration_count;           /* Number of T1 expirations   */
  word      ti_expiration_count;           /* Number of Ti expirations   */
  address   extended_status_table;         /* Address of extended status */
  word      number_of_free_ncbs;           /* Number of NCBs available   */
  word      max_configured_ncbs;           /* Configured NCB maximum     */
  word      max_allowed_ncbs;              /* Maximum NCBs (always 255)  */
  word      busy_condition_count;          /* Local station busy count   */
  word      max_datagram_size;             /* Maximum datagram packet    */
  word      pending_sessions;              /* Number of pending sessions */
  word      max_configured_sessions;       /* Configured session maximum */
  word      max_allowed_sessions;          /* Maximum sessions (254)     */
  word      max_data_packet_size;          /* Maximum session packet     */
  word      number_of_names_present;       /* Number of names in table   */
};
```

II

Network Programming

The following data structure defines the area of memory that NetBIOS fills with information when you use the Session Status NetBIOS command:

```
struct      ncb_session_status
{
  byte      name_number_of_sessions;   /* Name number for sessions   */
  byte      sessions_using_name;       /* # of sessions using name   */
  byte      active_rcv_datagrams;      /* # of receive datagrams out */
  byte      active_receive_anys;       /* # of RECEIVE.ANY cmnds out */
  byte      local_session_number;      /* Local session number       */
  byte      session_state;             /* State of session           */
  byte      local_name[16];            /* Local name                 */
  byte      remote_name[16];           /* Remote name                */
  byte      active_receives;           /* # of RECEIVE cmnds out     */
  byte      active_sends;              /* # of SEND, CHAIN.SEND out  */
};
```

The OS/2 NetBIOS reset command accepts a specially formatted NCB that contains information about the NetBIOS environment, as shown in the following definition:

```
struct      ncb_reset
{
  byte      ncb_command;               /* NetBIOS command code        */
  byte      ncb_retcode;               /* Return code                 */
  byte      ncb_lsn;                   /* Local session number        */
  byte      ncb_num;                   /* Number of application name  */
  address   dd_name_address;           /* Device drive name address   */
  byte      not_used1[2];              /* Not used                    */
  byte      req_sessions;              /* # of sessions requested     */
  byte      req_commands;              /* # of commands requested     */
  byte      req_names;                 /* # of names requested        */
  byte      req_name_one;              /* Name number one request     */
  byte      not_used2[12];             /* Not used                    */
  byte      act_sessions;              /* # of sessions obtained      */
  byte      act_commands;              /* # of commands obtained      */
  byte      act_names;                 /* # of names obtained         */
  byte      act_name_one;              /* Name number one response    */
  byte      not_used3[4];              /* Not used                    */
  byte      load_session;              /* Number of sessions at load  */
  byte      load_commands;             /* Number of commands at load  */
  byte      load_names;                /* Number of names at load     */
  byte      load_stations;             /* Number of stations at load  */
  byte      not_used4[2];              /* Not used                    */
  byte      load_remote_names;         /* Number of remote names      */
  byte      not_used5[5];              /* Not used                    */
  word      ncb_dd_id;                 /* NCB device driver ID        */
  byte      ncb_lana_num;              /* Adapter number              */
  byte      not_used6;                 /* Not used                    */
  byte      ncb_reserve[14];           /* NCB error information       */
};
```

Summary

This chapter explained how to program NetBIOS applications. You know how a network control block is constructed and what it is used for. You are now familiar with the NetBIOS commands for adding and deleting names, sending and receiving datagrams, creating sessions, and sending and receiving data messages within a session. You can use these NetBIOS commands in the DOS, Windows, and OS/2 environments. You have also picked up a useful set of design guidelines for PC-to-PC communications.

The next chapter covers the programming techniques that you use on NetWare LANs to do IPX and SPX peer-level communications.

II

Network Programming

Chapter 6

IPX and SPX Programming

In addition to NetBIOS (which is mandatory on LAN Server, LANtastic, and Windows for Workgroups LANs), NetWare offers the IPX and SPX protocols for PC-to-PC communications. Why would you want to use IPX or SPX rather than NetBIOS? For two reasons: speed and memory. Because Novell's NetBIOS software layer works by translating your NetBIOS function calls into IPX messages, you can "avoid the middleman" by coding your program to call IPX directly. IPX is faster than NetBIOS, and, if NetBIOS is not loaded, you have between 20K and 25K more DOS memory for your application.

This chapter explains both IPX and SPX and describes the techniques that you use to send and receive messages through these protocols. You first learn how to use IPX and SPX in a DOS environment. You then extend your programming skills by considering how to program IPX and SPX in the Windows and OS/2 environments.

Programming IPX

IPX (Internetwork Packet Exchange) is a datagram service available on NetWare LANs. The previous chapter showed how NetBIOS commands relate to disk file I/O options; table 6.1 compares IPX functions and equivalent DOS operations.

Table 6.1 File I/O Compared to IPX Functions	
File Operation	**IPX Equivalent**
Open	Open Socket
Read	Listen for Packet
Write	Send Packet
Seek	<none>
Close	Close Socket

Table 6.2 lists the sequence of events that you use to send and receive IPX packets.

Table 6.2 The Data Packet Sequence for IPX	
Workstation A	**Workstation B**
1. Open the socket	1. Open the socket
2. Get the network address of B	2. Get the network address of A
3. Send the packet to B	3. Receive the data packet
4. Receive the data packet	4. Send the packet to A
5. Close the socket	5. Close the socket

IPX is a datagram-based protocol. When you choose to use IPX to send and receive data packets, make sure that you design a scheme for verifying that the packets are delivered to the destination and received in the correct sequence. If you want to use a protocol that handles these details for you, use the SPX protocol discussed in the next section.

The IPX Installed Test

The test for the presence of IPX uses Interrupt 2F (hex), the multiplex interrupt. Put 0x7A, the multiplex number, in the AH register, put 0 in the AL register, and then do the Interrupt 2F. If IPX is installed, the Interrupt 2F call returns 0xFF in the AL register. As a side effect, the ES:DI register pair returns the entry point for IPX (and SPX) as a far pointer to a function. The following `ipx_installed()` function shows this technique. The function returns –1 if IPX is not installed and 1 if it is. The function also sets up a far function pointer, `*ipx_spx`, that you can use to call IPX.

```
/* Example in Borland C; note how MK_FP makes */
/* a far pointer from the ES:DI register pair */
/* in the example code.                       */

/* Also note that MK_FP works differently for */
/* some other compilers.                      */

void far    (*ipx_spx)(void);

int    ipx_installed(void)
       {
       union REGS      regs;
       struct SREGS    sregs;

       regs.x.ax = 0x7a00;
       int86x(0x2f, &regs, &regs, &sregs);
       if (regs.h.al != 0xff)
           return -1;

       ipx_spx = MK_FP(sregs.es, regs.x.di);
       return 1;
       }
```

Invoking IPX

There are two ways to call IPX, and each method has advantages and disadvantages. To use the first method, you set up the CPU registers as specified for a particular IPX function. You then call IPX using the ipx_spx function pointer obtained during the installed test. This first method is easy to do in Borland C, as long as you're careful about directly accessing CPU registers.

The following examples of IPX calls show how to invoke IPX. For now, simply study the part of the code that calls IPX; the functions being performed and the actual contents of the CPU registers are not important now.

```
/* example IPX call in Borland C */
/* note the direct access to the CPU registers */

void    ipx_listen_for_packet(struct ECB *ecb_ptr)
        {
        _ES = FP_SEG( (void far *) ecb_ptr);
        _SI = FP_OFF( (void far *) ecb_ptr);
        _BX = 0x0004;
        ipx_spx();             /* from the installed test */
        }
```

The second method uses Interrupt 7A (hex) to call IPX. This interrupt is a secondary entry point into IPX. Programmers who use a compiler that doesn't support inline assembler can use this method.

```
/* example call to IPX (Int 7A) */
void    close_socket(unsigned socket)
        {
```

```
union REGS regs;

regs.x.bx = 0x0001;
regs.x.dx = socket;
int86(0x7A, &regs, &regs);
}
```

Interrupt 7A has one major drawback: it is also used by the IBM 3270 Emulator product, and by a few other software products. Unless you can be absolutely certain of the environment in which your application will be used, you should avoid using the Interrupt 7A entry point into IPX.

Programmers who use a compiler that doesn't offer inline assembler, or those who simply want to understand the IPX interface from an assembler perspective, can benefit from the following assembler "helper" function. The call_ipx() function takes a single parameter: a pointer to a structure that contains register values to be passed to IPX. The function puts the indicated values in the CPU register, calls IPX, and returns the values of the AX and DX registers in the same structure.

Before you examine the assembler code, study this typical calling sequence:

```
/* first, the layout of the structure containing */
/* the registers */

struct IPX_REGS {
        unsigned  ax_reg;
        unsigned  bx_reg;
        unsigned  dx_reg;
        unsigned  si_reg;
        unsigned  di_reg;
        unsigned  es_reg;
        };

/* next, the prototype for the function */

extern void far call_ipx(struct IPX_REGS far *ipx_regs);


/* now use 'call_ipx' to receive a packet */

void    ipx_listen_for_packet(struct ECB far *ecb_ptr)
        {
        struct  IPX_REGS ipx_regs;

        ipx_regs.bx_reg = 0x04;
        ipx_regs.si_reg = FP_OFF(ecb_ptr);
        ipx_regs.es_reg = FP_SEG(ecb_ptr);
        call_ipx (&ipx_regs);
        }
```

The assembler routine itself follows:

```
; - - - - - - - - - - - - - - - - - - - - - - - - - - - - - - -
;        call_ipx()
;
;  Assembler function to set up the CPU registers
;  and call IPX:
;
;        1. Get IPX entry point, if not already set.
;        2. Load up the registers (AX, BX, DS, SI, DI, ES).
;        3. Call IPX via the IPX entry point (far call).
;        4. Return the AX and DX registers.
;
;  Code these statements early in your program:
;
;    struct IPX_REGS {
;        unsigned  ax_reg;
;        unsigned  bx_reg;
;        unsigned  dx_reg;
;        unsigned  si_reg;
;        unsigned  di_reg;
;        unsigned  es_reg;
;        };
;
;    extern void far call_ipx(struct IPX_REGS far *ipx_regs);
;
;
; - - - - - - - - - - - - - - - - - - - - - - - - - - - - - - -

;  Change the following line to match the memory model
;  you're using:

    .model small

    public _call_ipx

;  Symbolically map the stack area

parms   struc
sav_bp  dw      ?
ret_ip  dw      ?
ret_cs  dw      ?
reg_ofs dw      ?
reg_seg dw      ?
parms   ends


; Map the C structure in which the registers are passed

ipx_regs struc
ax_reg  dw      ?
bx_reg  dw      ?
dx_reg  dw      ?
si_reg  dw      ?
di_reg  dw      ?
es_reg  dw      ?
ipx_regs ends
```

```
            .data
ipx_epa dd      0

        .code
_call_ipx proc     far
        push    bp
        mov     bp, sp

; See if IPX Entry Point has been established yet

        cmp     word ptr ipx_epa, 0
        jne     set_up_regs

; Call Interrupt 2F to get entry point of IPX

        mov     ax, 7A00h
        int     2Fh
        cmp     al, 0FFh

; Just exit if IPX is not present (shouldn't be true!)

        jne     call_ipx_exit

; Set up far pointer to IPX

        mov     word ptr ipx_epa+2, es
        mov     word ptr ipx_epa, di

set_up_regs:
        push    ds
        mov     ds, [bp].reg_seg
        mov     bx, [bp].reg_ofs

        mov     es, ds:[bx].es_reg
        mov     di, ds:[bx].di_reg
        mov     si, ds:[bx].si_reg
        mov     dx, ds:[bx].dx_reg
        mov     ax, ds:[bx].ax_reg
        mov     bx, ds:[bx].bx_reg

        pop     ds
        call    far ptr ipx_epa

; Now hand back AX and DX

        push    ds
        mov     ds, [bp].reg_seg
        mov     bx, [bp].reg_ofs

        mov     ds:[bx].ax_reg, ax
        mov     ds:[bx].dx_reg, dx
        pop     ds
```

```
call_ipx_exit:
        pop     bp
    ret

_call_ipx endp
      end
```

The Event Control Block (ECB)

An event control block (ECB), like the network control block (NCB), is not transmitted across the network. Instead, the ECB merely serves as a set of directions to IPX and as an IPX storage area for the current operation. You should set up a separate ECB for each of the IPX operations that you plan to use in your application. The following code shows the layout of an ECB:

```
struct ECB
    {
    void far        *link_address;
    void far        (*event_service_routine)(void);
    unsigned char   in_use;
    unsigned char   completion_code;
    unsigned int    socket_number;
    unsigned char   ipx_workspace [4];
    unsigned char   driver_workspace  [12];
    unsigned char   immediate_address [ 6];
    unsigned int    packet_count;
    struct {
        void far    *address;
        unsigned int length;
        } packet [2];
    };
```

The event_service_routine (ESR) field, which this chapter discusses shortly, is a pointer to a function. The in_use flag is nonzero while IPX is processing a particular event in the background. You can poll for the completion of an event by looping until in_use becomes 0. When an event finishes, completion_code holds that event's return code from IPX. You use socket_number to identify a socket that you have opened and through which you are sending packets. For a Send Packet operation, you set the immediate_address field to the network address of a bridge that the packet must cross. The last items in the ECB, packet_count and the packet[].address and packet[].length fields, describe the data areas that IPX gathers into a single data packet or uses to break apart a received packet as the protocol hands the data back to your software.

The IPX Packet Header

The first 30 bytes of each IPX data packet that travels across the network contain an IPX packet header. IPX sets and manages some of the fields. The ones that you're responsible for are packet_type (set it to a value of 4) and the destination address fields `dest_network_number`, `dest_network_node`, and `dest_network_socket`. The destination address is discussed shortly.

```
struct IPXHEADER
    {
    unsigned int    checksum;
    unsigned int    length;
    unsigned char   transport_control;
    unsigned char   packet_type;
    unsigned char   dest_network_number [4];
    unsigned char   dest_network_node   [6];
    unsigned int    dest_network_socket;
    unsigned char   source_network_number [4];
    unsigned char   source_network_node   [6];
    unsigned int    source_network_socket;
    };
```

IPX Commands

When you call IPX, you put a value in the BX register that identifies the function that you want IPX to do. If an ECB is to be passed to IPX, you place a far pointer to the ECB in the ES:SI register pair. The following is a list of the IPX functions. Part III, "Reference," describes each of these in more detail.

```
#define ipx_open_socket              0x00
#define ipx_close_socket             0x01
#define ipx_get_local_target         0x02
#define ipx_send_packet              0x03
#define ipx_listen_for_packet        0x04
#define ipx_schedule_ipx_event       0x05
#define ipx_cancel_event             0x06
#define ipx_get_interval_marker      0x08
#define ipx_get_internetwork_address 0x09
#define ipx_relinquish_control       0x0A
#define ipx_disconnect_from_target   0x0B
```

The Event Service Routines (ESRs)

An event service routine (ESR) for IPX works much like a POST routine for NetBIOS. When the event finishes, IPX calls the ESR that you've coded. If you specify a NULL pointer in the `event_service_routine` function pointer in the ECB, IPX doesn't invoke an ESR when the event finishes. When you take this no-ESR approach, you must give IPX a chance to "breathe" while you poll for the completion of the operation.

The following example is a function that invokes the `relinquish_control` service in IPX:

```
/* example of ipx_relinquish_control in Borland C */

void    ipx_relinquish_control(void)
        {
```

```
_BX = 0x000A;
ipx_spx();
}
```

The following code demonstrates how to poll for the completion of an IPX operation. It uses the function example just coded.

```
/* assume a no-ESR IPX operation is started here */

while (receive_ecb.in_use)          /* poll */
    ipx_relinquish_control();
```

On the other hand, when you do specify an ESR in the associated ECB, your function is called, with the following conditions true:

■ Interrupts are disabled (masked off).

■ The routine has been invoked with a far call.

■ A far pointer to the ECB is in the ES:SI register pair.

■ The CPU registers have been saved.

■ The DS register does not necessarily point to your program's data area.

■ The ECB's in_use flag has been reset to 0.

■ Doing DOS function calls (disk file I/O, for instance) may not be safe.

An ESR is another case in which Borland C is convenient, because it enables you to access directly CPU registers inside the ESR. Therefore, you can set the DS register to point to your program's data area, and make a far pointer to the just-completed ECB from the ES:SI register pair, as shown in the following routine:

```
/* an Event Service Routine in Borland C */

struct      ECB far *completed_ecb_ptr;
int         event_completed_flag;

void    far receive_esr(void)
        {
        _AX = _ES;
        _DS = _AX;

        completed_ecb_ptr = MK_FP(_ES, _SI);
        event_completed_flag = TRUE;
        }
```

If you use a compiler that doesn't support inline assembler, you can use the following assembler function as the first statement in your ESR. The function sets up the DS register (by copying the ES register) and returns the ES:SI register pair in the parameter list.

II

Network Programming

```
;   - - - - - - - - - - - - - - - - - - - - - - - - - - - - -
;        esr_set()
;
;   Assembler function that sets DS equal to ES and returns
;   ES and SI.
;
;   extern void far esr_set(unsigned far *es_reg,
;                           unsigned far *si_reg);
;
;   - - - - - - - - - - - - - - - - - - - - - - - - - - - - -
;
;   A typical calling sequence:
;
;unsigned es_reg, si_reg;
;struct   ECB far *completed_ecb_ptr;
;
;void far receive_esr(void)
;        {
;        esr_set(&es_reg, &si_reg);
;        completed_ecb_ptr = MK_FP(es_reg, si_reg);
;        }
;
;   - - - - - - - - - - - - - - - - - - - - - - - - - - - - -

;   Change the following line to match the memory model
;   you're using:

        .model small

        public _esr_set

;   Symbolically map the stack area

parms    struc
sav_bp   dw      ?
ret_ip   dw      ?
ret_cs   dw      ?
es_ofs   dw      ?
es_seg   dw      ?
si_ofs   dw      ?
si_seg   dw      ?
parms    ends

        .code
_esr_set proc    far
        push    bp
        mov     bp, sp

        mov     ds, [bp].es_seg
        mov     bx, [bp].es_ofs
        mov     ds:[bx], es
        mov     ds, [bp].si_seg
        mov     bx, [bp].si_ofs
        mov     ds:[bx], si

        push    es
```

```
        pop     ds

        pop     bp
        ret

_esr_set endp
        end
```

Sockets

One of the first things you want to do in a program that uses IPX is open a socket, or perhaps more than one socket. You send a data packet through a socket to its destination, and receive a data packet through a socket.

Chapter 3, "PC-to-PC Communications Concepts," mentioned some guidelines and cautions for assigning socket numbers. You must avoid using the same socket numbers that NetWare is using. You also must assign them so that your application can easily determine the destination socket number when it wants to send a data packet. Another consideration is that NetWare defines the two bytes of a socket number "backward"—NetWare expects to see the most significant byte first (leftmost), which is contrary to the way that the PC's Intel-designed CPU chip usually stores numbers. Some creative programmers contrive to sidestep this issue altogether by using socket numbers such as 0x4545 or 0x6767. The two bytes of such a number have the same value, so it doesn't matter which comes first.

A socket may be short-lived or long-lived. Either kind of socket can be closed with a call to ipx_close_socket. A short-lived socket is also automatically closed when a program terminates. If you write terminate-and-stay-resident (TSR) programs, you should use long-lived sockets.

To open a socket, put the socket number in the DX register and set AL according to the longevity that you want the socket to have. Set AL to 0 for a short-lived socket, or set the register to 0xFF for a long-lived socket. The function code for open_socket is 0, which goes into the BX register.

The following code uses Borland C's direct access to CPU registers:

```
/* opening a socket in Borland C */

int     open_socket(unsigned int socket)
        {
        _DX = socket;
        _BX = 0x0000;
        _AL = 0x00;             /* short-lived */
        ipx_spx();
        _AH = 0;
        return _AX;
        }
```

The translation between the IPX calling conventions for both Borland C (just shown as the open_socket) and the call_ipx() ASM function (listed earlier) should be readily apparent. Both have conventions that are simply different ways of loading up the registers. For example, compare the following use of call_ipx() with the preceding Borland C function for opening a socket:

```
/* open_socket, using the call_ipx ASM function */

void    open_socket(unsigned int socket)
        {
        struct  IPX_REGS ipx_regs;

        ipx_regs.dx_reg = socket;
        ipx_regs.bx_reg = 0;
        ipx_regs.ax_reg = 0;
        call_ipx (&ipx_regs);
        }
```

To close a socket, put its value in the DX register and call IPX with a function code of 1 in BX. If a Send or Receive IPX operation is outstanding when you close the socket, IPX cancels that operation. The following function closes a socket:

```
void    close_socket(unsigned int socket)
        {
        _BX = 0x0001;
        _DX = socket;
        ipx_spx();
        }
```

The Destination Address

Chapter 3, "PC-to-PC Communications Concepts," listed three things that you must know to send a data packet to another workstation. The destination of a packet consists of a *network number*, *node address*, and *socket number*. The socket number is easy; you assign values yourself, as previously mentioned. The network number and node address, however, take a little more work. Recall from Chapter 3 that the network number identifies each segment of a multiserver NetWare LAN, and the node address identifies a particular work-station. Suppose, however, that all you know is the user ID logged on at the remote workstation. How do you turn the user ID into a network number and node address?

Each user or workstation is assigned a connection number at login time. To turn the user ID into a useful destination address, you first ask NetWare to give you the connection number for a particular user ID. You then ask NetWare for the network number and node address associated with that connection number. As a simple example to start with, the following NetWare function call obtains the connection number of the *local* user or workstation. You can code

```
my_connect_num = get_local_connection_num();
```

to invoke the following function:

```
/* get connection number for local workstation */

unsigned char get_local_connection_num(void)
        {
        _AH = 0xDC;
        geninterrupt(0x21);
        return _AL;
        }
```

Except through careful system administration, there's no way to guarantee that a user will not be logged on at multiple workstations on a NetWare LAN. For point-to-point message sending, you can usually just disregard any logins but the first. Given a particular user ID, the following function returns the first connection number for that user ID. You can call the function as follows:

```
unsigned    dest_connect_num;

dest_connect_num = get_1st_connection_num ("BARRY");
if (dest_connect_num == 0)
    printf("Not logged on.\n");
```

The following code is the get_1st_connection_num() function itself. It uses the NetWare function GetObjectConnectionNumbers, which returns an array of from 0 to 100 connection numbers for the given user ID. (Incidentally, Novell classifies GetObjectConnectionNumbers as a Connection Service, not as an IPX function.)

```
unsigned int    get_1st_connection_num (char *who)
        {
        union REGS      regs;
        struct SREGS    sregs;

        struct  {
                unsigned int    len;
                unsigned char   buffer_type;
                unsigned int    object_type;
                unsigned char   name_len;
                unsigned char   name [47];
                } request_buffer;

        struct  {
                unsigned int    len;
                unsigned char   number_connections;
```

II

```
                    unsigned char   connection_num [100];
                    } reply_buffer;

        regs.h.ah = 0xe3;

        request_buffer.len = 51;
        request_buffer.buffer_type = 0x15;
        request_buffer.object_type = 0x0100;
        request_buffer.name_len    = (unsigned char) strlen(who);
        strcpy(request_buffer.name, who);

        reply_buffer.len = 101;

        regs.x.si = FP_OFF( (void far *) &request_buffer);
        sregs.ds  = FP_SEG( (void far *) &request_buffer);
        regs.x.di = FP_OFF( (void far *) &reply_buffer);
        sregs.es  = FP_SEG( (void far *) &reply_buffer);

        int86x(0x21, &regs, &regs, &sregs);

        if (regs.h.al != 0) return 0;
        if (reply_buffer.number_connections == 0) return 0;

        regs.h.ah = 0;
        regs.h.al = reply_buffer.connection_num[0];
        return regs.x.ax;
        }
```

Now that you have obtained the connection number of the user ID to which you want to send packets, the final step is the translation of the connection number into a network number and node address. The following function is a call to the NetWare function GetInternetAddress, which Novell also classifies as a Connection Service. The call returns a connection's network number and node address, as well as the socket number through which the connection communicates with the file server. You are interested in the first two items, of course, but the returned socket number is one that you should avoid using!

```
int     get_internet_address(unsigned char connection_number,
                             unsigned char *network_number,
                             unsigned char *physical_node)
        {
        union REGS     regs;
        struct SREGS    sregs;

        struct {
                unsigned int    len;
                unsigned char   buffer_type;
                unsigned char   connection_number;
                } request_buffer;
```

```
struct  {
        unsigned int    len;
        unsigned char   network_number [4];
        unsigned char   physical_node  [6];
        unsigned int    server_socket;
        } reply_buffer;

regs.h.ah = 0xe3;
request_buffer.len = 2;
request_buffer.buffer_type = 0x13;
request_buffer.connection_number = connection_number;

reply_buffer.len = 12;

regs.x.si = FP_OFF( (void far *) &request_buffer);
sregs.ds  = FP_SEG( (void far *) &request_buffer);
regs.x.di = FP_OFF( (void far *) &reply_buffer);
sregs.es  = FP_SEG( (void far *) &reply_buffer);
int86x(0x21, &regs, &regs, &sregs);

memcpy(network_number, reply_buffer.network_number, 4);
memcpy(physical_node,  reply_buffer.physical_node,  6);
regs.h.ah = 0;
return regs.x.ax;
}
```

Finally, the following code demonstrates how to obtain the user ID for a given connection number. This function is sort of the reverse of the preceding procedure for turning a user ID into a connection number/destination. Suppose, for instance, that you want to find out the user ID logged in at the current (local) workstation. You first call get_local_connection_num() (shown earlier) to get the connection number of this workstation. Then you call the following get_user_id() function:

```
unsigned char   my_connect_num;
unsigned char   my_user_id[48];

my_connect_num = get_local_connection_num();
get_user_id(my_connect_num, my_user_id);
```

The get_user_id() function uses the NetWare GetConnectionInformation function (which is classified as a Connection Service):

```
/* get User ID for a given connection number */

void    get_user_id(unsigned char connection_number,
                unsigned char *user_id)
        {
        union REGS      regs;
        struct SREGS    sregs;
```

II

Network Programming

```
struct  {
        unsigned int    len;
        unsigned char   buffer_type;
        unsigned char   connection_number;
        } request_buffer;

struct  {
        unsigned int    len;
        unsigned char   object_id[4];
        unsigned char   object_type[2];
        char            object_name[48];
        char            login_time[7];
        } reply_buffer;

regs.h.ah = 0xe3;
request_buffer.len = 2;
request_buffer.buffer_type = 0x16;
request_buffer.connection_number = connection_number;

reply_buffer.len = 61;

regs.x.si = FP_OFF( (void far *) &request_buffer);
sregs.ds  = FP_SEG( (void far *) &request_buffer);
regs.x.di = FP_OFF( (void far *) &reply_buffer);
sregs.es  = FP_SEG( (void far *) &reply_buffer);
int86x(0x21, &regs, &regs, &sregs);
strncpy(user_id, reply_buffer.object_name, 48);
}
```

Receiving IPX Messages

You just did a lot of work to find out the destination address of the remote workstation. You can't relax yet, though. You now must receive a data packet from the remote workstation and then send a packet back. After you fill in the ECB for a Receive operation, you do the Receive by putting a value of 4 in the BX register, make the ES:SI register pair a far pointer to the ECB, and invoke IPX:

```
void    ipx_listen_for_packet(struct ECB *ecb_ptr)
        {
        _ES = FP_SEG( (void far *) ecb_ptr);
        _SI = FP_OFF( (void far *) ecb_ptr);
        _BX = 0x0004;
        ipx_spx();
        }
```

To receive a data packet, you fill in an ECB and pass it to IPX. As you fill in the ECB, you tell IPX the socket number that you're "listening on" (and which you previously opened). You also tell IPX where to put the received data. Because the incoming packet consists of an IPX header followed by the data message, you must set aside two areas to receive the packet. In the following example, packet_count is set to 2, which tells IPX that two data areas exist. The address and length fields of packet[0] express the IPX header, and the address and length fields of packet[1] describe the application's message buffer. After you set up the ECB, you call IPX. When the event finishes, the ECB's completion_code indicates whether the event succeeded.

```
struct ECB receive_ecb;
struct IPXHEADER receive_header;
char    message[81];

memset(&receive_ecb, 0, sizeof(struct ECB));
memset(&receive_header, 0, sizeof(struct IPXHEADER));

receive_ecb.socket_number = 0x4545;
receive_ecb.packet_count   = 2;
receive_ecb.packet[0].address = &receive_header;
receive_ecb.packet[0].length  = sizeof(struct IPXHEADER);
receive_ecb.packet[1].address = message;
receive_ecb.packet[1].length  = strlen(message);

ipx_listen_for_packet(&receive_ecb);

while (receive_ecb.in_use)
    ipx_relinquish_control();

if (receive_ecb.completion_code == 0)
    printf("Message received: %s\n", message);
else
    printf("Error occurred while receiving message\n");
```

Sending IPX Messages

When you receive an IPX data packet, you need to specify only the data areas into which the incoming packet goes and the socket number that you are listening on. Outbound, however, you must give IPX more information:

- The data areas to be sent, including an IPX header

- The socket number through which you're sending messages

- The "immediate address" of a bridge that will route the message

- A packet type (always 4 for IPX)

- A destination address, consisting of a network number, node address, and socket number

After you build the ECB and the IPX header for an IPX Send operation, you use the following function to invoke IPX:

```
void    ipx_send_packet(struct ECB *ecb_ptr)
        {
```

```
_ES = FP_SEG( (void far *) ecb_ptr);
_SI = FP_OFF( (void far *) ecb_ptr);
_BX = 0x0003;
ipx_spx();
}
```

The `immediate_address` field of the ECB needs to contain the six-byte node address of the bridge that will route the message. IPX provides a `get_local_target` function that returns the address of the bridge. If no bridge is involved in the sending of the message, `get_local_target` merely returns the node address of the destination workstation. In either case, the result goes into `immediate_address`. The following function shows how to use the IPX `get_local_target` function:

```
int get_local_target(unsigned char *dest_network,
                     unsigned char *dest_node,
                     unsigned int   dest_socket,
                     unsigned char *bridge_address)
{
unsigned int    temp_ax;

struct  {
        unsigned char    network_number [4];
        unsigned char    physical_node  [6];
        unsigned int     socket;
        } request_buffer;

struct  {
        unsigned char    local_target [6];
        } reply_buffer;

memcpy(request_buffer.network_number, dest_network, 4);
memcpy(request_buffer.physical_node, dest_node, 6);
request_buffer.socket = dest_socket;

_ES = FP_SEG( (void far *) &request_buffer);
_SI = FP_OFF( (void far *) &request_buffer);
_DI = FP_OFF( (void far *) &reply_buffer);
_BX = 0x0002;
ipx_spx();
_AH = 0;
temp_ax = _AX;
memcpy(bridge_address, reply_buffer.local_target, 6);
return temp_ax;
}
```

The following `send()` function shows how to send an IPX message. Its parameters are the destination (`dest_network`, `dest_node`, and `dest_socket`) and the data message to be sent (`packet_ptr` and `packet_len`). The `send()` function puts the socket number (the local one, not the the destination socket) into the ECB. After calling the preceding `get_local_target()` routine to set the immediate_address field, the function then puts into the ECB the address and length of two buffer areas: an IPX header and the data message.

The IPX header is the first 30 bytes of the packet that IPX transmits. The send() function inserts the destination address into the IPX header, sets the packet_type to 4, and calls IPX to send the message on its way.

```
struct ECB send_ecb;
struct IPXHEADER send_header;

void    send(char  *dest_network,
             char  *dest_node,
             int   dest_socket,
             void  *packet_ptr,
             int   packet_len)
        {
        int i;

        memset(&send_ecb, 0, sizeof(struct ECB));
        send_ecb.socket_number = our_socket;

        i = get_local_target(dest_network,
                             dest_node,
                             dest_socket,
                             send_ecb.immediate_address);
        if (i != 0) return;

        send_ecb.packet_count = 2;
        send_ecb.packet[0].address = &send_header;
        send_ecb.packet[0].length  = sizeof(struct IPXHEADER);
        send_ecb.packet[1].address = packet_ptr;
        send_ecb.packet[1].length  = packet_len;

        send_header.packet_type = 4;

        memcpy(send_header.dest_network_number,
                   dest_network, 4);
        memcpy(send_header.dest_network_node,
                   dest_node,    6);
        send_header.dest_network_socket = dest_socket;

        ipx_send_packet(&send_ecb);
        }
```

Programming SPX

Do not skip to this section without first reading the previous section on IPX programming. SPX uses IPX functions (SPX is a higher layer), and many of the IPX concepts and techniques just mentioned also apply to SPX. SPX creates connections (sessions) between workstations, monitors the exchange of application messages for the duration of the connection, and dismantles the connection when your application finishes. This section covers some of the trickier steps to establishing an SPX connection between two workstations. After you establish a connection, sending and receiving messages under SPX is similar to the operations that you perform under NetBIOS or IPX.

The SPX Installed Test

If your application is running on a NetWare LAN, you know that IPX is present. Not so with SPX. Novell added SPX to its LAN operating system software beginning with the 2.01–4 version of NetWare. Also, some workstations may be configured to save memory by not loading the SPX component of the network software. The following function uses the SPX Initialize service to determine whether SPX is present; the function returns 1 if SPX is available, and 0 if not. To enable SPX to initialize itself, you should always call this function once, early in your program.

```
int     spx_installed(void)
        {
        _BX = 0x0010;
        _AL = 0x00;
        ipx_spx();
        if (_AL == 0)
            return 0;

        return 1;
        }
```

Note that SPX uses the same entry point as IPX.

ECBs, ESRs, and Sockets

The ECB format provided previously in the discussion on IPX also applies to SPX. There are only a couple of differences in the way an ECB is used under SPX:

■ Your program does not have to set the immediate_address field before an SPX Send operation; SPX fills this field automatically.

■ The first two bytes of the ipx_workspace field contain the assigned connection ID after a successful SPXListenForConnection call.

For SPX, the following is a better definition of an ECB:

```
struct ECB
    {
    void far        *link_address;
    void far        (*event_service_routine)(void);
    unsigned char   in_use;
    unsigned char   completion_code;
```

```
unsigned int    socket_number;
unsigned int    connection_id;
unsigned char   reserved [2];
unsigned char   driver_workspace [12];
unsigned char   immediate_address [ 6];
unsigned int    packet_count;
struct {
    void far    *address;
    unsigned int length;
    } packet [2];
};
```

ESRs work the same for SPX as for IPX. The same environment exists when SPX invokes one of your program functions, and you code the ESR the same way. Socket numbers also have the same characteristics for SPX as for IPX. You must open a socket before doing SPX functions, and you must specify a socket number as part of the destination address when you establish an SPX connection.

The SPX Header

The first 30 bytes of an SPX header are actually an IPX header. The remaining 12 bytes are unique to SPX. The way that you treat the SPX header differs slightly from the way that you treat the IPX header. You don't have to set the packet_type field; SPX automatically gives it a value of 5 to identify an SPX packet. The destination address fields (dest_network_number, dest_network_node, and dest_network_socket) need to be set only before you issue an SPXEstablishConnection call. After the connection is created, you use an assigned connection ID to refer to the connection. The datastream_type field becomes important when the connection terminates. One workstation issues the termination request, and the other receives a data packet whose datastream_type field has been set to 0xFE by SPX.

```
struct SPXHEADER
    {
    unsigned int    checksum;
    unsigned int    length;
    unsigned char   transport_control;
    unsigned char   packet_type;
    unsigned char   dest_network_number [4];
    unsigned char   dest_network_node   [6];
    unsigned int    dest_network_socket;
    unsigned char   source_network_number [4];
    unsigned char   source_network_node   [6];
    unsigned int    source_network_socket;
    unsigned char   connection_control;
    unsigned char   datastream_type;
    unsigned int    source_connection_id;
    unsigned int    dest_connection_id;
    unsigned int    sequence_number;
```

II

Network Programming

```
unsigned int    acknowledge_number;
unsigned int    allocation_number;
};
```

SPX Commands

Just as with IPX functions, you specify an SPX command by setting the BX register to a certain value before calling SPX. The SPX functions are symbolically defined as follows:

```
#define spx_initialize                  0x10
#define spx_establish_connection        0x11
#define spx_listen_for_connection       0x12
#define spx_terminate_connection        0x13
#define spx_abort_connection            0x14
#define spx_get_connection_status       0x15
#define spx_send_sequenced_packet       0x16
#define spx_listen_for_sequenced_packet 0x17
```

Establishing a Connection

SPX assigns a connection ID to each connection that you establish, in much the same way that NetBIOS assigns local session numbers when you create NetBIOS sessions. You use the connection ID in subsequent Send and Receive operations to refer to the established connection.

The way that you use SPX to create a connection is similar to the way that you use NetBIOS to create a session. Under NetBIOS, one workstation issues a Listen command, while the other issues a Call command. Under SPX, the first workstation issues a *ListenForConnection* command, and the other workstation issues a subsequent *EstablishConnection* command. You must take some extra steps under SPX, however.

Under SPX, you must do at least a few (preferably five) calls to *SPXListenForSequencedPacket* before the call to either *ListenForConnection* or *EstablishConnection*. These calls give SPX a pool of ECBs and packet buffers that it can use. SPX uses some of these ECBs and packet buffers internally and thus transparently to your program. Some are used to receive incoming message packets after the connection is created. Later, when this chapter discusses receiving and sending SPX messages, you will learn how to handle these multiple outstanding events.

When you issue the set of *ListenForSequencedPacket* (receive) calls, fill in these ECB fields for each call:

event_service_routine	An ESR to handle incoming messages
socket	A socket that your application has opened

packet_count	2
packet[0].address	A pointer to an SPX header
packet[0].length	The length of an SPX header (42)
packet[1].address	A pointer to an incoming message buffer
packet[1].length	The length of the incoming message buffer

The ECB fields that you fill in before calling *ListenforConnection* are the
event_service_routine function pointer, socket, and the packet_count and
the packet address and length fields. You should set the packet_count field
to 2, the packet[0].address fields should point to an SPX header, and
packet[0].length should be set to 42 (the length of an SPX header).

Some of this will become clearer as you study the following code
examples. The first example shows how to issue the five receive
(*ListenforSequencedPacket*) operations. Note that this example declares
an array of five ECBs and an array of five SPX headers so that you can
conveniently use a program loop to issue the five commands.

```
for (i=0; i<5; i++)
    {
    memset(&ecb_list[i], 0, sizeof(struct ECB));
    memset(&spxheader_list[i], 0, sizeof(struct SPXHEADER));

    ecb_list[i].event_service_routine = receive_esr;
    ecb_list[i].socket_number       = socket;
    ecb_list[i].packet_count        = 2;
    ecb_list[i].packet[0].address = (void far *)
&spxheader_list[i];
    ecb_list[i].packet[0].length  = sizeof(struct SPXHEADER);
    ecb_list[i].packet[1].address = (void far *) packet_buffer;
    ecb_list[i].packet[1].length  = sizeof(packet_buffer);

    /* now issue a Listen For Sequenced Packet */
    _ES = FP_SEG( (void far *) ecb_list[i]);
    _SI = FP_OFF( (void far *) ecb_list[i]);
    _BX = 0x0017;
    ipx_spx();
    }
```

Next, the following code actually does the *ListenForConnection* call:

```
memset(&listen_ecb, 0, sizeof(struct ECB));
memset(&listen_header, 0, sizeof(struct SPXHEADER));
```

```
listen_ecb.event_service_routine = listen_esr;
listen_ecb.socket_number         = socket;
listen_ecb.packet_count          = 1;
listen_ecb.packet[0].address     = (void far *) &listen_header;
listen_ecb.packet[0].length      = sizeof(struct SPXHEADER);

/* do the listen_for_connection call */

_ES = FP_SEG( (void far *) &listen_ecb);
_SI = FP_OFF( (void far *) &listen_ecb);
_BX = 0x0012;
_AH = 0xFF;
_AL = 0;
ipx_spx();
```

Now one workstation has gone through the preceding steps and is waiting for another workstation to establish the connection. Before the other workstation can issue its *EstablishConnection* call, the workstation must also do a series of *ListenForSequencedPacket* calls:

```
for (i=0; i<5; i++)

    {
    memset(&ecb_list[i], 0, sizeof(struct ECB));
    memset(&spxheader_list[i], 0, sizeof(struct SPXHEADER));

    ecb_list[i].event_service_routine = receive_esr;
    ecb_list[i].socket_number      = our_socket;
    ecb_list[i].packet_count       = 2;
    ecb_list[i].packet[0].address = (void far *)&spxheader_list[i];
    ecb_list[i].packet[0].length  = sizeof(struct SPXHEADER);
    ecb_list[i].packet[1].address = (void far *) packet_buffer;
    ecb_list[i].packet[1].length  = sizeof(packet_buffer);

    /* now issue a Listen For Sequenced Packet */
    _ES = FP_SEG( (void far *) ecb_list[i]);
    _SI = FP_OFF( (void far *) ecb_list[i]);
    _BX = 0x0017;
    ipx_spx();
    }
```

Like IPX, SPX uses destination addresses (network number, node address, and socket number) to identify the target workstation. If you know the user ID but not the destination address, you can obtain the address by using the same NetWare Connection Services functions discussed earlier in this chapter for IPX. Notice that you let get_internet_address() put the network number and node address directly into the SPX header.

```
connection_number = get_1st_connection_num(dest_user_id);
if (connection_number == 0)
    return 1;                   /* not logged on */

memset(&call_header, 0, sizeof(struct SPXHEADER));
```

```
    get_internet_address(connection_number,
            call_header.dest_network_number,
            call_header.dest_network_node)
    call_header.dest_network_socket= dest_socket;
```

Now you're finally ready to establish the connection:

```
    memset(&call_ecb, 0, sizeof(struct ECB));

    call_ecb.event_service_routine = call_esr;
    call_ecb.socket_number         = our_socket;
    call_ecb.packet_count          = 1;
    call_ecb.packet[0].address     = (void far *) &call_header;
    call_ecb.packet[0].length      = sizeof(struct SPXHEADER);

    /* do the Establish Connection call */
    _ES = FP_SEG( (void far *) &call_ecb);
    _SI = FP_OFF( (void far *) &call_ecb);
    _BX = 0x0011;
    _AH = 0xFF;
    _AL = 0;
    ipx_spx();
```

After the *EstablishConnection* event completes, the assigned connection ID is
found in the DX register and also in the `call_header` SPX header (as
`call_header.source_connection_id`). On the other workstation, after the
ListenForConnection event completes, the assigned connection ID
for that connection partner is found inside the `listen_ecb` ECB,
`listen_ecb.connection_id`.

For both the *ListenForConnection* and *EstablishConnection* calls, you specify a
retry count and a watchdog flag. See the reference section "IPX and SPX
Functions," in Part III, "Reference," for a discussion of these fields.

Sending and Receiving Messages

To send a data message to a connection partner, you give SPX a connection
ID, an SPX header, and an ECB. Fill in the ECB with the ESR function pointer
(optional), the packet count, and the address and length of both the SPX
header and the data message that you want to send.

```
    void    send(unsigned connect_id, void *packet, int packet_length)
            {
            memset(&send_ecb, 0, sizeof(struct ECB));
            memset(&send_header, 0, sizeof(struct SPXHEADER));

            send_ecb.event_service_routine = send_esr;
            send_ecb.packet_count          = 2;
            send_ecb.packet[0].address     = (void far *) &send_header;
            send_ecb.packet[0].length      = sizeof(struct SPXHEADER);
```

```
send_ecb.packet[1].address     = (void far *) packet;
send_ecb.packet[1].length      = packet_length;

/* issue send_packet */
_ES = FP_SEG( (void far *) &send_ecb);
_SI = FP_OFF( (void far *) &send_ecb);
_DX = connection_id;
_BX = 0x0016;
ipx_spx();
}
```

Receiving an SPX data message is a little more complicated. SPX chooses one of the ECBs from the pool of five that you issued earlier and uses that ECB to signal that an incoming message has been received. Typically, you code a `receive_esr()` ESR that hands the data message to the main part of the program and then returns the ECB to the pool. To return the ECB to the pool, you issue another *ListenForSequencedPacket* call, using the same steps that originally put the ECB into the pool.

Terminating a Connection

When one connection partner issues an *SPXTerminateConnection* call, SPX processes the request by automatically sending a packet to the other workstation. This packet consists of just an SPX header with its `datastream_type` set to 0xFE. The other connection partner, on reception of this packet, should recognize that the connection no longer exists. Both partners should close any open sockets before returning to DOS.

The following code shows how to issue the SPX Terminate Connection function (0x0013). Note that the termination activity occurs in the background and you must wait for the function to finish. You can poll the `in_use` flag or set up an ESR to be invoked when the termination actually occurs.

```
struct ECB term_ecb;
struct SPXHEADER term_header;
unsigned int connection_id;


memset(&term_ecb, 0, sizeof(struct ECB));

term_ecb.packet_count     = 1;
term_ecb.packet[0].address = (void far *) &term_header;
term_ecb.packet[0].length  = sizeof(struct SPXHEADER);

_ES = FP_SEG( (void far *) &term_ecb);
_SI = FP_OFF( (void far *) &term_ecb);
_DX = connection_id;
_BX = 0x0013;
ipx_spx();

while (term_ecb.in_use)
    ;
```

Using IPX and SPX under Windows

Because you load DOS and the network software—including IPX and SPX—before you run Windows, you can use virtually all this chapter's preceding information about IPX and SPX programming in your Windows application software. However, the memory management and cooperative multitasking that are part of Windows present you with a few additional issues to consider.

> **Note**
>
> Novell offers the *NetWare Client SDK* for programmers who want to write software that uses IPX or NetWare services. The SDK includes online documentation, C language header files, import libraries, and other helpful tools. Although you can use the information in this book to access IPX and the NetWare services, you may find using the NetWare Client SDK convenient because it hides your program from the otherwise low-level assembler details of IPX and the NetWare services. The SDK is especially helpful in the Windows environment. In particular, the IPX and SPX functions supplied in the SDK enable NetWare to keep separate track of the ECB and socket resources that each Windows program might consume.

> **Note**
>
> For 386 Enhanced mode Windows, Novell supplies drivers in the VNETWARE.386, VIPX.386, and NETWARE.DRV files. The VNETWARE.386 and VIPX.386 files are virtual device drivers (VxDs). All three drivers help NetWare manage the multitasking environment of Windows. However, for Standard mode windows, you should run Novell's TBMI2 before starting Windows.

Chapter 5, "PC-to-PC NetBIOS Programming," in the section "Programming NetBIOS under Windows," explained the memory management and multitasking considerations that you face in the Windows environment. You might want to review that discussion now, because the same considerations affect how you write your IPX- and SPX-aware programs. In particular, you must make sure that your ESR functions and ECBs exist in fixed memory. You don't want Windows to move your ESR to the swap file when an incoming message arrives. Also, you should use the guidelines for calling `PeekMessage()` within the program loops that you code to watch for the completion of an ECB event.

II

Network Programming

Using IPX and SPX under OS/2

The NetWare Client SDK mentioned in the preceding section contains documentation, header files, import libraries, and other tools for OS/2 programmers as well as Windows programmers. Because IPX and SPX under OS/2 use a calling interface rather than a software interrupt interface, you will probably find the SDK necessary for most of your NetWare-related OS/2 programming. In general, however, the guidelines and concepts covered earlier in this chapter apply equally to the OS/2 environment.

The IPX and SPX device drivers that Novell supplies as part of the NetWare Requester for OS/2 are 16-bit modules. The following definitions will be helpful as you use IBM's 32-bit C/C++ Set/2 or C/C++ Tools compilers. These definitions use the _Far16 and _Seg16 compiler keywords to instruct the compiler to emit 16-bit pointers and calls.

```
#define IPXAPI    extern USHORT _Far16 _Pascal
#define FARPTR    * _Seg16
```

The following prototypes for IPX services, which you can use in your OS/2-based software, use the IPXAPI and FARPTR definitions:

```
/*
 *      IPX function prototypes
 */

IPXAPI IpxCheckReceive          (USHORT  Socket);
IPXAPI IpxCloseSocket           (USHORT  Socket);
IPXAPI IpxConnect               (IPX_ECB FARPTR ECB_Ptr);
IPXAPI IpxDisconnect            (IPX_ECB FARPTR ECB_Ptr);
IPXAPI IpxGetInternetworkAddress(UCHAR   FARPTR AddressPtr);
IPXAPI IpxGetLocalTarget        (UCHAR   FARPTR TargetPtr,
                                 IPX_ECB FARPTR ECB_Ptr,
                                 ULONG   FARPTR XMitTimePtr);
IPXAPI IpxGetVersion            (UCHAR   FARPTR MajorVersionPtr,
                                 UCHAR   FARPTR MinorVersionPtr,
                                 UCHAR   FARPTR RevisionPtr);
IPXAPI IpxOpenSocket            (USHORT  FARPTR SocketPtr);
IPXAPI IpxReceive               (USHORT  Socket,
                                 ULONG   Timeout,
                                 IPX_ECB FARPTR ECB_Ptr);
IPXAPI IpxSend                  (USHORT  Socket,
                                 IPX_ECB FARPTR ECB_Ptr);
```

The data definitions ECBFRAG, IPX_ECB, and IPX_HEADER also use the FARPTR definition to denote 16-bit pointers. Note that the ECB definition differs for OS/2; the OS/2 ECB doesn't include an ESR address.

```
typedef struct
    {
      void            FARPTR  FragAddress;
      USHORT                  FragSize;
    } ECBFRAG;


typedef struct IPX_ECBStruct
    {
      struct IPX_ECBStruct FARPTR Next;
      struct IPX_ECBStruct FARPTR Prev;
      USHORT                  Status;
      ULONG                   Reserved1;
      USHORT                  LProtID;
      UCHAR                   ProtID[6];
      USHORT                  BoardNumber;
      UCHAR                   ImmediateAddress[6];
      UCHAR                   DriverWS[4];
      UCHAR                   ProtocolWS[8];
      USHORT                  DataLen;
      USHORT                  FragmentCount;
      ECBFRAG                 FragmentList[2];
    } IPX_ECB;

typedef struct
    {
      USHORT            Checksum;
      USHORT            PacketLen;       /* High-low */
      UCHAR             TransportCtl;
      UCHAR             PacketType;
      UCHAR             DestNet[4];
      UCHAR             DestNode[6];
      USHORT            DestSocket;
      UCHAR             SourceNet[4];
      UCHAR             SourceNode[6];
      USHORT            SourceSocket;
    } IPX_HEADER;
```

The following code fragments show how to use these IPX services and data areas from within an OS/2 program. The first code fragment opens an IPX socket:

```
Socket = 0x2121;
IpxOpenSocket(&Socket);
```

The next code fragment closes a socket:

```
IpxCloseSocket(Socket);
```

To receive an IPX message packet, you can use program statements similar to those in the following code fragment:

```
memset(&ReceiveECB, 0, sizeof(IPX_ECB));
memset(&IpxHeader,  0, sizeof(IPX_HEADER));
ReceiveECB.Next = NULL;
ReceiveECB.Prev = NULL;
ReceiveECB.FragmentCount = 2;
ReceiveECB.FragmentList[0].FragAddress = &IpxHeader;
ReceiveECB.FragmentList[0].FragSize    = sizeof(IPX_HEADER);
ReceiveECB.FragmentList[1].FragAddress = MessageIn;
ReceiveECB.FragmentList[1].FragSize    = 600;
WaitTime = 10000L;

rc = IpxReceive(Socket, WaitTime, &ReceiveECB);
```

The last code fragment shows how to send an IPX message from within an OS/2 program:

```
memset(&SendECB, 0, sizeof(IPX_ECB));
memset(&IpxHeader, 0, sizeof(IPX_HEADER));
SendECB.Next = NULL;
SendECB.Prev = NULL;
SendECB.FragmentCount = 2;
SendECB.FragmentList[0].FragAddress = &IpxHeader;
SendECB.FragmentList[0].FragSize    = sizeof(IPX_HEADER);
SendECB.FragmentList[1].FragAddress = &MessageOut;
SendECB.FragmentList[1].FragSize    = sizeof(MessageOut);
memcpy(SendECB.ImmediateAddress, ReceiveECB.ImmediateAddress, 6);
IpxHeader.PacketType = 0;
memcpy(IpxHeader.DestNet,  IpxHeader.SourceNet,  4);
memcpy(IpxHeader.DestNode, IpxHeader.SourceNode, 6);
IpxHeader.DestSocket = 0x2121;

IpxSend(Socket, &SendECB);
```

Summary

In Chapter 5, "PC-to-PC NetBIOS Programming," and this chapter, "IPX and SPX Programming," you have acquired a solid, comprehensive set of communications tools. This chapter covered the IPX and SPX protocols that are present on NetWare LANs. You understand event control blocks (ECBs), IPX headers, and SPX headers. You can send and receive IPX datagrams, and you can create, use, and dismantle SPX connections. You know how to use the IPX and SPX protocols in the DOS, Windows, and OS/2 environments. You might want to consider writing a small "chat" facility using the techniques and code fragments from the last two chapters. It will be good practice and a lot of fun!

Chapter 7

Testing and Debugging Your Program

Testing your software is a matter of running it and verifying that it does what it's supposed to do. Having a test plan helps; most of my test plans are simply checklists that guide me through the testing. Debugging, on the other hand, is much less scientific. Most people think that finding and fixing bugs is a black art.

The information in this chapter is not intended to teach you how to test or debug your programs. Indeed, you should be able to apply most of the techniques that you have learned from your other programming adventures. Instead, this chapter describes network-related items that you can add to your test-plan checklists. These items are categorized according to whether they pertain to DOS-level program functions, such as file sharing and record locking, or to NetBIOS, IPX, and SPX PC-to-PC communications functions. Next, the chapter discusses debugging network-related program errors. For each of the techniques covered in the previous chapters, this chapter describes some of the things that can go wrong and ways to find and fix the errors.

Don't think of testing as a measure of your coding skills; that would be unrealistic, unfair, and counterproductive. Instead, treat the testing phase as a chance to find out new things about how the computer behaves. Especially when you're getting into a new area of software technology (networks, for instance), you need to realize that programming is a trial-and-error proposition.

When I try to do something new and it doesn't work the first time, I ask the following questions:

- Did I omit a statement?

- Do I have statements out of order?

- Did I misunderstand the concepts?

- Is there something else I should know that the reference manual is not telling me?

In each case, I check whether the code looks like it should do what I want. A careful rereading of the code often points out a minor discrepancy between what I want the code to do and what I actually coded. Sometimes, however, the code looks fine but still doesn't work. Then I start experimenting to see what I need to do differently. If I think major surgery is required, I first make a copy of the existing source file (it could have bugs, but it's a starting point to which I can always return). If I think I can try a different approach by making only a few small changes, I make the existing code a comment (by surrounding it with /* ... */) and then put some new code next to the old. If the new code works, I sigh in relief and quickly delete the old (commented out) code. If the new code doesn't work, I then go back through the same process. This time around, I have two routines that I can use as a base for further experimentation. I pick the routine that worked best, make a few changes, and try again.

DOS-Level Testing

You may develop software for in-house use in your company, or you might be an analyst or programmer whose efforts become products that get sold to other companies. In the first case, you can run tests on whatever sort of LAN you have at work and not worry about making your code widely compatible. However, if your software will be used on different kinds of LANs, you must test your code on as many LANs as possible.

The following example shows why this testing is necessary. (As a programmer and analyst, I have run into a few odd situations.)

The Record Locking function call in DOS (hex 5C) says Locking beyond end-of-file is not an error. I took this to mean that I could lock an entire file by using 0xFFFFFFFFl as the Length of Region to be locked. I knew from the description of the 5C Function Call that 0xFFFF would go into the SI register and 0xFFFF into the DI register, and this seemed to be exactly what I wanted to do. I put the code into the application, tested it under both IBM LAN Server and Novell NetWare, and the application worked just fine.

Later, a client said he wanted to use an IBM RS/6000, running AIX (IBM's flavor of UNIX) as a file server on a Token Ring LAN. IBM's AIX Access for DOS Users (AADU) was to redirect the DOS file. (AADU is actually Locus Computing's PC interface product, resold and relabeled by IBM.)

"Fine," I said, "But let's try it out first." With a borrowed RS/6000 computer, I tested the software. I discovered that AADU rejected the Record Locking function call because I used a Region Length of 0xFFFFFFFFl bytes. It took only a moment to change the code to a value that AADU would accept (I used 0x0FFFFFFFl, because AADU was obviously treating the value as a signed quantity). I was glad that I tested the software before sending it to the client.

This incident highlights the need to exercise your software in the presence of each different network operating system that your customers might use.

(Incidentally, I also found that AADU does not support the machine name; I had to put a small workaround in the code to make up for it.)

LAN Detection

The custom LAN-presence test described in Chapter 4, "Shared File Programming," is designed to work on any LAN. (The test even worked under AADU!) Testing should be simple—run your software on a stand-alone PC and your program should tell you immediately that the network is not active (or whatever). If clients say that they cannot run your LAN software product, you can confidently tell them to recheck their LAN configuration and setup. If that doesn't fix things, the client's "XYZ-Net LAN Operating System" is not quite as full-featured a LAN environment as the manufacturer claims.

Workstation IDs

If you're using the machine name or NetWare user IDs in your application, you should test to make sure that you're obtaining the string correctly and that your program is handling the string properly. Fortunately, both fields are normal, null-terminated C strings. Remember that the machine name is 16 bytes long (including the terminator) and that a user ID can be as much as 48 bytes long. I usually ignore long NetWare user IDs in my software. I initially acquire the user ID into a 50-byte string and drop a null terminator (\0) into the 16th byte. Thereafter, I treat the user ID just like a machine name.

II

Network Programming

If your program dies completely (crashes) when you obtain the workstation identifier (either the name or user ID), compare the code to the examples provided in this book. Probably something is wrong with the way that the registers are set up for the function call.

If your program fails to match the workstation identifier (or a substring of it) with some other string, check the case of both strings. To get the strings to match, you might have to use strupr() or strlwr().

In the previously mentioned situation with AADU, in which I found that AADU doesn't support the setting and obtaining of the machine name, I solved the problem with a small (400-byte) terminate-and-stay-ready (TSR) program called NAME and a couple of programs called GETNAME and SETNAME. NAME provides support for getting and setting the machine name. I had each user, at each workstation, put NAME and SETNAME into the AUTOEXEC.BAT file, as follows:

```
NAME
SETNAME 001_STATION    <different for each workstation>
```

In case you need them, NAME, GETNAME, and SETNAME are included on this book's companion disk.

File Sharing

Whether you open a file on the file server for shared (DENY_NONE) or exclusive (DENY_ALL) access, the test that you need to perform is to open the same file concurrently from two different workstations and see how your software behaves. If DOS sends the second workstation an Abort, Retry, or Ignore? message (or if your Interrupt 24, Critical Error Handler, is invoked), recheck the way that you are opening the file. If you omit the parameters in the open() call, or if you inadvertently used fopen() rather than open(), the second workstation may be opening the file in compatibility mode.

Don't forget to test your "Is SHARE loaded?" routine. You'll want to run your program on a just-booted workstation, without SHARE having been run, and look for your program to terminate with an error message.

The NETWORK.C program can be useful in your file-sharing tests (see Chapter 8, "Network Applications"). Appendix A, "Source Listing for File/Record Collision Tester," lists the program's source code, and the companion disk includes the program's source and executable code.

Record Locking

For record locks, you need to test essentially the same as you do for file sharing: cause a controlled, concurrent collision between two workstations. This test is not easy—a well-designed record lock lasts for only a brief moment. If you test by having two users at two workstations run your software and try to press the Enter key (to cause a record update) at exactly the same time, you'll quickly become frustrated; causing a collision this way is virtually impossible.

One approach is to change the copy of your program on the first workstation temporarily. Insert a "wait for keypress" function call (such as `getche()`) after acquiring the record locks. This approach lets you deliberately hold the lock longer. While the lock is present, the user at workstation B can attempt an update. You can then watch to see how your program behaves.

The NETWORK.C program (Chapter 8, "Network Applications") can also be helpful in your record-locking tests.

What can go wrong inside your record-locking routines? If the machine crashes when you issue the lock request, examine your function call carefully. If you call function 0x5C directly, check the way that the CPU registers get set.

If DOS returns an error to your lock request, look at the error code value. If it indicates the region is already locked (and you know that it shouldn't be), you may be encountering the residue of a lock that was issued (without an unlock) during an earlier test. You may be able to use NETWORK.C to unlock the file region so that you can proceed with your testing. Another possibility is that the flow of your program took you through the lock request twice, without an intervening unlock. If DOS indicates some other error (perhaps invalid handle or invalid function), carefully check your parameters in the call to the lock function.

DOS Function Call Tracking

If you have trouble determining what's wrong with an file open or lock/unlock request, you can run your program under a debugger and watch how the program reacts. In particular, you can set a breakpoint on the Interrupt 21 (hex) DOS entry point. The address of this entry point is in the interrupt vector table, in segment:offset form (four bytes, low-order byte first) at 0x0000:0x0084. Of course, if you set an unconditional breakpoint at the Interrupt 21 entry point, you'll see *every* DOS function call as it happens, which can become tedious. If your debugger supports conditional breakpoints, tell it to stop at the breakpoint when the AH register has a value of 0x5C (for record locks) or 0x3D (for file opens). When the debugger stops, inspect its display of the CPU registers to see whether they seem to be set correctly.

The File Server as a Debugging Tool

You can ask the NetWare file server to tell you about files and records that are currently locked. From a separate workstation connected to a NetWare 2.2 server, you can run the FCONSOLE utility to view a display of file activity. Make sure that you give yourself SUPERVISOR rights before using FCONSOLE, as well as rights to use the remote console facilities in FCONSOLE.

Sometimes you can use the file server itself as a debugging tool. Under NetWare 2.2, for example, you can use the MONITOR command to see file activity happen. Before you begin a test, use the NetWare utility USERLIST at your workstation to find out your connection number. Then, while a test is under way, issue the command MONITOR <connection number> at the file server. For NetWare 3.12 or 4.0, you load MONITOR as an NLM at the file server console and choose menu options to indicate the activity that you want the MONITOR NetWare loadable module (NLM) to reveal.

At the NetWare file server, you'll see each file operation happen. NetWare shows you a list of file names and a mnemonic for the most recent file activity. If your program issues a flurry of file operations, the display of activity whizzes by and you won't be able to read it. For the displays that you can read, however, be aware that the mnemonic for the file operation is NetWare-related, not DOS-related. After an unlock occurs, for example, you'll see Clr Phys Rec. To understand these mnemonics, see "Synchronization Services" in the reference section "NetWare's Extended DOS Services."

LAN Server and the IBM PC LAN Program have a similar facility, although the information is not presented in real-time. You can issue a NET FILE command at the file server to see which files are open. For each open file, LAN Server or the PC LAN Program displays the machine name of the workstation that opened the file as well as the number of locks in effect for that file. NET FILE can also be used to close an open file (but you should do this only if the application running at the workstation has crashed). If you want a continuous display of open files, create on the server a .BAT file that contains these statements:

```
ECHO OFF
:AGAIN
NET FILE
GOTO AGAIN
```

Although the file still isn't quite real-time, it does free you from having to type the command repeatedly. Press Ctrl-C to stop the display.

NetBIOS Debugging

The first time that you test a program that passes messages from workstation to workstation is exciting. You tell yourself that the program won't work the first time, but you're hopeful nevertheless. You start the programs, and—the two workstations refuse to talk to one another. It's a bit of a letdown. After you reboot the computers, you start wondering what might have gone wrong.

This section ("NetBIOS Debugging") and the next ("IPX and SPX Debugging") suggest some things that you can look for that might be the culprit.

Adding and Deleting Names

One of the first things you need to verify is that your program has added or deleted NetBIOS names correctly. If you actually have two workstations that seem to have gone out to lunch, don't reboot them quite yet. Go to a third workstation and run the NETTEST.C program. (Appendix B, "Source Listing for NetBIOS Microscope," shows the source code for NETTEST, which is also included on the companion disk.) Choose the Adapter Status menu option and specify that you want information about one of the test machines. If the computers are "alive" but unable to talk to one another, the display from the Adapter Status command tells you the contents of the local name table from one of the test machines. You'll then know whether your program at least performed a correct Add Name operation. You should check the return code from the Add Name operation and take appropriate action in your program if the call fails.

If the name isn't present in the test machine's local name table, or if the command times out, you can start looking for the problem in the part of the program that constructs the name and adds it to the local name table. If that code looks okay, you can try backtracking from there to see whether the problem occurred earlier in the execution of the program.

If the Adapter Status command times out, the Add Name operation may have executed properly but your program subsequently damaged NetBIOS or crashed the workstation entirely. If you can't find the problem in or before the code that does the Add Name operation, you might want to make what I call a "temporary assumption"—assume that the name was added correctly, and try looking for the problem later in the program.

Are there clues that you can look for to tell you whether the workstation has crashed completely? Yes. The following technique sounds strange, but it is well founded: press the Caps Lock, Scroll Lock, or Num Lock keys. If the green LEDs on the keyboard respond normally by toggling off and on, the computer is in a loop. The loop may well be in your program. If the LEDs don't respond, the computer has crashed. (You'll have to use the Red Switch to reboot the computer.) Of course, the loop (or the crash) may not be related to your calls to NetBIOS, but this technique can be informative.

Passing NetBIOS Datagrams

If your program is designed to pass datagram messages "silently," without some outward sign (such as an on-screen message) that you can use to tell what is going on, you should put into the program some temporary code that shows that messages are being transmitted or received. Testing on two workstations that are physically adjacent can be advantageous, so that so you can watch both at the same time.

Suppose that you determine that Workstation A is sending a datagram, but Workstation B is simply not getting the message. The first place to look is the code that does the Send Datagram operation. Does the code properly fill in the NCB_NUM field? Does the NCB_CALLNAME field contain the exact 16-byte name of the destination workstation? Is the NCB_LENGTH field nonzero? Are you getting a good return code from the Send Datagram call?

The next place to look is the Receive Datagram call. Is the NCB_NUM field properly filled in? Do NCB_BUFFER_PTR and NCB_LENGTH correctly express the address and length of the input buffer? Is the Receive Datagram call returning an error code? And, more generally, is the Receive Datagram call actually outstanding when the Send Datagram call is issued?

Another possible source of error is that the two workstations are on separate LANs, and the Bridge machine is not transferring NetBIOS messages from one LAN to the other. This error can happen, for example, if you have two separate Token Ring LANs, running Novell NetWare, that are bridged internally at the NetWare file server. If you are using the IBM NetBIOS device driver DXMT0MOD.SYS, NetWare will not transfer the IBM NetBIOS frames from one LAN to the other. In this instance, you can use the Novell NetBIOS emulator rather than DXMT0MOD.SYS.

Establishing Sessions

Again, to find out whether a session is being established correctly, you should put in your program some temporary code that gives you some sign that the

Call (or Listen) command has completed. Alternatively, you can use a debugger to trace through the code to find out exactly how the NetBIOS calls take place. In either case, make sure that you check return codes.

If you issued the Call and Listen commands on the two workstations but it appears that the session is not being established, you should first look in the NCB_CALLNAME field in both NCBs. For the Call command, make sure that the NCB_CALLNAME field contains the name of the listening workstation. For the Listen command, make sure that the first byte of NCB_CALLNAME is an asterisk (*) if you are listening for a call from anyone, or that NCB_CALLNAME is the exact name of the caller.

If you have a complicated design that generates multiple sessions, your program could exceed the number of available sessions. In this case, check the installation and configuration documentation for the NetBIOS software. You may be able to configure the software for a greater number of available sessions.

After a session is created successfully, make sure that you save the value of NCB_LSN. You will need this value in subsequent references to the session.

Sending and Receiving Session Messages

After you get the session under way, you can easily verify that messages are sent and received correctly—your program is working! If you encounter problems, however, their cause is probably either that the NCB_LSN (local session number) is not set properly, or that the NCB_BUFFER_PTR and NCB_LENGTH fields do not properly describe the input or output buffers. For the Receive operation, make sure that you set NCB_LENGTH to the size of the input buffer. Neglecting to set NCB_LENGTH is a common error; if the field is 0 when the Receive is issued, you cannot receive any data.

The Send and Receive operations time out according to the NCB_STO and NCB_RTO values given when the Call and Listen commands are issued. If your program seems to work only intermittently, you should check these fields to see whether they are set correctly. A Send operation that times out causes the session itself to be aborted.

Don't forget that both workstations should do a Hang Up command to dismantle the session. Unless you want to leave the names that you have added in the local name table, make sure that you do a Delete Name operation after the Hang Up operation finishes.

IPX and SPX Debugging

Many pitfalls of NetBIOS programming have counterparts in IPX and SPX.
One difference that you'll notice is that there are more things to keep track of
with IPX and SPX. This makes debugging a little tougher, because there are
more statements that can go wrong. As you test and debug a program that
uses IPX or SPX, watch for the following potential problems.

Opening Sockets

When you open one or more sockets in preparation for sending and receiving
data messages, always check the return code from the *OpenSocket* call to make
sure that the socket was opened successfully. If you write a TSR that uses IPX
or SPX, make sure that you set the Longevity flag appropriately when you
open a socket. NetWare closes any open sockets when the TSR operation
(DOS function call hex 31) occurs unless they are marked as "long-lived."
Trying to use a closed socket can result in strange behavior. When I encountered this bug, the program in error continued to run on some workstations,
but on other workstations the program would crash after putting stray gar-
bage on the screen.

Also remember that NetWare expects to see the socket value high-byte first,
in contrast to the way that the CPU normally represents integer-type items.
Finally, if you use both IPX and SPX in the same application, assign different
sockets to the operations that you do under each protocol.

Determining Destination Addresses

Chapter 6, "IPX and SPX Programming," introduced some programming
techniques for determining the destination address (network number and
node address) that assume you already know the destination user ID. Of
course, you can take another approach to obtain the destination address,
such as having your program maintain a table of target workstations. In either case, the FCONSOLE utility (which was mentioned previously) is useful
when you need to verify a workstation's destination address. If you want to
insert in your program some temporary code to display the value of the network number and node address, you can use the following technique:

```
for (i=0; i<4; i++)
    printf("%2.2X ", network_number[i]);

for (i=0; i<6; i++)
    printf("%2.2X ", node_address[i]);
```

The preceding statements let you see the network number and node address in hexadecimal notation, the same notation that FCONSOLE displays. Note that these fields can contain null bytes; a common error is to use strcpy() to move these fields around. Instead, use memcpy() or an equivalent.

In addition, if you are using the connection number to obtain the destination address, invoking the USERLIST utility from a separate workstation can help you verify whether you have the correct connection number.

Sending and Receiving IPX Messages

If you seem to be using the correct destination address for an IPX *SendPacket* call but the message still isn't being received, the problem could be that the IPX *ListenforPacket* call (the Receive operation) is not issued before the data packet is sent. Make sure that IPX always has an outstanding event control block (ECB) for receiving messages.

On the incoming side (a Receive operation), you should also check the contents of the ECB to make sure that the socket is correct and that you have properly expressed the length and address of the input buffers for both the IPX header and the data packet.

On the outbound side (a Send operation), check the value of packet_type, which should be 4. Make sure the immediate_address field is filled in with the result of a call to *GetLocalTarget*. The length and address of the output buffers (the IPX header and the data packet) should be properly set in the ECB.

Establishing an SPX Connection

If you are having trouble establishing an SPX connection, first check whether the listening workstation issued its *ListenForConnection* call before the other workstation issued an *EstablishConnection* call. Especially for the first test (no matter what retry logic you programmed), make sure that you start up the software on the listening workstation before you start up your software on the calling workstation.

As mentioned in Chapter 6, "IPX and SPX Programming," several *ListenForSequencedPacket* calls absolutely *must* be issued before you attempt to establish a connection. To make sure that the ECBs and input buffers are made available to SPX, compare your code to the examples I have provided. If a supply of these ECBs and buffers is not available for SPX to use as it creates the connection, SPX starves and crashes the workstation. As your program executes, check whether the completed ECBs (which you have used to receive incoming messages) are returned to the SPX pool of available ECBs.

Sending and Receiving SPX Messages

If you trace through your program and verify that the SPX connection is successfully established but the data packets don't seem to be reaching their destination, first check whether you are properly using the connection ID to refer to the connection. You might even want to code an *SPXGetConnectionStatus* call and display the result, just to make the whole process more visible during testing. If it appears that you are using the connection ID correctly, check the way that you are describing the input and output buffers. Make sure that the packet_count, packet[].address, and packet[].length fields of the ECBs are providing for both the SPX header and your data packet.

Before processing each received message, be sure to inspect the datastream_type field of the SPX header. A value of 0xFE indicates that the other workstation issued an *SPXTerminateConnection* call. When the dialog between the two machines finishes, don't forget to cancel any outstanding events and close any open sockets.

Summary

I wish that I could anticipate and help you with every bug you might encounter in your programs. Although I can't do that, this chapter has given you the basics of what to look for as well as ideas on how to approach each bug. Outlining many of the things that can go wrong with sharing files, locking records, and obtaining workstation IDs, this chapter discussed the kinds of problems that you are likely to encounter with NetBIOS, IPX, and SPX when you add names, use destination addresses, establish sessions (and connections), send and receive messages, and terminate the dialog.

Chapter 8

Network Applications

Sometimes code fragments alone aren't enough to explain how to use a new programming facility. If you are like me, you want to see a complete example that shows how to put the pieces together. With this thought in mind, I wrote six working programs, described in this chapter, that use the techniques discussed in previous chapters. Each of the six source code files is listed in an appendix at the end of this book, and the source and executable files are contained on the companion disk.

To compile the programs, I used the Borland C 3.1 compiler. (The EMAILNLM NetWare loadable module, however, required the Watcom 32-bit C compiler.) Some of the programs contain "inline" assembler code, so you also need an assembler (such as Microsoft's MASM or Borland's TASM) to compile and link the files yourself. You may also need to adjust the compiler command-line options to compile these programs successfully. The following lines from a TURBOC.CFG file show the options that you should use, where *x*: is the drive on which you installed the compiler:

```
-a- -f -C -i32 -K -d -G -N- -y -r -w -M -w-par -EMASM.EXE
-Ix:\BC\INCLUDE
-Lx:\BC\LIB
```

Most of the programs are discussed in two parts. The first part is a user guide that tells how to use the program. The second part is a programmer guide that shows how the program works and that highlights the program's network features.

I will have to gloss over some aspects of these programs. Details about PC interrupt vectors, terminate-and-stay-resident (TSR) techniques, or the ways that I manipulate the screen are beyond the scope of this book. For some detail on these non-network-related topics, I recommend the *MS-DOS Encyclopedia* (by Ray Duncan), *DOS Programmer's Reference*, 2nd Edition (by Terry Dettman), and *Undocumented DOS* (by Andrew Schulman). You can also use the Turbo Debugger, if you have it in your arsenal, to trace through the code. Even without these aids, however, you will learn much simply by studying the program listings.

File and Record Collision Tester

The Collision Tester is a terminate-and-stay-resident tool for causing deliberate file-sharing situations and record-locking collisions. Pressing Alt-Right Shift pops up a window. In that window, you open the same files that your application will open, or lock the same records that your application will lock. Then return to your application to watch how your software reacts when it encounters the already open file or already locked record. You can run your application and the Collision Tester on the same workstation. To use the Collision Tester, you do not have to be connected to a network.

User Guide

Installing the Collision Tester is easy; simply copy the NETWORK.EXE executable file to any one of the directories expressed by the path that you have set on your computer. If your computer already has a .COM, .BAT, or .EXE file named NETWORK, you should rename NETWORK.EXE during the installation. Renaming the file doesn't affect its operation.

To load the Collision Tester before testing the file-sharing and record-locking aspects of your application, enter **NETWORK** at the DOS prompt. The program then asks you to enter a drive letter for your network drive (which is important only if you are running the program on a stand-alone, non-LAN-attached computer). The Collision Tester then becomes a resident program and displays a message reminding you to press Alt-Right Shift to pop it up. While the Collision Tester is resident, it forces DOS to return a machine name of "01TEST   " to your application. It also forces DOS to return a Yes response to your application if it issues DOS function call *Is Drive Remote?* (0x4409) for the drive letter that you specified.

When you press Alt-Right Shift, the program displays the menu shown in figure 8.1.

To choose a menu option, you type its first letter. For example, to choose Open a file option, press O.

To unload the Collision Tester from memory when you finish testing your application, pop up the program and choose the menu option Remove Emulator from RAM. If another program is loaded on top of NETWORK.EXE when you choose this option, the Collision Tester waits until the other program is removed from memory before unloading itself.

```
┌─────────────────────────────────────┐
│                                     │
│   [ LAN EMULATOR ]                  │
│                                     │
│   E)xit to application              │
│   R)emove Emulator from RAM         │
│   O)pen a file                      │
│   C)lose a file                     │
│   L)ock a record                    │
│   U)nlock a record                  │
│   S)how current files/locks         │
│                                     │
│   (Select option by first letter)   │
│                                     │
└─────────────────────────────────────┘
```

Fig. 8.1
The main menu of the Collision Tester.

Before removing the Collision Tester from memory, you should unlock any locked records and close any open files (when you finish testing).

The Collision Tester works only in text mode. You should not use the program to test applications that put the computer into graphics mode.

Opening and Closing Files

Before you use the Collision Tester to see how your application handles file-sharing collisions, first put together a test plan. The plan should at least call each of the files that you open and give some information about how you open the file and how you expect the file to be shared. You need this plan to know which collisions you want to cause and how to specify them to the Collision Tester. This same information is useful also in your record-locking tests.

To open a file in the Collision Tester, pop up the program by pressing Alt-Right Shift and choose the Open a file option. When you choose this option, the program displays the menu shown in figure 8.2.

```
┌─────────────────────────────────────┐
│                                     │
│   [ OPEN A FILE ]                   │
│                                     │
│      Filename: c:network.c          │
│   Inheritance: N                    │
│        Sharing:                     │
│         Access:                     │
│    Record Len:                      │
│                                     │
│   1=Compatibility Mode; 2=Deny R/W; │
│   3=Deny Write; 4=Deny Read;        │
│   5=None                            │
│                                     │
└─────────────────────────────────────┘
```

Fig. 8.2
Opening a file.

The program prompts you to enter a file name. Specify a drive letter and path, if necessary. If you respond to the file name prompt by pressing the Esc key, the program returns to the main menu.

The program then asks whether the file is inheritable. Respond by typing Y for yes or N for no. At the Sharing prompt, specify which Sharing mode the Collision Tester should use by typing 1 for Compatibility mode, 2 for Deny Read/Write, 3 for Deny Write, 4 for Deny Read, or 5 for Deny None. The next prompt asks for the Access mode. Respond by typing 1 for Read Access, 2 for Write Access, or 3 for Read/Write Access. Finally, at the Record Len prompt, type a number that expresses the length of each of the logical records in the file. When you press the Enter key, an Open File request is issued to DOS. If the request succeeds, you see the message File successfully opened; otherwise, you see the message Failed. DOS error XX, where XX is the error code returned by DOS. In either case, you can press a key to return to the main menu. Unless you want to lock a record at this time, you can now choose the option Exit to application. As your program executes, the files that you opened remain open just as though another workstation were operating on the file.

Locking and Unlocking Records

Before locking a record in the Collision Tester window, you must first open it as described in the preceding section. You should use a Sharing mode of Deny None and an Access mode of Read-Write.

Choose the menu option Lock a record. You then see a numbered list of open files similar to that shown in figure 8.3.

Fig. 8.3

Locking a file.

```
[ LOCK A RECORD ]

1. c:network.c
2.
3.
4.
5.

Which record number? 2
(numbers start at 1)
```

Choose the file that you want by typing its number. The screen next asks for the record number that you want the Collision Tester to lock. Note that record numbers start at 1, not 0.

If the DOS function call 5C request (Lock Record) succeeds, you see the message Record X locked (*X* is the record number that you specified). If the call fails, you see the message Failed. DOS error XX, where *XX* is the error code returned by DOS. In either case, press a key to return to the main menu.

Programmer Guide

Appendix A, "Source Listing for File/Record Collision Tester," lists the source for the Collision Tester. If you put a bookmark or finger on Appendix A, you can trace through the code as the following text describes the program. The start of the program, main(), appears at the end of the program listing.

The main() function initializes the program, says hello, sets certain interrupt vectors to point to certain functions in the program, and then issues a TSR function call. Initialization consists of the following series of actions:

- Determine whether color or monochrone attributes should be used

- Detect whether the program is already loaded

- Check the DOS version

- Make sure that SHARE has been run

- Obtain pointers to variables inside DOS

- Allocate a private stack for later use

- Ask for a drive letter for the network drive

This program uses the following interrupt vectors (in hex):

08   *BIOS Timer Tick*—The computer hardware invokes this vector 18.2 times a second. The int08() function first calls the previous Interrupt 8 handler. The program then calls the do_popup() function if the hot key flag is on, the DOS variables and other flags indicate that the program can safely pop up, and the program is not already popped up.

09   *BIOS Keyboard*—Invoked by the computer hardware when a key is pressed or released, this vector detects when the hot key combination has been pressed. (The function int09() sets the hot key flag.)

10   *BIOS Video Functions*—A program that wants to perform screen-related events invokes this vector. While Interrupt 10 is active, a flag (in_int10) is set. This flag prevents the program from popping up inside Interrupt 10.

II

Network Programming

13   *BIOS Disk Functions*—DOS or a program that wants to do direct disk I/O invokes this interrupt, which is also flagged to prevent the program from popping up while active.

16   *BIOS Read Keyboard Functions*—DOS or a program that wants to read a character from the keyboard invokes this vector. (Interrupt 9, described previously, places keypresses in a buffer; Interrupt 16 gets a keypress from the buffer and returns that keypress to the caller.) Interrupt 16 is flagged (in_int16) and, if it must wait for a keypress to appear in the buffer, this interrupt is also used as an opportunity to pop up. This interrupt works similarly to the way that Interrupt 8 works, which was described previously.

21   *DOS Function Call Entry Point*—All function calls can flow directly into DOS except for *IsDriveRemote?* and *GetMachineName*. The following section, "Predetermined Network Environment," explains the interception of these functions.

24   *DOS Critical Error Handler*—DOS invokes Interrupt 24 to signal such things as Sector Not Found or Sharing Violation. The Interrupt 24 handler inside DOS displays the Abort, Retry, Ignore? message. By intercepting Interrupt 24, the program avoids this message.

28   *DOS Idle*—When DOS is idle, it periodically invokes this interrupt. These invocations happen mostly at the DOS prompt, when COMMAND.COM waits for you to enter a command or program name to execute. The Collision Tester uses Interrupt 28 as an opportunity to pop up. This interrupt works similarly to the way that Interrupt 8 works, which was described previously.

1B   Keyboard Ctrl-Break

1C   Auxiliary Timer Tick

23   DOS Ctrl-Break

      During the pop up, these interrupts are disabled. Each is essentially turned into a No Operation for the duration of the pop up.

Predetermined Network Environment

As mentioned in Chapter 2, "Multiuser Concepts," the SHARE.EXE program can be used to enable file sharing on a stand-alone machine as well as on a network workstation. The Collision Tester exploits this capability to enable you to test file sharing and record locking, obtain the machine name, and determine network drives on a stand-alone machine. In other words, you don't have to be on a network to use the Collision Tester.

Inside the int21() function, function 0x4409 is intercepted so that the Collision Tester can respond positively to the *IsDriveRemote?* call. Function 5E00 is intercepted so that the Collision Tester can return the machine name "01TEST   " to a request from your program. These "pretend network conditions" remain in effect until your program finishes running.

Files and Records

When you pop up the Collision Tester and tell it to open a file, the program prompts you for the file name, the Inheritance flag, the Sharing mode, the Access mode, and the record length. The program uses the first few items to issue DOS function call 3D, Open File. To construct the Open mode byte that this function requires, the Collision Tester uses your responses to set the fields file_inherit, file_sharing, and file_access to values that it simply ORs into the AL register for the call to function 3D. If the open succeeds, the file name, file handle, and other data are inserted into a table. The record length that you specify is used later if you tell the program to lock a record in the file. If the open fails, the DOS error code is displayed.

When you tell the Collision Tester to lock a record, the test program asks you Which file? and Which record number? The program uses your responses to issue to DOS a function call 5C request (*Lock/Unlock File Region*). The program calculates the starting file position of the file region as follows:

Record Length X (Record Number – 1)

NetBIOS Microscope

The NetBios Microscope (NETTEST.EXE) program is a simple test bed that you can use to explore NetBIOS PC-to-PC communications. From a menu, you choose the NetBIOS command that you want to execute. NETTEST issues the command and shows you the result. Using NETTEST, you can do the following:

■ Add and delete names to or from the local name table

■ Create and destroy sessions

■ Send and receive messages

■ Obtain session status and adapter status information

If you have a willing partner (or two physically adjacent workstations that you can operate), you can establish NETTEST sessions across the network. You can even establish sessions between two names within a single workstation.

User Guide

To install NETTEST, copy the executable file NETTEST.EXE into one of the directories expressed by the path that you have set up on your computer. To run the program, type **NETTEST** at the DOS prompt. NETTEST checks to make sure that NetBIOS is active and displays the menu shown in figure 8.4.

Fig. 8.4

The main menu of NetBIOS Microscope.

```
NET-TEST Menu:

 0...exit
 1...reset adapter
 2...adapter status
 3...add name
 4...add group name
 5...delete name
 6...call
 7...listen
 8...send
 9...receive
10...receive any
11...hang up
12...session status

    Choice?
```

To choose a NETTEST menu item, type its number and press Enter. Note that when you choose the Exit option, NETTEST does *not* perform any cleanup activity. When you exit the program, the sessions you created and the names you added remain intact. Use the Session Status and Adapter Status menu items to reveal the status of current sessions and names if you are in doubt about them. Unless you are deliberately doing something unusual, you should close sessions with the Hang Up command and clean up the local name table with the Delete Name command before exiting NETTEST.

When you select a NetBIOS command from the menu, NETTEST may ask you for additional information (such as the name that you want to add for an Add Name operation). NETTEST then issues the command in its no-wait form to NetBIOS and redisplays the main menu. While you look at the menu (and possibly issue another command), NetBIOS executes the command in the background. When the command finishes, a window pops up to show the results. The only command to execute immediately is Reset Adapter.

If a command fails to execute, NETTEST displays an error message in the pop-up window.

Session Status and Adapter Status

NETTEST displays the result of a Session Status command in the format shown in figure 8.5.

```
[NetTest POST results]
Command: SESSION STATUS
Immed: success,  Final: success,

Names: 255    sessions: 3
lsn = 3  (Active session)  recvcount = 0  sendcount = 0
localname = 'CHRIS          '    remotename = 'SCOTT          '
lsn = 2  (Active session)  recvcount = 0  sendcount = 0
localname = 'SCOTT          '    remotename = 'CHRIS          '
lsn = 1  (Active session)  recvcount = 0  sendcount = 0
localname = 'BARRY          '    remotename = 'SERVER1        '
```

Fig. 8.5
Session Status
results.

For an Adapter Status command, NETTEST displays the returned information in a series of screens. Figures 8.6 through 8.10 show these screens.

```
[NetTest POST results]
Command: ADAPTER STATUS
Immed: success,  Final: success,

Card ID (hex): A8 B3 00 5A 00 10

    Release level: 02

    Adapter type: FF

  Old/new parms: 13

            (Press any key)
```

Fig. 8.6
The first part of
Adapter Status
data.

II

Network Programming

Fig. 8.7

The second part of
Adapter Status
data.

```
[NetTest POST results]

     Reporting period (mins):     1501

   Frame rejections received:        0

       Frame rejections sent:        0

      Received I-frame errors:        0

 Unsuccessful transmissions:         0

            (Press any key)
```

Fig. 8.8

The third part of
Adapter Status
data.

```
[NetTest POST results]


   Good transmissions:      1596

     Good receptions:         74



            (Press any key)
```

Fig. 8.9

The fourth part of
Adapter Status
data.

```
[NetTest POST results]


          Retransmissions:      0
      Exhausted resources:      0
         Available NCB's:       0
    Max configured NCB's:       0
      Max possible NCB's:     255
         Pending sessions:      1
 Max configured sessions:       6
   Max possible sessions:     254
          Max frame size:    1020

            (Press any key)
```

```
[NetTest POST results]

MIDI            (#2)  Registered           Unique name
MIDI            (#3)  Registered           Unique name
MIDI            (#4)  Registered           Unique name

                (Press any key)
```

Fig. 8.10
The last part of
Adapter Status
data.

NETTEST Sessions

To create a session between two NetBIOS names (on the same workstation or on different workstations), first add the names to the local name tables. Choose the Add Name menu option for each name and watch for a successful completion of each command. For example, you could add the name SCOTT and then add the name CHRIS.

Next, issue a Listen command for one of the names. Specify one of the names as the listener (CHRIS) and specify the other name as the one being listened for (SCOTT). Alternatively, you can specify that CHRIS "listen for a call from anyone" by using an asterisk (*) rather than a specific name. You now have a Listen command outstanding.

Establish the session by having SCOTT call CHRIS. Choose the Call menu option and designate SCOTT as the caller (the local name) and CHRIS as the name to be called (the remote name).

If all goes according to plan, when both the Listen and Call commands complete the program will display screens similar to those in figures 8.11 and 8.12. Make a note of the local session number (LSN) assigned to each partner in the session. You need each LSN to send and receive messages.

```
[NetTest POST results]
Command: LISTEN
Immed: success,  Final: success,


Session established with 'SCOTT  ',  LSN = 3,

                (Press any key)
```

Fig. 8.11
POST result of a
Listen command.

II

Network Programming

Fig. 8.12
POST result of a
Call command.

```
[NetTest POST results]
Command: CALL
Immed: success,  Final: success,


Session established, LSN = 2,

              (Press any key)
```

Sending and Receiving Messages

Now that you have established a session, you can use the Send and Receive menu options to transfer text messages between the two workstations (or between the two names on the same workstation). Have one session partner issue a Receive (you'll be prompted for the LSN that you made a note of earlier). Then have the other session partner issue a Send. When you choose the Send menu option, you are prompted for both the LSN (use the one assigned to the sending session partner) and the text of a message. When the Receive command completes, NETTEST displays a screen similar to that shown in figure 8.13. You will also be notified when the Send command completes.

Fig. 8.13
A received
message.

```
[NetTest POST results]
Command: RECEIVE
Immed: success,  Final: success,


Message says:
This is a simple text message,

             (Press any key)
```

Programmer Guide

Appendix B, "Source Listing for NetBIOS Microscope," contains the source code for this program (each of the programs described in this chapter is listed in one of the appendixes). You can trace the code with a bookmark or finger as the text describes the program.

The user guide implied how the program functions. When you choose a menu option, the program issues the appropriate NetBIOS command in its no-wait form. A POST routine is used to signal the completion of each command. As many as 10 network control blocks (NCBs) may be outstanding at any one time. A wraparound (circular) buffer maintains these NCBs. After the 10th item is POSTed, the next item goes into the first slot. Each item consists of the segment and offset portions of the completed NCB's address.

While waiting for a menu selection to be typed at the keyboard, the program also awaits a signal from the POST routine indicating that a command has completed. Pressing a key sends the program into the code that processes each menu selection. The completion of a NetBIOS command, as signaled by the POST routine, sends the program into the report_result() function, where the results from a completed command are displayed. The Reset command, however, does not cause the POST routine to occur.

For any command but Reset, the program constructs an NCB, issues it to NetBIOS, and lets NetBIOS process the command in the background. For the Reset command, the program waits for the command to complete before continuing. To fill in the NCB, some of the commands require information (a name, a local session number, or a text message). These items are requested as necessary. Defaults are used for some of the NCB's parameters. In particular, the time-out values for the Call and Listen commands are hard-coded. If the defaults do not suit your needs, you may want to change some of these values and recompile the program.

The function post() is used as a POST routine. The completion of any command (except Reset) causes NetBIOS to call post(). The function inserts the address of the completed NCB into a table of far pointers (segments and offsets) and returns to NetBIOS.

The report_result() function interprets the NCB_COMMAND field as well as the NCB_RET_CODE and NCB_CMD_CPLT fields in the completed NCB. For each different command, this function then displays the data returned by NetBIOS. For the Adapter Status command, this display consists of a series of screens showing the information in the adapter_status structure. For an Add Name or Add Group Name operation, the assigned name number is shown. The Call and Listen commands cause the assigned local session number to be displayed. The contents of the text message are displayed when a Receive command completes. A Session Status results in a display of information about each of the sessions for a name in the local name table.

Remote Program Execution

With the Remote Program Execution (RPE) facility, you designate one of the workstations on the LAN as an unattended slave machine on which you run batch (noninteractive) programs. The programs (and DOS commands) executed on the slave machine are submitted remotely, through NetBIOS. One component of this facility, RPE.EXE, runs on the slave machine and executes the "jobs." You use the other component, REMOTE.EXE, to submit the jobs that RPE executes.

What sort of programs are good candidates for RPE to run as jobs? Compilers and linkers are obviously good examples, as are unattended tape backups. A good candidate program has the following attributes:

- Takes more than a few seconds to run

- Does not require keyboard interaction

- Terminates after running a finite length of time

RPE maintains a queue of as many as 50 jobs that are awaiting execution. Not only can you use REMOTE to submit jobs to RPE, you can issue Status, Cancel, and Quit commands to find out what is in the queue, cancel a job in the queue, or cause RPE to terminate when the queue is empty. A job can consist of a DOS command or a program. Output from the command or program that ordinarily would go to the screen is automatically redirected into a file that you can inspect when the job completes. RPE also maintains a log of all job activity.

User Guide

Install the RPE.EXE component by copying the executable file into one of the directories expressed by the PATH statement on the slave machine. To start up the facility on the slave machine, type **RPE** at a DOS prompt. The program asks you for a network (file server) drive letter and path where RPE should write its log file. If you answer, for example, H:\JOBS, the full name of the log file will be H:\JOBS\RPE.LOG. The redirected output of each program will be written to this same directory. When RPE is running, you can submit jobs remotely from one of the other workstations on the network.

The drive letter must represent a file server disk; otherwise, nobody on the network will be able to view either the log file or the redirected output files.

Install the REMOTE.EXE component by copying the executable file into one of the PATH directories on each workstation.

Submitting a Job Using REMOTE

To submit a job to RPE, type **REMOTE**, followed by a space, followed by the exact DOS command or program name that you want to execute on the RPE slave computer, as shown in the following examples:

```
remote chdir \compile

remote tcc bigprog
```

If RPE is not running, you see the following message:

```
Couldn't connect: no answer.
REMOTE ended (unsuccessfully).
```

If RPE is already running a job, REMOTE informs you that your job will go into the queue and asks you whether this is okay. If the queue is full (50 jobs are awaiting execution), you see the following message:

```
The queue is full at this time.  Try later.
```

Otherwise, REMOTE and RPE exchange a few data messages, and you should next see the following message:

```
Job # XXXX in queue on machine NNNNN
```

where XXXX is the assigned job number and NNNNN is the machine name of the slave computer.

RPE writes an entry in the log file RPE.LOG when each job starts and when it finishes. The elapsed time is shown for each job, and each entry in the log file carries a date-and-time stamp. When RPE initiates the job, it uses the angle bracket (<) notation on the DOS command line to cause STDOUT screen output to be redirected to a file named j*XXXX.out*, where *XXXX* is the assigned job number.

When the job completes, you can inspect the contents of the j*XXXX.out* file to see how the execution went.

Using Status, Cancel, and Quit Commands

You can find out what is in the queue by invoking REMOTE as follows:

```
remote status
```

After REMOTE and RPE exchange a few messages, you next see a display similar to the following example:

```
There are 3 jobs in MAINFRAME's queue.

JOB      COMMAND
-----    ------------------------------------
J0030    tcc bigfile        EXECUTING
J0031    tcc applic         PENDING
J0032    lc -L othprog      PENDING
```

You can cancel a job anytime before it begins executing. Use this syntax, for example, to cancel job number 31:

```
remote cancel j31
```

You can also tell RPE to stop. Type **remote quit,** and RPE terminates as soon as the queue is empty.

Programmer Guide

Appendix C, "Source Listing for RPE.C," and Appendix D, "Source Listing for REMOTE.C," contain the source code for these programs. If you're using a bookmark or finger to hold your place in the appendixes, note that the text discusses the RPE program first.

RPE (Program Launcher)

First, RPE creates a far pointer to the transient portion of COMMAND.COM, located in upper memory. You'll soon discover how this far pointer is used. Next, the job queue is initialized. RPE checks to make sure that the following conditions are true:

- The DOS version is 3.0 or later.

- SHARE.EXE is loaded.

- The machine name has been set.

- NetBIOS is active.

RPE asks NetBIOS to add its name (RPE) to the local name table. RPE then asks which network drive letter and path to use for the log file. The program attempts to create a new file with the name RPE.LOG. If the file already exists, the call fails and RPE then attempts to open the existing file for Read/Write access, using a Sharing mode of DENY_NONE. The file is opened in Append mode, so the existing contents of the file are not disturbed. If the file cannot be opened, RPE instructs NetBIOS to delete the name RPE from its name table before RPE displays an error message and terminates.

If RPE doesn't encounter any problems, it displays the message RPE Started and issues a NetBIOS Listen command. This command specifies the following:

- To listen for a call to RPE

- That the call can be from anyone

- That the POST routine is background_listen()

- To use a time-out value of 10 seconds for the Send and Receive commands issued in the upcoming session

RPE then goes into a loop, waiting for a user to stop it manually at the slave machine's keyboard or for a NetBIOS error to happen. Inside the loop, if RPE finds that the background processing established a session and placed an item in the queue, the program calls execute_program() to satisfy the request.

A call from another workstation triggers background (asynchronous) processing in RPE. A session is established (RPE saves the assigned local session number) and RPE begins the dialog by sending a message to the caller. The message contains the slave computer's machine name and an indicator of whether the queue is empty. RPE then receives from the caller a message that contains either a command line to be executed or a Status, Cancel, or Quit signal. If the message contains a command line, RPE puts the job in the queue, assigns a job number, sends this job number back to the caller in a NetBIOS message, and closes the session by doing a Hang Up. If the message contains a Status, Cancel, or Quit signal, RPE sends the caller the requested information (if appropriate) and closes the session. Unless RPE receives a Quit signal, the program restarts the process by reissuing a Listen command.

RPE executes a job by using the system() library function, which invokes a secondary copy of COMMAND.COM, and instructing COMMAND.COM to run the program represented by the job. Before executing this program, RPE zeros the transient portion of COMMAND.COM. (This step prevents an obscure bug in some versions of DOS by forcing COMMAND.COM to reload its upper-memory command processor.) An entry is written to the log file, the DOS command line is constructed, and the job is run. Elapsed time is measured and written to the log file when the job finishes.

REMOTE (Job Submission)

When you tell REMOTE to submit a job, the program begins processing by checking the DOS version and making sure that NetBIOS is active. REMOTE obtains the permanent node name from NetBIOS by performing an Adapter Status command and prefixing 10 binary 0s to the first six bytes of data that the command returns.

REMOTE then makes an exact copy of its command line and builds a data message to send to RPE. REMOTE issues to NetBIOS a Call command that specifies the following:

- A remote name of RPE

- A local name equal to the permanent node name

- Time-out values of 10 seconds each for Send and Receive commands issued in the upcoming session

Because RPE always starts the conversation by sending its machine name in a data message, REMOTE first issues a Receive command after the session is established. The data message also contains an indication of whether RPE's queue is empty. If the queue is not empty, REMOTE asks whether the submitted job can go into the queue.

REMOTE then sends its command line to the RPE machine. This command line might contain a DOS command, a program to be executed, the word cancel, the word status, or the word quit. REMOTE receives a reply from RPE and closes the session with a Hang Up command.

The reply from RPE is an assigned job number (a DOS command or program to run), the contents of the awaiting-execution queue (status), or confirmation of a cancel or quit request. REMOTE displays the information contained in the reply and terminates.

Dialog Design

The dialog between RPE and REMOTE is outlined as follows:

```
                    SESSION DIALOG DESIGN


        RPE (listener)                REMOTE (caller)
   ------------------------      -------------------------------
   1. Send:
      - machine name
      - idle/busy status

                                 1. Receive:
                                    - machine name
                                    - status

                                 2. Send:
                                    - command line
                                    if command line = 'quit',
                                    hang up

   2. Receive:
      - command line

      if command line = 'quit',
      hang up and don't take
      further job requests

   3. if command line = 'status', Send:
      - count of pending items
      - 0 to 50 pending items
      (then hang up)

                                 3. Receive:
                                    - queue status
                                    (then hang up)
```

```
4. If command line = 'cancel', Send:
   - job-not-found, or confirmation
   (then hang up)
```

```
                              4. Receive:
                                 - cancellation response
                                 (then hang up)
```

```
5. Send:
   - job number packet
   (then hang up)
```

```
                              5. Receive:
                                 - job number packet
                                 (then hang up)
```

Electronic Mail

The E-Mail application enables you to send memos to other users on your LAN. You can attach to each memo a binary or text file (such as a spreadsheet, a long letter, a report, or an .EXE), and you can send your memo to a list of people. E-Mail doesn't require any disk space or special rights on the file server; the memos are sent directly from user to user through NetBIOS.

User Guide

The E-Mail application consists of two programs. The first is the Postman. This small terminate-and-stay-resident (TSR) program, which has no user interface, simply receives and delivers mail. Postman places incoming mail in a specified directory and periodically checks whether your outbasket has any mail messages to be delivered.

The second program, Mail, is a somewhat larger TSR that contains the user interface for sending and receiving mail, including a simple text editor. You can pop up the Mail program to send a memo or to read your incoming mail. To send mail, you use the text editor to compose a memo and, when you finish, you specify a file attachment (if any) and a CC list (if any). The Postman is then triggered so that it can deliver your message. The text editor supports memos as much as one screen long. To pop up the Mail program, you press the Alt-Right Shift key combination. The Mail program is text-based. When you are running a program that has put your workstation into graphics mode and you try to pop up the Mail program, Mail beeps to let you know that it currently cannot use the screen.

To read a mail message, you scroll through your inbasket and choose the item that you want to read. After you read the message, you can then reply to the message, delete it, print it, or save it as a regular file.

Mail is delivered only if the recipients are running the Postman program at their workstation. If your Postman and the recipient's Postman cannot make a connection when you put the item in your outbasket, your Postman tries again every ten minutes thereafter. Presumably, the recipient will run his or her Postman program at some time during the day.

In addition to the NetBIOS version of these programs, this book's companion disk contains an IPX and SPX version of both Postman and Mail in the disk directory NETWARE. If you use Novell NetWare on your LAN, you can choose to load the Novell NetBIOS emulator (NETBIOS.EXE) and run the NetBIOS version of these programs, or you can choose to use the IPX or SPX version of Postman and Mail found in the NETWARE disk directory.

When you run the Postman, the program makes a note of the current drive and directory. All incoming mail and attached files are placed in this directory. The Postman also sets its "alarm clock" to wake up every ten minutes, at which time it checks your outbasket for undelivered mail. Before exiting to DOS as a TSR, the Postman displays a message reminding you to run the Mail program if you want to view your inbasket or outbasket. While the Postman is loaded, it is always ready to receive mail.

The Mail program is also a TSR. Although larger than the Postman program (Mail is 48K, Postman is 24K), Mail is easily unloaded from memory to give you room to run other applications. Unless you are *really* cramped for memory space, you should consider leaving Postman running for as long as you are on the network.

Installing the Mail Program and Popping Up

If you have a hard drive on your workstation, you should make a directory named MAIL on your C: drive and copy the POSTMAN.EXE and MAIL.EXE programs to that directory. If you don't have a hard drive, you can make a directory on the file server and copy the programs to it, but make sure that each user has his or her own directory for receiving mail. If two users try to share the same file server directory for E-Mail, the Postman program will get confused. The mail messages are not encrypted in any way, so for privacy, you should use the local hard disk installation method.

After you log on to the network, you run the Postman program and then the Mail program. You should first make your MAIL directory your current directory so that the Postman knows where to put your incoming mail. If you construct a .BAT file to load the Postman and Mail programs, the file should look like this:

```
C:
CD \MAIL
POSTMAN
MAIL
```

After the Postman is loaded, you can change drives and directories without affecting where the files containing your mail messages are placed.

When you pop up the Mail program by pressing Alt-Right Shift, the bottom line of the resultant screen shows the keys that you can press to tell the Mail program what to do:

- The F1 key to get help

- The S key to send a memo

- The I key to see what is in your inbasket

- The O key to view your outbasket (that is, any undelivered mail)

- The X key to exit E-Mail

- The F10 key to unload the Mail program from memory

Sending and receiving mail are described shortly. For now, note that the I and O keys toggle the display between the inbasket and the outbasket. The X key returns you to the foreground application (or to the DOS prompt). Not only can you press the F10 key to remove MAIL.EXE from memory, but, if you need the extra memory, you can press Alt-F10 to remove both MAIL.EXE and POSTMAN.EXE from memory. Remember, however, that you cannot receive mail from other users if the Postman is not running. After running your memory-intensive application, you should return to the C:\MAIL directory and reload the Postman.

For each item in your inbasket, Mail shows the sender's name, the subject of the memo, and the date and time that the memo was sent. For outbasket items, Mail shows the recipient's name, the subject, and the date and time that the memo was placed in the outbasket.

Sending Mail

Press the S key to send mail. You can practice sending mail by sending a message to yourself. From a DOS prompt, follow these steps to send the mail message:

1. Pop up the Mail program by pressing Alt-Right Shift. Make a note of your workstation name, which is displayed as XXXXXX in the E-Mail for XXXXXX message on the screen.

2. Press the S key.

3. Respond to the TO: prompt by typing the name by which your workstation is known on the network. Press Enter.

4. Respond to the SUBJECT: prompt by typing **Practice Test.** Press Enter.

5. You are now in the text editor. Type a couple of lines. (Remember that the editor does not have word wrap; press Enter before you get to the end of a line.) You can type anything you want; no one but you will see the message.

6. Press F2 when you finish composing the message.

7. When prompted for an attachment file name, press Enter.

8. To receive two copies of the message, respond to the CC: prompt by typing your workstation name again. Press Enter.

You then see the main screen for the Mail program. Soon afterward, you should hear a beep and see the message You have mail at the bottom of your screen. The message disappears by itself. You should then see your mail message in the inbasket on the screen. The beep and the momentary message repeat themselves when the CC message is also received and placed in your inbasket.

Don't read your mail yet. Press X to return to DOS, and find a file in another directory (not C:\MAIL) that you don't mind having two copies of. Note the drive, directory, and file name. Now pop up the Mail program again and follow the preceding steps to send another message to yourself. This time, when you see the Attach File: prompt, specify the drive, directory, and file name of the file that you just found. After the test, look in the C:\MAIL directory to see what the Postman delivered.

Reading and Disposing of Mail

If several items are in your inbasket (which holds as many as 50 memos), use the up-arrow and down-arrow cursor keys to select one item for reading. Press Enter when the item that you want is highlighted. The text of the selected mail message appears.

You can press the Esc key to leave the item in your inbasket; you can press D to delete it or press P to print it (make sure that your printer is ready). You can also press S to save the message as a regular text file, in which case Mail prompts you for a file name. Finally, you can press R if you want to reply to the mail message. Selecting this last option causes the Mail program automatically to switch the TO: and FROM: fields and put you in the text editor, where you can compose your reply.

In the display of your inbasket, an asterisk (*) before the sender's name identifies items that you have already read.

If an item sits in your outbasket for a long time, you may have misspelled the name of the recipient. To correct the name, press O to switch to the outbasket display, and then select the item by highlighting it with the up-arrow or down-arrow cursor keys. Then, when you press Enter, you see options for changing or deleting the message. If you press C to choose the Change option, you can retype the recipient's workstation name. The Postman can then successfully deliver the mail message.

The Text Editor

You can use the text editor to compose mail messages that are up to one screen long. If you want to send a longer memo, use a more powerful text editor or word processor to write the memo and attach the memo to a mail message.

The first two lines of the text editor screen are significant. The prompts TO: and SUBJECT: should not be modified. The Mail program looks for these phrases to identify the recipient and the subject of the mail message. The remainder of each line after the prompts TO: and SUBJECT:, however, can be modified. The name that you specify for the TO: prompt is used as the destination of the mail message. This name should contain the workstation name associated with the person who should receive the message. The phrase that you specify after the SUBJECT: is shown in the recipient's inbasket display to identify the message. If you inadvertently put in your outbasket an item that contains an invalid workstation name, you can use the previously described procedure to correct the name.

As with any text editor, certain keys cause certain things to happen. The general layout of the text editor screen looks like the following:

```
TO: <addressee>
SUBJECT: <subject phrase>

<body of message>

ESC-Quit  F2-Save  F4-Erase EOL  F5-Insert Line  F10-Delete Line
```

You can use the following keys to edit the text screen:

- Esc exits the text editor without actually sending the message.

- F2 schedules the message for delivery to the recipient.

- F4 erases the text from the cursor to the end of the line.

- F5 inserts a blank line between two existing lines.

- F10 deletes the line that the cursor is on.

- The up-arrow, down-arrow, left-arrow, and right-arrow keys move the cursor around the editor screen.

- The Tab key moves the cursor four spaces to the right.

- The Home key moves the cursor to the beginning of the line.

- The End key moves the cursor to the end of the line.

- The Delete key deletes the character that the cursor is on.

- The Backspace key moves the cursor to the left, just like the left-arrow cursor key. Backspace does not delete characters the cursor is on.

- The Ins key toggles Insert mode.

Word wrap is not supported. Make sure that you press Enter at the end of each line, before you reach the right side of the screen.

Programmer Guide

Appendix E, "Source Listing for the Postman Program," lists the source code for the Postman program, and Appendix F, "Source Listing for the Electronic Mail Program," lists the source code for the Mail program. This book does not present NetWare-specific (IPX/SPX version) program code, but such code is included in the NETWARE directory on the companion disk.

The Postman program occupies about 24K of memory when it is resident. The Mail program, on the other hand, occupies about 48K. Both programs began as a single program, but I split the functions into two programs after I realized that some users might want to unload the Mail program to have enough memory to run large applications. Leaving the smaller Postman program in memory just to receive incoming mail is a good compromise.

Much effort went into the TSR and interprocess communication techniques used by these two programs. I could write an entire book just on these techniques! However, because this book focuses on network programming techniques, the following program descriptions concentrate on the programs' PC-to-PC communications.

The Postman Program

Although smaller than the Mail program, Postman is easily the more complex of the two programs. At its outset, Postman performs the same sort of TSR initialization described earlier in the Collision Tester discussion. Postman also does a getcwd() call to find out the current working directory. Before making itself resident, Postman gets the machine name, prefixes the name with an exclamation point (!), and uses the result to do an Add Name operation. Postman uses the ! character to avoid conflicts with the IBM PC LAN Program, which is already using the machine name in its sessions with the file server. The program then issues a Receive Datagram call to NetBIOS and terminates to DOS with a TSR function call.

The mail messages (and optional attached files) that one Postman sends to another Postman are sent as a series of datagrams. Each datagram packet is formatted as follows:

```
typedef struct
    {
    char    type;
    int     sequence;
    int     data_length;
    char    data [500];
    }
    MAIL_PACKET;
```

The type field identifies the type of packet, as indicated in table 8.1.

Table 8.1 Values for the *type* Field

Value	Type	Definition
01	Acknowledgment	Returned by the recipient
10	Mail Header	First packet in each set
20	Mail Data	Carries the mail message text
30	Mail EOF	Signals the end of the mail message
50	File Header	First packet for an attached file
60	File Data	Carries parts of the attached file
70	File EOF	Signals the end of the attachment
99	Trailer	Last packet of each set

The sequence field is used to ensure that datagrams arrive in the proper order and that none are missed. The data_length field tells how long the data area is. Finally, the data field contains a portion of the mail message or attached file.

Each datagram received by the Postman is handled by the function POST_routine(). This function sets two flags, mail_flag (which triggers Postman to do background processing) and incoming_msg (which tells the background code that a datagram has been received and needs to be processed).

Several events trigger Postman to do background processing:

- The receipt of a datagram, as previously noted. (incoming_msg)

- The expiration of a 10-minute period of time, which causes Postman to look for outbasket items that it can attempt to deliver. Note that the Mail program can alter this time-out value so that mail is sent without waiting the full 10 minutes. (outbasket_alarm)

- The expiration of a 60-second time-out. Postman sets up this counter for incoming mail. Because a mail message (and optional attached file) are transmitted as several datagrams, this counter tells the Postman that 60 seconds have passed since the program last received the previous packet in a series of incoming packets. (incoming_alarm)

- The expiration of a five-second time-out. When Postman sends an initial datagram to a mail recipient, the program waits five seconds for an acknowledgment. If no acknowledgment is received, the sending Postman assumes that the recipient's Postman is not running and goes on to the next item in the outbasket. (no_answer_alarm)

When one of these events happens, Postman uses the next timer tick (Interrupt 8), the next keyboard idle time (Interrupt 16), or the next DOS idle time (Interrupt 28) to wake itself up. Background processing begins in the process_mail() function, which saves the current machine context, switches to a private stack, and calls the post_office() function. After post_office() finishes, process_mail() restores the machine context and stack and returns, through the interrupt handler, to the foreground process.

The post_office() function is the clearinghouse for all background activity. The function notes the reason that it was invoked, based on the event that has occurred (see the previous list). If Postman is sending a mail message to another workstation, and an Acknowledgment datagram packet is received from that workstation, send_next_packet() is called to send the next packet in the series.

If another workstation is sending mail (Postman is in the mode of recipient rather than the sender), and the datagram packet checks out okay (it is the expected type and the sequence number is valid), post_office() sends an Acknowledgment packet to the other workstation.

If post_office() is receiving mail and sees that 60 seconds have passed since it received the last datagram packet, the function cancels the receipt of incoming mail and assumes that the sender workstation will try again later.

If an exploratory mail header was sent to another workstation to check whether that workstation is ready to receive mail, and if five seconds pass without an acknowledgment of that mail header, post_office() assumes that the other workstation is not logged on or is not running the Postman program. The function leaves the item in the outbasket and goes on to the next item.

If post_office() detects that it is time to check the outbasket to see whether another item can be delivered (ten minutes have passed since the last attempt), the function invokes the send_mail() function to process whatever items are in the outbasket.

If an incoming datagram packet has been processed, post_office() issues another Receive Datagram call to NetBIOS.

The Mail Program

The Mail program creates outbasket files named *XXXXXX*.OUT, where *XXXXXX* is an ASCII representation for the number returned by the time() library function. Similarly, the inbasket files created by the Postman are named *XXXXXX*.IN. When you pop up Mail, the program looks in Postman's startup directory (usually C:\MAIL) for *.IN and *.OUT files. The information from the header portion of each of these files is placed in a table (which can include as many as 50 items). The contents of the tables are shown on the screen as inbasket or outbasket items.

Again, I hate to gloss over such things so quickly. The aspects of the Mail program dealing with becoming a TSR and popping up on a hot key are much like those described earlier for the Collision Tester. There are two important things to look for in the code, however.

The first is the way that Mail does an Interrupt 16 call early in the program, with AH set to PO. If the AH register is returned as po (notice the lowercase letters), Mail knows that Postman is active. From this call, Mail obtains pointers to certain variables inside Postman. One of these pointers is to the outbasket_alarm field. When you send a mail message, the Mail program sets Postman's outbasket_alarm field to 0 and thus causes Postman to wake up and send the mail. Otherwise, you would have to wait for a 10-minute period to elapse before the mail message got delivered. Another pointer that Mail obtains is that of a de_install flag inside Postman. When you press Alt-F10, which tells both the Mail program and the Postman program to remove themselves from memory, Mail uses its pointer to Postman's de_install flag to tell Postman to unload itself.

The other thing to look for is sort of subtle. When Mail knows that the keyboard is idle and that DOS is safe to use, the program does a dummy Interrupt 28 call from within its own Interrupt 16 handler. This extra DOS Idle Interrupt is important because it gives the Postman program a chance to "breathe"—Postman can take the opportunity to do some background processing even though the Mail program is popped up and active.

When you tell Mail that you want to send a memo, the program puts you in the text editor. When you finish composing the message, Mail asks you for the file name of an attachment file and the list of names to which carbon copies should be sent. This information goes into the header of the mail message. The CC list causes the Mail program to create one copy of the mail message file for each recipient. The copies are identified with an alphabetic suffix in the file name (*XXXXXX*A.OUT, *XXXXXX*B.OUT, and so on).

When you use Mail to read a mail message, the program loads the text of the mail message into the text editor work area and displays the memo on the screen.

The only network-related action that Mail performs is to obtain the machine name, which the program uses in the FROM: field of each mail message.

E-Mail Functional Design

The following is the functional specification used for the Postman and Mail programs. Notes regarding NetWare (IPX) calls appear in parentheses and refer to the source code listings on the companion disk rather than the listings shown in the appendixes.

```
A. Main routine

   1. Make sure the program is not already loaded
   2. Make sure that NetBIOS (or IPX) is loaded
   3. Do Add_Name (or IPX_Open_Socket)
   4. Install interrupt handlers
   5. Issue Receive_Datagram (or IPX_Listen_For_Packet)
   6. Terminate and stay resident

B. Deinstall routine (de_install flag ON)

   1. Do nothing until the program is last in memory
   2. Restore interrupt vectors
   3. Cancel Receive_Datagram (or IPX_Listen_For_Packet)
   4. Delete_Name (or IPX_Close_Socket)
   5. Deallocate memory
   6. Exit

C. Incoming mail routine, triggered by POST (or ESR) or timer tick

   1. If processing incoming mail:
      a. If the expected packet is not received (60 second timeout)
         1. Close files
         2. Delete files
         3. Reset sequence number, etc.
         4. Exit
      b. If not a packet-type that you logically expect
         1. Close files
         2. Delete files
         3. Reset the sequence number, etc.
         4. Reissue receive/listen
         5. Exit
      c. If duplicate packet
         1. Just resend the acknowledgment
         2. Reissue receive/listen
         3. Exit
      d. If missing packet
```

```
              1. Close files
              2. Delete files
              3. Reset sequence number, etc.
              4. Reissue receive/listen
              5. Exit
           e. Packet okay; process it
              1. Mail-Header packet
                 a. Determine local mail message file name
                 b. Create file
              2. Mail-Message-Data packet;
                 write to the mail message file
              3. Mail-Message-EOF packet;
                 close the mail message file
              4. Attached-File-Header packet;
                 create the new file
              5. Attached-File-Data packet;
                 write to the file
              6. Attached-File-EOF packet;
                 close file
              7. Mail-Trailer packet
                 a. Put item in the inbasket
                 b. Set the expected sequence number to 0
           f. Ask for the next packet
              1. Return an acknowledgment
              2. Increment the sequence number (0 if Trailer)
              3. Reissue Receive_Datagram (or IPX_Listen_For_Packet)
              4. Exit

        2. If receiving an acknowledgment for mail that you sent:
           a. Prepare to send the next packet, if any (see the following)

        Deliver an outbasket item

              1. Occurs every 10 minutes, or when a new item is
                 in the outbasket
              2. Send mail header for an outbasket item
              3. If no acknowledgment is received within five seconds,
                 go on to next item
              4. After checking the last item, go back to sleep
              5. If an acknowledgment is received, proceed
              6. Send packets
                 a. Mail-Message-Data (as many as needed)
                 b. Mail-Message-EOF
                 c. If no file is attached, send Mail-Trailer and exit
                 d. Attached-File-Header
                 e. Attached-File-Data (as many as needed)
                 f. Attached-File-EOF
                 g. Mail-Trailer
              7. For each packet sent, expect an acknowledgment
                 a. If ACK is not returned in five seconds, resend the
                    packet
                 b. If 10 errors in a row, cancel (leave item in the
                    outbasket)
              8. Exit

        Pop-up routine
```

1. Pop up on the hot key flag
2. Wait until DOS is safe to use
3. Switch contexts (just beep if the machine is in graph-ics mode)
4. Save the application screen
5. Determine the status of the inbasket
6. Determine the status of the outbasket (undelivered mail)
7. Put up our screen, including menu icons
8. Get the menu choice and perform a subroutine to handle it
   a. Send Mail
   b. Read Mail
   c. Change the outbasket item
   d. Remove from memory (sets de_install flag)
   e. Quit
9. If menu option isn't 'Remove', or 'Quit', go back to step 5
10. Restore the application screen
11. Restore the context
12. Exit from the pop-up routine

Send Mail subroutine

1. Clear the editor area
2. Ask "TO: "
3. Ask "SUBJECT: "
4. Invoke a simple text editor
5. After the edit session, ask:
   a. Attach file?
   b. Carbon copies?
6. If "attach file", ask for file name and verify that it exists
7. Put mail in the outbasket
8. Trigger mail-delivery routine
9. Exit

Read Mail routine

1. Read the mail message into the editor area
2. Show it on-screen
3. When done, show the submenu:
   a. Leave
   b. Delete
   c. Print
   d. Save as a regular file
   e. Reply
4. Mark the message as read
5. Exit

Change the outbasket item

1. Suspend mail delivery
2. Let the user withdraw or change the outbasket mail
3. Trigger the mail-delivery routine
4. Exit

Writing a NetWare Loadable Module

You can use a NetWare loadable module (NLM) to centralize functions on your NetWare LAN, such as tape backup, database retrieval, network management, or electronic mail post office. An NLM can also enable you to use spare CPU cycles on your NetWare file server PC so that you can process applications on your LAN. Most high-end 80486- and Pentium-based NetWare servers have plenty of spare CPU cycles. The server often expends most of its efforts accessing hard disks and network adapters, leaving the CPU to wait on these relatively slow I/O devices. An NLM can make use of some of the CPU processing power of an otherwise idle CPU server.

To demonstrate the techniques of NLM programming, I wrote a small NLM, EMAILNLM, that serves as a central post office for simple store-and-forward electronic-mail functions. E-mail provides a perfect opportunity to exploit the features and advantages of NLM technology. Although most commercial e-mail products work by reading and writing files in a post office directory on the server through redirected Open-Read-Write-Close I/O calls, EMAILNLM accesses its post office directly at the file server. The NLM uses IPX to receive outgoing mail through the LAN cable and stores mail items in a MAILBOX directory on the server. To read a mail item, a workstation sends an IPX message packet to EMAILNLM. The NLM delivers the mail item, as a series of LAN packets, to the workstation. Appendix N, "Source Listing for EMAILNLM.C," lists the source code for the NLM. The NLM also is included on this book's companion disk, but you must write the workstation software that interacts with the Post Office NLM.

> **Note**
>
> The Postman and Mail programs described earlier in this chapter are not designed to interact with EMAILNLM.

Understanding NLMs

NLMs are similar to ordinary computer programs, but have some unique characteristics that you need to consider when you're writing a program that will run in a NetWare file server. You shouldn't shy away from developing NLMs simply because your program runs on a file server rather than a workstation (although in some circumstances, described later, you don't want to burden your file server with additional processing loads). In fact, writing NLMs is in some ways simpler than writing DOS or Windows programs. For example, because an NLM runs in protected mode in a flat, 32-bit memory model, you don't have to concern yourself with segments, offsets, and 64K limitations. However, you must be aware of two significant considerations before you start writing your program.

First, NetWare 3.12 and 4.0 give your NLM a cooperative processing environment. Unlike preemptive environments such as OS/2 (running LAN Server), NetWare doesn't provide any built-in means of interrupting one task in favor of another. This approach has advantages and disadvantages. NetWare itself remains simpler because it doesn't have to handle the scheduling and dispatching of tasks in the computer. However, because this approach is used, the NLM developer is responsible for controlling how much the NLM uses the CPU.

Therefore, you must write your NLMs so that they relinquish control of the CPU occasionally to give other processes a chance to run. Fortunately, this responsibility isn't a burden if you keep in mind the file server environment in which your NLM will run. In fact, opportunities for NetWare to "take a breath"—that is, process file I/O requests from workstations—occur automatically when your NLM calls I/O functions to open, read, write, or close files, or when you send and receive messages to and from workstations.

Second, NetWare doesn't offer the kind of virtual memory management that an operating system such as OS/2 provides (OS/2 can overcommit memory by swapping not-recently-used pages of memory to a disk file). You cannot allocate or use more memory than physically exists in the file server, so you must ensure that the server has enough RAM for both NetWare and your NLM.

A NetWare loadable module has an extension of .NLM, .DSK, or .LAN rather than .EXE or .COM. An NLM runs in a NetWare 3.12 or 4.0 file server and uses the same memory, hard disk, network adapter, and library functions as NetWare itself. In fact, NetWare itself uses several NLMs, as documented in the NetWare manuals. For instance, the NE2000.LAN file provides support for NE-2000 (and compatible) network adapters. The TOKEN.LAN file supports IBM Token Ring adapters. The PS2SCSI.DSK file lets NetWare use SCSI disks on PS/2 computers. The MONITOR.NLM executable displays file server status information, and the PSERVER.NLM file enables a file server to act as a print server. You can find these and other examples of NLMs by changing to the SYS:SYSTEM directory from any workstation, using the DIR command, and looking for files with .NLM, .DSK, and .LAN extensions.

At a NetWare file server console, you can use the LOAD and UNLOAD commands to start and stop NLM programs. In fact, when an NLM finishes processing, it can terminate by unloading itself from memory. This capability to load and unload NLMs while the server is still running is what makes NLMs under NetWare 3.12 and 4.0 so powerful and easy to use. The NetWare 2.2 environment offers a similar type of server program, the value-added process (VAP), but to load and unload VAPs you have to stop and restart the file server.

Looking at Examples of NLMs

Recognizing that you might not want to buy a separate PC on which to run their software, a few commercial vendors of LAN-based software supply NLM versions of their products. In many cases, an NLM is a natural place to perform central LAN functions. In other cases, an NLM is the *only* way that the vendor can give you the functions and features of the product.

ORACLE sells an NLM version of its ORACLE database manager. Workstations issue Structured Query Language (SQL) requests to the ORACLE NLM, directly through the LAN cable, without having to open, read, write, and close files. The ORACLE NLM accesses the tables and rows of the database by performing file I/O operations inside the server and then returns only the requested information (the result of a SELECT query, for example) over the wire to the workstation.

Novell gives you a tape backup NLM (SBACKUP.NLM) with the NetWare 3.12 network operating system. This NLM enables you to back up copies of files on the server, if your file server PC has a tape drive attached. Novell also bundles its BTRIEVE file access method, in the form of an NLM, with the NetWare 3.12 NOS. Also, Frye's LAN Directory network management product uses an NLM to monitor a NetWare 3.12 file server's health. All these products are good examples of what you can accomplish with NLMs.

Exploring the NLM Development Environment

Novell supplies libraries of functions that your NLM program can use to perform its work. These functions enable NLMs to read and write files in the NetWare file system, communicate with workstations through the LAN cable, perform calculations, and do other types of information processing. With the functions, your NLM can allocate memory, spawn multiple processing threads, and advertise its presence to workstations on the LAN. An NLM can read and write objects in the NetWare Bindery, perform login and logout operations, create, change, or remove directories, add items to a NetWare queue, and become a queue processor or server. An NLM can even access files in a DOS partition on the server's hard disk. By using the AppleTalk Filing Protocol (AFP), an NLM also can access Macintosh files and their name spaces.

The CLIB NLM is important to developers because it contains most of the functions that an NLM calls. You link at compile-time with a CLIB import library and, at the file server console, you load the CLIB NLM before loading and running your own NLM. Other NLMs can also use the services and functions in the CLIB. The mechanism within NetWare for accessing CLIB and other NLM libraries works in much the same way that dynamic link libraries (DLLs) work in the Windows and OS/2 environments.

To compile and link your NLM, you need the Watcom 32-bit C compiler product (version 9.5 or later). Other compilers, such as Microsoft's, Borland's, Symantec's, and even IBM's 32-bit C Set/2, will not suffice. These other compilers either do not produce 32-bit code or cannot produce an executable file in NLM format. You can purchase the Watcom compiler from Watcom or Novell. Novell resells Watcom's 32-bit compiler—accompanied by the appropriate NLM programming technical reference manuals—as the Network C for NLMs Software Developer's Kit (NLM SDK).

To get up to speed in NLM development techniques, you will need some additional reading material. Novell's Developer Support Group in Austin, Texas publishes a set of technical reference manuals for NLM developers, as well as the *Bullets* newsletter. Novell Research publishes the helpful *NetWare Application Notes*, which often contains useful information about NLM development. Also, Novell Press publishes the book *NetWare 4.0 NLM Programming* to help you get started; much of the information in the book applies to NetWare 3.12 NLMs as well as 4.0 NLMs.

Setting Up Your E-Mail Server NLM

Before loading the E-Mail NLM the first time, a user with supervisor rights must run the SYSCON utility to establish a logon account named MAILBOX with a password of EMAIL. (If you want to maintain secrecy and security, you can change these values in the NLM, recompile the NLM, and change your installation procedures accordingly.) On the SYS: volume, create a directory named MAILBOX. In SYSCON, give the MAILBOX account all rights to SYS:MAILBOX and make sure that no other user has rights to the directory. Only the NLM will access files in the MAILBOX directory.

Copy the EMAILNLM.NLM file to the SYS:SYSTEM directory. To load the software, enter the command **LOAD EMAILNLM** at the file server console. If you want to load the software automatically each time that you start the server, you can put the LOAD EMAILNLM command in your AUTOEXEC.NCF file. You might want to make the SYSTEM directory off-limits from prying eyes; as currently coded, the password is a piece of text within the executable file, easily found with a file viewer.

This NLM relies on NetWare's own security mechanisms to ensure message privacy. The special logon account MAILBOX and users with supervisor-equivalent rights are the only entities who can access mail message files in the MAILBOX directory. As you customize and enhance the E-Mail NLM software, preserving the privacy of electronic mail in your organization should be easy. Just keep the logon account and password secret, and perhaps coordinate recompiles of the software with the network administrator so that you change the password on a regular basis.

Understanding How the NLM Works

The E-Mail Server program EMAILNLM does for e-mail requests from worksta-tions what NetWare itself does for file I/O requests from workstations. Work-stations use IPX to send mail request messages to the Post Office NLM, and the NLM responds by delivering the mail or taking some other requested action. Workstation software (that you write) sends and receives IPX mes-sages in a particular format to interact with EMAILNLM. The following C structure defines the format of mail message packets both sent and received by the NLM:

```
struct  {
        char    ActionCode;
        short   MailID;
        short   Sequence;
        char    LastPacketFlag;
        short   Length;
        short   Reserved;
        char    Packet [500];
        } Message;
```

EMAILNLM begins by logging in, preparing to receive IPX messages, and indexing any mail items in the post office. The ActionCode field within the mail message itself specifies the operation that the NLM should perform.

Based on the value of ActionCode (1–4), the NLM can do the following:

1. Give the user logged in to a workstation a list of items in his or her inbasket and outbasket

2. Let the user read a mail message

3. Delete a mail message

4. File an outgoing mail message for future delivery to another workstation

As the NLM receives LAN packets from workstations, it manages the files in the MAILBOX directory, where each file is a mail item. The NLM can return to the workstation a series of LAN messages, each an item in the user's inbasket or outbasket. The NLM can open a file for the workstation and send the mail item's contents as a series of IPX LAN messages. The NLM also can delete a mail item. Also, when it receives a request from a workstation, the NLM can create, write, and close a new outgoing mail item in the MAILBOX directory.

Examining the Detailed NLM Coding Techniques

When the E-Mail NLM begins running, it performs a NetWare LOGIN function with an account name of MAILBOX and a password of EMAIL. (You can change the account name and password in the source file and then recompile the source, if you're concerned about security.) The NLM does a change-directory operation to the SYS:MAILBOX directory. After opening an IPX socket (0x4545) for sending and receiving mail-request message packets, the NLM registers an `atexit()` function. If you issue an UNLOAD EMAILNLM command at the file server console, the registered `atexit()` function logs out and closes the IPX socket. The following fragment shows the C code that accomplishes these initial steps:

```
/* log in as user MAILBOX, password EMAIL */
    if (LoginToFileServer("mailbox", OT_USER, "EMAIL")) {
        printf("Could not log in as MAILBOX.  Aborting.\n");
        return 1; }

/* change to the SYS:\MAILBOX directory */
    if (chdir("SYS:\\MAILBOX")) {
        printf("Could not change to MAILBOX directory. Aborting.\n");
        return 1; }

/* open socket 0x4545 */
    Socket = 0x4545;
    IpxOpenSocket(&Socket);

/* register an atexit() function to happen at unload time */
    atexit(MailUnload);
```

Before processing any mail requests from workstations, the NLM creates an in-memory index of all the files in the MAILBOX directory. The program opens each file, stores information from the file's first (mail header) record in an in-memory array, and closes the file. The following C structure shows the layout of the mail header. The From, To, Date, Time, and Subject items should bring to mind standard interoffice mail.

```
struct  MailHeaderType {
        char    From [50];
        char    To [50];
        char    Date [10];
        char    Time [10];
        char    Subject [50];
        char    Reserved [4];
        char    FileName [15]; };
```

The FileName item in this structure is where the E-Mail NLM remembers the name of the file as the software creates the index of files in the MAILBOX directory. (With a slightly different design, the program could simply process the mail headers of all the files each time a workstation sends a mail request message. However, the NLM responds more quickly when it maintains an internal list of outstanding mail items.)

After indexing any outstanding mail, the NLM is almost ready to begin processing new mail requests from workstations. Because the NLM uses the IPX protocol to send and receive workstation mail requests, the E-Mail NLM issues a Listen ECB to the file server's IPX message handler:

```
        /* issue a Listen ECB */
IssueListen:
 memset(&EventControlBlock,0,sizeof(EventControlBlock));
 memset(&IpxHeader, 0, sizeof(IpxHeader));
 memset(&Message, 0, sizeof(Message));
 EventControlBlock.fragCount = 2L;
 EventControlBlock.fragList[0].fragAddress = &IpxHeader;
 EventControlBlock.fragList[0].fragSize = sizeof(IpxHeader);
 EventControlBlock.fragList[1].fragAddress = &Message;
 EventControlBlock.fragList[1].fragSize = sizeof(Message);

 IpxReceive(Socket, &EventControlBlock);
```

When an IPX message packet containing a socket value of 0x4545 arrives at the file server, the IPX message handler gives the packet to the E-Mail Server NLM. The NLM inspects the message packet's action code and performs the indicated operation. First, however, the NLM asks NetWare for the account name of the user logged in at the requesting workstation, by using the GetUserNameFromNetAddress() function:

```
GetUserNameFromNetAddress((BYTE *) IpxHeader.sourceNet,
                0, &User);
```

To ensure mail privacy, the NLM reads mail only for the user who is actually logged in at a workstation.

When users ask whether they have mail, the NLM searches its index and responds with a list of inbasket and outbasket mail items for that particular person. The returned list contains an identifying number for each mail item (the MailID field in the Message structure). The E-Mail NLM might send the workstation one or several messages, each corresponding to an inbasket or outbasket mail item. The last item in the list has a field (LastPacketFlag) set in the message packet to help the workstation determine whether to issue further IPX receive operations to get the entire list. Inside the Packet field of the Message structure, the NLM builds a MailHeaderType structure such as that shown earlier in this section. The complete list of returned mail header items contains enough information for the workstation to display a useful selection of inbasket and outbasket items. The workstation can then ask the NLM to read one of the items on the workstation's behalf.

```
Message.MailID = MailSub;
Message.Sequence++;
memcpy(&IpxHeader.destNet, &IpxHeader.sourceNet, 10);
IpxHeader.destSocket = Socket;
IpxHeader.packetType = 4;
EventControlBlock.fragCount = 2L;
EventControlBlock.fragList[0].fragAddress = &IpxHeader;
EventControlBlock.fragList[0].fragSize = sizeof(IpxHeader);
EventControlBlock.fragList[1].fragAddress = &Message;
EventControlBlock.fragList[1].fragSize=Message.Length+10;

IpxSend(Socket, &EventControlBlock);
```

When a workstation sends a mail message request with an action code of Read A Mail Item, along with the identifying number of that mail item, the NLM edits the request to make sure that it is legitimate (ensuring that the logged-in user is in fact the mail recipient for that numbered mail item). The NLM then reads, in 500-byte blocks, the file that contains the mail item. The NLM uses the IPXSend() function to send each block of the mail message to the requesting workstation. The last IPX packet contains a flag (LastPacketFlag) that tells the workstation that the mail delivery is finished. In the Packet field of the first block, the NLM stores the mail item's header (envelope) information. The NLM uses the Packet field for each subsequent block of data from the file for that mail item.

Workstation software can ask the E-Mail Server NLM to deliver an outgoing mail item with an appropriate action code. The NLM puts the mail header of the new item into the in-memory index of outstanding mail and writes in the MAILBOX directory a file that contains the mail item. The workstation sends as many 500-byte packets to the NLM as necessary to transfer the mail item to the server. When the E-Mail NLM receives a packet that has the LastPacketFlag set, the mail item sits in the post office (the MAILBOX directory) until the recipient accesses his or her mailbox with a Do I have any mail? request.

When the E-Mail NLM receives from a workstation an IPX message packet with an action code that tells the NLM to delete a mail item, the NLM simply deletes the file and removes the mail item's in-memory index entry. Of course, the NLM first verifies that the user who is logged in at the workstation is the user identified as the recipient of the mail item.

Because IPX is a datagram-based protocol and thus does not guarantee delivery of LAN packets, the E-Mail NLM inserts a sequence number into each packet to coordinate with the workstation. The workstation can then determine whether it has received a complete set of responses from the NLM.

Compiling and Linking the NLM

After you install the Watcom compiler at a DOS or OS/2 workstation and set a couple of environment variables (as explained in the Watcom *C/C++ User's Guide* manual), you are ready to produce an NLM. If you have several C source files, you may want to create a makefile to handle the compile and link steps. For small projects, a batch file (.BAT for DOS or .CMD for OS/2) suffices. On the compiler's command line, use the options -mf (32-bit, flat memory model) and -NETWARE to tell WCC386.EXE what kind of code to produce.

Testing and Debugging NLMs

After you compile your NLM and install the executable file in the SYS:SYSTEM directory, you can test your software by issuing a LOAD command at the file server console. Before you start the testing process, however, consider that LAN users may be using the file server when you want to run your new NLM. In particular, consider how embarrassing it would be if your NLM crashed the file server and you had to announce over the intercom that you need to reboot the server. You definitely want to make special plans regarding the testing of your NLM. Either schedule after-hours access to the server or arrange to use a server on which nobody minds having to log in a few times each day.

The NetWare 3.12 and 4.0 network operating systems both provide a built-in debugger that you can use to monitor the behavior of your NLM as it runs. In addition, you can debug your NLM remotely, from your workstation, using the Watcom WVIDEO debugger. This debugger is also included with the Novell's Network C for NLMs SDK. In the debugger's manual (entitled simply *VIDEO*), you can find details on how to set up and use these debugging facilities.

Knowing When To Avoid NLMs

NLMs are fun to write and easy to use. However, the preceding discussion on debugging NLMs should have set off warning bells in your head. You must consider two drawbacks to NLM development. One drawback is major, the other minor. The major drawback is that your NLM might contain a bug that will eventually crash the file server unexpectedly, when many users are using the server. The minor drawback is the cost of NLM development. If you don't already have the Watcom 32-bit C compiler, you might find the NLM development learning curve a bit steep.

On the bright side, you can use NLMs to create a LAN that has less network traffic and that uses fewer unattended PCs to achieve a useful client/server environment. NLMs give you more control over the access to files, as demonstrated in the E- Mail Server example. Also, NLMs enable you to centralize application and utility functions. Although PCs certainly are not terribly expensive these days, your organization doesn't want to buy an individual computer for each single application task or utility function.

Writing the Workstation Software

If you want to put the E-Mail Server to actual use, you must do a little programming first. Exactly how much is up to you, but you'll at least have to write workstation software that uses IPX to communicate with the E-Mail NLM, sending and receiving the `Message` C structure packets previously described.

You can use any kind of workstation and operating system you prefer—Macintosh System 7, DOS, DOS-and-Windows, OS/2, or UNIX—as long as the workstation is part of a NetWare LAN. Send packets that contain the appropriate action codes to the NLM and listen for and process the NLM's responses; you should have no trouble creating a useful e-mail environment that works the way that you want and that has the user interface of your choice.

You'll think of many customizations, extensions, and enhancements for the E-Mail NLM itself. In particular, you might want to explore making the NLM multithreaded so that you can better handle greater volumes of mail on large LANs. Otherwise, the main NLM thread might fall behind when trying to keep up with a sudden in-rush of mail requests from several workstations. You can use code similar to the following to launch new threads in your NLM:

```
/* open a dynamic socket for each thread */
  ThreadSocket = 0;
  IpxOpenSocket(&ThreadSocket);
  SocketTable[SocketCount++] = ThreadSocket;

/* start a thread for this workstation */
  BeginThread(WorkstationThread, NULL, 8192, &ThreadSocket);

/* tell the workstation the socket # it needs to use */
  memcpy(&IpxHeaderOut.destNet,&IpxHeaderSave.sourceNet,12);
  MessageOut.ThreadSocket = ThreadSocket;
  IpxSend(Socket, &EventControlBlockOut);
```

Then, in each thread (WorkstationThread(), in the preceding example), you handle mail messages for a particular workstation. When the dialog with the workstation finishes, the thread function can simply terminate after closing files and IPX sockets.

You can extend the NLM to handle and deliver attached binary files. Depending on how you want to design your mail attachment mechanism, you might insert a new field into the message packet to indicate that a series of packets contains binary file material. If your LAN is part of a larger network (a wide area network, or WAN), you could enhance the NLM so that it operates on each NetWare file server and automatically exchanges mail that belongs in a different post office. You can even customize the NLM to handle the forwarding of mail, sending mail to groups of people based on personal address lists and distinguishing between regular recipients and carbon copy recipients.

Viewing Token Ring MAC-Layer Frames

Media access control (MAC) layer frames exist on a Token Ring LAN solely to help the network adapters manage themselves and keep the ring healthy. These frames exist within the Data Link layer of the OSI Model. You find MAC-layer frames on Token Ring networks but not on Ethernet networks. The network operating system and transport layer software (NetWare or LANtastic; NetBIOS or IPX) do not access MAC-layer frames. However, computer software can intercept, translate, and display MAC-layer frames to help you monitor and diagnose your network.

An active (on the ring) Token Ring adapter sends and receives MAC-layer frames entirely from within itself, regardless of the type of computer, operating system, or network operating system. The IEEE 802.5 specification defines the MAC-layer activity on your Token Ring LAN. The adapters communicate with each other every few seconds, interspersing their MAC-layer frames with the ordinary network operating system "work-to-do" frames. The MAC-layer frames enable the adapters to tell each other which frame is in charge, which is present, which is merely coughing, and which is terminally ill. The MAC-layer frames even enable the Token Ring adapters to keep track of which adapters are neighbors on the ring.

On a Token Ring LAN, neighbor relationships have nothing to do with the physical location of the workstations and servers in your building. Two Token Ring devices are neighbors if they have adjacent connections at the multistation access unit (MAU, or hub). In the simplest case, two side-by-side MAU ports are neighbors if both ports are active (that is, both ports connect to devices that are members of the ring). If a device is not presently a ring member, the device's MAU port does not count in the determination of neighbor relationships. Therefore, the MAU ports of two Token Ring neighbors might not be next to each other physically, because the ports between them may belong to devices that aren't even on the LAN.

This discussion of neighbor relationships isn't purely academic. When a device sends an error message, the error often is the result of a garbled or missing transmission from the device's upstream neighbor (the "nearest active upstream neighbor," or NAUN). To find the error's cause, you need to know the NAUN of the device that is signaling the error.

The MAC-layer frames that you are interested in are active monitor frames, standby monitor frames, claim token frames, ring purge frames, soft error report (isolating and nonisolating) frames, and beacon frames.

Understanding the Token Ring Language

MAC-layer frames, like all other Token Ring data messages, contain the fields described in Chapter 3, "PC-to-PC Communications Concepts." As shown in figure 3.6, SD is the start delimiter field, AC is the access control field, FC is the frame control field, DA is the destination address, SA is the source address, INFO is the data that the frame carries (often an IPX packet to or from a NetWare file server), FCS is the frame check sequence, ED is the end delimiter, and FS is the frame status field. On most networks, the destination address and source address fields are six bytes long. The length of the INFO (data) field varies from packet to packet, but the field's maximum length is about 4K on 4-megabit-per-second LANs and about 17K on 16-megabit-per-second LANs. A non-MAC-layer frame does its work by carrying data in the INFO field (often a file service packet, or perhaps an account ID and password during a login attempt). A MAC-layer frame, on the other hand, carries ring-management data in the INFO field.

The one-byte frame control field contains two subfields: frame type and MAC control ID. The two frame type bits (FF) have a value of 00 for MAC frames and 01 for other frames. (Bits 11 and 10 are reserved.) The MAC control ID bits identify the type of ring-management frame.

The *active monitor present* MAC-layer frame identifies the network adapter that is presently in charge of the ring. The active monitor keeps the network running. For example, the active monitor detects when one of the ring's network adapters fumbles the token, in which case the active monitor restarts the ring by creating and transmitting a fresh token. The active monitor also watches for and corrects other error situations. On receiving the active monitor present frame, the other network adapters on the ring transmit *standby monitor present* frames. To ensure that its address is unique, a network adapter sends the *duplicate address test* frame when it first joins the ring.

If a standby monitor suspects that the active monitor may have died, it sends *claim token* frames. Sent in the event of a major network problem, such as a broken cable or a workstation that is transmitting without waiting for the token, the *beacon* frame is the network's loudest cry for help. By detecting which workstation is sending the beacon frame ("beaconing"), diagnostic software can localize the problem and tell you the identity of the nearest active upstream neighbor involved in the beaconing. Occasionally (particularly after ring initialization and after a new active monitor establishes itself), the active monitor circulates a *ring purge* frame to help the ring "clear its throat."

Normal Frame Activity

About every six seconds, the network adapter designated the active monitor transmits an active monitor present frame. The active monitor addresses the frame to all the other adapters on the network. The other adapters respond by transmitting standby monitor present frames. If the standby monitors do not receive an active monitor present frame for several seconds, they broadcast claim token frames. The standby monitors then negotiate with one another to determine which adapter will become the new active monitor. Ordinarily, however, the active monitor retains its status until a user powers off or reboots that workstation. The active monitor can be any one of the Token Ring adapters on the network, but tends to be the adapter in the PC that has been powered on the longest.

A healthy Token Ring LAN that is in a steady state—with no one joining or leaving the ring—exhibits simple MAC-layer activity. This activity usually consists of transmitting active monitor present frames, standby monitor present frames, and some neighbor-notification frames. When a workstation, server, or other Token Ring-connected device joins or leaves the ring, the joining causes a brief electrical disruption of the ring. The disruption occurs as a relay inside the MAU closes or opens. The downstream device (the one to receive a frame or token next) senses the disruption and transmits a *soft error report* (error notification) frame. Typically, the downstream device categorizes the error as a Burst error, Line error, or perhaps a Token error. When a device causes one of these errors by joining or leaving the ring, it is as though the ring suddenly coughed or sneezed. A healthy ring experiences Burst, Line, or Token errors as the membership of the ring changes over time. Normally, some soft error report frames occur on a properly running Token Ring LAN.

Abnormal Frames

A soft error report frame can signal other conditions besides Burst, Line, and Token errors. A downstream device also uses the soft error report frame to notify other ring stations that a Receiver Congestion, an Internal, a Lost Frame, a Frame-copied, a Frequency, or an Access Control error has occurred. Receiver Congestion errors on your network may indicate a failing network adapter or perhaps a network adapter that simply cannot keep up with the traffic flow. Receiver congestion happens when a Token Ring adapter's input buffers are full and the adapter cannot accept an incoming frame. An adapter that reports an Internal error is trying to tell you that it is not feeling well and may soon fail. When an adapter fails to receive one of its own frames that the adapter is sending, the adapter signals a Lost Frame error. A Frame-copied error happens when an adapter recognizes a frame addressed to itself that another device has already recognized. Frequency errors usually signify serious cabling problems. An adapter reports an Access Control (A/C) error when the adapter receives a standby monitor present frame without first receiving an active monitor present frame.

Beacon frames are a dreaded occurrence on a Token Ring LAN. An adapter transmits beacon frames (that is, the adapter is *beaconing*) when that adapter detects silence on the cable (no token or data frame) from its upstream neighbor. To alert the other devices, the adapter sends beacon frames downstream to all the other devices on the ring. The adapter that is upstream of the beaconing adapter receives the beacon alert and sees that its downstream neighbor is complaining. If the beaconing condition results from a momentary adapter fault, the adapter sensing the problem eventually gets a signal from its upstream neighbor and the ring resumes normal operation.

During the beaconing condition, the two adapters associated with the fault (the one beaconing and its upstream neighbor) remove themselves from the ring and then attempt to reattach to the ring. If the condition results from a cable break, one or both of the adapters will fail to reattach and the remainder of the ring resumes normal operation. Therefore, during a beaconing condition, a workstation or two usually drop from the ring, after which the other users on the LAN resume their normal work.

When a beaconing condition resolves itself successfully, users at most workstations experience what seems to be a momentary pause in network access. In fact, the users may not notice the event at all. (Of course, if a file server is involved in the fault and drops from the ring, everyone on the LAN may be affected.)

However, not all beaconing situations solve themselves automatically. For each case, you must determine which ring devices are faulty. The Token Ring Monitoring program offered in the next section helps you identify the failing devices. The software even enables you to associate names with the Token Ring adapters on your LAN so you don't have to remember which node address belongs to a particular computer. Appendix O, "Source Listing for TOKENRNG.C," lists the source code, which is also included on the companion disk.

User Guide

The Token Ring Monitoring program intercepts MAC-layer frames, decodes those frames, and displays the result. The top of the screen identifies the active monitor, shows the number of standby monitors, counts the number of MAC-layer frames that have been received, and lists the Token Ring nodes that have reported errors. The bottom half of the screen displays MAC-layer frames, one by one, as events. The program writes a log file of events and error statistics, appending to the file each time that a Token Ring device reports an error. The program updates the top half (the node list) of the screen every six seconds but shows events in the bottom half of the screen as they occur.

You install the program by creating a directory on a DOS workstation and copying all three files into the directory. The DOS workstation doesn't need to have expanded memory, extended memory, or a high-resolution monitor. However, the workstation must be running the IBM LAN Support Program (the DXMA0MOD.SYS and DXMC0MOD.SYS device drivers) or equivalent. Thomas Conrad, for example, provides a set of drivers for its Token Ring adapters, and these drivers behave the same as IBM's LAN Support Program (LSP) drivers. Madge and Xircom also provide LSP-compliant software with their adapters.

When the program begins running, it looks for a file named USER.LST and, if the file is present, loads workstation node addresses and logon names into memory. You can create a USER.LST file for your LAN, if your network operating system is NetWare, simply by running the USERLIST NetWare utility. Use the /a command line parameter to cause USERLIST to show node addresses in the utility's output, and use the > redirection character to redirect the output to a file. The following command does the job nicely:

```
USERLIST /A >USER.LST
```

If you use another network operating system besides NetWare, a sample USER.LST file accompanies the software. You can edit this file to add whatever names and node addresses exist on your LAN. Make sure that you use the same format as the existing lines in the sample USER.LST file. The Token Ring Monitoring program displays node addresses rather than names if you don't create a USER.LST file for your LAN or if the program receives a frame from a device that you haven't named in USER.LST.

As the program begins collecting MAC-layer frames, you see the screen update periodically with notifications of error events and statistics. On a healthy network, your screen will indicate a few Burst errors, Token errors, or Line errors as computers join or leave the ring. However, you won't see anything else happen on the screen and will get bored—which is good. The Token Ring Monitoring program is not a shoot-down-the-aliens video game; little or no screen activity means that your LAN is operating normally.

If serious errors occur, however, you'll see the error counts escalate and the events causing the errors begin to fill your screen. Also, for a beaconing condition, the monitoring software sounds an alert through the PC's speaker. For any error condition, you should note the node address or logon name of the node reporting the error, and the node address or logon name of the nearest active upstream neighbor. These pieces of information, along with the error message and the information in this chapter, should help you locate the problem. You might need to use a cable tester to verify the cables between the nodes involved in the error, and you might need to run network adapter diagnostic software at the nodes. But just knowing that a problem exists and knowing which nodes are involved in the problem go a long way toward helping you keep your LAN running smoothly.

The program clears the statistical error counts for a node that hasn't reported a problem in over ten minutes. Therefore, as time passes and the network operates normally, entries disappear from your screen. However, when you stop the program by pressing Q, the log file TOKENRNG.LOG contains all the events and statistical error counts.

II

Network Programming

Programmer Guide

The Token Ring Monitoring software is a DOS-based computer program written in the C language. If you want to make changes, you have to compile the program using Borland C/C++ 3.0 or later. However, to begin understanding the chattering of your Token Ring adapters, you don't have to change or recompile the program; simply run the program as described earlier.

The first approach I took in developing Token Ring MAC-layer monitoring software didn't work at all. Knowing that Novell's Open Datalink Interface (ODI) drivers are popular on DOS-based PCs, I tried to build a computer program that uses ODI to intercept MAC-layer frames. The ODI technical reference manual identifies a `RegisterReceiveMonitor()` function and describes a method of using the function to eavesdrop on all the packets destined for a particular workstation. Unfortunately, I discovered that not all ODI MLID (Multiple Link Interface Driver) modules implement the `RegisterReceiveMonitor()` function, especially for MAC-layer frames. In fact, only after writing an entire program based on the ODI packet-interception function did I discover the problem. I had to scrap the effort.

The second approach fared much better. IBM's LAN Support Program device drivers offer a programming interface that enables software to open a special "station ID" for a Token Ring adapter. The special station ID receives only MAC-layer frames—which is exactly what I wanted. The driver software predefines station ID 1 as the target for any MAC-layer frames that a program might want to receive.

When opening the network adapter, the program uses a value of 0x7880 for the options parameter. This parameter enables the program to specify, for example, how the network adapter driver software should behave when errors occur, whether the adapter should participate in the token-claiming process, and other characteristics. Network adapters send active monitor present and standby monitor present frames to all the other adapters on the ring. Similarly, a beaconing adapter broadcasts the beacon frame to all the other adapters. For soft error report frames, however, an adapter sends the error notification to a specially designated functional address, the ring error monitor (REM). The functional address of the REM is C00000000008. To receive soft error report frames, the monitoring program registers itself on the LAN with this functional address.

> **Note**
>
> The IBM *Token Ring Network Architecture Reference* (SC30-3374) and the IBM *Local Area Network Technical Reference* (SC30-3383) manuals contain much more detail about Token Ring errors, functional addresses, and MAC-layer frames than this chapter could possibly cover. I used both manuals as I coded and tested the Token Ring Monitoring software.

Each MAC-layer frame carries a variable-length data record, or *vector*, that in turn contains subvectors. The vector identifies the frame as a soft error report, active monitor present, or other frame. The subvectors contain the node address of the sending adapter's nearest active upstream neighbor, error counts, and other detailed information. The vector consists of a four-byte LLID followed by one or more subvectors. The LLID contains a two-byte length field, a half-byte destination class field, a half-byte source class field, and a command byte. The destination class and source class fields identify the functional class to which the frame pertains (ring station, DLC.LAN.MANAGER, configuration report server, ring parameter server, or ring error monitor). The command byte identifies the type of MAC-layer frame.

Each subvector consists of a one-byte-long field, a subcommand byte, and a value. For a NAUN subvector, the value field contains the node address of the nearest active upstream neighbor of the sending adapter. For soft error report frames, one subvector contains isolating error counts, and another subvector contains nonisolating error counts. *Isolating errors* (the Line, Internal, Burst, A/C, and Abort Delimiter Transmitted errors) specifically identify the node address of the adapter (and its neighbor) causing the error. On the other hand, *nonisolating errors* (the Lost Frame, Receiver Congestion, Frame-copied, Frequency, and Token errors), don't always point to a specific network adapter but indicate a general error condition on the ring. For example, an adapter reporting a Receiver Congestion error may be perfectly healthy; the problem may be that an upstream adapter is jabbering away and the reporting station simply cannot handle the large volumes of incoming messages.

One part of the monitoring program executes asynchronously (and concurrently) with the remainder of the program. After initializing and opening the network adapter, the program issues a receive operation and gives the address of a subroutine (`RecDataApp()`) that the driver software should call when the adapter receives a MAC-layer frame. The subroutine puts the incoming frame into a cumulative table of frames and immediately reissues a receive operation. Each incoming MAC-layer frame causes the subroutine to execute, perhaps even while the program is displaying or counting already received frames. The remainder of the program extracts from the cumulative table the frames that have been received but not yet processed. The program then decodes and displays those frames. This approach enables the program to receive incoming MAC-layer frames rapidly without concern for how long it might take to decode, count, or display the frames.

Summary

This chapter presented six complete applications for you to study and use. Each application is described from both a user perspective and a programmer perspective. The Collision Tester is a tool that shows how your program behaves when it encounters already open files and already locked records. The NetBIOS Microscope is a menu-driven interface to NetBIOS that enables you to explore PC-to-PC communications easily. The Remote Program Execution (RPE) facility runs batch-type jobs and lets you treat one of the workstations on the LAN almost as a mainframe computer. The E-Mail programs implement LAN-based interoffice mail with an attached-file feature. The Post Office NLM shows the coding techniques that you use when you develop NetWare loadable modules. Finally, the Token Ring Monitoring program shows how to intercept and decode MAC-layer frames on a Token Ring network.

As gently and nicely as I possibly can, let me mention something to you at this point. Buying this book gives you the equivalent of a single-user license of the software. If you use any or all of the software on your LAN, or a modified derivative of the software, you should (for both moral and legal reasons) arrange to purchase a copy of this book for each user. Thank you for your support!

This chapter ends the narrative portion of this book. When you turn the page, you will be in the Reference section. As its name suggests, the Reference section is intended to be a source of detailed programming information that you can use as you design and code your LAN-aware applications.

Part III

Reference

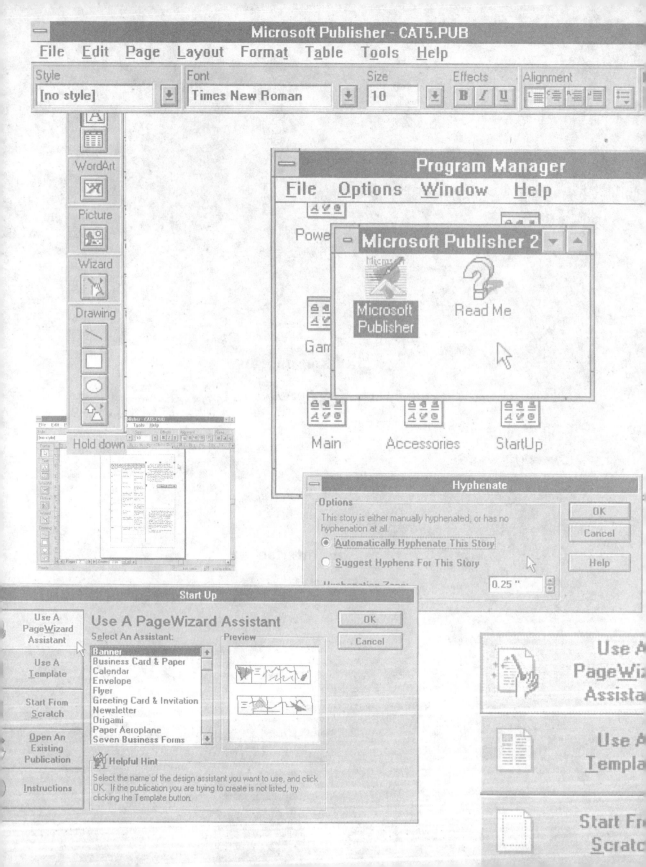

DOS Services for Network Programming

This section describes the DOS function calls that are related to network programming. Before issuing file-oriented function calls, you should make sure that SHARE.EXE, which enables file sharing in a DOS environment, is loaded. Chapter 4, "Shared File Programming," explains how to detect the presence of SHARE.

Create a File
0x3C

Description:

If the file does not exist, this function creates it. If the file exists, the function discards the existing contents by giving the file a length of 0 bytes. DOS then opens the file and returns a file handle. If specified in the CX register, a Read-Only file attribute takes effect only if the file did not previously exist. The Read-Only attribute also takes effect only after the file is closed; you can, of course, write to the file that you have just created. The file position is set to the first byte of the file.

Input Registers:

AH	0x3C
CX	File attributes
DS:DX	Far pointer to file name string

Output Registers:

Carry flag clear if successful

AX	File handle

Carry flag set if error

AX   Error codes:

03   Path Not Found

04   No Handles Left

05   Access Denied

Network Considerations:

If the file already exists and is marked Read-Only, an error is returned. If the file already exists and another workstation currently has it open, interrupt 24 (hex), the Critical-Error Handler, signals a sharing violation. You open the file with an Access mode of Read-Write and a Sharing mode of Compatibility. Under NetWare, the file is given the default attribute of NON-SHAREABLE. Also under NetWare, the user must have sufficient rights in the directory.

Invoked by C Library Functions:

creat(), open(), sopen(), and fopen()

Open a File
0x3D

Description:

If the file exists on the file server, and if there is no conflict among (1) how the file is already open by another workstation, (2) the file's current attribute, and (3) the intentions that you express in the Open mode field, the file is opened and a file handle is returned. The file position is set to the first byte of the file.

Input Registers:

AH   0x3D

DS:DX   Far pointer to file name string

AL   Open mode:

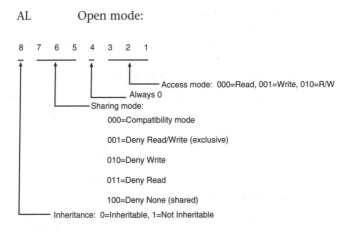

8   7   6   5   4   3   2   1

Access mode: 000=Read, 001=Write, 010=R/W
Always 0
Sharing mode:
    000=Compatibility mode
    001=Deny Read/Write (exclusive)
    010=Deny Write
    011=Deny Read
    100=Deny None (shared)
Inheritance: 0=Inheritable, 1=Not Inheritable

Output Registers:

Carry flag if clear

    AX   File handle

Carry flag set if error

    AX   Error codes:

        02   File Not Found

        03   Path Not Found

        04   No Handles Left

        05   Access Denied

Network Considerations:

If you try to open in Compatibility mode a file that another workstation has already opened in any other mode, Interrupt 24 (hex), the Critical-Error Handler, signals a sharing violation. Under NetWare, if you open a file marked Read-Only with an Access mode of Read-Write, an entry in the SHELL.CFG file controls whether an error is returned to your program when you try to open or write to the file. (This entry is the READ ONLY COMPATIBILITY = ON statement.)

Invoked by C Library Functions:

fopen(), open(), and sopen()

IOCTL—Is Drive Remote?
0x4409

Description:

This function returns an indication of whether a logical drive is local or remote.

Input Registers:

AH	0x44
AL	9
BL	Drive number (0 = default, 1 = A:, 3 = C:, and so on)

Output Registers:

DX	Bit 12 (bitmask 0x1000) = 1 if the drive is remote, 0 if local

Network Considerations:

CD-ROM drives also return a "drive is remote" indication (see Chapter 4, "Shared File Programming").

C Library Function:

The following function, is_drive_remote(), takes the single parameter drive_num and returns 1 if the drive is remote, or 0 if it is local:

```
#include <dos.h>

int     is_drive_remote(int drive_num)
        {
        union REGS regs;

        regs.x.ax = 0x4409;
        regs.h.bl = (unsigned char) drive_num;
        int86(0x21, &regs, &regs);
        if ((regs.x.dx & 0x1000) == 0x1000)
            return 1;
        return 0;
        }
```

IOCTL—Is Handle Remote?
0x440A

Description:

This function returns an indication of whether a file handle is for a local or remote file.

Input Registers:

AH	0x44
AL	0x0A
BX	File handle

Output Registers:

DX	Bit 15 (bitmask 0x8000) = 1 if handle is remote, 0 if local

Network Considerations:

Files on CD-ROM drives also return an indication that the handle is remote.

C Library Function:

The following function, is_handle_remote(), takes the single parameter file_handle and returns 1 if the handle is remote, 0 if it is local:

```
#include <dos.h>

int    is_handle_remote(int file_handle)
    {
    union REGS regs;

    regs.x.ax = 0x440A;
    regs.x.bx = file_handle;
    int86(0x21, &regs, &regs);
    if ((regs.x.dx & 0x8000) == 0x8000)
        return 1;
    return 0;
    }
```

III

Reference

Set Sharing Retry Count/Delay 0x440B

Description:

This function sets the number of retries that DOS performs, as well as the delay between tries, when a file-sharing or record-locking conflict occurs. If the condition persists after the specified number of retries, an error is returned to your program (or a sharing violation is handled as a critical error; see Chapter 2, "Multiuser Concepts"). Each delay loop consists of a simple "do-nothing" sequence:

```
XOR    CX, CX      ; zero the CX register
back:
LOOP back          ; cycle 64K times
```

DOS uses the following default values: 1 loop = 1 delay period, and retries = 3. Note that the loop is sensitive to the speed of the CPU on which it executes; faster workstations have shorter delay periods.

Input Registers:

AH	0x44
AL	0x0B
CX	Number of CPU loops (equals 1 delay period)
DX	Number of retries

Output Registers:

None	Error codes:
	None

Network Considerations:

See the Description.

C Library Function:

The following function, set_retries(), takes two parameters: retry_count and delay_loops. The function returns nothing.

```
#include <dos.h>

void    set_retries(unsigned retry_count, unsigned delay_loops)
    {
    union REGS regs;

    regs.x.ax = 0x440B;
    regs.x.cx = delay_loops;
    regs.x.dx = retry_count;
    int86(0x21, &regs, &regs);
    }
```

Create Unique File
0x5A

Description:

This function is exactly like Create a File (function 3C), except that the file
name is generated by DOS rather than by you, and the name is guaranteed to
be unique in the target directory. The same caveats as mentioned for Create a
File regarding permissions and Compatibility mode apply. You indicate the
directory in which the unique file should be created. This function is useful
for creating temporary files that must be specific to each workstation.

Input Registers:

AH   0x5A

CX   File attributes

DS:DX   Far pointer to the directory name string.
The final character of the string must be
a backslash, as in H:\\MYAPP\\. The string
area must be large enough to hold the directory
name plus the generated file name.

Output Registers:

Carry flag clear if successful

AX   File handle if the carry flag is clear

DS:DX Far pointer to the directory name string
to which the unique file name has been
appended

III

Reference

> Carry flag set if error
>
>> AX   Error codes:
>>
>>> 03   Path Not Found
>>>
>>> 04   No Handles Left

Network Considerations:

See Create a File (function 3C).

Invoked by C Library Functions:

creattemp(), tmpfile(), tmpnam(), and tempnam()

Create New File
0x5B

Description:

This function is exactly like Create a File (function 3C), except that 5B fails if the file already exists. The same caveats regarding permissions and Compatibility mode apply as for function 3C.

Input Registers:

> AH   0x5B
>
> CX   File attributes
>
> DS:DX   Far pointer to file name string

Output Registers:

> Carry flag clear if successful
>
>> AX   File handler
>
> Carry flag set if error
>
>> AX   Error codes:
>>
>>> 03   Path Not Found
>>>
>>> 04   No Handles Left
>>>
>>> 05   Access Denied

Network Considerations:
See Create a File (function 3C).

Invoked by C Library Functions:
creatnew( )

Lock/Unlock File Region
0x5C

Description:
This function locks or unlocks a given number of bytes in a file, starting at
a certain file position. Other workstations are denied access to the file region
from the time it is locked until the time it is unlocked. You can lock several regions, but they cannot overlap. Each locked region must be unlocked
individually; a single call cannot unlock physically adjacent locked areas.
If another workstation attempts to read from or write to the locked region,
Interrupt 24 (hex), the Critical-Error Handler, signals a sharing violation.
If another workstation attempts to lock all or any part of an already locked
region, Access Denied is returned to the program running on that workstation. You must unlock each locked region before your program terminates.
Locking beyond the end-of-file is not an error.

Input Registers:

AH	0x5C
AL	0 to lock, 1 to unlock
BX	File handle
CX:DX	File position (start of region)
SI:DI	Length of region

Output Registers:
Carry flag set if error

AX	Error code if carry flag is set:
	05 Access Denied

III

Reference

Network Considerations:

Some network operating systems clear dangling locks for you when your program terminates, but you should not rely on this behavior.

Invoked by C Library Functions:

lock(), lockf(), locking(), rlock(), and runlk()

Get Machine Name
0x5E00

Description:

This function obtains the workstation's machine name and NetBIOS name number, if they are available. The name, a 15-character string with a null byte in the 16th character, is padded on the right with spaces.

Input Registers:

AX	0x5E00
DS:DX	Far pointer to machine name string

Output Registers:

Carry flag clear if successful

CH	0 if name and number are not present
CL	NetBIOS name number
DS:DX	Far pointer to filled-in machine name

Carry flag set if error

AX	Error code:
	01 Invalid Function (if the network is not active)

Network Considerations:

The machine name may not be set in all cases. Duplicate machine names are possible.

Invoked by C Library Function:

Use the following library routine:

```
#include <dos.h>

/* pass back Machine Name and Name Number, if available, */
/* in the name/number fields. */
/* return 0 if not available, else return 1 */

int    get_machine_name(char *name, int *number)
    {
    union REGS regs;
    struct SREGS sregs;

    regs.x.ax = 0x5E00;
    regs.x.dx = FP_OFF( (void far *) name);
    sregs.ds  = FP_SEG( (void far *) name);
    int86x(0x21, &regs, &regs, &sregs);
    if (regs.h.ch == 0)
        return 0;
    number = (int) regs.h.cl;
    return 1;
    }
```

Set Machine Name
0x5E01

Description:

This undocumented function call sets the machine name and name number for later retrieval by Get Machine Name (function 5E00). Before calling this function, you must prepare the name carefully. Pad the name on the right with spaces, and make the string 15 characters long by putting a null byte in the 16th position.

Input Registers:

AX   0x5E01

CL   Name number

DS:DX   Far pointer to machine name string

Output Registers:

Carry flag set if error

     AX   Error code:

         01   Invalid Function (if the network is not active)

Network Considerations:

If NetBIOS is loaded, you should not need this function; it is useful only on non-NetBIOS LANs.

C Library Function:

The following set_machine_name() routine sets machine name and name number:

```
#include <dos.h>

void    set_machine_name(char *name, int number)
    {
    union REGS regs;
    struct SREGS sregs;

    regs.x.ax = 0x5E01;
    regs.x.dx = FP_OFF( (void far *) name);
    sregs.ds  = FP_SEG( (void far *) name);
    regs.h.cl = (unsigned char) number;
    int86x(0x21, &regs, &regs, &sregs);
    }
```

Set Printer Setup
0x5E02

Description:

This function call designates a printer Setup String of up to 64 bytes. These bytes are sent to the network printer each time the printer is opened as a file. With this function, each user of a shared printer can set the printer into a particular mode (character pitch, font, page orientation, and so on) for generating printouts from that user's workstation. Before you invoke this function, you must know the shared printer's Redirection List Index; you usually can obtain this list by calling Get Redirection List Entry (function 5F02).

Input Registers:

AX	0x5E02
BX	Redirection List Index for the specified printer
CX	Setup String length (0–64)
DS:SI	Far pointer to Setup String

Output Registers:

Carry flag set if error

AX   Error code:

01   Invalid Function (if the network is not active)

Network Considerations:

If one workstation uses this function, all workstations should use it.
Otherwise, the network printer is left as set by the most recent user of
this function.

Invoked by C Library Function:

Use the following:

```
#include <dos.h>

void    set_printer_setup(int index, char *setup, int len)
    {
    union REGS regs;
    struct SREGS sregs;

    regs.x.ax = 0x5E02;
    regs.x.bx = index;
    regs.x.cx = len;
    regs.x.si = FP_OFF( (void far *) setup);
    sregs.ds  = FP_SEG( (void far *) setup);
    int86x(0x21, &regs, &regs, &sregs);
    }
```

Get Printer Setup
0x5E03

Description:

This function obtains any Setup String specified in the latest Set Print Setup
call.

Input Registers:

AX   0x5E03

BX   Redirection List Index

ES:DI   Far pointer to Setup String buffer
          (maximum 64 bytes)

Output Registers:

Carry flag clear if successful

CX   Length of returned Setup String

ES:DI   Far pointer to Setup String
(now filled in)

Carry flag set if error

AX   Error code:

01   iInvalid Function (if the network is not active)

Network Considerations:

See Set Printer Setup (function 5E02).

Invoked by C Library Function:

Use the following:

```
#include <dos.h>

void    get_printer_setup(int index, char *setup, int *len_ptr)
    {
    union REGS regs;
    struct SREGS sregs;

    regs.x.ax = 0x5E03;
    regs.x.bx = index;
    regs.x.di = FP_OFF( (void far *) setup);
    sregs.es  = FP_SEG( (void far *) setup);
    int86x(0x21, &regs, &regs, &sregs);
    *len_ptr = regs.x.cx;
    }
```

Get Redirection List Entry
0x5F02

Description:

This function returns information about a particular redirected disk or printer device, for a given Redirection List Index value. A call establishes each entry to the Redirect Device function (5F03), which is normally issued only by network operating system software. You must perform a series of calls (one for each Redirection List Index value) to obtain all redirections. When the list is exhausted, error code 12 (hex) is returned. The information returned for each call consists of the following:

■ The local device name string (such as H:\)

- The network device name string (such as \\SERVER\C:)

- The device status flag

- The device type

- A user-defined parameter

Input Registers:

AX   0x5F02

BX   Redirection List Index

DS:SI   Far pointer to 128-byte local
device name

ES:DI   Far pointer to 128-byte network
device name

Output Registers:

Carry flag clear if successful

BH   Device status

76543210

............0 Device is valid

............1 Device is invalid

xxxxxxx.   Reserved

BL   Device type (3 = printer, 4 = file)

CX   Stored user-defined parameter

DX   Undefined (register not preserved)

DS:SI   Far pointer to filled-in local name

ES:DI   Far pointer to filled-in network name

III

Reference

Carry flag set if error

AX   Error codes:

0x01 Invalid function (if the network
is not active)

0x12 No more entries

01   Invalid Function (if the network is not active)

0x12 No more entries

Note that DX and BP are not preserved across the call.

Network Considerations:
Under the PC LAN Program, the user-defined two-byte parameter should not be used.

Invoked by C Library Function:
Use the following:

```
/* for a Redirection Index value, get local_name, */
/* network_name, et al.  Return 0 if successful,   */
/* else return DOS error code.                     */

#include <dos.h>

int    get_redirection_entry(int index,
                             char *local_name,
                             char *network_name,
                             int  *device_status,
                             int  *device_type,
                             int  *stored_parm)
    {
    union REGS regs;
    struct SREGS sregs;

    regs.x.ax = 0x5F02;
    regs.x.bx = index;
    regs.x.si = FP_OFF( (void far *) local_name);
    sregs.ds  = FP_SEG( (void far *) local_name);
    regs.x.di = FP_OFF( (void far *) network_name);
    sregs.es  = FP_SEG( (void far *) network name);
    int86x(0x21, &regs, &regs, &sregs);
    if (regs.x.cflag)
        return regs.x.ax;
    *device_type   = (int) regs.h.bl;
    *device_status = (int) regs.h.bh;
    *stored_parm   = (int) regs.x.cx;
    return 0;
    }
```

Redirect Device
0x5F03

Description:
This function sets up the relationship between a network device and its local workstation name, for both disk drives and printers. Application programs rarely should use this function; use existing redirections where possible.

Input Registers:

AX	0x5F03
BL	Device type (3 = printers, 4 = file)
CX	Parameter value (retrievable with Get Redirection ListEntry, function 5F02)
DS:SI	Far pointer to local name string
ES:DI	Far pointer to network name string

Output Registers:
Carry flag set if error

AX   Error code:

01   Invalid Function (if the network
is not active)

Network Considerations:
For compatibility with the PC LAN Program, the parameter value should always be 0. If you use this function to redirect a device, it is not visible in the display produced when you issue a NET USE command.

Invoked by C Library Function:
Use the following library code:

```
#include <dos.h>

int     redirect_device(int type,
                        char *local_name,
                        char *network_name)
    {
    union REGS regs;
    struct SREGS sregs;
```

III

Reference

```
regs.x.ax = 0x5F03;
regs.h.bl = (unsigned char) type;
regs.x.cx = 0;
regs.x.si = FP_OFF( (void far *) local_name);
sregs.ds  = FP_SEG( (void far *) local_name);
regs.x.di = FP_OFF( (void far *) network_name);
sregs.es  = FP_SEG( (void far *) network_name);
int86x(0x21, &regs, &regs, &sregs);
if (regs.x.cflag)
    return regs.x.ax;
return 0;
}
```

Cancel Redirection
0x5F04

Description:

This function terminates a logical local-name-to-network-name relationship established with the Redirect Device function call. You can cancel redirections only in the same program or process that created the redirection.

Input Registers:

AX   0x5F04

DS:SI   Far pointer to redirected local name string

Output Registers:

Carry flag set if error

AX   Error Code:

01   Invalid Function (if the network is not active)

Network Considerations:

After a redirection is terminated, the logical drive or device name (for example, F: or LPT1) reverts to whatever meaning it had before the redirection. For a disk drive, this usually means that DOS goes back to treating the drive as an "Invalid Drive Specification"; for a printer, printouts appear on the local printer if a local printer exists.

Invoked by C Library Function:

Use the following library code:

```
#include <dos.h>

int    cancel_redirection(char *local_name)
    {
    union REGS regs;
    struct SREGS sregs;

    regs.x.ax = 0x5F04;
    regs.x.si = FP_OFF( (void far *) local_name);
    sregs.ds  = FP_SEG( (void far *) local_name);
    int86x(0x21, &regs, &regs, &sregs);
    if (regs.x.cflag)
        return regs.x.ax;
    return 0;
    }
```

Commit File
0x68

Description:

This function causes file data in DOS buffers to be written to disk.

Input Registers:

AH	0x68
BX	File handle

Output Registers:

Carry flag set if error

AX	Error code:
	06 Invalid Handle

Network Considerations:

None.

C Library Function:

```
int    flush(int handle)
    {
    union REGS regs;

    regs.h.ah = 0x68;
    regs.x.bx = handle;
    int86(0x21, &regs, &regs);
    if (regs.x.cflag)
        return regs.x.ax;
    return 0;
    }
```

DLR and PCLP Programming Services

The programming services available under the IBM DOS LAN Requester (DLR) and PC LAN Program (PCLP) are explained in this section. Interrupts 2A (hex) and 2F (hex) are used to call these functions, rather than Interrupt 21 (hex). See the cautions in Chapter 4, "Shared File Programming," regarding the use of Interrupt 2F with DOS versions earlier than 3.0.

Interface Installation Check
Int 2A

Description:
This service returns an indication of whether the Int 2A Interface is installed.

Input Registers:

    AH   0

Output Registers:

    AH   0   Not installed

                1   Installed

Error Codes:
None

C Library Function Code:
isnet(), or use the following:

```
#include <dos.h>

int   int_2A_installed(void)
      {
      union REGS regs;
```

```
regs.h.ah = 0;
int86(0x2A, &regs, &regs);
if (regs.h.ah == 0)
return 0;
return 1;
}
```

Network Print Stream Control
Int 2A

Description:

This service sets the mode used by DOS LAN Requester or PC LAN Program to determine when one printout ends and another begins. The service also is used to indicate the end of a printout. In truncation mode (the default), the end of a print stream is indicated by any one of the following:

- End of program

- Opening and closing of the file names LPT1, LPT2, or LPT3

- Switching to or from printing through DOS and printing through Interrupt 17 (hex)

- Printing through Interrupt 17 (hex) from different programs (processes)

In concatenation mode, these conditions are ignored; the only delimiter or transition recognized in this mode is when COMMAND.COM issues a new DOS prompt after executing one complete program or complete .BAT file.

Input Registers:

AH	6	
AL	1	Set concatenation mode
	2	Set truncation mode
	3	Signal end-of-print-stream (truncate it)

Output Registers:

AX	DOS error code if carry flag set

C Library Function Code:

```
#include <dos.h>

int   print_stream_control(int flag)
    {
    union REGS regs;
```

```
regs.h.ah = 6;
regs.h.al = (unsigned char) flag;
int86(0x2A, &regs, &regs);
if (regs.x.cflag)
return regs.x.ax;
return 0;
}
```

Check Direct I/O
Int 2A

Description:
This service returns an indication of whether Interrupts 25 (hex), 26 (hex), or
13 (hex) can do direct disk I/O (at the sector level rather than the file level)
for a particular disk device.

Input Registers:
AH	3
AL	0
DS:SI	Far pointer to a disk device name string (example string: F:)

Output Registers:
Carry flag	0 (clear) if direct I/O allowed
	1 (set) if access through direct I/O is not allowed

C Library Function Code:
```
#include <dos.h>

int direct_io_allowed(char *device_name)
  {
  union REGS regs;
  struct SREGS sregs;

  regs.x.ax = 0x0300;
  regs.x.si = FP_OFF( (void far *) device_name);
  sregs.ds  = FP_SEG( (void far *) device_name);
  int86x(0x2A, &regs, &regs, &sregs);
  if (regs.x.cflag)
  return 0;
  return 1;
  }
```

III

Reference

Execute NetBIOS with Error Retry
Int 2A

Description:

This small, extra layer of software provides an additional interface to NetBIOS beyond that offered by the usual Interrupt 5C (hex) NetBIOS entry point. For these NetBIOS error codes, this interface performs automatic retries:

0x09	No Resource Available
0x12	Session Open Rejected
0x21	Interface Busy

Input Registers:

AH	4
AL	0
ES:BX	Far pointer to a network control block (see Chapter 5 for NCB definition)

Output Registers:

AH	0	No error occurred
	1	Error
AL		NetBIOS error code if AH = 1

C Library Function Code:

```c
#include <dos.h>

int   call_netbios_with_retry(void *ncb_ptr)
   {
   union REGS regs;
   struct SREGS sregs;

   regs.x.ax = 0x0400;
   regs.x.bx = FP_OFF( (void far *) ncb_ptr);
   sregs.es  = FP_SEG( (void far *) ncb_ptr);
   int86x(0x2A, &regs, &regs, &sregs);
   if (regs.h.ah == 0)
   return 0;
       regs.h.ah = 0;
   return regs.x.ax;
   }
```

Execute NetBIOS with No Error Retry
Int 2A

Description:

This small, extra layer of software provides an additional interface to NetBIOS beyond that offered by the usual Interrupt 5C (hex) NetBIOS entry point. No automatic error retry support is provided.

Input Registers:

AH	4
AL	1
ES:BX	Far pointer to a network control block (see Chapter 5 for NCB definition)

Output Registers:

AH	0	No error occurred
	1	Error
AL		NetBIOS error code if AH = 1

C Library Function Code:

```
#include <dos.h>

int        call_netbios_no_retry(void *ncb_ptr)
  {
  union REGS regs;
  struct SREGS sregs;

  regs.x.ax = 0x0401;
  regs.x.bx = FP_OFF( (void far *) ncb_ptr);
  sregs.es  = FP_SEG( (void far *) ncb_ptr);
  int86x(0x2A, &regs, &regs, &sregs);
  if (regs.h.ah == 0)
  return 0;
  regs.h.ah = 0;
  return regs.x.ax;
  }
```

Get Network Resource Information
Int 2A

Description:

This service asks PC LAN Program or DOS LAN Requester how many network resources remain for your use after PCLP or DLR has established its sessions with the file server. These resources are the number of network names, the number of network commands, and the number of network sessions. (See Chapter 5 for an explanation of these resources.)

Input Registers:

AH	5
AL	0

Output Registers:

AX	Reserved
BX	Number of network names available
CX	Number of network commands available
DX	Number of network sessions available

C Library Function Code:

```
#include <dos.h>

void        get_net_info(int *names, int *commands, int *sessions)
   {
   union REGS regs;

   regs.x.ax = 0x0500;
   int86(0x2A, &regs, &regs);
   *names    = regs.x.bx;
   *commands = regs.x.cx;
   *sessions = regs.x.dx;
   }
```

DOS LAN Requester Installed Check
Int 2F

Description:

This service returns whether PCLP or the DOS LAN Requester is installed, and, if it is installed, returns configuration information. This configuration information tells you whether PCLP or DLR is running on this workstation as a redirector or receiver.

Input Registers:

AH	0xB8 (multiplex number for PCLP and DLR)
AL	0

Output Registers:

AL   0 = PCLP or DLR is not installed

Nonzero = PCLP or DLR installed

BX   Bit flags for configuration information:

Bitmask	Configuration
0x0080	Receiver
0x0008	Redirector

C Library Function Code:

```
#include <dos.h>

int        dlr_installed(void)
   {
   union REGS regs;

   regs.x.ax = 0xB800;
   int86(0x2F, &regs, &regs)
   if (regs.h.al == 0)
   return 0;
   if ( (regs.x.bx & 0x0080) == 0x0080)
   return 2;
   if ( (regs.x.bx & 0x0008) == 0x0008)
   return 1;
   return -1;
   }
```

DOS LAN Requester Version Information
Int 2F

Description:

This service returns the Major and Minor version of the DOS LAN Requester, if it is installed. Do not use this service to determine the installed state of the DOS LAN Requester.

Input Registers:

AH   B8

AL   9

Output Registers:

AH   Minor version number

AL   Major version number

III

Reference

C Library Function Code:

```
#include <dos.h>

void        get_dlr_version(int *major, int *minor)
    {
    union REGS regs;

    regs.x.ax = 0xB809;
    int86(0x2F, &regs, &regs);
    *major = (int) regs.h.al;
    *minor = (int) regs.h.ah;
    }
```

DOS LAN Requester Logon ID
Int 2A

Description:

This function call provides the user ID and logon status information for the person currently logged on at this DLR workstation.

Input Registers:

AH	78
AL	2
ES:DI	Pointer to a nine-byte logon name buffer

Output Registers:

AL	Zero if no one logged on
	Nonzero if a logon is active
ES:DI	Points to a blank-padded, ASCIIZ logon name

C Library Function Code:

```
#include <dos.h>

void        get_logon_id(char *logon_name, int *status_ptr)
    {
    union REGS regs;
    struct SREGS sregs;

    regs.x.ax = 0x7802;
    regs.x.di = FP_OFF( (void far *) logon_name);
    sregs.es  = FP_SEG( (void far *) logon_name);
    int86x(0x2A, &regs, &regs, &sregs);
    *status_ptr = (int) regs.h.al;
    }
```

Novell's Extended DOS Services

Several categories of services are available to an application running on a NetWare workstation. This section explains each of the function calls in these frequently used categories:

- Bindery Services

- Connection Services

- Print Services

- Synchronization Services

- Transaction Tracking Services

- Workstation Services

NetWare's IPX and SPX services for PC-to-PC communications are described separately in their own section.

NetWare offers a few other categories of programmer services that this section does not cover. You probably won't need these services to develop your application programs. These other categories include the following:

- Accounting Services

- AppleTalk Services

- Diagnostic Services

- Directory Services

- File Server Services

- Server-based Message Services

- Queue Services

- Service Advertising Services

- Value Added Process (VAP) Services

If you want to use any of the services in these categories, Novell offers the NetWare Client SDK, the documentation of which explains these APIs in depth.

Numeric Formats and Buffer Lengths

NetWare defines the format of multibyte numeric items a little differently from the native representation internal to the PC. Instead of expecting the least significant byte first, NetWare looks for the most significant byte first. This means that you must swap the bytes of int and long items as you fill in the structures for each of the functions in this section.

The following typedefs denote these high-byte-first items:

```
typedef struct NW_INT
    {
    unsigned char high_byte;
    unsigned char low_byte;
    } nw_int;

typedef struct NW_LONG
    {
    unsigned char highest_byte;
    unsigned char higher_byte;
    unsigned char lower_byte;
    unsigned char lowest_byte;
    } nw_long;
```

Also note that the buffer_length field in each of the following request_buffer and reply_buffer data structures does not include itself as part of the length. Make sure that you set the buffer_length field in both the request_buffer and reply_buffer structures before you call a function.

Bindery Services

Not only can you use the information in this category in your applications, but the information also helps explain what goes on within NetWare itself. Although they function somewhat more abstractly than other NetWare services, Bindery Services reveal the interesting architecture of Novell's LAN operating system.

Two hidden files, NET$BIND.SYS and NET$BVAL.SYS, exist in the SYS:SYSTEM directory of each NetWare 2.x or 3.x file server. NetWare 4.x can optionally emulate the presence of the NET$BIND.SYS and NET$BVAL.SYS files, through *Bindery Emulation*. These files contain information about the users and other entities that can use the file server. The information is hierarchical, in three levels:

- Each entity (or *object*)

- Each object's *property* or *properties*

- Each property's *value* or *values*

NetWare versions 2.x, 3.x, and (through optional Bindery Services emulation) 4.x use the bindery internally to maintain the list of user IDs, passwords, groups, and security equivalences. If you follow the conventions discussed in this section, you can also use Bindery Services in your NetWare-specific applications.

Objects

The following information is maintained about each object:

- Object ID number

- Object name

- Object type

- Object flag

- Object security

- Properties flag

Object ID is a four-byte number that NetWare assigns to each object. The high-order byte is stored first (in contrast to the CPU's native representation for numeric items, which is low-byte first).

Object name is a 48-byte field that contains a null-terminated string of printable characters; for a user, this is the user ID.

Each entity is classed according to its *object type*:

Entity	Object Type
Unknown	0x0000
User	0x0001
User group	0x0002
Print queue	0x0003
File server	0x0004
Job server	0x0005
Gateway	0x0006
Print server	0x0007
Archive queue	0x0008
Archive server	0x0009
Job queue	0x000A
Administration	0x000B
Remote bridge	0x0026
Reserved	Up to 0x8000
Wild-card object type	0xFFFF (–1)

Object flag defines an object as being either static (0x00) or dynamic (0x01). Static objects are explicitly created and deleted, but dynamic objects exist only until the file server is rebooted (or until the object is deleted).

The *object security* field expresses which users are granted access for the following:

- ■ Viewing the information in the bindery for an object

- ■ Modifying the information

Security permission levels for both types of access are encoded in four bits (one nibble) each:

Access Level	Object Security
Anyone	0 0 0 0
Logged in	0 0 0 1

Access Level	Object Security
Object itself	0 0 1 0
Supervisor	0 0 1 1
NetWare only	0 1 0 0

The *properties Flag* indicates whether the object has one or more properties associated with it (0 = no properties; 0xFF = at least one property).

Properties of an Object

The following information is maintained for each property of an object:

- Property name
- Property flags
- Property security
- Property values flag

Property flags indicate two things: whether the property is static or dynamic, and whether the property is an item or a set, as defined by the two low-order bits of the field:

Bit Position	Meaning
76543210	
.......0	Static
.......1	Dynamic
......0.	Item
......1.	Set
xxxxxx..	Reserved

An item property has a value that is maintained inside the bindery but not recognized by Bindery Services. The user name is an example of an item property. On the other hand, Bindery Services defines a set property as a list of object ID numbers. An example of set property is the list of users (object names) in a user group, where the group is an *object* with a *set property* whose *property value* consists of the list (set) of member users.

III

Reference

Property name identifies the property and can be from 1 to 15 characters long. Programmers can define their own names; however, Novell defines the following names:

    LOGIN_CONTROL
    ACCOUNT_SERVERS
    ACCOUNT_BALANCE
    PASSWORD
    SECURITY_EQUALS
    GROUP_MEMBERS
    GROUPS_I'M_IN
    NET_ADDRESS
    IDENTIFICATION
    OPERATORS

Property security determines who can access the property for either viewing or updating. It is similar to object security and has the same encoding.

The *property values flag* indicates whether a property has a value (0x00 = no value present, 0xFF = value present).

Values of a Property

The values of a property are maintained in 128-byte segment records. More than one segment can exist. Each segment is numbered, and each Read or Write operation that you specify deals with one entire segment.

Filling in the Structs

Many of the structs used by the Bindery Services functions include a name field preceded by a name_length field, as in the following example:

```
typedef unsigned int    word;
typedef unsigned char   byte;

struct  {
        word buffer_len
        byte name_length;      /* Set to 48 */
        char name [48];
        byte object_flag;
        } request_buffer;
```

For each of these "name-length" fields, the length value tells NetWare the size of the next field (name). For example, if you put a value of 6 in the name_length field, NetWare expects the name field to be declared as follows:

```
char      name [6];
```

If you want to use the same struct to refer to any possible name, you should always set the name_length field to a value that represents the maximum size of the name field:

```
request_buffer.name_length = 48;
strcpy(request_buffer.name, "BARRY");
```

Because the string that you put in the name field is null-terminated (that is, it is a normal C string), NetWare properly uses only the portion of the name up to the terminating (/0) byte. The length field tells NetWare where the next field begins (not necessarily the length of the name string itself). The alternative is not to use a struct at all, but to build a memory area "on the fly." This alternative approach is more difficult to code. The simpler approach is shown here.

Finally, to set the buffer_len field, you can code

```
request_buffer.buffer_len = sizeof(request_buffer) - 2;
```

because the buffer_len field expresses the total length of the struct, but does not include itself.

Add Bindery Object to Set
0xE3, type 0x41

Description:
This service adds an object to a set property. The member_object_type and member_object_name that you specify are used to check that object's object ID, and the result is added to the set of values for the specified property.

Request Buffer:
```
struct
    {
    word     buffer_length;
    byte     type;
    nw_int   object_type;
    byte     object_name_length;
    char     object_name[48];
    byte     property_name_length;
    char     property_name[16];
    nw_int   member_object_type;
    byte     member_object_length;
    char     member_object_name[48];
    } request_buffer;
```

Reply Buffer:
```
struct
    {
    word     buffer_length;
    } reply_buffer;
```

III

Reference

Input Registers:

AH	0xE3
DS:SI	Far pointer to `request_buffer`
ES:DI	Far pointer to `reply_buffer`

Output Registers:

AL   Completion codes:

0x00 Success

0x96 Server out of memory

0xE9 Member already exists

0xEB Not a set property

0xF0 Wild card not allowed

0xF8 No privilege to modify property

0xFB No such property

0xFC No such object

0xFE Server bindery locked

0xFF Bindery failure

Change Bindery Object Password
0xE3, type 0x40

Description:

This service changes the password of an object. If the object does not already have a property named PASSWORD, one is added to the object with a property security of 0x44 (NetWare-only, Read-Write). Both the old and new passwords can be zero length; both must be uppercase.

Request Buffer:

```
struct
    {
    word     buffer_length;
    byte type;
    nw_int object_type;
    byte     object_name_length;
    char     object_name[48];
    byte old_password_length;
    char old_password[127];
```

```
        byte new_password_length;
        char new_password[127];
        } request_buffer;
```

Reply Buffer:
```
    struct
        {
        word buffer_length;
        } reply_buffer;
```

Input Registers:

AH   0xE3

DS:SI   Far pointer to `request_buffer`

ES:DI   Far pointer to `reply_buffer`

Output Registers:

AL   Completion codes:

            0x00 Success

            0x96 Server out of memory

            0xF0 Wild card not allowed

            0xF8 No privilege to modify property

            0xFC No such object

            0xFE Server bindery locked

            0xFF Password error

Change Bindery Object Security
0xE3, type 0x38

Description:
You can modify object security with this service. It requires SUPERVISOR
rights, and cannot be used to set or clear NetWare-only, Read-Write security.

Request Buffer:
```
    struct
        {
        word    buffer_length;
        byte type;
        byte new_object_security;
        nw_int object_type;
```

III

Reference

```
byte     object_name_length;
char     object_name[48];
} request_buffer;
```

Reply Buffer:
```
struct
    {
    word buffer_length;
    } reply_buffer;
```

Input Registers:

AH   0xE3

DS:SI   Far pointer to `request_buffer`

ES:DI   Far pointer to `reply_buffer`

Output Registers:

AL   Completion codes:

        0x00 Success

        0x96 Server out of memory

        0xF0 Wild card not allowed

        0xF1 Invalid bindery security

        0xFC No such object

        0xFE Server bindery locked

        0xFF Bindery failure

Change Property Security 0xE3, type 0x3B

Description:

This service updates the property security of a particular object's property. You cannot set a property's security mask to a level greater than the workstation currently holds.

Request Buffer:
```
struct
    {
    word     buffer_length;
    byte type;
    nw_int object_type;
```

```
byte      object_name_length;
char      object_name[48];
byte new_property_security;
byte      property_name_length;
char      property_name[16];
} request_buffer;
```

Reply Buffer:

```
struct
    {
    word buffer_length;
    } reply_buffer;
```

Input Registers:

AH   0xE3

DS:SI   Far pointer to request_buffer

ES:DI   Far pointer to reply_buffer

Output Registers:

AL   Completion codes:

            0x00 Success

            0x96 Server out of memory

            0xF0 Wild card not allowed

            0xF1 Invalid bindery security

            0xFB No such property

            0xFC No such object

            0xFE Server bindery locked

            0xFF Bindery failure

Close Bindery
0xE3, type 0x44

Description:

This service closes both bindery files (NET$BIND.SYS and NET$BVAL.SYS).
These files are normally open and locked; you must close them, however,
before performing a global operation such as backing up (archiving) the
bindery. You do not have to close the bindery to do any of the update actions
described in this section. Close Bindery requires SUPERVISOR privileges.

III

Reference

Caution: While the bindery is closed, the network is effectively asleep, so do not keep the bindery closed any longer than necessary.

Request Buffer:
```
struct
    {
    word      buffer_length;
    byte type;
    } request_buffer;
```

Reply Buffer:
```
struct
    {
    word buffer_length;
    } reply_buffer;
```

Input Registers:

AH   0xE3

DS:SI   Far pointer to `request_buffer`

ES:DI   Far pointer to `reply_buffer`

Output Registers:

AL   Completion code:

            0x00 Success

Create Bindery Object
0xE3, type 0x32

Description:

This service creates an object and gives it its object-level characteristics. It requires SUPERVISOR-level rights.

Request Buffer:
```
struct
    {
    word      buffer_length;
    byte type;
    byte object_flag;
    byte object_security;
    nw_int object_type;
    byte      object_name_length;
    char      object_name[48];
    } request_buffer;
```

Reply Buffer:
```
struct
    {
    word buffer_length;
    } reply_buffer;
```

Input Registers:

AH   0xE3

DS:SI   Far pointer to request_buffer

ES:DI   Far pointer to reply_buffer

Output Registers:

AL   Completion codes:

         0x00 Success

         0x96 Server out of memory

         0xEE Object already exists

         0xEF Invalid name

         0xF0 Wild card not allowed

         0xF1 Invalid bindery security

         0xF5 No privilege to create object

         0xFE Server bindery locked

         0xFF Bindery failure

Create Property
0xE3, type 0x39

Description:

This service adds a property to an object and gives the property its characteristics. To use this service, you must have Read-Write access to the object.

Request Buffer:
```
struct
    {
    word      buffer_length;
    byte type;
    nw_int object_type;
    byte      object_name_length;
```

III

Reference

```
    char    object_name[48];
    byte new_property_flags;
    byte new_property_security;
    byte    property_name_length;
    char    property_name[16];
    } request_buffer;
```

Reply Buffer:
```
    struct
        {
        word buffer_length;
        } reply_buffer;
```

Input Registers:

AH   0xE3

DS:SI   Far pointer to `request_buffer`

ES:DI   Far pointer to `reply_buffer`

Output Registers:

AL   Completion codes:

0x00 Success

0x96 Server out of memory

0xED Property already exists

0xEF Invalid name

0xF0 Wild card not allowed

0xF1 Invalid bindery security

0xF7 No property create privilege

0xFC No such object

0xFE Server bindery locked

0xFF Bindery failure

Delete Bindery Object
0xE3, type 0x33

Description:

This service deletes an object. To use this service, you must have SUPERVISOR-level rights.

Request Buffer:

```
struct
    {
    word    buffer_length;
    byte type;
    nw_int object_type;
    byte    object_name_length;
    char    object_name[48];
    } request_buffer;
```

Reply Buffer:

```
struct
    {
    word buffer_length;
    } reply_buffer;
```

Input Registers:

AH	0xE3
DS:SI	Far pointer to request_buffer
ES:DI	Far pointer to reply_buffer

Output Registers:

AH   Completion codes:

0x00 Success

0x96 Server out of memory

0xEF Invalid name

0xF0 Wild card not allowed

0xF4 No object delete privilege

0xFC No such object

0xFE Server bindery locked

0xFF Bindery error

Delete Bindery Object from Set
0xE3, type 0x42

Description:

This service, which requires Write privilege at the property level, deletes an object ID (corresponding to the given object name and object type) from a set property.

Reference

Request Buffer:

```
struct
    {
    word    buffer_length;
    byte    type;
    nw_int object_type;
    byte    object_name_length;
    char    object_name[48];
    byte    property_name_length;
    char    property_name[16];
    nw_int member_object_type;
    byte    member_object_name_length;
    char    member_object_name[48];
    } request_buffer;
```

Reply Buffer:

```
struct
    {
    word buffer_length;
    } reply_buffer;
```

Input Registers:

AH	0xE3
DS:SI	Far pointer to request_buffer
ES:DI	Far pointer to reply_buffer

Output Registers:

AL   Completion codes:

0x00 Success

0x96 Server out of memory

0xEA No such member

0xEB Not a set property

0xF0 Wild card not allowed

0xF8 No property write privilege

0xFB No such property

0xFC No such object

0xFE Server bindery locked

0xFF Bindery error

Delete Property
0xE3, type 0x3A

Description:
This service, which requires Write access to both the object and the property, deletes one or more properties from an object. The property name may contain wild-card characters.

Request Buffer:
```
struct
    {
    word      buffer_length;
    byte      type;
    nw_int  object_type;
    byte      object_name_length;
    char      object_name[48];
    byte      property_name_length;
    char      property_name[16];
    } request_buffer;
```

Reply Buffer:
```
struct
    {
    word buffer_length;
    } reply_buffer;
```

Input Registers:
AH   0xE3

DS:SI   Far pointer to request_buffer

ES:DI   Far pointer to reply_buffer

Output Registers:
AL   Completion codes:

      0x00 Success

      0x96 Server out of memory

      0xF1 Invalid bindery security

      0xF6 No property delete privilege

      0xFB No such property

      0xFC No such object

      0xFE Server bindery locked

      0xFF Bindery failure

III

Reference

Get Bindery Access Level
0xE3, type 0x46

Description:

This service returns this workstation's access level to the bindery. It also returns the workstation's (user's) object ID.

Request Buffer:

```
struct
    {
    word      buffer_length;
    byte      type;
    } request_buffer;
```

Reply Buffer:

```
struct
    {
    word      buffer_length;
    byte      access_level;
    nw_long object_id;
    } reply_buffer;
```

Input Registers:

AH	0xE3
DS:SI	Far pointer to `request_buffer`
ES:DI	Far pointer to `reply_buffer`

Output Registers:

AL	Completion code:
	0x00 Success

Get Bindery Object ID
0xE3, type 0x35

Description:

This service, which requires Read access to the object, returns an object's unique object ID number.

Request Buffer:

```
struct
    {
    word      buffer_length;
    byte      type;
```

```
        nw_int object_type;
        byte   object_name_length;
        char   object_name[48];
        } request_buffer;
```

Reply Buffer:
```
    struct
        {
        word   buffer_length;
        nw_long object_id;
        nw_int object_type;
        char   object_name[48];
        } reply_buffer;
```

Input Registers:

AH   0xE3

DS:SI   Far pointer to request_buffer

ES:DI   Far pointer to reply_buffer

Output Registers:

AL   Completion codes:

0x00 Success

0x96 Server out of memory

0xEF Invalid name

0xF0 Wild card not allowed

0xFC No such object

0xFE Server bindery locked

0xFF Bindery failure

Get Bindery Object Name
0xE3, type 0x36

Description:

This service, which requires Read access to the object, returns the object name and object type that correspond to a particular object ID number.

Request Buffer:
```
struct
    {
    word     buffer_length;
    byte     type;
    nw_long object_id;
    } request_buffer;
```

Reply Buffer:
```
struct
    {
    word     buffer_length;
    nw_long object_id;
    nw_int object_type;
    char     object_name[48];
    } reply_buffer;
```

Input Registers:

AH   0xE3

DS:SI   Far pointer to `request_buffer`

ES:DI   Far pointer to `reply_buffer`

Output Registers:

AL   Completion codes:

0x00 Success

0x96 Server out of memory

0xFC No such object

0xFE Server bindery locked

0xFF Bindery failure

Is Bindery Object in Set?
0xE3, type 0x43

Description:

This service returns an indication of whether one object (specified by its object name and object type) is in a particular set property for another given object. The candidate member object is first searched for in the bindery. If it exists, its corresponding object ID number is then used as a search argument in a scan of the values of the given property of the given object. If the object is found, a completion code of 0x00 is returned. If the candidate member object doesn't exist, a completion code of 0xFC is returned. If the candidate member object exists but is not in the set of object ID numbers for the given object or property, a completion code of 0xEA is returned. This service requires Read access to the property.

Request Buffer:
```
struct
    {
    word      buffer_length;
    byte      type;
    nw_int object_type;
    byte      object_name_length;
    char      object_name[48];
    byte      property_name_length;
    char      property_name[16];
    nw_int member_object_type;
    byte      member_object_length;
    char      member_object_name[48];
    } request_buffer;
```

Reply Buffer:
```
struct
    {
    word buffer_length;
    } reply_buffer;
```

Input Registers:

AH   0xE3

DS:SI   Far pointer to request_buffer

ES:DI   Far pointer to reply_buffer

Output Registers:

AL   Completion codes:

            0x00 Success

            0x96 Server out of memory

            0xEA No such member

            0xEB Not a set property

            0xF0 Wild card not allowed

            0xF9 No privilege to read property

            0xFB No such property

III

Reference

0xFC No such object

0xFE Server bindery locked

0xFF Bindery failure

Open Bindery
0xE3, type 0x45

Description:
This service, which requires SUPERVISOR-level rights, reopens the bindery after a previous Close Bindery call.

Request Buffer:
```
struct
    {
    word    buffer_length;
    byte    type;
    } request_buffer;
```

Reply Buffer:
```
struct
    {
    word    buffer_length;
    } reply_buffer;
```

Input Registers:
AH	0xE3
DS:SI	Far pointer to request_buffer
ES:DI	Far pointer to reply_buffer

Output Registers:
AL	Completion code:
	0x00 Success

Read Property Value
0xE3, type 0x3D

Description:
This service returns the value (or part of the value) of a given property for a given object, as a 128-byte segment. You should set the field request_buffer.segment_number to 1 for the first call and increment the field

for each subsequent call. The field `reply_buffer.more_segments` is set to 0 when the last (or only) segment is returned; the field is 0xFF for all intermediate segments. A request for a nonexistent segment returns a completion code of 0xEC. This function requires Read access to the property.

Request Buffer:

```
struct
    {
    word      buffer_length;
    byte      type;
    nw_int object_type;
    byte      object_name_length;
    char      object_name[48];
    byte      segment_number;
    byte      property_name_length;
    char      property_name[16];
    } request_buffer;
```

Reply Buffer:

```
struct
    {
    word buffer_length;
    byte property_value[128];
    byte more_segments;
    byte      property_flags;
    } reply_buffer;
```

Input Registers:

AH	0xE3
DS:SI	Far pointer to `request_buffer`
ES:DI	Far pointer to `reply_buffer`

Output Registers:

AL   Completion codes:

0x00 Success

0x96 Server out of memory

0xEC No such segment

0xF0 Wild card not allowed

0xF1 Invalid security

0xF9 No privilege to read property

III

Reference

0xFB No such property

0xFC No such object

0xFE Server bindery locked

0xFF Bindery failure

Rename Bindery Object
0xE3, type 0x34

Description:
This service, which requires SUPERVISOR-level rights, renames an object.
The object ID number is not changed.

Request Buffer:
```
struct
    {
    word     buffer_length;
    byte     type;
    nw_int object_type;
    byte     old_object_name_length;
    char     old_object_name[48];
    byte     new_object_name_length;
    char     new_object_name[48];
    } request_buffer;
```

Reply Buffer:
```
struct
    {
    word     buffer_length;
    } reply_buffer;
```

Input Registers:

AH   0xE3

DS:SI   Far pointer to request_buffer

ES:DI   Far pointer to reply_buffer

Output Registers:

AL   Completion codes:

          0x00 Success

          0x96 Server out of memory

          0xEF Invalid name

0xF0 Wild card not allowed

0xF3 No privilege to rename objects

0xFC No such object

0xFE Server bindery locked

0xFF Bindery failure

Scan Bindery Object
0xE3, type 0x37

Description:
This service searches the bindery for an object (by its type and name)
and returns information about the object. You can use wild cards in
both the type and name fields, in which case this service may be called
repeatedly to obtain all matching objects. For the first call, the field
`request_buffer.last_object_id` should be set to 0xFFFFFFFF. For subsequent
calls, this field should be set to the value of `reply_buffer.object_id` returned
by the previous call. When there are no more matching entries, this service
returns a completion code of 0xFC (no such object).

Request Buffer:
```
struct
    {
    word      buffer_length;
    byte      type;
    nw_long last_object_id;
    nw_int object_type;
    byte      object_name_length;
    char      object_name[48];
    } request_buffer;
```

Reply Buffer:
```
struct
    {
    word      buffer_length;
    nw_long object_id;
    nw_int object_type;
    char      object_name[48];
    byte      object_flag;
    byte      object_security;
    byte      object_has_properties;
    } reply_buffer;
```

III

Reference

Input Registers:

AH	0xE3
DS:SI	Far pointer to `request_buffer`
ES:DI	Far pointer to `reply_buffer`

Output Registers:

AL   Completion codes:

0x00 Success

0x96 Server out of memory

0xEF Invalid name

0xFC No such object

0xFE Server bindery locked

0xFF Bindery failure

Scan Property
0xE3, type 0x3C

Description:

This service retrieves each property (one per call) for a given object. Wild cards are not allowed in the object name or the object type. For the first call, the field `request_buffer.sequence_number` should be set to 0xFFFFFFFF. For subsequent calls, this field should be set to the value of `reply_buffer.sequence_number` returned by the previous call. The field `reply_buffer.more_properties` is set to 0x00 for the last entry; this field is 0xFF for all intermediate entries. This service returns a completion code of 0xFB (no such property) when there are no more matching entries. This function requires Read access to the object and the property.

Request Buffer:

```
struct
    {
    word    buffer_length;
    byte    type;
    nw_int object_type;
    byte    object_name_length;
    char    object_name[48];
    nw_long sequence_number;
    byte    property_name_length;
    char    property_name[16];
    } request_buffer;
```

Reply Buffer:

```
struct
    {
    word      buffer_length;
    char      property_name[16];
    byte      property_flags;
    byte      property_security;
    nw_long   sequence_number;
    byte      property_has_value;
    byte      more_properties;
    } reply_buffer;
```

Input Registers:

AH	0xE3
DS:SI	Far pointer to `request_buffer`
ES:DI	Far pointer to `reply_buffer`

Output Registers:

AL   Completion codes:

0x00 Success

0x96 Server out of memory

0xF1 Invalid security

0xFB No such property

0xFC No such object

0xFE Server bindery locked

0xFF Bindery failure

Verify Bindery Object Password
0xE3, type 0x3F

Description:

This service compares the password supplied in the `request_buffer` to the password stored in the bindery for an object. It then returns a completion code that indicates whether the two passwords are equal. The password stored in the bindery is a value of the predefined PASSWORD property, which is a required property for any object intended to log in to a file server. The property value can be null. The password supplied in the `request_buffer` must be uppercase or null (an empty string). This call does not require that the requesting workstation be logged in to the file server.

Request Buffer:
```
struct
    {
    word     buffer_length;
    byte     type;
    nw_int object_type;
    byte     object_name_length;
    char     object_name[48];
    byte     password_length;
    char     password[128];
    } request_buffer;
```

Reply Buffer:
```
struct
    {
    word     buffer_length;
    } reply_buffer;
```

Input Registers:

AH	0xE3
DS:SI	Far pointer to `request_buffer`
ES:DI	Far pointer to `reply_buffer`

Output Registers:

AL   Completion codes:

0x00 Success (passwords are equal)

0x96 Server out of memory

0xF0 Wild card not allowed

0xFB No such property

0xFC No such object

0xFE Server bindery locked

0xFF Bad password

Write Property Value
0xE3, type 0x3E

Description:
This service writes as a 128-byte segment the value (or part of the value) of a given property for a given object. The value can span from 1 to 255 segments. Each segment is numbered and the segments must be created in sequence.

This is done by setting the field `request_buffer.segment_number` to 1 for the first call and incrementing it for each subsequent call. Therefore, a value longer than 128 bytes can be split into multiple segments. Of course, the value that you store can fit into one 128-byte segment. If the value is shorter than 128 bytes, you use only the first sequence of bytes (however many are requested); the remainder is unused.

This call is useful only for Item properties; the values of set properties should be managed only with the Add Bindery Object to Set function. If you are overwriting existing segments and want to truncate the overall length of the value at the current segment, you can set the field `request_buffer.erase_remaining_segments` to 0. If you set this field to 0xFF, subsequent segments can continue to exist. This service requires Write privileges at the property level.

Request Buffer:
```
struct
    {
    word       buffer_length;
    byte       type;
    nw_int object_type;
    byte       object_name_length;
    char       object_name[48];
    byte       segment_number;
    byte       erase_remaining_segments;
    byte       property_name_length;
    char       property_name[16];
    byte       property_value_segment[128];
    } request_buffer;
```

Reply Buffer:
```
struct
    {
    word       buffer_length;
    } reply_buffer;
```

Input Registers:

AH	0xE3
DS:SI	Far pointer to `request_buffer`
ES:DI	Far pointer to `reply_buffer`

III

Reference

Output Registers:

AL   Completion codes:

0x00 Success

0x96 Server out of memory

0xE8 Not item property

0xEC No such segment

0xF0 Wild card not allowed

0xF1 Invalid security

0xF8 No privilege to write property

0xFB No such property

0xFC No such object

0xFE Server bindery locked

0xFF Bindery failure

Connection Services

The services in this category enable you to perform login, attach, and logout operations from within your application.

The NetWare shell program running on each workstation maintains two internal tables, the *Server Name Table* and the *Connection ID Table*. Each table can hold as many as eight entries. The number of the table entry (1–8) identifies that file server. Each entry in the Server Name Table is simply a 48-byte string that contains the name of a file server. Each corresponding entry in the Connection ID Table looks like this:

```
struct
    {
    byte      in_use_flag;
    byte      order_number;
    byte      network_number[4];
    byte      node_address[6];
    byte      socket_number[2];
    byte      receive_timeout[2];
    byte      routing_node[6];
    byte      packet_sequence_number;
    byte      connection_number;
    byte      connection_status;
```

```
byte      maximum_timeout[2];
byte      reserved[5];
} connect_id_table[8];
```

Attach to File Server
0xF1, type 0x00

Description:
This service attaches the workstation to the specified file server. The workstation must already be logged into at least one file server, and can be attached to as many as eight file servers.

Input Registers:
AH	0xF1
AL	0
DL	Server connection ID (1–8)

Output Registers:
AL   Completion codes:

0x00 Success

0xF8 Already attached

0xF9 No free connection slots at the file server

0xFA More server slots

0xFC Unknown file server

0xFE Server bindery locked

0xFF No response from the server
       (illegal server address)

Detach from File Server
0xF1, type 0x01

Description:
This service detaches this workstation from the specified file server.

Input Registers:

AH	0xF1
AL	1
DL	Server connection ID (1–8)

Output Registers:

AL   Completion codes:

0x00 Success

0xFF Connection does not exist

Enter Login Area
0xE3, type 0x0A

Description:

This service puts the workstation in the SYS:LOGIN directory on the file server and tells NetWare the name of the subdirectory beneath SYS:LOGIN in which the LOGIN utility exists. This call is not particularly useful in application programs; it is used mostly by the Boot ROM chips found in diskless workstations.

Request Buffer:

```
struct
    {
    word    buffer_length;
    byte    type;
    byte    number_of_local_drives;
    byte    subdirectory_name_length;
    char    subdirectory_name[255];
    } request_buffer;
```

Reply Buffer:

```
struct
    {
    word    buffer_length;
    } reply_buffer;
```

Input Registers:

AH	0xE3
DS:SI	Far pointer to `request_buffer`
ES:DI	Far pointer to `reply_buffer`

Output Registers:

AL   Completion code:

0x00 Success

Get Connection Information
0xE3, type 0x16

Description:

This service returns information about the object that is logged in as the specified connection number. The connection number ranges from 1 to 100. You can obtain this number with a call to either Get Connection Number or Get Object Connection Numbers. The login_time field returned in the reply_buffer is a seven-byte character array:

```
login_time[0] - year, in the range 0-99 (0=1980)
login_time[1] - month, 1-12
login_time[2] - day, 1-31
login_time[3] - hour, 0-23
login_time[4] - minute, 0-59
login_time[5] - second, 0-59
login_time[6] - day of week, 0-6 (0=Sunday)
```

Request Buffer:

```
struct
    {
    word      buffer_length;
    byte      type;
    byte      connection_number;
    } request_buffer;
```

Reply Buffer:

```
struct
    {
    word      buffer_length;
    nw_long object_id;
    nw_int  object_type;
    char      object_name[48];
    char      login_time[7]
    word      reserved;
    } reply_buffer;
```

Input Registers:

AH   0xE3

DS:SI   Far pointer to request_buffer

ES:DI   Far pointer to reply_buffer

III

Reference

Output Registers:

AL   Completion code:

            0x00 Success

Get Connection Number
0xDC

Description:
This service returns the connection number that the workstation uses to communicate with the default file server.

Input Registers:

AH   0xDC

Output Registers:

AL   Connection number (1–100)

CL   First digit of the connection number

CH   Second digit of the connection number

Get Internet Address
0xE3, type 0x13

Description:
This service obtains a connection's internetwork address, consisting of network number, node address, and socket number (see Chapter 3, "PC-to-PC Communications Concepts"). The socket number that this function returns is the one that the workstation uses to communicate with the file server; do not use it yourself.

Request Buffer:
```
struct
    {
    word    buffer_length;
    byte    type;
    byte    connection_number;
    } request_buffer;
```

Reply Buffer:
```
struct
    {
    word    buffer_length;
    byte    network_number[4];
```

```
byte    node_address[6];
byte    socket_number[2];
} reply_buffer;
```

Input Registers:

AH	0xE3

DS:SI   Far pointer to `request_buffer`

ES:DI   Far pointer to `reply_buffer`

Output Registers:

AL   Completion code:

0x00 Success

Get Object Connection Numbers
0xE3, type 0x15

Description:

This service returns an array of from 0 to 100 connection numbers under
which the given object is logged on. Objects are defined in the Bindery Services reference section.

Request Buffer:

```
struct
    {
    word    buffer_length;
    byte    type;
    nw_int object_type;
    byte    object_name_length;
    char    object_name[48];
    } request_buffer;
```

Reply Buffer:

```
struct
    {
    word    buffer_length;
    byte    number_of_connections;
    byte    connection_numbers[100];
    } reply_buffer;
```

Input Registers:

AH   0xE3

DS:SI	Far pointer to `request_buffer`
ES:DI	Far pointer to `reply_buffer`

Output Registers:

AL   Completion code:

0x00 Success

Login to File Server
0xE3, type 0x14

Description:

This service logs an object (normally a user) in to the default file server.

Request Buffer:

```
struct
    {
    word      buffer_length;
    byte      type;
    nw_int object_type;
    byte      object_name_length;
    char      object_name[48];
    byte      password_length;
    char      password[128];
    } request_buffer;
```

Reply Buffer:

```
struct
    {
    word      buffer_length;
    } reply_buffer;
```

Input Registers:

AH	0xE3
DS:SI	Far pointer to `request_buffer`
ES:DI	Far pointer to `reply_buffer`

Output Registers:

AL   Completion codes:

0x00 Success

0xFF Bad password

Logout
0xD7

Description:
This service performs a logout action. The object at this workstation is logged off all file servers, detached from all file servers except for the default, and placed in the SYS:LOGIN directory.

Input Registers:
>   AH   0xD7

Logout from File Server
0xF1, type 0x02

Description:
This service logs out a workstation (object) from the specified file server.

Input Registers:
>   AH   0xF1
>
>   AL   2
>
>   DL   Server connection ID (1–8)

Print Services

As was discussed in Chapter 4, "Shared File Programming," the functions offered by NetWare under the category of Print Services provide a variety of controls over how things are printed. Your application can switch between the local and network printer or printers, and can specify the number of copies, the tab expansion factor, the form type, the banner page text, and other parameters. When NetWare intercepts print data (from Interrupt hex 17) and sends it instead to a network printer, the process is called *capturing*.

Many of the functions in this category use the following data structure; if your software uses certain Print Services functions, you can modify the structure's first 42 bytes (up through form_name) except for status:

```
struct     PRINT_CONTROL_DATA
    {
    unsigned char status;
```

III

Reference

```
        unsigned char print_flags;
        unsigned char tab_size;
        unsigned char server_printer;
        unsigned char number_copies;
        unsigned char form_type;
        unsigned char reserved1;
        unsigned char banner_text[13];
        unsigned char reserved2;
        unsigned char local_lpt_device;
        unsigned int  flush_timeout_count;
        unsigned char flush_on_close;
        unsigned int  maximum_lines;
        unsigned int  maximum_chars
        unsigned char form_name[13];
        unsigned char lpt_flag;
        unsigned char file_flag;
        unsigned char timeout_flag;
        char far      *setup_string_ptr;
        char far      *reset_string_ptr;
        unsigned char connect_id_queue_print_job;
        unsigned char in_progress;
        unsigned char print_queue_flag;
        unsigned char print_job_valid;
        unsigned long print_queue_id;
        unsigned int  print_job_number;
        };
```

Cancel LPT Capture
0xDF, type 0x02

Description:

This service cancels the capturing of print stream data to the default printer. The print queue item is deleted and capturing is turned off (the local printer regains control).

Input Registers:

AH   0xDF

DL   2

Output Registers:

AL   Completion code:

0x00 Success

Cancel Specific LPT Capture
0xDF, type 0x06

Description:

This service cancels the capturing of print stream data to a specific printer. The print queue item is deleted and capturing is turned off (the local printer regains control).

Input Registers:

AH	0xDF
DL	6
DH	LPT device (0 = LPT1, 1= LPT2, 2 = LPT3)

Output Registers:

AL	Completion code:
	0x00 Success

End Print Capture
0xDF, type 0x01

Description:

This service releases the print queue item for printing and ends capturing for the default print device (the local printer regains control).

Input Registers:

AH	0xDF
DL	1

Output Registers:

AL	Completion code:
	0x00 Success

End Specific Print Capture
0xDF, type 0x05

Description:

This service releases the print queue item for the specific printer for printing and ends capturing (the local printer regains control).

Input Registers:

AH	0xDF
DL	5
DH	LPT device (0 = LPT1, 1 = LPT2, 2 = LPT3)

Output Registers:

AL	Completion code:
	0x00 Success

Flush Capture
0xDF, type 0x03

Description:

This service releases the print queue item for the default printer for printing but continues the capturing of print data.

Input Registers:

AH	0xDF
DL	5

Output Registers:

AL	Completion code:
	0x00 Success

Flush Specific Capture
0xDF, type 0x07

Description:

This service releases the print queue item for the specified printer for printing but continues capturing print data.

Input Registers:

AH	0xDF
DL	7
DH	LPT device (0 = LPT1, 1 = LPT2, 2 = LPT3)

Output Registers:

AL   Completion code:

0x00 Success

Get Banner User Name
0xB8, type 0x08

Description:
This service returns the user name that is printed on the banner pages, if set; otherwise, the name of the user logged in at the workstation is returned.

Reply Buffer:
```
char     banner_user_name[12];
```

Input Registers:

AH   0xB8

AL   8

ES:BX   Far pointer to `reply_buffer`

Output Registers:

AL   Completion code:

0x00 Success

Get Default Printer Capture Data
0xB8, type 0x00

Description:
This service returns a filled-in PRINT_CONTROL_DATA structure, as defined earlier.

Reply Buffer:
```
struct    PRINT_CONTROL_DATA     reply_buffer;
```

Input Registers:

AH   0xB8

AL   0

CX   Length of `reply_buffer`

ES:BX   Far pointer to `reply_buffer`

III

Reference

Output Registers:

AL   Completion code:

            0x00 Success

Get Default Local Printer
0xB8, type 0x04

Description:
This service returns a number that corresponds to the default print device currently set up for capturing print data.

Input Registers:

AH   0xB8

AL   4

Output Registers:

DH   Default LPT device (0 = LPT1, 1 = LPT2, 2 = LPT3)

Get Capture Status
0xF0, type 0x03

Description:
This service indicates whether capturing is currently active for the default print device.

Input Registers:

AH   0xF0

AL   3

Output Registers:

AH   Completion codes:

            0x00 Capturing not active

            0xFF Capturing is active

AL   Connection ID (1–8) (only returned if capturing is active)

Get Printer Status
0xE0, type 0x06

Description:

This service returns the current status of a specified network printer. A file server can manage as many as five print devices (three parallel and two serial), so the printer_number field can range from 0 to 4.

Request Buffer:
```
struct
    {
    word      buffer_length;
    byte      type;
    byte      printer_number; /* 0-4 */
    } request_buffer;
```

Reply Buffer:
```
struct
    {
    word      buffer_length;
    byte      printer_halted;         /* 0=active, 0xFF=stopped */
    byte      printer_offline;        /* 1=offline */
    byte      form_type;              /* 0-255 */
    byte      target_printer_number;  /* same as above, unless */
                                      /* re-routed */
    } reply_buffer;
```

Input Registers:

AH   0xE0

DS:SI   Far pointer to request_buffer

ES:DI   Far pointer to reply_buffer

Output Registers:

AL   Completion codes:

          0x00 Success

          0xFF No such printer

Get Specified Printer Capture Data
0xB8, type 0x02

Description:

This service returns a filled-in PRINT_CONTROL_DATA structure, as defined earlier, for a specific print device.

Reply Buffer:
```
struct PRINT_CONTROL_DATA     reply_buffer;
```

Input Registers:

AH	0xB8
AL	2
CX	Length of reply_buffer
ES:BX	Far pointer to reply_buffer
DH	Printer number (0 = LPT1, 1 = LPT2, 2 = LPT3)

Output Registers:

AL	Completion code:
	0x00 Success

Set Banner User Name
0xB8, type 0x09

Description:

This service sets the user name that is printed on banner pages.

Request Buffer:
```
char    banner_user_name[12];
```

Input Registers:

AH	0xB8
AL	9
ES:BX	Far pointer to request_buffer

Output Registers:

AL	Completion code:
	0x00 Success

Set Capture Print Queue
0xB8, type 0x06

Description:

This service targets the next print capture to a specified print queue.

Input Registers:

AH	0xB8
AL	6
DH	Print device (0 = LPT1, 1 = LPT2, 2 = LPT3)
BX:CX	Queue ID (the bindery object ID number)

Output Registers:

AL	Completion codes:
	0x00 Success
	0xFF Print job already queued

Set Default Printer Capture Data
0xB8, type 0x01

Description:

This service enables you to change any of the first 42 bytes (up through form_name, except for the status field) of the print_control data structure for the default print device.

Reply Buffer:
```
struct PRINT_CONTROL_DATA reply_buffer;
```

Input Registers:

AH	0xB8
AL	1
CX	reply_buffer length (1–42)
ES:BX	Far pointer to reply_buffer

Output Registers:

AL	Completion code:
	0x00 Success

Set Default Local Printer
0xB8, type 0x05

Description:
This service designates the default local print device (LPT1, LPT2, or LPT3) and remains in effect until this function is called again or the workstation is rebooted. The designated device becomes the selected printer for the default print capture functions in this category.

Input Registers:

AH	0xB8
AL	5
DH	Print device (0 = LPT1, 1 = LPT2, 2 = LPT3)

Output Registers:

AL	Completion code:
	0x00 Success

Set Specified Printer Capture Data
0xB8, type 0x03

Description:
This service enables you to change any of the first 42 bytes (up through form_name, except for the status field) of the print_control data structure for the specified print device.

Request Buffer:
```
struct PRINT_CONTROL_DATA request_buffer;
```

Input Registers:

AH	0xB8
AL	3
CX	request_buffer length (1–42)
DH	Print device (0 = LPT1, 1 = LPT2, 2 = LPT3)
ES:BX	Far pointer to request_buffer

Output Registers:

AL   Completion code:

            0x00 Success

Specify Capture File
0xE0, type 0x09

Description:

This service creates a disk file and directs that the next capture of print stream
data go into the file. The previous contents of the file, if any, are lost. This
service must be used for the default print device, not a specific print device.
The file is closed when the application invokes a Cancel Capture, End Capture, or Flush Capture function call. This service requires Read, Write, and
Create rights in the target directory.

Request Buffer:

```
struct
    {
    word     buffer_length;
    byte     type;
    byte     directory_handle;   /* 0 */
    byte     file_path_length;   /* 1-255 */
    char     file_path[255];     /* full path and file name */
    } request_buffer;
```

Reply Buffer:

```
struct
    {
    word     buffer_length;
    } reply_buffer;
```

Input Registers:

AH   0xE0

AL   9

DS:SI   Far pointer to `request_buffer`

ES:DI   Far pointer to `reply_buffer`

Output Registers:

AL   Completion codes:

            0x00 Success

            0x9C Invalid path

III

Reference

Start LPT Capture
0xDF, type 0x00

Description:

This service starts a capture of print data to the default print device. Subsequent characters sent to the default printer are redirected to a network printer. The current settings in the `print_control_data` structure for the default printer are used to manage the printout.

Input Registers:

AH	0xDF
AL	0

Output Registers:

AL	Completion code:
	0x00 Success

Start Specific LPT Capture
0xDF, type 0x04

Description:

This service starts a capture of print data to the specified print device. Subsequent characters sent to that printer are redirected to a network printer. The current settings in the `print_control_data` structure for the specified printer are used to manage the printout. The print material is sent to its final destination when the application issues an End Specific Capture call or a Flush Specific Capture call.

Input Registers:

AH	0xDF
AL	4
DH	Print device (0 = LPT1, 1 = LPT2, 2 = LPT3

Output Registers:

AL	Completion code:
	0x00 Success

Synchronization Services

You can consider the services in this category as extensions to the PC DOS file-sharing and record-locking services. However, these services actually exist at a lower level than the DOS functions. The sharing and locking calls that you issue to DOS are translated into equivalent Synchronization Services calls as part of the redirection of DOS functions that occurs in the NetWare redirector/shell software. Therefore, the file server doesn't have to know anything about PC DOS function calls (even redirected ones); it only has to be able to handle the NetWare-specific functions that it receives from the shell/redirector or directly from your application.

This section focuses on the Synchronization Services that handle physical file or record locks. See Chapters 2, "Multiuser Concepts," and 4, "Shared File Programming," for further discussion of these services.

Clear File
0xED

Description:
This service unlocks the specified file and removes it from the log table for a workstation.

Request Buffer:
```
char     file_path[255];     /* drive, path, and file name */
```

Input Registers:

AH   0xED

DS:DX   Far pointer to the `request_buffer` string

Output Registers:

AL   Completion codes:

0x00 Success

0xFF File not found

Clear File Set
0xCF

Description:
This service unlocks all files in the log table for a workstation and removes them from the log table.

III

Reference

Input Registers:

AH	0xCF

Clear Physical Record
0xBE

Description:

This service unlocks the specified physical record and removes it from the log table.

Input Registers:

AH	0xBE
BX	File handle (from DOS function 3C, 3D, or 5B)
CX:DX	The record's location in the file
SI:DI	The record's length (file region)

Output Registers:

AL	Completion codes:
	0x00 Success
	0xFF No locked record found

Clear Physical Record Set
0xC4

Description:

This service unlocks all physical records in the log table and removes them from the log table.

Input Registers:

AH	0xC4

Get Lock Mode
0xC6, type 0x02

Description:

This service returns the current lock mode flag. This flag indicates whether NetWare should recognize the time-out value specified for certain function calls. Set the flag to 0 for versions of NetWare prior to release 4.61. NetWare

4.61 and all versions of Advanced NetWare 286 and 386 require a lock flag value of 1. The default is 0.

Input Registers:

AH	0xC6
AL	2

Output Registers:

AL	Current lock mode

Lock File Set
0xCB

Description:
This service attempts to lock all files in the log table. The time-out value indicates how long NetWare will wait for an already locked file to become unlocked (available). A value of 0 means no wait.

Input Registers:

AH	0xCB
BP	Time-out limit, in 1/18ths of a second

Output Registers:

AL	Completion codes:
	0x00 Success
	0xFE Timed out (could not acquire all locks)
	0xFF Failure

Lock Physical Record Set
0xC2

Description:
This service attempts to lock all physical records in the log table. The time-out value indicates how long NetWare will wait for an already locked file to become unlocked (available). A value of 0 means no wait. The lock directive denotes the type of locking to be performed:

| 00 | Lock records with exclusive locks |
| 01 | Lock with SHAREABLE, Read-Only locks |

Input Registers:

AH	0xC2
AL	Lock directive
BP	Time-out limit, in 1/18ths of a second

Output Registers:

| AL | Completion codes: |

0x00 Success

0xFE Timed out (could not acquire all locks)

0xFF Failure

Log File
0xEB

Description:

This service puts a file in the log table. Optionally, you can use this service to attempt to lock the file.

Request Buffer:

```
char    file_path[255];   /* drive, path, and file name */
```

Input Registers:

| AH | 0xEB |
| AL | Lock directive: |

0 Log file

1 Log and lock file

| BP | Time-out limit (needed only if the lock directive = 1) |
| DS:DX | Far pointer to request_buffer |

Output Registers:

AL   Completion codes:

0x00 Success

0x96 Server out of memory

0xFE Timed out (lock not acquired)

0xFF Hardware failure

Log Physical Record
0xBC

Description:

This service logs a physical record in the log table. Optionally, you also can attempt to lock the record using this service.

Input Registers:

AH   0xBC

AL   Lock directive:

0   Log the record

1   Log and lock record with an exclusive lock

3   Log and lock record with a SHAREABLE, Read Only lock

BX   File handle (from DOS function 3C, 3D, or 5B)

BP   Time-out limit, in 1/18ths of a second

CX:DX   File position of the record

SI:DI   Record length

Output Registers:

AL   Completion codes:

0x00 Success

0x96 Server out of memory

0xFE Timed out (lock not acquired)

0xFF Failure

III

Reference

Release File
0xEC

Description:
This service unlocks a file that was previously logged and locked. The entry in the log table is not removed.

Request Buffer:
```
char    file_path[255]          /* drive, path, and file name */
```

Input Registers:
AH   0xEC

DS:DX   Far pointer to request_buffer

Output Registers:
AL   Completion codes:

    0x00   Success

    0xFF   File not found

Release File Set
0xCD

Description:
This service unlocks all files logged in the log table, but doesn't remove the entries from the table.

Input Registers:
AH   0xCD

Output Registers:
None

Release Physical Record
0xBD

Description:
This service unlocks a physical record in the log table, but does not remove the entry from the table.

Input Registers:

AH	0xBD
BX	File handle (from DOS function 3C, 3D, or 5B)
CX:DX	File position of the record
SI:DI	Record length

Output Registers:

AL   Completion codes:

0x00 Success

0xFF Locked record not found

Release Physical Record Set
0xC3

Description:
This service unlocks all physical records in the log table, but does not remove the entries from the table.

Input Registers:

AH   0xC3

Output Registers:

None

Set Lock Mode
0xC6

Description:
This service sets the current lock mode flag. This flag indicates whether NetWare should recognize the time-out value specified for certain function calls. Set the flag to 0 for versions of NetWare prior to release 4.61. NetWare 4.61 and all versions of Advanced NetWare 286 and 386 require a lock flag value of 1. The default is 0.

Input Registers:

AH	0xC6
AL	Lock mode (0 or 1)

III

Reference

Transaction Tracking Services

Chapter 4, "Shared File Programming," discusses related file updates and the need for a mechanism for maintaining consistency among the data in two or more related files. I mapped out in pseudocode such a mechanism, involving journaling and rollback, that you can develop yourself. However, if you don't mind writing your application in a Novell-specific fashion, such a mechanism called *Transaction Tracking Services* (TTS) is provided for you. When enabled and properly used, TTS guarantees that all related updates take place or that none of them do.

TTS is available only on file servers that use the SFT Advanced NetWare and NetWare 386 products. Also, the server must be configured to use TTS at the time it is "NETGEN'd." Finally, to enable TTS to treat a file specially, the file must be marked *Transactional* with the Set Extended File Attributes service. (With all these prerequisites, you might think that TTS is seldom used; this is not the case, however, primarily because applications that make TTS calls still function on non-TTS networks—except, of course, that transaction tracking is not performed on such networks.)

TTS performs both implicit and explicit transaction tracking. *Implicit* means that activity to a Transactional file is tracked on a record-by-record basis without the need for TTS-aware programming. *Explicit* means that TTS (as Novell puts it) "allows applications to neatly bracket file update sequences with locking and TTS system calls." You incorporate TTS calls in your application to delimit updates to related files. TTS then ensures that half-finished operations do not corrupt the relationships and consistencies in the data.

The server can monitor 1 to 200 transactions at a time; exactly how many transactions is specified when the server is "NETGEN'd." Because the server keeps a "before" image of each update, TTS requires more disk space. Also, because journaling requires extra I/O, TTS can slow down the process just a little. The extra data protection that TTS provides, however, can well justify the extra disk space and I/O time.

Get Extended File Attributes
0xB6, type 0x00

Description:
This service returns the NetWare-specific *Extended File Attributes* for a named file. (See the Set Extended File Attributes call.)

Request Buffer:
```
char    file_path[255]          /* drive, path, and file name */
```

Input Registers:

AH	0xB6
AL	0
DS:DX	Far pointer to `request_buffer`

Output Registers:

AL	Completion codes:
	0x00 Success
	0xFE No privilege
	0xFF File not found
CL	Extended file attributes

Set Extended File Attributes
0xB6, type 0x01

Description:
This service sets the NetWare-specific Extended File Attributes for a named file. Bit 5 (bitmask 0x10) of the attribute byte defines whether the file is transactional. Setting the attribute to 0x10 informs TTS of the file. While this bit is set, the file cannot be deleted or renamed. Bit 6 (bitmask 0x20) of the attribute byte determines whether NetWare indexes the file. Indexing makes accessing different records within the file take less time. Usually, if a file is accessed randomly at the record level and is greater than 2M, you should index it.

Request Buffer:
```
char    file_path[255]          /* drive, path, and file name */
```

Input Registers:

AH	0xB6
AL	1
CL	Extended file attributes
DS:DX	Far pointer to `request_buffer`

Output Registers:

AL   Completion codes:

               0x00 Success

               0xFE No privilege

               0xFF File not found

TTS Abort Transaction
0xC7, type 0x03

Description:

This service enables you to manually abort a transaction. This process restores the files involved in the current transaction to their original state before the transaction started. If TTS acquires automatic physical record locks while the transaction is active, they are released.

Input Registers:

AH   0xC7

AL   3

Output Registers:

Carry flag clear

    AL   Completion codes:

                  0x00 Success

Carry flag set

    AL   0xFD TTS is presently disabled

                  0xFE Transaction ended; records locked

                  0xFF No explicit transaction is active

TTS Begin Transaction
0xC7, type 0x00

Description:

This service is used to start an explicit transaction. When this call is made, TTS begins tracking writes to transactional files. TTS automatically acquires a physical record lock on each record being written, unless it is already locked.

If TTS places the lock, the lock stays in place until a TTS End Transaction call or a TTS Abort Transaction call.

Input Registers:

AH   0xC7

AL   0

Output Registers:

Carry flag clear

AL   Completion codes:

0x00 Success

Carry flag set

AL   0x96 Out of dynamic work space

0xFE Implicit transaction is already active (is now con
verted to an explicit transaction)

0xFF Explicit transaction is already active
(it continues normally)

TTS End Transaction
0xC7, type 0x01

Description:

This service is used to end an explicit transaction. File server I/O continues even after this call returns. TTS supplies a transaction reference number that you can use to determine when the transaction actually finishes. To obtain the transaction reference number, you call the TTS Transaction Status function. Any automatically acquired physical record locks are released.

Input Registers:

AH   0xC7

AL   1

Output Registers:
>Carry flag clear

>>AL   Completion codes:

>>>0x00 Success

>>>0xFD Transaction tracking disabled

>>>0xFE Transaction ended; records still locked (transaction is backed out)

>>CX:DX Transaction reference number

>Carry flag set

>>0xFF   No explicit transaction active

TTS Get Application Thresholds
0xC7, type 0x05

Description:

This service returns threshold information about application-level logical or physical record locks. TTS uses this information for implicit transactions. (See the TTS Set Application Thresholds call.)

Input Registers:
>AH   0xC7

>AL   5

Output Registers:
>AL   Completion codes:

>>0x00 Success

>CL   Logical record lock threshold (0–225)

>CH   Physical record lock threshold (0–225)

TTS Get Workstation Thresholds
0xC7, type 0x07

Description:

This service returns information about workstation-level logical or physical record locks. TTS uses this information for implicit transactions. (See the TTS Set Workstation Thresholds call.)

Input Registers:

AH	0xC7
AL	7

Output Registers:

AL	Completion code:
	0x00 Success
CL	Logical record lock threshold (0–225)
CH	Physical record lock threshold (0–225)

TTS Is Available
0xC7, type 0x02

Description:

This service returns an indication of whether TTS is available and active on the default file server.

Input Registers:

AH	0xC7
AL	2

Output Registers:

AL	Completion codes:
	0x00 TTS not available
	0x01 TTS available
	0xFD TTS currently disabled

TTS Set Application Thresholds
0xC7, type 0x06

Description:

This service sets application-level logical and physical record lock thresholds. TTS starts an implicit transaction if the number of logical or physical record locks exceed these thresholds. The default for both is 0. A threshold of 0xFF turns off the generation of implicit transactions for that lock type. Turn off implicit transaction tracking if your application is designed to use explicit

III

Reference

transactions but sometimes generates unwanted implicit transactions just because of the way that it locks records. The threshold values that you specify with this function are in effect only temporarily, until your application terminates.

Input Registers:

AH	0xC7
AL	6
CL	Logical record lock threshold (0–225)
CH	Physical record lock threshold (0–225)

Output Registers:

AL	Completion code:
	0x00 Success

TTS Set Workstation Thresholds
0xC7, type 0x08

Description:

This service sets workstation-level logical and physical record lock thresholds. TTS starts an implicit transaction if the number of logical and physical record locks exceed these thresholds. The default for both is 0. A threshold of 0xFF turns off the generation of implicit transactions for that lock type. Turn off implicit transaction tracking if your application is designed to use explicit transactions but sometimes generates unwanted implicit transactions just because of the way that it locks records. The threshold values that you set with this function survive the termination of your application; they are reset only by another call to this function or the rebooting of the workstation.

Input Registers:

AH	0xC7
AL	8
CL	Logical record lock threshold (0–225)
CH	Physical record lock threshold (0–225)

Output Registers:

AL	Completion code:
	0x00 Success

TTS Transaction Status
0xC7, type 0x04

Description:
This service returns an indication of whether a transaction has been completely written to disk. Because NetWare uses a "lazy-write" caching algorithm in the file server, several seconds may pass before the transaction is actually recorded on the surface of the network disk.

Input Registers:

AH	0xC7
AL	4
CX:DX	Transaction reference number (returned by a TTS End Transaction call)

Output Registers:

AL	Completion codes:
	0x00 Success
	0xFF Not yet completely written to disk

Workstation Services

The services in this category provide information about the NetWare shell/redirector program running on the workstation. These services also enable you to control certain workstation environmental factors, such as the following:

- Whether NetWare performs cleanup actions when a program terminates

- Whether critical errors should be returned to your program or cause an Abort, Retry, Fail? message to appear

The NetWare shell program running on each workstation maintains two internal tables: the Server Name Table and the Connection ID Table. Each table can hold as many as eight entries. The number of the table entry (1–8)

III

Reference

identifies the file server. Each entry in the Server Name Table is simply a 48-byte string that contains the name of a file server. Each corresponding entry in the Connection ID Table looks like this:

```
struct
    {
    byte    in_use_flag;
    byte    order_number;
    byte    network_number[4];
    byte    node_address[6];
    byte    socket_number[2];
    byte    receive_timeout[2];
    byte    routing_node[6];
    byte    packet_sequence_number;
    byte    connection_number;
    byte    connection_status;
    byte    maximum_timeout[2];
    byte    reserved[5];
    } connect_id_table[8];
```

The addresses (returned as far pointers) of these two tables are available through the function calls in this category.

End Of Job
0xD6

Description:

This service causes certain cleanup actions at both the workstation and the file server. File and record locks are released; network and local files are closed; and Error mode and Lock mode are reset. The Synchronization Services section discusses Lock mode. Error mode is discussed later in this section as part of the Set Error mode call. Unless you call Set End of Job Status, the NetWare shell automatically calls this function when your application terminates and returns to DOS.

Input Registers:

AH	0xD6
BX	0x0000 For the current process only
	0xFFFF For all processes on the workstation

Get Connection ID Table Pointer
0xEF, type 0x03

Description:
This service returns a far pointer to the Connection ID Table within the NetWare shell program.

Input Registers:

AH	0xEF
AL	3

Output Registers:

ES:SI	Far pointer to the workstation's Connection ID Table

Get File Server Name Table Pointer
0xEF, type 0x04

Description:

This service returns a far pointer to the File Server Name Table within the NetWare shell program.

Input Registers:

AH	0xEF
AL	4

Output Registers:

ES:SI	Far pointer to the workstation's Server Name Table

Get Shell Version Information
0xEA, type 0x01

Description:

This service returns information about the workstation's environment.

Reply Buffer:

```
byte reply_buffer[40]
     (is filled with four concatenated, null-terminated
     strings.  The first string contains the name of the
     workstation's operating system (e.g., "MS DOS").
     The second string contains the version of the
     operating system.  The third string contains an
     identification of the type of computer (e.g, "IBM PC").
     And the fourth string contains a more generic
     identification of the type of computer (e.g, "IBM").)
```

III

Reference

Input Registers:

AH	0xEA
AL	1
BX	0
ES:DI	Far pointer to `reply_buffer`

Output Registers:

AH	Workstation operating system (0 = PC DOS)
AL	Customization code
BH	Major NetWare shell version
BL	Minor NetWare shell version
CL	Shell revision number
ES:SI	Far pointer to `reply_buffer`

Set End of Job Status
0xBB

Description:

This service turns on or off the automatic cleanup actions that the NetWare shell program performs when an application terminates.

Input Registers:

AH	0xBB
AL	End of Job flag
	0 Disabled
	1 Enabled

Output Registers:

AL	Previous setting of the End of Job flag

Set NetWare Error Mode
0xDD

Description:

This service enables you to tell NetWare how you want it to handle critical errors (the kind that normally invoke Interrupt 24 [hex]). Error mode 0 is the default. Note that the setting of Error mode affects only DOS function calls; direct calls to NetWare services return completion codes as outlined in this section. Also note that you can choose to install your own Interrupt 24 handler.

Input Registers:

AH	0xDD

DL   Error mode:

    0   Ask the user Abort, Retry, Fail?

    1   Don't do Interrupt 24; return NetWare error to program

    2   Don't do Interrupt 24; return the DOS error to program

Output Registers:

AL   Previous setting of the Error mode

OS/2 Services

This section includes reference material on the `DosOpen()`, `DosClose()`, `DosFileLocks()`, and `DosBufReset()` functions, as well as material on the O/S kernel API calls that deal with named pipes.

In addition to the file-oriented programmer services described in this section, OS/2 also offers a protected-mode implementation of NetBIOS that applications can use for PC-to-PC communications. OS/2 NetBIOS is very similar to the DOS-based NetBIOS, which is described in Chapter 5, "PC-to-PC NetBIOS Programming."

Recall from Chapter 1, "The Basics of Networking," that an application that wants to create a named pipe is the *server* (not to be confused with the *file server*) and the application at the other end of the pipe is the *client*. A *named pipe* is a file whose name has a particular format (the path and extension are optional):

```
\PIPE\path\name.ext
```

You typically use a named pipe as follows: the server application calls `DosMakeNmPipe()` to create a named pipe, and then uses `DosConnectNmPipe()` to wait until the client opens the pipe with a call to `DosOpen()`. The communication link is bidirectional; both the server and client can use `DosWrite()` and `DosRead()` calls to put data in the pipe or to remove data from it. You can use `DosPeekNmPipe()` to inspect data in the pipe without removing the data. At the end of the pipe's lifetime, the server can close the pipe with a `DosClose()` call and destroy the pipe with `DosDisConnectNmPipe()`. You can treat named pipes as simple data streams or message pipes. In the latter case, each call to `DosRead()` fetches one message at a time from the pipe.

In the function definitions that follow, the data types `byte`, `word`, and `dword` are used as though the following `#define` statements are in effect:

```
#define byte    unsigned char
#define word    unsigned int
#define dword   unsigned long
```

III

DosBufReset

Description:

This function takes data that has been written to a file but is still sitting in OS/2's internal buffers, and flushes the data to the output device (usually a disk). The directory entry for the file is updated. If the `handle` parameter is –1, all buffers for all open files associated with the current process are written to disk.

Prototype:

```
word  DosBufReset(word handle);
```

Returns:

0 on success, nonzero on error.

DosCallNmPipe

Description:

Using this function, a client workstation can perform a series of actions in one fell swoop: the workstation opens the named pipe, writes a message record to the pipe, reads a message from the pipe, and closes the pipe. The server workstation must have opened the pipe in message mode. If you specify an input buffer too small to hold the entire incoming message, you can call this function again to receive the remainder of the message.

As was mentioned earlier, you must specify the `pipename` parameter in the form \PIPE*path**filename.ext*. The `write_length` parameter indicates how many bytes to write from `write_buffer`. The `input_length` parameter gives the length of the `input_buffer` area. The parameter `actual_length_ptr` points to an item that is set to the length of the incoming message. Finally, the `timeout_interval` parameter specifies the number of milliseconds to wait for the incoming message before returning an error. You can also set `timeout_interval` to 0 to tell OS/2 to use its default time-out value, or you can set `timeout_value` to –1 to indicate that you want to wait indefinitely.

Prototype:

```
word DosCallNmPipe( char *pipename,
                    char *write_buffer,
                    word write_length,
                    char *input_buffer,
                    word input_length,
                    word *actual_length_ptr,
                    long timeout_interval);
```

Returns:
0 on success, nonzero on error.

DosClose

Description:
This function does the following:

- Closes the file associated with the file or pipe handle

- Flushes to disk any buffered, written data

- Updates the directory entry

If either the server or the client closes a named pipe handle that is in the "connected" state, the state of the pipe changes to "closing." If the pipe is not in the "connected" state and the server (pipe creator) closes the pipe, this function destroys the pipe.

Prototype:
```
word DosClose(word handle);
```

Returns:
0 on success, nonzero on error.

DosConnectNmPipe

Description:
This function is used by the server workstation, never by the client. If the pipe is opened in blocking mode, this function waits until the client workstation opens the pipe with a call to DosOpen(). If the server workstation opens the pipe in nonblocking mode and the client workstation has not yet opened the other end of the pipe, this function returns an error code; if the client workstation opens the pipe, the function returns a 0. If the pipe is opened n nonblocking mode, you can use this function inside a loop to poll for the client to open the pipe; however, you should use DosSleep() in the polling loop to ensure that you do not drain CPU resources while waiting. The DosMakeNmPipe() function returns the parameter handle.

Prototype:
```
word DosConnectNmPipe(word handle);
```

III

Reference

Returns:

0 if the client workstation opened the pipe, otherwise a nonzero error code.

DosDisConnectNmPipe

Description:

A server workstation uses this function to "break the pipe" (terminate the connection) abruptly. When this call finishes, the client workstation can no longer read from or write to the named pipe. Any unread data remaining in the pipe is abandoned.

Prototype:

```
word DosDisConnectNmPipe(word handle);
```

Returns:

0 on success, nonzero on error.

DosSetFileLocks

Description:

This function locks or unlocks a file region. If you specify a null pointer for either LOCK_INFO parameter, this function does not perform the corresponding action (lock or unlock). However, if both parameters are present, the function performs the unlock action before the lock action. Locking beyond the end-of-file is not an error. Do not overlap regions. A child process does not inherit access to a locked region of a file. The time-out parameter specifies how many milliseconds the operating system should retry the function if the lock or unlock cannot be immediately performed. The flags parameter indicates the type of lock that you want to place on the region of the file:

Bit	Description
31–2	Reserved
1	Atomic lock
0	Shared lock

Bit 1 defines a request for atomic locking. If this bit is set to 1 and the lock range is equal to the unlock range, an atomic lock occurs. If this bit is set to 1 and the lock range is not equal to the unlock range, an error is returned. If this bit is set to 0, then the lock may or may not occur atomically with the unlock.

Bit 0 defines the type of access that other processes may have to the file range that is being locked. If this bit is set to 0, other processes have no access to the locked file range. The current process has exclusive access to the locked file range. If this bit is set to 1, the current process and other processes have shared Read-Only access to the locked file range. A file range with shared access may overlap any other file range with shared access, but must not overlap any other file range with exclusive access.

Prototype:

```
struct LOCK_INFO
    {
    dword file_offset;
    dword region_length;
    };

word DosSetFileLocks(word handle,
                     struct LOCK_INFO *unlock_info,
                     struct LOCK_INFO *lock_info,
                     word timeout,
                     word flags);
```

Returns:

0 on success, nonzero on error.

DosCreateNPipe

Description:

This function creates a new named pipe. The workstation that calls this function is the *server*. If successful, this function returns a handle that you use in other functions to refer to the pipe.

The pipename parameter must be a string in the following format:

\PIPE*path**filename.ext*

The open_mode parameter specifies the following:

For the open_mode's high byte:

Bits	Meaning
FEDCBA98	
..xxxxxx	Reserved
.x......	write_through flag
x.......	Reserved

For the open_mode's low byte:

Bits	Meaning
76543210	
.....xxx	access_mode
.xxxx...	Reserved
x.......	Inheritance

If the write_through flag is a 0, DosMakeNmPipe buffers write operations. If the flag is a 1, write operations cause data to flow immediately into the pipe. The access_mode bits indicate whether the pipe is bidirectional (010), server-to-client (001), or client-to-server (000). The inheritance bit indicates whether a child process can inherit the pipe handle (0 = inheritable, 1 = not inheritable).

The pipe_mode parameter specifies the following:

Bits	Meaning
FEDCBA98 76543210	
.... xxxxxxxx	max_instance_count
.......x	read_mode
......x.	Reserved
.....x..	write_mode
.xxxx...	Reserved
x.......	blocking_mode

These parameters are defined as follows:

- max_instance_count denotes the maximum number of instances of the pipe that can exist (255 = no limit).

- read_mode specifies whether the pipe is to be read as a simple stream of bytes (0) or as either a series of distinct messages or a stream of bytes (1).

- write_mode identifies whether data is to be written to the pipe as a stream of bytes (0) or as a series of distinct messages (1).

■ `blocking_mode` indicates that a read or write operation should wait (block) until the specified number of bytes are read or written (0), or that the read or write operation should return immediately to the application if it cannot be completely satisfied (1).

The `outbound_size` field specifies how many bytes to allocate for the pipe's output buffer. `inbound_size` does the same for the pipe's input buffer. If you specify 0 for either of these parameters, a default buffer size of 1,024 bytes is used.

Set the `timeout_interval` to the number of milliseconds that `DosWaitNmPipe()` and `DosConnectNmPipe()` wait before returning to your application (specifying 0 tells OS/2 to use its default, 50 milliseconds).

Prototype:

```
word DosCreateNPipe(char   *pipename,
                    word   *handle,
                    word   open_mode,
                    word   pipe_mode,
                    word   outbound_size,
                    word   inbound_size,
                    dword  timeout_interval);
```

Returns:
0 on success, nonzero on error.

DosOpen

Description:
This function opens a file or an existing named pipe or creates a new file, and returns a handle that you use in subsequent references to the file. When creating a new file, set the `attribute` and `initial_filesize` parameters to indicate the file's attribute and initial size allocation. The current file position is set to 0 (the first byte). A client workstation uses this function to open a named pipe; the pipe defaults to *blocking* and *byte stream* modes. If you want to change these default characteristics, issue a call to `DosSetNmPHandState()`. The `open_mode` parameter has a slightly different definition for named pipes; see the description of the `open_mode` bit fields that follows.

The `action` parameter returned indicates one of the following:

■ That the file exists and is open

■ That the file did not exist and was created

■ That the file existed and was replaced

III

Reference

Code the `attribute` parameter for a new file as follows:

Bits	Meaning
FEDCBA98 76543210	
....x	Read-only
....x.	Hidden
....x..	System
....xx...	Reserved
....x.....	Archive
xxxxxxxx xx......	Reserved

The bits of `open_flag` have the following meanings:

Bits	Meaning
FEDCBA98 76543210	
....0000	Fail if the file exists
....0001	Open if the file exists
....0010	Replace if the file exists
.... 0000....	Fail if the file does not exist
.... 0001....	Create if the file does not exist
xxxxxxxx	Reserved

Except for named pipes, code `open_mode` according to the following bit fields:

Bits	Meaning
FEDCBA98 76543210	
....000	Access mode: Read-Only
....001	Access mode: Write-Only
....010	Access mode: Read-Write
....x...	Reserved

Bits	Meaning
.... .001....	Sharing mode: deny read/write (exclusive)
.... .010....	Sharing mode: deny write
.... .011....	Sharing mode: deny read
.... .100....	Sharing mode: deny none (fully shared)
.... 0.......	Inheritable by a child process
.... 1.......	Not inheritable by child
...XXXXX	Reserved
..0.....	Let the system handle critical errors
..1.....	Return the error to the program
.0......	Okay if writes are buffered
.1......	Do not buffer writes
0.......	Normal file open
1.......	Open entire volume as a file (don't use on network disks)

For a named pipe, bits 3 through D and bit F of open_mode must be 0. Also, bits 0 through 2 are defined as pipe_mode rather than access_mode:

Bits	Meaning
76543210	
.....000	Inbound pipe (client to server)
.....001	Outbound pipe (server to client)
.....010	Bidirectional

Prototype:
```
word DosOpen(char *filename,
             word *handle,
             word *action,
             dword initial_filesize,
             word attribute,
             word open_flag,
             word open_mode,
             dword reserved);
```

III

Reference

Returns:

0 on success, nonzero on error.

DosPeekNmPipe

Description:

As its name implies, this function lets you peek at the data in the named pipe without actually removing the data from the pipe. `DosPeekNmPipe()` attempts to transfer `buffer_size` bytes into `buffer`, but does not block (wait) if it cannot fill the buffer. The actual number of bytes is placed in `actual_size`, and the `pipe_data_ptr` structure receives the number of bytes remaining in the pipe and the number of bytes remaining in the current message. Finally, `pipe_status` returns one of following statuses of the named pipe:

1. Disconnected

2. Listening

3. Connected

4. Closing

Prototype:

```
struct PIPE_DATA
    {
    word bytes_left_in_pipe;
    word bytes_left_in_message;
    };

word DosPeekNmPipe(word handle,
                   char *buffer,
                   word buffer_size,
                   word *actual_size,
                   struct PIPE_DATA *pipe_data_ptr,
                   word *pipe_status);
```

Returns:

0 on success, nonzero on error.

DosQNmPHandState

Description:

This function returns information about a named pipe in the `state` variable:

Bits	Meaning
FEDCBA98 76543210	
.... xxxxxxxx	max_instance_count
.......x	read_mode
......x.	Reserved
.....x..	write_mode
..xxx...	Reserved
.x......	server_client
x.......	blocking_mode

server_client is 0 if the workstation making the call is the client, and 1 if the workstation is the server. The other bit fields are described under DosMakeNmPipe().

Prototype:
```
word DosQNmPHandState(word handle, word *state);
```

Returns:
0 on success, nonzero on error.

DosQNmPipeInfo

Description:
This function returns information about a named pipe. You should set the info_level parameter to 1 before calling this function. The function returns information in a structure called PIPE_INFO. You specify the size of this structure in the last parameter, pipe_info_size.

Prototype:
```
struct PIPE_INFO
    {
    word output buffer size (outbound data);
    word input buffer size (inbound data);
    byte max_instances;
    byte actual_instance_count;
    byte pipe_name_length;
    char pipe_name[255];
    };
```

III

Reference

```
word DosQNmPipeInfo(word handle,
                    word info_level,
                    struct PIPE_INFO *pipe_info_ptr,
                    word pipe_info_size);
```

Returns:

0 on success, nonzero on error.

DosQNmPipeSemState

Description:

This function provides information about a named pipe associated with a given system semaphore (see DosSetNmPipeSem()). The information is returned in the SEM_INFO structure as a series of six-byte entries:

```
struct SEM_INFO
    {
    byte pipe_status;
    byte wait_status;
    word semaphore_key;
    word bytes_available;
    } [xx];
```

The entries provide the following information:

- pipe_status is 0 if the pipe is empty, 1 if data is available in the pipe, 2 if the pipe has some free space, or 3 if the pipe is closing.

- wait_status is 0 if the other workstation is not waiting for pipe data, or 1 if the other workstation is waiting for data.

- semaphore_key is the key associated with the semaphore handle.

- bytes_available represents the number of bytes available to be read (if pipe_status is 1) or the free space inside the pipe (if pipe_status is 2).

OS/2 returns information about all named pipes related to the given semaphore, unless sem_info_size specifies an array of SEM_INFO structures too small to receive the information.

Prototype:

```
word DosQNmPipeSemState(dword sem_handle,
                        struct SEM_INFO *sem_info,
                        word sem_info_size);
```

Returns:

0 on success, nonzero on error.

DosSetNmPHandState

Description:

This function establishes a new `read_mode` and `blocking_mode` for an open named pipe. Code `state` as follows:

Bits	Meaning
FEDCBA98 76543210	
.... xxxxxxxx	Reserved
.......0	read_mode: byte stream only
.......1	read_mode: byte stream or message stream
.xxxxxx.	Reserved
0.......	blocking_mode: wait for read or write complete
1.......	blocking_mode: return from read or write (with an error code) if the read or write operation cannot be immediately satisfied

Prototype:

```
word DosSetNmPHandState(word handle, word state);
```

Returns:

0 on success, nonzero on error.

DosSetNmPipeSem

Description:

This function attaches a system semaphore to a named pipe, or replaces a semaphore already attached. The semaphore is cleared when either the other workstation places data in the pipe to be read, or the pipe becomes less than full (so that more data can be written). The semaphore key that you assign returns when you later call `DosQNmPipeSemState()`. Several named pipes can be associated with a single semaphore, so you can use the semaphore key to distinguish which pipe needs to be serviced.

Prototype:

```
word DosSetNmPipeSem(word handle,
                     dword semaphore_handle,
                     word  semaphore_key);
```

Returns:

0 on success, nonzero on error.

DosTransactNmPipe

Description:

This function sends a message to another workstation and then receives a message from that workstation. `DosTransactNmPipe()` waits for the incoming message regardless of how the pipe's blocking mode is set. The parameter `actual_bytes` specifies the actual number of bytes received. If the read buffer is too small, this function returns an error; however, you can obtain the remainder of the message by calling `DosTransactNmPipe()` again. This function also returns an error if the pipe is in byte-stream-only mode, or if the pipe is not empty when you call this function.

Prototype:

```
word DosTransactNmPipe(word handle,
                       char *write_buffer,
                       word write_buffer_size,
                       char *read_buffer,
                       word read_buffer_size,
                       word *actual_bytes);
```

Returns:

0 on success, nonzero on error.

DosWaitNmPipe

Description:

A client workstation uses this function to wait until an instance of a named pipe is available. If you call `DosOpen()` and receive an error telling you that the pipe is busy (that is, the maximum number of instances of the pipe is already in use), you can use this function to wait until you can open the named pipe. When an instance of the pipe becomes available, `DosWaitNmPipe()` returns 0. The `timeout` parameter specifies, in milliseconds, how long to wait for the pipe to become available. Code a `timeout` value of 0 to use the pipe default (50 milliseconds); code a value of –1 to wait indefinitely.

Prototype:

```
word DosWaitNmPipe(char *pipename, dword timeout);
```

Returns:

0 on success, nonzero on error.

NetBIOS Functions (DOS)

This section contains reference information on the NetBIOS functions for PC-to-PC communications.

You invoke a NetBIOS function in three steps:

1. Fill in the proper fields of a network control block (NCB)

2. Set up the ES:BX register pair as a far pointer to the NCB

3. Perform an Interrupt 5C (hex)

Many commands have both wait and no-wait options. When you specify the wait option, or if the command does not have a no-wait option, the call to NetBIOS (Interrupt 5C) does not return to your program until the command is executed. With some commands, the wait option can be risky, because an unforeseen error situation (such as a hardware error or power loss at the other workstation) can cause your program to wait forever for a response that never comes. NetBIOS does the following when you specify the no-wait option:

- Initiates the operation, sets the final return code to 0xff, and returns to your program with an immediate return code

- Continues the operation in the background

- Detects the completion of the event

- Sets the final return code to the proper value

- Calls the POST routine (if the NCB specifies one)

A POST routine must function exactly like an interrupt service routine. NetBIOS invokes the routine when a no-wait command is executed and the POST_FUNC field in the NCB is not NULL. The following conditions are true at the outset of the POST routine:

- Interrupts are OFF.

- ES:BX forms a far pointer to the NCB associated with the completed event.

- AL contains a copy of the final return code (the same as that within the NCB).

- The other registers (DS and so on) have no particular value.

- DOS function calls may or may not be safe to perform from within the POST routine.

The POST routine should save the registers, set DS (and any other registers) as necessary, process as quickly as possible the NCB to which ES:BX points, restore the registers, and finish by executing an IRET instruction. (Accomplishing these steps in Borland C is not that difficult; Chapter 5, "PC-to-PC NetBIOS Programming," shows how to code a POST routine.)

The following definition of an NCB is used throughout the reference section:

```c
typedef unsigned char byte;
typedef unsigned int  word;

/* Network Control Block (NCB)  */

typedef struct
    {
    byte NCB_COMMAND;               /* command id for this NCB   */
    byte NCB_RETCODE;               /* immediate return code     */
    byte NCB_LSN;                   /* local session number      */
    byte NCB_NUM;                   /* network name number       */
    void far *NCB_BUFFER_PTR;       /* pointer to message packet */
    word NCB_LENGTH;                /* length of message packet  */
    byte NCB_CALLNAME[16];          /* name of the other computer */
    byte NCB_NAME[16];              /* our network name          */
    byte NCB_RTO;                   /* receive time-out, 1/2 secs.*/
    byte NCB_STO;                   /* send time-out, in 1/2 secs.*/
    void interrupt (*NCB_POST)(); /* POST function pointer       */
    byte NCB_LANA_NUM;              /* adapter number (0 or 1)   */
    byte NCB_CMD_CPLT;              /* final return code         */
    byte NCB_RESERVE[14];           /* reserved area             */
    }
    NCB;
```

Reset Adapter
0x32 (wait)

Description:

This command resets NetBIOS, erasing and clearing all session information, deleting all names (except for the permanent node name) from the name table, and resetting the maximum number of sessions and the maximum number of outstanding NCBs. New values for these maximums can be supplied as part of the Reset command.

If you want to alter the default maximums for number of sessions and number of outstanding NCBs, code the new values in the NCB_LSN and NCB_NUM fields, respectively, before performing the Reset command. If these NCB fields are zero (0x00) when you issue the Reset command, the defaults of 6 sessions and 12 NCBs are used. For best performance, code these values to be as small as possible.

If a workstation has two adapters, this command resets NetBIOS only as it affects the adapter specified in the NCB_LANA_NUM field.

The Reset command does not affect the traffic and error statistics (see the Adapter Status command).

Caution
Do not use this command when running under the IBM PC LAN Program. The command clears the PCLP sessions and deletes the PCLP names, resulting in errors.

NCB Input Fields:

NCB_COMMAND	0x32
NCB_LSN	Maximum sessions, or 0x00 for default
NCB_NUM	Maximum NCBs, or 0x00 for default
NCB_LANA_NUM	0 = adapter 1, 1 = adapter 2

NCB Output Fields:

NCB_CMD_CPLT	Final return code

Immediate Return Code:

None

III

Reference

Final Return Code:

0x00	Success
0x03	Invalid command
0x23	Invalid NCB_LANA_NUM
0x40–0x4F	Unusual network condition
0x50–0xFE	Adapter malfunction

Cancel
0x35 (wait)

Description:

This command cancels an outstanding NetBIOS command. Place the address of the NCB whose pending command is to be canceled in the NCB_BUFFER_PTR field (it requires a far pointer). The return code from the Cancel command pertains only to the Cancel operation, indicating nothing about the command being canceled. The NCB_CMD_CPLT field in the NCB being canceled identifies the return code of the canceled command.

The following commands cannot be canceled:

Add Name
Add Group Name
Delete Name
Send Datagram
Send Broadcast Datagram
Session Status
Reset Adapter
Another Cancel command

NCB Input Fields:

NCB_COMMAND	0x35
NCB_BUFFER_PTR	Far pointer to the NCB to be canceled
NCB_LANA_NUM	0 = adapter 1, 1 = adapter 2

NCB Output Fields:

NCB_CMD_CPLT	Final return code

Immediate Return Code:
None

Final Return Code:

0x00	Success
0x03	Invalid command
0x23	Invalid LAN adapter number
0x24	Command executed during cancellation
0x26	Command cannot be canceled
0x40–0x4F	Unusual network condition
0x50–0xFE	Adapter malfunction

Get Adapter Status
0x33 (wait), 0xB3 (no-wait)

Description:
This command obtains status information about any workstation's network adapter, local or remote, currently active on the network. You specify the workstation by placing in the NCB_CALLNAME field any one of the names by which it is known. To obtain status information about the local workstation, you can put an asterisk (*) in the first byte of NCB_CALLNAME. Tell NetBIOS where to put the returned data by placing a far pointer to the following structure in the NCB_BUFFER_PTR field and then placing the structure length in the NCB_LENGTH field. The returned area must be at least 60 bytes.

After the call, NCB_LENGTH contains the actual number of bytes returned. The returned data is in three distinct parts:

- 6 bytes of network adapter ID

- 52 bytes of error or traffic information

- 2 bytes that contain a count of the names in the name table plus 18 bytes of information about each name table entry, repeated as many times as necessary for the number of names in the name table

III

Reference

```
/*      The following structures describe the layout      */
/*      of Adapter Status information returned by the      */
/*      DXMT0MOD.SYS implementation of NetBIOS.  Other     */
/*      implementations may return slightly different      */
/*      data.                                              */

typedef struct {
        char            tbl_name[16];
        unsigned char   tbl_name_number;
        unsigned char   tbl_name_status;
        }
        NAME_TABLE;

typedef struct {
        unsigned char   network_card_id[6];
        unsigned char   external_option;
        unsigned char   self_test_result;
        unsigned char   type_of_adapter;
        unsigned char   old_or_new_parameters;
        unsigned int    reporting_period_minutes;
        unsigned int    crc_errors;
        unsigned int    alignment_errors;
        unsigned int    collision_errors;
        unsigned int    unsuccessful_transmissions;
        unsigned long   good_transmissions;
        unsigned long   good_receptions;
        unsigned int    retransmissions;
        unsigned int    exhausted_resource_count;
        char            reserved1[8];
        unsigned int    available_ncbs;
        unsigned int    max_ncbs_configured;
        unsigned int    max_ncbs_possible;
        char            reserved2[4];
        unsigned int    pending_sessions;
        unsigned int    max_sessions_configured;
        unsigned int    max_sessions_possible;
        unsigned int    max_frame_size;
        int             name_count;
        NAME_TABLE      name_table[20];
        }
        ADAPTER_DATA;
```

You construct a permanent node name by prefixing the 6 bytes of network_card_id (returned in the preceding structure) with 10 bytes of binary zeros. Note that the resulting 16-byte character array is *not* a normal C string, because it is not null-terminated. For example, you can use memcpy() on it, but not strcpy().

NCB Input Fields:

NCB_COMMAND	0x33 or 0xB3
NCB_BUFFER_PTR	Far pointer to the ADAPTER_DATA area
NCB_LENGTH	Size of the ADAPTER_DATA area

NCB_CALLNAME	Name of the other workstation, or *
NCB_LANA_NUM	0 = adapter 1, 1 = adapter 2
NCB_POST	Far POST routine pointer, or NULL

NCB Output Fields:

NCB_LENGTH	Actual bytes returned
NCB_RETCODE	Immediate return code
NCB_CMD_CPLT	Final return code

Immediate Return Code:

0x00	No immediate error
0x03	Invalid command
0x21	Interface busy
0x22	Too many commands outstanding
0x23	Invalid NCB_LANA_NUM
0x40–0x4F	Unusual network condition
0x50–0xFE	Adapter malfunction

Final Return Code:

0x00	Success
0x01	Invalid buffer length
0x03	Invalid command
0x05	Command timed out
0x06	Buffer is too small (the remaining data is lost)
0x0B	Command canceled
0x15	Invalid name
0x19	Name conflict detected
0x21	Interface busy
0x22	Too many commands outstanding
0x23	Invalid NCB_LANA_NUM

III

Reference

0x40–0x4F	Unusual network condition
0x50–0xFE	Adapter malfunction

Unlink
0x70 (wait)

Description:

A workstation that has booted from the network rather than from its own disk or disk drives uses this command to disconnect itself effectively from the network. This command does not apply to normal workstations; it is intended to be used by system software running on diskless workstations.

If a special ROM chip is installed on the network adapter card (the Remote Program Load feature), the workstation at power-on time loads PC DOS from the file server. The workstation also establishes a special session with the file server. When this command is issued, the special session is dropped and redirection of disk I/O to and from the file server is terminated.

NCB Input Fields:

NCB_COMMAND	0x70
NCB_LANA_NUM	Adapter to unlink

NCB Output Fields:

NCB_CMD_CPLT	Final return code

Immediate Return Code:
None

Final Return Code:

0x00	Success
0x03	Invalid command
0x21	Interface busy
0x23	Invalid NCB_LANA_NUM
0x40–0x4F	Unusual network condition
0x50–0xFE	Adapter malfunction

Add Name
0x30 (wait), 0xB0 (no-wait)

Description:

This commands adds the 16-byte name specified in NCB_NAME to the name table as a unique name. An error is returned if any other workstation is already using the name either as a name or a group name. You build the name string by padding on the right with spaces and inserting a null character (\0) in the last character position, as shown in the following example:

```
char netbios_name[16];

strcpy(netbios_name, "BARRY");
while (strlen(netbios_name) < 15)
    strcat(netbios_name, " ");
```

NetBIOS assigns a number to the name that you add and returns this number in the NCB_NUM field. Use this number in datagram commands and in Receive Any commands.

NCB Input Fields:

NCB_COMMAND	0x30 or 0xB0
NCB_NAME	Name that you want to add
NCB_POST	Far pointer to POST routine, or NULL
NCB_LANA_NUM	0 = adapter 1, 1 = adapter 2

NCB Output Fields:

NCB_NUM	Assigned name number
NCB_RETCODE	Immediate return code
NCB_CMD_CPLT	Final return code

Immediate Return Code:

0x00	No immediate error
0x03	Invalid command
0x21	Interface busy
0x22	Too many commands outstanding
0x23	Invalid NCB_LANA_NUM

III

Reference

0x40–0x4F	Unusual network condition
0x50–0xFE	Adapter malfunction

Final Return Code:

0x00	Success
0x03	Invalid command
0x09	No resource available
0x0D	Name already in use by this workstation
0x0E	Name table is full
0x15	Invalid name
0x16	Name already in use by another workstation
0x19	Name conflict (NetBIOS internal error)
0x21	Interface busy
0x22	Too many commands outstanding
0x23	Invalid NCB_LANA_NUM
0x40–0x4F	Unusual network condition
0x50–0xFE	Adapter malfunction

Add Group Name
0x36 (wait), 0xB6 (no-wait)

Description:

This command adds the 16-byte name specified in NCB_NAME to the name table as a group name. If any other workstation is already using the name as a unique name, an error is returned. However, no error is returned if other workstations are using the name as a group name. You build the name string by padding on the right with spaces and inserting a null character (\0) in the last character position, as in the following example:

```
char netbios_name[16];

strcpy(netbios_name, "TEAM_ONE");
while (strlen(netbios_name) < 15)
     strcat(netbios_name, " ");
```

NetBIOS assigns a number to the name that you add and returns this number in the NCB_NUM field. Use this number in datagram commands and in Receive Any commands.

NCB Input Fields:

NCB_COMMAND	0x36 or 0xB6
NCB_NAME	Group name that you want to add
NCB_POST	Far pointer to POST routine, or NULL
NCB_LANA_NUM	0 = adapter 1, 1 = adapter 2

NCB Output Fields:

NCB_NUM	Assigned name number
NCB_RETCODE	Immediate return code
NCB_CMD_CPLT	Final return code

Immediate Return Code:

0x00	No immediate error
0x03	Invalid command
0x21	Interface busy
0x22	Too many commands outstanding
0x23	Invalid NCB_LANA_NUM
0x40–0x4F	Unusual network condition
0x50–0xFE	Adapter malfunction

Final Return Code:

0x00	Success
0x03	Invalid command
0x09	No resource available
0x0D	Name already in use by this workstation
0x0E	Name table is full
0x15	Invalid name
0x16	Name already in use by another workstation

III

Reference

0x21	Interface busy
0x22	Too many commands outstanding
0x23	Invalid NCB_LANA_NUM
0x40–0x4F	Unusual network condition
0x50–0xFE	Adapter malfunction

Delete Name
0x31 (wait), 0xB1 (no-wait)

Description:

This command deletes from the name table the 16-byte name specified in NCB_NAME. An error is returned if the name has an active session; the name is marked as deregistered and the name isn't actually deleted until its sessions are closed. Before you delete the name, you should use the Hang Up command to terminate any active sessions. If the name has a Listen, Receive Any, Receive Datagram, or Receive Broadcast Datagram command pending when the Delete Name command is issued, the name is deleted but the pending command is terminated with a name was deleted error code. Before you issue the Delete Name command, you should use the Cancel command to terminate the outstanding Listen or other outstanding command explicitly.

NCB Input Fields:

NCB_COMMAND	0x31 or 0xB1
NCB_NAME	Name to be deleted
NCB_POST	Far POST routine pointer, or NULL
NCB_LANA_NUM	0 = adapter 1, 1 = adapter 2

NCB Output Fields:

| NCB_RETCODE | Immediate return code |
| NCB_CMD_CPLT | Final return code |

Immediate Return Code:

| 0x00 | No immediate error |
| 0x03 | Invalid command |

0x21	Interface busy
0x22	Too many commands outstanding
0x23	Invalid NCB_LANA_NUM
0x40–0x4F	Unusual network condition
0x50–0xFE	Adapter malfunction

Final Return Code:

0x00	Success
0x03	Invalid command
0x0F	Name marked `deregistered` (active sessions)
0x15	Invalid name
0x21	Interface busy
0x22	Too many commands outstanding
0x23	Invalid NCB_LANA_NUM
0x40–0x4F	Unusual network condition
0x50–0xFE	Adapter malfunction

Call
0x10 (wait), 0x90 (no-wait)

Description:

This command establishes a session with the workstation named in
NCB_CALLNAME. A session can be established between names on two different workstations or between two names on a single workstation.

If multiple workstations are using the name as a group name and have issued
Listen commands, the Call command establishes only one session. However,
multiple sessions can be opened between the same pair of names (by issuing
multiple Call or Listen sequences). The name specified in NCB_NAME identifies the local side of the session. The name must be one of the names in the
local name table.

III

Reference

If the named workstation does not have an outstanding Listen command pending, the Call command is retried several times before your program receives an error. If the Call command succeeds, your program receives a local session number (LSN). Subsequent session activities (Send, Receive, and Hang Up commands) use the assigned LSN to refer to this session.

Time-out intervals for subsequent Send and Receive commands are specified in the Call NCB, not in the individual Send and Receive commands. The NCB_STO (Send Time Out) and NCB_RTO (Receive Time Out) fields are given in 500-millisecond (1/2 second) increments. If you set either to a value of zero, no time occurs for the corresponding command.

NCB Input Fields:

NCB_COMMAND	0x10 or 0x90
NCB_CALLNAME	Name of the Listening workstation
NCB_NAME	Local name performing the call
NCB_RTO	Receive time-out, in 1/2 seconds
NCB_STO	Send time-out, in 1/2 seconds
NCB_POST	Far POST routine pointer, or NULL
NCB_LANA_NUM	0 = adapter 1, 1 = adapter 2

NCB Output Fields:

NCB_LSN	The assigned local session number
NCB_RETCODE	Immediate return code
NCB_CMD_CPLT	Final return code

Immediate Return Code:

0x00	No immediate error
0x03	Invalid command
0x09	No resource available
0x15	Invalid name
0x21	Interface busy
0x22	Too many commands outstanding

0x23	Invalid NCB_LANA_NUM
0x40–0x4F	Unusual network condition
0x50–0xFE	Adapter malfunction

Final Return Code:

0x00	Success
0x03	Invalid command
0x09	No resource available
0x0B	Command canceled
0x11	Local session table full
0x12	Session open rejected
0x14	No answer, or no such name
0x15	Invalid name
0x18	Session ended abnormally
0x19	Name conflict
0x21	Interface busy
0x22	Too many commands outstanding
0x23	Invalid NCB_LANA_NUM
0x40–0x4F	Unusual network condition
0x50–0xFE	Adapter malfunction

Listen
0x11 (wait), 0x91 (no-wait)

Description:

This command answers a Call command and opens a session with the workstation named in NCB_CALLNAME. If the first byte of NCB_CALLNAME is an asterisk (*), it means "Listen for a call to our name (NCB_NAME) from any user." A session can be established between names on two different workstations or between two names on a single workstation.

III

Reference

If you have multiple Listens outstanding, a Listen command for a specific name takes priority over a Listen command for any name. You can open multiple sessions between the same pair of names (by issuing multiple Call and Listen sequences). The name specified in NCB_NAME identifies the local side of the session. The name must be one of those in the local name table.

If the Listen command succeeds, your program receives a local session number (LSN). Subsequent session activities (Send, Receive, and Hang Up commands) use the assigned LSN to refer to this session. Also, if you are listening for a call from any user, the name of the calling workstation is returned in the NCB_CALLNAME field.

Time-out intervals for subsequent Send and Receive commands are specified in the Listen NCB, not in the individual Send and Receive commands. The NCB_STO (Send Time Out) and NCB_RTO (Receive Time Out) fields are given in 500-millisecond (1/2 second) increments. If you set either to a value of zero, no time-out occurs for the corresponding command. Note that the Listen command itself does not time out. Use the wait option carefully.

NCB Input Fields:

NCB_COMMAND	0x11 or 0x91
NCB_CALLNAME	Name to Listen for (* = any user)
NCB_NAME	Local (Listening) name
NCB_RTO	Receive time-out, in 1/2 seconds
NCB_STO	Send time-out, in 1/2 seconds
NCB_POST	Far POST routine pointer, or NULL
NCB_LANA_NUM	0 = adapter 1, 1 = adapter 2

NCB Output Fields:

NCB_LSN	The assigned local session number
NCB_CALLNAME	Caller's name if "Listening for any user"
NCB_RETCODE	Immediate return code
NCB_CMD_CPLT	Final return code

Immediate Return Code:

0x00	No immediate error
0x03	Invalid command
0x09	No resource available
0x15	Invalid name
0x21	Interface busy
0x22	Too many commands outstanding
0x23	Invalid NCB_LANA_NUM
0x40–0x4F	Unusual network condition
0x50–0xFE	Adapter malfunction

Final Return Code:

0x00	Success
0x03	Invalid command
0x09	No resource available
0x0B	Command canceled
0x11	Local session table full
0x15	Invalid name
0x17	Name was deleted
0x18	Session ended abnormally
0x19	Name conflict
0x21	Interface busy
0x22	Too many commands outstanding
0x23	Invalid NCB_LANA_NUM
0x40–0x4F	Unusual network condition
0x50–0xFE	Adapter malfunction

III

Reference

Hang Up
0x12 (wait), 0x92 (no-wait)

Description:

This command closes the session identified by the local session number (NCB_LSN). Both partners in the session should issue this call at the end of the session.

Any pending Receive commands for this LSN are terminated and their NCB_CMD_CPLT fields are set to 0x0A (session closed). Pending Send commands, however, are given roughly 20 seconds in which to complete, after which they too are terminated with error code 0x0A (unless, of course, they complete successfully). If a pending Send command does not complete during the 20-second time period, the Hang Up command itself is returned with an error code 0x05 (timed out), and the session ends. Finally, if one or more Receive Any commands are outstanding when the Hang Up command is issued, one of those Receive Any commands is returned with error code 0x0A (session closed). Any other commands outstanding when the Hang Up command is issued are returned with error code 0x18 (session ended abnormally).

As the preceding discussion suggests, you should coordinate the commands issued by both partners so that none are outstanding when the Hang Up is issued.

NCB Input Fields:

NCB_COMMAND	0x12 or 0x92
NCB_LSN	Local session number
NCB_POST	Far POST routine pointer, or NULL
NCB_LANA_NUM	0 = adapter 1, 1 = adapter 2

NCB Output Fields:

NCB_RETCODE	Immediate return code
NCB_CMD_CPLT	Final return code

Immediate Return Code:

0x00	No immediate error
0x03	Invalid command
0x21	Interface busy

0x22	Too many commands outstanding
0x23	Invalid NCB_LANA_NUM
0x40–0x4F	Unusual network condition
0x50–0xFE	Adapter malfunction

Final Return Code:

0x00	Success
0x03	Invalid command
0x05	Timed out
0x08	Invalid local session number
0x0A	Session closed
0x0B	Command canceled
0x18	Session ended abnormally
0x21	Interface busy
0x22	Too many commands outstanding
0x23	Invalid NCB_LANA_NUM
0x40–0x4F	Unusual network condition
0x50–0xFE	Adapter malfunction

Send
0x14 (wait), 0x94 (no-wait)

Description:

This command sends from 1 to 65,535 bytes of data to the NetBIOS session partner associated with the local session number specified in NCB_LSN. You place the address of the data in NCB_BUFFER_PTR as a far pointer, and you set the length in NCB_LENGTH.

Issuing a Hang Up command while Send commands are pending results in the error situations discussed in the Hang Up command description. The period of time in which the Send must complete successfully (Send Time Out) is given in the corresponding Call or Listen command, not by the Send command itself. If this time period expires before the other workstation receives the data, the session terminates abnormally and the Send NCB returns error 0x05 (timed out). (This differs with a Receive command that times out, for which the session does not terminate.) Furthermore, if the Send command cannot complete successfully for *any* reason, the session is terminated.

If multiple Send commands are outstanding, the other workstation receives them in the proper order (first-in, first-out).

Avoid issuing a Send command unless the other workstation has issued a corresponding Receive command.

NCB Input Fields:

NCB_COMMAND	0x14 or 0x94
NCB_LSN	Local session number
NCB_BUFFER_PTR	Far pointer to the data to be sent
NCB_LENGTH	Number of bytes to send
NCB_POST	Far POST routine pointer, or NULL
NCB_LANA_NUM	0 = adapter 1, 1 = adapter 2

NCB Output Fields:

NCB_RETCODE	Immediate return code
NCB_CMD_CPLT	Final return code

Immediate Return Code:

0x00	No immediate error
0x03	Invalid command
0x21	Interface busy
0x22	Too many commands outstanding
0x23	Invalid NCB_LANA_NUM
0x40–0x4F	Unusual network condition
0x50–0xFE	Adapter malfunction

Final Return Code:

0x00	Success
0x03	Invalid command
0x05	Timed out
0x08	Invalid local session number
0x0A	Session closed
0x0B	Command canceled
0x18	Session ended abnormally
0x21	Interface busy
0x22	Too many commands outstanding
0x23	Invalid NCB_LANA_NUM
0x40–0x4F	Unusual network condition
0x50–0xFE	Adapter malfunction

Send No ACK
0x71 (wait), 0xF1 (no-wait)

Description:

This command works exactly like the Send command, except that it does not require an acknowledgment from the receiving workstation and therefore operates a little quicker.

NCB Input Fields:

NCB_COMMAND	0x71 or 0xf1
NCB_LSN	Local session number
NCB_BUFFER_PTR	Far pointer to the data to be sent
NCB_LENGTH	Number of bytes to send
NCB_POST	Far POST routine pointer, or NULL
NCB_LANA_NUM	0 = adapter 1, 1 = adapter 2

III

Reference

NCB Output Fields:

NCB_RETCODE	Immediate return code
NCB_CMD_CPLT	Final return code

Immediate Return Code:

0x00	No immediate error
0x03	Invalid command
0x21	Interface busy
0x22	Too many commands outstanding
0x23	Invalid NCB_LANA_NUM
0x40–0x4F	Unusual network condition
0x50–0xFE	Adapter malfunction

Final Return Code:

0x00	Success
0x03	Invalid command
0x05	Timed out
0x08	Invalid local session number
0x0A	Session closed
0x0B	Command canceled
0x18	Session ended abnormally
0x21	Interface busy
0x22	Too many commands outstanding
0x23	Invalid NCB_LANA_NUM
0x40–0x4F	Unusual network condition
0x50–0xFE	Adapter malfunction

Chain Send
0x17 (wait), 0x97 (no-wait)

Description:

This command behaves exactly like the Send command, except that it sends two data buffers rather than one. The two data buffers are concatenated and sent as a single message. The first two bytes of NCB_CALLNAME are used to specify the length of the second buffer and the next four bytes of NCB_CALLNAME are used as a far pointer to the second buffer. The maximum number of bytes for both buffers is 131,070.

NCB Input Fields:

NCB_COMMAND	0x17 or 0x97
NCB_LSN	Local session number
NCB_BUFFER_PTR	Far pointer to the first data buffer
NCB_LENGTH	Length of the first data buffer
NCB_CALLNAME	Length of the second buffer in the first two bytes; address (far pointer) of the buffer in following four bytes
NCB_POST	Far POST routine pointer, or NULL
NCB_LANA_NUM	0 = adapter 1, 1 = adapter 2

NCB Output Fields:

NCB_RETCODE	Immediate return code
NCB_CMD_CPLT	Final return code

Immediate Return Code:

0x00	No immediate error
0x03	Invalid command
0x21	Interface busy
0x22	Too many commands outstanding
0x23	Invalid NCB_LANA_NUM
0x40–0x4F	Unusual network condition
0x50–0xFE	Adapter malfunction

III

Reference

Final Return Code:

0x00	Success
0x03	Invalid command
0x05	Timed out
0x08	Invalid local session number
0x0A	Session closed
0x0B	Command canceled
0x18	Session ended abnormally
0x21	Interface busy
0x22	Too many commands outstanding
0x23	Invalid NCB_LANA_NUM
0x40–0x4F	Unusual network condition
0x50–0xFE	Adapter malfunction

Chain Send No ACK
0x72 (wait), 0xf2 (no-wait)

Description:

This command behaves exactly like the Chain Send command, except that it does not require an acknowledgment from the receiving workstation, and therefore operates a little quicker than its more reliable counterpart.

NCB Input Fields:

NCB_COMMAND	0x72 or 0xf2
NCB_LSN	Local session number
NCB_BUFFER_PTR	Far pointer to the first data buffer
NCB_LENGTH	Length of the first data buffer
NCB_CALLNAME	Length of the second buffer in the first two bytes; address (far pointer) of the buffer in the following four bytes

| NCB_POST | Far POST routine pointer, or NULL |
| NCB_LANA_NUM | 0 = adapter 1, 1 = adapter 2 |

NCB Output Fields:

| NCB_RETCODE | Immediate return code |
| NCB_CMD_CPLT | Final return code |

Immediate Return Code:

0x00	No immediate error
0x03	Invalid command
0x21	Interface busy
0x22	Too many commands outstanding
0x23	Invalid NCB_LANA_NUM
0x40–0x4F	Unusual network condition
0x50–0xFE	Adapter malfunction

Final Return Code:

0x00	Success
0x03	Invalid command
0x05	Timed out
0x08	Invalid local session number
0x0A	Session closed
0x0B	Command canceled
0x18	Session ended abnormally
0x21	Interface busy
0x22	Too many commands outstanding
0x23	Invalid NCB_LANA_NUM
0x40–0x4F	Unusual network condition
0x50–0xFE	Adapter malfunction

III

Reference

Receive
0x15 (wait), 0x95 (no-wait)

Description:

The command receives data that the other session-partner workstation has sent with the Sent or Chain Sent command. If different types of Receive commands are outstanding, they are processed in the following order: Receive, Receive Any for a specified name, and Receive Any for any name. The time-out interval for the Receive command is specified in the Call or Listen command and not in the Receive command. Note that a time-out error (0x05) does not cause the session to be aborted. See the discussion of the Hang Up command for a description of what happens when a Hang Up command is issued even though outstanding Receive commands are pending.

If you give NetBIOS a receive buffer that is too small for the incoming message, you receive error code 0x06. However, to read the remainder of the data (before the end of the time-out interval), you can issue another Receive command. NCB_LENGTH returns the number of bytes actually received.

NCB Input Fields:

NCB_COMMAND	0x15 or 0x95
NCB_LSN	Local session number
NCB_BUFFER_PTR	Far pointer to the input buffer
NCB_LENGTH	Length of the input buffer
NCB_POST	Far POST routine pointer, or NULL
NCB_LANA_NUM	0 = adapter 1, 1 = adapter 2

NCB Output Fields:

NCB_LENGTH	Actual number of bytes received
NCB_RETCODE	Immediate return code
NCB_CMD_CPLT	Final return code

Immediate Return Code:

0x00	No immediate error
0x03	Invalid command

0x21	Interface busy
0x22	Too many commands outstanding
0x23	Invalid NCB_LANA_NUM
0x40–0x4F	Unusual network condition
0x50–0xFE	Adapter malfunction

Final Return Code:

0x00	Success
0x03	Invalid command
0x05	Timed out
0x06	Receive buffer is too small
0x08	Invalid local session number
0x0A	Session closed
0x0B	Command canceled
0x18	Session ended abnormally
0x21	Interface busy
0x22	Too many commands outstanding
0x23	Invalid NCB_LANA_NUM
0x40–0x4F	Unusual network condition
0x50–0xFE	Adapter malfunction

Receive Any
0x16 (wait), 0x96 (no-wait)

Description:

This command receives data from any of your session partners. You specify your name number (which NetBIOS assigns when the Add Name or Add Group Name commands were performed) rather than the local session number in this call. If you set the NCB_NUM field to 0xFF, this command receives data from any session partner for any of your names.

III

Reference

See the description of the Hang Up command for an explanation of what happens when you issue a Hang Up command and outstanding Receive Any commands are pending. Also, note that this command does not time-out; use the wait option carefully.

If you give NetBIOS a receive buffer that is too small for the incoming message, you receive error code 0x06. However, to read the remainder of the data (before the end of the time-out interval), you can issue another Receive Any command. NCB_LENGTH returns the number of bytes actually received.

Caution

Do not use the Receive Any command when running under the IBM PC LAN Program. This command blocks PCLP from receiving messages properly.

NCB Input Fields:

NCB_COMMAND	0x16 or 0x96
NCB_NUM	Name number (0xFF = receive from any partner)
NCB_BUFFER_PTR	Far pointer to the input buffer
NCB_LENGTH	Length of the input buffer
NCB_POST	Far POST routine pointer, or NULL
NCB_LANA_NUM	0 = adapter 1, 1 = adapter 2

NCB Output Fields:

NCB_LENGTH	Actual number of bytes received
NCB_NUM	Name number of the name receiving the data
NCB_RETCODE	Immediate return code
NCB_CMD_CPLT	Final return code

Immediate Return Code:

0x00	No immediate error
0x03	Invalid command
0x21	Interface busy
0x22	Too many commands outstanding

0x23	Invalid NCB_LANA_NUM
0x40–0x4F	Unusual network condition
0x50–0xFE	Adapter malfunction

Final Return Code:

0x00	Success
0x03	Invalid command
0x06	Receive buffer is too small
0x0A	Session closed
0x0B	Command canceled
0x13	Invalid name number
0x17	Name deleted
0x18	Session ended abnormally
0x19	Name conflict
0x21	Interface busy
0x22	Too many commands outstanding
0x23	Invalid NCB_LANA_NUM
0x40–0x4F	Unusual network condition
0x50–0xFE	Adapter malfunction

Session Status
0x34 (wait), 0xB4 (no-wait)

Description:

Use this command to obtain status information about the sessions, if any, that are associated with a given NCB_NAME. If the first byte of NCB_NAME is an asterisk (*), this command returns information about names in the local name table.

A return code of 0x06 (buffer too small) causes any data that could not fit in the input buffer to be discarded.

III

Reference

The following structures show the layout of the information that this command returns:

```
/* information about each session:              */
/*     local session number                     */
/*     session state:                           */
/*          1 - Listen pending                   */
/*          2 - Call pending                     */
/*          3 - Session established              */
/*          4 - Hang Up pending                  */
/*          5 - Hang Up complete                 */
/*          6 - Session ended abnormally         */
/*     local workstation name                   */
/*     remote (partner) workstation name        */
/*     number of Receive cmds outstanding       */
/*     number of Send cmds outstanding          */

typedef struct {
    byte lsn;
    byte state;
    char local_name[16];
    char remote_name[16];
    byte recv_count;
    byte send_count;
    }
    A_SESSION;


/* information about the specified name:         */
/*     name number, number of sessions,          */
/*     number of outstanding Receive Datagrams,  */
/*     number of outstanding Receive Any cmds,   */
/*     and data about each session.              */

typedef struct {
    byte name_num;
    byte session_count;
    byte datagrams_outstanding;
    byte receive_any_outstanding;
    A_SESSION session_data[40];
    }
    STATUS_INFO;
```

NCB Input Fields:

NCB_COMMAND	0x34 or 0xB4
NCB_BUFFER_PTR	Address (far pointer) of the status buffer
NCB_LENGTH	Size of the status buffer
NCB_NAME	* = all local names
NCB_POST	Far POST routine pointer, or NULL
NCB_LANA_NUM	0 = adapter 1, 1 = adapter 2

NCB Output Fields:

NCB_LENGTH	Actual number of bytes returned
NCB_RETCODE	Immediate return code
NCB_CMD_CPLT	Final return code

Immediate Return Code:

0x00	No immediate error
0x03	Invalid command
0x15	Invalid name
0x21	Interface busy
0x22	Too many commands outstanding
0x23	Invalid NCB_LANA_NUM
0x40–0x4F	Unusual network condition
0x50–0xFE	Adapter malfunction

Final Return Code:

0x00	Success
0x01	Invalid buffer length
0x03	Invalid command
0x06	Receive buffer is too small
0x19	Name conflict
0x21	Interface busy
0x22	Too many commands outstanding
0x23	Invalid NCB_LANA_NUM
0x40–0x4F	Unusual network condition
0x50–0xFE	Adapter malfunction

III

Reference

Send Datagram
0x20 (wait), 0xA0 (no-wait)

Description:

This command sends a datagram to a unique name or to a group name. The datagram can be from 1 to 512 bytes long. You do not have to have a session already established before using this command; however, the command does not guarantee that the datagram will be received.

NCB Input Fields:

NCB_COMMAND	0x20 or 0xA0
NCB_NUM	Name number assigned when the name was added
NCB_CALLNAME	Destination workstation name
NCB_BUFFER_PTR	Far pointer to the output buffer
NCB_LENGTH	Size of the output buffer (1–512)
NCB_POST	Far POST routine pointer, or NULL
NCB_LANA_NUM	0 = adapter 1, 1 = adapter 2

NCB Output Fields:

NCB_RETCODE	Immediate return code
NCB_CMD_CPLT	Final return code

Immediate Return Code:

0x00	No immediate error
0x03	Invalid command
0x21	Interface busy
0x22	Too many commands outstanding
0x23	Invalid NCB_LANA_NUM
0x40–0x4F	Unusual network condition
0x50–0xFE	Adapter malfunction

Final Return Code:

0x00	Success
0x01	Invalid buffer length
0x03	Invalid command
0x13	Name number
0x19	Name conflict
0x21	Interface busy
0x22	Too many commands outstanding
0x23	Invalid NCB_LANA_NUM
0x40–0x4F	Unusual network condition
0x50–0xFE	Adapter malfunction

Send Broadcast Datagram
0x22 (wait), 0xA2 (no-wait)

Description:

This command sends a datagram to all workstations that have issued an outstanding Receive Broadcast Datagram command (other workstations do not receive the message). If a Receive Broadcast Datagram command is outstanding at the local workstation, it also receives the message. If multiple Receive Broadcast Datagram commands are outstanding at a workstation, they all receive the message.

NCB Input Fields:

NCB_COMMAND	0x22 or 0xA2
NCB_NUM	Name number assigned when the name was added
NCB_BUFFER_PTR	Far pointer to the output buffer
NCB_LENGTH	Size of the output buffer (1–512)
NCB_POST	Far POST routine pointer, or NULL
NCB_LANA_NUM	0 = adapter 1, 1 = adapter 2

III

Reference

NCB Output Fields:

NCB_RETCODE	Immediate return code
NCB_CMD_CPLT	Final return code

Immediate Return Code:

0x00	No immediate error
0x03	Invalid command
0x21	Interface busy
0x22	Too many commands outstanding
0x23	Invalid NCB_LANA_NUM
0x40–0x4F	Unusual network condition
0x50–0xFE	Adapter malfunction

Final Return Code:

0x00	Success
0x01	Invalid buffer length
0x03	Invalid command
0x13	Invalid name number
0x21	Interface busy
0x22	Too many commands outstanding
0x23	Invalid NCB_LANA_NUM
0x40–0x4F	Unusual network condition
0x50–0xFE	Adapter malfunction

Receive Datagram
0x21 (wait), 0xA1 (no-wait)

Description:

This command receives a datagram (but not Broadcast Datagrams) sent by any user to a unique name or to a group name in the local name table. The datagram can be up to 512 bytes long. You do not have to have a session already established to use this command. If set to 0xFF, the NCB_NUM field signifies that a datagram can be received from any user for any of the names in the local name table. If the size of the datagram is longer than specified in NCB_LENGTH, the remainder of the message data is discarded.

Note that this command does not time out. Use the wait option carefully.

NCB Input Fields:

NCB_COMMAND	0x21 or 0xA1
NCB_NUM	Name number or 0xFF
NCB_BUFFER_PTR	Far pointer to the input buffer
NCB_LENGTH	Size of the input buffer (1–512)
NCB_POST	Far POST routine pointer, or NULL
NCB_LANA_NUM	0 = adapter 1, 1 = adapter 2

NCB Output Fields:

NCB_CALLNAME	Name of the other workstation
NCB_LENGTH	Actual number of bytes received
NCB_RETCODE	Immediate return code
NCB_CMD_CPLT	Final return code

Immediate Return Code:

0x00	No immediate error
0x03	Invalid command
0x21	Interface busy
0x22	Too many commands outstanding
0x23	Invalid NCB_LANA_NUM
0x40–0x4F	Unusual network condition
0x50–0xFE	Adapter malfunction

Final Return Code:

0x00	Success
0x01	Invalid buffer length

III

0x03	Invalid command
0x06	Buffer is too small
0x0B	Command canceled
0x13	Invalid name number
0x17	Name deleted
0x19	Name conflict
0x21	Interface busy
0x22	Too many commands outstanding
0x23	Invalid NCB_LANA_NUM
0x40–0x4F	Unusual network condition
0x50–0xFE	Adapter malfunction

Receive Broadcast Datagram
0x23 (wait), 0xA3 (no-wait)

Description:

This command receives a broadcast datagram (but no regular datagrams) sent by any user. The datagram can be as much as 512 bytes long. You do not need to have a session established before you use this command. If the datagram is longer than specified in the NCB_LENGTH field, the remainder of the message data is discarded.

Note that this command does not time out. Use the wait option carefully.

NCB Input Fields:

NCB_COMMAND	0x23 or 0xA3
NCB_NUM	Name number or 0xFF
NCB_BUFFER_PTR	Far pointer to the input buffer
NCB_LENGTH	Size of the input buffer (1–512)
NCB_POST	Far POST routine pointer, or NULL
NCB_LANA_NUM	0 = adapter 1, 1 = adapter 2

NCB Output Fields:

NCB_CALLNAME	Name of the other workstation
NCB_LENGTH	Actual number of bytes received
NCB_RETCODE	Immediate return code
NCB_CMD_CPLT	Final return code

Immediate Return Code:

0x00	No immediate error
0x03	Invalid command
0x21	Interface busy
0x22	Too many commands outstanding
0x23	Invalid NCB_LANA_NUM
0x40–0x4F	Unusual network condition
0x50–0xFE	Adapter malfunction

Final Return Code:

0x00	Success
0x01	Invalid buffer length
0x03	Invalid command
0x06	Buffer is too small
0x0B	Command canceled
0x13	Invalid name number
0x17	Name deleted
0x19	Name conflict
0x21	Interface busy
0x22	Too many commands outstanding
0x23	Invalid NCB_LANA_NUM
0x40–0x4F	Unusual network condition
0x50–0xFE	Adapter malfunction

III

Reference

IPX and SPX Functions

This section contains reference information regarding the IPX and SPX protocols, available under Novell NetWare. Some general reminders about important techniques are mentioned here, but you should refer to Chapter 6, "IPX and SPX Programming," for details on accessing the functions and their data structures, especially when direct access to CPU registers is required.

There are two ways to call IPX/SPX. The first method entails setting up the CPU registers (as specified for the given function) and performing a far call to an address that you have previously obtained. After calling Interrupt 2F (hex) with a multiplex number of 7A (hex) and a function code of 0, the entry point for this method is returned in the ES:DI register pair. The entry point itself is a far pointer to a function. The following example demonstrates how to obtain the function pointer (the first method's entry point):

```
void far (*ipx_spx)(void);      /* far pointer to function */

int  get_ipx_spx_pointer(void)
     {
     union REGS regs;
     struct SREGS sregs;

     regs.x.ax = 0x7A00;
     int86x(0x2F, &regs, &regs, &sregs);
     if (regs.h.al != 0xFF)
          return -1;            /* IPX/SPX not installed! */

     ipx_spx = MK_FP(sregs.es, regs.x.di);

     return 0;                  /* entry point established */
     }
```

When this function pointer is known, calling IPX or SPX is a matter of setting up certain CPU registers (as specified in this section) and calling the function. This is easy to do in Borland C (because it allows direct access to CPU registers) but requires some assembler coding if you're using Microsoft C. The following is an example of how to call IPX/SPX in Borland C:

```
void close_socket(unsigned socket)
{
_BX = 0x0001;
_DX = socket;
ipx_spx();      /* compiler generates a "far call" */
}
```

The second method uses the older (but still supported) Interrupt 7A (hex)
entry point into IPX/SPX. This entry point is easier for Microsoft C users to
invoke:

```
void close_socket(unsigned socket)
{
union REGS regs;

regs.x.bx = 0x0001;
regs.x.dx = socket;
int86(0x7A, &regs, &regs);
}
```

The one drawback to using Interrupt 7A is that the IBM 3270 Emulation
product also uses this interrupt. If you're using the Microsoft C compiler and
want to avoid potential interrupt vector conflicts, see the discussion in Chapter 6, "IPX and SPX Programming," on constructing a custom assembler interface to IPX/SPX.

An event control block (ECB) is associated with almost every IPX or SPX function. SPX in particular must draw from a pool of available ECBs that you
submit. IPX/SPX uses some of the items internally in an ECB. However, you
specify some items, which are described for each function call in this section
and are marked /* you set */ in the following code. An ECB looks like this:

```
struct ECB
{
void far          *link_address;
void far          (*event_svc_routine)();      /* you set */
unsigned char     in_use;
unsigned char     completion_code;
unsigned char     socket_number[2];            /* you set */
unsigned int      connection_id;
unsigned int      reserved1;
unsigned char     reserved2 [12];
unsigned char     immediate_address [6];       /* you set */
unsigned int      fragment_count;              /* you set */
struct {
    void far      *address;                    /* you set */
    unsigned int length;                       /* you set */
    } fragment [2];
};
```

IPX/SPX uses the `link_address` field internally. When you submit the ECB, IPX/SPX sets the `in_use` item to a nonzero value, which remains nonzero while the ECB is being processed and then is set to zero when the event completes. (You can use the setting of this item to poll for the completion of the event.) After the event completes, you can inspect the `completion_code` field to determine the event's success or failure. You set `socket_number` to identify the socket that you have opened and through which you are sending and receiving packets. The high-order byte of `socket_number` occurs first. SPX returns the `connection_id` field after a successful `SPXListenForConnection()` call.

Before each `IPXSendPacket()` call, you use `IPXGetLocalTarget()` to set the `immediate_address` field, which represents the node address of a bridge that the packet must cross to reach its destination. You set `fragment_count` to tell IPX/SPX how many packet fragments it must "gather" to form a complete packet. `fragment[].address` and `fragment[].length` describe the packet fragments themselves. The first fragment is always an IPX header (30 bytes) or an SPX header (42 bytes). The second fragment is usually one entire data buffer (as much as 546 bytes for IPX, or as much as 534 bytes for SPX).

If you specify an event service routine (ESR) by putting a non-NULL function pointer in the ECB's `event_svc_routine` field, IPX/SPX calls that function when the event associated with the ECB finishes. When the ESR is called, the following conditions are true:

- Interrupts are disabled.

- A far call invokes the ESR; you must declare the far call as follows: `void far event_handler(void)`.

- A far pointer to the associated ECB is in the ES:SI register pair.

- The CPU registers are saved.

- The DS register does not necessarily point to your program's data area.

- The ECB's `in_use` field has been reset to 0.

To show what these conditions mean to a C program, an example of an ESR in Borland C follows. Notice that direct access to the CPU registers is needed to set up the ESR properly.

```
void far event_handler(void)
    {
    struct ECB far *ecb_ptr;
```

```
                        _AX = _ES;
                        _DS = _AX;        /* establish addressability */
                        ecb_ptr = MK_FP(_ES, _SI);
                        global_return_code = ecb_ptr->completion_code;
                        ecb_attention_flag = 1;      /* signal the main pgm */
                        }
```

The format of an IPX header follows:

```
            struct IPXHEADER
                {
                unsigned int      checksum;
                unsigned int      length;
                unsigned char     transport_control;
                unsigned char     packet_type;                  /* you set */
                unsigned char     dest_network_number[4];       /* you set */
                unsigned char     dest_network_node[6];         /* you set */
                unsigned char     dest_network_socket[2];       /* you set */
                unsigned char     source_network_number[4];
                unsigned char     source_network_node[6];
                unsigned char     source_network_socket[2];
                };
```

IPX sets the checksum, length, and transport_control fields, as well as the source_network fields (number, node, and socket). To distinguish an IPX packet from an SPX packet, you set packet_type to 4. You set the dest_network fields (number, node, and socket) to identify a packet's destination (see Chapter 6, "IPX and SPX Programming"). The destination can be a single workstation or (if *node* = 0xFF 0xFF 0xFF 0xFF 0xFF 0xFF) all workstations on the network. *Note:* You represent a socket number with its high-order byte first. An IPX header is 30 bytes long. If you mix IPX and SPX calls in your program, you must not use the same socket for both.

The following is an SPX header:

```
            struct SPXHEADER
                {
                unsigned int      checksum;
                unsigned int      length;
                unsigned char     transport_control;
                unsigned char     packet_type;
                unsigned char     dest_network_number[4];       /* you set */
                unsigned char     dest_network_node[6];         /* you set */
                unsigned char     dest_network_socket[2];       /* you set */
                unsigned char     source_network_number[4];
                unsigned char     source_network_node[6];
                unsigned char     source_network_socket[2];
                unsigned char     connection_control;
                unsigned char     datastream_type;              /* you set */
                unsigned int      source_connection_id;
                unsigned int      dest_connection_id;
                unsigned int      sequence_number;
                unsigned int      acknowledge_number;
                unsigned int      allocation_number;
                };
```

The first 30 bytes of the 42-byte SPX header have the same layout as for an IPX header. You don't have to set packet_type; SPX does that for you automatically. The dest_network fields (number, node, and socket) identify a packet's destination, just as with IPX, except that *node* cannot contain a broadcast address. *Note*: A socket number is represented with its high-order byte first. datastream_type is a dual-purpose field that both you and SPX can use (see Chapter 6, "IPX and SPX Programming"). SPX sets and manages the other fields in the SPX header. As was previously mentioned, do not use the same socket for IPX and SPX calls if you use both protocols in your program.

IPX Functions

IPXCancelEvent
0x06

Description:
This function cancels a pending IPX or SPX event that is associated with a particular ECB. Note that IPX returns a completion code in the canceled ECB but does not invoke the ESR, if the ECB specifies one. If the cancellation succeeds, the completion code in the canceled ECB is set to 0xFC (event canceled). This completion code is distinct from the completion code returned in the AL register (see the output registers for this function).

The event to be canceled must not have been started yet (it must still be pending). IPXCancelEvent must not cancel ECBs related to the following two SPX functions (use SPXAbortConnection instead):

- SPXEstablishConnection

- SPXSendSequencedPacket

Input Registers:

BX	0x06
ES:SI	Far pointer to event control block

III

Reference

Output Registers:

AL   Completion codes:

     0x00   Success

     0xF9   ECB cannot be canceled

     0xFF   ECB is not in use

IPXCloseSocket
0x01

Description:

This function closes a socket. Any events associated with the socket are canceled. Closing a socket that is already closed is harmless. If you terminate your program without closing a socket, and if a pending ECB tries to call an ESR after your program is no longer in memory, your workstation probably will crash.

Input Registers:

BX   0x01

DX   Socket number

IPXDisconnectFromTarget
0x0B

Description:

Network communications software drivers use this function to notify a listening node that communications to a specified socket are being terminated. The driver on the destination node reacts by deallocating any virtual connection that it has with the originating node. Do not call this function from within an ESR.

Request Buffer:

```
struct
      {
      byte dest_network_number[4];
      byte dest_node_address[6];
      byte dest_socket[2];
      } request_buffer;
```

Input Registers:

BX	0x0B
ES:SI	Far pointer to `request_buffer`

IPXGetInternetworkAddress
0x09

Description:

This function returns the network number and node address of the work-station calling this function.

Reply Buffer:
```
struct
    {
    byte network_number[4];
    byte node_address[6];
    } reply_buffer;
```

Input Registers:

BX	0x09
ES:SI	Far pointer to `reply_buffer`

Output Registers:

ES:SI	Far pointer to `reply_buffer`

IPXGetIntervalMarker
0x08

Description:

This function returns a time marker that is measured in timer ticks. Each second, 18.2 timer ticks occur. A subsequent call to this function returns a time marker with a greater value; you can subtract the first marker value from the later one to get an idea of how much time has passed. You cannot use the returned field to measure periods of time longer than about one hour, because the returned interval marker is a 16-bit quantity with a maximum value of 65,535.

III

Reference

Input Registers:

    BX   0x08

Output Registers:

    AX   Interval marker

Special Note:

A better way to "mark time" in your program is to create a far pointer to the doubleword timer tick, which the computer maintains automatically. You create the far pointer as follows:

```
unsigned long far *tick_ptr;
unsigned long then, now, interval;


tick_ptr = MK_FP(0x0040, 0x006C);    /* valid for IBM and */
                                     /* compatibles      */
then = *tick_ptr;

/* do something here that takes up some time */

now = *tick_ptr;
interval = now - then;
```

IPXGetLocalTarget
0x02

Description:

This function provides routing information for a given destination workstation. You need to use this information when constructing an IPXSendPacket() ECB. This function returns the node_address, which you copy into the immediate_address field of the ECB before calling IPXSendPacket(). Use the memcpy() library function (or an equivalent function) to copy the six bytes.

The returned node_address value is either the identification of the nearest bridge if the packet must cross a bridge on its way to the destination, or the node address of the destination workstation itself if there is no intervening bridge. In either case, copy the returned value to the immediate_address field.

If performance is a concern, you can expedite the process by using the necessary routing information contained in the ECB of a received packet. After an IPXListenForPacket() call finishes, save the immediate_address field from its ECB. Use this value to construct the ECB for your next IPXSendPacket() call to that same destination.

This function also returns an estimate of how much time a packet takes to reach the destination workstation. This value is represented in timer ticks (18.2 ticks per second).

You can call this function from within an ESR.

Request Buffer:
```
struct
    {
    byte dest_network_number[4];
    byte dest_node_address[6];
    byte dest_socket[2];
    } request_buffer;
```

Reply Buffer:
```
struct
    {
    byte node_address[6];
    } reply_buffer;
```

Input Registers:

BX	0x02
ES:SI	Far pointer to request_buffer
ES:DI	Far pointer to reply_buffer

Output Registers:

AL	Completion codes:
	0x00 Success
	0xFA No path to destination
CX	Estimated transport time
ES:DI	Far pointer to reply_buffer

IPXListenForPacket
0x04

Description:
To give IPX the address of a buffer in which it should place the next incoming message packet for a particular open socket, you issue one or more calls to this function. Each call gives IPX an ECB that the protocol places in a pool of listening ECBs. IPX returns immediately to your program after each call, but waits in the background for incoming packets.

On receiving a packet, IPX selects one of the listening ECBs that has a socket number matching that of the incoming packet. If multiple ECBs are outstanding for the socket number, IPX can choose any one of the listening ECBs. Still processing in background mode, IPX does the following:

- Sets the completion code in the ECB

- Places the node address of the sender, or the local bridge that routed this packet, in the immediate_address field of the ECB

- Sets the in_use flag to 0

- Invokes the ESR associated with the ECB, if one is specified

You must have previously opened the socket with a call to IPXOpenSocket(). Before calling this function, you should set the fields in each ECB as follows:

socket_number -	The socket number that you opened.
event_svc_routine	A function pointer, or NULL.
fragment_count	Typically a value of 2, to express both the incoming IPX header and the incoming data message.
fragment[0].address	A far pointer to an IPX header buffer.
fragment[0].length	The length of the IPX header buffer (30 bytes).
fragment[1].address	A far pointer to a data area that will receive the incoming message. The data area can be as long as 546 bytes.
fragment[1].length	The length of the data area.

Input Registers:

BX   0x04

ES:SI   Far pointer to an ECB

Output Registers:

AL   Immediate completion codes:

0x00   Success (the ECB was added to the pool)

x   Listening socket does not exist

ECB Completion Codes:

0x00	Packet successfully received
0xFC	This event has been canceled
0xFD	Buffer is too small
0xFF	Socket is not open

IPXOpenSocket
0x00

Description:

This function opens a socket for use by either IPX or SPX. If you specify a 0 value, IPX assigns a socket number in the range of 0x4000 to 0x8000. You use the open socket when sending or receiving message packets. Also, to send message packets, you must know the socket number at the destination workstation.

If you specify the socket number, do not use values in the range of 0x0000 to 0x0BB9 or higher than 0x8000. These values are reserved or already assigned by Novell. To obtain registered socket number assignments for your applications, you can contact Novell.

> ### Note
>
> The high-order byte of socket number occurs first. This differs from the CPU's native, internal representation of numbers, so you must swap the bytes.

A socket can be short-lived or long-lived. If short-lived, the socket is closed when a program terminates or when an explicit call to IPXCloseSocket() is made. If long-lived, the socket is closed only by an explicit call to IPXCloseSocket(), which is particularly useful in terminate-and-stay-resident (TSR) programs.

You can configure the maximum number of open sockets (as many as 150) at each workstation when you load the IPX software. The default is 20.

III

Reference

Input Registers:

BX	0x00
AL	Socket longevity flag:
	0x00 Short-lived
	0xFF Long-lived
DX	Requested socket number (high byte first)

Output Registers:

AL	Completion codes:
	0x00 Success
	0xFE Socket table is full
	0xFF Socket is already open
DX	Assigned socket number

IPXRelinquishControl
0x0A

Description:
You call this function inside your polling loops (while waiting for an IPX or SPX event to complete) to give IPX the CPU time it needs to process the event.

Input Registers:

BX	0x0A

IPXScheduleIPXEvent
0x05

Description:
This function tells IPX to schedule the processing of the specified ECB for a later time. The delay period is specified in timer ticks (18.2 timer ticks per second). Setting the delay period to the maximum of 0xFFFF (65,535) causes a delay of about one hour. IPX returns to your application immediately after this call and then waits in the background until the delay period is exhausted. When the time expires, IPX initiates the event, sets the ECB's in_use field to 0, and invokes the ESR associated with the ECB (if non-NULL).

You use this function for events that involve sending or receiving packets. You do *not* use this function to delay SPXEstablishConnection() from establishing a connection, for example. The function is particularly useful inside an ESR when you want to process the completed ECB at a later time.

The associated ECB must contain a function pointer to an ESR (or a NULL pointer) and an open socket number.

Input Registers:

BX	0x05
AX	Delay ticks
ES:SI	Far pointer to an ECB

IPXSendPacket
0x03

Description:
This function instructs IPX to gather the data fragments described in the ECB into a message packet and send the packet to the destination expressed in the ECB. IPX returns immediately to your program and performs the actual send operation in the background. The delivery of the message packet is not guaranteed (because IPX is a datagram-based protocol). When the send attempt completes, IPX does the following:

- Sets the completion code in the ECB

- Sets the in_use flag to 0

- Invokes the ESR associated with the ECB, if one is specified (non-NULL function pointer)

If you know the user ID that is logged on at the destination workstation but not the destination network and node address information, you can call GetObjectConnectionNumbers() and GetInternetAddress(). Both of these functions are described under Connection Services in the "Novell's Extended DOS Services" reference section.

You must have previously opened the source socket, through which the message packet will be sent, with a call to IPXOpenSocket(). Similarly, the application running on the destination workstation must have opened a socket (which you specify as dest_network_socket in the IPX header) and must have issued one or more IPXListenForPacket() calls.

III

Reference

You should set the following fields in the ECB before calling this function:

socket_number	The (source) socket that you have opened
event_svc_routine	A function pointer, or NULL
immediate_address	See IPXGetLocalTarget
fragment_count	Typically a value of 2, to express both the outgoing IPX header and the outgoing data message
fragment[0].address	A far pointer to an IPX header buffer
fragment[0].length	The length of the IPX header buffer (30 bytes)
fragment[1].address	A far pointer to a data area to be sent to the destination (the data area can be as much as 546 bytes)
fragment[1].length	The length of the data area

In addition, you must set the following fields in the IPX header that the first fragment address and fragment length reference:

packet_type	A value of 4
dest_network_number and dest_network_node	The workstation to which the message packet will be sent
dest_network_socket	A socket that the application running on the destination workstation has opened

Input Registers:

BX	0x03
ES:SI	Far pointer to an ECB

ECB (Final) Completion Codes:

0x00	Message sent (delivery is not guaranteed)
0xFC	This event has been canceled
0xFD	Bad packet (the packet size is less than 30 or greater than 576; the first fragment is less than 30 bytes; or the fragment count is 0)

0xFE	Undeliverable (the destination workstation doesn't exist; there is no bridge or path to destination; the destination socket is not open; or destination is not listening)
0xFF	Hardware or network failure

SPX Functions

SPXAbortConnection
0x14

Description:
This function aborts an SPX connection by abnormally terminating any outstanding SPX events. No notification of the abnormal termination is sent to the other workstation; it learns of the broken connection when error codes are returned to the application running on the other workstation.

The abnormal termination occurs in the background. SPX invokes the ESR of each terminated ECB (unless the ESR function pointer is NULL) after setting the ECB completion code to 0xED (abnormal termination).

To terminate an SPX connection orderly and gracefully, use the SPXTerminateConnection() function rather than this function.

Input Registers:

BX	0x14
DX	Connection ID

SPXInitialize
0x10

Description:
This function determines whether SPX is running on this workstation; if it is, this function returns version and configuration information. SPX is not available in earlier versions of NetWare. Detecting the presence of IPX does not automatically imply that SPX is loaded.

III

Reference

Input Registers:

BX	0x10
AL	0x00

Output Registers:

AL	SPX installation flag:
	0x00 Not installed
	0xFF Installed
BH	SPX major version
BL	SPX minor version
CX	Maximum number of connections supported
DX	Available number of connections

SPXEstablishConnection
0x11

Description:

This function creates a connection between this workstation and the speci-fied destination workstation. The destination workstation must be ready and waiting for the connection to be made, by having already called SPXListenForConnection(). To create the connection, follow these steps at the originating workstation:

1. Open a socket by calling IPXOpenSocket().

2. Do five SPXListenForSequencedPacket() calls, to give SPX a pool of ECBs and packet buffers that it can use. SPX uses some of these ECBs and buffers internally, and this usage is transparent to your program. Some are used to receive incoming message packets after the connection is created; the best way to process these ECBs and buffers is with an ESR. Fill in these ECB fields for each call:

ESR function pointer

Socket Number—set in step 1

Fragment Count—set to a value of 2

First Fragment Pointer—the address of an SPX header

First Fragment Length—the length of the SPX header

Second Fragment Pointer—the address of a packet buffer

Second Fragment Length—the size of the buffer, which must be in the range of 1 to 534 bytes

3. Issue the `SPXEstablishConnection()` call. Fill in these ECB fields for this call:

ESR function pointer

Socket Number—set in step 1

Fragment Count—set to a value of 1

First Fragment Pointer—the address of an SPX header

First Fragment Length—the length of the SPX header

The SPX header referenced by the first fragment pointer and length should be initialized with the network number, node, and socket that identify the destination workstation.

You specify a retry count and a watchdog flag when you call `SPXEstablishConnection()`. A retry count tells SPX how many times to attempt to send a packet to the other workstation before returning an error to your program. Setting Retry Count to 0 tells SPX to use its default retry count. The watchdog flag tells SPX whether to monitor the connection by sending periodic "Are you there?" packets to the other workstation. A value of 0 disables monitoring; a value of 1 enables it. If monitoring is enabled and SPX detects that the connection has been broken, the protocol signals the error by using one of the ECBs associated with an outstanding `SPXListenForSequencedPacket()` call. The chosen ECB's `in_use` flag is set to 0, its `completion_code` is set to `0xED` (failed connection), and its ESR is invoked.

SPX returns to your program immediately after each of the calls to `SPXListenForSequencedPacket()` and after the call to `SPXEstablishConnection()`. SPX returning a completion code of 0 in the AL register signifies that SPX is

III

Reference

processing the connection request in the background. Any other immediate completion code value indicates that SPX found something wrong and could not process the connection request.

The connection ID returned in the DX register after the call to SPXEstablishConnection() was assigned by SPX but cannot be used until the connection is actually created. SPX signals the establishment of the connection by setting the in_use flag of the SPXEstablishConnection() ECB to 0 and invoking the ESR associated with that ECB. SPX also returns the assigned connection ID in the source_connection_id field of the SPX header pointed to by the SPXEstablishConnection() ECB's first fragment address. If SPX cannot create the connection, the completion_code field of the SPXEstablishConnection() ECB returns an error code.

To cancel a pending SPXEstablishConnection() call, use SPXAbortConnection(), not IPXCancelEvent().

Input Registers:

BX	0x11
AL	Retry count:

	0	Use SPX default
	1–255	User specified retry count

AH	Watchdog flag:

	0	Disable
	1	Enable

ES:SI	Far pointer to an ECB

Output Registers:

AL	Completion codes:

	0x00	Success (SPX is attempting to make the connection)
	0xEF	Local connection table is full
	0xFD	Error in the ECB; the fragment count is not 1, or the fragment length is not 42
	0xFF	Sending socket is not open

DX	Connection ID

ECB Completion Codes:

0x00   Success (connection established)

0xED   No answer from the destination

0xEF   Connection table became full

0xFC   Sending socket closed during background processing

0xFD   Error in the ECB; the fragment count is not 1, or the fragment length is not 42

0xFF   Sending socket is not open

SPXGetConnectionStatus
0x15

Description:

This function returns status information about an existing SPX connection, as defined by the following `reply_buffer` structure declaration.

Reply Buffer:

```
struct
{
byte connect_status;
        /* 1=waiting;          2=starting;       */
        /* 3=established;       4=terminating     */
byte watchdog;
        /* if the second bit is 1, monitoring is active */
word local_connect_id;
        /* this workstation's connection id */
word remote_connect_id;
        /* the other computer's connection id */
word sequence_num;
        /* the number of the next packet to be sent */
word local_acknowledge_num;
        /* the number of the next packet to receive */
word local_allocation_num;
        /* number of listen ECBs in SPX's pool */
word remote_acknowledge_num;
        /* other computer's next packet number */
word remote_allocation_num;
        /* other computer's number of listen ECBs */
byte local_socket[2];
        /* local socket number for this connection */
byte immediate_address[6];
        /* address of bridge or of destination node */
byte remote_network[4];
        /* other computer's network number */
```

III

Reference

```
byte remote_node[6];
        /* other computer's node address */
byte remote_socket[2];
        /* socket being used by the other computer */
word retransmit_count;
        /* the retry count that SPX is using */
word est_roundtrip_time;
        /* packet-send time-out value, in timer ticks */
word retransmitted_packets;
        /* number of resent packets */
word suppressed_packets;
        /* number of duplicate packets received */
} reply_buffer;
```

Input Registers:

BX	0x15
DX	Connection ID
ES:SI	Far pointer to reply_buffer

Output Registers:

AL   Completion codes:

0x00   Success

0xEE   No such connection

SPXListenForConnection
0x12

Description:

This function tells SPX to expect an Establish Connection request from another workstation. SPX returns immediately to your program and waits in the background for the request packet. If the packet is received, SPX assigns a connection ID and signals the creation of the connection by setting the in_use flag of the SPXListenForConnection() ECB to 0, setting the ECB's completion_code, and invoking its ESR.

To enable SPX to create the connection successfully, follow these steps:

1. Open a socket by calling IPXOpenSocket().

2. Do five SPXListenForSequencedPacket() calls to give SPX a pool of ECBs and packet buffers that it can use. SPX uses some of these ECBs and buffers internally, and this usage is transparent to your program. Some are used to receive incoming message packets after the connection is

created; the best way to process the ECBs and buffers is with an ESR. Fill in these ECB fields for each of the five calls:

ESR function pointer

Socket Number—set in step 1

Fragment Count—set to a value of 2

First Fragment Pointer—the address of an SPX header

First Fragment Length—the length of the SPX header

Second Fragment Pointer—the address of a packet buffer

Second Fragment Length—the size of the buffer, which must be in the range of 1 to 534 bytes

3. Issue the SPXListenForConnection() call. The ECB fields to fill in for this call are the following:

ESR function pointer

Socket Number—set in step 1

Fragment Count—set to a value of 1

First Fragment Pointer—the address of an SPX header

First Fragment Length—the length of the SPX header

When you call SPXListenForConnection(), you specify a retry count and a watchdog flag. The retry count tells SPX how many times to try to send a packet to the other workstation before returning an error to your program. Setting the retry count to 0 lets SPX use its default retry count. The watchdog flag tells SPX whether to monitor the connection by sending periodic "Are you there?" packets to the other workstation. A value of 0 disables monitoring; a value of 1 enables it. If monitoring is enabled and SPX detects that the connection has been broken, the protocol signals the error by using one of the ECBs associated with an outstanding SPXListenForSequencedPacket() call. The chosen ECB's in_use flag is set to 0, its completion_code is set to 0xED (failed connection), and its ESR is invoked.

When the connection is created, SPX returns a connection ID to your program in the connection_id field of the ECB associated with the SPXListenForConnection() call. The ECB's in_use flag is set to 0, its completion_code is set, and the ESR specified in the ECB is invoked.

If SPX cannot create the connection, the completion_code field of the SPXListenForConnection() ECB returns an error code.

To cancel a pending SPXListenForConnection() call, use IPXCancelEvent().

Input Registers:

BX	0x12
AL	Retry count:
	0 Use SPX default
	1–255 User specified the retry count
AH	Watchdog flag:
	0 Disable
	1 Enable
ES:SI	Far pointer to an ECB

ECB Completion Codes:

0x00	Success
0xEF	Local connection table is full
0xFC	Canceled by IPXCancelEvent
0xFF	Socket is not open

SPXListenForSequencedPacket
0x17

Description:

This function gives SPX an ECB and a packet buffer to use when an incoming message packet is received. SPX places the ECB or buffer in a pool of listening ECBs and returns immediately to your program. On receiving a message packet, SPX selects one of the available listening ECBs for the specified socket number. The in_use flag of that ECB is set to 0, the completion_code is set, and the ESR is invoked.

Before calling this function, you should initialize the ECB as follows:

ESR function pointer

Socket Number

Fragment Count—set to 2

First Fragment Address—must point to an SPX header

First Fragment Length—must be 42 bytes

In addition, make the second Fragment Address point to a data buffer and make the second Fragment Length express the length of that buffer. The buffer can be as long as 534 bytes.

When an application receives a packet with a datastream_type field of 0xFE, the application should recognize that the connection has been terminated and finish up its processing accordingly. (See SPXTerminateConnection.)

Input Registers:

BX   0x17

ES:SI   Far pointer to an ECB

ECB Completion Codes:

0x00   Success

0xED   Connection failed

0xFC   Canceled by IPXCancelEvent

0xFD   Buffer is too small

0xFF   Socket is not open, the fragment count is 0, or the first fragment is not at least 42 bytes

SPXSendSequencedPacket
0x16

Description:

This function tells SPX to send a message packet to the other workstation involved in this connection. SPX returns immediately to your program and performs the actual send operation in the background. When the operation finishes, the in_use flag of the associated ECB is set to 0, the completion_code is set, and the ESR is invoked.

Before calling this function, you should initialize the ECB as follows:

ESR function pointer

Fragment Count—set to 2

First Fragment Address—must point to an SPX header

First Fragment Length—must be 42 bytes

In addition, make the second Fragment Address point to a data buffer (that you want to transmit) and make the second Fragment Length express the length of that buffer. The buffer can be as long as 534 bytes.

Before you call this function, the connection_control field and the datastream_type field of the SPX header should both be set to 0.

Input Registers:

BX	0x16
DX	Connection ID
ES:SI	Far pointer to an ECB

ECB Completion Codes:

0x00	Success
0xEC	The other workstation ended the connection (the packet may not have been received)
0xED	Connection aborted or failed
0xEE	No such connection
0xFC	Socket is not open
0xFD	Fragment count is 0, the packet is too large, or the first fragment is not at least 42 bytes (the connection is aborted)

SPXTerminateConnection
0x13

Description:

This function terminates a connection. SPX returns immediately to your program. The termination operation occurs in the background.

Before calling this function, you should initialize the ECB as follows:

ESR function pointer

Fragment Count—must be 1

First Fragment Address—must point to an SPX header

First Fragment Length—must be 42 bytes

SPX sets the `datastream_type` field in the SPX header to 0xFE and sends the SPX header as a packet to the other workstation. When the send operation finishes, the `in_use` flag of the associated ECB is set to 0, the `completion_code` is set, and the ESR is invoked.

When the application running at the other workstation receives a packet with a `datastream_type` field of 0xFE, the application should recognize that the connection is terminated and finish its processing accordingly.

Input Registers:

BX	0x13
DX	Connection ID
ES:SI	Far pointer to an ECB

ECB Completion Codes:

0x00	Success
0xEC	The other workstation ended the connection (the packet may not have been received)
0xED	Connection aborted or failed
0xEE	No such connection
0xFC	Socket is not open
0xFD	Fragment count is 0, the packet is too large, or the first fragment is not at least 42 bytes (the connection is aborted)

III

Reference

The LANtastic Programming Interface

LANtastic offers a programming interface that extends the Interrupt 21h DOS function call interface just as NetWare does. However, the services available through the LANtastic interface differ somewhat from those available from NetWare, and the programming interface itself differs. This section provides the details of the LANtastic programming interface.

> **Note**
>
> For some of the LANtastic programming services, you supply a string that contains multiple components, such as the server name, user name, and password. You insert a single byte with a zero value between the components to indicate to LANtastic which component is which. In the descriptions of the programming services, this book identifies such strings with the following syntax:
>
> \\server\username<NULLBYTE>password<NULLBYTE>
>
> The <NULLBYTE> notation signifies the zero-value byte you use to separate the components of the string.

To issue one of the following LANtastic functions, set the specified CPU register values and perform an Interrupt 21h:

Number	Function Name	Purpose
5E00H	GetMachineName()	Get the machine name
5E02H	SetPrinterSetup()	Set the printer setup
5E03H	GetPrinterSetup()	Get the printer setup

Number	Function Name	Purpose
5F02H	GetRedirDevice()	Gets the redirected device entry
5F03H	RedirDevice()	Redirects a device
5F04H	CancelRedir()	Cancels device redirection
5F80H	GetLogin()	Gets the login entry
5F81H	Login()	Logs in to a server
5F82H	Logout()	Logs out of a server
5F83H	GetUserName()	Gets the user name entry
5F84H	GetServer()	Gets the inactive server entry
5F85H	ChangePassword()	Changes the password
5F86H	Disable()	Disables an account
5F87H	GetAccount()	Gets an account
5F88H	LogoutAll()	Logs out from all servers
5F97H	CopyFile()	Copies a file
5F98H	SendMsg()	Sends an unsolicited message
5F99H	GetMsg()	Gets the last unsolicited message received
5F9AH	GetMsgFlag()	Gets a message processing flag
5F9BH	SetMsgFlag()	Sets a message processing flag
5F9CH	PopUpMsg()	Pops up the last received message
5FA0H	GetQueue()	Gets the queue entry
5FA1H	SetQueue()	Sets the queue entry
5FA2H	ControlQueue()	Controls the queue
5FA3H	GetStatus()	Gets the printer status
5FA4H	GetStreamInfo()	Gets stream information
5FA5H	SetStreamInfo()	Sets stream information
5FA7H	CreateAudit()	Creates a user audit entry
5FB0H	GetUserInfo()	Gets active user information

Number	Function Name	Purpose
5FB1H	GetDirInfo()	Gets shared directory information
5FB2H	GetUserAcct()	Gets a user name from an account file
5FB3H	TranslatePath()	Translates a path
5FB4H	CreateIndir()	Creates an indirect file
5FB5H	GetIndir()	Gets the indirect file contents
5FC0H	GetTime()	Gets the server's time
5FC8H	Shutdown()	Schedules the server's shutdown
5FC9H	CancelShutdown()	Cancels the server's shutdown
5FCAH	StuffServerBuffer()	Stuffs the server keyboard buffer
5FD0H	GetLPTTimeout()	Gets a redirected printer time-out
5FD1H	SetLPTTimeout()	Sets redirected printer time-outs
5FE0H	GetDOSVector()	Gets the DOS service vector
5FE1H	SetDOSVector()	Sets the DOS service vector
5FE2H	GetMsgVector()	Gets the message service vector
5FE3H	SetMsgVector()	Sets the message service vector

LANtastic Error Codes

The following is a list of error codes that LANtastic may return:

Error Number	Meaning
01H	Invalid function number
02H	File not found
03H	Path not found
04H	File open limit has been exceeded or no handles are left
05H	Access denied
06H	Invalid handle

Error Number	Meaning
07H	Memory-control blocks destroyed
08H	The memory limit has been exceeded
09H	Invalid memory-block address
0AH	Invalid environment
0BH	Invalid format
0CH	Invalid access code
0DH	Invalid data
0EH	Reserved
0FH	Invalid drive was specified
10H	Attempt to remove the current directory
11H	Not the same device
12H	No more files
13H	Attempt to write on write-protected disk
14H	Unknown unit
15H	Drive was not ready
16H	Unknown command
17H	Data CRC (Cyclic Redundancy Checksum) error
18H	Bad request structure length
19H	Seek error
1AH	Unknown media
1BH	Sector was not found
1CH	No paper
1DH	Write fault
1EH	Read fault
1FH	General failure
20H	Sharing violation
21H	Lock violation

Error Number	Meaning
22H	Invalid disk change
23H	File control block (FCB) unavailable
24H	Sharing buffer overflow
25H	Reserved
26H	Cannot complete the file operation
27H–31H	Reserved
32H	Network request is not supported
33H	Network node ??????????????? is not listening
34H	The name already exists on the network
35H	Cannot locate the network name
36H	The network is busy
37H	Connection to the network node ??????????????? was broken
38H	The NetBIOS command limit has been exceeded
39H	The network adapter has malfunctioned
3AH	Incorrect response from the network node ???????????????
3BH	Unexpected network error from the node ???????????????
3CH	Incompatible network node ???????????????
3DH	Print queue is full on the network node ???????????????
3EH	No room for the print file on the network node ???????????????
3FH	Print file deleted on the network node ???????????????
40H	The network name has been deleted
41H	Denied access on the network node ???????????????
42H	Invalid network device
43H	The network name was not found
44H	The network name limit has been exceeded

Error Number	Meaning
45H	The session limit has been exceeded
46H	Network node ??????????????? temporarily paused
47H	Request to network node ??????????????? was denied
48H	Print or disk services paused on the node ???????????????
49H	Invalid network version
4AH	Account has expired
4BH	Password has expired
4CH	Login attempt is invalid at this time
4DH	Disk limit exceeded on the network node ???????????????
4EH	Not logged into the network node ???????????????
4FH	Reserved
50H	The file already exists
51H	Reserved
52H	Cannot make the directory entry
53H	Failure on critical error
54H	Maximum redirections or logins to the node ???????????????
55H	Duplicate redirection or login to the node ???????????????
56H	Invalid user name or password
57H	Invalid parameter
58H	Network data fault
59H	Function is not supported on network
5AH	Required system component is not installed

If LANtastic detects an error condition while executing a LANtastic network function, it sets the carry flag and puts an error code into the AX register.

LANtastic Functions

Retrieve LANtastic Error Message

Description:
While expanding the error code into a text string, LANtastic substitutes the network node name for the question marks in the error message. To expand an error code into a text string, you issue the multiplex interrupt (Int 2FH) with the following input registers.

Input Registers:

AH	5
AL	0 for installation check
BX	Error code

Output Registers:

ES:DI	Points to null-terminated error text
	Carry flag set if the error code cannot be converted

Test for the Existence of the Redirector, Server, and LANPUP

Description:
You issue the multiplex interrupt (2FH) to determine whether the redirector, server, or LANPUP software is loaded.

Input Registers:

AX	B800H

Output Registers:

AL	0 if neither the redirector or server is installed	
BL	Bits set to indicate that the software is installed	
	10000000b	Redirector has pop-up receive-message capability
	01000000b	Server is installed
	00001000b	Redirector is installed
	00000010b	LANPUP is installed

III

Reference

Get Network Software Version

Description:

You issue the multiplex interrupt (2FH) to determine which version of LANtastic is running.

Input Registers:

AX   B809H

Output Registers:

AH   Major version number

AL   Minor version number

Control Redirected Printer Stream

Description:

To control how LANtastic sends output to redirected printers, you can do any of the following:

- Set a *combine-output* mode that instructs LANtastic to continue building a single print job even when programs terminate or when a program opens the printer device.

- Set a *separate* mode that instructs LANtastic to create new print jobs when a program terminates or when the printer device is opened and closed.

- Flush redirected printer output, which causes LANtastic to end a print job and begin sending the print job to the printer.

Input Registers:

AX   5D08H

DL   0   Set combine-output mode

          1   Set separate mode

Flush Printer Output

Input Registers:

AX   5D09H

Output Registers:
None

Return Redirected Printer Mode

Description:
This function returns the current printer mode.

Input Registers:

AX   5D07H

Output Registers:

DL   0   Combined mode

          1   Separate mode

Get Login Entry

Description:
This function identifies the servers to which a workstation is logged in.

Input Registers:

AX   5F80H

BX   Login entry index (0 based)

ES:DI   Pointer to a 16-byte buffer (which receives the logged-in server name)

Output Registers:

DL   Adapter number used for login

ES:DI   Pointer to an ASCIIZ server name; does not include the \\ prefix

Log In to a Server

Description:
This function logs in to a particular server.

Input Registers:

AX   5F81H

ES:DI	Pointer to a string that contains the server, user name, and password, in the following form: *server**username*<NULLBYTE>*password*<NULLBYTE>
BL	Adapter number to use for the login attempt

Output Registers:

AX	Error code if an error occurs

Log Out from a Server

Description:
This function notifies a file server that this workstation no longer needs its services.

Input Registers:

AX	5F82H
ES:DI	Pointer to an ASCIIZ server name, in the form *server*

Output Registers:

AX	Error code if an error occurs

Get Username Entry

Description:
This function returns the logon account in effect at this workstation.

Input Registers:

AX	5F83H
BX	User name entry index (0 based)
ES:DI	Pointer to a 16-byte buffer to receive the user name used for this login

Output Registers:

AX	Error code if an error occurs
DL	Adapter number used for login
ES:DI	Pointer to an ASCIIZ user name

Get Inactive Server Entry

Description:

This function returns the name of a server that is available on the network but not logged in to by the workstation.

Input Registers:

AX	5F84H
BX	Index to the available but not-logged-in-to server
ES:DI	Pointer to a 16-byte buffer to receive a server name that you are not logged in to, but that is available for logging in

Output Registers:

AX	Error code if an error occurs
DL	Adapter number for the inactive server connection
ES:DI	Pointer to an ASCIIZ server name (does not include the \\ prefix)

Change Password

Description:

This function changes the user's password. The user must be logged in to the server when this call is issued.

Input Registers:

AX	5F85H
ES:DI	Pointer to a string, in the following form: *server\old-password*<NULLBYTE>*new-password*<NULLBYTE>

Output Registers:

AX	Error code if an error occurs

Disable Account

Description:

This function disables the currently logged-in account. The function applies only when concurrent login entries have a value of 1 (set by NET_MGR). The system manager must then reenable the account. After a DISABLE

III

Reference

ACCOUNT operation, a logged-in user can continue to use the current session. Logging out triggers the disabling of the account.

Input Registers:

AX	5F86H
ES:DI	Pointer to an ASCIIZ server and password string, in the form *server\password;* the user must be logged in to the server

Output Registers:

AX	Error code if an error occurs

Get Account

Description:
This function returns information for the currently logged-in account.

Input Registers:

AX	5F87H
DS:SI	Pointer to a 128-byte account information data structure
ES:DI	Pointer to an ASCIIZ server string, in the form *server;* the user must be logged in to the server

Output Registers:

AX	Error code if an error occurs
BX	Destroyed (not an input parameter)

The Account Information Data Structure:

```
user_account          struc
UA_name               db  16 dup (?)   ; Zero-padded user name
UA_internal           db  16 dup (0)
UA_description        db  32 dup (?)   ; Full user description
UA_privilege          db  ?            ; Privilege bits (see bit mask
                                       ; definitions at the end of this
                                       ; structure)
UA_concurrent         db  ?            ; Maximum concurrent logins
UA_allowed_times      db  42 dup (?)   ; 1 bit for each half hour for
                                       ; 7 day week beginning on Sunday
                                       ; 0 = allowed, 1 = not allowed
UA_internal2          dw  ?
UA_last_login_time    dw  2 dup (?)    ; Last time logged in
UA_account_expiration dw  2 dup (?)    ; Expiration date (DOS-format)
                                       ; Year, Month:Day
```

```
UA_password_expiration dw  2 dup (?)     ; Expiration date (DOS-format)
                                         ; 0 means no expiration date
UA_password_extension  db  ?             ; 1-31; number days to reextend
                                         ; password after change
                                         ; 0 No extension required
UA_undelete_char       db  ?             ; First letter of UA_name when
                                         ; account is deleted (first
                                         ; character of UA_name is replaced
                                         ; with a 0.)
UA_xprivilege          db  ?             ; Extended privilege
UA_future              db  128 - UA_future dup (?)
user_account           ends
```

Privilege bits for UA_privilege:

```
UA_privilege_superACL   equ 10000000b ; Bypass ACLs
UA_privilege_superqueue equ 01000000b ; Bypass queue protection
UA_privilege_peer       equ 00100000b ; Treat as local process
UA_privilege_supermail  equ 00010000b ; Bypass mail protection
UA_privilege_audit      equ 00001000b ; The user can create audit entries
UA_privilege_system     equ 00000100b ; The user has system manager
                                      ; privileges
UA_xprivilege_nopwchange equ 00000001b; User cannot change password
```

Log Out from All Servers

Description:

This call is equivalent to performing a logout call for all the servers that the user is currently logged in to.

Input Registers:

AX   5F88H

Output Registers:

AX   Error code if an error occurs

Copy File

Description:

This call copies the source file (designated by the source handle) to the destination file (designated by the destination handle). The server performs the copy, which requires no workstation resources. Both files must reside on the same server.

Input Registers:

AX	5F97H
CX:DX	Bytes to copy (0xFFFF:0xFFFF copies the entire file)
SI	Source handle
DI	Destination handle

Output Registers:

AX	Error code if an error occurs
DX:AX	Bytes copied if successful

Send Unsolicited Message

Description:

This function uses the LANtastic message service to transmit messages across the network. The messages have a fixed format. The 16-byte name fields (MB_machine, MB_server, and MB_user) are null-terminated and contain the characters to be matched. A null string matches any other string. The server names should not contain leading backslashes (\\). The names are case sensitive. You should convert any strings to be uppercase only to match LANtastic conventions. You can use the MB_server and MB_user fields to restrict the message recipients.

Input Registers:

AX	5F98H
DS:SI	Pointer to message_buffer

Output Registers:

AX	Error code if an error occurs

The Message Data Structure:

```
message_buffer      struc
MB_reserved         db  ?       : Reserved field used by system call
MB_type             db  ?       ; User-defined message type (see bit mask
                                ; definitions at the end of this structure)
MB_machine    db  16 dup (?) ; Machine name destination
MB_server     db  16 dup (?) ; User must be logged into this server
MB_user       db  16 dup (?) ; User must be using this user name
MB_originator db  16 dup (?) ; Originator's machine name. Filled in
                                ; when message is received
```

```
MB_text          db  80 dup (?) ; Message text
message_buffer             ends
```

Bit mask definitions for MB_type:

```
MBT_general     equ  0   ; General message used by NET, LANPUP, and others
MBT_warning     equ  1   ; Server warning message
```

Get Last Received Unsolicited Message

Description:

This function enables you to retrieve a copy of the last message received on a machine.

Input Registers:

AX   5F99H

ES:DI   Pointer to message_buffer (see the Send Unsolicited Message function for the data structure format)

Output Registers:

AX   Error code if an error occurs

Get Message Processing Flag

Description:

This function returns a flag indicating the current status of the LANtastic message service on the machine.

Input Registers:

AX   5F9AH

Output Registers:

DL   Flag describing what processing to do when an unsolicited message is received

AX   Error code if an error occurs

Format of Returned Message Processing Flag:

```
MPB_beep        equ 00000001b  ; Beep before the message delivered
MPB_deliver     equ 00000010b  ; Deliver message to message service
MPB_auto_pop_up equ 00000100b  ; Pop up messages automatically
```

III

Reference

Set Message Processing Flag

Description:
This function controls the status of the LANtastic message service.

Input Registers:

AX   5F9BH

DL   Bits describing what processing to do when an unsolicited
          message is received (see the Get Message Processing Flag
          function for the format)

Output Registers:

AX   Error code if an error occurs

Pop Up Last Received Message

Description:
This function uses the LANtastic message service to display the last received
message on the screen. The message is placed on the specified line for the
specified time. When LANtastic removes the message, the original screen
contents are restored. By pressing the Esc key, the user can remove the message before the display time elapses.

Input Registers:

AX   5F9CH

CX   Amount of time, in ticks, to leave message on the screen
          (there are 18.2 ticks per second)

DH   Line number where the message will be placed (the top line
          is 0; no validity checking is done)

Output Registers:

AX   Error code if an error occurs

Get Queue Entry

Description:
This function returns information about a spool queue entry.

Input Registers:

AX	5FA0H
BX	Queue entry index (0 for the first entry)
DS:SI	Pointer to a 162-byte buffer to receive queue entry information
ES:DI	Pointer to an ASCIIZ server name, in the form *server*

Output Registers:

AX	Error code if an error occurs
BX	Next queue entry index
DS:SI	Filled queue entry information buffer

Data Structure for a Queue Entry:

```
queue_entry         struc
QE_status           db   ?            ; Status of queue entry
QE_size             dd   ?            ; Size of spooled file
QE_type             db   ?            ; Type of queue entry
QE_output_control   db   ?            ; Control of the despooled file
QE_copies           dw   1            ; Number of copies
QE_sequence         dd   ?            ; Sequence number of the queue entry
QE_spooled_file     db   48 dup (?) ; Pathname of spooled file
QE_user             db   16 dup (?) ; User name who spooled the file
QE_machine          db   16 dup (?) ; Machine name that the user was on
QE_date             dw   ?            ; Date file spooled (DOS format)
QE_time             dw   ?            ; Time file spooled (DOS format)
QE_destination      db   17 dup (?) ; ASCIIZ device name or user name
                                     ; destination
QE_comment          db   48 dup (?) ; Comment field
queue_entry         ends
```

The Queue Entry Status:

```
QE_status_free        equ   0  ; The queue entry is empty
QE_status_update      equ   1  ; The queue entry is being updated
QE_status_hold        equ   2  ; The queue entry is held
QE_status_wait        equ   3  ; The queue entry is waiting for despool
QE_status_active      equ   4  ; The queue entry is being despooled
QE_status_cancel      equ   5  ; The queue has been canceled
QE_status_file_error  equ   6  ; The spooled file could not be accessed
QE_status_spool_error equ   7  ; The destination could not be accessed
QE_status_rush        equ   8  ; Rush this job
```

Type of Queue Entry:

```
QE_type_print       equ   0  ; Spooled printer queue file
QE_type_message     equ   1  ; Spooled message (mail)
QE_type_local_file  equ   2  ; Spooled local file
```

III

Reference

```
QE_type_remote_file   equ   3   ; Spooled remote file
QE_type_modem         equ   4   ; Spooled to remote modem
QE_type_batch         equ   5   ; Spooled batch processor file
```

Output Control Settings:
```
QE_OC_keep    equ 01000000b  ; Keep after despooling (don't delete)
                             ; let only the owner delete mail
QE_OC_voice   equ 00100000b  ; Mail file contains voice data
QE_OC_opened  equ 00010000b  ; Mail message has been read
QE_OC_request_response equ 00001000b
                             ; For mail, a response is requested
```

Set Queue Entry

Description:

This call enables you to set fields in a newly created queue entry. You create a queue entry by performing an open or create call on the file *server*\@MAIL (for mail messages) or *server*\@*resource* (for printer queue entries). You then use the returned handle in the Set Queue Entry call. The fields that a Set Queue Entry call can alter are the following:

■ QE_output_control

■ QE_copies

■ QE_destination (only for @MAIL queue entries)

■ QE_comment

Input Registers:

AX	5FA1H
BX	Handle of the queue entry
DS:SI	Pointer to the queue information buffer (see the Get Queue Info function for buffer format)

Output Registers:

AX	Error code if an error occurs

Control Queue

Description:

This call enables you to manipulate print jobs and physical printer despooling. The following table lists the operations that this call performs.

You must have the proper privilege (Q) to execute the commands marked with an asterisk (*).

```
CQ_start      equ   0   ;*Start despooling
CQ_halt       equ   1   ;*Halt despooling
CQ_halt_EOJ   equ   2   ;*Halt despooling at end of job
CQ_pause      equ   3   ;*Pause the despooler at end of job
CQ_single     equ   4   ;*Print single job
CQ_restart    equ   5   ;*Restart the current queue entry
CQ_cancel     equ   6   ; Cancel the current queue entry
CQ_hold       equ   7   ; Hold the queue entry
CQ_release    equ   8   ; Release a held queue entry
CQ_rush       equ   9   ;*Make the queue entry a rushed job
```

Input Registers:

AX   5FA2H

BL   Queue control command

ES:DI   Pointer to an ASCIIZ server, in the form \\server

For Cancel, Hold, Release, and Rush commands:

CX:DX   Queue sequence number to the control

For Start, Halt, Halt_EOJ, Pause, Single, and Restart commands:

DX   Physical printer number:

          0   LPT1

          1   LPT2

          2   LPT3

          3   COM1

          4   COM2

Output Registers:

AX   Error code if an error occurs

Get Printer Status

Description:
This function returns printer status information. If the printer is actively printing, this function returns more detailed information.

Input Registers:

AX	5FA3H
BX	Physical printer number:

      0 LPT1

      1 LPT2

      2 LPT3

      3 COM1

      4 COM2

DS:SI	Pointer to the 15-byte buffer to receive printer status information
ES:DI	Pointer to an ASCIIZ server, in the form \\server<0>; the user must be logged into the server

Output Registers:

AX	Error code if an error occurs
BX	Next physical printer number
DS:SI	Filled-in printer status buffer

Definition of a Printer Status Entry:

```
PS              struc
PS_state        db  ?   ; Printer state (defined in the next definition)
PS_index        dw  ?   ; Queue index corresponding to print job being
                        ; despooled. (-1 if not despooling: ignore rest
                        ; of the fields)
PS_CPS          dw  ?   ; Actual characters per second being output
PS_output_chars dd  ?   ; Characters actually output so far
PS_read_chars   dd  ?   ; Characters actually read from the despooled
                        ; file so far. Can be used to compute percentage
                        : completed.
PS_copies       dw  ?   ; Copies remaining to print
PS              ends
```

Definition of Printer States:

```
printer_state        record  PS_state_pause:1, PS_state_value:7
PS_state_disabled    equ 0   ; Printer is disabled
PS_state_single_job  equ 1   ; Printer will stop at the end of job
PS_state_multijob    equ 2   ; Printer should print multiple jobs
```

Get Stream Info

Description:

This function returns information about a printer stream entry. Each stream contains a logical printer resource template and a flag that indicates whether jobs destined for that logical printer resource should be queued.

Input Registers:

AX	5FA4H
BX	Stream index number (0 based)
DS:SI	Pointer to a 13-byte buffer to receive stream information
ES:DI	Pointer to an ASCIIZ server, in the form *server*<0>; the user must be logged in to the server

Output Registers:

AX	Error code if an error occurs
BX	Next stream number

Definition of a Logical Stream Entry:

```
logical_stream struc
LS_queue      db  ?            ; 0 Disabled, nonzero Enabled
LS_template   db  12 dup (?) ; Template may contain ?s
logical_stream ends
```

Set Stream Info

Description:

This function sets information about a printer stream entry.

Input Registers:

AX	5FA5H
BX	Stream index number (0 based)
DS:SI	Pointer to a 13-byte buffer that contains stream information (see the Get Stream Info function for the Logical Stream Entry format)
ES:DI	Pointer to an ASCIIZ server, in the form *server*<0>; the user must be logged in to the server

III

Reference

Output Registers:

AX   Error code if an error occurs

Create User Audit Entry

Description:

You can use this function, if you have the U privilege, to perform the Net Audit command.

Input Registers:

AX   5FA7H

DS:DX   Pointer to an eight-byte ASCIIZ reason code

DS:SI   Pointer to a 128-byte ASCIIZ reason string

ES:DI   Pointer to ASCIIZ server, in the form *server*<0>; the user must be logged in to the server

Output Registers:

AX   Error code if an error occurs

Get Active User Information

Description:

This function returns information about a workstation session.

Input Registers:

AX   5FB0H

BX   Login entry index of a server (0 based)

DS:SI   Pointer to a 44-byte buffer to receive a server login entry

ES:DI   Pointer to an ASCIIZ server, in the form *server*

Output Registers:

AX   Error code if an error occurs

BX   Next login entry index

DS:SI   Filled buffer with login entry information

Definition of an Active User Entry:

```
active_user_entry           struc
AUE_VCID        dw    0           ; Virtual circuit number
AUE_state       db    ?           ; Login state (defined next)
AUE_command     db    ?           ; Last command issued
AUE_IO          db    5 dup (?)   ; Number of I/O bytes (40-bit number)
AUE_requests    db    3 dup (?)   ; Number of server requests
                                  ; (24-bit number)
AUE_name        db    16 dup (?)  ; Name of the logged-in user
AUE_machine     db    16 dup (?)  ; Name of the remote logged-in machine
AUE_xprivilege  db    ?           ; Extended privileges
AUE_time_left   dw    ?           ; Time left in minutes (0 is unlimited)
active_user_entry           ends
```

Definition of the Various Login States and Privileges:

```
AUE_state_starting        equ   00000000b ; We are in the middle of a login
AUE_state_in              equ   00000001b ; We are fully logged in
AUE_state_RPL             equ   00000010b ; Remote program load login

AUE_privilege_superACL    equ   10000000b ; Bypass ACLs
AUE_privilege_superqueue  equ   01000000b ; Bypass queue protection
AUE_privilege_peer        equ   00100000b ; Treat as a local process
AUE_privilege_supermail   equ   00010000b ; Bypass mail protection
AUE_privilege_audit       equ   00001000b ; User can create audit entries
AUE_privilege_system      equ   00000100b ; User has system manager
                                          ; privileges
AUE_xprivilege_nopwchange equ 000000001b; User cannot change password
```

Active User Entry Commands:

```
AUEC_login          equ   0    ; Log in to a server
AUEC_terminate      equ   1    ; Process termination
AUEC_open           equ   2    ; Open a file
AUEC_close          equ   3    ; Close a file
AUEC_create         equ   4    ; Create a file whether it exists or not
AUEC_new            equ   5    ; Create a new file that doesn't exist
AUEC_unique         equ   6    ; Create a unique file
AUEC_commit         equ   7    ; Commit disk data to a disk
AUEC_read           equ   8    ; Read from a file
AUEC_write          equ   9    ; Write to a file
AUEC_delete         equ   10   ; Delete a file
AUEC_set_attr       equ   11   ; Set file attributes
AUEC_lock           equ   12   ; Lock the byte range
AUEC_unlock         equ   13   ; Unlock the byte range
AUEC_create_dir     equ   14   ; Create a subdirectory
AUEC_delete_dir     equ   15   ; Delete a subdirectory
AUEC_rename_file    equ   16   ; Rename a file
AUEC_find_first     equ   17   ; Find the first matching file
AUEC_find_next      equ   18   ; Find the next matching file
AUEC_disk_free      equ   19   ; Get the disk free space
AUEC_get_queue      equ   20   ; Get a queue entry
AUEC_set_queue      equ   21   ; Set a queue entry
AUEC_control_queue  equ   22   ; Control the queue
AUEC_get_login      equ   23   ; Return login information
AUEC_get_link       equ   24   ; Return link description
```

III

Reference

```
AUEC_seek              equ  25   ; Seek to a file position
AUEC_get_time          equ  26   ; Get the server's time
AUEC_audit             equ  27   ; Create an audit entry
AUEC_multi_open        equ  28   ; Open the file in multiple modes
AUEC_change_password   equ  29   ; Change a password
AUEC_disable_account   equ  30   ; Disable the account from further logins
AUEC_copy_file         equ  31   ; Local server file copy
AUEC_get_username      equ  32   ; Get a user name from the account file
AUEC_translate_path    equ  33   ; Translate a server's logical path
AUEC_create_indirect   equ  34   ; Make an indirect file
AUEC_get_indirect      equ  35   ; Get indirect file text
AUEC_printer_status    equ  36   ; Printer status obtained
AUEC_get_stream        equ  37   ; Get logical print stream information
AUEC_set_stream        equ  38   ; Set logical print stream information
AUEC_get_account       equ  39   ; Get an account record
AUEC_shutdown          equ  40   ; Request server shutdown
AUEC_cancel_shutdown   equ  41   ; Cancel server shutdown
AUEC_stuff             equ  42   ; Stuff server's keyboard
AUEC_write_with_commit equ 43   ; Write and then commit data to disk
```

Get Shared Directory Information

Description:

This function returns rights and permissions information about a shared resource.

Input Registers:

AX   5FB1H

DS:SI   Pointer to a 64-byte buffer to receive a shared-resource description

ES:DI   Pointer to an ASCIIZ server and a resource, in the form \\server\shared-resource

Output Registers:

AX   Error code if an error occurs

CX   ACL (Access Control List) privilege bits for the requesting user

DS:SI   ASCIIZ description of a shared resource

ACL Bit Definitions:

```
ACL_read        equ 1000000000000000b  ; (R) Allow open for read
                                       ;     and reading
ACL_write       equ 0100000000000000b  ; (W) Allow open for write
                                       ;     and writing
ACL_create_file equ 0010000000000000b  ; (C) Allow file creation
ACL_create_dir  equ 0001000000000000b  ; (M) Allow directory creation
ACL_lookup      equ 0000100000000000b  ; (L) Allow file/directory
                                       ;     lookups
ACL_delete_file equ 0000010000000000b  ; (D) Allow file deletion
ACL_delete_dir  equ 0000001000000000b  ; (K) Allow directory deletion
ACL_rename      equ 0000000100000000b  ; (N) Allow file renaming
ACL_execute     equ 0000000010000000b  ; (E) Allow program execution
ACL_physical    equ 0000000001000000b  ; (P) Allow physical access
                                       ;     to device
ACL_attribute   equ 0000000000100000b  ; (A) Allow attribute changing
ACL_indirect    equ 0000000000010000b  ; (I) Allow expansion
                                       ;     of indirect files
```

Get Username from Account File

Description:

This function extracts a user name from a server's list of valid logon accounts.

Input Registers:

AX	5FB2H
BX	User name entry index (0 for first entry)
DS:SI	Pointer to a 16-byte buffer to receive the user name
ES:DI	Pointer to ASCIIZ server, in the form *server*

Output Registers:

AX	Error code if an error occurs
BX	Next user name entry index (updated)
DS:SI	A 16-character user name retrieved from server's account file (not in ASCIIZ form)

Translate Path

Description:

This function translates an indirect file into a full network path or translates the given path into the path relative to the server.

Input Registers:

AX	5FB3H
DS:SI	Pointer to a 128-byte partial path string
ES:DI	Pointer to a full ASCIIZ path
DX	Type of translation to be performed:

00000001b   Recursively expand indirect files until all are resolved

00000010b   Translate to the server's physical path

Output Registers:

AX	Error code if an error occurs
DS:SI	ASCIIZ-translated path

Create Indirect File

Description:

This function enables you to create an indirect file on a LANtastic server.

Input Registers:

AX	5FB4H
DS:SI	Pointer to a 128-byte ASCIIZ server relative path that will be the indirect file's contents
ES:DI	Pointer to an indirect file's full ASCIIZ path

Output Registers:

AX	Error code if an error occurs

Get Indirect File Contents

Description:

This function returns the contents of an indirect file.

Input Registers:

AX	5FB5H

DS:SI	Pointer to a 128-byte buffer to receive indirect file contents
ES:DI	Pointer to a full network path of an indirect file

Output Registers:

AX	Error code if an error occurs
DS:SI	ASCIIZ contents of an indirect file (a path)

Get Server's Time

Description:

This function returns the current date and time from a specified server.

Input Registers:

AX	5FC0H
DS:SI	Pointer to an eight-byte buffer to receive time information
ES:DI	Pointer to an ASCIIZ server, in the form \\server; the user must be logged in to the server

Output Registers:

AX	Error code if an error occurs
DS:SI	Points to a buffer with time information

Definition of the Time Buffer:

```
time_block      struc
TB_year         dw  ?   ; Year
TB_day          db  ?   ; Day of month (1-31)
TB_month        db  ?   ; Month (1-12)
TB_minutes      db  ?   ; Minutes (0-59)
TB_hour         db  ?   ; Hour (0-23)
TB_hundredths   db  ?   ; Hundredths of seconds (0-99)
TB_seconds      db  ?   ; Seconds (0-59)
time_block      ends
```

Schedule Server Shutdown

Description:

This function schedules the termination of server activities on a specified file server.

III

Reference

Input Registers:

AX	5FC8H
DS:SI	Pointer to an 80-character ASCIIZ reason string
ES:DI	Pointer to an ASCIIZ server, in the form *server*
CX	Number of minutes after which to shut down (0 results in an immediate shutdown)
DX	Option flags

Output Registers:

AX	Error code if an error occurs

Shutdown Option Flags:

```
SHUTDOWN_option_reboot      equ 0000000000000001b ; Auto reboot
SHUTDOWN_option_silent      equ 0000000000000010b ; Do not notify users
SHUTDOWN_option_halt        equ 0000000000000100b ; Halt after shutdown
SHUTDOWN_option_powerfail   equ 0000000000001000b ; Power fail
                                                  ; (Used by UPS.)
SHUTDOWN_option_reserved1   equ 0000000000010000b ; Reserved
SHUTDOWN_option_reserved2   equ 0000000000100000b ; Reserved
SHUTDOWN_option_reserved3   equ 0000000001000000b ; Reserved
SHUTDOWN_option_reserved4   equ 0000000010000000b ; Reserved
SHUTDOWN_option_user1       equ 0000000100000000b ; User-definable
SHUTDOWN_option_user2       equ 0000001000000000b ; User-definable
SHUTDOWN_option_user3       equ 0000010000000000b ; User-definable
SHUTDOWN_option_user4       equ 0000100000000000b ; User-definable
SHUTDOWN_option_user5       equ 0001000000000000b ; User-definable
SHUTDOWN_option_user6       equ 0010000000000000b ; User-definable
SHUTDOWN_option_user7       equ 0100000000000000b ; User-definable
SHUTDOWN_option_reserved5   equ 1000000000000000b ; Reserved
```

Cancel Server Shutdown

Description:

This function cancels a previously issued Schedule Server Shutdown function call.

Input Registers:

AX	5FC9H
ES:DI	Pointer to an ASCIIZ server, in the form \\server

Output Registers:

AX	Error code if an error occurs

Stuff Server Keyboard Buffer

Description:

This function causes a specified string of characters to appear in the keyboard buffer of a particular file server.

Input Registers:

AX	5FCAH
ES:DI	Pointer to an ASCIIZ server, in the form *server*
DS:SI	Pointer to a 128-byte ASCIIZ string to stuff into buffer

Output Registers:

AX	Error code if an error occurs

Get Redirected Printer Time-out

Description:

This function returns the print redirection time-out value. This value represents the number of 55-millisecond ticks that LANtastic will wait before signaling the end of a print job.

Input Registers:

AX	5FD0H

Output Registers:

AX	Error code if an error occurs
CX	Redirected printer time-out in ticks (18.2 ticks = 1 second); a value of 0 means that time-outs are disabled

Set Redirected Printer Time-out

Description:

This function sets the print redirection time-out value. This value represents the number of 55-millisecond ticks that LANtastic will wait before signaling the end of a print job.

III

Reference

Input Registers:

AX   5FD1H

CX   Printer time-out in ticks (18.2 ticks = 1 second); a value of 0 disables the time-out

Output Registers:

AX   Error code if an error occurs

Part IV

Appendixes

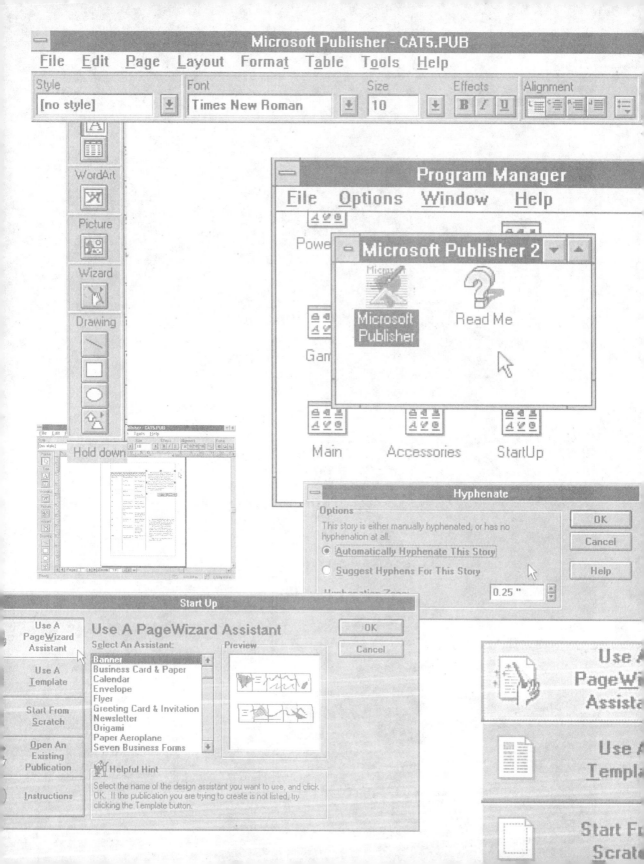

Appendix A

Source Listing for File/ Record Collision Tester

See Chapter 8, "Network Applications," for a discussion about what the following program does, how it works, and how to use it.

```c
/*   NETWORK.C   */

/*   a Local Area Network emulator   */
/*   written in Borland C            */

#pragma   inline

#include <stdio.h>
#include <dos.h>
#include <fcntl.h>
#include <conio.h>
#include <io.h>
#include <bios.h>
#include <stdlib.h>
#include <string.h>
#include <stddef.h>
#include <stdarg.h>
#include <dir.h>
#include <mem.h>
#include <process.h>


void    main(int argc, char *argv[]);
void    init_program(void);
void    do_popup(void);
void    actual_popup(void);

void    open_file(void);
void    close_file(void);
void    lock_record(void);
void    unlock_record(void);
void    show_file(void);
```

```
void      show_status(void);

void      getkey(void);
int       kbdstring(char buff[], int max_chars);
int       get_vid_mode(void);
void      save_cursor(struct csavetype *csave);
void      restore_cursor(struct csavetype *csave);

void interrupt   int08 (void);
void interrupt   int09 (void);
void interrupt   int10 (unsigned bp,
                        unsigned di,
                        unsigned si,
                        unsigned ds,
                        unsigned es,
                        unsigned dx,
                        unsigned cx,
                        unsigned bx,
                        unsigned ax,
                        unsigned ip,
                        unsigned cs,
                        unsigned flags);
        void interrupt   int13 (unsigned bp,
                        unsigned di,
                        unsigned si,
                        unsigned ds,
                        unsigned es,
                        unsigned dx,
                        unsigned cx,
                        unsigned bx,
                        unsigned ax,
                        unsigned ip,
                        unsigned cs,
                        unsigned flags);
        void interrupt   int16 (unsigned bp,
                        unsigned di,
                        unsigned si,
                        unsigned ds,
                        unsigned es,
                        unsigned dx,
                        unsigned cx,
                        unsigned bx,
                        unsigned ax,
                        unsigned ip,
                        unsigned cs,
                        unsigned flags);
        void interrupt   int1b  (void);
        void interrupt   int1c  (void);
        void      interrupt int21(unsigned bp,
                        unsigned di,
                        unsigned si,
                        unsigned ds,
                        unsigned es,
                        unsigned dx,
                        unsigned cx,
                        unsigned bx,
```

IV

Appendixes

```c
                             unsigned ax,
                             unsigned ip,
                             unsigned cs,
                             unsigned flags);
    void interrupt   int23  (void);
    void interrupt   int24  (unsigned bp,
                             unsigned di,
                             unsigned si,
                             unsigned ds,
                             unsigned es,
                             unsigned dx,
                             unsigned cx,
                             unsigned bx,
                             unsigned ax,
                             unsigned ip,
                             unsigned cs,
                             unsigned flags);
    void interrupt   int28  (void);

    #define    TRUE         1
    #define    FALSE        0
    #define    LT           <0
    #define    EQ           ==0
    #define    GT           >0
    #define    NE           !=0
    #define    MY_STK_SIZE  1500
    #define    LINE_LENGTH  81
    #define    MAX_LINES    100
    #define    FOUR_SECS    73


    #define    BELL         7
    #define    BS           8
    #define    LINEFEED     10
    #define    FORMFEED     12
    #define    CR           13
    #define    BACKTAB      15
    #define    CTRLQ        17
    #define    CTRLS        19
    #define    CTRLX        24
    #define    CTRLZ        26
    #define    ESC          27

    #define    ALTX         45
    #define    ALTC         46
    #define    ALTD         32
    #define    ALTE         18
    #define    ALTF         33
    #define    ALTT         20
    #define    ALTM         50
    #define    ALTH         35
    #define    HOMEKEY      71
    #define    ENDKEY       79
    #define    UPKEY        72
    #define    DOWNKEY      80
    #define    PGUPKEY      73
```

```
#define     PGDNKEY      81
#define     LEFTKEY      75
#define     INSKEY       82
#define     RIGHTKEY     77
#define     DELKEY       83
#define     CTRLLEFTKEY  115
#define     CTRLRIGHTKEY 116


#define     ALT          56
#define     RIGHT_SHIFT  54
#define     F1           59
#define     F2           60
#define     F3           61
#define     F4           62
#define     F5           63
#define     F6           64
#define     F7           65
#define     F8           66
#define     F9           67
#define     F10          68


struct      csavetype
            {
            unsigned int curloc;
            unsigned int curmode;
            };

struct      FILE_DATA
            {
            char name[81];
            int  handle;
            int  rec_length;
            int  lock_count;
            unsigned char inherit_flag;
            unsigned char sharing_flag;
            unsigned char access_flag;
            };

struct  FILE_DATA file_data[5];

char            filename[81];
unsigned char   file_inherit;
unsigned char   file_sharing;
unsigned char   file_access;
int             file_rec_len;
int             open_count;

unsigned int    paragraphs;
unsigned int    temp1, temp2;
unsigned int    current_ss;
unsigned int    current_sp;
unsigned int    save_ss;
unsigned int    save_sp;

unsigned int    far *our_mcb_size;
```

```
unsigned int      far *next_mcb_owner;
unsigned char     far *ourdta_ptr;
unsigned char     far *olddta_ptr;
unsigned char     far *our_mcb;
unsigned char     far *next_mcb;
unsigned char     far *prtsc_flag_ptr;
unsigned char     far *indos_ptr;
unsigned char     far *indos2_ptr;
unsigned char     far *kbd_flag_ptr;

unsigned int      ourpsp;
unsigned int      oldpsp;
unsigned int      break_state;

union    REGS     regs;
struct   SREGS    sregs;

void     interrupt (*oldint08)(void);
void     interrupt (*oldint09)(void);
void     interrupt (*oldint10)(void);
void     interrupt (*oldint13)(void);
void     interrupt (*oldint16)(void);
void     interrupt (*oldint1b)(void);
void     interrupt (*oldint1c)(void);
void     interrupt (*oldint21)(void);
void     interrupt (*oldint23)(void);
void     interrupt (*oldint24)(void);
void     interrupt (*oldint28)(void);
void     interrupt (*vectsave)(void);
void     interrupt (*vecthold)(void);

unsigned int      in_int08        = FALSE;
unsigned int      in_int09        = FALSE;
unsigned int      in_int10        = FALSE;
unsigned int      in_int13        = FALSE;
unsigned int      in_int16        = FALSE;
unsigned int      in_int21        = FALSE;
unsigned int      in_int28        = FALSE;
unsigned int      in_popup        = FALSE;
unsigned int      hot_flag        = FALSE;
unsigned int      de_install      = FALSE;
unsigned int      break_flag      = FALSE;
unsigned int      crit_err_flag   = FALSE;
unsigned int      we_are_last     = FALSE;
unsigned int      first_time      = TRUE;

unsigned int      tick_counter    = 0;
char              machine_name [16] = "01TEST          ";
unsigned char     network_drive;
char              string1 [LINE_LENGTH];

unsigned char     key_char;
unsigned char     extended_char;
unsigned int      i, j;
unsigned int      temp_ax;
unsigned int      temp_bx;
```

```
unsigned char     temp_ah;
unsigned char     temp_bl;

unsigned int      low_inten;
unsigned int      hi_inten;


unsigned char     *box_lines1[] =
                     {
                  "- [ LAN EMULATOR ]----------------------",
                  "                                        ",
                  "   E)xit to application                 ",
                  "   R)emove Emulator from RAM            ",
                  "   O)pen a file                         ",
                  "   C)lose a file                        ",
                  "   L)ock a record                       ",
                  "   U)nlock a record                     ",
                  "   S)how current files/locks            ",
                  "                                        ",
                  "                                        ",
                  "- (Select option by first letter)-------"
                     };

unsigned char     *box_lines2[] =
                     {
                  "----------------------------------------",
                  "                                        ",
                  "                                        ",
                  "                                        ",
                  "                                        ",
                  "                                        ",
                  "                                        ",
                  "                                        ",
                  "                                        ",
                  "                                        ",
                  "                                        ",
                  "----------------------------------------"
                     };

unsigned char     app_window_save [42*12*2];
struct csavetype app_cursor;
unsigned int      *our_stack;

/************************************/

void     interrupt int08(void)
     {
     in_int08 = TRUE;
     oldint08();
     enable();
     tick_counter++;

int08_p1:
     if (!hot_flag && !de_install)
         goto exit08;
```

```
int08_p2:
    if (in_int09 || in_int10 || in_int13
        || in_int16 || in_int21 || in_int28 || in_popup)
        goto exit08;

    if (*indos_ptr != 0)
        goto exit08;

    if (*indos2_ptr != 0)
        goto exit08;

    if (*prtsc_flag_ptr == 1)
        goto exit08;

    outportb(0x20, 0x0b);
    if (inportb(0x20)) goto exit08;

    in_popup = TRUE;
    do_popup();
    in_popup = FALSE;

exit08:
    in_int08 = FALSE;
    }

/***********************************/

void interrupt  int09 (void)
    {
    in_int09 = TRUE;
    oldint09();
    enable();

    if ( (*kbd_flag_ptr & 0x09) == 0x09 )
        {
        de_install = FALSE;
        hot_flag   = TRUE;
        }

    in_int09 = FALSE;
    }

/***********************************/

void     interrupt int10(unsigned bp,
                         unsigned di,
                         unsigned si,
                         unsigned ds,
                         unsigned es,
                         unsigned dx,
                         unsigned cx,
                         unsigned bx,
                         unsigned ax,
                         unsigned ip,
                         unsigned cs,
                         unsigned flags)
```

```
     {
     in_int10 = TRUE;
     enable();

     asm     push bp
      asm     pushf
     asm     CLI
      asm     call dword ptr _oldint10
     asm     pop  bp

     asm     pushf
     asm     pop flags
     ax      = _AX;
     bx      = _BX;
     cx      = _CX;
     dx      = _DX;
     in_int10 = FALSE;
     }

/************************************/

void    interrupt int13(unsigned bp,
                        unsigned di,
                        unsigned si,
                        unsigned ds,
                        unsigned es,
                        unsigned dx,
                        unsigned cx,
                        unsigned bx,
                        unsigned ax,
                        unsigned ip,
                        unsigned cs,
                        unsigned flags)
     {
     in_int13 = TRUE;

     oldint13();
     enable();
     asm     pushf
     asm     pop flags
     ax      = _AX;

     in_int13 = FALSE;
     }

/************************************/

void    interrupt int16(unsigned bp,
                        unsigned di,
                        unsigned si,
                        unsigned ds,
                        unsigned es,
                        unsigned dx,
                        unsigned cx,
                        unsigned bx,
                        unsigned ax,
```

```
                        unsigned ip,
                        unsigned cs,
                        unsigned flags)
    {
    temp_ax  = _AX;
    temp_bx  = _BX;
    temp_ah  = _AH;
    in_int16 = TRUE;
    enable();

    if (temp_ax == 'BN')
        {
        temp_ax = 'bn';
        goto int16_exit;
        }

    if (in_popup)
        goto do_old16;

    if (temp_ah != 0)
        goto do_old16;

wait_for_key:
    _AH = 1;
    oldint16();
    asm     jz    popup_16

    goto do_old16;

popup_16:
    if (!hot_flag && !de_install)
        goto wait_for_key;

    if (in_int08 || in_int09 || in_int10 || in_int13
        || in_int21 || in_int28 || in_popup)
        goto wait_for_key;

    if (*indos_ptr != 0)
        goto wait_for_key;

    if (*indos2_ptr != 0)
        goto wait_for_key;

    if (*prtsc_flag_ptr == 1)
        goto wait_for_key;

    outportb(0x20, 0x0b);
    if (inportb(0x20))
        goto wait_for_key;

    in_popup = TRUE;
    do_popup();
    in_popup = FALSE;

    goto wait_for_key;
```

```
do_old16:
    _AX = temp_ax;
    oldint16();
    asm       pushf
    asm       pop flags
    temp_ax = _AX;
    temp_bx = _BX;

int16_exit:
    ax = temp_ax;
    bx = temp_bx;
    in_int16 = FALSE;
    }

/**********************************/

void interrupt  int1b (void)
    {
    enable();
    break_flag = TRUE;
    }

/**********************************/

void interrupt  int1c (void)
    {
    enable();
    }

/**********************************/

void    interrupt int21(unsigned bp,
                        unsigned di,
                        unsigned si,
                        unsigned ds,
                        unsigned es,
                        unsigned dx,
                        unsigned cx,
                        unsigned bx,
                        unsigned ax,
                        unsigned ip,
                        unsigned cs,
                        unsigned flags)
    {
    if (ax == 0x4409 ¦¦ ax == 0x5e00)
        goto carry_on;

    asm       mov    sp, bp
    asm       pop    bp
    asm       pop    di
    asm       pop    si
    asm       pop    ds
    asm       pop    es
    asm       pop    dx
```

```c
    asm     pop     cx
    asm     pop     bx
    asm     pop     ax

/*  jmp dword ptr cs:[0]  */
    asm     db      02eh,0ffh,02eh,0000h,000h


carry_on:
    in_int21        = TRUE;

    if (ax == 0x4409)       /* network drives */
        {
        if (temp_bl == network_drive)
            dx = 0x1000;
        else
            dx = 0x0000;
        ax = 0;
        goto int21exit;
        }
    else                    /* machine name */
        {
        movedata(_DS, (unsigned) machine_name, ds, dx, 16);
        cx = 0x0101;
        ax = 0;
        }

int21exit:
    flags &= 0xfffe;        /* clear the carry flag */
    in_int21 = FALSE;
    }

/***********************************/
void interrupt  int23 (void)
    {
    enable();
    }

/***********************************/
void interrupt  int28 (void)
    {
    in_int28 = TRUE;
    enable();
    oldint28();

    if (!hot_flag && !de_install)
        goto exit28;

    if (in_int08 || in_int09 || in_int10 || in_int13
        || in_int16 || in_popup)
        goto exit28;

    if (*indos_ptr > 1)
        goto exit28;
```

```c
        if (*indos2_ptr != 0)
            goto exit28;

        if (*prtsc_flag_ptr == 1)
            goto exit28;

        outportb(0x20, 0x0b);
        if (inportb(0x20)) goto exit28;

        in_popup = TRUE;
        do_popup();
        in_popup = FALSE;

exit28:
        in_int28 = FALSE;
        }

/*************************************/

void    interrupt int24(unsigned bp,
                        unsigned di,
                        unsigned si,
                        unsigned ds,
                        unsigned es,
                        unsigned dx,
                        unsigned cx,
                        unsigned bx,
                        unsigned ax,
                        unsigned ip,
                        unsigned cs,
                        unsigned flags)
    {
    temp1 = _AX;
    crit_err_flag = TRUE;

    if (_osmajor < 3)
        ax = (temp1 & 0xFF00);
    else
        ax = (temp1 & 0xFF00) | 0x03;
    }

/*************************************/

void    do_popup (void)
        {
        disable();
        current_ss = _SS;
        current_sp = _SP;
        _SS = save_ss;
        _SP = save_sp;
        enable();

        next_mcb       = MK_FP( (ourpsp) + *our_mcb_size, 0);
        next_mcb_owner = MK_FP(  ourpsp  + *our_mcb_size, 1);
```

```
        if (   *next_mcb_owner == 0x0000
           || *next_mcb_owner == 0xffff
           || *next_mcb_owner <  ourpsp  )
               we_are_last = TRUE;
        else
               we_are_last = FALSE;

        if (!de_install)
            goto process_popup;

        if (!we_are_last)
            goto do_popup_exit;

        regs.x.ax = 0x5000;
        regs.x.bx = ourpsp;
        intdos(&regs, &regs);
        setvect(0x08, oldint08);
        setvect(0x09, oldint09);
        setvect(0x10, oldint10);
        setvect(0x13, oldint13);
        setvect(0x16, oldint16);
        setvect(0x21, oldint21);
        setvect(0x28, oldint28);
        _AX = _CS;
        _ES = _AX;
        _AH = 0x49;
        geninterrupt(0x21);
        _ES = ourpsp;
        _BX = 0x2c;
        asm   mov es, es:[bx]
        _AH = 0x49;
        geninterrupt(0x21);
        _AX = 0x4c00;
        geninterrupt(0x21);


process_popup:
        break_state = getcbrk();
        oldint1b = getvect(0x1b);
        setvect(0x1b, int1b);
        oldint1c = getvect(0x1c);
        setvect(0x1c, int1c);
        oldint23 = getvect(0x23);
        setvect(0x23, int23);
        oldint24 = getvect(0x24);
        setvect(0x24, int24);
        olddta_ptr = getdta();
        setdta(ourdta_ptr);
        regs.x.ax = 0x5100;
        intdos(&regs, &regs);
        oldpsp = regs.x.bx;
        regs.x.ax = 0x5000;
        regs.x.bx = ourpsp;
        intdos(&regs, &regs);
```

```
        if (hot_flag)
            {
            save_cursor(&app_cursor);
            gettext(19, 7, 59, 18, app_window_save);
            actual_popup();
            puttext(19, 7, 59, 18, app_window_save);
            restore_cursor(&app_cursor);
            }

        regs.x.ax = 0x5000;
        regs.x.bx = oldpsp;
        intdos(&regs, &regs);
        setdta(olddta_ptr);
        setvect(0x24, oldint24);
        setvect(0x23, oldint23);
        setvect(0x1c, oldint1c);
        setvect(0x1b, oldint1b);
        setcbrk(break_state);

do_popup_exit:
        disable();
        _SS = current_ss;
        _SP = current_sp;
        enable();
        }

/************************************/

void    actual_popup(void)
        {
        de_install     = FALSE;
        hot_flag       = FALSE;

show_menu1:
        window(1, 1, 80, 25);
        textattr(low_inten);
        for (i=0; i<12; i++)
            {
            gotoxy(19, i+7);
            cprintf("%s", box_lines1[i]);
            }
        window(20, 8, 58, 17);

win_key:
        gotoxy(1, 1);
        getkey();

        if (key_char == ESC)
            {
            goto exit_popup;
            }

        if (key_char == 'e' || key_char == 'E')
            goto exit_popup;
```

```
        if (key_char == 'r' || key_char == 'R')
             {
             de_install = TRUE;
             goto exit_popup;
             }

        if (key_char == 'o' || key_char == 'O')
             {
             open_file();
             goto show_menu1;
             }

        if (key_char == 'c' || key_char == 'C')
             {
             close_file();
             goto show_menu1;
             }

        if (key_char == 'l' || key_char == 'L')
             {
             lock_record();
             goto show_menu1;
             }

        if (key_char == 'u' || key_char == 'U')
             {
             unlock_record();
             goto show_menu1;
             }

        if (key_char == 's' || key_char == 'S')
             {
             show_status();
             goto show_menu1;
             }

        goto win_key;

exit_popup:
        window(1, 1, 80, 25);
        }

/**********************************/
void    open_file(void)
        {
        window(1, 1, 80, 25);
        textattr(low_inten);
        for (i=0; i<12; i++)
             {
             gotoxy(19, i+7);
             cprintf("%s", box_lines2[i]);
             }

        gotoxy(21, 7);
        cprintf("[ OPEN A FILE ]");
        window(20, 8, 58, 18);
```

```
                    if (open_count == 5)
                        {
                        gotoxy(1, 8);
                        textattr(hi_inten);
                        cprintf("Whoops. 5 files already open.");
                        gotoxy(1, 9);
                        cprintf("   (Press a key)");
                        textattr(low_inten);
                        gotoxy(1, 1);
                        getkey();
                        goto open_exit;
                        }

                    gotoxy(1, 2);
                    cprintf("   Filename: ");
                    gotoxy(1, 3);
                    cprintf("Inheritance: ");
                    gotoxy(1, 4);
                    cprintf("    Sharing: ");
                    gotoxy(1, 5);
                    cprintf("     Access: ");
                    gotoxy(1, 6);
                    cprintf(" Record Len: ");

                    gotoxy(1, 8);
                    textattr(hi_inten);
                    cprintf("Enter filename and press <enter>");
                    gotoxy(1, 9);
                    cprintf("(ESC if none)");
                    textattr(low_inten);
                    gotoxy(14, 2);
                    memset(filename, 0, 80);
                    kbdstring(filename, 20);
                    if (filename[0] == '\0')
                        goto open_exit;

    get_inherit:
                    gotoxy(1, 8);
                    textattr(hi_inten);
                    cprintf("File is inheritable? (Y or N)     ");
                    gotoxy(1, 9);
                    cprintf("                              ");
                    textattr(low_inten);
                    gotoxy(14, 3);
                    getkey();

                    if (key_char == 'y' || key_char == 'Y')
                        file_inherit = 0x00;
                    else
                    if (key_char == 'n' || key_char == 'N')
                        file_inherit = 0x80;
                    else
                        goto get_inherit;
                    cprintf("%c", key_char);
```

```
get_sharing:
        gotoxy(1, 8);
        textattr(hi_inten);
        cprintf("1=Compatibility Mode; 2=Deny R/W;");
        gotoxy(1, 9);
        cprintf("3=Deny Write; 4=Deny Read; 5=None");
        textattr(low_inten);
        gotoxy(14, 4);
        getkey();

        if (key_char == '1')
            {
            file_sharing = 0x00;
            cprintf("Compatibility Mode");
            }
        else
        if (key_char == '2')
            {
            file_sharing = 0x10;
            cprintf("Deny Read/Write");
            }
        else
        if (key_char == '3')
            {
            file_sharing = 0x20;
            cprintf("Deny Write");
            }
        else
        if (key_char == '4')
            {
            file_sharing = 0x30;
            cprintf("Deny Read");
            }
        else
        if (key_char == '5')
            {
            file_sharing = 0x40;
            cprintf("Deny None");
            }
        else
            goto get_sharing;

        gotoxy(1, 8);
        cprintf("                              ");
        gotoxy(1, 9);
        cprintf("                              ");

get_access:
        gotoxy(1, 8);
        textattr(hi_inten);
        cprintf("1=Read access;  2=Write access   ");
        gotoxy(1, 9);
        cprintf("3=Read/Write access              ");
        textattr(low_inten);
        gotoxy(14, 5);
        getkey();
```

```
            if (key_char == '1')
                {
                file_access = 0x00;
                cprintf("Read access");
                }
            else
            if (key_char == '2')
                {
                file_access = 0x01;
                cprintf("Write access");
                }
            else
            if (key_char == '3')
                {
                file_access = 0x02;
                cprintf("Read/Write access");
                }
            else
                goto get_access;

            gotoxy(1, 8);
            cprintf("                              ");
            gotoxy(1, 9);
            cprintf("                              ");

get_rec_len:
            gotoxy(1, 8);
            textattr(hi_inten);
            cprintf("Enter record length (1-32767)");
            gotoxy(1, 9);
            cprintf("and press <enter>");
            textattr(low_inten);
            gotoxy(14, 6);
            file_rec_len = 0;
            memset(string1, 0, 80);
            kbdstring(string1, 7);
            if (string1[0] == '\0')
                goto get_rec_len;
            file_rec_len = atoi(string1);
            if (file_rec_len < 1)
                goto get_rec_len;

            gotoxy(1, 8);
            cprintf("                              ");
            gotoxy(1, 9);
            cprintf("                              ");

            regs.h.ah = 0x3d;
            regs.h.al = file_inherit | file_sharing | file_access;
            regs.x.dx = (unsigned) filename;
            intdos(&regs, &regs);

            if (regs.x.cflag)
                {
                gotoxy(1, 8);
```

```
                    textattr(hi_inten);
                    cprintf("Failed.  DOS error %d", regs.x.ax);
                    gotoxy(1, 9);
                    cprintf("   (Press a key)");
                    textattr(low_inten);
                    }
                else
                    {
                    open_count++;
                    i = 0;
                    while (file_data[i].handle != 0)
                        i++;
                    strcpy(file_data[i].name, filename);
                    file_data[i].handle       = regs.x.ax;
                    file_data[i].lock_count   = 0;
                    file_data[i].rec_length   = file_rec_len;
                    file_data[i].inherit_flag = file_inherit;
                    file_data[i].sharing_flag = file_sharing;
                    file_data[i].access_flag  = file_access;
                    gotoxy(1, 8);
                    textattr(hi_inten);
                    cprintf("File successfully opened");
                    gotoxy(1, 9);
                    cprintf("   (Press a key)");
                    textattr(low_inten);
                    }

            gotoxy(1, 1);
            getkey();

    open_exit:
            window(1, 1, 80, 25);
            }

    void    close_file(void)
            {
            window(1, 1, 80, 25);
            textattr(low_inten);
            for (i=0; i<12; i++)
                {
                gotoxy(19, i+7);
                cprintf("%s", box_lines2[i]);
                }

            gotoxy(21, 7);
            cprintf("[ CLOSE A FILE ]");
            window(20, 8, 58, 18);

            if (open_count == 0)
                {
                gotoxy(1, 8);
                textattr(hi_inten);
                cprintf("Whoops. No files are open.");
                gotoxy(1, 9);
                cprintf("   (Press a key)");
                textattr(low_inten);
```

```
                        gotoxy(1, 1);
                        getkey();
                        goto close_exit;
                        }

                for (i=0; i<5; i++)
                        {
                        gotoxy(1, i+2);
                        cprintf(" %d. ", i+1);
                        if (file_data[i].handle)
                                cprintf("%s", file_data[i].name);
                        }

get_close:
                gotoxy(1, 8);
                textattr(hi_inten);
                cprintf("Which file? (1-5) ");
                gotoxy(1, 9);
                cprintf("(ESC if none)");
                textattr(low_inten);
                gotoxy(19, 8);
                getkey();

                if (key_char == ESC)
                        goto close_exit;

                i = (int) key_char - '1';
                if (i < 0 || i > 4)
                        goto get_close;

                if (file_data[i].handle == 0)
                        goto get_close;

                if (file_data[i].lock_count != 0)
                        {
                        gotoxy(1, 8);
                        textattr(hi_inten);
                        cprintf("%d records are still locked!",
                        file_data[i].lock_count);
                        gotoxy(1, 9);
                        cprintf("File not closed.  (Press a key)");
                        textattr(low_inten);
                        gotoxy(1, 1);
                        getkey();
                        goto close_exit;
                        }

                regs.h.ah = 0x3e;
                regs.x.bx = file_data[i].handle;
                intdos(&regs, &regs);

                if (regs.x.cflag)
                        {
                        gotoxy(1, 8);
                        textattr(hi_inten);
                        cprintf("Failed.  DOS error %d", regs.x.ax);
```

```
        gotoxy(1, 9);
        cprintf("   (Press a key)");
        textattr(low_inten);
        }
    else
        {
        open_count--;
        file_data[i].handle = 0;
        gotoxy(1, 8);
        textattr(hi_inten);
        cprintf("%s closed", file_data[i].name);
        gotoxy(1, 9);
        cprintf("   (Press a key)");
        textattr(low_inten);
        }

    gotoxy(1, 1);
    getkey();

close_exit:
    window(1, 1, 80, 25);
    }

void    lock_record(void)
    {
    window(1, 1, 80, 25);
    textattr(low_inten);
    for (i=0; i<12; i++)
        {
        gotoxy(19, i+7);
        cprintf("%s", box_lines2[i]);
        }

    gotoxy(21, 7);
    cprintf("[ LOCK A RECORD ]");
    window(20, 8, 58, 18);

    if (open_count == 0)
        {
        gotoxy(1, 8);
        textattr(hi_inten);
        cprintf("Whoops. No files are open.");
        gotoxy(1, 9);
        cprintf("   (Press a key)");
        textattr(low_inten);
        gotoxy(1, 1);
        getkey();
        goto lock_exit;
        }

    for (i=0; i<5; i++)
        {
        gotoxy(1, i+2);
        cprintf(" %d. ", i+1);
        if (file_data[i].handle)
            cprintf("%s", file_data[i].name);
        }
```

```
get_lock_file:
        gotoxy(1, 8);
        textattr(hi_inten);
        cprintf("Which file? (1-5) ");
        gotoxy(1, 9);
        cprintf("(ESC if none)");
        textattr(low_inten);
        gotoxy(19, 8);
        getkey();

        if (key_char == ESC)
            goto lock_exit;

        i = (int) key_char - '1';
        if (i < 0 || i > 4)
            goto get_lock_file;

        if (file_data[i].handle == 0)
            goto get_lock_file;

get_lock_rec:
        gotoxy(1, 8);
        textattr(hi_inten);
        cprintf("Which record number? ");
        gotoxy(1, 9);
        cprintf("(numbers start at 1) ");
        textattr(low_inten);

        j = 0;
        gotoxy(22, 8);
        memset(string1, 0, 80);
        kbdstring(string1, 5);
        j = atoi(string1);
        if (j < 1)
            goto get_lock_rec;

        regs.h.ah = 0x5c;
        regs.h.al = 0x00;
        regs.x.bx = file_data[i].handle;
        regs.x.di = file_data[i].rec_length;
        regs.x.si = 0;
        regs.x.cx = 0;
        regs.x.dx = (j - 1) * file_data[i].rec_length;
        intdos(&regs, &regs);

        if (regs.x.cflag)
            {
            gotoxy(1, 8);
            textattr(hi_inten);
            cprintf("Failed.  DOS error %d      ", regs.x.ax);
            gotoxy(1, 9);
            cprintf("    (Press a key)              ");
            textattr(low_inten);
            }
```

```
        else
            {
            file_data[i].lock_count++;
            gotoxy(1, 8);
            textattr(hi_inten);
            cprintf("record %d locked             ", j);
            gotoxy(1, 9);
            cprintf("    (Press a key)            ");
            textattr(low_inten);
            }

        gotoxy(1, 1);
        getkey();

lock_exit:
        window(1, 1, 80, 25);
        }

void    unlock_record(void)
        {
        window(1, 1, 80, 25);
        textattr(low_inten);
        for (i=0; i<12; i++)
            {
            gotoxy(19, i+7);
            cprintf("%s", box_lines2[i]);
            }

        gotoxy(21, 7);
        cprintf("[ UNLOCK A RECORD ]");
        window(20, 8, 58, 18);

        if (open_count == 0)
            {
            gotoxy(1, 8);
            textattr(hi_inten);
            cprintf("Whoops. No files are open.");
            gotoxy(1, 9);
            cprintf("    (Press a key)");
            textattr(low_inten);
            gotoxy(1, 1);
            getkey();
            goto unlock_exit;
            }

        for (i=0; i<5; i++)
            {
            gotoxy(1, i+2);
            cprintf(" %d. ", i+1);
            if (file_data[i].handle)
                cprintf("%s", file_data[i].name);
            }

get_unlock_file:
        gotoxy(1, 8);
        textattr(hi_inten);
```

```
            cprintf("Which file? (1-5) ");
            gotoxy(1, 9);
            cprintf("(ESC if none)");
            textattr(low_inten);
            gotoxy(19, 8);
            getkey();

            if (key_char == ESC)
                goto unlock_exit;

            i = (int) key_char - '1';
            if (i < 0 || i > 4)
                goto get_unlock_file;

            if (file_data[i].handle == 0)
                goto get_unlock_file;

            if (file_data[i].lock_count == 0)
                {
                gotoxy(1, 8);
                textattr(hi_inten);
                cprintf("No records are locked!");
                gotoxy(1, 9);
                cprintf("  (Press a key)");
                textattr(low_inten);
                gotoxy(1, 1);
                getkey();
                goto unlock_exit;
                }

get_unlock_rec:
            gotoxy(1, 8);
            textattr(hi_inten);
            cprintf("Which record number? ");
            gotoxy(1, 9);
            cprintf("(numbers start at 1) ");
            textattr(low_inten);

            j = 0;
            gotoxy(22, 8);
            memset(string1, 0, 80);
            kbdstring(string1, 5);
            j = atoi(string1);
            if (j < 1)
                goto get_unlock_rec;

            regs.h.ah = 0x5c;
            regs.h.al = 0x01;
            regs.x.bx = file_data[i].handle;
            regs.x.di = file_data[i].rec_length;
            regs.x.si = 0;
            regs.x.cx = 0;
            regs.x.dx = (j - 1) * file_data[i].rec_length;
            intdos(&regs, &regs);

            if (regs.x.cflag)
                {
```

```
            gotoxy(1, 8);
            textattr(hi_inten);
            cprintf("Failed.  DOS error %d     ", regs.x.ax);
            gotoxy(1, 9);
            cprintf("    (Press a key)              ");
            textattr(low_inten);
            }
        else
            {
            file_data[i].lock_count--;
            gotoxy(1, 8);
            textattr(hi_inten);
            cprintf("record %d unlocked           ", j);
            gotoxy(1, 9);
            cprintf("    (Press a key)              ");
            textattr(low_inten);
            }

        gotoxy(1, 1);
        getkey();

unlock_exit:
        window(1, 1, 80, 25);
        }

void    show_file(void)
        {
        j = i;

        window(1, 1, 80, 25);
        textattr(low_inten);
        for (i=0; i<12; i++)
            {
            gotoxy(19, i+7);
            cprintf("%s", box_lines2[i]);
            }

        gotoxy(21, 7);
        cprintf("[ FILE/LOCK STATUS ]");
        window(20, 8, 58, 18);

        i = j;
        gotoxy(1, 2);
        cprintf("      Name: %s", file_data[i].name);
        gotoxy(1, 3);
        cprintf("    Handle: %5d", file_data[i].handle);
        gotoxy(1, 4);
        cprintf("Rec Length: %5d", file_data[i].rec_length);
        gotoxy(1, 5);
        cprintf("Lock Count: %5d", file_data[i].lock_count);
        gotoxy(1, 6);
        j =   file_data[i].inherit_flag
            | file_data[i].sharing_flag
            | file_data[i].access_flag;
        cprintf(" Open Mode:   %2.2x (hex)", j);
```

```
                    gotoxy(1, 8);
                    textattr(hi_inten);
                    cprintf("(Press a key) ");
                    textattr(low_inten);
                    gotoxy(1, 1);
                    getkey();
                    }

        void    show_status(void)
                {
                window(1, 1, 80, 25);
                textattr(low_inten);
                for (i=0; i<12; i++)
                    {
                    gotoxy(19, i+7);
                    cprintf("%s", box_lines2[i]);
                    }

                gotoxy(21, 7);
                cprintf("[ FILE/LOCK STATUS ]");
                window(20, 8, 58, 18);

                if (open_count == 0)
                    {
                    gotoxy(1, 8);
                    textattr(hi_inten);
                    cprintf("Whoops. No files are open.");
                    gotoxy(1, 9);
                    cprintf("    (Press a key)");
                    textattr(low_inten);
                    gotoxy(1, 1);
                    getkey();
                    goto status_exit;
                    }

                for (i=0; i<5; i++)
                    {
                    gotoxy(1, i+2);
                    cprintf(" %d. ", i+1);
                    if (file_data[i].handle)
                        cprintf("%s", file_data[i].name);
                    }

        get_status_file:
                gotoxy(1, 8);
                textattr(hi_inten);
                cprintf("Which file? (1-5) ");
                gotoxy(1, 9);
                cprintf("(ESC if none)");
                textattr(low_inten);
                gotoxy(19, 8);
                getkey();

                if (key_char == ESC)
                    goto status_exit;
```

```
                    i = (int) key_char - '1';
                    if (i < 0 || i > 4)
                        goto get_status_file;

                    if (file_data[i].handle == 0)
                        goto get_status_file;

                    show_file();

status_exit:
                    window(1, 1, 80, 25);
                    }
/************************************/

int     kbdstring(char buff[], int max_chars)
                {
                unsigned int    i, j, insert_mode, ctype, res;
                unsigned char   row, col, trow, tcol;
                unsigned int    cblock;

                i = j = insert_mode = 0;
                if (get_vid_mode() == 7)
                    cblock = 0x000D;
                else
                    cblock = 0x0007;

                _AH = 3;
                _BH = 0;
                geninterrupt(0x10);
                ctype = _CX;
                col = wherex();
                row = wherey();
                cprintf("%-*s", max_chars-1, buff);
                gotoxy(col, row);

ks1:        getkey();
                tcol = wherex();
                trow = wherey();
                if (key_char == ESC)
                    {
                    buff[0] = '\0';
                    res = 0;
                    goto kbdstring_exit;
                    }

                if (key_char == 0)
                    {
                    if (extended_char == INSKEY)
                        {
                        if (insert_mode)
                            {
                            insert_mode = FALSE;
                            _CX = ctype;
                            _AH = 1;
                            geninterrupt(0x10);
                            }
```

```
            else
                {
                insert_mode = TRUE;
                _CX = cblock;
                _AH = 1;
                geninterrupt(0x10);
                }
            }
        else
        if (extended_char == HOMEKEY)
            {
            i = 0;
            gotoxy(col, row);
            }
        else
        if (extended_char == ENDKEY)
            {
            i = strlen(buff);
            gotoxy(col+strlen(buff), row);
            }
        else
        if (extended_char == DELKEY)
            {
            for (j = i; j < strlen(buff); j++)
                buff[j] = buff[j+1];
            gotoxy(col, row);
            cprintf("%-*s", max_chars-1, buff);
            gotoxy(tcol, trow);
            }
        else
        if (extended_char == RIGHTKEY)
            {
            if (i < strlen(buff))
                {
                i++;
                gotoxy(tcol+1, trow);
                }
            }
        else
        if (extended_char == LEFTKEY)
            {
            if (i > 0)
                {
                i--;
                gotoxy(tcol-1, trow);
                }
            }
        }

    if (key_char == 0)
        goto ks1;

    if (key_char == BS)
        {
        if (i > 0)
            {
```

```
                    i--;
                    gotoxy(tcol-1, trow);
                    }
                }

        if (key_char == CR)
            {
            res = 0;
            goto kbdstring_exit;
            }
        if (key_char < 32)
            goto ks1;
        if (i == max_chars-1)
            goto ks1;

        if (insert_mode)
            {
            for (j = strlen(buff)-1; j >= i; j--)
                if (j < max_chars-2)
                    buff[j+1] = buff[j];
            buff[i++] = key_char;
            _CX = ctype;
            _AH = 1;
            geninterrupt(0x10);
            gotoxy(col, row);
            cprintf("%-*s", max_chars-1, buff);
            gotoxy(++tcol, trow);
            _CX = cblock;
            _AH = 1;
            geninterrupt(0x10);
            }
        else
            {
            buff[i++] = key_char;
            cprintf("%c", key_char);
            }

        goto ks1;


kbdstring_exit:
        _CX = ctype;
        _AH = 1;
        geninterrupt(0x10);
        return(res);
        }

/**********************************/

void    getkey(void)
        {
        unsigned int    k;

        k             = bioskey(0);
        key_char      = k & 0x00FF;
        extended_char = (k & 0xFF00) >> 8;
        }
```

```
/***********************************/

int     get_vid_mode(void)
        {
        regs.h.ah = 15;
        int86(0x10, &regs, &regs);
        regs.h.ah = 0;
        return(regs.x.ax);
        }

/***********************************/

void    save_cursor(struct csavetype *csave)
        {
        _AH = 3;
        _BH = 0;
        geninterrupt(0x10);
        csave->curloc  = _DX;
        csave->curmode = _CX;
        }

/***********************************/

void    restore_cursor(struct csavetype *csave)
        {
        _DX = csave->curloc;
        _AH = 2;
        _BH = 0;
        geninterrupt(0x10);

        _CX = csave->curmode;
        _AH = 1;
        geninterrupt(0x10);
        }

/***********************************/

void    init_program(void)
        {
        if (get_vid_mode() == 7)
            {
            low_inten = 0x07;
            hi_inten  = 0x0f;
            }
        else
            {
            low_inten = 0x17;
            hi_inten  = 0x1f;
            }

        file_data[0].handle = 0;
        file_data[1].handle = 0;
        file_data[2].handle = 0;
        file_data[3].handle = 0;
        file_data[4].handle = 0;
        file_data[0].lock_count = 0;
        file_data[1].lock_count = 0;
```

```
file_data[2].lock_count = 0;
file_data[3].lock_count = 0;
file_data[4].lock_count = 0;
open_count = 0;

clrscr();

_AX = 'BN';
geninterrupt(0x16);
if (_AX == 'bn')
    {
    gotoxy(1, 2);
    cprintf("The Local Area Network Emulator is already loaded.");
    gotoxy(1, 3);
    cprintf("Use ALT/RIGHT-SHIFT to activate it.");
    gotoxy(1, 5);
    exit(1);
    }

if (_osmajor < 3)
    {
    gotoxy(1, 2);
    cprintf("Early versions of DOS not supported...");
    gotoxy(1, 4);
    exit(1);
    }

regs.x.ax = 0x1000;
int86(0x2f, &regs, &regs);
if (regs.h.al != 0xff)
    {
    gotoxy(1, 2);
cprintf("You must run SHARE.EXE before using the LAN Emulator.");
    gotoxy(1, 4);
    exit(1);
    }

sregs.ds = _DS;
regs.x.ax = 0x3400;
intdosx(&regs, &regs, &sregs);
indos_ptr = MK_FP(sregs.es, regs.x.bx);
if (_osmajor == 2)
    indos2_ptr = MK_FP(sregs.es, regs.x.bx + 1);
else
    indos2_ptr = MK_FP(sregs.es, regs.x.bx - 1);

prtsc_flag_ptr = MK_FP(0x0050, 0x0000);
kbd_flag_ptr   = MK_FP(0x0040, 0x0017);

if ( (our_stack = malloc(MY_STK_SIZE)) == NULL)
    {
    gotoxy(1, 2);
    cprintf("Insufficient memory.");
    gotoxy(1, 5);
    exit(1);
    }
```

```
get_net_drive:
        gotoxy(1, 24);
        cprintf("Drive letter that will be your network drive: ");
        network_drive = 0;
        gotoxy(1, 25);
        memset(string1, 0, 80);
        kbdstring(string1, 5);
        strupr(string1);
        network_drive = string1[0] - '@';
        if (network_drive < 1 || network_drive > 20)
            goto get_net_drive;


        }
/************************************/


void    main(int argc, char *argv[])
        {
        init_program();

        clrscr();
        gotoxy(1, 3);
cprintf("NETWORK--a LAN Emulator.  Copyright (c) 1988 Barry R. Nance");
        gotoxy(1, 4);
        cprintf("Press ALT/RIGHT-SHIFT to activate this program.");
        gotoxy(1, 6);
cprintf("As you test, the following conditions will exist:");
        gotoxy(1, 7);
        cprintf("     Machine Name: %s", machine_name);
        gotoxy(1, 8);
        cprintf("    Network Drive: %c:", network_drive + '@');
        gotoxy(1, 12);

        save_ss  = _SS;
        save_sp  = ( (unsigned) our_stack + MY_STK_SIZE ) - 2;

        ourdta_ptr = getdta();
        regs.x.ax = 0x5100;
        intdos(&regs, &regs);
        ourpsp = regs.x.bx;

        our_mcb       = MK_FP(ourpsp-1, 0);
        our_mcb_size  = MK_FP(ourpsp-1, 3);

        oldint08 = getvect(0x08);
        oldint09 = getvect(0x09);
        oldint10 = getvect(0x10);
        oldint13 = getvect(0x13);
        oldint16 = getvect(0x16);
        oldint28 = getvect(0x28);
        oldint21 = getvect(0x21);
        asm     mov ax, word ptr oldint21
        asm     mov word ptr cs:[0000], ax
        asm     mov ax, word ptr oldint21+2
        asm     mov word ptr cs:[0002], ax
```

```
    setvect(0x10, int10);
    setvect(0x13, int13);
    setvect(0x16, int16);
    setvect(0x21, int21);
    setvect(0x28, int28);
    setvect(0x09, int09);
    setvect(0x08, int08);

    paragraphs = (save_ss + (save_sp >> 4) + 0x10) - ourpsp;
    keep(0, paragraphs);
    }

/************************************/
```

Appendix B

Source Listing for NetBIOS Microscope

See Chapter 8, "Network Applications," for a discussion of the following program.

```c
#include <stdio.h>
#include <stdlib.h>
#include <dos.h>
#include <mem.h>
#include <bios.h>
#include <conio.h>
#include <string.h>
#include <process.h>
#include <netbios.h>

#define  MSG_SIZE  1001

/* - - - - - - - - - - - - - - - - - - - - - - - - */

char           message_out[MSG_SIZE];
char           message_in [MSG_SIZE];
char           string     [MSG_SIZE];
char           string2    [MSG_SIZE];
char           localname  [17];
char           remotename [17];
unsigned char  lsn;
unsigned char  name_number;
int            choice;
int            x;
int            cursor_x;
int            cursor_y;

/* - - - - - - - - - - - - - - - - - - - - - - - - */

unsigned            ncb_segments[10];
unsigned            ncb_offsets [10];
unsigned volatile   ncb_head  = 0;
unsigned            ncb_tail  = 0;
```

```
/* - - - - - - - - - - - - - - - - - - - - - - - - */

NCB      reset_ncb;
NCB      adapter_status_ncb;
NCB      session_status_ncb;
NCB      call_ncb;
NCB      listen_ncb;
NCB      add_name_ncb;
NCB      add_group_name_ncb;
NCB      delete_name_ncb;
NCB      send_ncb;
NCB      receive_ncb;
NCB      receive_any_ncb;
NCB      hangup_ncb;
NCB      temp_ncb;

/* - - - - - - - - - - - - - - - - - - - - - - - - */

typedef struct {
        unsigned char    card_id[6];
        unsigned char    release_level;
        unsigned char    reserved1;
        unsigned char    type_of_adapter;
        unsigned char    old_or_new_parameters;
        unsigned int     reporting_period_minutes;

        unsigned int     frame_reject_recvd_count;
        unsigned int     frame_reject_sent_count;
        unsigned int     recvd_I_frame_errors;

        unsigned int     unsuccessful_transmissions;
        unsigned long    good_transmissions;
        unsigned long    good_receptions;
        unsigned int     retransmissions;
        unsigned int     exhausted_resource_count;
        unsigned int     t1_timer_expired_count;
        unsigned int     ti_timer_expired_count;
        char             reserved2[4];
        unsigned int     available_ncbs;
        unsigned int     max_ncbs_configured;
        unsigned int     max_ncbs_possible;
        unsigned int     buffer_or_station_busy_count;
        unsigned int     max_datagram_size;
        unsigned int     pending_sessions;
        unsigned int     max_sessions_configured;
        unsigned int     max_sessions_possible;
        unsigned int     max_frame_size;
        int              name_count;
        struct {
            char             tbl_name[16];
            unsigned char    tbl_name_number;
            unsigned char    tbl_name_status;
            } name_table[20];
        }
        ADAPTER_DATA;
```

```
typedef struct {
        unsigned char  lsn;
        unsigned char  state;
        char           local_name[16];
        char           remote_name[16];
        unsigned char  recv_count;
        unsigned char  send_count;
        }
        A_SESSION;

typedef struct {
        unsigned char  name_num;
        unsigned char  session_count;
        unsigned char  junk1;
        unsigned char  junk2;
        A_SESSION      session_data[40];
        }
        STATUS_INFO;

ADAPTER_DATA    adapter_data;
STATUS_INFO     session_info;

/* - - - - - - - - - - - - - - - - - - - - - - - - - */

unsigned        es_reg, bx_reg;
void interrupt  (*int_5C_vector)(void);
char            screen_save[4000];

char    *state_msg [7] = {
        "                    ",
        "LISTEN pending",
        "CALL pending",
        "Active session",
        "HANG UP pending",
        "HANG UP complete",
        "Session abort"
        };

int     name_type;
char    *name_type_msg [2] = {
        "Unique name",
        "Group name "
        };

int     name_status;
char    *name_status_msg [8] = {
        "Reg. in progress   ",
        "                   ",
        "                   ",
        "                   ",
        "Registered         ",
        "De-registered      ",
        "Dupl detected      ",
        "Dupl; dereg pend.  "
        };
```

```
unsigned char    *box[18] = {
   " [NetTest POST results]---------------------",
   "                                            ",
   "                                            ",
   "                                            ",
   "                                            ",
   "                                            ",
   "                                            ",
   "                                            ",
   "                                            ",
   "                                            ",
   "                                            ",
   "                                            ",
   "                                            ",
   "                                            ",
   "                                            ",
   "                                            ",
   "                                            ",
   "---------------------"
      };


/* - - - - - - - - - - - - - - - - - - - - - - */

void    NetBios(NCB far *ncb_ptr)
        {
        _ES    = FP_SEG(ncb_ptr);
        _BX    = FP_OFF(ncb_ptr);
        _AX    = 0x0100;
        geninterrupt(0x5c);
        }

/* - - - - - - - - - - - - - - - - - - - - - - */

void    expand_to_16_chars(char *name)
        {
        char *p;
        char tmp[17];
        int  i;

        memset(tmp, ' ', 15);
        p = name;
        i = 0;
        while (i < 15 && *p)
            {
            tmp[i] = *p;
            i++;
            p++;
            }
        tmp[15] = '\0';
        strcpy(name, tmp);
        }

/* - - - - - - - - - - - - - - - - - - - - - - */
```

```
void     show_traffic_and_errors(void)
         {
       gotoxy(1, 6);
       cprintf("    Release level: %2.2X ",
                  (int) adapter_data.release_level);
       gotoxy(1, 8);
       cprintf("     Adapter type: %2.2X ",
                  (int) adapter_data.type_of_adapter);
       gotoxy(1, 10);
       cprintf("   Old/new parms: %2.2X ",
                  (int) adapter_data.old_or_new_parameters);
       gotoxy(15, 16);
       cprintf("(Press a key)");
       bioskey(0);
       clrscr();

       gotoxy(1, 6);
       cprintf("   Reporting period (mins): %6u ",
                  adapter_data.reporting_period_minutes);
       gotoxy(1, 8);
       cprintf(" Frame rejections received: %6u ",
                  adapter_data.frame_reject_recvd_count);
       gotoxy(1, 10);
       cprintf("     Frame rejections sent: %6u ",
                  adapter_data.frame_reject_sent_count);
       gotoxy(1, 12);
       cprintf("   Received I-frame errors: %6u ",
                  adapter_data.recvd_I_frame_errors);
       gotoxy(1, 14);
       cprintf("Unsuccessful transmissions: %6u ",
                  adapter_data.unsuccessful_transmissions);
       gotoxy(15, 16);
       cprintf("(Press a key)");
       bioskey(0);
       clrscr();

       gotoxy(1, 6);
       cprintf("Good transmissions: %10lu ",
                  adapter_data.good_transmissions);
       gotoxy(1, 8);
       cprintf("   Good receptions: %10lu ",
                  adapter_data.good_receptions);
       gotoxy(15, 16);
       cprintf("(Press a key)");
       bioskey(0);
       clrscr();

       gotoxy(1, 6);
       cprintf("          Retransmissions: %6u ",
                  adapter_data.retransmissions);
       gotoxy(1, 7);
       cprintf("     Exhausted resources: %6u ",
                  adapter_data.exhausted_resource_count);
       gotoxy(1, 8);
       cprintf("          Available NCB's: %6u ",
                  adapter_data.available_ncbs);
```

```
                gotoxy(1, 9);
                cprintf("    Max configured NCB's: %6u ",
                          adapter_data.max_ncbs_configured);
                gotoxy(1, 10);
                cprintf("      Max possible NCB's: %6u ",
                          adapter_data.max_ncbs_possible);
                gotoxy(1, 11);
                cprintf("        Pending sessions: %6u ",
                          adapter_data.pending_sessions);
                gotoxy(1, 12);
                cprintf("Max configured sessions: %6u ",
                          adapter_data.max_sessions_configured);
                gotoxy(1, 13);
                cprintf("  Max possible sessions: %6u ",
                          adapter_data.max_sessions_possible);
                gotoxy(1, 14);
                cprintf("          Max frame size: %6u ",
                          adapter_data.max_frame_size);
                gotoxy(15, 16);
                cprintf("(Press a key)");
                bioskey(0);
                clrscr();
                }

/* - - - - - - - - - - - - - - - - - - - - - - - - - */

void    report_result(void)
        {
        int i, j;

        gettext(1, 1, 80, 25, screen_save);
        cursor_x = wherex();
        cursor_y = wherey();
        for (i=0; i<18; i++)
            {
            gotoxy(5, i+1);
            cprintf("%s", box[i]);
            }
        window(6, 2, 70, 17);

        movedata(ncb_segments[ncb_tail], ncb_offsets[ncb_tail],
                FP_SEG(&temp_ncb), FP_OFF(&temp_ncb),
                sizeof(NCB));
        ncb_tail++;
        if (ncb_tail == 10)
            ncb_tail = 0;

        if (temp_ncb.NCB_LENGTH == MSG_SIZE - 1)
            temp_ncb.NCB_LENGTH = 0;

        if (temp_ncb.NCB_LENGTH >  320)
            temp_ncb.NCB_LENGTH = 320;

        switch (temp_ncb.NCB_COMMAND)
            {
            case RESET         : {strcpy(string, "RESET ADAPTER"); break;}
```

```
      case STATUS        : {strcpy(string, "ADAPTER STATUS");break;}
      case ADD_NAME       : {strcpy(string, "ADD NAME");      break;}
      case ADD_GROUP_NAME: {strcpy(string, "ADD GRP NAME");  break;}
      case DELETE_NAME   : {strcpy(string, "DELETE NAME");   break;}
      case LISTEN        : {strcpy(string, "LISTEN");        break;}
      case CALL          : {strcpy(string, "CALL");          break;}
      case HANG_UP       : {strcpy(string, "HANG UP");       break;}
      case SEND          : {strcpy(string, "SEND");          break;}
      case RECEIVE       : {strcpy(string, "RECEIVE");       break;}
      case RECEIVE_ANY   : {strcpy(string, "RECEIVE ANY");   break;}
      case SESSION_STATUS: {strcpy(string, "SESSION STATUS");break;}
      default            : {strcpy(string, "<unknown>");     break;}
      }

gotoxy(1, 1);
cprintf("Command: %s", string);

if (temp_ncb.NCB_RETCODE <= 0x26)
    strcpy(string, net_error_message[temp_ncb.NCB_RETCODE]);
else
if (temp_ncb.NCB_RETCODE == 0xff)
    strcpy(string, "command pending");
else
    strcpy(string, "adapter malfunction");

if (temp_ncb.NCB_CMD_CPLT <= 0x26)
strcpy(string2,
    net_error_message[temp_ncb.NCB_CMD_CPLT]);
else
if (temp_ncb.NCB_CMD_CPLT == 0xff)
    strcpy(string2, "command pending");
else
    strcpy(string2, "adapter malfunction");

gotoxy(1, 2);
cprintf("Immed: %s.  Final: %s.", string, string2);

if (temp_ncb.NCB_RETCODE > 0 || temp_ncb.NCB_CMD_CPLT > 0)
    goto report_exit;


if (temp_ncb.NCB_COMMAND == STATUS)
    {
    gotoxy(1, 4);
    cprintf("Card ID (hex): ");
    for (i=0; i<6; i++)
        cprintf("%2.2X ", (int) adapter_data.card_id[i]);
    show_traffic_and_errors();
    gotoxy(1, 14);
    cprintf("Local name table items: %d",
        adapter_data.name_count);
    gotoxy(15, 16);
    cprintf("(Press a key)");
    bioskey(0);
    if (adapter_data.name_count == 0) goto report_exit;
```

```
        clrscr();
        for (i=0, j=2; i<adapter_data.name_count; i++)
            {
adapter_data.name_table[i].tbl_name[15] = '\0';
name_status = (init) adapter_data.name_ table[i]. tbl_name_status;
name_status &= 0x0007;
name_type = (int) adapter_data.name_table[i].tbl_ name_status;
name_type &= 0x0080;
name_type = (name_type == 0x0080)? 1 : 0;
            if (i > 9)
                {
                gotoxy(15, 16);
                cprintf("(Press a key)");
                bioskey(0);
                clrscr();
                j = 2;
                }
            gotoxy(1, j++);
            cprintf("%s   (#%d)   %s   %s",
                adapter_data.name_table[i].tbl_name,
                (int)
            adapter_data.name_table[i].tbl_name_number,
                name_status_msg [name_status],
                name_type_msg   [name_type]);
            }
        }
    else
    if (temp_ncb.NCB_COMMAND == ADD_NAME
      || temp_ncb.NCB_COMMAND == ADD_GROUP_NAME)
        {
        gotoxy(1, 5);
        cprintf("Name number = %d.", (int) temp_ncb.NCB_NUM);
        }
    else
    if (temp_ncb.NCB_COMMAND == CALL)
        {
        gotoxy(1, 5);
        cprintf("Session established.  LSN = %d.",
            (int) temp_ncb.NCB_LSN);
        }
    else
    if (temp_ncb.NCB_COMMAND == LISTEN)
        {
        gotoxy(1, 5);
        strncpy(string, temp_ncb.NCB_CALLNAME, 16);
        string[16] = '\0';
        cprintf("Session established with '%s'.  LSN = %d.",
                string, (int) temp_ncb.NCB_LSN);
        }
    else
    if (temp_ncb.NCB_COMMAND == RECEIVE
      || temp_ncb.NCB_COMMAND == RECEIVE_ANY)
        {
        gotoxy(1, 5);
        cprintf("Message says: ");
        for (i=0, j=6; i<temp_ncb.NCB_LENGTH; i++)
            {
```

```
                if (i % 60 == 0)
                    gotoxy(1, j++);
                cprintf("%c", message_in[i]);
                }
            }
        else
        if (temp_ncb.NCB_COMMAND == SESSION_STATUS)
            {
            gotoxy(1, 4);
            cprintf("Names: %d    sessions: %d",
                (int) session_info.name_num,
                (int) session_info.session_count);
            if (session_info.session_count == 0) goto report_exit;
            j = 5;
            for (i=0; i<session_info.session_count; i++)
                {
                if (i > 5)
                    {
                    gotoxy(15, 16);
                    cprintf("(Press a key)");
                    bioskey(0);
                    clrscr();
                    j = 5;
                    }
                gotoxy(1, j++);
                cprintf("lsn = %d  (%s)  recvcount = %d  sendcount = %d",
                        (int) session_info.session_data[i].lsn,
                        state_msg[(int) session_info.session_data[i].state],
                        (int) session_info.session_data[i].recv_count,
                        (int) session_info.session_data[i].send_count );
                gotoxy(1, j++);
                session_info.session_data[i].local_name[15] = '\0';
                session_info.session_data[i].remote_name[15] = '\0';
                cprintf("localname = '%s'   remotename = '%s'",
                        session_info.session_data[i].local_name,
                        session_info.session_data[i].remote_name);
                }
            }
        else
        if (temp_ncb.NCB_COMMAND == HANG_UP)
            {
            gotoxy(1, 5);
            cprintf("Session closed.");
            }

report_exit:
        gotoxy(15, 16);
        cprintf("(Press a key)");
        bioskey(0);
        window(1, 1, 80, 25);
        gotoxy(cursor_x, cursor_y);
        puttext(1, 1, 80, 25, screen_save);
        }

/* - - - - - - - - - - - - - - - - - - - - - - - - - - - */
```

```
void interrupt     post(void)
        {
        es_reg  = _ES;
        bx_reg  = _BX;

        ncb_segments[ncb_head] = es_reg;
        ncb_offsets [ncb_head] = bx_reg;
        ncb_head++;

        if (ncb_head == 10)
            ncb_head = 0;
        }

/* - - - - - - - - - - - - - - - - - - - - - - - - - */

void    main(int argc, char *argv[])
        {
        int_5C_vector = getvect(0x5C);
        if (int_5C_vector == (void far *) NULL)
            {
            printf("NetBios not loaded (Int5C not present).\n");
            exit(0);
            }

        memset(&temp_ncb, 0, sizeof(NCB));
        temp_ncb.NCB_COMMAND = 0x7F;
        NetBios(&temp_ncb);
        if (temp_ncb.NCB_RETCODE != 03)
            {
            printf("NetBios not loaded (No response from Int5C).\n");
            exit(0);
            }

show_menu:
        clrscr();
        choice = 0;

        printf("NET-TEST Menu:\n\n");
        printf(" 0...exit\n");
        printf(" 1...reset adapter\n");
        printf(" 2...adapter status\n");
        printf(" 3...add name\n");
        printf(" 4...add group name\n");
        printf(" 5...delete name\n");
        printf(" 6...call\n");
        printf(" 7...listen\n");
        printf(" 8...send\n");
        printf(" 9...receive\n");
        printf("10...receive any\n");
        printf("11...hang up\n");
        printf("12...session status\n\n");
        printf("    Choice? ");

get_choice:
        if (ncb_head != ncb_tail)
            report_result();
```

```
if (!bioskey(1))
    goto get_choice;

gets(string);
printf("\n");
if (strlen(string) == 0) goto show_menu;

choice = atoi(string);
if (choice < 0 || choice > 12) goto show_menu;

switch (choice)
    {
    case 0 :{printf("Exiting.\n"); exit(0);}
    case 1 :{
            printf("Are you sure (Y/N)? ");
            gets(string);
            strlwr(string);
            if (string[0] != 'y') break;
            printf("Resetting adapter...\n");
            memset(&reset_ncb, 0, sizeof(NCB));
            reset_ncb.NCB_COMMAND = RESET;
            NetBios(&reset_ncb);
            printf("Return Code = %d.   (press a key)",
                (int) reset_ncb.NCB_RETCODE);
            bioskey(0);
            break;
            }
    case 2 :{
            printf("GET STATUS -- Enter name of adapter: ");
            gets(remotename);
            if (strlen(remotename) == 0) break;
            expand_to_16_chars(remotename);
            memset(&adapter_status_ncb, 0, sizeof(NCB));
            adapter_status_ncb.NCB_COMMAND = STATUS;
            adapter_status_ncb.POST_FUNC = post;
            strcpy(adapter_status_ncb.NCB_CALLNAME,remotename);
            adapter_status_ncb.NCB_BUFFER_PTR = &adapter_data;
            adapter_status_ncb.NCB_LENGTH  = sizeof(ADAPTER_DATA);
            memset(&adapter_data, 0, sizeof(ADAPTER_DATA));
            NetBios(&adapter_status_ncb);
            break;
            }
    case 3 :{
            printf("ADD NAME -- Enter name: ");
            gets(localname);
            if (strlen(localname) == 0) break;
            expand_to_16_chars(localname);
            memset(&add_name_ncb, 0, sizeof(NCB));
            add_name_ncb.NCB_COMMAND = ADD_NAME;
            strcpy(add_name_ncb.NCB_NAME, localname);
            add_name_ncb.POST_FUNC = post;
            NetBios(&add_name_ncb);
            break;
            }
```

```
            case 4 :{
                    printf("ADD GROUP NAME -- Enter name: ");
                    gets(localname);
                    if (strlen(localname) == 0) break;
                    expand_to_16_chars(localname);
                    memset(&add_group_name_ncb, 0, sizeof(NCB));
                    add_group_name_ncb.NCB_COMMAND = ADD_GROUP_NAME;
                    strcpy(add_group_name_ncb.NCB_NAME, localname);
                    add_group_name_ncb.POST_FUNC = post;
                    NetBios(&add_group_name_ncb);
                    break;
                    }
            case 5 :{
                    printf("DELETE NAME -- Enter name: ");
                    gets(localname);
                    if (strlen(localname) == 0) break;
                    expand_to_16_chars(localname);
                    memset(&delete_name_ncb, 0, sizeof(NCB));
                    delete_name_ncb.NCB_COMMAND = DELETE_NAME;
                    strcpy(delete_name_ncb.NCB_NAME, localname);
                    delete_name_ncb.POST_FUNC = post;
                    NetBios(&delete_name_ncb);
                    break;
                    }
            case 6 :{
                    printf("CALL -- Enter remote name to call: ");
                    gets(remotename);
                    if (strlen(remotename) == 0) break;
                    printf("        Enter local (calling) name: ");
                    gets(localname);
                    if (strlen(localname) == 0) break;
                    expand_to_16_chars(remotename);
                    expand_to_16_chars(localname);
                    memset(&call_ncb, 0, sizeof(NCB));
                    call_ncb.NCB_COMMAND = CALL;
                    strcpy(call_ncb.NCB_NAME,     localname);
                    strcpy(call_ncb.NCB_CALLNAME, remotename);
                    call_ncb.NCB_RTO = 0;
                    call_ncb.NCB_STO = 0;
                    call_ncb.POST_FUNC = post;
                    NetBios(&call_ncb);
                    break;
                    }
            case 7 :{
                    printf("LISTEN -- Enter remote name to listen for: ");
                    gets(remotename);
                    if (strlen(remotename) == 0) break;
                    printf("            Enter local (listening) name: ");
                    gets(localname);
                    if (strlen(localname) == 0) break;
                    expand_to_16_chars(remotename);
                    expand_to_16_chars(localname);
                    memset(&listen_ncb, 0, sizeof(NCB));
                    listen_ncb.NCB_COMMAND = LISTEN;
                    strcpy(listen_ncb.NCB_NAME,     localname);
                    strcpy(listen_ncb.NCB_CALLNAME, remotename);
```

```
        listen_ncb.NCB_RTO = 60;
        listen_ncb.NCB_STO = 0;
        listen_ncb.POST_FUNC = post;
        NetBios(&listen_ncb);
        break;
        }
case 8 :{
        printf("SEND -- Enter message to be sent: ");
        gets(message_out);
        if (strlen(message_out) == 0) break;
        printf("           Enter session number: ");
        gets(string);
        if (strlen(string) == 0) break;
        x = atoi(string);
        if (x < 1 ¦¦ x > 254) break;
        lsn = (unsigned char) x;
        memset(&send_ncb, 0, sizeof(NCB));
        send_ncb.NCB_COMMAND = SEND;
        send_ncb.NCB_LSN     = lsn;
        send_ncb.NCB_LENGTH  = strlen(message_out) + 1;
        send_ncb.NCB_BUFFER_PTR = message_out;
        send_ncb.POST_FUNC = post;
        NetBios(&send_ncb);
        break;
        }
case 9 :{
        printf("RECEIVE -- Enter session number: ");
        gets(string);
        if (strlen(string) == 0) break;
        x = atoi(string);
        if (x < 1 ¦¦ x > 254) break;
        lsn = (unsigned char) x;
        memset(&receive_ncb, 0, sizeof(NCB));
        receive_ncb.NCB_COMMAND = RECEIVE;
        receive_ncb.NCB_LSN     = lsn;
        receive_ncb.NCB_LENGTH  = MSG_SIZE - 1;
        receive_ncb.NCB_BUFFER_PTR = message_in;
        receive_ncb.POST_FUNC = post;
        NetBios(&receive_ncb);
        break;
        }
case 10:{
        printf("RECEIVE ANY -- Enter name number: ");
        gets(string);
        if (strlen(string) == 0) break;
        x = atoi(string);
        if (x < 1 ¦¦ x > 255) break;
        name_number = (unsigned char) x;
        memset(&receive_any_ncb, 0, sizeof(NCB));
        receive_any_ncb.NCB_COMMAND = RECEIVE_ANY;
        receive_any_ncb.NCB_NUM     = name_number;
        receive_any_ncb.NCB_LENGTH  = MSG_SIZE - 1;
        receive_any_ncb.NCB_BUFFER_PTR = message_in;
        receive_any_ncb.POST_FUNC = post;
        NetBios(&receive_any_ncb);
        break;
```

```
                                }
                      case 11:{
                                printf("HANG UP -- Enter session number: ");
                                gets(string);
                                if (strlen(string) == 0) break;
                                x = atoi(string);
                                if (x < 1 || x > 254) break;
                                lsn = (unsigned char) x;
                                memset(&hangup_ncb, 0, sizeof(NCB));
                                hangup_ncb.NCB_COMMAND = HANG_UP;
                                hangup_ncb.NCB_LSN      = lsn;
                                hangup_ncb.POST_FUNC    = post;
                                NetBios(&hangup_ncb);
                                break;
                                }
                      case 12:{
                                printf("GET SESSION STATUS -- Enter name:");
                                gets(localname);
                                if (strlen(localname) == 0) break;
                                expand_to_16_chars(localname);
                                memset(&session_status_ncb, 0, sizeof(NCB));
                                session_status_ncb.NCB_COMMAND = SESSION_STATUS;
                                strcpy(session_status_ncb.NCB_NAME, localname);
                                session_status_ncb.NCB_LENGTH  = sizeof(STATUS_INFO);
                                session_status_ncb.NCB_BUFFER_PTR = &session_info;
                                session_status_ncb.POST_FUNC = post;
                                NetBios(&session_status_ncb);
                                break;
                                }
                      default : break;
                      }

                 goto show_menu;
                 }

      /* - - - - - - - - - - - - - - - - - - - - - - - - - */
```

Appendix C

Source Listing for RPE.C

A discussion about how this program works is in Chapter 8, "Network Applications." Its companion, REMOTE.C, is in Appendix D.

```c
/*
 *          Remote Program Executioner  (RPE)
 *
 *  The "Executioner" takes from other workstations calls that consist
 *  of messages that tell it to execute programs or DOS commands.
 *  It returns a "job ticket" to each caller.  A queue of up to 50
 *  pending jobs is maintained.
 *
 *  Copyright (c) 1989, 1994 Barry Nance
 *  All Rights Reserved
 *
 *
 *  Written for Borland C.
 *  Use the HUGE memory model to compile this program.
 *
 */

/* - - - - - - - - - - - - - - - - - - - - - - - - - - */
#include <stdio.h>
#include <stdlib.h>
#include <dos.h>
#include <bios.h>
#include <mem.h>
#include <fcntl.h>
#include <io.h>
#include <conio.h>
#include <string.h>
#include <time.h>
#include <process.h>
#include <alloc.h>

#include <netbios.h>
void    interrupt background_listen(void);

#define  TRUE    1
#define  FALSE   0
```

```
/* - - - - - - - - - - - - - - - - - - - - - - - */

unsigned extern _stklen = 2000;

NCB     cancel_ncb;
NCB     listen_ncb;
NCB     add_name_ncb;
NCB     delete_name_ncb;
NCB     send_ncb;
NCB     receive_ncb;
NCB     hangup_ncb;

NCB     temp_ncb;

void interrupt  (*int_5C_vector)(void);

char    ch;
char    string[201];
char    *exec_prog;
char    *exec_parms;
char    path[81];
char    logname[81];
char    outname[81];
char    machine_name[16];
int     log_handle;
int     job_number;
int     background_activity;
int     executing;
int     i;
unsigned u;
unsigned char general_error;

struct  RUN_PACKET
        {
        char    packet_flag;
        char    program_and_commandline[133];
        };

struct  RUN_PACKET run_packet;

struct  QUEUE_INFO
        {
        int     queue_count;
        int     queue_head;
        int     queue_tail;
        struct  RUN_PACKET run_queue[50];
        int     next_jobnum[50];
        };

struct  QUEUE_INFO queue_info;

struct  JOB_PACKET
        {
        char    status_flag;
        char    our_name[16];
        char    job[9];
        };
```

```
struct  JOB_PACKET job_packet;

long    start_time;
long    stop_time;

unsigned paragraphs;
char    *transient;

/* - - - - - - - - - - - - - - - - - - - - - - - - */
/*
 *  A function to call NetBIOS (via Int 5C).
 *
 *
 */
void    NetBios(NCB *ncb_ptr)
        {
        ncb_ptr->NCB_CMD_CPLT = 0xFF;

        _ES     = FP_SEG(ncb_ptr);
        _BX     = FP_OFF(ncb_ptr);
        _AX     = 0x0100;

        geninterrupt(0x5c);
        }

/* - - - - - - - - - - - - - - - - - - - - - - - - */
/*
 *  Expand 'name' to be a 16 byte string, padded
 *  on the right with spaces, and null-terminated.
 *  (Doesn't work with 'permanent node names'.)
 */
void    expand_to_16_chars(char *name)
        {
        char *p;
        char tmp[17];
        int  i;

        memset(tmp, ' ', 15);
        p = name;
        i = 0;
        while (i < 15 && *p)
            {
            tmp[i] = *p;
            i++;
            p++;
            }
        tmp[15] = '\0';
        strcpy(name, tmp);
        }

/* - - - - - - - - - - - - - - - - - - - - - - - - */
/*
 *  Format a log file entry, lock the file, write
 *  the entry, and unlock the file.  Abort if a serious
 *  error occurs.
 */
```

```
void    log(char *log_message)
        {
        char    line[201];
        char    *str_time;
        long    now;
        int     retry_count;

        time(&now);
        str_time = ctime(&now);
        str_time[strlen(str_time) - 1] = '\0';
        sprintf(line, "%s <%s> ==> %s\n",
                str_time,
                machine_name,
                log_message);

        printf("%s", line);

        retry_count = 0;
        while ( lock(log_handle, 0x00000001, 0x0FFFFFF1) )
            if (++retry_count > 100)
                {
                printf("SYSTEM ERROR.  Could not lock the log file.\n");
                close(log_handle);
                exit(1);
                }

        write(log_handle, line, strlen(line));

        retry_count = 0;
        while ( unlock(log_handle, 0x00000001, 0x0FFFFFF1) )
            if (++retry_count > 100)
                {
                printf("SYSTEM ERROR.  Could not unlock the log file.\n");
                close(log_handle);
                exit(1);
                }

        close(dup(log_handle));
        }

/* - - - - - - - - - - - - - - - - - - - - - - - - - */
/*
 * Build the 'add_name' NCB and send it out
 * across the network.
 *
 */
void    net_add_name(char *name)
        {
        memset(&add_name_ncb, 0, sizeof(NCB));
        add_name_ncb.NCB_COMMAND = ADD_NAME;
        strcpy(add_name_ncb.NCB_NAME, name);
        expand_to_16_chars(add_name_ncb.NCB_NAME);
        NetBios(&add_name_ncb);
        }

/* - - - - - - - - - - - - - - - - - - - - - - - - - */
/*
```

```
 *     Build the 'delete_name' NCB
 *
 */
void    net_delete_name(char *name)
        {
        memset(&delete_name_ncb, 0, sizeof(NCB));
        delete_name_ncb.NCB_COMMAND = DELETE_NAME;
        strcpy(delete_name_ncb.NCB_NAME, name);
        expand_to_16_chars(delete_name_ncb.NCB_NAME);
        NetBios(&delete_name_ncb);
        }

/* - - - - - - - - - - - - - - - - - - - - - - - */
/*
 *     Build the 'listen' NCB and send it out
 *     across the network.  Set the POST address to
 *     point to a 'background' routine to handle a caller.
 */
void    net_listen_post(char *caller, char *us,
                        void interrupt (*post_function)(),
                        unsigned char rto, unsigned char sto)

        {
        memset(&listen_ncb, 0, sizeof(NCB));
        listen_ncb.NCB_COMMAND = LISTEN;
        strcpy(listen_ncb.NCB_NAME,      us);
        strcpy(listen_ncb.NCB_CALLNAME, caller);
        expand_to_16_chars(listen_ncb.NCB_NAME);
        expand_to_16_chars(listen_ncb.NCB_CALLNAME);
        listen_ncb.POST_FUNC = post_function;
        listen_ncb.NCB_RTO = rto;
        listen_ncb.NCB_STO = sto;
        NetBios(&listen_ncb);
        }

/* - - - - - - - - - - - - - - - - - - - - - - - */
/*
 *     Build the 'cancel' NCB and send it out
 *     across the network.
 *
 */
void    net_cancel(NCB *np)
        {
        memset(&cancel_ncb, 0, sizeof(NCB));
        cancel_ncb.NCB_COMMAND = CANCEL;
        cancel_ncb.NCB_BUFFER_PTR = np;
        NetBios(&cancel_ncb);
        }

/* - - - - - - - - - - - - - - - - - - - - - - - */
/*
 *     Build the 'receive' NCB and send it out
 *     across the network.  When the operation completes,
 *     let NetBIOS call the POST routine to handle it.
 */
void    net_receive_post(unsigned char lsn,
                         void interrupt (*post_function)(),
```

```
                              void *packet_ptr, int packet_len)
                {
            memset(&receive_ncb, 0, sizeof(NCB));
            receive_ncb.NCB_COMMAND = RECEIVE;
            receive_ncb.NCB_LSN = lsn;
            receive_ncb.NCB_LENGTH = packet_len;
            receive_ncb.NCB_BUFFER_PTR = packet_ptr;
            receive_ncb.POST_FUNC = post_function;
            NetBios(&receive_ncb);
                }

/* - - - - - - - - - - - - - - - - - - - - - - - - - */
/*
 *    Build the 'send' NCB and send it out
 *    across the network.
 *
 */
void    net_send(unsigned char lsn,void *packet_ptr, int packet_len)
                {
            memset(&send_ncb, 0, sizeof(NCB));
            send_ncb.NCB_COMMAND = SEND;
            send_ncb.NCB_LSN = lsn;
            send_ncb.NCB_LENGTH = packet_len;
            send_ncb.NCB_BUFFER_PTR = packet_ptr;
            NetBios(&send_ncb);
                }

/* - - - - - - - - - - - - - - - - - - - - - - - - */
/*
 *    Build the 'hang up' NCB and send it out
 *    across the network.  Wait for completion.
 *
 */
void    net_hangup(unsigned char lsn)
                {
            memset(&hangup_ncb, 0, sizeof(NCB));
            hangup_ncb.NCB_COMMAND = HANG_UP;
            hangup_ncb.NCB_LSN = lsn;
            NetBios(&hangup_ncb);
                }

/* - - - - - - - - - - - - - - - - - - - - - - - - - */
/*
 *  Find job in the pending queue and remove it
 *  by marking it with a packet flag of 'C'
 *  (or return a 'job not found' indication).
 */

void    cancel_job (int job)
                {
            int  x;

            sprintf(job_packet.job, "J%4.4d", job);
            x = queue_info.queue_tail;
            while (x != queue_info.queue_head)
                {
```

```
                if (queue_info.next_jobnum[x] == job)
                    {
                    queue_info.run_queue[x].packet_flag = 'C';
                    job_packet.status_flag = 'C';
                    return;
                    }
                if (++x == 50) x = 0;
                }
            job_packet.status_flag = 'E';
            }

/* - - - - - - - - - - - - - - - - - - - - - - - */
/*
 *  This function is called by NetBIOS when a POSTed
 *  receive completes (meaning that someone sent us a
 *  status packet, a cancel packet, or a run packet
 *  that goes into the queue).
 *
 */
void      interrupt background_receive(void)
          {
          char *job_token;

          general_error = receive_ncb.NCB_CMD_CPLT;
          if (general_error != 0)
              goto bg_receive_exit;

forget_it:
          if (run_packet.packet_flag == 'X')
              goto bg_close_session;

          if (queue_info.queue_count > 45)
              {
              job_packet.status_flag = 'Z';
              net_send(listen_ncb.NCB_LSN, &job_packet,
                  sizeof(job_packet));
              goto bg_close_session;
              }

status_response:
          if (strnicmp(run_packet.program_and_commandline, "status",
              6) == 0)
              {
              net_send(listen_ncb.NCB_LSN, &queue_info,
                  sizeof(queue_info));
              goto bg_close_session;
              }

cancel_a_job:
          if (strnicmp(run_packet.program_and_commandline, "cancel",
              6) == 0)
              {
              job_token = strtok(run_packet.program_and_commandline,
                  "Jj");
              if (job_token != NULL)
```

```
                                i = atoi( strtok(NULL, " \n") );
                        cancel_job(i);
                        net_send(listen_ncb.NCB_LSN, &job_packet,
                            sizeof(job_packet));
                        goto bg_close_session;
                        }

        queue_the_job:
                strcpy(queue_info.run_queue
                            [queue_info.queue_head].program_and_commandline,
                        run_packet.program_and_commandline);
                queue_info.run_queue[queue_info.queue_head].packet_flag = 'Q';
                sprintf(job_packet.job, "J%4.4d", ++job_number);
                job_packet.status_flag = 'J';
                queue_info.next_jobnum[queue_info.queue_head] = job_number;

                if (++queue_info.queue_head == 50) queue_info.queue_head = 0;
                queue_info.queue_count++;

                net_send(listen_ncb.NCB_LSN, &job_packet,
                            sizeof(job_packet));

        bg_close_session:
                net_hangup(listen_ncb.NCB_LSN);
                if (strnicmp(run_packet.program_and_commandline, "quit", 4) == 0)
                    goto bg_receive_exit;

        reissue_listen:
                net_listen_post("*", "RPE", background_listen, 20, 20);

        bg_receive_exit:
                background_activity = FALSE;
                }

        /* - - - - - - - - - - - - - - - - - - - - - - - - - */
        /*
         *  This function is activated when a 'call RPE' command
         *  is issued by another workstation.
         *
         */
        void    interrupt background_listen(void)
                {
                general_error = listen_ncb.NCB_CMD_CPLT;
                if (general_error != 0)
                    goto bg_listen_exit;

                background_activity = TRUE;

                strcpy(job_packet.our_name, machine_name);
                strcpy(job_packet.job, "          ");

                if (executing)
                    job_packet.status_flag = 'Q';
                else
                    job_packet.status_flag = 'J';
```

```
        net_send(listen_ncb.NCB_LSN, &job_packet,
            sizeof(job_packet));

        net_receive_post(listen_ncb.NCB_LSN,
                        background_receive,
                        &run_packet, sizeof(run_packet));

bg_listen_exit:
        ;
        }

/* - - - - - - - - - - - - - - - - - - - - - - - - */
/*
 *  Execute the next item in the queue.
*/

void    execute_program(int job)
        {
/*
 *
 *  if a call is still under way, let it finish.
 *
*/

        while (background_activity)
            ;

/*
 *  As mentioned below, we want to force Command.Com to reload
 *  its transient (high-memory) portion.  This avoids an obscure
 *  DOS bug and makes RPE a little more bullet-proof.
*/
        for (i=0; i<8000; i++)
            transient[i] = 0;

/*
 *
 *  Mention how many jobs are awaiting execution.  Log this job.
 *
*/

        if (queue_info.queue_count != 0)
            {
            sprintf(string, "%d job(s) awaiting execution",
                    queue_info.queue_count);
            log(string);
            }

        sprintf(job_packet.job, "J%4.4d", job);
        log(job_packet.job);


/*
 *  If the caller is instructing us to quit (remotely), we do so.
 *
 *
*/
```

```
            if (strnicmp(run_packet.program_and_commandline, "quit", 4) == 0)
                {
                log("RPE ended remotely.");
                close(log_handle);
                net_hangup(listen_ncb.NCB_LSN);
                while (hangup_ncb.NCB_CMD_CPLT == 0xFF)
                    ;
                net_delete_name("RPE");
                while (delete_name_ncb.NCB_CMD_CPLT == 0xFF)
                    ;
                exit(0);
                }

/*
 *  Now construct the DOS command line that we'll pass to the
 *  system() function, just as if it were to be executed at a
 *  DOS prompt.  Redirect 'stdout' output to a job-specific file.
 */

            sprintf(string, "%s >%sJ%4.4d.OUT",
                run_packet.program_and_commandline,
                path,
                job);
            log(string);

/*
 *  Execute the program (or DOS command).  For statistical purposes,
 *  keep track of elapsed time.
 *
 */

            executing = TRUE;
            time(&start_time);
            system(string);
            time(&stop_time);
            executing = FALSE;

/*
 *  Log the completion of the program/command.
 *
 */

            sprintf(string, "Job %4.4d completed.  %ld elapsed second(s).",
                    job, (long) stop_time - start_time );
            log(string);
            }

/* - - - - - - - - - - - - - - - - - - - - - - - - */
/*
 *  The program starts here.
 *
 *  Initialize job_number, then figure out where the transient
 *  portion of Command.Com is located.  We'll use this later to
 *  zero that area, because we want to force Command.Com to
 *  reload it.  This avoids an obscure bug in PC-DOS.
 *
 */
```

```c
void    main (int argc, char *argv[])
        {
        general_error = 0;

        job_number = 0;
        paragraphs = (biosmemory() - 8) * 64;
        transient  = MK_FP(paragraphs, 0);

        background_activity = FALSE;
        queue_info.queue_head = 0;
        queue_info.queue_tail = 0;

/*
 *  Abort if we're running on top of a DOS version earlier than 3.0.
 *  Also, check to see if SHARE.EXE has been run (to support file-
 *  sharing).  Finally, make sure NetBIOS is present.
 */
Step_1:
        if (_osmajor < 3)
            {
            printf("ERROR. Early versions of DOS not supported.\n");
            exit(1);
            }

        _AX = 0x1000;
        geninterrupt(0x2F);
        if (_AL != 0xFF)
            {
        printf("ERROR. 'Share.Exe' (file sharing support) not loaded.\n");
            exit(1);
            }

        _DX = (unsigned) &machine_name[0];
        _AX = 0x5E00;
        geninterrupt(0x21);
        if (_CH == 0)
            {
            printf("ERROR.  Machine name not set.\n");
            exit(1);
            }

        i = strlen(machine_name) - 1;
        while (i > 0 && machine_name[i] == ' ')
            {
            machine_name[i] = '\0';
            i—;
            }

        int_5C_vector = getvect(0x5C);
        if (int_5C_vector == (void far *) NULL)
            {
            printf("ERROR. NetBios not loaded (Int5C not present).\n");
            exit(1);
            }
```

```
        memset(&temp_ncb, 0, sizeof(NCB));
        temp_ncb.NCB_COMMAND = 0x7F;
        NetBios(&temp_ncb);
        if (temp_ncb.NCB_RETCODE != 03)
            {
        printf("ERROR. NetBios not loaded (No response from Int5C).\n");
            exit(1);
            }

/*
 *  Do an 'Add Name' call, to make us available on
 *  the network.
 *
 */
Step_2:
        printf("Adding name 'RPE' to the network...");

        net_add_name("RPE");
        while (add_name_ncb.NCB_CMD_CPLT == 0xFF)
            ;

        printf("\n");
        if (add_name_ncb.NCB_CMD_CPLT != 0)
            {
            printf("ERROR.  NetBios said: %s.\n",
                net_error_message[(int)add_name_ncb.NCB_CMD_CPLT]);
            exit(1);
            }

/*
 *  Now find out the drive and directory in which the log file
 *  should be written.  Open it for shared access (if it's
 *  necessary to create it, we'll have to close it and reopen
 *  it because file-creation confers exclusive access, which we
 *  don't want).
 */
Step_3:
        printf("Specify network Drive:\\Path for log file: ");
        gets(path);
        if (strlen(path) == 0)
            goto Step_3;

        if (path[strlen(path)-1] != '\\')
            strcat(path, "\\");
        strcpy(logname, path);
        strcat(logname, "RPE.LOG");
        strupr(logname);

        printf("Log file is %s (append/shared)\n", logname);

        if ( (log_handle = creatnew(logname, 0)) != -1)
            close(log_handle);
        log_handle = open(logname,
            O_RDWR ¦ O_APPEND ¦ O_TEXT ¦ O_DENYNONE);
```

```
            if (log_handle == -1)
                {
                net_delete_name("RPE");
                while (delete_name_ncb.NCB_CMD_CPLT == 0xFF)
                    ;
                printf("ERROR. Could not open log file.\n");
                exit(1);
                }

        log("RPE started.");

/*
 *   Issue a Listen-to-anyone command.  Set the receive-timeout
 *   and send-timeout fields to 20 500-ms periods (10 seconds)
 *   each.  If someone calls, invoke the 'background_listen()'
 *   routine.
 */
Step_4:
        net_listen_post("*", "RPE", background_listen, 20, 20);


/*
 *   Let people know we're waiting for something to do,
 *   and tell how to stop the program.
 */

Step_5:
        log("Waiting for work.  Press 'ESC' to stop RPE. ");

/*
 *   While we're waiting for a call, look for a press of the
 *   ESCape key, to see if someone wants to stop the program.
 *   Confirm their response.  To stop RPE, we need to leave
 *   things the way we found them, so we cancel the
 *   outstanding 'listen' command, delete our name from the
 *   name table, and then go back to DOS.
 *
 */
Step_6:
        while (!general_error)
            {
            if (bioskey(1))
                if ( (ch = (char) getch()) == 27 )
                    {
                    log("Terminate RPE (Yes/No)? ");
                    gets(string);
                    if (string[0] == 'Y' || string[0] == 'y')
                        {
                        log("RPE ended.");
                        close(log_handle);
                        net_cancel(&listen_ncb);
                        while (cancel_ncb.NCB_CMD_CPLT == 0xFF)
                            ;
                        net_delete_name("RPE");
                        while (delete_name_ncb.NCB_CMD_CPLT == 0xFF)
                            ;
```

```
                                    exit(0);
                                    }
                            goto Step_5;
                            }
                if (queue_info.queue_head != queue_info.queue_tail)
                    {
                    strcpy(run_packet.program_and_commandline,
                            queue_info.run_queue
                                [queue_info.queue_tail].program_and_commandline);
                    job_number = queue_info.next_jobnum[queue_info.queue_tail];
                    if (queue_info.run_queue
                            [queue_info.queue_tail].packet_flag != 'C')
                        {
                        queue_info.run_queue
                            [queue_info.queue_tail].packet_flag = 'E';
                        execute_program(job_number);
                        }
                    queue_info.queue_count--;
                    if (++queue_info.queue_tail == 50) queue_info.queue_tail = 0;
                    }
                }


    /*
     *  If an error occurs, we want to stop the program as
     *  gracefully as possible.  So, we make sure we cancel
     *  any outstanding 'listen' and delete the name 'RPE'
     *  before going back to DOS.
     */

            sprintf(string, "RPE aborted--%s",
                    net_error_message[general_error]);
            log(string);
            close(log_handle);
            net_cancel(&listen_ncb);
            while (cancel_ncb.NCB_CMD_CPLT == 0xFF)
                ;
            net_delete_name("RPE");
            while (delete_name_ncb.NCB_CMD_CPLT == 0xFF)
                ;
            exit(1);
            }
```

Appendix D

Source Listing for REMOTE.C

A discussion about how this program works is in Chapter 8, "Network Applications." Its companion, RPE.C, is in Appendix C.

```
/*
 *          Remote -- A "Job" Dispatcher
 *
 *   "Remote" sends messages to "RPE" (which you run on a separate
 *   workstation), telling it to execute programs or DOS commands.
 *   A "job ticket" is issued back to REMOTE by RPE for each job.
 *
 *   Since the program or DOS command runs remotely, your computer
 *   is freed up immediately to do other work.
 *
 *   Copyright (c) 1989, 1994 Barry Nance
 *   All Rights Reserved
 *
 *
 *   Written for Borland C.
 *   Use the SMALL memory model to compile this program.
 *
 */

/* - - - - - - - - - - - - - - - - - - - - - - - - */
#include <stdio.h>
#include <conio.h>
#include <stdlib.h>
#include <string.h>
#include <process.h>
#include <dos.h>

#include <netbios.h>

NCB     status_ncb;
NCB     call_ncb;
NCB     send_ncb;
NCB     receive_ncb;
NCB     hangup_ncb;
NCB     temp_ncb;
```

```c
void interrupt  (*int_5C_vector)(void);

char    string[201];
char    our_name[16];
char    other_name[16];
char    i;
int     j;

char far *command_line;
char far *byte_count;

struct  RUN_PACKET
        {
        char    packet_flag;
        char    program_and_commandline[133];
        };

struct  RUN_PACKET run_packet;

struct  QUEUE_INFO
        {
        int     queue_count;
        int     queue_head;
        int     queue_tail;
        struct  RUN_PACKET run_queue[50];
        int     next_jobnum[50];
        };

struct  QUEUE_INFO queue_info;

struct  JOB_PACKET
        {
        char    status_flag;
        char    machine_name[16];
        char    job[9];
        };

struct  JOB_PACKET job_packet;

/* - - - - - - - - - - - - - - - - - - - - - - - - */
/*
 *  Call NetBIOS, via Interrupt 5C.
 */
void    NetBios(NCB far *ncb_ptr)
        {
        ncb_ptr->NCB_CMD_CPLT = 0xFF;

        _ES     = FP_SEG(ncb_ptr);
        _BX     = FP_OFF(ncb_ptr);
        _AX     = 0x0100;

        geninterrupt(0x5c);
        }

/* - - - - - - - - - - - - - - - - - - - - - - - - */
/*
 *  Expand a NetBIOS name by padding on the right
```

```
 *  with spaces.
 */
void     expand_to_16_chars(char *name)
         {
         char *p;
         char tmp[17];
         int  i;

         memset(tmp, ' ', 15);
         p = name;
         i = 0;
         while (i < 15 && *p)
             {
             tmp[i] = *p;
             i++;
             p++;
             }
         tmp[15] = '\0';
         strcpy(name, tmp);
         }

/* - - - - - - - - - - - - - - - - - - - - - - - */
/*
 *  Build and send an 'adapter status' command
 */
void     net_status(char far *buffer, int len)
         {
         memset(&status_ncb, 0, sizeof(NCB));
         status_ncb.NCB_COMMAND = STATUS;
         strcpy(status_ncb.NCB_CALLNAME, "*");
         expand_to_16_chars(status_ncb.NCB_CALLNAME);
         status_ncb.NCB_LENGTH = len;
         status_ncb.NCB_BUFFER_PTR = buffer;
         NetBios(&status_ncb);
         }

/* - - - - - - - - - - - - - - - - - - - - - - - */
/*
 *  "Call" another workstation.
 */
void     net_call(char *who, char *us, unsigned char rto,
    unsigned char sto)
         {
         memset(&call_ncb, 0, sizeof(NCB));
         call_ncb.NCB_COMMAND = CALL;
         memcpy(call_ncb.NCB_NAME,     us, 16);
         strcpy(call_ncb.NCB_CALLNAME, who);
         expand_to_16_chars(call_ncb.NCB_CALLNAME);
         call_ncb.NCB_RTO = rto;
         call_ncb.NCB_STO = sto;
         NetBios(&call_ncb);
         }

/* - - - - - - - - - - - - - - - - - - - - - - - */
/*
 *  Issue a "receive" command to NetBIOS.
```

```
*/
void    net_receive(unsigned char lsn, void far *packet_ptr,
    int packet_len)
        {
        memset(&receive_ncb, 0, sizeof(NCB));
        receive_ncb.NCB_COMMAND = RECEIVE;
        receive_ncb.NCB_LSN = lsn;
        receive_ncb.NCB_LENGTH = packet_len;
        receive_ncb.NCB_BUFFER_PTR = packet_ptr;
        NetBios(&receive_ncb);
        }

/* - - - - - - - - - - - - - - - - - - - - - - - */
/*
 *  Build and send a message packet via NetBIOS.
 */
void    net_send(unsigned char lsn, void far *packet_ptr,
    int packet_len)
        {
        memset(&send_ncb, 0, sizeof(NCB));
        send_ncb.NCB_COMMAND = SEND;
        send_ncb.NCB_LSN = lsn;
        send_ncb.NCB_LENGTH = packet_len;
        send_ncb.NCB_BUFFER_PTR = packet_ptr;
        NetBios(&send_ncb);
        }

/* - - - - - - - - - - - - - - - - - - - - - - - */
/*
 *  Close a session with a "hang up" command.
 */
void    net_hangup(unsigned char lsn)
        {
        memset(&hangup_ncb, 0, sizeof(NCB));
        hangup_ncb.NCB_COMMAND = HANG_UP;
        hangup_ncb.NCB_LSN = lsn;
        NetBios(&hangup_ncb);
        }

/* - - - - - - - - - - - - - - - - - - - - - - - */
/*
 *  The program starts here.
 *
 *  Basically, all we do is send our command line to "RPE"
 *  so that it can treat it as a program (or DOS command)
 *  to be executed remotely.
 *
 */
void    main(int argc, char *argv[])
        {
/*
 *  First, make sure that we're running under DOS 3.0 or later.
 *  Then check to make sure that SHARE.EXE has been run and that
 *  NetBIOS is active.
 */
```

```
Step_1:
        if (_osmajor < 3)
            {
            printf("ERROR. Early versions of DOS not supported.\n");
            exit(1);
            }

        _AX = 0x1000;
        geninterrupt(0x2F);
        if (_AL != 0xFF)
            {
    printf("ERROR. 'Share.Exe' (file-sharing support) not loaded.\n");
            exit(1);
            }

        int_5C_vector = getvect(0x5C);
        if (int_5C_vector == (void far *) NULL)
            {
    printf("ERROR. NetBios not loaded (Int5C not present).\n");
            exit(1);
            }

        memset(&temp_ncb, 0, sizeof(NCB));
        temp_ncb.NCB_COMMAND = 0x7F;
        NetBios(&temp_ncb);
        if (temp_ncb.NCB_RETCODE != 03)
            {
    printf("ERROR. NetBios not loaded (No response from Int5C).\n");
            exit(1);
            }

/*
 *  We need a name to identify ourselves when we later issue the
 *  "call" command.  Let's use the "Permanent Node Name"...we build
 *  it by getting the first six bytes of the data area returned by
 *  the "adapter status" command, and prefixing them with ten bytes
 *  of binary zeroes.
 *
 *  Note that we only give the 'adapter status' command a buffer of
 *  60 bytes to fill.  We then deliberately ignore the almost certain
 *  NCB_CMD_CPLT return code of 6 ("data area too small").
 */
Step_2:
        net_status(string, 60);
        while (status_ncb.NCB_CMD_CPLT == 0xFF)
            ;
if (status_ncb.NCB_CMD_CPLT != 0x00 && status_ncb.NCB_CMD_CPLT != 0x06)
            {
            printf("ERROR.  NetBios said: %s.\n",
                net_error_message[(int)status_ncb.NCB_CMD_CPLT]);
            exit(1);
            }
```

```
        memset(our_name, 0, 16);
        for (i=0; i<6; i++)
            our_name[i+10] = string[i];

/*
 *  REMOTE expects to be invoked like this:
 *
 *      C:> remote <progname> <command line parameters>
 *
 *  or this:
 *
 *      C:> remote <dos command> <command parameters>
 *
 *  So we go down inside the Program Segment Prefix to pick up
 *  REMOTE's command line, which will be sent to RPE.  If REMOTE
 *  is run without a command line, it simply exits after reminding
 *  the user that a command line is required.
 *
 *  The length of the command line is found in byte 0x80 (byte 128)
 *  of the PSP.  The bytes following the length are the command
 *  line, terminated by a carriage return.  For example:
 *
 *  (11)    C   O   P   Y       A   :   *   .   *   (13)
 *  --- --- --- --- --- --- --- --- --- --- --- --- ---
 *  0x80  81  82  83  84  85  86  87  88  89  8A  8B  8C
 *
 *  Note that the first byte following the length byte is normally
 *  a space character.  We bypass it.
 *
 */
Step_3:
        byte_count   = MK_FP(_psp, 0x0080);
        command_line = MK_FP(_psp, 0x0081);

        if (*byte_count == 0)
            {
            printf("Usage: REMOTE <progname> <command line>\n");
            printf("    or REMOTE <dos command> <parms>\n");
            exit(1);
            }

        memset(run_packet.program_and_commandline, 0, 133);
        while (*command_line == ' ')
            ++command_line;

        i = 0;
        while (*command_line != 13 && *command_line != 0)
            {
            run_packet.program_and_commandline[i] = *command_line;
            ++command_line;
            ++i;
            }

/*
 *  Issue a NetBIOS 'call' to establish a session with "RPE".
 *
```

```
        *
*/
Step_5:
        net_call("RPE", our_name, 20, 20);
        while (call_ncb.NCB_CMD_CPLT == 0xFF)
            ;

        if (call_ncb.NCB_CMD_CPLT != 0)
            {
            printf("Couldn't connect: %s\n",
                    net_error_message[call_ncb.NCB_CMD_CPLT]);
            printf("'Remote' ended (unsuccessfully).\n");
            exit(1);
            }

/*
 *  "RPE" always starts the conversation by sending us the machine-
 *  name of the computer it's running on (as part of 'job_packet').
 *  So the first thing we do is issue a 'receive' command in order
 *  to get that first message.
 */
Step_6:
        net_receive(call_ncb.NCB_LSN, &job_packet,
            sizeof(job_packet));
        while (receive_ncb.NCB_CMD_CPLT == 0xFF)
            ;

        if (receive_ncb.NCB_CMD_CPLT != 0)
            {
            printf("RPE aborted—%s\n",
                    net_error_message[receive_ncb.NCB_CMD_CPLT]);
            net_hangup(call_ncb.NCB_LSN);
            while (hangup_ncb.NCB_CMD_CPLT == 0xFF)
                ;
            printf("Remote ended due to error.\n");
            exit(1);
            }

        strcpy(other_name, job_packet.machine_name);
        j = strlen(other_name) - 1;
        while (j > 0 && other_name[j] == ' ')
            {
            other_name[j] = '\0';
            j--;
            }

/*
 *  If the job packet returned by "RPE" contains a 'packet_flag'
 *  of 'Q', it means that our job request will go into the queue.
 *  Let's ask if this is okay.
 *
 *  If 'packet_flag' is a 'Z', the queue is full.
 *
 *  If the user doesn't want the job placed in the awaiting-
 *  execution queue, we'll tell "RPE" to forget it.
 *
```

```
              *  If the command line contains 'quit', 'status', or 'cancel',
              *  pass it immediately to "RPE".
              *
              */
          Step_7:
                  if (strnicmp(run_packet.program_and_commandline, "quit",
                      4) == 0)
                     goto Step_8;
                  if (strnicmp(run_packet.program_and_commandline, "status",
                      6) == 0)
                     goto Step_8;
                  if (strnicmp(run_packet.program_and_commandline, "cancel",
                      6) == 0)
                     goto Step_8;

                  if (job_packet.status_flag == 'Z')
                      {
                      printf("The queue is full at this time.  Try later.\n");
                      net_hangup(call_ncb.NCB_LSN);
                      while (hangup_ncb.NCB_CMD_CPLT == 0xFF)
                          ;
                      printf("'Remote' ended due to error.\n");
                      exit(1);
                      }

                  if (job_packet.status_flag == 'Q')
                      {
                      printf("\n");
                  printf("RPE (%s) is busy...your request will go into the queue.\n",
                          other_name);
                      printf("Is this okay (Yes/No)? ");
                      do
                          i = (char) getch();
                          while (i != 'N' && i != 'n' && i != 'Y' && i != 'y');
                      if (i == 'y' || i == 'Y')
                          {
                          printf("Yes...\n");
                          goto Step_8;
                          }
                      printf("No...\n");
                      printf("Job request cancelled.\n");
                      run_packet.packet_flag = 'X';
                      net_send(call_ncb.NCB_LSN, &run_packet,
                          sizeof(run_packet));
                      while (send_ncb.NCB_CMD_CPLT == 0xFF)
                          ;
                      if (send_ncb.NCB_CMD_CPLT != 0)
                          {
                          printf("NetBios error msg: %s\n",
                                  net_error_message[send_ncb.NCB_CMD_CPLT]);
                          net_hangup(call_ncb.NCB_LSN);
                          while (hangup_ncb.NCB_CMD_CPLT == 0xFF)
                              ;
                          printf("'Remote' ended due to error.\n");
                          exit(1);
                          }
```

```
                net_hangup(call_ncb.NCB_LSN);
                while (hangup_ncb.NCB_CMD_CPLT == 0xFF)
                    ;
                exit(0);
                }

/*
 *  Send "RPE" a message containing REMOTE's command line.
 *
 */
Step_8:
        run_packet.packet_flag = 'P';

        net_send(call_ncb.NCB_LSN, &run_packet,
            sizeof(run_packet));
        while (send_ncb.NCB_CMD_CPLT == 0xFF)
            ;

        if (send_ncb.NCB_CMD_CPLT != 0)
            {
            printf("NetBios error msg: %s\n",
                    net_error_message[send_ncb.NCB_CMD_CPLT]);
            net_hangup(call_ncb.NCB_LSN);
            while (hangup_ncb.NCB_CMD_CPLT == 0xFF)
                ;
            printf("'Remote' ended due to error.\n");
            exit(1);
            }


/*
 *  If we sent a 'quit' command, we're stopping "RPE".  So we can
 *  quit, too.
 *
 */
Step_9:
        if (strnicmp(run_packet.program_and_commandline, "quit",
            4) == 0)
            {
            printf("RPE (%s) will stop when the queue is empty.\n",
                    other_name);
            net_hangup(call_ncb.NCB_LSN);
            while (hangup_ncb.NCB_CMD_CPLT == 0xFF)
                ;
            exit(0);
            }

/*
 *  Receive a response from "RPE".
 *
 */
Step_10:
        if (strnicmp(run_packet.program_and_commandline, "status",
            6) == 0)
```

```
                net_receive(call_ncb.NCB_LSN, &queue_info, sizeof(queue_info));
            else
            if (strnicmp(run_packet.program_and_commandline, "cancel",
                6) == 0)
                net_receive(call_ncb.NCB_LSN, &job_packet,
                    sizeof(job_packet));
            else
                net_receive(call_ncb.NCB_LSN, &job_packet,
                    sizeof(job_packet));


            while (receive_ncb.NCB_CMD_CPLT == 0xFF)
                ;

            if (receive_ncb.NCB_CMD_CPLT != 0)
                {
                printf("RPE aborted--%s\n",
                        net_error_message[receive_ncb.NCB_CMD_CPLT]);
                net_hangup(call_ncb.NCB_LSN);
                while (hangup_ncb.NCB_CMD_CPLT == 0xFF)
                    ;
                printf("Remote ended due to error.\n");
                exit(1);
                }

/*
 *  The dialog is finished; hang up on "RPE".
 *
 */

            net_hangup(call_ncb.NCB_LSN);
            while (hangup_ncb.NCB_CMD_CPLT == 0xFF)
                ;


/*
 *  Display the awaiting-execution queue.
 *
 */
Step_11:
            if (strnicmp(run_packet.program_and_commandline, "status",
                6) == 0)
                {
                printf("\n");
                printf("There are %d job(s) in %s's queue.\n\n",
                        queue_info.queue_count,
                        other_name);
                if (queue_info.queue_count > 0)
                    {
                    printf("  JOB   COMMAND\n");
                    printf("  -----  --------------------------------------\n");
                    for (j=0; j<queue_info.queue_count; j++)
                        {
                        if (queue_info.run_queue
                                [queue_info.queue_tail].packet_flag == 'C')
```

```
                            strcpy(string, "CANCELLED");
                    else
                    if (queue_info.run_queue
                            [queue_info.queue_tail].packet_flag == 'E')
                        strcpy(string, "EXECUTING");
                    else
                        strcpy(string, "PENDING");
                    printf(" J%4.4d  %-40.40s  %s\n",
                        queue_info.next_jobnum[queue_info.queue_tail],
                        queue_info.run_queue
                            [queue_info.queue_tail].program_and_commandline,
                        string);
                    if (++queue_info.queue_tail == 50)
                        queue_info.queue_tail = 0;
                    }
                printf("\n");
                }
            printf("Remote ended successfully.\n");
            exit(0);
            }


/*
 *  Display whether the job was cancelled or not found in the queue.
 *
 */
Step_12:
            if (strnicmp(run_packet.program_and_commandline, "cancel",
                6) == 0)
                {
            if (job_packet.status_flag == 'E')
                printf("Job %s not found in %s's queue.\n",
                        job_packet.job,
                        other_name);
            else
                printf("Job %s cancelled in %s's queue.\n",
                        job_packet.job,
                        other_name);
            printf("Remote ended successfully.\n");
            exit(0);
            }


/*
 *  Display the assigned job number.
 *
 */
Step_13:
        printf("\n");
        printf("Job # %s in queue on machine %s.\n",
            job_packet.job,
            other_name);
        printf("Remote ended successfully.\n");
        exit(0);
        }
```

Appendix E

Source Listing for the PostMan Program

See Chapter 8, "Network Applications," for a discussion of what this program does, how it works, and how to use it.

```c
/*      E-Mail  V1.00   (PostMan)              */
/*      Copyright (c) 1989, 1994 Barry R. Nance */

#pragma  inline

#include <stdio.h>
#include <dos.h>
#include <dir.h>
#include <mem.h>
#include <io.h>
#include <fcntl.h>
#include <errno.h>
#include <conio.h>
#include <bios.h>
#include <stdlib.h>
#include <string.h>
#include <stddef.h>
#include <stdarg.h>
#include <time.h>
#include <netbios.h>

void    interrupt POST_receive(void);
void    interrupt POST_send(void);

void    send_mail(int first_item);
void    process_mail(void);
int     fgetbuf(int fh);
int     fgetstring(int fh, char buff[], int max_chars);
void    beep(void);

#define TRUE        1
#define FALSE       0
```

```c
#define LINEFEED     10
#define CR           13

#define ACK           1
#define HEADER       10
#define MAIL_DATA    20
#define MAIL_EOF     30
#define FILE_HDR     50
#define FILE_DATA    60
#define FILE_EOF     70
#define TRAILER      99

NCB      cancel_ncb;
NCB      add_name_ncb;
NCB      delete_name_ncb;
NCB      send_dg_ncb;
NCB      receive_dg_ncb;
NCB      temp_ncb;

void interrupt  (*int_5C_vector)(void);

char     machine_name[16];
char     mail_name[16];
char     caller[16];
char     addressee[16];
char     subject[31];
unsigned char name_number;

typedef struct
        {
        char    type;
        int     sequence;
        int     data_length;
        char    data[500];
        } MAIL_PACKET;

MAIL_PACKET packet_in;
MAIL_PACKET packet_out;

typedef struct
        {
        char    addressee[16];
        char    to_name[16];
        char    sender[16];
        char    maildate[17];
        char    subject[31];
        char    copy_flag;
        char    attachment_flag;
        char    attachment_name[66];
        char    cc_list[66];
        char    read_flag;
        char    crlf[2];
        } ENVELOPE;

ENVELOPE    envelope_in;
ENVELOPE    envelope_out;
```

```
int      errors_this_packet = 0;
int      send_handle = -1;
int      mail_handle = -1;
int      file_handle = -1;
int      expected_sequence = 1;
char     state = 0;

unsigned      paragraphs;
char          critical_error = FALSE;
int           i, j, k;
unsigned      temp1, temp2;
unsigned      temp_ax;
unsigned char temp_ah;
unsigned      old_ss, old_sp, our_ss, our_sp;
char          far *ourdta_ptr;
char          far *olddta_ptr;
char          far *our_mcb;
unsigned      far *our_mcb_size;
char          far *next_mcb;
unsigned      far *next_mcb_owner;
unsigned      ourpsp;
unsigned      oldpsp;
int           break_state;
void     interrupt (*oldint08)(void);
void     interrupt (*oldint09)(void);
void     interrupt (*oldint10)(void);
void     interrupt (*oldint13)(void);
void     interrupt (*oldint16)(void);
void     interrupt (*oldint1b)(void);
void     interrupt (*oldint1c)(void);
void     interrupt (*oldint23)(void);
void     interrupt (*oldint24)(void);
void     interrupt (*oldint28)(void);
char far            *kbd_flag_ptr;
unsigned char far   *indos_ptr;
unsigned char far   *indos2_ptr;
unsigned char    in_int08 = FALSE;
unsigned char    in_int09 = FALSE;
unsigned char    in_int10 = FALSE;
unsigned char    in_int13 = FALSE;
unsigned char    in_int16 = FALSE;
unsigned char    in_int28 = FALSE;
unsigned char    in_popup = FALSE;
unsigned char    de_install = FALSE;
unsigned char    mail_flag = FALSE;
unsigned char    new_mail  = FALSE;
unsigned char    incoming_msg = FALSE;
unsigned char    send_complete = TRUE;
unsigned char    break_flag = FALSE;

unsigned char    trigger_outbasket= FALSE;
unsigned char    incoming_timeout = FALSE;
unsigned char    no_answer        = FALSE;

unsigned char   first_packet = FALSE;
```

```
long            tick_counter = 01;

long            outbasket_alarm = 109201;
long            incoming_alarm  = 0x0FFFFFFF1;
long            no_answer_alarm = 0x0FFFFFFF1;

long            t;
char            filepart[10];
char            extpart[6];

char            mail_path[65];
char            io_buffer[512];
char            outname[81];
char            mailname[81];
char            filename[81];
char            string[101];

struct ffblk    find_block;
int             io_len   = 0;
unsigned int    fbufndx  = 2000;
unsigned int    fbufbytes = 0;
unsigned        *our_stack;

/* - - - - - - - - - - - - - - - - - - - - - - - - - */

void    interrupt int08(void)
    {
    in_int08 = TRUE;
    oldint08();
    tick_counter++;
    enable();

    if (tick_counter > outbasket_alarm)
        {
        mail_flag = TRUE;
        trigger_outbasket = TRUE;
        }

    if (tick_counter > incoming_alarm)
        {
        mail_flag = TRUE;
        incoming_timeout = TRUE;
        }

    if (tick_counter > no_answer_alarm)
        {
        mail_flag = TRUE;
        no_answer = TRUE;
        }

    if (!de_install && !mail_flag)
        goto exit08;

    if (!send_complete)
        goto exit08;
```

```
    if (in_popup)
        goto exit08;

    if (in_int09 || in_int10 || in_int13 || in_int16 || in_int28)
        goto exit08;

    if (*indos_ptr != 0)
        goto exit08;

    if (*indos2_ptr != 0)
        goto exit08;

    outportb(0x20, 0x0b);
    if (inportb(0x20)) goto exit08;

    in_popup = TRUE;
    process_mail();
    in_popup = FALSE;

exit08:
    in_int08 = FALSE;
    }

void interrupt  int09 (void)
    {
    in_int09 = TRUE;
    oldint09();
    enable();
    in_int09 = FALSE;
    }

void    far int10(unsigned flags)
    {
    asm     pop  bp

    asm     push ax
    asm     push ds
    asm     mov  ax, DGROUP
    asm     mov  ds, ax
    asm     mov  _in_int10, 1
    asm     pop  ds
    asm     pop  ax

    asm     pushf
    asm     call    dword ptr cs:[0000h]
    asm     sti

    asm     push bp
    asm     mov  bp, sp
    asm     pushf
    asm     pop  flags
    asm     pop  bp

    asm     push ax
    asm     push ds
    asm     mov  ax, DGROUP
```

```
asm     mov  ds, ax
asm     mov  _in_int10, 0
asm     pop  ds
asm     pop  ax

asm     iret
}

void    far int13(unsigned flags)
{
asm     pop  bp

asm     push ax
asm     push ds
asm     mov  ax, DGROUP
asm     mov  ds, ax
asm     mov  _in_int13, 1
asm     pop  ds
asm     pop  ax

asm     pushf
asm     call      dword ptr cs:[0004h]
asm     sti

asm     push bp
asm     mov  bp, sp
asm     pushf
asm     pop  flags
asm     pop  bp

asm     push ax
asm     push ds
asm     mov  ax, DGROUP
asm     mov  ds, ax
asm     mov  _in_int13, 0
asm     pop  ds
asm     pop  ax

asm     iret
}

void    interrupt int16(unsigned bp,
                        unsigned di,
                        unsigned si,
                        unsigned ds,
                        unsigned es,
                        unsigned dx,
                        unsigned cx,
                        unsigned bx,
                        unsigned ax,
                        unsigned ip,
                        unsigned cs,
                        unsigned flags)
{
in_int16 = TRUE;
enable();
```

```
    temp_ax = _AX;
    temp_ah = _AH;

    if (temp_ax == 'PO')
        {
        ax = 'po';
        es = FP_SEG( (void far *) mail_path);
        bx = FP_OFF( (void far *) mail_path);
        si = FP_OFF( (void far *) &outbasket_alarm);
        di = FP_OFF( (void far *) &new_mail);
        dx = FP_OFF( (void far *) &de_install);
        goto int16_exit;
        }

    if (temp_ah != 0)
        goto do_old16;

wait_for_key:
    _AH = 1;
    oldint16();
    asm     jz    check_flags

    goto do_old16;

check_flags:
    if (in_popup)
        oldint28();

    if (!mail_flag && !de_install)
        goto wait_for_key;

    if (!send_complete)
        goto wait_for_key;

    if (*indos_ptr != 0)
        goto wait_for_key;

    if (*indos2_ptr != 0)
        goto wait_for_key;

    outportb(0x20, 0x0b);
    if (inportb(0x20)) goto wait_for_key;

    in_popup = TRUE;
    process_mail();
    in_popup = FALSE;

    goto wait_for_key;


do_old16:
    _AX = temp_ax;
    oldint16();
    asm     pushf
    asm     pop flags
    ax    = _AX;
```

```
        bx   = _BX;
        cx   = _CX;
        dx   = _DX;

int16_exit:
    in_int16 = FALSE;
    }

void interrupt  int1b (void)
    {
    enable();
    break_flag = TRUE;
    }

void interrupt  int1c (void)
    {
    enable();
    }

void interrupt  int23 (void)
    {
    enable();
    }


void     interrupt int24(unsigned bp,
                         unsigned di,
                         unsigned si,
                         unsigned ds,
                         unsigned es,
                         unsigned dx,
                         unsigned cx,
                         unsigned bx,
                         unsigned ax,
                         unsigned ip,
                         unsigned cs,
                         unsigned flags)
    {
    temp1 = _AX;
    critical_error = TRUE;

    if (_osmajor < 3)
        ax = (temp1 & 0xFF00);
    else
        ax = (temp1 & 0xFF00) ¦ 0x03;
    }


void     interrupt int28(void)
    {
    in_int28 = TRUE;
    oldint28();
    enable();

    if (!mail_flag && !de_install)
        goto exit28;
```

```
        if (!send_complete)
            goto exit28;

        if (in_popup)
            goto exit28;

        if (*indos_ptr > 1)
            goto exit28;

        if (*indos2_ptr != 0)
            goto exit28;

        outportb(0x20, 0x0b);
        if (inportb(0x20))
            goto exit28;

        in_popup = TRUE;
        process_mail();
        in_popup = FALSE;

exit28:
        in_int28 = FALSE;
        }

/* ---------------------------------------------- */


/* - - - - - - - - - - - - - - - - - - - - - - - */
/*
 *  A function to call NetBIOS (via Int 5C).
 *
 *
 */
void    NetBios(NCB *ncb_ptr)
        {
        ncb_ptr->NCB_CMD_CPLT = 0xFF;

        _ES   = FP_SEG(ncb_ptr);
        _BX   = FP_OFF(ncb_ptr);
        _AX   = 0x0100;

        geninterrupt(0x5c);
        }

/* - - - - - - - - - - - - - - - - - - - - - - - */
/*
 *  Expand 'name' to be a 16 byte string, padded
 *  on the right with spaces, and null-terminated.
 *  (Doesn't work with 'permanent node names'.)
 */
void    expand_to_16_chars(char *name)
        {
        char *p;
        char tmp[17];
        int  i;
```

```
                    memset(tmp, ' ', 15);
                    p = name;
                    i = 0;
                    while (i < 15 && *p)
                        {
                        tmp[i] = *p;
                        i++;
                        p++;
                        }
                    tmp[15] = '\0';
                    strcpy(name, tmp);
                    }

/* - - - - - - - - - - - - - - - - - - - - - - - - */
/*
 *  Build the 'add_name' NCB and send it out
 *  across the network.
 *
 */
void    net_add_name(char *name)
        {
        memset(&add_name_ncb, 0, sizeof(NCB));
        add_name_ncb.NCB_COMMAND = ADD_NAME;
        strcpy(add_name_ncb.NCB_NAME, name);
        expand_to_16_chars(add_name_ncb.NCB_NAME);
        NetBios(&add_name_ncb);
        }

/* - - - - - - - - - - - - - - - - - - - - - - - - */
/*
 *    Build the 'delete_name' NCB
 *
 */
void    net_delete_name(char *name)
        {
        memset(&delete_name_ncb, 0, sizeof(NCB));
        delete_name_ncb.NCB_COMMAND = DELETE_NAME;
        strcpy(delete_name_ncb.NCB_NAME, name);
        expand_to_16_chars(delete_name_ncb.NCB_NAME);
        NetBios(&delete_name_ncb);
        }


/* - - - - - - - - - - - - - - - - - - - - - - - - */
/*
 *    Build the 'cancel' NCB and send it out
 *    across the network.
 *
 */
void    net_cancel(NCB *np)
        {
        memset(&cancel_ncb, 0, sizeof(NCB));
        cancel_ncb.NCB_COMMAND = CANCEL;
        cancel_ncb.NCB_BUFFER_PTR = np;
        NetBios(&cancel_ncb);
        }
```

```
/* - - - - - - - - - - - - - - - - - - - - - - - */
/*
 *    Build the 'receive datagram' NCB and send it out
 *    across the network.
 */
void    net_receive_dg_post(unsigned char name_num,
                            void *packet_ptr, int packet_len)
        {
        memset(&receive_dg_ncb, 0, sizeof(NCB));
        receive_dg_ncb.NCB_COMMAND = RECEIVE_DATAGRAM;
        receive_dg_ncb.NCB_NUM = name_num;
        receive_dg_ncb.NCB_LENGTH = packet_len;
        receive_dg_ncb.NCB_BUFFER_PTR = packet_ptr;
        receive_dg_ncb.POST_FUNC = POST_receive;
        NetBios(&receive_dg_ncb);
        }

/* - - - - - - - - - - - - - - - - - - - - - - - */
/*
 *    Build the 'send datagram' NCB and send it out
 *    across the network.
 *
 */
void    net_send_dg(char *destination,
                    unsigned char name_num,
                    void *packet_ptr,
                    int packet_len)

        {
        while (!send_complete)
            ;

        send_complete = FALSE;

        memset(&send_dg_ncb, 0, sizeof(NCB));
        send_dg_ncb.NCB_COMMAND = SEND_DATAGRAM;
        send_dg_ncb.POST_FUNC = POST_send;
        send_dg_ncb.NCB_NUM = name_num;
        strcpy(send_dg_ncb.NCB_CALLNAME, destination);
        expand_to_16_chars(send_dg_ncb.NCB_CALLNAME);
        send_dg_ncb.NCB_LENGTH = packet_len;
        send_dg_ncb.NCB_BUFFER_PTR = packet_ptr;
        NetBios(&send_dg_ncb);
        }

/* - - - - - - - - - - - - - - - - - - - - - - - */

int     okay_to_unload(void)
        {
        next_mcb       = MK_FP( (ourpsp) + *our_mcb_size, 0);
        next_mcb_owner = MK_FP(  ourpsp  + *our_mcb_size, 1);

        if (   *next_mcb_owner == 0x0000
            || *next_mcb_owner == 0xffff
            || *next_mcb_owner <  ourpsp  )
                return TRUE;
```

```
                return FALSE;
                }

void    beep(void)
        {
        sound(880);
        delay(100);
        nosound();
        }

/* ---------------------------------------------- */

void    announce_mail(void)
        {
        char    linsav[160];
        int     n, cpos, ctype, vid_mode;

        _AH = 15;
        geninterrupt(0x10);
        _AH = 0;
        vid_mode = _AX;
        if (vid_mode != 2
            && vid_mode != 3
            && vid_mode != 7)
                {
                beep();
                delay(100);
                beep();
                delay(10);
                beep();
                return;
                }

        gettext(1, 25, 80, 25, linsav);
        _AH = 3;
        _BH = 0;
        geninterrupt(0x10);
        cpos  = _DX;
        ctype = _CX;

        gotoxy(1, 25);
        textcolor(BLACK);
        textbackground(LIGHTGRAY);
        cprintf("%-79.79s", "                    You have mail.");
        beep();

        for (n=0; n<20; n++)
            {
            delay(100);
            if (bioskey(1))
                {
                bioskey(0);
                break;
                }
            }
```

```
        puttext(1, 25, 80, 25, linsav);
        _DX = cpos;
        _AH = 2;
        _BH = 0;
        geninterrupt(0x10);
        _CX = ctype;
        _AH = 1;
        geninterrupt(0x10);
        }

void    send_ack(void)
        {
        packet_in.type = ACK;
        packet_in.data_length = 0;
        net_send_dg(caller, name_number, &packet_in, 5);
        }

void    receive_incoming_mail(void)
        {
        incoming_alarm = tick_counter + 10921;

        switch (packet_in.type)
            {
            case HEADER :
                {
                strcpy(caller, receive_dg_ncb.NCB_CALLNAME);
                state = 1;
                first_packet = TRUE;
                time(&t);
                sprintf(string, "%ld", t);
                strcpy(mailname, mail_path);
                strcat(mailname, &string[3]);
                strcat(mailname, ".IN");
                mail_handle = _creat(mailname, 0);
                if (mail_handle == -1)
                    return;
                send_ack();
                break;
                }
            case MAIL_DATA :
                {
                write(mail_handle, packet_in.data,
                        packet_in.data_length);
                if (first_packet)
                    {
                    memcpy(&envelope_in,
                            &packet_in.data, sizeof(ENVELOPE));
                    first_packet = FALSE;
                    }
                send_ack();
                break;
                }
            case MAIL_EOF :
                {
                close(mail_handle);
```

```
                    mail_handle = -1;
                    send_ack();
                    break;
                    }
              case FILE_HDR :
                    {
                    fnsplit(envelope_in.attachment_name,
                            NULL, NULL, filepart, extpart);
                    strcpy(filename, mail_path);
                    strcat(filename, filepart);
                    strcat(filename, extpart);
                    file_handle = _creat(filename, 0);
                    if (file_handle != -1)
                        send_ack();
                    break;
                    }
              case FILE_DATA :
                    {
                    write(file_handle, packet_in.data,
                            packet_in.data_length);
                    send_ack();
                    break;
                    }
              case FILE_EOF :
                    {
                    close(file_handle);
                    file_handle = -1;
                    send_ack();
                    break;
                    }
              case TRAILER :
                    {
                    new_mail = TRUE;
                    incoming_alarm = 0x0FFFFFFFl;
                    state = 0;
                    expected_sequence = 0;
                    send_ack();
                    announce_mail();
                    break;
                    }
              default :
                    {
                    return;
                    }
              };

        expected_sequence++;
        }

void    cancel_incoming_mail(void)
        {
        if (mail_handle != -1)
            {
            close(mail_handle);
            unlink(mailname);
            mail_handle = -1;
```

```
            }
        if (file_handle != -1)
            {
            close(file_handle);
            unlink(filename);
            file_handle = -1;
            }
        state = 0;
        expected_sequence = 1;
        }

void    send_next_packet(void)
        {
        int rc, retry_count;

        no_answer_alarm = tick_counter + 91;
        errors_this_packet = 0;
        packet_out.sequence++;

        if (packet_out.type == TRAILER)
            {
            packet_out.type = HEADER;
            send_mail(0);
            return;
            }

        if (packet_out.type == FILE_EOF)
            {
            retry_count = 0;
            do  rc = unlink(outname);
                while (rc != 0 && ++retry_count < 10);
            packet_out.type = TRAILER;
            net_send_dg(addressee, name_number, &packet_out, 5);
            return;
            }

        if (packet_out.type == MAIL_EOF)
            {
            if (envelope_out.attachment_flag == 'N'
                || strcmp(envelope_out.addressee,
                        envelope_out.sender) == 0)
                {
                retry_count = 0;
                do  rc = unlink(outname);
                    while (rc != 0 && ++retry_count < 10);
                packet_out.type = TRAILER;
                net_send_dg(addressee, name_number, &packet_out, 5);
                return;
                }
            send_handle =
                    open(envelope_out.attachment_name,
                    O_RDWR | O_DENYALL);
            if (send_handle == -1)
                {
                retry_count = 0;
                do  rc = unlink(outname);
```

```
                        while (rc != 0 && ++retry_count < 10);
                    packet_out.type = TRAILER;
                    net_send_dg(addressee, name_number, &packet_out, 5);
                    return;
                    }
                packet_out.type = FILE_HDR;
                packet_out.data_length = 0;
                net_send_dg(addressee, name_number, &packet_out, 5);
                return;
                }

            if (packet_out.type == FILE_DATA
                ¦¦ packet_out.type == FILE_HDR)
                {
                packet_out.type = FILE_DATA;
                packet_out.data_length
                    = read(send_handle, packet_out.data, 500);
                if (packet_out.data_length == 0)
                    {
                    close(send_handle);
                    send_handle = -1;
                    packet_out.type = FILE_EOF;
                    }
                net_send_dg(addressee, name_number,
                            &packet_out, packet_out.data_length+5);
                return;
                }

            if (packet_out.type == HEADER)
                {
                send_handle = open(outname, O_RDWR ¦ O_DENYALL);
                if (send_handle == -1)
                    return;
                }

            packet_out.type = MAIL_DATA;
            packet_out.data_length
                = read(send_handle, packet_out.data, 500);
            if (packet_out.data_length == 0)
                {
                close(send_handle);
                send_handle = -1;
                packet_out.type = MAIL_EOF;
                }

            net_send_dg(addressee, name_number,
                        &packet_out, packet_out.data_length+5);
            }

void    send_mail(int first_item)
        {
        int i, flag;

        if (!first_item && packet_out.type != HEADER)
            {
```

```
        if (++errors_this_packet < 10)
            {
            outbasket_alarm = tick_counter + 109201;
            no_answer_alarm = tick_counter + 91;
            net_send_dg(addressee, name_number,
                        &packet_out, packet_out.data_length+5);
            return;
            }
        if (send_handle != -1)
            close(send_handle);
        }

    if (first_item)
        {
        strcpy(outname, mail_path);
        strcat(outname, "*.out");
        flag = findfirst(outname, &find_block, 0);
        }
    else
        flag = findnext(&find_block);

    if (flag != 0)
        {
        no_answer_alarm = 0x0FFFFFFF1;
        return;
        }

    outbasket_alarm = tick_counter + 109201;
    no_answer_alarm = tick_counter + 91;
    errors_this_packet = 0;

    packet_out.type = HEADER;
    packet_out.sequence = 1;
    packet_out.data_length = 0;

    strcpy(outname, mail_path);
    strcat(outname, find_block.ff_name);
    send_handle = open(outname, O_RDWR | O_DENYALL);
    if (send_handle == -1)
        return;
    i = read(send_handle, &envelope_out, sizeof(ENVELOPE));
    close(send_handle);
    send_handle = -1;
    if (i != sizeof(ENVELOPE))
        return;
    strcpy(addressee, envelope_out.addressee);
    strupr(addressee);

    if (strcmp(addressee, mail_name) == 0)
        {
        no_answer_alarm = 0x0FFFFFFF1;
        time(&t);
        sprintf(string, "%ld", t);
        strcpy(mailname, mail_path);
        strcat(mailname, &string[3]);
        strcat(mailname, ".IN");
```

```
                    rename(outname, mailname);
                    }
            else
                net_send_dg(addressee, name_number, &packet_out, 5);
            }

    void    post_office(void)
            {
            mail_flag = FALSE;

            if (incoming_msg)
                {
                incoming_msg = FALSE;
                if (receive_dg_ncb.NCB_CMD_CPLT != 0)
                    {
                    gotoxy(50, 1);
                    cprintf("Mail error!  code = %d.",
                        (int) receive_dg_ncb.NCB_CMD_CPLT);
                    gotoxy(1,1);
                    cancel_incoming_mail();
                    net_receive_dg_post(name_number,
                                        &packet_in,
                                        sizeof(MAIL_PACKET));
                    }
                else
                if (packet_in.type == ACK)
                    {
                    send_next_packet();
                    net_receive_dg_post(name_number,
                                        &packet_in,
                                        sizeof(MAIL_PACKET));
                    }
                else
                if (packet_in.type == HEADER && state != 0)
                    {
                    net_receive_dg_post(name_number,
                                        &packet_in,
                                        sizeof(MAIL_PACKET));
                    }
                else
                if (packet_in.sequence == expected_sequence)
                    {
                    receive_incoming_mail();
                    net_receive_dg_post(name_number,
                                        &packet_in,
                                        sizeof(MAIL_PACKET));
                    }
                else
                if (packet_in.sequence == expected_sequence - 1)
                    {
                    send_ack();
                    net_receive_dg_post(name_number,
                                        &packet_in,
                                        sizeof(MAIL_PACKET));
                    }
```

```
            else
                {
                cancel_incoming_mail();
                net_receive_dg_post(name_number,
                                    &packet_in,
                                    sizeof(MAIL_PACKET));
                }
            goto post_office_exit;
            }

        if (incoming_timeout)
            {
            incoming_timeout = FALSE;
            incoming_alarm   = 0x0FFFFFFFl;
            cancel_incoming_mail();
            goto post_office_exit;
            }

        if (no_answer)
            {
            no_answer = FALSE;
            send_mail(0);
            goto post_office_exit;
            }

        if (trigger_outbasket)
            {
            trigger_outbasket = FALSE;
            outbasket_alarm   = tick_counter + 109201;
            send_mail(1);
            }

post_office_exit:
        ;
        }

void    process_mail(void)
        {
        disable();
        old_ss = _SS;
        old_sp = _SP;
        _SS = our_ss;
        _SP = our_sp;
        enable();

        if (!send_complete)
            goto process_mail_exit;

        if (de_install)
            {
            if (!okay_to_unload())
                goto process_mail_exit;
            _AX = 0x5000;
            _BX = ourpsp;
            geninterrupt(0x21);
            setvect(0x08, oldint08);
```

```
            setvect(0x28, oldint28);
            setvect(0x09, oldint09);
            setvect(0x10, oldint10);
            setvect(0x13, oldint13);
            setvect(0x16, oldint16);
            net_cancel(&receive_dg_ncb);
            net_delete_name(mail_name);
            _ES = ourpsp;
            _BX = 0x2c;
            asm    mov es, es:[bx]
            _AH = 0x49;
            geninterrupt(0x21);
            _ES = ourpsp;
            _AH = 0x49;
            geninterrupt(0x21);
            asm    mov ax, word ptr next_mcb+2
            asm    inc ax
            asm    mov es, ax
            _AH = 0x49;
            geninterrupt(0x21);
            _AX = 0x4c00;
            geninterrupt(0x21);
            }

        break_state = getcbrk();
        oldint1b = getvect(0x1b);
        setvect(0x1b, int1b);
        oldint1c = getvect(0x1c);
        setvect(0x1c, int1c);
        oldint23 = getvect(0x23);
        setvect(0x23, int23);
        oldint24 = getvect(0x24);
        setvect(0x24, int24);
        olddta_ptr = getdta();
        setdta(ourdta_ptr);
        _AX = 0x5100;
        geninterrupt(0x21);
        oldpsp = _BX;
        _AX = 0x5000;
        _BX = ourpsp;
        geninterrupt(0x21);

        post_office();

        _AX = 0x5000;
        _BX = oldpsp;
        geninterrupt(0x21);
        setdta(olddta_ptr);
        setvect(0x24, oldint24);
        setvect(0x23, oldint23);
        setvect(0x1c, oldint1c);
        setvect(0x1b, oldint1b);
        setcbrk(break_state);

process_mail_exit:
        disable();
```

```
          _SS = old_ss;
          _SP = old_sp;
          enable();
          }

/* ------------------------------------------------ */
void    interrupt POST_send(void)
          {
          send_complete = TRUE;
          }

void    interrupt POST_receive(void)
          {
          incoming_msg = TRUE;
          mail_flag   = TRUE;
          }

/* ------------------------------------------------ */
void    main(int argc, char *argv[])
          {
          _fmode = O_BINARY;

          if (_osmajor < 2)
              {
              cprintf("\r\n");
              cprintf("Early versions of DOS not supported...\r\n");
              exit(1);
              }

          _AX = 'PO';
          geninterrupt(0x16);
          if (_AX == 'po')
              {
              cprintf("\r\n");
              cprintf("The PostMan program was already loaded.\r\n");
              exit(1);
              }

          if ( (our_stack = malloc(1000)) == NULL)
              {
              cprintf("\r\n");
              cprintf("Insufficient memory...\r\n");
              exit(1);
              }

          getcwd(mail_path, 64);
          if (mail_path[strlen(mail_path) - 1] != '\\')
              strcat(mail_path, "\\");

          our_ss    = _DS;
          our_sp    = FP_OFF( (void far *) our_stack) + 998;

          _AX = 0x3400;
          geninterrupt(0x21);
          temp2 = _BX;
```

```
temp1 = _ES;
indos_ptr = MK_FP(temp1, temp2);
if (_osmajor == 2)
    indos2_ptr = MK_FP(temp1, temp2 + 1);
else
    indos2_ptr = MK_FP(temp1, temp2 - 1);

delay(10);
kbd_flag_ptr   = MK_FP(0x0040, 0x0017);

_DX = FP_OFF( (void far *) machine_name);
_AX = 0x5E00;
geninterrupt(0x21);
if (_CH == 0)
    {
 printf("Error...machine name not set.\n");
 printf("If you are on a NetWare LAN, you should use the SETNAME\n");
 printf("utility that comes with Que-Mail to set a unique machine\n");
 printf("name for each workstation.\n");
 printf("Then restart Que-Mail by re-running POSTMAN.\n");
 exit(1);
    }
machine_name[14] = '\0';
strupr(machine_name);
strcpy(mail_name, "!");
strcat(mail_name, machine_name);

i = strlen(machine_name) - 1;
while (i > 0 && machine_name[i] == ' ')
    {
    machine_name[i] = '\0';
    i--;
    }

int_5C_vector = getvect(0x5C);
if (int_5C_vector == NULL)
    {
    printf("ERROR. NetBios not loaded (Int5C not present).\n");
    exit(1);
    }

memset(&temp_ncb, 0, sizeof(NCB));
temp_ncb.NCB_COMMAND = 0x7F;
NetBios(&temp_ncb);
if (temp_ncb.NCB_RETCODE != 03)
    {
    printf("ERROR. NetBios not loaded (No response from Int5C).\n");
    exit(1);
    }

printf("Adding mailing address (%s) to the network...", machine_name);
net_add_name(mail_name);
while (add_name_ncb.NCB_CMD_CPLT == 0xFF)
    ;
printf("\n");
if (add_name_ncb.NCB_CMD_CPLT != 0)
    {
```

```
        printf("ERROR.  NetBios said: %s.\n",
            net_error_message[(int)add_name_ncb.NCB_CMD_CPLT]);
        exit(1);
        }

name_number = add_name_ncb.NCB_NUM;
cprintf("\r\n\r\n");
cprintf("PostMan is loaded.\r\n");
cprintf("Run the 'MAIL' program to see your IN/OUT baskets.\r\n");

ourdta_ptr = getdta();
_AX = 0x5100;
geninterrupt(0x21);
ourpsp = _BX;
our_mcb        = MK_FP(ourpsp-1, 0);
our_mcb_size  = MK_FP(ourpsp-1, 3);
oldint08 = getvect(0x08);
oldint09 = getvect(0x09);
oldint10 = getvect(0x10);
oldint13 = getvect(0x13);
oldint16 = getvect(0x16);
oldint28 = getvect(0x28);

asm     mov ax, word ptr oldint10
asm     mov word ptr cs:[0000h], ax
asm     mov ax, word ptr oldint10+2
asm     mov word ptr cs:[0002h], ax
asm     mov ax, word ptr oldint13
asm     mov word ptr cs:[0004h], ax
asm     mov ax, word ptr oldint13+2
asm     mov word ptr cs:[0006h], ax

setvect(0x10, (void interrupt (*)()) int10);
setvect(0x13, (void interrupt (*)()) int13);
setvect(0x16, int16);
setvect(0x09, int09);
setvect(0x28, int28);
setvect(0x08, int08);

net_receive_dg_post(name_number,
                    &packet_in,
                    sizeof(MAIL_PACKET));

paragraphs = (our_ss + (our_sp >> 4) + 1) - ourpsp;
keep(0, paragraphs);
}
```

Appendix F

Source Listing for the Electronic Mail Program

See Chapter 8, "Network Applications," for a discussion of what this program does, how it works, and how to use it.

```c
/*      E-Mail  V1.00  (Mail)                   */
/*      Copyright © 1989, 1994 Barry R. Nance   */

#pragma  inline

#include <stdio.h>
#include <dos.h>
#include <dir.h>
#include <mem.h>
#include <io.h>
#include <fcntl.h>
#include <errno.h>
#include <conio.h>
#include <bios.h>
#include <stdlib.h>
#include <string.h>
#include <stddef.h>
#include <stdarg.h>
#include <time.h>

void    do_popup(void);
void    actual_popup(void);
int     get_vid_mode(void);
void    getkey(void);
void    vidtype(void);
int     kbdstring(char buff[], int max_chars);
int     fgetbuf(int fh);
int     fgetstring(int fh, char buff[], int max_chars);
void    message(char *s);
void    ask_yn(char *s);
void    beep(void);
```

```
#define    TRUE           1
#define    FALSE          0
#define    LT            <0
#define    EQ           ==0
#define    GT            >0
#define    NE           !=0
#define    ALT           56
#define    RIGHT_SHIFT   54
#define    BELL           7
#define    BS             8
#define    LINEFEED      10
#define    FORMFEED      12
#define    CR            13
#define    TAB            9
#define    BACKTAB       15
#define    CTRLQ         17
#define    CTRLS         19
#define    CTRLX         24
#define    CTRLZ         26
#define    ESC           27
#define    ALTX          45
#define    ALTC          46
#define    ALTS          31
#define    ALTD          32
#define    ALTE          18
#define    ALTF          33
#define    ALTT          20
#define    ALTM          50
#define    ALTH          35
#define    ALT1         120
#define    ALT2         121
#define    ALT3         122
#define    ALT4         123
#define    ALT5         124
#define    ALT6         125
#define    ALT7         126
#define    ALT8         127
#define    ALT9         128
#define    HOMEKEY       71
#define    ENDKEY        79
#define    UPKEY         72
#define    DOWNKEY       80
#define    PGUPKEY       73
#define    PGDNKEY       81
#define    LEFTKEY       75
#define    INSKEY        82
#define    RIGHTKEY      77
#define    DELKEY        83
#define    CTRLLEFTKEY  115
#define    CTRLRIGHTKEY 116
#define    F1            59
#define    F2            60
#define    F3            61
#define    F4            62
#define    F5            63
#define    F6            64
```

```
#define     F7               65
#define     F8               66
#define     F9               67
#define     F10              68
#define     ALT_F10          113


/* ----------------------------------------- */
char    machine_name[16];
char    mail_name[16];
char    addressee[16];
char    subject[31];

typedef struct
        {
        char    mailfile[13];
        char    mailname[16];
        char    maildate[17];
        char    subject[31];
        char    read_flag;
        } BASKET;

BASKET outbasket[50];
BASKET inbasket[50];

typedef struct
        {
        char    addressee[16];
        char    to_name[16];
        char    sender[16];
        char    maildate[17];
        char    subject[31];
        char    copy_flag;
        char    attachment_flag;
        char    attachment_name[66];
        char    cc_list[66];
        char    read_flag;
        char    crlf[2];
        } ENVELOPE;

ENVELOPE    envelope;

char    edit_area[1920];
char    *edit_line[24];

unsigned    paragraphs;
char        critical_error = FALSE;
int         i, j, k;
unsigned    temp1, temp2, temp3, temp4, temp5;
unsigned    temp_ax;
unsigned char temp_ah;
unsigned    old_ss, old_sp, our_ss, our_sp;
char        far *ourdta_ptr;
char        far *olddta_ptr;
char        far *our_mcb;
unsigned    far *our_mcb_size;
char        far *next_mcb;
```

```
unsigned    far *next_mcb_owner;
unsigned    ourpsp;
unsigned    oldpsp;
int         break_state;
void    interrupt (*oldint08)(void);
void    interrupt (*oldint09)(void);
void    interrupt (*oldint10)(void);
void    interrupt (*oldint13)(void);
void    interrupt (*oldint16)(void);
void    interrupt (*oldint1b)(void);
void    interrupt (*oldint1c)(void);
void    interrupt (*oldint23)(void);
void    interrupt (*oldint24)(void);
void    interrupt (*oldint28)(void);
char far            *kbd_flag_ptr;
unsigned char far    *indos_ptr;
unsigned char far    *indos2_ptr;
unsigned char    in_int08 = FALSE;
unsigned char    in_int09 = FALSE;
unsigned char    in_int10 = FALSE;
unsigned char    in_int13 = FALSE;
unsigned char    in_int16 = FALSE;
unsigned char    in_int28 = FALSE;
unsigned char    in_popup = FALSE;
unsigned char    hotkey_flag = FALSE;
unsigned char    de_install = FALSE;
unsigned char    break_flag = FALSE;

long far        *outbasket_alarm_ptr;
unsigned char far *postman_deinstall_ptr;
unsigned char far *new_mail_ptr;

char            mail_path[65];
int             in_count, out_count;
int             top_inbasket, top_outbasket;
int             inbasket_choice;
int             outbasket_choice;
int             which_basket;
int             redraw_list;
char            io_buffer[512];
char            filename[81];
char            string[101];
int             handle   = 0;
int             io_len   = 0;
unsigned int    fbufndx  = 2000;
unsigned int    fbufbytes = 0;

int             curr_item, old_item;
unsigned char   reg_fg = LIGHTGRAY;
unsigned char   reg_bg = BLUE;
unsigned char   msg_fg = BLACK;
unsigned char   msg_bg = CYAN;
```

```c
int             cursor_save;
int             cursor_type;
unsigned        vidmode;
unsigned char   curr_vid_mode;
unsigned char   key_char;
unsigned char   extended_char;
char            app_screen [4000];
unsigned long   file_bytes;

char    *empty_basket[7] =
    {
    "                    ",
    "                    ",
    "                    ",
    "                    ",
    "                    ",
    "                    ",
    "                    "
    };

char    *one_letter[7] =
    {
    "                    ",
    "                    ",
    "                    ",
    "                    ",
    "                    ",
    "                    ",
    "                    "
    };

char    *multiple_letters[7] =
    {
    "                    ",
    "                    ",
    "                    ",
    "                    ",
    "                    ",
    "                    ",
    "                    "
    };

char    *send_icon[7] =
    {
    "                    ",
    "                    ",
    "                    ",
    "                    ",
    "                    ",
    "                    ",
    "                    "
    };
```

```c
char    *list_icon[11] =
    {
"┌                              ┐",
"│ o                          o │",
"│ o                          o │",
"│ o                          o │",
"│ o                          o │",
"│ o                          o │",
"│ o                          o │",
"│ o                          o │",
"│ o                          o │",
"│ o                          o │",
"└                              ┘",
    };


unsigned                    *our_stack;

/* - - - - - - - - - - - - - - - - - - - - - - - */

void    interrupt int08(void)
    {
    in_int08 = TRUE;
    oldint08();
    enable();

    if (!hotkey_flag && !de_install)
        goto exit08;

    if (in_popup)
        goto exit08;

    if (in_int09 || in_int10 || in_int13 || in_int16 || in_int28)
        goto exit08;

    if (*indos_ptr != 0)
        goto exit08;

    if (*indos2_ptr != 0)
        goto exit08;

    outportb(0x20, 0x0b);
    if (inportb(0x20)) goto exit08;

    in_popup = TRUE;
    do_popup();
    in_popup = FALSE;

exit08:
    in_int08 = FALSE;
    }

void interrupt  int09 (void)
    {
    in_int09 = TRUE;
    oldint09();
    enable();
```

```c
    if ( (*kbd_flag_ptr & 0x09) == 0x09 )
        {
        de_install = FALSE;
        hotkey_flag= TRUE;
        }
    in_int09 = FALSE;
    }

void    far int10(unsigned flags)
    {
    asm     pop  bp

    asm     push ax
    asm     push ds
    asm     mov  ax, DGROUP
    asm     mov  ds, ax
    asm     mov  _in_int10, 1
    asm     pop  ds
    asm     pop  ax

    asm     pushf
    asm     call    dword ptr cs:[0000h]
    asm     sti

    asm     push bp
    asm     mov  bp, sp
    asm     pushf
    asm     pop  flags
    asm     pop  bp

    asm     push ax
    asm     push ds
    asm     mov  ax, DGROUP
    asm     mov  ds, ax
    asm     mov  _in_int10, 0
    asm     pop  ds
    asm     pop  ax

    asm     iret
    }

void    far int13(unsigned flags)
    {
    asm     pop  bp

    asm     push ax
    asm     push ds
    asm     mov  ax, DGROUP
    asm     mov  ds, ax
    asm     mov  _in_int13, 1
    asm     pop  ds
    asm     pop  ax

    asm     pushf
    asm     call    dword ptr cs:[0004h]
    asm     sti
```

```
        asm     push bp
        asm     mov  bp, sp
        asm     pushf
        asm     pop  flags
        asm     pop  bp

        asm     push ax
        asm     push ds
        asm     mov  ax, DGROUP
        asm     mov  ds, ax
        asm     mov  _in_int13, 0
        asm     pop  ds
        asm     pop  ax

        asm     iret
        }

void    interrupt int16(unsigned bp,
                        unsigned di,
                        unsigned si,
                        unsigned ds,
                        unsigned es,
                        unsigned dx,
                        unsigned cx,
                        unsigned bx,
                        unsigned ax,
                        unsigned ip,
                        unsigned cs,
                        unsigned flags)
    {
    in_int16 = TRUE;
    enable();
    temp_ax = _AX;
    temp_ah = _AH;

    if (temp_ax == 'MA')
        {
        ax = 'ma';
        goto int16_exit;
        }

    if (temp_ah != 0)
        goto do_old16;

wait_for_key:
    _AH = 1;
    oldint16();
    asm     jz   popup_16
    goto do_old16;

popup_16:
    if (in_popup)
        {
        if (*new_mail_ptr)
            {
            ax = 0x0000;
```

```c
                goto int16_exit;
                }
        oldint28();
        goto wait_for_key;
        }

    if (!hotkey_flag && !de_install)
        goto wait_for_key;

    if (*indos_ptr != 0)
        goto wait_for_key;

    if (*indos2_ptr != 0)
        goto wait_for_key;

    outportb(0x20, 0x0b);
    if (inportb(0x20)) goto wait_for_key;

    in_popup = TRUE;
    do_popup();
    in_popup = FALSE;

    goto wait_for_key;

do_old16:
    _AX = temp_ax;
    oldint16();
    asm     pushf
    asm     pop flags
    ax    = _AX;
    bx    = _BX;
    cx    = _CX;
    dx    = _DX;

int16_exit:
    in_int16 = FALSE;
    }

void interrupt  int1b (void)
    {
    enable();
    break_flag = TRUE;
    }

void interrupt  int1c (void)
    {
    enable();
    }

void interrupt  int23 (void)
    {
    enable();
    }

void    interrupt int24(unsigned bp,
                        unsigned di,
```

```
                        unsigned si,
                        unsigned ds,
                        unsigned es,
                        unsigned dx,
                        unsigned cx,
                        unsigned bx,
                        unsigned ax,
                        unsigned ip,
                        unsigned cs,
                        unsigned flags)
    {
    temp1 = _AX;
    critical_error = TRUE;

    if (_osmajor < 3)
        ax = (temp1 & 0xFF00);
    else
        ax = (temp1 & 0xFF00) | 0x03;
    }


void    interrupt int28(void)
    {
    in_int28 = TRUE;
    oldint28();
    enable();

    if (!hotkey_flag && !de_install)
        goto exit28;

    if (in_popup)
        goto exit28;

    if (*indos_ptr > 1)
        goto exit28;

    if (*indos2_ptr != 0)
        goto exit28;

    outportb(0x20, 0x0b);
    if (inportb(0x20)) goto exit28;

    in_popup = TRUE;
    do_popup();
    in_popup = FALSE;

exit28:
    in_int28 = FALSE;
    }

/* ---------------------------------------- */

void    beep(void)
        {
        sound(880);
        delay(100);
```

```
        nosound();
        }

void    save_screen(unsigned left, unsigned top,
                    unsigned right, unsigned bottom, char *buf,
                    int *curpos, int *curtype)
        {
        gettext(left, top, right, bottom, buf);

        _AH = 3;
        _BH = 0;
        geninterrupt(0x10);
        *curpos  = _DX;
        *curtype = _CX;
        }

void    restore_screen(unsigned left, unsigned top,
                       unsigned right, unsigned bottom, char *buf,
                       int *curpos, int *curtype)
        {
        puttext(left, top, right, bottom, buf);

        _DX = *curpos;
        _AH = 2;
        _BH = 0;
        geninterrupt(0x10);
        _CX = *curtype;
        _AH = 1;
        geninterrupt(0x10);
        }

void    getkey(void)
        {
        int     k;

        k             = bioskey(0);
        key_char      = k & 0x00FF;
        extended_char = (k & 0xFF00) >> 8;
        }


int     kbdstring(char buff[], int max_chars)
        {
        int             i, j, insert_mode, ctype, res;
        unsigned char   row, col, trow, tcol;
        unsigned int    cblock;

        i = j = insert_mode = 0;
        if (get_vid_mode() == 7)
            cblock = 0x000D;
        else
            cblock = 0x0007;

        _AH = 3;
        _BH = 0;
        geninterrupt(0x10);
```

```
                ctype = _CX;
                col = wherex();
                row = wherey();

                textcolor(msg_fg);
                textbackground(msg_bg);
                cprintf("%-*s", max_chars-1, buff);
                gotoxy(col, row);

ks1:    getkey();
                tcol = wherex();
                trow = wherey();

                if (key_char == ESC)
                    {
                    memset(buff, 0, max_chars);
                    res = 0;
                    goto kbdstring_exit;
                    }

                if (key_char == 0)
                    {
                    if (extended_char == INSKEY)
                        {
                        if (insert_mode)
                            {
                            insert_mode = FALSE;
                            _CX = ctype;
                            _AH = 1;
                            geninterrupt(0x10);
                            }
                        else
                            {
                            insert_mode = TRUE;
                            _CX = cblock;
                            _AH = 1;
                            geninterrupt(0x10);
                            }
                        }
                    else
                    if (extended_char == HOMEKEY)
                        {
                        i = 0;
                        gotoxy(col, row);
                        }
                    else
                    if (extended_char == ENDKEY)
                        {
                        i = strlen(buff);
                        gotoxy(col+strlen(buff), row);
                        }
                    else
                    if (extended_char == DELKEY)
                        {
                        for (j = i; j < strlen(buff); j++)
                            buff[j] = buff[j+1];
```

```
            buff[max_chars] = '\0';
            gotoxy(col, row);
            textcolor(msg_fg);
            textbackground(msg_bg);
            cprintf("%-*s", max_chars-1, buff);
            gotoxy(tcol, trow);
            }
    else
    if (extended_char == RIGHTKEY)
        {
        if (i < strlen(buff))
            {
            i++;
            gotoxy(tcol+1, trow);
            }
        }
    else
    if (extended_char == LEFTKEY)
        {
        if (i > 0)
            {
            i--;
            gotoxy(tcol-1, trow);
            }
        }
    }

if (key_char == 0)
    goto ks1;

if (key_char == BS)
    {
    if (i > 0)
        {
        i--;
        gotoxy(tcol-1, trow);
        }
    }

if (key_char == CR)
    {
    res = 0;
    goto kbdstring_exit;
    }

if (key_char < 32)
    goto ks1;

if (i == max_chars-1)
    goto ks1;

if (insert_mode)
    {
    for (j = strlen(buff)-1; j >= i; j--)
        if (j < max_chars-2)
            buff[j+1] = buff[j];
```

```
            buff[i++] = key_char;
            buff[max_chars] = '\0';
            _CX = ctype;
            _AH = 1;
            geninterrupt(0x10);
            gotoxy(col, row);
            textcolor(msg_fg);
            textbackground(msg_bg);
            cprintf("%-*s", max_chars-1, buff);
            gotoxy(++tcol, trow);
            _CX = cblock;
            _AH = 1;
            geninterrupt(0x10);
            }
        else
            {
            buff[i++] = key_char;
            textcolor(msg_fg);
            textbackground(msg_bg);
            cprintf("%c", key_char);
            }

        goto ks1;


kbdstring_exit:
        _CX = ctype;
        _AH = 1;
        geninterrupt(0x10);

        return(res);
        }

/***********************************/

int     fgetbuf(int fh)
        {
fgetbuf01:
        if (fbufndx < fbufbytes)
            return( (int) io_buffer[fbufndx++]);

        io_len = read(fh, io_buffer, 512);
        if (io_len == -1)
            {
            fbufndx = 2000;
            return(-1);
            }

        fbufbytes = io_len;
        if (fbufbytes == 0)
            {
            fbufndx = 2000;
            return(-1);
            }

        fbufndx = 0;
```

```
                goto fgetbuf01;
                }

/***********************************/

int     fgetstring(int fh, char buff[], int max_chars)
                {
                int i, c;
                char ch;

                setmem(buff, max_chars, 0);
                i = 0;

fgs1:   if (i == max_chars - 1)
                    {
                    buff[i] = '\0';
                    return(0);
                    }
                if ( (c = fgetbuf(fh)) == -1 )
                    {
                    buff[i] = '\0';
                    return(-1);
                    }
                ch = (char) c;
                if (ch == CR)
                    goto fgs1;
                if (ch == LINEFEED)
                    {
                    buff[i] = '\0';
                    return(0);
                    }

                buff[i++] = ch;
                goto fgs1;
                }


void    ask_yn(char *s)
                {
                char    linsav[160];
                int     cpos, ctype;

                save_screen(1,25,80,25, linsav, &cpos, &ctype);
                gotoxy(1, 25);
                cprintf("%-79.79s", " ");
                gotoxy(1, 25);
                cprintf("%s (y/n) ", s);

ask10:
                getkey();
                if ( key_char != 'y' && key_char != 'Y'
                  && key_char != 'n' && key_char != 'N' )
                    goto ask10;

                key_char |= 0x20;
                restore_screen(1,25,80,25, linsav, &cpos, &ctype);
                }
```

```
void      message(char *s)
          {
          char    linsav[160];
          int     cpos, ctype;

          save_screen(1,25,80,25, linsav, &cpos, &ctype);
          gotoxy(1, 25);
          cprintf("%-64.64s<Press a key.> ", s);
          getkey();
          restore_screen(1,25,80,25, linsav, &cpos, &ctype);
          }

int       okay_to_unload(void)
          {
          next_mcb       = MK_FP( (ourpsp) + *our_mcb_size, 0);
          next_mcb_owner = MK_FP(  ourpsp  + *our_mcb_size, 1);

          if (  *next_mcb_owner == 0x0000
             || *next_mcb_owner == 0xffff
             || *next_mcb_owner <  ourpsp  )
                  return TRUE;

          return FALSE;
          }


void      show_help(int context)
          {
          int     help_handle, row, j;
          char    *p;
          char    str80[81];
          char    itemid[4];
          char    pageid[4];

          if ( (p = searchpath("mail.hlp")) == NULL || critical_error )
              {
              critical_error = FALSE;
              beep();
              message("ERROR.  'MAIL.HLP' not found.");
              return;
              }

          strcpy(str80, p);
          help_handle = open(str80, O_RDONLY | O_DENYNONE);
          if (help_handle < 1)
              {
              beep();
              message("ERROR.  'MAIL.HLP' not found.");
              return;
              }

          sprintf(itemid, "%1d", context);
          strcpy(pageid, "pg");
          strcat(pageid, itemid);
          i = fgetstring(help_handle, str80, 80);
          while (strcmp(str80, pageid) NE && i != -1)
              i = fgetstring(help_handle, str80, 80);
```

```
another_one:
        i = fgetstring(help_handle, str80, 80);
        row = 0;
        textcolor(msg_fg);
        textbackground(msg_bg);
        clrscr();

        while (strchr(str80, FORMFEED) == NULL && i != -1 && row < 24)
            {
            gotoxy(1, ++row);
            for (j=0; j<strlen(str80); j++)
                {
                if (str80[j] == 01)
                    {
                    textcolor(msg_bg);
                    textbackground(msg_fg);
                    }
                else
                if (str80[j] == 02)
                    {
                    textcolor(msg_fg);
                    textbackground(msg_bg);
                    }
                else
                    cprintf("%c", str80[j]);
                }
            i = fgetstring(help_handle, str80, 80);
            }

        if (i != -1)
            {
          message(" ESC to leave Help; any other key to see more Help. ");
            if (key_char != ESC)
                {
                i = fgetstring(help_handle, str80, 80);
                goto another_one;
                }
            }
        else
            message(" ");

        close(help_handle);
        }

int     get_vid_mode(void)
        {
        _AH = 15;
        geninterrupt(0x10);
        _AH = 0;
        return _AX;
        }

void    sort_basket(BASKET basket[], int count)
        {
        int     i, n1, n2;
        BASKET  temp;
```

```
            i = 0;
            while (i < count - 1)
                {
                n1 = atoi(basket[i].mailfile);
                n2 = atoi(basket[i+1].mailfile);
                if (n2 < n1)
                    {
                    temp = basket[i];
                    basket[i] = basket[i+1];
                    basket[i+1] = temp;
                    i = 0;
                    }
                else
                    {
                    i++;
                    }
                }
            }

void     check_inbasket(void)
         {
         int  i, flag;
         struct ffblk findblock;

         for (i=0; i<50; i++)
             memset(&inbasket[i], 0, sizeof(BASKET));

         in_count = 0;
         strcpy(filename, mail_path);
         strcat(filename, "*.in");
         flag = findfirst(filename, &findblock, 0);
         while (flag == 0 && in_count < 50)
             {
             strcpy(inbasket[in_count].mailfile, findblock.ff_name);
             strcpy(filename, mail_path);
             strcat(filename, findblock.ff_name);
             handle = open(filename, O_RDWR | O_DENYALL);
             if (handle == -1)
                 return;
             i = read(handle, &envelope, sizeof(ENVELOPE));
             if (i == sizeof(ENVELOPE))
                 {
                 strcpy(inbasket[in_count].mailname,
                        &envelope.sender[1]);
                 strcpy(inbasket[in_count].maildate,
                        envelope.maildate);
                 strcpy(inbasket[in_count].subject,
                        envelope.subject);
                 inbasket[in_count].read_flag = envelope.read_flag;
                 }
             close(handle);
             in_count++;
             flag = findnext(&findblock);
             }
         sort_basket(inbasket, in_count);
         }
```

```c
void    check_outbasket(void)
        {
        int  i, flag;
        struct ffblk findblock;

        for (i=0; i<50; i++)
            memset(&outbasket[i], 0, sizeof(BASKET));

        out_count = 0;
        strcpy(filename, mail_path);
        strcat(filename, "*.out");
        flag = findfirst(filename, &findblock, 0);
        while (flag == 0 && out_count < 50)
            {
            strcpy(outbasket[out_count].mailfile, findblock.ff_name);
            strcpy(filename, mail_path);
            strcat(filename, findblock.ff_name);
            handle = open(filename, O_RDWR | O_DENYALL);
            if (handle == -1)
                return;
            i = read(handle, &envelope, sizeof(ENVELOPE));
            if (i == sizeof(ENVELOPE))
                {
                strcpy(outbasket[out_count].mailname,
                        &envelope.addressee[1]);
                strcpy(outbasket[out_count].maildate,
                        envelope.maildate);
                strcpy(outbasket[out_count].subject,
                        envelope.subject);
                outbasket[out_count].read_flag = envelope.read_flag;
                }
            close(handle);
            out_count++;
            flag = findnext(&findblock);
            }
        sort_basket(outbasket, out_count);
        }

void    get_attached_filename(void)
        {
        int h;

get_name:
        textcolor(reg_fg);
        textbackground(reg_bg);
        clrscr();

        textcolor(msg_fg);
        textbackground(msg_bg);
        gotoxy(1, 25);
        cprintf(
" Enter filename to attach (if any), including drive:\path.
➥Then press enter. ");

        gotoxy(1, 1);
        envelope.attachment_flag = 'N';
```

```
                        cprintf("Attach file: ");
                        kbdstring(envelope.attachment_name, 65);

                        textcolor(reg_fg);
                        textbackground(reg_bg);
                        gotoxy(1, 25);
                        clreol();

                        if (strlen(envelope.attachment_name) > 0)
                            {
                            h = open(envelope.attachment_name, O_RDONLY);
                            if (h == -1)
                                {
                                textcolor(msg_fg);
                                textbackground(msg_bg);
                                gotoxy(2, 25);
                                if (errno == ENOENT)
                                    cprintf("ERROR. No file by that name (press a key)");
                                else
                                    cprintf("ERROR. Cannot access file.  (press a key)");
                                getkey();
                                goto get_name;
                                }
                            close(h);
                            envelope.attachment_flag = 'Y';
                            }
                        }

            void    editor(char *filename)
                    {
                    int     i, column, row, ed_handle, count, insert_mode;
                    char    CRLF[3] = {13, 10, 0};
                    char    cc_sequence[2] = {'A', 0};
                    char    cc_string[66];
                    char    current_date[30];
                    char    cc_filename[81];
                    long    t;
                    char    *p;

                    textcolor(reg_fg);
                    textbackground(reg_bg);
                    clrscr();

                    for (row=0; row<24; row++)
                        memset(edit_line[row], 0, 80);
                    ed_handle = open(filename, O_RDWR ¦ O_DENYALL);
                    fbufndx = 2000;
                    if (ed_handle == -1)
                        {
                        if (errno != ENOENT)
                            {
                            clrscr();
                            gotoxy(1, 1);
                            cprintf("I/O Error; can't open file.  (Press a key)");
                            getkey();
                            return;
                            }
```

```
            memset(&envelope, 0, sizeof(ENVELOPE));
            gotoxy(1, 1);
            cprintf("TO: ");
            memset(addressee, 0, 16);
            kbdstring(addressee, 15);
            if (strlen(addressee) == 0)
                {
                textcolor(reg_fg);
                textbackground(reg_bg);
                clrscr();
                return;
                }
            textcolor(reg_fg);
            textbackground(reg_bg);
            gotoxy(1, 3);
            cprintf("SUBJECT: ");
            memset(subject, 0, 31);
            kbdstring(subject, 30);
            strcpy(edit_line[0], "TO: ");
            strcat(edit_line[0], addressee);
            strcpy(edit_line[1], "SUBJECT: ");
            strcat(edit_line[1], subject);
            textcolor(reg_fg);
            textbackground(reg_bg);
            clrscr();
            gotoxy(1, 1);
            cprintf("%s", edit_line[0]);
            gotoxy(1, 2);
            cprintf("%s", edit_line[1]);
            }
        else
            {
            i = read(ed_handle, &envelope, sizeof(ENVELOPE));
            if (i != sizeof(ENVELOPE))
                {
                close(ed_handle);
                clrscr();
                gotoxy(1, 1);
                cprintf("Error...can't read envelope. (Press a key)");
                getkey();
                return;
                }
            if (envelope.copy_flag == 'Y')
                {
                textcolor(reg_fg);
                textbackground(reg_bg);
                clrscr();
                textcolor(msg_fg);
                textbackground(msg_bg);
                gotoxy(1, 25);
                cprintf(
" This is a CC: copy.  Respecify the destination name,
➥then press enter. ");
                gotoxy(1, 3);
                cprintf("Destination: ");
                memset(addressee, 0, 16);
```

```
                              strcpy(addressee, &envelope.addressee[1]);
                              kbdstring(addressee, 15);
                              textcolor(reg_fg);
                              textbackground(reg_bg);
                              gotoxy(1, 25);
                              clreol();
                              if (strlen(addressee) == 0)
                                  {
                                  close(ed_handle);
                                  return;
                                  }
                              memset(envelope.addressee, 0, 16);
                              strcpy(envelope.addressee, "!");
                              strcat(envelope.addressee, addressee);
                              while (strlen(envelope.addressee) < 15)
                                  strcat(envelope.addressee, " ");
                              strupr(envelope.addressee);
                              lseek(ed_handle, 01, SEEK_SET);
                              write(ed_handle, &envelope, sizeof(ENVELOPE));
                              close(ed_handle);
                              return;
                              }
                          strcpy(edit_line[0], "TO: ");
                          strcat(edit_line[0], &envelope.addressee[1]);
                          strcpy(edit_line[1], "SUBJECT: ");
                          strcat(edit_line[1], envelope.subject);
                          textcolor(reg_fg);
                          textbackground(reg_bg);
                          clrscr();
                          gotoxy(1, 1);
                          cprintf("%s", edit_line[0]);
                          gotoxy(1, 2);
                          cprintf("%s", edit_line[1]);
                          fbufndx = 2000;
                          for (row=2; row<24; row++)
                              {
                              i = fgetstring(ed_handle, edit_line[row], 80);
                              if (i == -1) break;
                              gotoxy(1, row + 1);
                              cprintf("%s", edit_line[row]);
                              }
                          close(ed_handle);
                          }
                      row = 4; column = 1; insert_mode = 0;

                      textcolor(msg_fg);
                      textbackground(msg_bg);
                      gotoxy(2, 25);
                      cprintf(
           "ESC-Quit  F2-Save   F4-Erase EOL    F5-Insert Line
            ➡F10-Delete Line               ");
                      textcolor(reg_fg);
                      textbackground(reg_bg);

                      window(1, 1, 80, 24);
```

```
editor_keypress:
        gotoxy(column, row);
        getkey();

        if (key_char == ESC)
            {
            window(1, 1, 80, 25);
            gotoxy(1, 25);
            clreol();
            gotoxy(2, 25);
            textcolor(msg_fg);
            textbackground(msg_bg);
            cprintf("Are you sure? (y/n) ");
            getkey();
            if (key_char == 'Y' || key_char == 'y')
                {
                textcolor(reg_fg);
                textbackground(reg_bg);
                clrscr();
                return;
                }
            textcolor(msg_fg);
            textbackground(msg_bg);
            gotoxy(2, 25);
            cprintf(
"ESC-Quit  F2-Save    F4-Erase EOL    F5-Insert Line
➥F10-Delete Line            ");
            insert_mode = 0;
            textcolor(reg_fg);
            textbackground(reg_bg);
            window(1, 1, 80, 24);
            }
        else
        if (key_char >= 32 && key_char <= 127)
            {
            if (row == 1 && column < 5)
                goto editor_keypress;
            if (row == 2 && column < 10)
                goto editor_keypress;
            if (row == 24 && column == 80)
                goto editor_keypress;
            while (strlen(edit_line[row-1]) < column - 1)
                strcat(edit_line[row-1], " ");
            if (insert_mode)
                {
                if (edit_line[row-1][78] != ' '
                    && edit_line[row-1][78] != '\0')
                    goto editor_keypress;
                for (i=78; i>=column-1; i--)
                    edit_line[row-1][i+1] = edit_line[row-1][i];
                edit_line[row-1][column-1] = key_char;
                edit_line[row-1][79] = '\0';
                gotoxy(1, row);
                cprintf("%s", edit_line[row-1]);
                }
```

```
            else
                {
                edit_line[row-1][column-1] = key_char;
                cprintf("%c", key_char);
                }
            if (column < 80)
                {
                column++;
                }
            else
            if (row < 24)
                {
                column = 1;
                row++;
                }
            }
        else
        if (key_char == CR)
            {
            if (insert_mode && row < 24)
                {
                if (row == 1 && column < 5)
                    goto editor_keypress;
                if (row == 2 && column < 10)
                    goto editor_keypress;
                for (i=23; i>row; i--)
                    strcpy(edit_line[i], edit_line[i-1]);
                memset(edit_line[row], 0, 80);
                if (edit_line[row-1][column-1] != '\0')
                    strcpy(edit_line[row], &edit_line[row-1][column-1]);
                for (i=column-1; i<80; i++)
                    edit_line[row-1][i] = '\0';
                clreol();
                row++;
                column = 1;
                gotoxy(1, row);
                insline();
                gotoxy(1, row);
                cprintf("%s", edit_line[row-1]);
                }
            else
                {
                if (row < 24)
                    {
                    column = 1;
                    row++;
                    }
                }
            }
        else
        if (key_char == BS)
            {
            key_char = 0;
            extended_char = LEFTKEY;
            }
        else
```

```
        if (key_char == TAB && column < 72)
            {
            column += 4;
            }

        if (key_char == 0)
            {
            if (extended_char == F2)
                {
                window(1, 1, 80, 25);
                ed_handle = _creat(filename, 0);
                if (ed_handle == -1)
                    {
                    clrscr();
                    gotoxy(1, 1);
                    cprintf("I/O Error; can't open file.(Press a key)");
                    getkey();
                    return;
                    }
                count = 24;
                for (row=23; row >1; row--)
                    {
                    if (strlen(edit_line[row]) > 0)
                        break;
                    count--;
                    }
                edit_line[0][19] = '\0';
                strupr(edit_line[0]);
                time(&t);
                strcpy(current_date, ctime(&t));
                current_date[16] = '\0';
                edit_line[1][39] = '\0';
                get_attached_filename();
                textcolor(msg_fg);
                textbackground(msg_bg);
                gotoxy(1, 25);
                cprintf(
"Enter CC: names (if any) separated by commas or spaces.
➡Then press enter. ");
                gotoxy(1, 3);
                cprintf("CC: ");
                kbdstring(envelope.cc_list, 65);
                textcolor(reg_fg);
                textbackground(reg_bg);
                gotoxy(1, 25);
                clreol();
                strcpy(envelope.addressee, "!");
                strcat(envelope.addressee, &edit_line[0][4]);
                while (strlen(envelope.addressee) < 15)
                    strcat(envelope.addressee, " ");
                strcpy(envelope.to_name, &envelope.addressee[1]);
                strcpy(envelope.sender, mail_name);
                strcpy(envelope.maildate, current_date);
                strcpy(envelope.subject, &edit_line[1][9]);
                envelope.read_flag = 'N';
                envelope.copy_flag = 'N';
```

```
                    envelope.crlf[0] = 13;
                    envelope.crlf[1] = 10;
                    i = write(ed_handle, &envelope, sizeof(ENVELOPE));
                    for (row=2; row<count; row++)
                        {
                        i = strlen(edit_line[row]);
                        if (i > 0)
                            write(ed_handle, edit_line[row], i);
                        write(ed_handle, CRLF, 2);
                        }
                    write(ed_handle, CRLF, 2);
                    close(ed_handle);
                    strcpy(cc_string, envelope.cc_list);
                    cc_sequence[0] = 'A';
                    time(&t);
                    p = strtok(cc_string, " ,");
                    while (p != NULL && strlen(p) < 16)
                        {
                        strcpy(envelope.addressee, "!");
                        strcat(envelope.addressee, p);
                        while (strlen(envelope.addressee) < 15)
                            strcat(envelope.addressee, " ");
                        strupr(envelope.addressee);
                        envelope.copy_flag = 'Y';
                        sprintf(current_date, "%ld", t);
                        strcpy(cc_filename, mail_path);
                        strcat(cc_filename, &current_date[3]);
                        strcat(cc_filename, cc_sequence);
                        cc_sequence[0]++;
                        strcat(cc_filename, ".OUT");
                        ed_handle = _creat(cc_filename, 0);
                        write(ed_handle, &envelope, sizeof(ENVELOPE));
                        for (row=2; row<count; row++)
                            {
                            i = strlen(edit_line[row]);
                            if (i > 0)
                                write(ed_handle, edit_line[row], i);
                            write(ed_handle, CRLF, 2);
                            }
                        write(ed_handle, CRLF, 2);
                        close(ed_handle);
                        p = strtok(NULL, " ,");
                        }
                    which_basket = 0;
                    redraw_list = TRUE;
                    *outbasket_alarm_ptr = 01;
                    clrscr();
                    return;
                    }
                else
                if (extended_char == F4)
                    {
                    if (row == 1 && column < 5)
                        goto editor_keypress;
                    if (row == 2 && column < 10)
                        goto editor_keypress;
```

IV

Appendixes

```
            for (i=column-1; i<80; i++)
                edit_line[row-1][i] = '\0';
            clreol();
            }
        else
        if (extended_char == F5)
            {
            if (row < 3)
                goto editor_keypress;
            for (i=23; i>row-1; i--)
                strcpy(edit_line[i], edit_line[i-1]);
            memset(edit_line[row-1], 0, 80);
            insline();
            }
        else
        if (extended_char == F10)
            {
            if (row < 3)
                goto editor_keypress;
            for (i=row-1; i<24; i++)
                strcpy(edit_line[i], edit_line[i+1]);
            memset(edit_line[23], 0, 80);
            delline();
            }
        else
        if (extended_char == INSKEY)
            {
            insert_mode = ~insert_mode;
            window(1, 1, 80, 25);
            gotoxy(72, 25);
            textcolor(msg_fg);
            textbackground(msg_bg);
            if (insert_mode)
                cprintf("INSERT");
            else
                cprintf("      ");
            textcolor(reg_fg);
            textbackground(reg_bg);
            window(1, 1, 80, 24);
            }
        else
        if (extended_char == HOMEKEY)
            {
            if (row == 1)
                column = 5;
            else
            if (row == 2)
                column = 10;
            else
            column = 1;
            }
        else
        if (extended_char == ENDKEY)
            {
            column = strlen(edit_line[row-1]) + 1;
            }
```

```
else
if (extended_char == DELKEY)
    {
    if (row == 1 && column < 5)
        goto editor_keypress;
    if (row == 2 && column < 10)
        goto editor_keypress;
    for (i=column-1; i<79; i++)
        edit_line[row-1][i] = edit_line[row-1][i+1];
    edit_line[row-1][79] = '\0';
    gotoxy(1, row);
    clreol();
    cprintf("%s", edit_line[row-1]);
    }
else
if (extended_char == RIGHTKEY)
    {
    if (column < 80)
        {
        column++;
        }
    else
        {
        if (row < 24)
            {
            column = 1;
            row++;
            }
        }
    }
else
if (extended_char == LEFTKEY)
    {
    if (column > 1)
        {
        column--;
        }
    else
        {
        if (row > 1)
            {
            row--;
            column = strlen(edit_line[row-1]) + 1;
            }
        }
    }
else
if (extended_char == UPKEY)
    {
    if (row > 1)
        row--;
    }
else
if (extended_char == DOWNKEY)
    {
    if (row < 24)
```

```
                            row++;
                    }
                }

            goto editor_keypress;
            }


void    browse(char *filename)
        {
        int     i, j, count, row, browse_handle;
        char    formfeed = 12;
        char    CRLF[3] = {13, 10, 0};
        long    t;

open_browse:
        textcolor(reg_fg);
        textbackground(reg_bg);
        clrscr();

        for (row=0; row<24; row++)
            memset(edit_line[row], 0, 80);
        browse_handle = open(filename, O_RDWR ¦ O_DENYALL);
        if (browse_handle == -1)
            {
            clrscr();
            gotoxy(1, 1);
            cprintf("I/O Error; can't open file.  (Press a key)");
            getkey();
            return;
            }
        i = read(browse_handle, &envelope, sizeof(ENVELOPE));
        if (i != sizeof(ENVELOPE))
            {
            clrscr();
            gotoxy(1, 1);
            cprintf("Error...can't read envelope. (Press a key)");
            getkey();
            return;
            }
        sprintf(edit_line[0],
            "TO: %-16.16s   FROM: %-16.16s   DATE: %-16.16s",
                    envelope.to_name,
                    &envelope.sender[1],
                    envelope.maildate);
        sprintf(edit_line[1], "SUBJECT: %s", envelope.subject);
        textcolor(reg_fg);
        textbackground(reg_bg);
        clrscr();
        gotoxy(1, 1);
        cprintf("%s", edit_line[0]);
        gotoxy(1, 2);
        cprintf("%s", edit_line[1]);
        fbufndx = 2000;
        for (row=2; row<24; row++)
            {
```

```
                        i = fgetstring(browse_handle, edit_line[row], 80);
                        if (i == -1) break;
                        gotoxy(1, row + 1);
                        cprintf("%s", edit_line[row]);
                        }
                if (envelope.read_flag == 'N')
                        {
                        envelope.read_flag = 'Y';
                        lseek(browse_handle, 0l, SEEK_SET);
                        write(browse_handle, &envelope, sizeof(ENVELOPE));
                        }
                close(browse_handle);

                gotoxy(1, 24);
                if (strlen(envelope.cc_list) > 0)
                        cprintf("CC: %s", envelope.cc_list);

                gotoxy(70, 24);
                if (envelope.attachment_flag == 'Y')
                        cprintf("ATTACHMENT");

browse_prompt:
                textcolor(msg_fg);
                textbackground(msg_bg);
                gotoxy(2, 25);

                if (which_basket == 0)
                        {
                        cprintf(
" ESC - Exit     D - Delete Mail     S - Save as file
 ➥P - Print   R - Reply  ");
                        }
                else
                        {
                        cprintf(
"     ESC - Exit          C - Change Contents
 ➥D - Delete This Mail        ");
                        }

                textcolor(reg_fg);
                textbackground(reg_bg);

browse_key:
                gotoxy(80, 25);
                getkey();

                if (key_char == ESC)
                        {
                        clrscr();
                        return;
                        }

                if (key_char == 'd' || key_char == 'D')
                        {
                        unlink(filename);
                        clrscr();
```

```
        return;
        }

if (which_basket == 1)
    if (key_char == 'c' || key_char == 'C')
        {
        editor(filename);
        clrscr();
        return;
        }

if (which_basket == 0)
    {
    if (key_char == 'r' || key_char == 'R')
        {
        strcpy(string, envelope.addressee);
        strcpy(envelope.addressee, envelope.sender);
        strcpy(envelope.sender, string);
        envelope.attachment_flag = 'N';
        memset(envelope.attachment_name, 0, 66);
        time(&t);
        sprintf(string, "%ld", t);
        strcpy(io_buffer, mail_path);
        strcat(io_buffer, &string[3]);
        strcat(io_buffer, ".OUT");
        strcpy(string, io_buffer);
        handle = _creat(string, 0);
        if (handle == -1)
            {
            textcolor(msg_fg);
            textbackground(msg_bg);
            gotoxy(2, 25);
            clreol();
            cprintf(" Error.  Could not create file. ");
            textcolor(reg_fg);
            textbackground(reg_bg);
            getkey();
            goto open_browse;
            }
        write(handle, &envelope, sizeof(ENVELOPE));
        close(handle);
        editor(string);
        goto open_browse;
        }
    if (key_char == 's' || key_char == 'S')
        {
        textcolor(reg_fg);
        textbackground(reg_bg);
        memset(filename, 0, 81);
        gotoxy(2, 25);
        clreol();
        cprintf("Save as: ");
        kbdstring(filename, 65);
        textcolor(reg_fg);
        textbackground(reg_bg);
        if (strlen(filename) == 0)
```

```
                        goto browse_prompt;
                handle = _creat(filename, 0);
                if (handle == -1)
                    {
                    textcolor(msg_fg);
                    textbackground(msg_bg);
                    gotoxy(2, 25);
                    clreol();
                    cprintf(" Error.  Could not create file. ");
                    textcolor(reg_fg);
                    textbackground(reg_bg);
                    getkey();
                    goto browse_prompt;
                    }
                count = 24;
                for (i=23; i>1; i--)
                    {
                    if (strlen(edit_line[i]) > 0)
                        break;
                    count--;
                    }
                for (i=0; i<count; i++)
                    {
                    j = strlen(edit_line[i]);
                    if (j > 0)
                        write(handle, edit_line[i], j);
                    write(handle, CRLF, 2);
                    }
                write(handle, CRLF, 2);
                close(handle);
                goto browse_prompt;
                }
            if (key_char == 'p' || key_char == 'P')
                {
                handle = open("LPT1", O_WRONLY);
                if (handle == -1)
                    {
                    textcolor(msg_fg);
                    textbackground(msg_bg);
                    gotoxy(2, 25);
                    clreol();
                    cprintf(" Error.  Could not open printer. ");
                    textcolor(reg_fg);
                    textbackground(reg_bg);
                    getkey();
                    goto browse_prompt;
                    }
                count = 24;
                for (i=23; i>1; i--)
                    {
                    if (strlen(edit_line[i]) > 0)
                        break;
                    count--;
                    }
                for (i=0; i<count; i++)
                    {
```

```
                        j = strlen(edit_line[i]);
                        if (j > 0)
                            write(handle, edit_line[i], j);
                        write(handle, CRLF, 2);
                        }
                    write(handle, CRLF, 2);
                    write(handle, &formfeed, 1);
                    close(handle);
                    goto browse_prompt;
                    }
                }

        goto browse_key;
        }


void    show_icon(int x, int y, char *icon[])
        {
        int i;

        for (i=0; i<7; i++)
            {
            gotoxy(x, y++);
            cprintf("%s", icon[i]);
            }
        }


void    actual_popup(void)
        {
        long t;

        de_install = FALSE;
        hotkey_flag= FALSE;

reset_trays:
        redraw_list= TRUE;
        inbasket_choice = 0;
        outbasket_choice = 0;
        top_inbasket = 0;
        top_outbasket = 0;

show_menu:
        textcolor(reg_fg);
        textbackground(reg_bg);
        clrscr();
        gotoxy(2, 1);
        cprintf(
"          , (cursor keys) move light bar.  selects item.          ");
        gotoxy(2, 2);
        cprintf(
"------------------------------------------------------
➡--------------------");
```

```
show_prompts:
        textcolor(reg_fg);
        textbackground(reg_bg);
        gotoxy(2, 24);
        cprintf(
"-------------------------------------------------------
➥-------------------");
        gotoxy(2, 25);
        cprintf(
" F1-Help    S-Send Mail    I-Inbasket    O-Outbasket    X-Exit
➥    F10-Unload ");
show_send_item:
        show_icon(2, 3, send_icon);
        gotoxy(9, 10);
        cprintf("S)end");

show_list:
        for (i=0, j=12; i<11; i++)
            {
            gotoxy(4, j++);
            cprintf("%s", list_icon[i]);
            }

show_baskets:
        *new_mail_ptr = FALSE;
        check_inbasket();
        check_outbasket();
        textcolor(reg_fg);
        textbackground(reg_bg);

        if (in_count == 0)
            show_icon(25, 3, empty_basket);
        else
        if (in_count == 1)
            show_icon(25, 3, one_letter);
        else
            show_icon(25, 3, multiple_letters);
        gotoxy(28, 10);
        cprintf("I)n (%2d items)", in_count);

        if (out_count == 0)
            show_icon(52, 3, empty_basket);
        else
        if (out_count == 1)
            show_icon(52, 3, one_letter);
        else
            show_icon(52, 3, multiple_letters);
        gotoxy(54, 10);
        cprintf("O)ut (%2d undeliv.)", out_count);

        textcolor(reg_bg);
        textbackground(reg_fg);
        gotoxy(30, 3);
        cprintf("E-Mail for %s", machine_name);
```

```c
if (which_basket == 0)
    {
    textcolor(reg_fg);
    textbackground(reg_bg);
    gotoxy(2, 23);
    cprintf("%-79.79s", " ");
    gotoxy(6, 13);
    textcolor(reg_bg);
    textbackground(reg_fg);
    cprintf(" %-16.16s   %-30.30s    %-17.17s",
        "FROM", "SUBJECT", "DATE");
    gotoxy(6, 21);
    cprintf("%-25.25s %-44.44s",
        " ", "INBASKET STATUS");
    window(6, 14, 75, 20);
    textcolor(msg_fg);
    textbackground(msg_bg);
    if (redraw_list) clrscr();
    if (in_count == 0)
        {
        gotoxy(28, 1);
        cprintf("<empty>");
        }
    else
        {
        for (i=0, j=1; i<7; i++)
            {
            k = i + top_inbasket;
            if (k == in_count) break;
            gotoxy(1, j++);
            if (k == inbasket_choice)
                {
                textcolor(msg_bg);
                textbackground(msg_fg);
                }
            else
                {
                textcolor(msg_fg);
                textbackground(msg_bg);
                }
            if (inbasket[k].read_flag == 'Y')
                cprintf("*");
            else
                cprintf(" ");
            cprintf("%-16.16s    %-30.30s    %-16.16s",
                inbasket[k].mailname,
                inbasket[k].subject,
                inbasket[k].maildate);
            }
        }
    }
else
    {
    textcolor(reg_bg);
    textbackground(reg_fg);
    gotoxy(2, 23);
```

```
                cprintf(
        "   Delivery of outbasket items is deferred while you browse
➡  the outbasket.    ");
                gotoxy(6, 13);
                cprintf("  %-16.16s     %-30.30s     %-17.17s",
                    "TO", "SUBJECT", "DATE");
                gotoxy(6, 21);
                cprintf("%-25.25s %-44.44s",
                    " ", "OUTBASKET STATUS");
                window(6, 14, 75, 20);
                textcolor(msg_fg);
                textbackground(msg_bg);
                if (redraw_list) clrscr();
                if (out_count == 0)
                    {
                    gotoxy(28, 1);
                    cprintf("<empty>");
                    }
                else
                    {
                    for (i=0, j=1; i<7; i++)
                        {
                        k = i + top_outbasket;
                        if (k == out_count) break;
                        gotoxy(1, j++);
                        if (k == outbasket_choice)
                            {
                            textcolor(msg_bg);
                            textbackground(msg_fg);
                            }
                        else
                            {
                            textcolor(msg_fg);
                            textbackground(msg_bg);
                            }
                        cprintf("  %-16.16s     %-30.30s     %-16.16s",
                            outbasket[k].mailname,
                            outbasket[k].subject,
                            outbasket[k].maildate);
                        }
                    }
                }

            textcolor(reg_fg);
            textbackground(reg_bg);
            window(1, 1, 80, 25);
            redraw_list = FALSE;
            gotoxy(80, 25);

get_menu_key:
            getkey();
            if (*new_mail_ptr)
                {
                *new_mail_ptr = FALSE;
                redraw_list   = TRUE;
                goto show_baskets;
                }
```

```
if (key_char == CR)
    {
    if (which_basket == 0 && in_count > 0)
        {
        strcpy(filename, mail_path);
        strcat(filename,
            inbasket[inbasket_choice].mailfile);
        browse(filename);
        goto reset_trays;
        }
    else
    if (which_basket == 1 && out_count > 0)
        {
        strcpy(filename, mail_path);
        strcat(filename,
            outbasket[outbasket_choice].mailfile);
        browse(filename);
        goto reset_trays;
        }
    }

if (key_char == 0 && extended_char == DOWNKEY)
    {
    if (which_basket == 0)
        {
        if (inbasket_choice < in_count - 1)
            inbasket_choice++;
        if (inbasket_choice > top_inbasket + 6)
            top_inbasket++;
        }
    else
        {
        if (outbasket_choice < out_count - 1)
            outbasket_choice++;
        if (outbasket_choice > top_outbasket + 6)
            top_outbasket++;
        }
    goto show_baskets;
    }

if (key_char == 0 && extended_char == UPKEY)
    {
    if (which_basket == 0)
        {
        if (inbasket_choice > 0)
            inbasket_choice--;
        if (inbasket_choice < top_inbasket)
            top_inbasket--;
        }
    else
        {
        if (outbasket_choice > 0)
            outbasket_choice--;
        if (outbasket_choice < top_outbasket)
            top_outbasket--;
        }
```

```
                    goto show_baskets;
                    }

            if (key_char == 's' || key_char == 'S')
                    {
                    time(&t);
                    sprintf(string, "%ld", t);
                    strcpy(filename, mail_path);
                    strcat(filename, &string[3]);
                    strcat(filename, ".OUT");
                    editor(filename);
                    goto reset_trays;
                    }

            if (key_char == 'i' || key_char == 'I')
                    {
                    if (*outbasket_alarm_ptr == 0x0FFFFFFFl)
                        *outbasket_alarm_ptr = 0l;
                    which_basket = 0;
                    redraw_list  = TRUE;
                    goto show_baskets;
                    }

            if (key_char == 'o' || key_char == 'O')
                    {
                    *outbasket_alarm_ptr = 0x0FFFFFFFl;
                    which_basket = 1;
                    redraw_list  = TRUE;
                    goto show_baskets;
                    }

            if (key_char == 'x' || key_char == 'X')
                    goto exit_popup;

            if (key_char == 0 && extended_char == F1)
                    {
                    show_help(1);
                    redraw_list  = TRUE;
                    goto show_menu;
                    }

            if (key_char == 0 && extended_char == F10)
                    {
                    de_install = TRUE;
                    goto exit_popup;
                    }

            if (key_char == 0 && extended_char == ALT_F10)
                    {
                    *postman_deinstall_ptr = TRUE;
                    de_install = TRUE;
                    goto exit_popup;
                    }

        goto get_menu_key;
```

```
exit_popup:
        hotkey_flag,  = FALSE;
        if (*outbasket_alarm_ptr == 0x0FFFFFFFl)
            *outbasket_alarm_ptr = 0l;
        }


void    do_popup(void)
        {
        disable();
        old_ss = _SS;
        old_sp = _SP;
        _SS = our_ss;
        _SP = our_sp;
        enable();

        if (de_install)
            {
            if (!okay_to_unload()) goto do_popup_exit;
            _AX = 0x5000;
            _BX = ourpsp;
            geninterrupt(0x21);
            setvect(0x08, oldint08);
            setvect(0x28, oldint28);
            setvect(0x09, oldint09);
            setvect(0x10, oldint10);
            setvect(0x13, oldint13);
            setvect(0x16, oldint16);
            _ES = ourpsp;
            _BX = 0x2c;
            asm   mov es, es:[bx]
            _AH = 0x49;
            geninterrupt(0x21);
            _ES = ourpsp;
            _AH = 0x49;
            geninterrupt(0x21);
            asm   mov ax, word ptr next_mcb+2
            asm   inc ax
            asm   mov es, ax
            _AH = 0x49;
            geninterrupt(0x21);
            _AX = 0x4c00;
            geninterrupt(0x21);
            }

process_popup:
        curr_vid_mode = get_vid_mode();
        if (curr_vid_mode != 2
            && curr_vid_mode != 3
            && curr_vid_mode != 7)
                {
                beep();
                delay(100);
                beep();
                hotkey_flag = FALSE;
                goto do_popup_exit;
                }
```

```
                    break_state = getcbrk();
                    oldint1b = getvect(0x1b);
                    setvect(0x1b, int1b);
                    oldint1c = getvect(0x1c);
                    setvect(0x1c, int1c);
                    oldint23 = getvect(0x23);
                    setvect(0x23, int23);
                    oldint24 = getvect(0x24);
                    setvect(0x24, int24);
                    olddta_ptr = getdta();
                    setdta(ourdta_ptr);
                    _AX = 0x5100;
                    geninterrupt(0x21);
                    oldpsp = _BX;
                    _AX = 0x5000;
                    _BX = ourpsp;
                    geninterrupt(0x21);

                    save_screen(1,1,80,25, app_screen,
                                        &cursor_save, &cursor_type);
                    actual_popup();
                    restore_screen(1,1,80,25, app_screen,
                                        &cursor_save, &cursor_type);

                    _AX = 0x5000;
                    _BX = oldpsp;
                    geninterrupt(0x21);
                    setdta(olddta_ptr);
                    setvect(0x24, oldint24);
                    setvect(0x23, oldint23);
                    setvect(0x1c, oldint1c);
                    setvect(0x1b, oldint1b);
                    setcbrk(break_state);

            do_popup_exit:
                    disable();
                    _SS = old_ss;
                    _SP = old_sp;
                    enable();
                    }

            /* ---------------------------------------- */

            void    main(int argc, char *argv[])
                    {
                    char far *path_ptr;

                    _fmode = O_BINARY;
                    if (_osmajor < 2)
                        {
                        cprintf("\r\n");
                        cprintf("Early versions of DOS not supported...\r\n");
                        exit(1);
                        }
```

```
_AX = 'PO';
geninterrupt(0x16);
temp_ax = _AX;
temp2   = _BX;
temp1   = _ES;
temp3   = _SI;
temp4   = _DX;
temp5   = _DI;
if (temp_ax == 'po')
    {
    path_ptr = MK_FP(temp1, temp2);
    for (i=0; i<65; i++)
        {
        mail_path[i] = *path_ptr;
        path_ptr++;
        }
    outbasket_alarm_ptr = MK_FP(temp1, temp3);
    postman_deinstall_ptr = MK_FP(temp1, temp4);
    new_mail_ptr = MK_FP(temp1, temp5);
    }
else
    {
    cprintf("\r\n");
    cprintf("You must run the PostMan program\r\n");
    cprintf("before you can send/receive mail.\r\n");
    exit(1);
    }

_AX = 'MA';
geninterrupt(0x16);
if (_AX == 'ma')
    {
    cprintf("\r\n");
    cprintf("The E-Mail program was already loaded.\r\n");
    cprintf("Use ALT/RIGHT-SHIFT to activate it.\r\n");
    exit(1);
    }

if ( (our_stack = malloc(1000)) == NULL)
    {
    cprintf("\r\n");
    cprintf("Insufficient memory...\r\n");
    exit(1);
    }

curr_vid_mode = get_vid_mode();
if (curr_vid_mode == 7)
    {
    reg_fg = LIGHTGRAY;
    reg_bg = BLACK;
    msg_fg = WHITE;
    msg_bg = BLACK;
    }
```

```
for (i=0; i<24; i++)
    edit_line[i] = &edit_area[i*80];

our_ss   = _DS;
our_sp   = FP_OFF( (void far *) our_stack) + 998;

_AX = 0x3400;
geninterrupt(0x21);
temp2 = _BX;
temp1 = _ES;
indos_ptr = MK_FP(temp1, temp2);
if (_osmajor == 2)
    indos2_ptr = MK_FP(temp1, temp2 + 1);
else
    indos2_ptr = MK_FP(temp1, temp2 - 1);

delay(10);
kbd_flag_ptr   = MK_FP(0x0040, 0x0017);
cprintf("\r\n\r\n");
cprintf("E-Mail Program is loaded.\r\n");
cprintf("Press ALT/RIGHT-SHIFT to activate the program.\r\n\r\n");

_DX = FP_OFF( (void far *) machine_name);
_AX = 0x5E00;
geninterrupt(0x21);
if (_CH == 0)
    {
    printf("ERROR.  Machine name not set.\n");
    exit(1);
    }
machine_name[14] = '\0';
strupr(machine_name);
strcpy(mail_name, "!");
strcat(mail_name, machine_name);

i = strlen(machine_name) - 1;
while (i > 0 && machine_name[i] == ' ')
    {
    machine_name[i] = '\0';
    i--;
    }

ourdta_ptr = getdta();
_AX = 0x5100;
geninterrupt(0x21);
ourpsp = _BX;
our_mcb        = MK_FP(ourpsp-1, 0);
our_mcb_size = MK_FP(ourpsp-1, 3);
oldint08 = getvect(0x08);
oldint09 = getvect(0x09);
oldint10 = getvect(0x10);
oldint13 = getvect(0x13);
oldint16 = getvect(0x16);
oldint28 = getvect(0x28);
```

```
asm     mov ax, word ptr oldint10
asm     mov word ptr cs:[0000h], ax
asm     mov ax, word ptr oldint10+2
asm     mov word ptr cs:[0002h], ax
asm     mov ax, word ptr oldint13
asm     mov word ptr cs:[0004h], ax
asm     mov ax, word ptr oldint13+2
asm     mov word ptr cs:[0006h], ax

setvect(0x10, (void interrupt (*)()) int10);
setvect(0x13, (void interrupt (*)()) int13);
setvect(0x16, int16);
setvect(0x09, int09);
setvect(0x28, int28);
setvect(0x08, int08);

de_install = FALSE;
hotkey_flag= TRUE;

paragraphs = (our_ss + (our_sp >> 4) + 1) - ourpsp;
keep(0, paragraphs);
}
```

Appendix G

Source Listing for NETBIOS.H

The following header file is used by C programmers whose source code listings appear in these appendixes.

```c
/* NETBIOS.H */

typedef unsigned char byte;
typedef unsigned int  word;

/* Network Control Block (NCB)   */

typedef struct
    {
    byte NCB_COMMAND;               /* command id                        */
    byte NCB_RETCODE;               /* immediate return code             */
    byte NCB_LSN;                   /* local session number              */
    byte NCB_NUM;                   /* network name number               */
    void far *NCB_BUFFER_PTR;       /* address of message packet         */
    word NCB_LENGTH;                /* length of message packet          */
    byte NCB_CALLNAME[16];          /* name of the other computer        */
    byte NCB_NAME[16];              /* our network name                  */
    byte NCB_RTO;                   /* receive time-out in 500 ms. incrs */
    byte NCB_STO;                   /* send time-out - 500 ms. increments */
    void interrupt (*POST_FUNC)(void); /* address of POST routine        */
    byte NCB_LANA_NUM;              /* adapter number (0 or 1)           */
    byte NCB_CMD_CPLT;              /* final return code                 */
    byte NCB_RESERVE[14];           /* Reserved area                     */
    }
    NCB;
```

```c
/* NetBIOS error return messages  */

char    *net_error_message[] = {
        "success",                      /*  00  */
        "invalid buffer length",        /*  01  */
        "ret code 02",                  /*  02  */
        "invalid command",              /*  03  */
        "ret code 04",                  /*  04  */
        "timed out",                    /*  05  */
        "buffer too small",             /*  06  */
        "ret code 07",                  /*  07  */
        "invalid session num",          /*  08  */
        "no resource",                  /*  09  */
        "session closed",               /*  0A  */
        "command cancelled",            /*  0B  */
        "ret code 0C",                  /*  0C  */
        "dupl. local name",             /*  0D  */
        "name table full",              /*  0E  */
        "active session",               /*  0F  */
        "ret code 10",                  /*  10  */
        "session table full",           /*  11  */
        "no one listening",             /*  12  */
        "invalid name num",             /*  13  */
        "no answer",                    /*  14  */
        "no local name",                /*  15  */
        "name in use",                  /*  16  */
        "name is deleted",              /*  17  */
        "abnormal end",                 /*  18  */
        "name conflict",                /*  19  */
        "ret code 1A",                  /*  1A  */
        "ret code 1B",                  /*  1B  */
        "ret code 1C",                  /*  1C  */
        "ret code 1D",                  /*  1D  */
        "ret code 1E",                  /*  1E  */
        "ret code 1F",                  /*  1F  */
        "ret code 20",                  /*  20  */
        "card busy",                    /*  21  */
        "too many cmds",                /*  22  */
        "invalid card num",             /*  23  */
        "cancel done",                  /*  24  */
        "ret code 25",                  /*  25  */
        "cannot cancel"                 /*  26  */
        };
```

```
/* Symbolic names for NetBIOS commands  */

#define RESET                           0x32
#define CANCEL                          0x35
#define STATUS                          0xb3
#define STATUS_WAIT                     0x33
#define TRACE                           0xf9
#define TRACE_WAIT                      0x79
#define UNLINK                          0x70
#define ADD_NAME                        0xb0
#define ADD_NAME_WAIT                   0x30
#define ADD_GROUP_NAME                  0xb6
#define ADD_GROUP_NAME_WAIT             0x36
#define DELETE_NAME                     0xb1
#define DELETE_NAME_WAIT                0x31
#define CALL                            0x90
#define CALL_WAIT                       0x10
#define LISTEN                          0x91
#define LISTEN_WAIT                     0x11
#define HANG_UP                         0x92
#define HANG_UP_WAIT                    0x12
#define SEND                            0x94
#define SEND_WAIT                       0x14
#define SEND_NO_ACK                     0xf1
#define SEND_NO_ACK_WAIT                0x71
#define CHAIN_SEND                      0x97
#define CHAIN_SEND_WAIT                 0x17
#define CHAIN_SEND_NO_ACK               0xf2
#define CHAIN_SEND_NO_ACK_WAIT          0x72
#define RECEIVE                         0x95
#define RECEIVE_WAIT                    0x15
#define RECEIVE_ANY                     0x96
#define RECEIVE_ANY_WAIT                0x16
#define SESSION_STATUS                  0xb4
#define SESSION_STATUS_WAIT             0x34
#define SEND_DATAGRAM                   0xa0
#define SEND_DATAGRAM_WAIT              0x20
#define SEND_BCST_DATAGRAM              0xa2
#define SEND_BCST_DATAGRAM_WAIT         0x22
#define RECEIVE_DATAGRAM                0xa1
#define RECEIVE_DATAGRAM_WAIT           0x21
#define RECEIVE_BCST_DATAGRAM           0xa3
#define RECEIVE_BCST_DATAGRAM_WAIT      0x23
```

Appendix H

Source Listing for IPX.C

The following Borland C code calls IPX functions. The code is explained in Chapter 6, "IPX and SPX Programming."

```c
/*
 *  IPX.C -- helper routines for accessing IPX services
 */

#include <stdlib.h>
#include <dos.h>
#include <mem.h>
#include <string.h>
#include <ipx.h>

void far          (*ipx_spx)(void);

int     ipx_spx_installed(void)
        {
        union REGS      regs;
        struct SREGS    sregs;

        regs.x.ax = 0x7a00;
        int86x(0x2f, &regs, &regs, &sregs);
        if (regs.h.al != 0xff) return -1;

        ipx_spx = MK_FP(sregs.es, regs.x.di);
        _BX = 0x0010;
        _AL = 0x00;
        ipx_spx();
        if (_AL == 0x00) return 0;

        return 1;
        }

int     ipx_cancel_event(struct ECB *ecb_ptr)
        {
        _ES = FP_SEG( (void far *) ecb_ptr);
        _SI = FP_OFF( (void far *) ecb_ptr);
        _BX = 0x0006;
        ipx_spx();
```

```
                    _AH = 0;
                    return _AX;
                    }

        void        close_socket(unsigned int socket)
                    {
                    if (ipx_spx_installed() < 1) return;
                    _BX = 0x0001;
                    _DX = socket;
                    ipx_spx();
                    }

        int         open_socket(unsigned int socket)
                    {
                    if (ipx_spx_installed() < 1) return -1;
                    _DX = socket;
                    _BX = 0x0000;
                    _AL = 0xFF;
                    ipx_spx();
                    _AH = 0;
                    return _AX;
                    }

        int         get_local_target(unsigned char *dest_network,
                                     unsigned char *dest_node,
                                     unsigned int   dest_socket,
                                     unsigned char *bridge_address)
                    {
                    unsigned int    temp_ax;

                    struct {
                            unsigned char   network_number [4];
                            unsigned char   physical_node  [6];
                            unsigned int    socket;
                            } request_buffer;

                    struct {
                            unsigned char   local_target [6];
                            } reply_buffer;

                    memcpy(request_buffer.network_number, dest_network, 4);
                    memcpy(request_buffer.physical_node, dest_node, 6);
                    request_buffer.socket = dest_socket;

                    _ES = FP_SEG( (void far *) &request_buffer);
                    _SI = FP_OFF( (void far *) &request_buffer);
                    _DI = FP_OFF( (void far *) &reply_buffer);
                    _BX = 0x0002;
                    ipx_spx();
                    _AH = 0;
                    temp_ax = _AX;
                    memcpy(bridge_address, reply_buffer.local_target, 6);
                    return temp_ax;
                    }
```

```
void    let_ipx_breath(void)
        {
        _BX = 0x000A;
        ipx_spx();
        }

void    ipx_listen_for_packet(struct ECB *ecb_ptr)
        {
        _ES = FP_SEG( (void far *) ecb_ptr);
        _SI = FP_OFF( (void far *) ecb_ptr);
        _BX = 0x0004;
        ipx_spx();
        }

void    ipx_send_packet(struct ECB *ecb_ptr)
        {
        _ES = FP_SEG( (void far *) ecb_ptr);
        _SI = FP_OFF( (void far *) ecb_ptr);
        _BX = 0x0003;
        ipx_spx();
        }

void    ipx_get_sizes(int *max_size, int *r_w_cycles)
        {
        unsigned int ax, cx;

        _BX = 0x000D;
        ipx_spx();
        ax = _AX;
        cx = _CX;
        *max_size = ax;
        *r_w_cycles = cx;
        }

int     get_internet_address(unsigned char connection_number,
                        unsigned char *network_number,
                        unsigned char *physical_node)
        {
        union REGS      regs;
        struct SREGS    sregs;

        struct  {
                unsigned int    len;
                unsigned char   buffer_type;
                unsigned char   connection_number;
                } request_buffer;

        struct  {
                unsigned int    len;
                unsigned char   network_number [4];
                unsigned char   physical_node  [6];
                unsigned int    server_socket;
                } reply_buffer;
```

```
        regs.h.ah = 0xe3;
        request_buffer.len = 2;
        request_buffer.buffer_type = 0x13;
        request_buffer.connection_number = connection_number;

        reply_buffer.len = 12;

        regs.x.si = FP_OFF( (void far *) &request_buffer);
        sregs.ds  = FP_SEG( (void far *) &request_buffer);
        regs.x.di = FP_OFF( (void far *) &reply_buffer);
        sregs.es  = FP_SEG( (void far *) &reply_buffer);
        int86x(0x21, &regs, &regs, &sregs);

        memcpy(network_number, reply_buffer.network_number, 4);
        memcpy(physical_node,  reply_buffer.physical_node,  6);
        regs.h.ah = 0;
        return regs.x.ax;
        }

unsigned int    get_1st_connection_num (char *who)
        {
        union REGS      regs;
        struct SREGS    sregs;

        struct  {
                unsigned int    len;
                unsigned char   buffer_type;
                unsigned int    object_type;
                unsigned char   name_len;
                unsigned char   name [48];
                unsigned int    reserved;
                } request_buffer;

        struct  {
                unsigned int    len;
                unsigned char   number_connections;
                unsigned char   connection_num [100];
                unsigned int    reserved[2];
                } reply_buffer;

        regs.h.ah = 0xe3;

        request_buffer.len = strlen(who) + 5;
        request_buffer.buffer_type = 0x15;
        request_buffer.object_type = 0x0100;
        request_buffer.name_len    = (unsigned char) strlen(who);
        strcpy(request_buffer.name, who);

        reply_buffer.len = 101;

        regs.x.si = FP_OFF( (void far *) &request_buffer);
        sregs.ds  = FP_SEG( (void far *) &request_buffer);
        regs.x.di = FP_OFF( (void far *) &reply_buffer);
        sregs.es  = FP_SEG( (void far *) &reply_buffer);

        int86x(0x21, &regs, &regs, &sregs);
```

```
        if (regs.h.al != 0) return 0;
        if (reply_buffer.number_connections == 0) return 0;

        regs.h.ah = 0;
        regs.h.al = reply_buffer.connection_num[0];
        return regs.x.ax;
        }

unsigned char get_connection_number(void)
        {
        _AH = 0xDC;
        geninterrupt(0x21);
        return _AL;
        }

void    get_user_id(unsigned char connection_number,
                    unsigned char *user_id)
        {
        union REGS      regs;
        struct SREGS    sregs;

        struct {
                unsigned int    len;
                unsigned char   buffer_type;
                unsigned char   connection_number;
                } request_buffer;

        struct {
                unsigned int    len;
                unsigned char   object_id[4];
                unsigned char   object_type[2];
                char            object_name[48];
                char            login_time[7];
                unsigned int    reserved;
                } reply_buffer;

        regs.h.ah = 0xe3;
        request_buffer.len = 2;
        request_buffer.buffer_type = 0x16;
        request_buffer.connection_number = connection_number;

        reply_buffer.len = sizeof(reply_buffer) - 2;

        regs.x.si = FP_OFF( (void far *) &request_buffer);
        sregs.ds  = FP_SEG( (void far *) &request_buffer);
        regs.x.di = FP_OFF( (void far *) &reply_buffer);
        sregs.es  = FP_SEG( (void far *) &reply_buffer);
        int86x(0x21, &regs, &regs, &sregs);

        strncpy(user_id, reply_buffer.object_name, 48);
        }
```

Appendix I

Header Source Listing for Use with IPX.C

The following header is for use with the Borland C++ code in Appendix H, "Source Listing for IPX.C."

```
/*
 *  IPX.H
 *
 */

struct IPXHEADER
    {
    unsigned int    checksum;
    unsigned int    length;
    unsigned char   transport_control;
    unsigned char   packet_type;
    unsigned char   dest_network_number [4];
    unsigned char   dest_network_node   [6];
    unsigned int    dest_network_socket;
    unsigned char   source_network_number [4];
    unsigned char   source_network_node   [6];
    unsigned int    source_network_socket;
    };

struct ECB
    {
    void far        *link_address;
    void far        (*event_service_routine)(void);
    unsigned char   in_use;
    unsigned char   completion_code;
    unsigned int    socket_number;
    unsigned int    connection_id;        /* returned by Listen */
    unsigned int    rest_of_workspace;
    unsigned char   driver_workspace [12];
    unsigned char   immediate_address [ 6];
    unsigned int    packet_count;
    struct {
```

```
                    void far    *address;
                    unsigned int length;
                    } packet [2];
            };


    int     ipx_spx_installed(void);
    int     ipx_cancel_event(struct ECB *ecb_ptr);
    void    close_socket(unsigned int socket);
    int     open_socket(unsigned int socket);
    int     get_local_target(unsigned char *dest_network,
                                unsigned char *dest_node,
                                unsigned int   dest_socket,
                                unsigned char *bridge_address);
    void    let_ipx_breath(void);
    void    ipx_listen_for_packet(struct ECB *ecb_ptr);
    void    ipx_get_sizes(int *max_size, int *r_w_cycles);
    void    ipx_send_packet(struct ECB *ecb_ptr);
    int     get_internet_address(unsigned char connection_number,
                                    unsigned char *network_number,
                                    unsigned char *physical_node);
    unsigned int    get_1st_connection_num (char *who);
    unsigned char get_connection_number(void);
    void    get_user_id(unsigned char connection_number,
                            unsigned char *user_id);
```

Appendix J

DOS Error Codes

The following error codes are given in hexadecimal:

Code	Error
01	Invalid function
02	File not found
03	Path not found
04	No more file handles (too many open files)
05	Access denied
06	Invalid handle
07	Memory control blocks damaged
08	Insufficient memory
09	Invalid memory block address
0A	Invalid environment
0B	Invalid format
0C	Invalid access code
0D	Invalid data
0E	Reserved
0F	Invalid drive specified
10	Attempt to remove current directory
11	Not the same device

Code	Error
12	No more files
13	Attempt to write on write-protected disk
14	Unknown unit
15	Drive not ready
16	Unknown command
17	Data (CRC) error
18	Bad request structure length
19	Seek error
1A	Unknown media error
1B	Sector not found
1C	Printer out of paper
1D	Write fault
1E	Read fault
1F	General failure
20	Sharing violation
21	Lock violation
22	Invalid disk change
23	File control block (FCB) unavailable
24	Sharing buffer overflow
25–31	Reserved
32	Network request not supported
33	Remote computer not listening
34	Duplicate name on network
35	Network name not found
36	Network busy
37	Network device no longer exists
38	NetBIOS command limit exceeded

Code	Error
39	Network adapter hardware error
3A	Incorrect response from network
3B	Unexpected network error
3C	Incompatible remote adapter
3D	Print queue full
3E	Not enough disk space for the print file
3F	Print file was deleted
40	Network name was deleted
41	Access denied
42	Incorrect network device type
43	Network name not found
44	Network name limit exceeded
45	NetBIOS session limit exceeded
46	Temporarily paused
47	Network request not accepted
48	Print or disk redirection is paused
49–4F	Reserved
50	File exists
51	Reserved
52	Cannot make directory entry
53	Fail on Interrupt 24 (critical error handler)
54	Too many redirections
55	Duplicate redirection
56	Invalid password
57	Invalid parameter
58	Network data fault

IV

Appendixes

Appendix K

OS/2 Error Codes

The following error codes are given in decimal:

Code	Error	Meaning
0	NO_ERROR	No error occurred
1	INVALID_FUNCTION	Invalid function number
2	FILE_NOT_FOUND	File not found
3	PATH_NOT_FOUND	Path not found
4	TOO_MANY_OPEN_FILES	Too many open files
5	ACCESS_DENIED	Access denied
6	INVALID_HANDLE	Invalid handle
7	ARENA_TRASHED	Memory control blocks destroyed
8	NOT_ENOUGH_MEMORY	Insufficient memory
9	INVALID_BLOCK	Invalid memory-block address
10	BAD_ENVIRONMENT	Invalid environment
11	BAD_FORMAT	Invalid format
12	INVALID_ACCESS	Invalid access code
13	INVALID_DATA	Invalid data
14		Reserved
15	INVALID_DRIVE	Invalid drive specified

Code	Error	Meaning
16	CURRENT_DIRECTORY	Attempt to remove current directory
17	NOT_SAME_DEVICE	Not same device
18	NO_MORE_FILES	No more files
19	WRITE_PROTECT	Attempt to write on write-protected disk
20	BAD_UNIT	Unknown unit
21	NOT_READY	Drive not ready
22	BAD_COMMAND	Unknown command
23	CRC	Data error—cyclic redundancy check
24	BAD_LENGTH	Invalid request structure length
25	SEEK	Seek error
26	NOT_DOS_DISK	Unknown media type
27	SECTOR_NOT_FOUND	Sector not found
28	OUT_OF_PAPER	Printer is out of paper
29	WRITE FAULT	Write fault
30	READ_FAULT	Read fault
31	GEN_FAILURE	General failure
32	SHARING_VIOLATION	Sharing violation
33	LOCK_VIOLATION	Lock violation
34	WRONG_DISK	Invalid disk change
35	FCB_UNAVAILABLE	File control block unavailable
36	SHARING_BUFFER_EXCEEDED	Sharing buffer overflow
37	CODE_PAGE_MISMATCHED	Code page does not match
38	HANDLE_EOF	End of file reached
39	HANDLE_DISK_FULL	Disk is full
40–49		Reserved

Code	Error	Meaning
50	NOT_SUPPORTED	Network request is not supported
51	REM_NOT_LIST	Remote network node is not on-line
52	DUP_NAME	Duplicate file name in network
53	BAD_NETPATH	Network path was not found
54	NETWORK_BUSY	Network is busy
55	DEV_NOT_EXIST	Device is not installed in the network
56	TOO_MANY_CMDS	Network command limit reached
57	ADAP_HDW_ERR	Network adapter hardware error
58	BAD_NET_RESP	Incorrect response in network
59	UNEXP_NET_ERR	Unexpected error in network
60	BAD_REM_ADAPTER	Remote network adapter error
61	PRINTQ_FULL	Network printer queue is full
62	NO_SPOOL_SPACE	No space in print spool file
63	PRINT_CANCELLED	Print spool file was deleted
64	NETNAME_DELETED	Network name was deleted
65	NETWORK_ACCESS_DENIED	Access to network is denied
66	BAD_DEV_TYPE	Device type is invalid for network
67	BAD_NET_NAME	Network name was not found
68	TOO_MANY_NAMES	Network name limit exceeded
69	TOO_MANY_SESS	Network session limit exceeded
70	SHARING_PAUSED	Temporary pause in network
71	REQ_NOT_ACCEPTED	Network request is denied
72	REDIR_PAUSED	Pause in network print disk redirection

IV

Appendixes

Code	Error	Meaning
73	SBCS_ATT_WRITE_PROT	Attempt to write on a protected disk
74	SBCS_GENERAL_FAILURE	General failure, single-byte character set
75–79		Reserved
80	FILE_EXISTS	File exists
81		Reserved
82	CANNOT_MAKE	Cannot make directory entry
83	FAIL_I24	Failure on Int 24
84	OUT_OF_STRUCTURES	Too many redirections
85	ALREADY_ASSIGNED	Duplicate redirection
86	INVALID_PASSWORD	Invalid password
87	INVALID_PARAMETER	Invalid parameter
88	NET_WRITE_FAULT	Network device fault
89	NO_PROC_SLOTS	No process slots available
90	NOT_FROZEN	System error
91	ERR_TSTOVFL	Timer service table overflow
92	ERR_TSTDUP	Timer service table duplicate
93	NO_ITEMS	No items to work on
95	INTERRUPT	Interrupted system call
99	DEVICE_IN_USE	Device in use
100	TOO_MANY_SEMAPHORES	User/system open semaphore limit was reached
101	EXCL_SEM_ALREADY_OWNED	Exclusive semaphore is already owned
102	SEM_IS_SET	DosCloseSem found the semaphore set
103	TOO_MANY_SEM_REQUESTS	Too many exclusive semaphore requests
104	INVALID_AT_INTERRUPT_TIME	Operation is invalid at interrupt time

Code	Error	Meaning
105	SEM_OWNER_DIED	Previous semaphore owner was terminated without freeing semaphore
106	SEM_USER_LIMIT	Semaphore limit was exceeded
107	DISK_CHANGE	Insert drive B disk into drive A
108	DRIVE_LOCKED	Drive locked by another process
109	BROKEN_PIPE	Write on a pipe with no reader
110	OPEN_FAILED	Open or create failed due to an explicit fail command
111	BUFFER_OVERFLOW	Buffer passed to a system call is too small to hold return data
112	DISK_FULL	Not enough space on the disk
113	NO_MORE_SEARCH_HANDLES	Cannot allocate another search structure and handle
114	INVALID_TARGET_HANDLE	Target handle in `DosDupHandle` is invalid
115	PROTECTION_VIOLATION	Invalid user virtual address
116	VIOKBD_REQUEST	Error on display write or keyboard read
117	INVALID_CATEGORY	Category for `DevIOCtl` is not defined
118	INVALID_VERIFY_SWITCH	Invalid value passed for verify flag
119	BAD_DRIVER_LEVEL	Level four driver was not found
120	CALL_NOT_IMPLEMENTED	Invalid function was called
121	SEM_TIMEOUT	Time-out occurred from semaphore API function
122	INSUFFICIENT_BUFFER	Data buffer is too small
123	INVALID_NAME	Illegal character or invalid file-system name
124	INVALID_LEVEL	Nonimplemented level for information retrieval or setting

Code	Error	Meaning
125	NO_VOLUME_LABEL	No volume label was found with `DosQueryFSInfo` function
126	MOD_NOT_FOUND	Module handle was not found with `DosQueryProcAddr()` or `DosQueryModAddr()`
127	PROC_NOT_FOUND	Procedure address was not found with `DosQueryProcAddr()`
128	WAIT_NO_CHILDREN	`DosWaitChild` finds no children
129	CHILD_NOT_COMPLETE	`DosWaitChild` children were not terminated
130	DIRECT_ACCESS_HANDLE	Handle operation is invalid for direct disk-access handles
131	NEGATIVE_SEEK	Attempting seek to negative offset
132	SEEK_ON_DEVICE	Application trying to seek on a device or pipe
133	IS_JOIN_TARGET	Drive has previously joined drives
134	IS_JOINED	Drive is already joined
135	IS_SUBSTED	Drive is already substituted
136	NOT_JOINED	Cannot delete a drive that is not joined
137	NOT_SUBSTED	Cannot delete a drive that is not substituted
138	JOIN_TO_JOIN	Cannot join to a joined drive
139	SUBST_TO_SUBST	Cannot substitute to a substituted drive
140	JOIN_TO_SUBST	Cannot join to a substituted drive
141	SUBST_TO_JOIN	Cannot substitute to a joined drive
142	BUSY_DRIVE	Specified drive is busy

Code	Error	Meaning
143	SAME_DRIVE	Cannot join or substitute a drive to a directory on the same drive
144	DIR_NOT_ROOT	Directory must be a subdirectory of the root
145	DIR_NOT_EMPTY	Directory must be empty to use the join command
146	IS_SUBST_PATH	Specified path is being used in a substitute
147	IS_JOIN_PATH	Specified path is being used in a join
148	PATH_BUSY	Specified path is being used by another process
149	IS_SUBST_TARGET	Cannot join or substitute a drive that has a directory that is the target of a previous substitute
150	SYSTEM_TRACE	System trace error
151	INVALID_EVENT_COUNT	DosWaitMuxWaitSem errors
152	TOO_MANY_MUXWAITERS	System limit of 100 entries was reached
153	INVALID_LIST_FORMAT	Invalid list format
154	LABEL_TOO_LONG	Volume label is too big
155	TOO_MANY_TCBS	Cannot create another TCB
156	SIGNAL_REFUSED	Signal was refused
157	DISCARDED	Segment is discarded
158	NOT_LOCKED	Segment is not locked
159	BAD_THREADID_ADDR	Invalid thread-identity address
160	BAD_ARGUMENTS	Invalid environment pointer
161	BAD_PATHNAME	Invalid path name passed to exec
162	SIGNAL_PENDING	Signal already pending
163	UNCERTAIN_MEDIA	Error with Int 24 mapping

IV

Appendixes

Code	Error	Meaning
164	MAX_THRDS_REACHED	No more process slots
165	MONITORS_NOT_SUPPORTED	Error with Int 24 mapping
166	UNC_DRIVER_NOT_INSTALLED	Default redirection return code
167	LOCK_FAILED	Locking failed
168	SWAPIO_FAILED	Swap I/O failed
169	SWAPIN_FAILED	Swap in failed
170	BUSY	Segment is busy
171–172		Reserved
173	CANCEL_VIOLATION	A lock request is not outstanding for the specified file range, or the range length is 0
174	ATOMIC_LOCK_NOT_SUPPORTED	The file-system driver (FSD) does not support atomic lock operations
175	READ_LOCKS_NOT_SUPPORTED	The file system driver (FSD) does not support shared read locks
176–179		Reserved
180	INVALID_SEGMENT_NUMBER	Invalid segment number
181	INVALID_CALLGATE	Invalid call gate
182	INVALID_ORDINAL	Invalid ordinal
183	ALREADY_EXISTS	Shared segment already exists
184	NO_CHILD_PROCESS	No child process to wait for
185	CHILD_ALIVE_NOWAIT	No-wait was specified and child is alive
186	INVALID_FLAG_NUMBER	Invalid flag number
187	SEM_NOT_FOUND	Semaphore does not exist
188	INVALID_STARTING_CODESEG	Invalid starting code segment
189	INVALID_STACKSEG	Invalid stack segment

Code	Error	Meaning
190	INVALID_MODULETYPE	Invalid module type; a dynamic-link library file cannot be used as an application, and an application cannot be used as a dynamic-link library
191	INVALID_EXE_SIGNATURE	Invalid EXE signature; the file is a DOS mode program or an improper program
192	EXE_MARKED_INVALID	EXE marked invalid; the link detected errors when the application was created
193	BAD_EXE_FORMAT	Invalid EXE format; the file is a DOS mode program or an improper program
194	ITERATED_DATA_EXCEEDS_64k	Iterated data exceeds 64K; one of the file's segments has more than 64K of data
195	INVALID_MINALLOCSIZE	Invalid minimum allocation size; the size is specified to be less than the size of the segment data in the file
196	DYNLINK_FROM_INVALID_RING	Dynamic link from invalid privilege level; a privilege-level-2 routine cannot link to dynamic-link libraries
197	IOPL_NOT_ENABLED	IOPL is not enabled; IOPL set to NO in CONFIGSYS
198	INVALID_SEGDPL	Invalid segment descriptor privilege level; can only have privilege levels of 2 and 3
199	AUTODATASEG_EXCEEDS_64k	Automatic data segment exceeds 64K
200	RING2SEG_MUST_BE_MOVABLE	Privilege-level-2 segment must be movable
201	RELOC_CHAIN_XEEDS_SEGLIM	Relocation chain exceeds segment limit
202	INFLOOP_IN_RELOC_CHAIN	Infinite loop in relocation chain segment
203	ENVVAR_NOT_FOUND	Environment variable not found

IV

Appendixes

Code	Error	Meaning
204	NOT_CURRENT_CTRY	Not the current country
205	NO_SIGNAL_SENT	No signal sent; no process in the command subtree has a signal handler
206	FILENAME_EXCED_RANGE	File name or extension is greater than 83 characters
207	RING2_STACK_IN_USE	Privilege-level-2 stack is in use
208	META_EXPANSION_TOO_LONG	Meta (global) expansion is too long
209	INVALID_SIGNAL_NUMBER	Invalid signal number
210	THREAD_1_INACTIVE	Inactive thread
211	INFO_NOT_AVAIL	File system information is not available for this file
212	LOCKED	Locked error
213	BAD_DYNALINK	Attempted to execute a nonfamily API in DOS mode
214	TOO_MANY_MODULES	Too many modules
215	NESTING_NOT_ALLOWED	Nesting is not allowed
217	ZOMBIE_PROCESS	Zombie process
218	STACK_IN_HIGH_MEMORY	Stack is in high memory
219	INVALID_EXITROUTINE_RING	Invalid exit routine ring
220	GETBUF_FAILED	Get buffer failed
221	FLUSHBUF_FAILED	Flush buffer failed
222	TRANSFER_TOO_LONG	Transfer is too long
224	SMG_NO_TARGET_WINDOW	The application window was created without the FCF_TASKLIST style, or the application window has not yet been created or has already been destroyed
228	NO_CHILDREN	No child process
229	INVALID_SCREEN_GROUP	Invalid session

Code	Error	Meaning
230	BAD_PIPE	Nonexistent pipe or invalid operation
231	PIPE_BUSY	Pipe is busy
232	NO_DATA	No data available on nonblocking read
233	PIPE_NOT_CONNECTED	Pipe was disconnected by server
234	MORE_DATA	More data is available
240	VC_DISCONNECTED	Session was dropped due to errors
250	CIRCULARITY_REQUESTED	Renaming a directory that would cause a circularity problem
251	DIRECTORY_IN_CDS	Renaming a directory that is in use
252	INVALID_FSD_NAME	Trying to access nonexistent FSD
253	INVALID_PATH	Invalid pseudo device
254	INVALID_EA_NAME	Invalid character in name, or invalid cbName
255	EA_LIST_INCONSISTENT	List does not match its size, or there are invalid EAs in the list
256	EA_LIST_TOO_LONG	EA list is longer than 64K bytes
257	NO_META_MATCH	String does not match expression
259	NO_MORE_ITEMS	DosQueryFSAttach ordinal query
260	SEARCH_STRUC_REUSED	DOS mode "find first or next" search structure reused
261	CHAR_NOT_FOUND	Character not found
262	TOO_MUCH_STACK	Stack request exceeds system limit
263	INVALID_ATTR	Invalid attribute
264	INVALID_STARTING_RING	Invalid starting ring

Code	Error	Meaning
265	INVALID_DLL_INIT_RING	Invalid DLL INIT ring
266	CANNOT_COPY	Cannot copy
267	DIRECTORY	Used by DOSCOPY in doscall1
268	OPLOCKED_FILE	Oplocked file
269	OPLOCK_THREAD_EXISTS	Oplock thread exists
270	VOLUME_CHANGED	Volume changed
271–273		Reserved
274	ALREADY_SHUTDOWN	System is already shut down
275	EAS_DIDNT_FIT	Buffer is not big enough to hold the EAs
276	EA_FILE_CORRUPT	EA file has been damaged
277	EA_TABLE_FULL	EA table is full
278	INVALID_EA_HANDLE	EA handle is invalid
279	NO_CLUSTER	No cluster
280	CREATE_EA_FILE	Cannot create the EA file
281	CANNOT_OPEN_EA_FILE	Cannot open the EA file
282	EAS_NOT_SUPPORTED	Destination file system does not support EAs
283	NEED_EAS_FOUND	Destination file system does not support EAs, and the source file's EAs contain a needed EA
284	DUPLICATE_HANDLE	The handle already exists
285	DUPLICATE_NAME	The name already exists
286	EMPTY_MUXWAIT	The list of semaphores in a muxwait semaphore is empty
287	MUTEX_OWNED	The calling thread owns one or more of the mutex semaphores in the list
288	NOT_OWNER	Caller does not own the semaphore

IV

Code	Error	Meaning
289	PARAM_TOO_SMALL	Parameter is not large enough to contain all the semaphore records in the muxwait semaphore
290	TOO_MANY_HANDLES	Limit reached for number of handles
291	TOO_MANY_OPENS	Too many files or semaphores are open
292	WRONG_TYPE	Attempted to create the wrong type of semaphore
294	THREAD_NOT_TERMINATED	Thread has not terminated
295	INIT_ROUTINE_FAILED	Initialization routine failed
296	MODULE_IN_USE	Module is in use
297	NOT_ENOUGH_WATCHPOINTS	There are not enough watchpoints
298	TOO_MANY_POSTS	Post count limit was reached for an event semaphore
299	ALREADY_POSTED	Event semaphore is already posted
300	ALREADY_RESET	Event semaphore is already reset
301	SEM_BUSY	Semaphore is busy
302		Reserved
303	INVALID_PROCID	Invalid process identity
304	INVALID_PDELTA	Invalid priority delta
305	NOT_DESCENDANT	Not descendant
306	NOT_SESSION_MANAGER	Requester is not a session manager
307	INVALID_PCLASS	Invalid P class
308	INVALID_SCOPE	Invalid scope
309	INVALID_THREADID	Invalid thread identity
310	DOSSUB_SHRINK	Cannot shrink segment (DosSubSetMem)

Code	Error	Meaning
311	DOSSUB_NOMEM	No memory to satisfy request (`DosSubAllocMem`)
312	DOSSUB_OVERLAP	Overlap of the specified block with a block of allocated memory (`DosSubFreeMem`)
313	DOSSUB_BADSIZE	Invalid size parameter (`DosSubAllocMem` or `DosSubFreeMem`)
314	DOSSUB_BADFLAG	Invalid flag parameter (`DosSubSetMem`)
315	DOSSUB_BADSELECTOR	Invalid segment selector
316	MR_MSG_TOO_LONG	Message is too long for the buffer
317	MR_MID_NOT_FOUND	Message identity number was not found
318	MR_UN_ACC_MSGF	Unable to access message file
319	MR_INV_MSGF_FORMAT	Invalid message file format
320	MR_INV_IVCOUNT	Invalid insertion variable count
321	MR_UN_PERFORM	Unable to perform the function
322	TS_WAKEUP	Unable to wake up
323	TS_SEMHANDLE	Invalid system semaphore
324	TS_NOTIMER	No timers available
326	TS_HANDLE	Invalid timer handle
327	TS_DATETIME	Invalid date or time
328	SYS_INTERNAL	Internal system error
329	QUE_CURRENT_NAME	Current queue name does not exist
330	QUE_PROC_NOT_OWNED	Current process does not own the queue
331	QUE_PROC_OWNED	Current process owns the queue
332	QUE_DUPLICATE	Duplicate queue name

Code	Error	Meaning
333	QUE_ELEMENT_NOT_EXIST	Queue element does not exist
334	QUE_NO_MEMORY	Inadequate queue memory
335	QUE_INVALID_NAME	Invalid queue name
336	QUE_INVALID_PRIORITY	Invalid queue priority parameter
337	QUE_INVALID_HANDLE	Invalid queue handle
338	QUE_LINK_NOT_FOUND	Queue link was not found
339	QUE_MEMORY_ERROR	Queue memory error
340	QUE_PREV_AT_END	Previous queue element was at the end of the queue
341	QUE_PROC_NO_ACCESS	Process does not have access to queues
342	QUE_EMPTY	Queue is empty
343	QUE_NAME_NOT_EXIST	Queue name does not exist
344	QUE_NOT_INITIALIZED	Queues are not initialized
345	QUE_UNABLE_TO_ACCESS	Unable to access queues
346	QUE_UNABLE_TO_ADD	Unable to add new queue
347	QUE_UNABLE_TO_INIT	Unable to initialize queues
349	VIO_INVALID_MASK	Invalid function replaced
350	VIO_PTR	Invalid pointer to a parameter
351	VIO_APTR	Invalid pointer to an attribute
352	VIO_RPTR	Invalid pointer to a row
353	VIO_CPTR	Invalid pointer to a column
354	VIO_LPTR	Invalid pointer to a length
355	VIO_MODE	Unsupported screen mode
356	VIO_WIDTH	Invalid cursor width value
357	VIO_ATTR	Invalid cursor attribute value
358	VIO_ROW	Invalid row value

Code	Error	Meaning
359	VIO_COL	Invalid column value
360	VIO_TOPROW	Invalid top row value
361	VIO_BOTROW	Invalid bottom row value
362	VIO_RIGHTCOL	Invalid right column value
363	VIO_LEFTCOL	Invalid left column value
364	SCS_CALL	Call issued by other than session manager
365	SCS_VALUE	Value is not for save or restore
366	VIO_WAIT_FLAG	Invalid wait-flag setting
367	VIO_UNLOCK	Screen was not previously locked
368	SGS_NOT_SESSION_MGR	Caller is not the session manager
369	SMG_INVALID_SGID	Invalid session identity
369	SMG_INVALID_SESSION_ID	Invalid session ID
370	SMG_NOSG	No sessions available
370	SMG_NO_SESSIONS	No sessions available
371	SMG_GRP_NOT_FOUND	Session was not found
371	SMG_SESSION_NOT_FOUND	Session was not found
372	SMG_SET_TITLE	Title set by the shell or parent cannot be changed
373	KBD_PARAMETER	Invalid parameter to the keyboard
374	KBD_NO_DEVICE	No device
375	KBD_INVALID_IOWAIT	Invalid I/O wait specified
376	KBD_INVALID_LENGTH	Invalid length for the keyboard
377	KBD_INVALID_ECHO_MASK	Invalid echo mode mask
378	KBD_INVALID_INPUT_MASK	Invalid input mode mask
379	MON_INVALID_PARMS	Invalid parameters to DosMon

Code	Error	Meaning
380	MON_INVALID_DEVNAME	Invalid device name string
381	MON_INVALID_HANDLE	Invalid device handle
382	MON_BUFFER_TOO_SMALL	Buffer is too small
383	MON_BUFFER_EMPTY	Buffer is empty
384	MON_DATA_TOO_LARGE	Data record is too large
385	MOUSE_NO_DEVICE	Mouse device is closed (invalid device handle)
386	MOUSE_INV_HANDLE	Mouse device is closed (invalid device handle)
387	MOUSE_INV_PARMS	Parameters invalid for display mode
388	MOUSE_CANT_RESET	Functions are assigned and cannot be reset
389	MOUSE_DISPLAY_PARMS	Parameters are invalid for display mode
390	MOUSE_INV_MODULE	Module is invalid
391	MOUSE_INV_ENTRY_PT	Entry point is invalid
392	MOUSE_INV_MASK	Function mask is invalid
393	NO_MOUSE_NO_DATA	No valid data
394	NO_MOUSE_PTR_DRAWN	Pointer was drawn
395	INVALID_FREQUENCY	Invalid frequency for a beep
396	NLS_NO_COUNTRY_FILE	Cannot find the COUNTRY.SYS file
397	NLS_OPEN_FAILED	Cannot open the COUNTRY.SYS file
398	NLS_NO_CTRY_CODE	Country code was not found
398	NO_COUNTRY_OR_CODEPAGE	Country code was not found
399	NLS_TABLE_TRUNCATED	Table returned information truncated; the buffer is too small
400	NLS_BAD_TYPE	Selected type does not exist

Code	Error	Meaning
401	NLS_TYPE_NOT_FOUND	Selected type is not in the file
402	VIO_SMG_ONLY	Valid from the session manager only
403	VIO_INVALID_ASCIIZ	Invalid ASCIIZ length
404	VIO_DEREGISTER	VioDeRegister is not allowed
405	VIO_NO_POPUP	Pop-up window is not allocated
406	VIO_EXISTING_POPUP	Pop-up window is on-screen
407	KBD_SMG_ONLY	Valid from the session manager only
408	KBD_INVALID_ASCIIZ	Invalid ASCIIZ length
409	KBD_INVALID_MASK	Invalid replacement mask
410	KBD_REGISTER	KbdRegister is not allowed
411	KBD_DEREGISTER	KbdDeRegister is not allowed
412	MOUSE_SMG_ONLY	Valid from the session manager only
413	MOUSE_INVALID_ASCIIZ	Invalid ASCIIZ length
414	MOUSE_INVALID_MASK	Invalid replacement mask
415	MOUSE_REGISTER	Mouse register is not allowed
416	MOUSE_DEREGISTER	Mouse deregister is not allowed
417	SMG_BAD_ACTION	Invalid action was specified
418	SMG_INVALID_CALL	INIT called more than once, or invalid session identity
419	SCS_SG_NOTFOUND	New session number
420	SCS_NOT_SHELL	Caller is not the shell
421	VIO_INVALID_PARMS	Invalid parameters passed
422	VIO_FUNCTION_OWNED	Save or restore already owned
423	VIO_RETURN	Nondestruct return (undo)
424	SCS_INVALID_FUNCTION	Caller invalid function

Code	Error	Meaning
425	SCS_NOT_SESSION_MGR	Caller is not the session manager
426	VIO_REGISTER	VioRegister is not allowed
427	VIO_NO_MODE_THREAD	No mode restore thread in SG
428	VIO_NO_SAVE_RESTORE_THD	No save or restore thread in SG
429	VIO_IN_BG	Function is invalid in the background
430	VIO_ILLEGAL_DURING_POPUP	Function is not allowed during a pop-up window
431	SMG_NOT_BASESHELL	Caller is not the base shell
432	SMG_BAD_STATUSREQ	Invalid status was requested
433	QUE_INVALID_WAIT	NoWait parameter is out of bounds
434	VIO_LOCK	Error returned from Scroll Lock
435	MOUSE_INVALID_IOWAIT	Invalid parameters for IOWait
436	VIO_INVALID_HANDLE	Invalid VIO handle
437	VIO_ILLEGAL_DURING_LOCK	Function is not allowed during a screen lock
438	VIO_INVALID_LENGTH	Invalid VIO length
439	KBD_INVALID_HANDLE	Invalid KBD handle
440	KBD_NO_MORE_HANDLE	Ran out of handles
441	KBD_CANNOT_CREATE_KCB	Unable to create KCB
442	KBD_CODEPAGE_LOAD_INCOMPL	Unsuccessful code-page load
443	KBD_INVALID_CODEPAGE_ID	Invalid code-page identity
444	KBD_NO_CODEPAGE_SUPPORT	No code-page support
445	KBD_FOCUS_REQUIRED	Keyboard focus is required
446	KBD_FOCUS_ALREADY_ACTIVE	Calling thread has an outstanding focus
447	KBD_KEYBOARD_BUSY	Keyboard is busy
448	KBD_INVALID_CODEPAGE	Invalid code page

IV

Appendixes

Code	Error	Meaning
449	KBD_UNABLE_TO_FOCUS	Focus attempt failed
450	SMG_SESSION_NON_SELECT	Session is not selectable
451	SMG_SESSION_NOT_FOREGRND	Parent or child session is not in the foreground
452	SMG_SESSION_NOT_PARENT	Not the parent of the requested child
453	SMG_INVALID_START_MODE	Invalid session-start mode
454	SMG_INVALID_RELATED_OPT	Invalid session-start related option
455	SMG_INVALID_BOND_OPTION	Invalid session-bond option
456	SMG_INVALID_SELECT_OPT	Invalid session-select option
457	SMG_START_IN_BACKGROUND	Session started in the background
458	SMG_INVALID_STOP_OPTION	Invalid session-stop option
459	SMG_BAD_RESERVE	Reserved parameters are not zero
460	SMG_PROCESS_NOT_PARENT	Session-parent process already exists
461	SMG_INVALID_DATA_LENGTH	Invalid data length
462	SMG_NOT_BOUND	Parent is not bound
463	SMG_RETRY_SUB_ALLOC	Retry request-block allocation
464	KBD_DETACHED	Call is not allowed for a detached PID
465	VIO_DETACHED	Call is not allowed for a detached PID
466	MOU_DETACHED	Call is not allowed for a detached PID
467	VIO_FONT	No font is available to support the mode
468	VIO_USER_FONT	User font is active
469	VIO_BAD_CP	Invalid code page was specified
470	VIO_NO_CP	System display does not support the code page

Code	Error	Meaning
471	VIO_NA_CP	Current display does not support the code page
472	INVALID_CODE_PAGE	Invalid code page
473	CPLIST_TOO_SMALL	Code page list is too small
474	CP_NOT_MOVED	Code page was not moved
475	MODE_SWITCH_INIT	Mode switch initialization error
476	CODE_PAGE_NOT_FOUND	Code page was not found
477	UNEXPECTED_SLOT_RETURNED	Internal error
478	SMG_INVALID_TRACE_OPTION	Invalid start-session trace indicator
479	VIO_INTERNAL_RESOURCE	VIO internal resource error
480	VIO_SHELL_INIT	VIO shell initialization error
481	SMG_NO_HARD_ERRORS	No session manager hard errors
482	CP_SWITCH_INCOMPLETE	DosSetProcessCp cannot set a KBD or VIO code page
483	VIO_TRANSPARENT_POPUP	Error during a VIO pop-up window
484	CRITSEC_OVERFLOW	Critical section overflow
485	CRITSEC_UNDERFLOW	Critical section underflow
486	VIO_BAD_RESERVE	Reserved parameter is not zero
487	INVALID_ADDRESS	Invalid physical address
488	ZERO_SELECTORS_REQUESTED	At least one selector must be requested
489	NOT_ENOUGH_SELECTORS_AVA	Not enough GDT selectors to satisfy request
490	INVALID_SELECTOR	Not a GDT selector
491	SMG_INVALID_PROGRAM_TYPE	Invalid program type
492	SMG_INVALID_PGM_CONTROL	Invalid program control
493	SMG_INVALID_INHERIT_OPT	Invalid inherit option

IV

Appendixes

Appendix L

NetBIOS Error Codes

The following error codes are given in hexadecimal:

Code	Error
01	Illegal buffer length
03	Invalid command
05	Timed out
06	Message incomplete
07	Send No ACK—data was not received
08	Invalid local session number
09	No resource available (temporary condition)
0A	Session closed
0B	Command canceled
0D	Duplicate name in local name table
0E	Local session table is full
0F	Name has active sessions; is deregistered
11	Local session table is full
12	Session open was rejected
13	Invalid name number
14	Can't find the name called
15	Name not found, or illegal name

Code	Error
16	Name in use on a remote adapter
17	Name was deleted
18	Session abnormal termination
19	Name conflict detected
21	Interface busy
22	Too many outstanding commands
23	Invalid adapter number
24	Command completed while cancel occurred
26	Command not valid to cancel
30	Name defined by another environment
34	Environment not defined; must issue Reset
35	Resources exhausted; try later
36	Maximum applications exceeded
37	No service access points available
38	Requested resource not available
39	Invalid NCB address
3A	Reset may not be issued inside POST routine
3B	Invalid NCB_DD_ID value
3C	NetBIOS attempt to lock user storage failed
3F	NetBIOS device driver open error
40	OS/2 error detected
4E–4F	Network status error
F6–FA	Adapter error
FB	NetBIOS program is not loaded
FC	Adapter open failed
FD	Unexpected adapter close
FE	NetBIOS not active

Appendix M

IPX and SPX Error Codes

The following error codes are given in hexadecimal:

Code	Error
EC	Connection severed by remote workstation
ED	No answer from destination, or connection failed
EE	No such connection
EF	Local connection table is full
F9	ECB cannot be canceled
FA	No path to destination
FC	ECB not active, or has been canceled
FD	Invalid packet length
FE	Socket table is full, or packet is undeliverable
FF	Destination socket not open, local socket already open, or network failure

Appendix N

Source Listing for EMAILNLM.C

This program, written in 32-bit Watcom C, is a NetWare loadable module. Chapter 8, "Network Applications," discusses this program in detail.

```
/*
 *   EMAILNLM.C
 *
 *   An example NLM for NetWare 3.1x. This program maintains
 *   mail files on the server in a special subdirectory. For
 *   privacy, only this NLM has rights to that subdirectory.
 *
 *       1. Before loading this NLM, use SYSCON to establish
 *          user id "MAILBOX", password "EMAIL".  At a DOS
 *          prompt, use MKDIR to create a directory named
 *          "MAILBOX" on the SYS: volume.  Ensure the user
 *          "MAILBOX" has all rights to the directory.
 *
 *       2. On the workstation side, you need to create a
 *          program that communicates with this NLM through
 *          IPX, using the packet/message structures given
 *          below in this listing.
 *
 *
 *   Barry Nance
 *   released to the public domain
 *
 */

#include <nwtypes.h>
#include <nwbindry.h>
#include <nwipxspx.h>
#include <nwconn.h>
#include <nwdir.h>
#include <conio.h>
#include <process.h>
#include <string.h>
```

35638.

```c
#include <fcntl.h>
#include <io.h>
#include <stdio.h>
#include <stdlib.h>
#include <errno.h>

struct  MailHeaderType
        {
        char    From[50];
        char    To[50];
        char    Date[10];
        char    Time[10];
        char    Subject[50];
        char    Reserved[4];
        char    FileName[15];
        };

unsigned short Socket;
DIR     *MailDirPtr;
DIR     *DirEntryPtr;
FILE    *MailFile;
struct  MailHeaderType   MailHeader;
struct  MailHeaderType   MailTable[500];
int     MailSub;
int     MailCount;
IPX_ECB EventControlBlock;
IPX_HEADER IpxHeader;
struct  {
        char    ActionCode;
        short   MailID;
        short   Sequence;
        char    LastPacketFlag;
        short   Length;
        short   Reserved;
        char    Packet[500];
        } Message;

struct UserNameStruct User;

/* - - - - - - - - - - - - - - - - - - - - - - - - - - - - - - - - - - */

void    MailUnload(void)
        {
        Logout();
        IpxCloseSocket(Socket);
        }

/* - - - - - - - - - - - - - - - - - - - - - - - - - - - - - - - - - - */
int     main(int argc, char *argv[])
        {
        /* login as user MAILBOX, password EMAIL */
        if (LoginToFileServer("mailbox", OT_USER, "EMAIL"))
            {
            printf("Could not login as MAILBOX.  Aborting.\n");
            return 1;
            }
```

```
/* change to the SYS:\MAILBOX directory */
if (chdir("SYS:\\MAILBOX"))
    {
    printf("Could not change to MAILBOX directory. Aborting.\n");
    return 1;
    }

/* open socket 0x4545 */
Socket = 0x4545;
IpxOpenSocket(&Socket);

/* register an atexit() function to happen at unload time */
atexit(MailUnload);

printf("Mail Server is now active.\n");

/* index any outstanding mail files */
MailSub = 0;
MailDirPtr = opendir("*.*");
if (MailDirPtr != NULL)
    {
    DirEntryPtr = readdir(MailDirPtr);
    while (DirEntryPtr != NULL)
        {
        MailFile = fopen(DirEntryPtr->d_name, "rb");
        fread(&MailHeader, sizeof(MailHeader), 1, MailFile);
        fclose(MailFile);
        strcpy(MailHeader.FileName, DirEntryPtr->d_name);
        MailTable[MailSub] = MailHeader;
        MailSub++;
        DirEntryPtr = readdir(MailDirPtr);
        }
    closedir(MailDirPtr);
    }
MailCount = MailSub;

/* issue a Listen ECB */
IssueListen:
    memset(&EventControlBlock, 0, sizeof(EventControlBlock));
    memset(&IpxHeader, 0, sizeof(IpxHeader));
    memset(&Message, 0, sizeof(Message));
    EventControlBlock.fragCount = 2L;
    EventControlBlock.fragList[0].fragAddress = &IpxHeader;
    EventControlBlock.fragList[0].fragSize    = sizeof(IpxHeader);
    EventControlBlock.fragList[1].fragAddress = &Message;
    EventControlBlock.fragList[1].fragSize    = sizeof(Message);
    IpxReceive(Socket, &EventControlBlock);

    /* wait for a message */
    while (EventControlBlock.status)
        delay(100);

    GetUserNameFromNetAddress( (BYTE *) &IpxHeader.sourceNet,
                                0, &User);
```

35638.

```c
                       /* Action Code 1 is "Do I have any mail?" */
                       if (Message.ActionCode == '1')
                           {
                           if (Message.Sequence == 1)
                              MailSub = 0;
                           while (strcmp(User.UserName, MailTable[MailSub].To) != 0
                             && MailSub < 500)
                                MailSub++;
                           if (MailSub == 500)
                               {
                               Message.LastPacketFlag = 'Y';
                               Message.Length = 0;
                               }
                           else
                               {
                               Message.LastPacketFlag = 'N';
                               memcpy(Message.Packet, &MailTable[MailSub],
                                      sizeof(MailHeader));
                               Message.Length = sizeof(MailHeader);
                               }
                           Message.MailID = MailSub;
                           Message.Sequence++;
                           memcpy(&IpxHeader.destNet, &IpxHeader.sourceNet, 10);
                           IpxHeader.destSocket = Socket;
                           IpxHeader.packetType = 4;
                           EventControlBlock.fragCount = 2L;
                           EventControlBlock.fragList[0].fragAddress = &IpxHeader;
                           EventControlBlock.fragList[0].fragSize = sizeof(IpxHeader);
                           EventControlBlock.fragList[1].fragAddress = &Message;
                           EventControlBlock.fragList[1].fragSize = Message.Length+10;
                           IpxSend(Socket, &EventControlBlock);
                           goto IssueListen;
                           }

                       /* Action Code 2 is "Give me that mail item" */
                       if (Message.ActionCode == '2')
                           {
                           MailSub = Message.MailID;
                           if (strcmp(User.UserName, MailTable[MailSub].To) != 0)
                              goto IssueListen;
                           if (Message.Sequence == 1)
                               {
                               MailFile = fopen(MailTable[Message.MailID].FileName,
                                    "rb");
                               if (MailFile == NULL)
                                   goto IssueListen;
                               }
                           if (fread(Message.Packet, 500, 1, MailFile) != 1)
                               {
                               Message.LastPacketFlag = 'Y';
                               fclose(MailFile);
                               }
                           else
                               {
                               Message.LastPacketFlag = 'N';
                               }
```

```
    Message.Sequence++;
    Message.Length = 500;
    memcpy(&IpxHeader.destNet, &IpxHeader.sourceNet, 10);
    IpxHeader.destSocket = Socket;
    IpxHeader.packetType = 4;
    EventControlBlock.fragCount = 2L;
    EventControlBlock.fragList[0].fragAddress = &IpxHeader;
    EventControlBlock.fragList[0].fragSize = sizeof(IpxHeader);
    EventControlBlock.fragList[1].fragAddress = &Message;
    EventControlBlock.fragList[1].fragSize    = 510;
    IpxSend(Socket, &EventControlBlock);
    goto IssueListen;
    }

/* Action Code 3 is "Delete mail item" */
if (Message.ActionCode == '3')
    {
    MailSub = Message.MailID;
    if (strcmp(User.UserName, MailTable[MailSub].To) != 0)
        goto IssueListen;
    unlink(MailTable[MailSub].FileName);
    strcpy(MailTable[MailSub].To, "");
    goto IssueListen;
    }

/* Action Code 4 is "Send this mail item" */
if (Message.ActionCode == '4')
    {
    if (Message.Sequence == 1)
        {
        MailSub = 0;
        while (strlen(MailTable[MailSub].To) > 0
          && MailSub < 500)
            MailSub++;
        if (MailSub == 500)
            goto IssueListen;
        sprintf(MailTable[MailSub].FileName, "%5.5d", MailSub);
        MailFile = fopen(MailTable[MailSub].FileName, "wb");
        if (MailFile == NULL)
            goto IssueListen;
        }
    fwrite(Message.Packet, Message.Length, 1, MailFile);
    if (Message.LastPacketFlag == 'Y')
        fclose(MailFile);
    Message.Sequence++;
    Message.Length = 0;
    memcpy(&IpxHeader.destNet, &IpxHeader.sourceNet, 10);
    IpxHeader.destSocket = Socket;
    IpxHeader.packetType = 4;
    EventControlBlock.fragCount = 2L;
    EventControlBlock.fragList[0].fragAddress = &IpxHeader;
    EventControlBlock.fragList[0].fragSize = sizeof(IpxHeader);
    EventControlBlock.fragList[1].fragAddress = &Message;
    EventControlBlock.fragList[1].fragSize    = 10;
    IpxSend(Socket, &EventControlBlock);
    }
```

35638.

```
        goto IssueListen;
        }
/* - - - - - - - - - - - - - - - - - - - - - - - - - - - - - - - - */
```

Appendix O

Source Listing for TOKENRNG.C

This program, written in Borland C, uses the LAN Support Program interface to intercept and display MAC-layer Token Ring frames. Chapter 8, "Network Applications," discusses this program in detail.

```
/*
 *   TOKENRNG.C
 *
 *   Intercepts Media Access Control (MAC) token ring frames
 *   and displays data from the frames.
 *
 *   You must load the IBM "LAN Support Program" or equivalent
 *   before running this program. LSP consists of device drivers
 *   named DXMA0MOD, DXMC0MOD, etc. An equivalent would be the
 *   SMARTLSP program for Madge or Xircom adapters.
 *
 *   Compile with Borland C/C++ 3.0 or later.
 *   Use the "LARGE" (-ml command line option) memory model.
 *
 *
 */

#include <stdio.h>
#include <stdlib.h>
#include <conio.h>
#include <dos.h>
#include <ctype.h>
#include <string.h>
#include <process.h>
#include <time.h>
#include <math.h>
#include <graphics.h>


/* - - - - - - - - - - - - - - - - - - - - - - - - - - - - - */
```

```
#define DIR_INTERRUPT        0x00
#define DIR_OPEN_ADAPTER     0x03
#define DIR_INITIALIZE       0x20
#define RECEIVE              0x28
#define RECEIVE_CANCEL       0x29
#define BUFFER_FREE          0x27
#define DLC_MAX_SAP          2
#define DLC_MAX_STATIONS     4
#define STANDBY_MONITOR      0x06
#define ACTIVE_MONITOR       0x05
#define BEACON               0x02
#define CLAIM_TOKEN          0x03
#define ERROR_REPORT         0x00
#define RING_PURGE           0x04
#define FALSE                0
#define TRUE                 1


/* - - - - - - - - - - - - - - - - - - - - - - - - - - - - - - */

typedef unsigned char        BYTE;
typedef unsigned int         WORD;
typedef unsigned long        ULONG;

typedef struct  {
        BYTE    Name [21];
        BYTE    StringAddress [15];
        BYTE    Address [6];
        } USERLIST;

typedef struct  {
        BYTE    Length;
        BYTE    Command;
        BYTE    Value [46];
        } VECTOR;

typedef struct  {
        BYTE    Length;
        BYTE    Command;
        BYTE    Address [6];
        } NAUN;

typedef struct  {
        BYTE    Length;
        BYTE    Command;
        BYTE    PhysicalLocation [4];
        } PHYSICAL_LOCATION;

typedef struct  {
        BYTE    Length;
        BYTE    Command;
        BYTE    LineErrors;
        BYTE    InternalErrors;
        BYTE    BurstErrors;
        BYTE    ACErrors;
        BYTE    AbortDelimiterErrors;
        BYTE    Reserved;
```

```c
        } ISOLATING_ERRORS;

typedef struct  {
        BYTE    Length;
        BYTE    Command;
        BYTE    LostFrameErrors;
        BYTE    ReceiverCongestionErrors;
        BYTE    FrameCopiedErrors;
        BYTE    FrequencyErrors;
        BYTE    TokenErrors;
        BYTE    Reserved;
        } NON_ISOLATING_ERRORS;

typedef struct  {
        BYTE    Length;
        BYTE    Command;
        WORD    BeaconType;
        } BEACON_TYPE;

typedef struct  {
        BYTE    AccessControl;
        BYTE    FrameControl;
        BYTE    Destination[6];
        BYTE    Source[6];
        WORD    MajorVectorLen;
        BYTE    Class;
        BYTE    Command;
        union   {
                VECTOR                  Vector;
                NAUN                    Vect02;
                PHYSICAL_LOCATION       Vect0B;
                ISOLATING_ERRORS        Vect2D;
                NON_ISOLATING_ERRORS    Vect2E;
                BEACON_TYPE             Vect01;
                } SubV;
        } MACFRAME;

typedef struct  {
        BYTE    EventCode;
        BYTE    EventTime [10];
        BYTE    EventVector [46];
        } EVENT;

typedef struct      {
    BYTE    adapter;
    BYTE    command;
    BYTE    retcode;
    BYTE    work;
    void    *pointer;
    void    *cmd_cplt;
    void        *parm_tab;
    } CCB;

typedef struct {
    WORD    bring_up_err;
    WORD    sram_addr;
```

```
     BYTE     reserved[4];
     void     *adptr_chk_exit;
     void        *ring_status_exit;
     void        *pc_error_exit;
     } DIR_INIT_PT;

typedef struct {
     void     *adapter_parms;
     void     *direct_parms;
     void     *dlc_parms;
     void     *msg_parms;
     } DIR_OPEN_PT;

typedef struct {
     WORD     open_error_code;
     WORD     open_options;
     BYTE     node_addr[6];
     BYTE     group_addr[4];
     BYTE     func_addr[4];
     WORD     num_rcv_buffers;
     WORD     rcv_buffer_len;
     WORD     dhb_length;
     BYTE     dhb_number;
     BYTE     reserved;
     WORD     lock_code;
     void     *prod_id_addr;
     } DIR_OPEN_AD_PT;

typedef struct {
     WORD     dir_buf_size;
     WORD     dir_pool_blocks;
     void        *dir_pool_address;
     void        *adpt_chk_exit;
     void        *ring_status_exit;
     void        *pc_error_exit;
     void        *work_addr;
     WORD     work_len_req;
     WORD     work_len_act;
     } DIR_OPEN_DIR_PT;

typedef struct {
     BYTE     max_sap;
     BYTE     max_sta;
     BYTE     max_gsap;
     BYTE     max_gmem;
     BYTE     t1_tick_one;
     BYTE     t2_tick_one;
     BYTE     ti_tick_one;
     BYTE     t1_tick_two;
     BYTE     t2_tick_two;
     BYTE     ti_tick_two;
     } DIR_OPEN_DLC_PT;

typedef struct {
     WORD     station_id;
     WORD     buffers_left;
```

```c
        BYTE    numbuffs;
        BYTE    reserved[3];
        BYTE    *first_buffer;
        } BUFFER_PT;

struct Lanheader  {
    BYTE access_ctl;
        BYTE frame_ctl;
        BYTE destaddr[6];
        BYTE srcaddr[6];
        BYTE rinfo[18];
    };

struct Dlcheader  {
    BYTE dsap;
    BYTE ssap;
    WORD control;
    };

typedef struct {
    BYTE    *next_buf_ptr;
    BYTE    data[1];
    } BUFFER;

typedef struct {
    BUFFER *next_buf_ptr;
    WORD    rcv_len;
    WORD    len_in_buffer;
    WORD    adapter_offset;
    WORD    user_length;
    WORD    station_id;
    BYTE    options;
    BYTE    msg_type;
    WORD    buffers_left;
    BYTE    receive_fs;
    BYTE    adapter_num;
    BYTE    lan_hdr_len;
    BYTE    dlc_hdr_len;
    struct Lanheader lan_hdr;
    struct Dlcheader dlc_hdr;
    } RECV_BUFFER_ONE;

typedef struct {
    BUFFER *next_buf_ptr;
    WORD    rcv_len;
    WORD    len_in_buffer;
    WORD    adapter_offset;
    WORD    user_length;
    WORD    station_id;
    BYTE    options;
    BYTE    msg_type;
    WORD    buffers_left;
    BYTE    receive_fs;
    BYTE    adapter_num;
    BYTE    recvd_data[1];
    } BUF1_CONTIG;
```

```
typedef struct {
    WORD        station_id;
    WORD        user_length;
    void        *recv_exit;
    RECV_BUFFER_ONE  *first_buffer;
    BYTE        recv_options;
    } RECV_PT;

typedef struct {
    BYTE        Address [6];
    BYTE        Name [15];
    BYTE        NeighborAddr [6];
    BYTE        NeighborName [15];
    BYTE        FirstSeenTime [10];
    WORD        X;
    WORD        Y;
    BYTE        HeardFromFlag;
    BYTE        Status;
    BYTE        ErrorTime [10];
    BYTE        ErrorFlag;
    long        SecondsSinceError;
    WORD        LineError;
    WORD        InternalError;
    WORD        BurstError;
    WORD        ACError;
    WORD        AbortDelimError;
    WORD        LostFrameError;
    WORD        ReceiverCongestionError;
    WORD        FrameCopiedError;
    WORD        FrequencyError;
    WORD        TokenError;
    WORD        BeaconError;
    } NODE;

/* - - - - - - - - - - - - - - - - - - - - - - - - - - - - - */

void    interrupt CCBCpltApp(void);
void    interrupt RecDataApp(void);
int     DoInt5C(void *cmdptr);
void    Terminate(BYTE *message, int code);
int     AdapterInterrupt(CCB *ccbptr);
int     AdapterInitialize(CCB *ccbptr);
int     AdapterOpen(CCB *ccbptr);
int     ReceiveMACFrames(CCB *ccbptr, WORD stationid);
int     ReceiveCancel(CCB *ccbptr, WORD stationid);
int     FreeBuffer(CCB *ccbptr, WORD stationid, void *BufPtr);
void    ReportError(char *Message);

/* - - - - - - - - - - - - - - - - - - - - - - - - - - - - - */

unsigned char   Buffers[4096];
unsigned char   FrameTable[64 * 256];
int             HeadCount, TailCount;
BYTE            *HeadPtr, *TailPtr;
int             StandbyCount;
```

```
int             BeaconFlag;
long            TotalFrames;
long            Now, Then;
int             FrameLen;
int             VectorLen;

FILE            *TextFile;
char            String [1024];
char            String2 [32];
USERLIST        UserList [255];
int             UserCount;

NODE            Node [255];
int             NodeCount;
int             ThisNode;

EVENT           Events [50];
int             EventCount;
int             EventFlag;

unsigned int    SaveSS;
unsigned int    SaveSP;
unsigned int    OurSS;
unsigned int    OurSP;
unsigned char   OurStack [512];

CCB             *CCBPtr;
BUF1_CONTIG     *DataPtr;
BUF1_CONTIG     *MACPtr;
BUF1_CONTIG     *RecvBuff;

union   {
        VECTOR                  Vector;
        NAUN                    Naun;
        PHYSICAL_LOCATION       PhysicalLocation;
        ISOLATING_ERRORS        IsolatingErrors;
        NON_ISOLATING_ERRORS    NonIsolatingErrors;
        BEACON_TYPE             BeaconType;
        } SubVector;

CCB             workccb;
CCB             recvccb;
BYTE            funcaddr[4] = {0x80, 0x00, 0x00, 0x08};
MACFRAME        *MACframeptr;
WORD            Stationid;
WORD            i, j;

int             rc;
int             intrrc;
int             initrc;
int             openrc;
int             FirstTimeFlag;
BYTE            ch;
BYTE            ch1;
BYTE            ch2;
BYTE            *ch_ptr;
WORD            RegES, RegBX;
double          Dummy;
```

```
DIR_INIT_PT      InitParms;
DIR_OPEN_PT      openpt;
DIR_OPEN_AD_PT adpt;
DIR_OPEN_DIR_PT dirpt;
DIR_OPEN_DLC_PT dlcpt;
RECV_PT          RecvParms;
RECV_PT          RecvCancel;
BUFFER_PT        BufferPoolPT;

/* - - - - - - - - - - - - - - - - - - - - - - - - - - - - - */
void    interrupt CCBCpltApp(void)
        {
        disable();
        RegES = _ES;
        RegBX = _BX;
        CCBPtr = MK_FP(RegES, RegBX);
        enable();
        }

/* - - - - - - - - - - - - - - - - - - - - - - - - - - - - - */
void    interrupt RecDataApp(void)
        {
        disable();

        RegES  = _ES;
        RegBX  = _BX;
        MACPtr = MK_FP(RegES, RegBX);

        SaveSS = _SS;
        SaveSP = _SP;
        _SS = OurSS;
        _SP = OurSP;
        enable();

        memcpy(HeadPtr, MACPtr, 64);
        HeadPtr += 64;
        HeadCount++;
        if (HeadCount > 255)
            {
            HeadCount = 0;
            HeadPtr  = FrameTable;
            }

        FreeBuffer(&workccb, Stationid, MACPtr);
        ReceiveMACFrames(&recvccb, Stationid);

        disable();
        _SS = SaveSS;
        _SP = SaveSP;
        enable();
        }
```

```
/* - - - - - - - - - - - - - - - - - - - - - - - - - - - - - */
int     DoInt5C(void *cmdptr)
        {
        _ES = FP_SEG(cmdptr);
        _BX = FP_OFF(cmdptr);
        geninterrupt(0x5C);
        _BX = _AX;
        _BH = 0;
        return _BX;
        }

/* - - - - - - - - - - - - - - - - - - - - - - - - - - - - - */
void    Terminate(BYTE *message, int code)
        {
        clrscr();
        gotoxy(1, 2);
        cprintf("ERROR: %s. return code = %d", message, code);
        gotoxy(1, 5);
        exit(code);
        }

/* - - - - - - - - - - - - - - - - - - - - - - - - - - - - - */
int     AdapterInterrupt(CCB *ccbptr)
        {
        ccbptr->command  = DIR_INTERRUPT;
        ccbptr->adapter  = 0;
        ccbptr->parm_tab = ccbptr->pointer = ccbptr->cmd_cplt = NULL;
        DoInt5C(ccbptr);
        while( ccbptr->retcode == 0xFF )
            ;
        return (int) ccbptr->retcode;
        }

/* - - - - - - - - - - - - - - - - - - - - - - - - - - - - - */
int     AdapterInitialize(CCB *ccbptr)
        {
        ccbptr->command  = DIR_INITIALIZE;
        ccbptr->adapter  = 0;
        ccbptr->retcode  = 0xFF;
        ccbptr->parm_tab = (void *) &InitParms;
        ccbptr->cmd_cplt = ccbptr->pointer = NULL;
        memset(&InitParms, 0, sizeof(DIR_INIT_PT));
        return (DoInt5C(ccbptr));
        }

/* - - - - - - - - - - - - - - - - - - - - - - - - - - - - - */
int     AdapterOpen(CCB *ccbptr)
        {
        ccbptr->command  = DIR_OPEN_ADAPTER;
        ccbptr->adapter  = 0;
        ccbptr->parm_tab = (void *) &openpt;
        ccbptr->pointer  = NULL;
        ccbptr->cmd_cplt = (void *) CCBCpltApp;
        openpt.adapter_parms = (void *) &adpt;
        openpt.direct_parms  = (void *) &dirpt;
        openpt.dlc_parms     = (void *) &dlcpt;
```

```c
        openpt.msg_parms     = NULL;
        memset(&adpt,  0, sizeof(DIR_OPEN_AD_PT));
        memset(&dirpt, 0, sizeof(DIR_OPEN_DIR_PT));
        memset(&dlcpt, 0, sizeof(DIR_OPEN_DLC_PT));
        dlcpt.max_sap    = DLC_MAX_SAP;
        dlcpt.max_sta    = DLC_MAX_STATIONS;
        dirpt.dir_buf_size    = 160;
        dirpt.dir_pool_blocks = 20;
        dirpt.dir_pool_address = Buffers;
        adpt.open_options = 0x7880;              /* for MAC frames */
        memcpy(adpt.func_addr, funcaddr, 4);
        CCBPtr = NULL;
        DoInt5C(ccbptr);
        while (CCBPtr == NULL)
            ;
        return CCBPtr->retcode;
        }

/* - - - - - - - - - - - - - - - - - - - - - - - - - - - - - - - - */
int     ReceiveMACFrames(CCB *ccbptr, WORD stationid)
        {
        ccbptr->command = RECEIVE;
        ccbptr->adapter = 0;
        ccbptr->pointer = NULL;
        ccbptr->parm_tab = (void *) &RecvParms;
        ccbptr->cmd_cplt = (void *) CCBCpltApp;
        memset( &RecvParms, 0, sizeof(RECV_PT) );
        RecvParms.station_id  = stationid;
        RecvParms.recv_exit   = (void *) RecDataApp;
        RecvParms.recv_options = 0x80;              /* MAC frames */
        return (DoInt5C(ccbptr));
        }

/* - - - - - - - - - - - - - - - - - - - - - - - - - - - - - - - - */
int     ReceiveCancel(CCB *ccbptr, WORD stationid)
        {
        memset(&RecvCancel, 0, sizeof(RECV_PT));
        ccbptr->command = RECEIVE_CANCEL;
        ccbptr->adapter = 0;
        ccbptr->pointer = NULL;
        ccbptr->cmd_cplt = NULL;
        ccbptr->parm_tab = MK_FP(0x0000, stationid);
        RecvCancel.station_id  = stationid;
        RecvCancel.recv_exit   = NULL;
        return (DoInt5C(ccbptr));
        }

/* - - - - - - - - - - - - - - - - - - - - - - - - - - - - - - - - */
int     FreeBuffer(CCB *ccbptr, WORD stationid, void *BufPtr)
        {
        memset(&BufferPoolPT, 0, sizeof(BUFFER_PT));
        ccbptr->command = BUFFER_FREE;
        ccbptr->adapter = 0;
        ccbptr->pointer = NULL;
        ccbptr->parm_tab = (void *) &BufferPoolPT;
        ccbptr->cmd_cplt = NULL;
```

```c
        BufferPoolPT.station_id   = stationid;
        BufferPoolPT.first_buffer = BufPtr;
        return (DoInt5C(ccbptr));
        }

/* - - - - - - - - - - - - - - - - - - - - - - - - - - - - - - */
int     GetSubVector(BYTE SubCommand)
        {
        int    ByteCount;
        int    VectorLen;
        BYTE   VectorID;

        swab((char *) &MACframeptr->MajorVectorLen,
            (char *) &ByteCount, 2);
        ByteCount -= 4;
        ch_ptr = (BYTE *) &MACframeptr->SubV;

        while (ByteCount > 0)
            {
            VectorLen = (int) *ch_ptr;
            VectorID  = *(ch_ptr+1);
            if (VectorID == SubCommand)
                {
                memcpy(&SubVector, ch_ptr, VectorLen);
                return TRUE;
                }
            ch_ptr     += VectorLen;
            ByteCount -= VectorLen;
            }

        return FALSE;
        }

/* - - - - - - - - - - - - - - - - - - - - - - - - - - - - - - */
void    InitErrorTotals(int Sub)
        {
        Node[Sub].ErrorFlag = FALSE;

        strcpy(Node[i].ErrorTime, " ");
        Node[Sub].SecondsSinceError = 0;

        Node[Sub].LineError = 0;
        Node[Sub].InternalError = 0;
        Node[Sub].BurstError = 0;
        Node[Sub].ACError = 0;
        Node[Sub].AbortDelimError = 0;
        Node[Sub].LostFrameError = 0;
        Node[Sub].ReceiverCongestionError = 0;
        Node[Sub].FrameCopiedError = 0;
        Node[Sub].FrequencyError = 0;
        Node[Sub].TokenError = 0;
        Node[Sub].BeaconError = 0;
        }
```

```
/* - - - - - - - - - - - - - - - - - - - - - - - - - - - - - - */
void    UpdateNodeList(void)
        {
        int i, j;

        i = 0;
        while (i < NodeCount)
            {
            if (memcmp(Node[i].Address, MACframeptr->Source, 6) == 0)
                goto Update;
            i++;
            }

        i = 0;
        while (i < NodeCount)
            {
            if (memcmp(Node[i].Address, SubVector.Naun.Address, 6) == 0)
                {
                i++;
                for (j=NodeCount; j>i; j--)
                    Node[j] = Node[j-1];
                goto Insert;
                }
            i++;
            }

AddToList:
        i = NodeCount;

Insert:
        memcpy(Node[i].Address,       MACframeptr->Source, 6);
        strcpy(Node[i].Name, " ");
        for (j=0; j<UserCount; j++)
            {
            if (memcmp(Node[i].Address, UserList[j].Address, 6) == 0)
                {
                strcpy(Node[i].Name, UserList[j].Name);
                break;
                }
            }

        if (FirstTimeFlag)
            _strtime(Node[i].FirstSeenTime);
        else
            _strtime(Node[i].FirstSeenTime);

        Node[i].X = 0;
        Node[i].Y = 0;
        Node[i].HeardFromFlag = 4;

        InitErrorTotals(i);
        NodeCount++;

Update:
        ThisNode = i;
        memcpy(Node[i].NeighborAddr, SubVector.Naun.Address, 6);
```

```
        strcpy(Node[i].NeighborName, " ");
        for (j=0; j<UserCount; j++)
            {
          if (memcmp(Node[i].NeighborAddr, UserList[j].Address, 6) == 0)
                {
                strcpy(Node[i].NeighborName, UserList[j].Name);
                break;
                }
            }

        Node[i].HeardFromFlag = 4;
        if (MACframeptr->FrameControl == STANDBY_MONITOR)
            Node[i].Status = 'S';
        else
            Node[i].Status = 'A';
        }

/* - - - - - - - - - - - - - - - - - - - - - - - - - - - - - - */
void    ProcessActiveMonitor(void)
        {
        StandbyCount = 0;
        if (GetSubVector(0x02))
            UpdateNodeList();
        }

/* - - - - - - - - - - - - - - - - - - - - - - - - - - - - - - */
void    ProcessStandbyMonitor(void)
        {
        StandbyCount++;
        if (GetSubVector(0x02))
            UpdateNodeList();
        }

/* - - - - - - - - - - - - - - - - - - - - - - - - - - - - - - */
void    ReportError(char *Message)
        {
        BYTE    CurrentTime [15];

        EventFlag = TRUE;
        window(1, 13, 80, 25);
        gotoxy(1, 1);
        cprintf(
"-- EVENTS ----------------------------------------------------------");

        i = ThisNode;
        _strtime(CurrentTime);

        gotoxy(1, 2);
        delline();

        if (Node[i].Name[0] == ' ')
            sprintf(String, "%2.2X%2.2X%2.2X %2.2X%2.2X%2.2X",
                (int) Node[i].Address[0],
                (int) Node[i].Address[1],
                (int) Node[i].Address[2],
                (int) Node[i].Address[3],
                (int) Node[i].Address[4],
                (int) Node[i].Address[5]);
```

```
                    else
                        strcpy(String, Node[i].Name);

                    if (Node[i].NeighborName[0] == ' ')
                        sprintf(String2, "%2.2X%2.2X%2.2X %2.2X%2.2X%2.2X",
                            (int) Node[i].NeighborAddr[0],
                            (int) Node[i].NeighborAddr[1],
                            (int) Node[i].NeighborAddr[2],
                            (int) Node[i].NeighborAddr[3],
                            (int) Node[i].NeighborAddr[4],
                            (int) Node[i].NeighborAddr[5]);
                    else
                        strcpy(String2, Node[i].NeighborName);

                    gotoxy(1, 12);
                    cprintf("%-9.9s  %-13.13s  %-30.30s   NAUN: %-13.13s",
                            CurrentTime,
                            String,
                            Message,
                            String2);

                    time(&Node[i].SecondsSinceError);
                    _strtime(Node[i].ErrorTime);

                    TextFile = fopen("TOKENRNG.LOG", "a+");
                    if (TextFile != NULL)
                        {
                        fprintf(TextFile,
                            "%-9.9s  %-13.13s  %-30.30s   NAUN: %-13.13s\n",
                                    CurrentTime,
                                    String,
                                    Message,
                                    String2);
                        fclose(TextFile);
                        }

                    window(1, 1, 80, 25);
                    }

/* - - - - - - - - - - - - - - - - - - - - - - - - - - - - - - */
void    ProcessRingPurge(void)
        {
        i = 0;
        while (i < NodeCount)
            {
            if (memcmp(Node[i].Address, MACframeptr->Source, 6) == 0)
                goto RecordRingPurge;
            i++;
            }

        return;

RecordRingPurge:
        ThisNode = i;
        ReportError("Ring purge");
        }
```

IV

```c
/* - - - - - - - - - - - - - - - - - - - - - - - - - - - - - */
void    ProcessClaimToken(void)
        {
        i = 0;
        while (i < NodeCount)
            {
            if (memcmp(Node[i].Address, MACframeptr->Source, 6) == 0)
                goto RecordClaimToken;
            i++;
            }

        return;

RecordClaimToken:
        ThisNode = i;
        ReportError("Claim token");
        }

/* - - - - - - - - - - - - - - - - - - - - - - - - - - - - - */
void    ProcessBeacon(void)
        {
        BeaconFlag = TRUE;

        sound(440);
        delay(75);
        nosound();
        sound(660);
        delay(50);
        nosound();

        i = 0;
        while (i < NodeCount)
            {
            if (memcmp(Node[i].Address, MACframeptr->Source, 6) == 0)
                goto RecordBeacon;
            i++;
            }

        return;

RecordBeacon:
        ThisNode = i;
        Node[i].ErrorFlag = TRUE;
        Node[i].BeaconError++;

        ReportError("BEACON error!");
        }

/* - - - - - - - - - - - - - - - - - - - - - - - - - - - - - */
void    ProcessErrorReport(void)
        {
        i = 0;
        while (i < NodeCount)
            {
            if (memcmp(Node[i].Address, MACframeptr->Source, 6) == 0)
                goto RecordError;
            i++;
            }
```

```
            return;

    RecordError:
            ThisNode = i;
            if (GetSubVector(0x2D))
                {
                Node[i].LineError
                ➥+= SubVector.IsolatingErrors.LineErrors;
                Node[i].InternalError
                ➥+= SubVector.IsolatingErrors.InternalErrors;
                Node[i].BurstError
                ➥+= SubVector.IsolatingErrors.BurstErrors;
                Node[i].ACError += SubVector.IsolatingErrors.ACErrors;
                Node[i].AbortDelimError
                ➥+= SubVector.IsolatingErrors.AbortDelimiterErrors;
                }

            if (GetSubVector(0x2E))
                {
                Node[i].LostFrameError
                ➥+= SubVector.NonIsolatingErrors.LostFrameErrors;
                Node[i].ReceiverCongestionError
                ➥+= SubVector.NonIsolatingErrors.ReceiverCongestionErrors;
                Node[i].FrameCopiedError
                ➥+= SubVector.NonIsolatingErrors.FrameCopiedErrors;
                Node[i].FrequencyError
                ➥+= SubVector.NonIsolatingErrors.FrequencyErrors;
                Node[i].TokenError
                ➥+= SubVector.NonIsolatingErrors.TokenErrors;
                }

            Node[i].ErrorFlag = TRUE;

            if (GetSubVector(0x2D))
                {
                if (SubVector.IsolatingErrors.LineErrors != 0)
                    ReportError("Line error");
                if (SubVector.IsolatingErrors.InternalErrors != 0)
                    ReportError("Internal error");
                if (SubVector.IsolatingErrors.BurstErrors != 0)
                    ReportError("Burst error");
                if (SubVector.IsolatingErrors.ACErrors != 0)
                    ReportError("A-C error");
                if (SubVector.IsolatingErrors.AbortDelimiterErrors != 0)
                    ReportError("Abort Delim. error");
                }
            if (GetSubVector(0x2E))
                {
                if (SubVector.NonIsolatingErrors.LostFrameErrors != 0)
                    ReportError("Lost frame error");
                if (SubVector.NonIsolatingErrors.ReceiverCongestionErrors != 0)
                    ReportError("Receiver congestion error");
                if (SubVector.NonIsolatingErrors.FrameCopiedErrors != 0)
                    ReportError("Frame copied error");
                if (SubVector.NonIsolatingErrors.FrequencyErrors != 0)
                    ReportError("Frequency error");
                if (SubVector.NonIsolatingErrors.TokenErrors != 0)
```

```
                    ReportError("Token error");
                }
            }

/* - - - - - - - - - - - - - - - - - - - - - - - - - - - - - - */
void    DrawRing(void)
        {
        int   row;

        if (!EventFlag)
            goto ShowRingData;

        TextFile = fopen("TOKENRNG.LOG", "a+");
        if (TextFile == NULL)
            goto ShowRingData;

        _strtime(String);
        _strdate(String2);
        fprintf(TextFile, "\n\nToken Ring log entries @ %s on %s\n\n",
                String, String2);

        fprintf(TextFile,
    "   On at St Line Brst  A/C  Abt Lost Cong Cpd Freq Tok Beac\n");
        fprintf(TextFile,
    "   ----- -- ---- ---- ---- ---- ---- ---- ---- ---- ---- ----\n");

        for (i=0; i<NodeCount; i++)
            {
            if (Node[i].NeighborName[0] == ' ')
                sprintf(String2, "%2.2X%2.2X%2.2X %2.2X%2.2X%2.2X",
                    (int) Node[i].NeighborAddr[0],
                    (int) Node[i].NeighborAddr[1],
                    (int) Node[i].NeighborAddr[2],
                    (int) Node[i].NeighborAddr[3],
                    (int) Node[i].NeighborAddr[4],
                    (int) Node[i].NeighborAddr[5]);
            else
                strcpy(String2, Node[i].NeighborName);
            fprintf(TextFile,
                "%-10.10s [%2.2X%2.2X%2.2X %2.2X%2.2X%2.2X]   ",
                    Node[i].Name,
                    (int) Node[i].Address[0],
                    (int) Node[i].Address[1],
                    (int) Node[i].Address[2],
                    (int) Node[i].Address[3],
                    (int) Node[i].Address[4],
                    (int) Node[i].Address[5]);
            fprintf(TextFile, " NAUN: %s\n", String2);
            fprintf(TextFile, "     %s (%c)",
                    Node[i].FirstSeenTime,
                    Node[i].Status);
           fprintf(TextFile, "%4d %4d %4d %4d %4d %4d %4d %4d %4d %4d\n",
                    Node[i].LineError,
                    Node[i].BurstError,
                    Node[i].ACError,
                    Node[i].AbortDelimError,
```

```c
                             Node[i].LostFrameError,
                             Node[i].ReceiverCongestionError,
                             Node[i].FrameCopiedError,
                             Node[i].FrequencyError,
                             Node[i].TokenError,
                             Node[i].BeaconError);
                }

        fclose(TextFile);

ShowRingData:
        window(1, 1, 80, 12);
        clrscr();
        for (i=0; i<NodeCount; i++)
            if (Node[i].Status == 'A')
                {
                gotoxy(1, 1);
    cprintf("Active monitor is %-10.10s
➥[%2.2X%2.2X%2.2X %2.2X%2.2X%2.2X]",
                         Node[i].Name,
                         (int) Node[i].Address[0],
                         (int) Node[i].Address[1],
                         (int) Node[i].Address[2],
                         (int) Node[i].Address[3],
                         (int) Node[i].Address[4],
                         (int) Node[i].Address[5]);
                }

        gotoxy(50, 1);
        cprintf("    Total standby monitors: %d", StandbyCount);
        gotoxy(60, 2);
        cprintf("Total frames: %ld", TotalFrames);

        gotoxy(1, 3);
        cprintf(
"In Error        NAUN          Line Brst  A/C  Abt Lost Cong  Cpd Freq
➥  Tok Beac");
        gotoxy(1, 4);
        cprintf(
".............. ............. .... .... .... .... .... .... .... ....
➥ .... ....");

        row = 5;
        for (i=0; i<NodeCount; i++)
            {
            if (Node[i].ErrorFlag)
                {
                if (Node[i].Name[0] == ' ')
                    sprintf(String2, "%2.2X%2.2X%2.2X %2.2X%2.2X%2.2X",
                        (int) Node[i].Address[0],
                        (int) Node[i].Address[1],
                        (int) Node[i].Address[2],
                        (int) Node[i].Address[3],
                        (int) Node[i].Address[4],
                        (int) Node[i].Address[5]);
```

```
            else
                strcpy(String2, Node[i].Name);
            gotoxy(1, row);
            cprintf("%-13.13s", String2);
            if (Node[i].NeighborName[0] == ' ')
                sprintf(String2, "%2.2X%2.2X%2.2X %2.2X%2.2X%2.2X",
                    (int) Node[i].NeighborAddr[0],
                    (int) Node[i].NeighborAddr[1],
                    (int) Node[i].NeighborAddr[2],
                    (int) Node[i].NeighborAddr[3],
                    (int) Node[i].NeighborAddr[4],
                    (int) Node[i].NeighborAddr[5]);
            else
                strcpy(String2, Node[i].NeighborName);
            gotoxy(15, row);
            cprintf("%-13.13s", String2);
            gotoxy(29, row);
            cprintf("%4d %4d %4d %4d %4d %4d %4d %4d %4d %4d",
                Node[i].LineError,
                Node[i].BurstError,
                Node[i].ACError,
                Node[i].AbortDelimError,
                Node[i].LostFrameError,
                Node[i].ReceiverCongestionError,
                Node[i].FrameCopiedError,
                Node[i].FrequencyError,
                Node[i].TokenError,
                Node[i].BeaconError);
            row++;
            if (row > 12)
                break;
            }
        }
    window(1, 1, 80, 25);
    EventFlag = FALSE;
    }

/* - - - - - - - - - - - - - - - - - - - - - - - - - - - - - - */
void    main(int argc, char *argv[])
    {
    _AH = 15;
    geninterrupt(0x10);
    _AH = 0;
    i = _AX;
    if (i == 7)
        textattr(0x07);
    else
        textattr(0x02);

    clrscr();
    gotoxy(1, 1);
    cprintf("Starting Token Ring Monitor...");
    gotoxy(1, 5);
```

```
TextFile = fopen("TOKENRNG.LOG", "a+");
if (TextFile != NULL)
    {
    _strtime(String);
    _strdate(String2);
    fprintf(TextFile,
        "\nToken Ring monitor started @ %s on %s\n\n",
        String, String2);
    fclose(TextFile);
    }

FirstTimeFlag = TRUE;
EventFlag    = TRUE;

TextFile = fopen("USER.LST", "r");
UserCount = 0;
if (TextFile != NULL)
    {
    while ( (fgets(String, 1000, TextFile)) != NULL)
        {
        if (strlen(String) < 5)
            continue;
        if (strchr(String, '[') == NULL)
            continue;
        ch_ptr = &String[12];
        i = 0;
        while (*ch_ptr != ' ' && i < 10)
            {
            UserList[UserCount].Name[i] = *ch_ptr;
            ch_ptr++;
            i++;
            }
        strupr(String);
        ch_ptr = &String[40];
        i = 0;
        while (*ch_ptr != ']' && i < 12)
            {
            if (*ch_ptr == ' ')
                *ch_ptr = '0';
            UserList[UserCount].StringAddress[i] = *ch_ptr;
            ch_ptr++;
            i++;
            }
        j = 40;
        for (i=0; i<6; i++)
            {
            ch1 = String[j];
            if (ch1 >= '0' && ch1 <= '9')
                ch1 -= '0';
            else
                {
                ch1 -= 'A';
                ch1 += 10;
                }
            j++;
```

IV

Appendixes

```
                    ch2 = String[j];
                    if (ch2 >= '0' && ch2 <= '9')
                        ch2 -= '0';
                    else
                        {
                        ch2 -= 'A';
                        ch2 += 10;
                        }
                    ch = (BYTE) (ch1 << 4) ¦ ch2;
                    UserList[UserCount].Address[i] = ch;
                    j++;
                    }
                UserCount++;
                }
            fclose(TextFile);
            }

        OurSP    = FP_OFF( (void *) &OurStack[510] );
        OurSS    = FP_SEG( (void *) &OurStack[510] );

        Stationid = 1;
        TotalFrames = 0;
        HeadCount = 0;
        HeadPtr   = FrameTable;
        TailCount = 0;
        TailPtr   = FrameTable;

        if (getvect(0x5C) == NULL)
            Terminate("Adapter handler not installed.", 16);

        intrrc = AdapterInterrupt(&workccb);
        if ( (intrrc != 0) && (intrrc != 0x09) )
            Terminate( "Could not communicate with network adapter",
                    intrrc);

        initrc = AdapterInitialize(&workccb);
        if (initrc)
            Terminate( "Could not initialize network adapter", initrc);

        openrc = AdapterOpen(&workccb);
        if (openrc && openrc != 0x10)
            Terminate("Could not open network adapter", openrc);

        time(&Then);
        ReceiveMACFrames(&recvccb, Stationid);

CheckActivity:
        if (kbhit())
            {
            ch = getch();
            if (ch != 'q' && ch != 'Q')
                goto GetFrameFromTable;
            TextFile = fopen("TOKENRNG.LOG", "a+");
            if (TextFile != NULL)
                {
                _strtime(String);
```

```
                        _strdate(String2);
                        fprintf(TextFile,
                            "\nToken Ring monitor ended @ %s on %s\n\n",
                            String, String2);
                        fclose(TextFile);
                        }
                ReceiveCancel(&recvccb, Stationid);
                gotoxy(1,24);
                clreol();
                cprintf("Ring Error Monitor completed.");
                while (recvccb.retcode == 0xFF)
                    ;
                exit(0);
                }

GetFrameFromTable:
        if (HeadCount == TailCount)
            goto TimeToDisplay;

        RecvBuff = (void *) TailPtr;
        TailPtr += 64;
        TailCount++;
        if (TailCount > 255)
            {
            TailCount = 0;
            TailPtr   = FrameTable;
            }

        MACframeptr = (MACFRAME *) &RecvBuff->recvd_data[0];
        TotalFrames++;

        if (MACframeptr->FrameControl == STANDBY_MONITOR)
            {
            ProcessStandbyMonitor();
            goto TimeToDisplay;
            }

        if (MACframeptr->FrameControl == ACTIVE_MONITOR)
            {
            ProcessActiveMonitor();
            goto TimeToDisplay;
            }

        if (MACframeptr->FrameControl == BEACON)
            {
            ProcessBeacon();
            goto TimeToDisplay;
            }

        if (MACframeptr->FrameControl == CLAIM_TOKEN)
            {
            ProcessClaimToken();
            goto TimeToDisplay;
            }
```

```
        if (MACframeptr->FrameControl == ERROR_REPORT)
            {
            ProcessErrorReport();
            goto TimeToDisplay;
            }

        if (MACframeptr->FrameControl == RING_PURGE)
            {
            ProcessRingPurge();
            goto TimeToDisplay;
            }

        goto CheckActivity;


TimeToDisplay:
        time(&Now);
        if (Now < Then + 6 && !BeaconFlag)
            goto CheckActivity;
        Then = Now;

        for (ThisNode=0; ThisNode<NodeCount; ThisNode++)
            {
            Node[ThisNode].HeardFromFlag--;
            if (Node[ThisNode].HeardFromFlag == 0)
                Node[ThisNode].Status = 'O';
            if (Node[ThisNode].SecondsSinceError < Now - 600)
                InitErrorTotals(ThisNode);
            }

        DrawRing();

        BeaconFlag = FALSE;
        FirstTimeFlag = FALSE;
        goto CheckActivity;
        }

/* - - - - - - - - - - - - - - - - - - - - - - - - - - - - - - - - */
```

Index

S